Good luck in Leeds

lots of love

# NEANDERTHALS IN WALES

*The Main Entrance of Pontnewydd Cave.*

# NEANDERTHALS IN WALES

## PONTNEWYDD AND THE ELWY VALLEY CAVES

*edited by*

Stephen Aldhouse-Green, Rick Peterson
and Elizabeth A. Walker

*in association with*
Amgueddfa Cymru – National Museum Wales

OXBOW BOOKS
*Oxford and Oakville*

*Published by*
Oxbow Books, Oxford, UK
*in association with*
Amgueddfa Cymru – National Museum Wales

ISBN 978-1-84217-460-9


*This book is available direct from:*

Oxbow Books, Oxford, UK
(Phone: 01865-241249; Fax: 01865-794449)

*and*

The David Brown Book Company
PO Box 511, Oakville, CT 06779, USA
(Phone: 860-945-9329; Fax: 860-945-9468)

*or from our website*

www.oxbowbooks.com

*Front cover: Excavations in progress in the Main East Passage, Pontnewydd Cave.*
*Back cover: The interior of Pontnewydd Cave. Area G looking into the New Passage.*

A CIP record for this book is available from the British Library

Library of Congress Cataloging-in-Publication Data

Neanderthals in Wales : Pontnewydd and the Elwy valley caves / edited by Stephen Aldhouse-Green, Rick Peterson and Elizabeth A. Walker.
   p. cm.
 Includes bibliographical references.
 ISBN 978-1-84217-460-9
 1. Neanderthals--Wales. 2. Excavations (Archaeology)--Wales. 3. Antiquities, Prehistoric--Wales. I. Aldhouse-Green, Stephen. II. Peterson, Rick. III. Walker, Elizabeth A.
 GN285.N457 2012
 569.9'8609429--dc23
                          2012002767


Printed and bound at
Gomer Press, Llandysul, Wales

# Contents

# Foreword

## David Anderson

Amgueddfa Cymru – National Museum Wales commenced the Palaeolithic Settlement of Wales research project in 1978 with a first season of excavation at Pontnewydd Cave, Denbighshire under the direction of Stephen Aldhouse-Green who became Keeper of Archaeology and Numismatics 1988–1996. The research project led to the investigation and publication of a further six caves across Wales.

Prior to the commencement of the Pontnewydd Cave excavations our knowledge and understanding of the Palaeolithic occupation of Wales was very patchy. Archaeological evidence was scanty with just a handful of surface finds and a limited number of excavated site assemblages including Paviland Cave, Hoyle's Mouth and the Tremeirchion caves. With the National Museum's research programme this was all to change, as it pushed back the knowledge of a human presence in Wales from 50,000 to 230,000 years ago. The discovery in 1980 of a tooth that Chris Stringer was to identify as Neanderthal transformed the whole nature of the project. The research now attracted funding from many international research bodies and drew together a team of scientists from across the globe who, as the contributors list for this volume demonstrates, are all leaders and highly regarded in their respective fields. In 1984 the first interim report published by the National Museum provided the taster for this long-awaited volume and it is to Stephen and his team's credit that the research commenced over thirty years ago is now drawn together into this new book. Inevitably scientific knowledge has developed in leaps and bounds after three decades, and the editors of this book have involved the original scientists as well as embracing a new generation along the way.

Since its foundation in 1907 the National Museum has been engaged in archaeological excavation of key sites around Wales in order to discover, preserve and reveal to the public the heritage of the whole of Wales. Heritage now forms part of the nation's self construction. For a time, particularly during the 1940s until the foundation of the Welsh Archaeological Trusts in the early 1970s the Museum undertook rescue archaeology. Since 1974, the staff has once more focused on research programmes with a range of aims unique to archaeology in Wales. The Department of Archaeology and Numismatics delivers the complete virtuous ark of activities – fieldwork and collecting, research and interpretation, publication, delivery and public engagement. Above all archaeology is about people and their lives and the past environments in which they lived, the challenge being to place the social lives of these people into a framework that is based on material culture and archaeological evidence rather than on language. Projects such as Pontnewydd have captured the public and press imagination along the way; the cave even entered the Guinness Book of Records in 1984 for being the oldest known occupied site in Wales and, at that time, for producing the oldest human tooth found in Britain as well as for being the furthest north-westerly earlier Palaeolithic site known in Europe. All this helps us to demonstrate the ability of our Museum's curators to be archaeological scientists using modern techniques to explore and elucidate the lives of the people whose remains they are studying and to be effective communicators of this knowledge.

A book such as this is always the work of many people. Above all Stephen Aldhouse-Green, whose research this has been, deserves great credit for seeing a very large and complex research project through to fruition. Everyone who has been involved with the preparation of the reports that follow is thanked for their patience and willingness to persevere with its long duration. Rick Peterson and Elizabeth Walker have both played key roles in assisting Stephen with editing and bringing this book to completion. Lastly I would like to acknowledge here the contribution that the landowner, Sir Watkin Williams Wynn Bt, has made to this project, and thank him for his generosity in donating all the finds discovered by this research to Amgueddfa Cymru – National Museum Wales. On behalf of the people of Wales the Museum will continue to curate and use these finds to inform and inspire future generations.

*David Anderson*
*Director General*
*Amgueddfa Cymru – National Museum Wales*

# Contributors

STEPHEN ALDHOUSE-GREEN

Stephen Aldhouse-Green is an honorary professor in the Department of Archaeology at Cardiff University and an Emeritus Professor at Newport University. He began his career as a Lecturer in Archaeology, University of Khartoum 1968–69. He was a Field Archaeologist, Milton Keynes New City 1971–76. In 1976, he moved to the National Museum of Wales as Assistant Keeper where he became Keeper of Archaeology from 1988–96. In 1996, he moved to Newport University where he taught human origins. He has been Director of the Palaeolithic Settlement of Wales Research Programme from 1978 to the present. This has involved excavation at cave-sites in Wales, namely Pontnewydd, Cefn, Cae Gronw, Hoyle's Mouth and Little Hoyle, and publication of the work of the late Professor Charles McBurney at Coygan Cave. The project was expanded to embrace the definitive publication of Paviland Cave in 2000. The Palaeolithic Settlement of Wales research programme has involved several related but discrete projects. It has now moved to a post-excavation and interpretative stage. Its projects may be grouped under two headings:

- Pontnewydd and the Elwy valley caves: early Neanderthal archaeology *c.* 250 ka;
- Paviland, Pembrokeshire and the Vale of Clwyd: late Neanderthals and anatomically modern humans *c.* 50–10 ka.

c/o Department of Archaeology, Cardiff University, Cathays Park, Cardiff, CF10 3EU, U.K.
aldhousegreen@btinternet.com

TIM ATKINSON

Tim Atkinson is a Principal Research Associate and Honorary Professor of Environmental Geoscience at University College London. However, most of his work relating to Pontnewydd Cave was done in collaboration with Peter Rowe while he was Reader in Environmental Sciences at the University of East Anglia.

Department of Earth Sciences, University College London, Gower Street, London, WC1E 6BT, U.K.
t.atkinson@ucl.ac.uk

RICHARD E. BEVINS

Dr Richard Bevins is Keeper of Geology at the National Museum of Wales. His expertise lies in the igneous and metamorphic history of Wales and he has published over 75 papers on this area in peer-reviewed journals and books. He has provided provenancing input to a number of archaeological projects, including not only Pontnewydd Cave but also Alderley Edge hammerstone studies and lithic artefacts from excavations of the Bronze Age site at Oversley Bank, discovered during construction of the second runway at Manchester Airport. His most recent research has been on the Stonehenge bluestone assemblage, which has led to the first ever identification of the source of one of the rhyolite lithologies.

Department of Geology, Amgueddfa Cymru – National Museum Wales, Cathays Park, Cardiff, CF10 3NP, U.K.
Richard.Bevins@museumwales.ac.uk

DAVID Q. BOWEN

David Quentin Bowen was born and raised in Llanelli, Carmarthenshire, and was an undergraduate and postgraduate at University College London. He has been Professor of Physical Geography at Aberystwyth, Professor of Geography in London University and Professor of Quaternary Geology at Cardiff University where he is now Professor Emeritus. He is an honorary life member of the International Union for Quaternary Research and was President of the Quaternary Research Association. His book *Quaternary Geology* was translated into Russian. He was founder and editor of *Quaternary Science Reviews* and he edited the Geological Society of London's *Correlation of Quaternary Deposits* in the British Isles. He also served as a member of the Nature Conservancy Council, member of the Joint Nature Conservation Committee and vice-chairman of the Countryside Council for Wales.

School of Earth and Ocean Sciences, Cardiff University, Cardiff, CF10 3YE, U.K.
bowendq@cardiff.ac.uk

PETER BULL

Dr Peter Bull obtained his degrees (BSc MSc and PhD)

from the University of Wales, Swansea and has taught and undertaken research at the University of Oxford since 1978. He is a Fellow and Tutor at Hertford College and University Lecturer in Physical Geography. His main research interests include environmental reconstruction of cave sediments by scanning electron microscopy and provenance studies of sediments in forensic geoscience.

School of Geography and the Environment, South Parks Road, Oxford, OX1 3QY, U.K.

peter.bull@hertford.ox.ac.uk

DAVID CASE

Dr David J. Case is Principal Lecturer in the Department of Geography and Environmental Management at the University of the West of England, Bristol. With a background in geology and geomorphology from the Universities of Reading and Aberystwyth, he has worked on Quaternary sediments and landforms in Wales and south-west England, including the cave sites of Pontnewydd, Paviland, Hoyle's Mouth, Little Hoyle and the Wye Valley.

Principal Lecturer, Department of Geography and Environmental Management, Faculty of Environment and Technology, University of the West of England, Coldharbour Lane, Bristol, BS16 1QY, U.K.

David.Case@uwe.ac.uk

BRYONY COLES

Bryony Coles is an Emeritus Professor of the University of Exeter. Following her postgraduate training at the Institute of Archaeology in London, she was appointed Lecturer in Prehistory at Exeter, where she specialised in wetland archeology and wood-based material culture. Her interest in the archaeology of beavers developed out of her research in the Somerset Levels with John Coles, and has led to fieldwork in present-day beaver territories in Europe and a multi-period study of the beaver evidence from Britain.

Department of Archaeology, Laver Building, North Park Road, Exeter, EX4 4QE, U.K.

b.j.coles@ex.ac.uk

TIM COMPTON

Tim Compton is a dental anthropologist and is a research associate in the Human Origins Group at the Natural History Museum, London. His present research interests are the teeth of Pleistocene hominins, in particular their morphology. He has previously worked on Middle Eastern material from Tel Abu Hureyra, Çatal Hüyük, and Jericho and has also studied the variation of less frequently recorded dental traits in South East Asian populations. He is an associate member of the Ancient Human Occupation of Britain Project. His background is in archaeology, having studied at the Institute of Archaeology in London.

Human Origins Group, Department of Palaeontology, Natural History Museum, Cromwell Road, London, SW7 5BD, U.K.

tim.compton10@btinternet.com

ANDY CURRANT

Andy Currant has worked on the fossil mammal collection at the Natural History Museum, London for around forty years. During that time he has become a specialist cave excavator and been involved in fieldwork projects all over the world. His research interests are very much directed towards mammalian biostratigraphy, establishing the true history of faunal changes through time.

Andy is first and foremost a curator – someone who arranges and interprets the collections under his care and makes them available to other people in a whole range of ways. He took on the initial identification of the Pontnewydd material 'in the field' and he is acutely aware of the shortcomings of giving this kind of treatment to fragmented remains from complex environments, but he is happy that his overall interpretation of the Pontnewydd material is sound. He has been fascinated by the interpretation of this site since he first saw it and has sought to find a means of making sense of the finds through details of their preservation and their identity.

Department of Palaeontology, Natural History Museum, Cromwell Road, London, SW7 5BD, U.K.

a.currant@nhm.ac.uk

NICK DEBENHAM

Dr Nick Debenham is a freelance scientific consultant specialising in archaeological and geological applications of thermoluminescence (TL) dating. Having gained his doctorate in physics at Imperial College, London, he joined the Research Laboratory for Archaeology and History of Art, Oxford, in 1978 to work on the TL dating of stalagmitic calcite and, three years later, stayed to carry out a further research programme on dating sedimentary deposits. From 1985, he worked at the British Museum Department of Scientific Research, applying TL techniques to a variety of heated and unheated archaeological materials. He moved to Nottingham in 1993 to set up Quaternary TL Surveys.

Quaternary TL Surveys Ltd. 19 Leonard Avenue, Nottingham, NG5 2LW, U.K.

n.debenham@qtls.globalnet.co.uk

ANNE EASTHAM

Anne Eastham studied environmental archaeology at the Institute of Archaeology, University of London. At the Institute and subsequently whilst teaching, she embarked upon a long-term study, interpretation and publication of bird faunas from archaeological sites, initially covering mainly Spain and Britain but currently including French and Near Eastern material. Her publications aim to show how bird remains indicate many aspects of the contemporary environment in relation to human behaviour. In 2004 she was appointed as a Commissioner on the Royal Commission for the Ancient and Historical Monuments of Wales.

Cleddau Laboratory for Archaeozoological Analysis, Dolau, Dwrbach, Fishguard, Pembrokeshire, SA65 9RN, U.K.

TRISTAN GRAY HULSE
Pen-y-Bont, Bont Newydd, St Asaph, Denbighshire, LL17 0HH, U.K.

VAUGHAN GRIMES
Dr Vaughan Grimes is a bioarchaeologist and Assistant Professor in the Department of Archaeology, Memorial University, Canada, whose research focuses on using bone and tooth chemistry to reconstruct human and animal behaviour, mobility and diet. He obtained his PhD from the University of Bradford and was an affiliated member of the Ancient Human Occupation of Britain (AHOB) project. Following this, he spent three years as a post-doctoral researcher at the Max Planck Institute for Evolutionary Anthropology, Leipzig, Germany, where he was responsible for the development of new analytical methods to measure strontium isotopes in biological tissues for mobility studies.

Department of Archaeology, Memorial University, St John's, Newfoundland, A1C 5S7, Canada.
vgrimes@mun.ca

PROF. RAINER GRÜN
Earth Environment, Research School of Earth Sciences, The Australian National University, Canberra 0200, Australia.
rainer.grun@anu.edu.au

THOMAS HIGHAM
Dr Thomas Higham is the Deputy Director of the Oxford Radiocarbon Accelerator Unit at the RLAHA, University of Oxford. He was previously Deputy Director of the Waikato Radiocarbon Laboratory in New Zealand, where he obtained his D.Phil. His research interests revolve around the radiocarbon dating of bone, radiocarbon reservoir effects, the application of Bayesian calibration methods to archaeological dating, dating novel sample types and sample pretreatment chemistry. With colleagues including the late Roger Jacobi, he has worked on the application of ultrafiltration preparative methods for improving the extraction of collagen from Palaeolithic bone for more reliable AMS dating.

Research Laboratory for Archaeology, Dyson Perrins Building, South Parks Road, Oxford, OX1 3QY, U.K.
thomas.higham@rlaha.ox.ac.uk

RUPERT HOUSLEY
Dr Rupert Housley is currently in the Department of Geography at Royal Holloway, University of London as Project Manager for the RESET Consortium, a 5-year NERC funded major research programme which commenced in January 2008.

Rupert obtained a BSc degree in Archaeological Studies from the University of Leicester and an MSc in Archaeological Science from the University of Southampton. His PhD from the University of Cambridge was awarded in 1987 for a thesis which focused on the palaeo-environment of the Somerset Levels. His first academic appointment was as Senior Archaeologist to the Radiocarbon Accelerator Unit, Oxford University – the post he held until 1995, when he joined the Department of Archaeology in the University of Glasgow as a Lecturer. In 2003 Rupert was Visiting Research Associate at the Department of Geology, Colgate University (NY, USA) and in 2006 held the Snell Visiting Fellowship at Balliol College, Oxford.

Rupert's research interests include botanical aspects of environmental archaeology; Quaternary dating methods – specifically radiocarbon, tephrochronology and luminescence dating; and the more scientific aspects of archaeology. In terms of time periods his interests have ranged from historical periods to the Middle/Upper Palaeolithic Transition.

Department of Geography, Royal Holloway, University of London, Egham, Surrey, TW20 0EX, U.K.
rupert.housley@rhul.ac.uk

HEATHER JACKSON
Department of Learning, Amgueddfa Cymru – National Museum Wales, Cathays Park, Cardiff, CF10 3NP, U.K.
heather.jackson@museumwales.ac.uk

MANDY JAY
Dr Mandy Jay became interested in working with isotopes as a mature archaeology undergraduate and undertook research in this area both for her undergraduate dissertation and for her PhD, both at the University of Bradford. She went on to do post-doctoral research for Mike Richards, first on the Ancient Human Occupation of Britain (AHOB) project and then on the Beaker People Project (Principal Investigator Mike Parker Pearson, University of Sheffield, co-Principal Investigators Mike Richards and Andrew Chamberlain), working out of the Max Planck Institute for Evolutionary Anthropology in Leipzig and Durham University. Her main interests lie in the isotopic analysis of organic collagen (carbon, nitrogen and sulphur) and in British prehistory. She is currently undertaking post-doctoral research through the University of Sheffield for Mike Parker Pearson's Feeding Stonehenge project.

Department of Archaeology, University of Sheffield, Northgate House, West Street, Sheffield, S1 4ET, U.K.
mandy.jay@sheffield.ac.uk

WILLIAM JONES
Dr William Jones is geologist with a BA from Cambridge and a PhD from London Universities. He has worked as a university lecturer, school teacher, geological consultant and civil servant as well as a geophysicist in the oil exploration industry. As a native of North Wales, William has a long standing interest in the geology and archaeology of Wales and has advised on the geological aspects of several archaeological investigations. At present he is a geophysicist with Petroleum Geo-Services in Perth, Australia.

Petroleum Geo-Services, 4 The Heights, Brooklands, Weybridge, Surrey, KT13 0NY, U.K.
william.jones@pgs.com

HELEN LIVINGSTON

Dr Helen Livingston studied the glacial geomorphology of the Elwy valley and Vale of Clwyd at King's College, London, under the supervision of the late Clifford Embleton and was awarded her doctorate in 1986. She continued her geomorphological research at Cardiff University and Hatfield Polytechnic, working mostly on the Quaternary in Wales. Since the mid 1990s she has been a freelance writer producing several books and numerous articles on various subjects while maintaining an active interest in the history of the landscape.

Orchard Cottage, Wineham Lane, Wineham, Near Henfield, West Sussex, BN5 9AY, U.K.

RICHARD MOURNE

Dr Richard Mourne is Senior Lecturer in the Department of Geography and Environmental Management at the University of the West of England, Bristol. With a background in physical geography and environmental physics from Manchester Polytechnic and the University of Edinburgh, and a research interest in geoarchaeology, he has participated in the excavations at Pontnewydd, Paviland, Burry Holms and the Wye Valley, and has carried out extensive post-excavation sedimentological work.

Department of Geography and Environmental Management, Faculty of Environment and Technology, University of the West of England, Coldharbour Lane, Bristol, BS16 1QY, U.K.

richard.mourne@uwe.ac.uk

PAUL PETTITT

Dr Paul Pettitt is Reader in Palaeolithic Archaeology at the University of Sheffield, U.K. He has degrees from the Universities of Birmingham (BA), London (MA) and Cambridge (PhD). He was Senior Archaeologist in the Radiocarbon Accelerator Unit at Oxford from 1995–2001, and was Research Fellow and Tutor in Archaeology and Anthropology at Keble College, Oxford, from 1997–2003. His research interests focus on the European Middle and Upper Palaeolithic, and he has worked in particular on the application of radiocarbon dating to Palaeolithic archaeology, the origin of human mortuary activity, and Palaeolithic art. In 2003 he co-discovered Britain's first known examples of Palaeolithic cave art at Creswell Crags, where he has been directing excavations since 2006. In 2008 he was elected a Fellow of the Society of Antiquaries of London.

Department of Archaeology, University of Sheffield, Northgate House, West Street, Sheffield, S1 4ET, U.K.

P.Pettitt@sheffield.ac.uk

RICK PETERSON

Rick Peterson is Senior Lecturer in Archaeology at the University of Central Lancashire. He was educated at Cardiff and Southampton Universities and is a Fellow of the Society of Antiquaries. His research focuses on the Holocene prehistory of caves and rock-shelters and on material culture, particularly Neolithic ceramics. He was co-director (with Professor Aldhouse-Green) of cave excavations at Goldsland Wood in the Vale of Glamorgan; which uncovered evidence of ritual activity and burial from the Late Mesolithic and Early Neolithic periods. He has just begun a new field project looking at caves and rock-shelters in the Forest of Bowland in Lancashire.

School of Forensic & Investigative Sciences, University of Central Lancashire, Preston, PR1 2HE, U.K.

rpeterson@uclan.ac.uk

ED RHODES

Ed Rhodes is Professor of Geology in Earth and Space Sciences, University of California, Los Angeles. Besides applying ESR dating to a range of Quaternary fauna, he was instrumental in developing OSL dating from its earliest days, and has been involved in the dating of many Quaternary sites in the U.K., Australia, Europe and beyond, with archaeological, geological and environmental foci. Ed has worked at Oxford, Cambridge, Royal Holloway, The Australian National University and Manchester Metropolitan University.

Department of Earth and Space Sciences, University of California, Los Angeles, 595 Charles Young Drive East, Box 951567, Los Angeles, CA 90095-1567, U.S.A.

erhodes@ess.ucla.edu

MIKE RICHARDS

Mike Richards is a Professor in the Department of Anthropology at the University of British Columbia in Canada, and at the Department of Human Evolution at the Max Planck Institute for Evolutionary Anthropology in Leipzig, Germany. His main research interests are in reconstructing past human diets, especially Neanderthal and modern human diets in Palaeolithic Europe, and across the European Mesolithic/Neolithic transition. His main area of expertise is in the application of isotope analysis to reconstruct past human and animal diets, migration, and movement patterns.

Department of Archaeology, Durham University, South Road, Durham, DH1 3LE, U.K.

michael.richards@durham.ac.uk

PETER ROWE

Dr Peter Rowe is a Quaternary geologist and isotope geochemist with strong interests in palaeoclimate reconstruction, and especially the interpretation of stable isotopic records in speleothems. He has many years experience of uranium-series dating and as well as speleothems has worked on tufas, lake deposits, calcretes and corals. Previous archaeological dating work has helped to unravel the stratigraphy of the deposits in Pin Hole Cave and Robin Hood's Cave in Creswell Crags, England. He is currently involved in isotopic studies of speleothems from the East and West Mediterranean regions.

School of Environmental Sciences, University of East Anglia, Norwich, NR4 7TJ, U.K.

p.rowe@uea.ac.uk

Dr Kate Scott
St Cross College, St Giles, Oxford, OX1 3LZ, U.K.

Chris Stringer
Professor Chris Stringer has worked at The Natural History Museum since 1973, and is now Research Leader in Human Origins and an FRS. His early research was on the relationship of Neanderthals and early modern humans in Europe, but through his work on the 'Out of Africa' theory of modern human origins, he now collaborates with archaeologists, dating specialists and geneticists in attempting to reconstruct the evolution of modern humans globally. He has excavated at sites in Britain and abroad, and is currently leading the Ancient Human Occupation of Britain project in its third phase (AHOB3), funded by the Leverhulme Trust. He has published over 200 scientific papers and his recent books include *The Complete World of Human Evolution* (2005, with Peter Andrews), the award-winning *Homo Britannicus* (2006), and *The Origin of Our Species* (2011).

Human Origins Unit, Department of Palaeontology, Natural History Museum, Cromwell Road, London, SW7 5BD, U.K.
c.stringer@nhm.ac.uk

Heather Viles
Professor Heather Viles is a geomorphologist at the University of Oxford who specializes in research on biological interactions with geomorphological processes and applications of geomorphology to understanding and conserving cultural heritage.

School of Geography and the Environment, University of Oxford, South Parks Road, Oxford, OX1 3QY, U.K.
heather.viles@ouce.ox.ac.uk

Elizabeth A. Walker
Elizabeth Walker is Curator of Palaeolithic and Mesolithic Archaeology at Amgueddfa Cymru – National Museum Wales, where she has worked since 1986. She has been involved with the Pontnewydd Cave project since volunteering for the Museum during her years as a student at the University of Lancaster. Her first paid employment was four weeks measuring the Pontnewydd Cave artefacts in 1986, following which she joined the Museum permanently and as part of her role became Finds Supervisor for the Pontnewydd Cave excavations. Since the excavations ended she has curated the collections and archive for the Museum.

Elizabeth has worked on many cave excavations across Wales and beyond, and has directed her own excavations of an early Mesolithic site on Burry Holms, Gower, Swansea. She has particular interests and expertise in Prehistoric lithic artefacts and in the history of collecting.

Department of Archaeology & Numismatics, Amgueddfa Cymru – National Museum Wales, Cathays Park, Cardiff, CF10 3NP, U.K.
Elizabeth.Walker@museumwales.ac.uk

Tim Young
Tim graduated with a degree in Natural Sciences in Cambridge. During a PhD project at Sheffield University he developed a research interest in iron ores. He was National Correspondent and a member of the International Steering Committee of IGCP Project 277 – Phanerozoic Ironstones (1989–1992) and Secretary of the International Subcommission on the Systematics of Sedimentary Rocks (1992–1996). Since 1997 Tim has run the consultancy GeoArch, specializing in archaeometallurgy and archaeogeophysics. He is particularly interested in early iron-making and iron-working in Britain and Ireland. This work involves both the interpretation of early technology and the provenancing of the iron ore. He was a member of Council of the Historical Metallurgy Society (2002–2006) and more recently its Chairman.

GeoArch, Unit 6, Western Industrial Estate, Caerphilly, CF83 1BQ, U.K.
Tim.Young@geoarch.co.uk

Prof. Li-Ping Zhou
Ministry of Education Laboratory for Earth Surface Processes, Department of Geography, Peking University, Beijing 100871, China.
lpzhou@pku.edu.cn

# Acknowledgements

The Pontnewydd Cave project commenced in 1978 so there are very many people who have had an involvement in some way or other with this work. It is impossible to name them all here. Special thanks must go to Sir Watkin Williams Wynn for permission to undertake the excavations in the caves and for generously donating all the resulting finds to the National Museum of Wales. Cadw and the Countryside Council for Wales are thanked for permitting the work to take place in Scheduled Ancient Monuments and Sites of Special Scientific Interest. The funding for the work has originated from many sources. The majority of this came from the National Museum of Wales who funded all stages of the work. Grants from the L. S. B. Leakey Foundation, the Board of Celtic Studies, the Cambrian Archaeological Association, the British Academy, the Prehistoric Society, The Society of Antiquaries of London, The Royal Archaeological Institute, the Natural Environment Research Council (N.E.R.C.) and the University of Wales College, Newport have all been gratefully received and have funded some of the specialist reports that follow in this volume.

In the field Kenneth Brassil, Brian Milton, Elizabeth Walker, Sue Stallibrass, Yolanda Stanton, Stephen Hartgroves and Angela Fussell were the key supervisory staff for many seasons; and particular thanks go to them, as well as to Simon Collcutt, Jill Cook, Sheila Coulson and Tony Valdemar who were involved at the very beginning of the project. The Cefn Estate Team who facilitated much of the groundwork ahead of excavation seasons are also thanked. In particular Denis Matheson, the former Farm Manager, Mark the woodman, Sid and Bill for providing their skills with a JCB and dumper truck to dig out the New Entrance and re-bury it before and after each season.

All the specialists who have been involved with the project are owed many thanks indeed for all their work and time. The staff of the National Museum have provided support in many ways; particularly the late George Boon who encouraged the project from its inception. Thanks are due to those who have undertaken work to prepare this volume. The photographs are the work of the former National Museum of Wales photographers, Kevin Thomas and James Wild, and of the Natural History Museum's Photographic Unit. The illustrations were drawn by Anne Leaver, Rick Peterson and Tony Daly. The artefact drawings are the work of Hazel Martingell. Tara Bowen, Rachel Eames and Alison Brookes are thanked for their work on the archive. Editorial assistance has been provided by Elizabeth Clapham. The staff at Oxbow have been a pleasure, as always, to work with. Particular thanks must be given to Julie Blackmore, Julie Gardiner and Clare Litt.

Stephen Aldhouse-Green particularly wishes to thank Derek Roe and the late John Wymer who wrote so many letters of support to accompany the many grant applications, and who were so supportive of the project throughout. Special visitors to the project were Kate Scott, Joan Taylor, Clive Gamble, Rob Foley, Richard Brewer, Mike Corfield, the late Rhys Jones, Miro Ivanovich, Clifford Embleton and Jeffrey May. I wish to make special acknowledgement to Elizabeth Walker. In 1999, I was diagnosed with Parkinson's disease and the work of getting the Pontnewydd volume together became progressively more difficult. I am pleased now to acknowledge Liz's role in ensuring the publication of the report, supported by her National Museum colleagues. I cannot express my thanks fully enough to such a remarkable person.

Finally, I wish to thank Miranda Aldhouse-Green who shared in the 'Pontnewydd experience' (particularly in the early days) and without whose support this volume would have been very different.

David Bowen wishes to acknowledge the shrewd advice throughout of Dr David Case. Also the following for reading different parts of the chapter and offering their expert advice: Professors Marshall McCabe, Darrel Maddy, Mike O'Hara F.R.S. and Dr Peter Walsh. Thanks are also due to Professor John Ludden, Director of the British Geological Survey, Alun Rogers of Cardiff University and Tony Daly of the National Museum for their expertise with the diagrams.

William Jones is grateful to Sir Watkin Williams-Wynn for permission to visit sites on the Cefn Estate, to Peter Appleton for introducing him to the caving literature on the Elwy valley and to Professor D. Q. Bowen for a helpful review of this contribution.

Richard Mourne and David Case would like to acknowledge the support of the Faculty of the Built Environment, and the School of Geography and Environmental Management, University of the West of England, Bristol for funding elements of their work. They also acknowledge the help of Chris Wade and Jan Major in preparing the figures, and Malcolm Skinner for support in laboratory work.

Andy Currant would like to express his thanks for the excellent working facilities at the National Museum of Wales and to the members of staff who made his stay so pleasant. He would like to give special thanks to Elizabeth Walker for her hospitality, care and patience during his visit and for the phenomenal amount of work she has done and continues to do in documenting and curating the Pontnewydd fauna.

Anne Eastham would like to thank Elizabeth Walker for making it possible to study the Pontnewydd bird bones and for her kindness and patience during the process.

Chris Stringer and Tim Compton would like to thank Robert Kruszynski (Natural History Museum, London) and Elizabeth Walker (National Museum of Wales, Cardiff) for allowing access to fossils and casts in their care and for their kind help. We would also like to thank Tim Atkinson, Shara Bailey, José María Bermúdez de Castro, Alfredo Coppa, Chris Dean, Yolanda Fernández Jalvo, David Frayer, Simon Hillson, Louise Humphrey, Joel Irish, Tania King, Helen Liversidge, Maria Martinón-Torres, Theya Molleson, Tanya Smith, Daris Swindler and Peter Ungar for all their contributions and comments and especially José María Bermúdez de Castro and Simon Hillson for reviewing and commenting on the draft. We would like, in addition, to thank Mary Davis at the National Museum of Wales and the Natural History Museum Photography Unit for taking the photographs of the Pontnewydd teeth, and Shara Bailey for her kind donation of photographs of other original specimens. Thanks are also due to Select Business Centre for typing the original draft, to Marilynne Raybould and Rick Peterson for their help with editing it and to Rob Symmons for drawing three of the figures. Chris Stringer is a member of the Ancient Human Occupation of Britain project (AHOB), funded by the Leverhulme Trust.

Paul Pettitt, Rupert Housley and Tom Higham are grateful to Stephen Aldhouse-Green for inviting us to make this contribution to the Pontnewydd project; to Elizabeth Walker for her assistance (and patience) and to Andrew Currant for faunal identifications. Funding for the study was provided by the Natural Environmental Research Council (NERC) through a grant to the ORADS.

# Preface

## Derek Roe

It is a privilege to be asked to contribute a brief introduction to this volume, whose publication brings to a close an extraordinary project begun a little over thirty years ago. In that time, the name of Pontnewydd Cave, of which few had heard in the 1970s, has entered the Hall of Fame of Palaeolithic Archaeology, and a mass of information has been gathered, ranging across most of the sciences that make up Quaternary Research. Stephen Aldhouse-Green and his remarkable team deserve the highest praise for what they have achieved.

Readers will be aware that a comprehensive interim account of the work was published in 1984, and this new volume brings that up to date and adds various fresh individual contributions. Although in 1984 the field work still had several more seasons to run, it was never anticipated that such a long period would elapse before the final report could be completed. Many however will be aware that for much of the last decade Stephen has been fighting a serious debilitating illness, and it is an extraordinary triumph that he has been able to see the work through to completion, with the dedicated and loyal support of his co-authors. He makes no mention of this himself in his personal Prologue, and you will certainly find no sign of it in the sections he has himself contributed, which show all his usual scholarly qualities – the precision, breadth, thoroughness and, yes, imperturbability, which his friends and colleagues know and expect. The finished product is surely a fitting reward for all those who have laboured so patiently to ensure its completion.

Pontnewydd is the most important, archaeologically, of the many caves that lie in the parish of Cefn Meriadog, Denbighshire, mainly exposed where the River Elwy has cut its course through Carboniferous Limestone. Within the project, some of the other caves were also briefly excavated, but only Pontnewydd produced significant finds of Middle Pleistocene age, including artefacts, faunal remains and no less than 17 Early Neanderthal teeth. If your heart, like mine, is in the artefacts side of Palaeolithic archaeology, you might think it a little unfair that the human teeth have stolen the limelight, but you will not be surprised, for it is hominid fossils (or hominin, as it has become

fashionable to say) that grab the public interest these days, and bring the grant money rolling in. All these categories of the Pontnewydd finds are considered in detail in this volume, as are the geological setting of the site and its own stratigraphy and sedimentology, and the dating evidence, which is based on several quite separate methods. It is not the role of a Preface writer, I am assured, to preview the conclusions that the various contributors reach – and that is just as well, or my Preface would be as long as one of the other chapters. Instead, I would like just to comment very briefly at the significance of the Pontnewydd project more generally, and to view it in the context of the time when it was carried out.

The number is diminishing of those who held teaching and research posts in Britain in the 1970s, and younger scholars may not realise how short we then were of what is now regarded as basic information in Palaeolithic Archaeology and Pleistocene chronology. The methods which were to fill the gaps and change our thinking radically were at best in their infancy, or else not yet dreamed of. Archaeologists seemed to catch on only slowly to the significance of the Marine Isotope stages, or Oxygen Isotope Stages as they were then called, although there was good literature about them available from quite early in the decade. We speculated rather daringly that loyalty to our familiar named British Pleistocene stages, based on the East Anglian sequence, might be causing us to miss out a whole interglacial somewhere, but we had no inkling of the true complexity of the Pleistocene climatic succession, and could only guess what its driving forces were. As for Neanderthals, most people viewed them as a rather late evolutionary development of mainly European significance, and their real business was to make Mousterian industries in France and other parts of Continental Europe. Indeed, if you read Christopher Stringer's Introduction to Human Evolution in this volume, you will soon realise that the clear picture on a world scale, which he is able to set out, depends mainly on finds which were made many years later on – those of the Atapuerca sites, including Sima de los Huesos, are a good example. Far too often, in the 1970s, the archaeologists were working in their own world, treating the geologists and the human palaeontologists as not very accessible scholars in other disciplines. One of the very best things about the Pontnewydd dig was that, right from the start, Stephen Aldhouse-Green was determined to make it an interdisciplinary project of Quaternary Research, and I wanted to emphasise here that in the late 1970s that was something rare and visionary in Britain, though well enough known in some other contexts – for example, amongst those working on the earliest Palaeolithic sites in East Africa. The work at Pontnewydd reaped rich rewards from its interdisciplinary nature: history shows that the field seasons there between 1978 and 1995 coincided with a period of explosive development in Archaeological Science, to which British researchers made important contributions, and also with an unprecedented level of new discoveries of Palaeolithic sites and hominid fossils, all over the world. Both of these revolutions, as one can reasonably call them, have continued, with no slackening of pace, throughout Pontnewydd's phase of post-excavation study. Stephen set out in 1978 to examine a small and not very easy cave site in a remote area of north Wales, of which little more was known than that, a hundred years earlier, antiquarians digging there had recovered stone tools, Pleistocene faunal remains, and an archaic looking human tooth (which – can you believe it? – was subsequently lost). This volume shows the real significance and context of Pontnewydd Cave and its contents, which simply could not have been predicted at the outset, and along the way the site became a testing ground for several of the new techniques.

I make these points, with no space to develop them further, simply as something the reader may like to keep in mind when following the detailed exposition in this volume of the archaeological, geological, faunal and human palaeontological evidence from Pontnewydd Cave. In the final outcome, we see a very specific human community, living at one of the remotest points of the whole Palaeolithic world as we know it at present, and we learn that the people had admirable resources of game, and some unusual but very serviceable rocks from which to make their tools. They did not come here frequently or stay long, and many of the detailed questions we would like to ask are unanswerable, because the archaeological material is very far from being in a primary context. Throughout the text, however, Stephen Aldhouse-Green and his co-authors are concerned to keep the people themselves clearly in mind. We have learned quite a lot about the local landscape in which they dwelt, but we can say little or nothing about the precise route by which they arrived, and we do not know whether they pushed on further: is it too much to hope that other traces of them may have survived in North Wales or in those areas of north-west England that are at present a blank on the Lower and Middle Palaeolithic distribution map?

I warmly commend the chapters which follow to the reader, not least those at the beginning and end, which give a real sense of how much this long project has meant to all those who were involved in it over so many years. I visited many of the field seasons myself, and various students of ours at Oxford took an active part: I remember with great pleasure my annual pilgrimages to the beautiful Elwy valley, and watching the work expand and unfold. Quite apart from the excitement of the archaeological operation, and the latest finds, one could not make even a short visit without getting some sense of the aura of Pontnewydd Cave and its surroundings. The Cefn caves have been regarded as special places by many people in recent centuries, and it may well be that they were special in much the same way to a group of Early Neanderthals, a quarter of a million years or so ago.

# Pontnewydd – A Personal Prologue

## Stephen Aldhouse-Green

*But I was in search of love in those days, and went full of curiosity and the faint, unrecognized apprehension that here, at last, I should find that low door in the wall ... which opened on an enclosed and enchanted garden[1]*
Evelyn Waugh – *Brideshead Revisited.*

### The *Traumfahrt* ends

A *Traumfahrt* is a dream journey. Such journeys to far off places and to the world of ancient myth were one of the literary devices used by the Czech writer Franz Kafka (Urzidil 1968, 62). For me, the work at Pontnewydd was just such a journey. Indeed, I know that many of my colleagues who worked at the site were similarly entranced by its remarkable aura. It seems appropriate, therefore, to offer the reader a brief personal statement of the reasons that led me to Pontnewydd and kept me there for so long.

### Poetry and prose

I cannot begin to describe the pleasure I have drawn from Gladys Mary Coles's poem on my excavations of Pontnewydd Cave, here reproduced with her permission. Her theme is that the hunters are no longer the Neanderthals, but the archaeologists.

#### Pontnewydd Cave, Valley of the Elwy
*These trowels unlock the earth*
*deftly lift wedges like chocolate gateau*
*chink on clinker, cola cans*
*the flat tongues of flint.*

*Within the cave's cool dark, again*
*men and women cluster, crouch*
*over prehistoric fires, forage*
*for likely bones, appropriate stones.*

*Excited by a possibility, they chunter*
*sifting the soil tenderly, harvesting*
*fragments of something, someone –*
*the worn milk tooth of a child, born*
*a quarter of a million years before the Nazarene,*
*an adult's ground-down molar*

*bones of a bear's forearm*
*the flakes of tools, leaf-shaped spearheads.*

*Satisfied, they seal the sepulchre,*
*depart with their hunting equipment:*
*silence reclaims the hillside*
*where, high above the wooded valley,*
*limestone reflects sunlight, signals*
*to the tawny Elwy, as it slides*
*seeking the once-carboniferous sea.*
Gladys Mary Coles 1992.

### Silbury Hill, where it all began

Silbury was the place where my fascination with worlds of darkness began. It is the largest artificial mound in Neolithic Europe but no-one knew its purpose. Nobody knows it now. Richard Atkinson thought he knew, believing it to be the burial place of the builder of Stonehenge. His words are:

*Yet who but he should sleep, like Arthur or Barbarossa, in the quiet darkness of a sarsen vault beneath the mountainous pile of Silbury Hill? And is not Stonehenge itself his memorial?*
Atkinson 1956, 165.

Atkinson undoubtedly believed in the existence of a 'barbarian British king, whose voice and gifts spoke loudly enough to be heard even in the cities of the Mediterranean' (1956, 164). It all now seems a little oversimplified and improbable, but the development of a sound theoretical framework for archaeology was still awaited.

I was a student of Richard's and so naturally took part in the first two seasons of the Silbury excavations in 1968 before leaving to take up my first archaeological appointment in the University of Khartoum. Silbury was a huge project in its day but my interest in it was as much experiential as academic. Our strategy was to access the very centre of the hill by locating and making safe a tunnel dug by John Merewether, Dean of Hereford, in 1849. Three shifts of three people – each shift composed of two mining students and one archaeologist – covered the 24 hour day. There was normally only room for three

*Figure 1. Silbury Hill 2007, the Merewether/Atkinson tunnel.*

people to work in the tunnel at any one time, and under such circumstances, one developed considerable intimacy with the hill, especially in the dark and magical hours of the night.

Silbury created my passion for working underground. But there is a sequel to this tale. In 2007, the hill was opened up again in order to consolidate it. As part of this work, the Merewether/Atkinson tunnel was reopened (Figure 1). On 21st July, I revisited Silbury and was shocked to find that none of the joy and excitement came back to me. I saw instead a decayed tunnel with its massive steel rings rusted and leaning. The planks that had formed its roof and walls had totally decomposed. Moreover, the tunnel's metal structure, for the most part, now stood proud of the chalk hill into which it once had fitted so tightly. What I saw was a metaphor for old age, impotence and death. The Silbury that I had known in 1968 was the focus for a series of academic enquiries, full of excitement, possibility, and the challenge of the unknown. By contrast, in 2007, the concern lay instead with consolidation and conservation, safety and security. These concerns did not speak to me.

In truth, I was just as glad to leave the tunnel on this occasion as I used to be when, after a demanding night shift, I left the hill to have breakfast with the other members of my team. It was normally already day when we emerged from the darkness of that twentieth century passage grave but sometimes I imagined that I had encountered Dawn as

she entered the tunnel, when:

> *... down the long and silent street,*
> *The dawn, with silver-sandalled feet,*
> *Crept like a frightened girl.*
> Oscar Wilde – *The Harlot's House.*

On 21st September 2007, word reached me that the Atkinson tunnel had collapsed on the day after my visit. The dream was over.

## In praise of darkness

Whether modern twenty-first century humans can see the world through Neanderthal eyes is undoubtedly arguable. I would, however, join with many scholars in believing that Neanderthals were more like us than not and that, if they can be described as 'other', this is more likely to have arisen from differing historical trajectories than from inherent differences. It may be, however, that many Neanderthals lived lives reminiscent of the childhood of Jean-Paul Sartre (1964, 96), that were solitary, lacking both 'hearth and home':

> *Je viellissais dans les ténèbres, je devenais un adulte solitaire, sans père et sans mère, sans feu ni lieu, presque sans nom.*
> Jean-Paul Sartre – *Les Mots.*

Neanderthals lived in an unconstructed landscape. Their closest approach to a built environment was probably the natural 'architecture' of caves, I have argued elsewhere that Neanderthals possessed a 'sense of place' and that caves may, in consequence, have been recognized as landmarks, even as 'home'. It may be that the growing use of caves by Neanderthals left to a conceptualization not only of the worlds of light and darkness but also of the terrors that waited in the depths.

The poet and writer Jorge Luis Borges (1899–1986) was an Argentinian with family roots in England and Spain. Fluent in English and Spanish, he wrote in a kind of Spanish baroque. The feature which led me to him was his disability, his blindness. When I was digging Pontnewydd Cave in the 1980s, I brought with me, one season, a collection of poems called *In Praise of Darkness* (*Elogio de la Sombra*). In the darkness of a cave which once had been both home to hibernating bears and, at times, the den of such carnivores as the lion, wolf and leopard, these poems took on a new meaning. The poem that spoke to me most directly was simply called *Labyrinth*:

> *Forget the onslaught of a bull that is a man ... He does not exist.*
> *Hope for nothing: not even the wild beast in the darkness.*
> *No aguardes la embestida del toro que es un hombre ... No existe.*
> *Nada esperes.*
> *Ni siquiera en el negro crepsculo la fiera.*
> Jorge Luis Borges – *Labyrinth/Laberinto.*

It was somehow very easy to believe that something lurked in the darkness of the recesses of Pontnewydd Cave. But deep and dark caves were certainly special places in the later Palaeolithic as at the painted cave of Chauvet, or, again, in numerous Magdalenian cave-sanctuaries.

Caves and other monuments lend themselves to hierophanies and to myth. We see this in Borges's story of the *Circular Ruins* in which a man travels to the site of an ancient temple where he 'dreams' another human being. The dénouement comes unexpectedly at the very end of the story when the dreamer finally understands that he himself was just a character in someone else's dream.

> *Con terror, que el tambien era una apariencia, que otro estaba soñandolo*
> > Jorge Luis Borges – *Circular Ruins.*

## MacNeice and Kafka

I had grown up in the 1940s and 50s, a child of the urban blitz-scapes of post-war Bristol and also, of a failed marriage, separation and divorce. Reading Louis MacNiece's poem *Autobiography* still takes me back to that unhappy world.

> *In my childhood trees were green.*
> *And there were plenty to be seen.*
>
> *My mother wore a yellow dress;*
> *Gentle, gently, gentleness.*
>
> *When I was five the black dreams came;*
> *Nothing after was quite the same.*
>
> *The dark was talking to the dead;*
> *The lamp was dark beside my bed.*
> > Louis MacNiece – *Autobiography*

The Czech writer Franz Kafka is often attributed with the creation of a nightmare world. But when I discovered Kafka at about the age of fourteen through his books *The Trial* and *The Castle* (*Der Prozess* and *Das Schloss*) I found that they spoke to me not of an unreal world of nightmare but of a very real world of disempowerment. As Kafka put it '*alles geht vom Schloss aus*', meaning that all power emanated from unknown, unknowable and unreachable officials residing in the centres of authority symbolized in this case by the eponymous Castle (Wood 2003, 69). In Kafka's short story *Before the Law*, successive doors are guarded by doorkeepers, 'each more powerful than the last', but these keepers may know 'nothing of the law' that they are guarding (Kafka 1978, 127–129; Wood 2003, 58). In all of these stories, the important part of Kafka's literary creation lies not in his scenes of nightmare but rather, in the apparent perception by those involved in these oneiric experiences, these *Traumfährten*, of their normality (Wood 1924, 24).

## Miranda

I want to pay homage here to my wonderful wife Miranda. We studied archaeology together at Cardiff under Richard Atkinson and married on 3rd January 1970. Every day together has been a day of great happiness and the pleasure increases with time. Miranda was in at the start of Pontnewydd and was a key member of the small group who visited the then Major David Williams Wynn at Plas-yn-Cefn on spec. in order to gain permission to excavate. In the early years of the dig Miranda worked on site, in charge of processing the finds, but later her rapidly developing career frequently took her away from the cave. Miranda has enriched my life in many ways but particularly with early music and Shakespeare. The following quotation will recall to all who took part in the dig, and perhaps even the Neanderthal one-time residents, just how bad the weather can be at Pontnewydd:

> *Things that love night*
> *Love not such nights as these; the wrathful skies*
> *Gallow[2] the very wanderers of the dark,*
> *And make them keep their caves.*
> > William Shakespeare *King Lear* Act III, scene ii.

## The changing social world

The Bank Holiday walk to Cefn Caves was a rural institution that lasted until well into the twentieth century. Set against the wider British scene, this can be viewed as part of a series of changes starting from the movement of population from the countryside to the cities which began with the onset of the 'Industrial Revolution' in the latter half of the eighteenth century. The concomitant development of steam technology led to the growth of the railways in the middle of the nineteenth century. Even so, for many, if not perhaps even for most, 'life was local'. The real change came in the 1920s with the growth of motorized transport replacing the horse and horse-drawn carriage; the arrival of rural bus services, in the form of the replacement of the wagon by the charabanc; and through the appearance of the radio which brought news of a 'world elsewhere' to remote rural communities.

Such a situation is well-documented in Laurie Lee's *Cider with Rosie*, set in the Slad valley near Stroud in Gloucestershire. When I began work at Pontnewydd in the late 1970s, Cefn had become a minor tourist attraction and visitors regularly availed themselves of the free car park generously provided by the landowner and, just as regularly emptied the collection box provided there for the upkeep of the paths. Graffiti began to appear on the trees – particularly the mysterious acronym 'L.F.C.' – and some visitors (who had probably never previously climbed anything higher than the top floor of a double-decker bus) for reasons plausibly connected with establishing themselves as alpha-males, began to perform displays of the 'human fly act' on the dangerous and towering cliffs known as Cefn Rocks. It had to come to an end and the need for a site on which to dump spoil from the deep New Entrance excavations eventually provided the means of closure.

## Pontnewydd revisited

I began this Prologue with a quotation from Waugh's *Brideshead Revisited* and, so, I will end. But first I will recall first my departure from the site. I left Cefn Village Hall (the *Neuadd Owen*) and travelled downhill to the bridge (*y bont*) on the valley floor. My route lay down the 'new road' of 1820, with the old 'hollow way' on its left, I passed the cave and, lower down the Old Post Office where Hughie Jones who had visited the excavations in 1978, was born eighty years earlier and had lived as a child. Hughie had known Professor William Boyd Dawkins between about 1903 and 1908 when he used to visit Cefn School in order to talk to the children about the caves. On the other side of the bridge lay the Dolben Arms, where A. D. Lacaille had stayed during his reconnaissance of Welsh caves in 1948. Beyond the Dolben, the road ran on the far side of the valley and presented spectacular views of Cefn Rocks. At Pont-y-Trap the road moved steeply up the valley-side into the woodland where I had once disturbed a herd of fallow deer at dawn. On and up the vale of Cyfreddin I continued until finally:

> *... I turned back ... to take ... my last view ... [and] felt that I was leaving part of myself behind, and that wherever I went afterwards I should feel the lack of it, and search for it hopelessly, as ghosts are said to do ... A door had shut, the low door in the wall I had sought and found [before]; open it now and I should find no enchanted garden.*
>
> Evelyn Waugh – *Brideshead Revisited*.

*Notes*

1 It is interesting that Waugh refers to an enclosed garden as a place of enchantment, for the etymology of the word 'paradise' derives from the Greek words παρα and τειχος, meaning 'walled around'.

2 The word means 'frighten' and is an obsolete form of 'gally'; the words are spoken by Kent on the heath.

# Key

|  |  |
|---|---|
| (black filled) | in situ stalagmite (stal A) |
| (cross-hatched) | slumped in situ stalagmite (stal B) |
| (stippled) | derived/rafted stalagmite |
| (oval) | boss |
| (diagonal) | flowstone on wall |
| (curve) | wall |
| (empty) | dripline |
| (grid) | cemented layer |
| (hatched) | exotic |
| (pattern) | clay |
| (grey) | corroded limestone |
| (irregular) | bedrock |
| (vertical lines) | laminated travertine |

| Boundary | |
|---|---|
| ———————— | sharp boundary |
| – – – – – – – – | diffuse boundary |
| ·················· | extrapolated boundary |
| —·—·—·—·—· | edge of excavation |

| | | |
|---|---|---|
| LT | — | Laminated Travertine |
| UCS | — | Upper Clays and Sands |
| UB | — | Upper Breccia |
| UB/UCSm | — | Upper Breccia with UCS matrix |
| UB/Sbm | — | Upper Breccia with Silt beds matrix |
| uSb | — | unstructured Silt beds |
| sSb | — | structured Silt beds |
| LB | — | Lower Breccia |
| BI | — | Buff Intermediate |
| OI | — | Orange Intermediate |
| Ic | — | Intermediate Complex |
| USG | — | Upper Sands and Gravels |
| LSG | — | Lower Sands and Gravels |

## Site Recording System

Excavated areas of the cave are differentiated using an alphabetical prefix A, B, C *etc.* (see Figure 6.1) and are differentiated in the text by being named Area A, Area B *etc.* All finds are numbered within the site areas and accordingly carry the area prefixes.

Two horizontal recording systems were used at the site. The first, used principally during excavation, is a single system of numbered one metre squares (*e.g.* K21, G4). The second used during surveying and in the figures in this book is a metric co-ordinate system which locates squares by their north-west corners: for example H20 is also 197/99 and the square centimetre at its north-west corner, is 197.00/99.00. The horizontal co-ordinates are permanently marked on site by metal hooks set into the cave-roof.

The vertical co-ordinate system was measured from two metal rawlbolts located in the cave-wall. Site datum was taken to be 100.00 m this equates to 90.473 m O.D.

All artefacts, identifiable bones, stalagmite and all flint (whether worked or not) were three-dimensionally recorded within metre squares using x, y and z co-ordinates where:

x = the distance from north to south

y = the distance from west to east.

z = the levelled height relative to site datum.

See Green 1984a, 20–21 for a more detailed account of the recording system used.

# 1. An Introduction to Human Evolution, and the Place of the Pontnewydd Cave Human Fossils

## Chris Stringer

The earliest stages of human evolution took place in Africa between about 7 million and 2 million years ago, and it was there that typical hominin features such as bipedalism, canine reduction, carnivory and stone tool technology had their beginnings. The term hominin refers to the lineage of human and human-like species post-dating our divergence from the lineage of our closest living relatives, the chimpanzees. Genetic data suggest that the human lineage diverged from that of chimpanzees around 6 million years ago, but until recently there was little relevant fossil evidence from this time period. Now, with the finds of *Ardipithecus* from Ethiopia, *Orrorin* from Kenya, and *Sahelanthropus* from Chad, we have material that may lie close to the ultimate origins of humanity. However, it is not yet clear how these finds relate to humans, chimpanzees, and to each other, and it is not until about 4 million years ago, with the appearance of australopithecines ('Southern apes'), that the picture becomes somewhat clearer (Wood and Lonergan 2008; Klein 2009; Stringer and Andrews 2011).

At least eight species of australopithecines are now known, stretching from Chad and Ethiopia to the location of the first discoveries, South Africa. These different species are sometimes grouped into 'gracile' and 'robust' forms, with the latter showing a range of specializations, especially in powerful jaws and enlarged molar teeth. Some experts prefer to formalize this distinction by grouping the gracile species in the genus *Australopithecus*, and the robust forms into the separate genus *Paranthropus* ('Beside humans'). Even though it is known from fossils and ancient tracks that the australopithecines were bipedal, like humans, they still showed many skeletal differences from us, and hence they are not usually regarded as true humans – that is, members of our genus, *Homo*. For that status, a brain size above the 350–550 millilitre volume of australopithecines and modern African apes would be expected, along with features such as a less projecting face, a more prominent nose, smaller teeth, and a human-like body shape. Where it could be determined, it might also be expected that other human features such as regular tool production, high levels of carnivory, and a relatively long period of growth and development, might be present. For the australopithecines, these human features cannot definitely be recognized. But while the last australopithecines still lived in southern and eastern Africa, more advanced hominins had appeared and were living alongside them; these are usually regarded as the first humans and are often assigned to the species *Homo habilis* ('Handy Man').

By about 2.3 million years ago, these new types of hominin had appeared in the fossil record of eastern and southern Africa. The finds are isolated and rather incomplete, but include a lower jaw from Uraha in Malawi, the side of a cranium from Chemeron in Kenya, and an upper jaw from Hadar in Ethiopia. At the slightly earlier date of about 2.5 million years ago, the first recognized stone tools were being manufactured, and these evolutionary and behavioural events may have marked the advent of the earliest true humans, who are often assigned to the species *Homo habilis*. This member of the genus *Homo* was named in 1964 by Louis Leakey and colleagues on the basis of fossils found at Olduvai Gorge in Tanzania, now known to date to between 1.5 and 1.8 million years ago. *Homo habilis* was regarded as intermediate between australopithecines and later humans, and fragments of skull were used to estimate a brain size of about 700 millilitres, above the values for australopithecines and the largest-brained apes. The back teeth were large, but narrow, compared with those of earlier hominins. Further material attributed to *Homo habilis* has been recovered from Koobi Fora in northern Kenya and neighbouring areas since 1969. These include a number of partial skulls, mandibles, and, from the same sites, a hip bone and various limb bones. In addition, there were simple stone tools, all dating from the period between about 1.5 and 2.0 million years ago. The specimens are generally known from their Kenya National Museum catalogue numbers, and the initials of the original site name, East Rudolf (later renamed East Turkana).

Probably the most famous of these fossils is KNM-ER 1470, found in 1972. This skull had a large brain (volume about 750 millilitres) and was originally dated to more than 2.5 million years ago, subsequently revised to about 1.9 million years. The braincase had a more human shape than is found in australopithecines, but the face was flat and very high, with prominent and wide australopithecine-like cheekbones. Although no teeth were preserved, the spaces for them were large by human standards. There are correspondingly large jaws and teeth in other specimens from the same levels at Koobi Fora, and some skull fragments indicate an even larger brain than in KNM-ER 1470. If hip and leg bones found in the same deposits belong to the species, they indicate that some of these very early humans were large and apparently rather similar to the later species *Homo erectus* in aspects of their body structure. The specimens from Koobi Fora discussed so far have often been assigned to *Homo habilis*. However, there are further finds from Koobi Fora that complicate the picture of early human evolution. These include specimen KNM-ER 1813, a small skull with a brain volume of only 510 millilitres, which nevertheless looks more 'human' in its face and upper jaw than does the 1470 skull, and KNM-ER 1805, which has teeth like 1813, a face more like 1470, a brain capacity of about 580 millilitres, and a braincase with a primitive crest along the midline – a feature otherwise only found in large australopithecines among early hominins. The meaning of this great variation in morphology is still unclear, but it may be that *Homo habilis* was not the only human-like inhabitant of eastern and southern Africa about 2 million years ago.

Further evidence of this complexity has come from a subsequent discovery at Olduvai of parts of a skull and a skeleton of a small-bodied hominin (OH 62) from the lowest levels, which had previously yielded *Homo habilis* fossils. Features of the fragmentary skull are similar to those of some *Homo habilis* fossils, yet the rest of the skeleton more closely resembles those of much more ancient australopithecines. While some experts still believe that *Homo habilis* had a very variable body size, it now seems more likely that there were at least two forms of early *Homo*, one large and the other small, with the small species retaining australopithecine features in the limbs. One suggestion is that the large forms, such as 1470, represent a distinct species, *Homo rudolfensis*, while the smaller ones would still be classified in the original species, *Homo habilis*. If this view is accepted, the oldest finds mentioned, from Uraha and Chemeron, would represent *Homo rudolfensis,* while the Hadar upper jaw would be a genuine *habilis* (Wood and Lonergan 2008).

However, although many experts regard the *Homo habilis* and *Homo rudolfensis* fossils as belonging to the genus *Homo*, they still lacked several 'human' features. These include our distinctive long-legged and linear body shape, an extension of childhood growth and development, and higher levels of encephalization (enlargement of brain relative to body size). These only really become evident around 1.8 million years ago, and are manifested in the species *Homo erectus* ('Erect Man'). This species is currently first recognized in the fossil record of eastern Africa, and it persisted for well over a million years

in some parts of the world. *Homo erectus* was the first human species known to have spread out of Africa to Asia (although *Homo floresiensis*, discussed below, may provide evidence of an even earlier dispersal) (Figure 1.1). Most scientists believe that the African and Asian fossils assigned to *Homo erectus* represent a single species, but a minority feel that the earliest African fossils represent a more primitive, and presumably ancestral, species called *Homo ergaster* (Wood and Lonergan 2008; Klein 2009; Stringer and Andrews 2011).

If we accept the majority view, early examples of *Homo erectus* are known from northern Kenya, on the east side (Koobi Fora and Ileret) and west side (Nariokotome) of Lake Turkana. At the eastern sites skulls (*e.g.* KNM-ER 3733, 3883 and 42700) and various other fragments have been found, while at Nariokotome the nearly complete skeleton of a boy (KNM-WT 15000) was discovered in 1984. These fossils are characterized by brain sizes of some 700–900 millilitres (averaging well above those of earlier African fossils), but the braincase was relatively long, flattened, and angular. The brow ridges were prominent, whilst the face was less projecting than in earlier human-like species, with evidence of a more prominent nose (another typical human feature). The Nariokotome boy's skeleton shows that although he was only about 9 years old at death, he was already about 168 centimetres (5 ft 6 in.) tall and well built. He had the long-legged but narrow-bodied build found in many of today's tropical humans, but there were also some unusual features in his spinal column and rib cage. Nevertheless, his skeleton below the neck was unmistakably that of a human.

Other examples of early *Homo erectus* are known from Olduvai Gorge, where a skull dated to about 1.2 million years ago was discovered in 1960. This strongly built skull (OH 9) has a brain volume of about 1,050 millilitres, a flat forehead, and a very thick brow ridge. Later finds from Olduvai (less than 1 million years old) include jaw fragments, a robustly built hip bone and partial thigh bone (OH 28), and a small and more lightly built skull (OH 12), which represents either an extreme variant of the *Homo erectus* type or perhaps even an entirely separate species. Elsewhere in Africa, fossils attributed to *Homo erectus* have been found in Kenya (*e.g.* Baringo), and further afield at localities such as Buia (Eritrea), Algeria (Tighenif), Morocco (*e.g.* Aïn Marouf and the Thomas quarries), Ethiopia (*e.g.* Daka and Melka Kontoure), and South Africa (*e.g.* Swartkrans).

By 1.6 million years ago, *Homo erectus* was also present in western and eastern Asia, with particularly rich finds dating from about 1.75 million years ago from Dmanisi in Georgia (Rightmire *et al.* 2006; Lordkipanidze *et al.* 2007). These latter specimens are primitive and varied enough to raise fundamental issues about the origins of the species. Some researchers have even used them and the enigmatic fossil material assigned to *Homo floresiensis,* from Liang Bua, on the Indonesian island of Flores, to question the orthodox view that *Homo erectus* originated in Africa and dispersed from there. Instead, they have argued that a

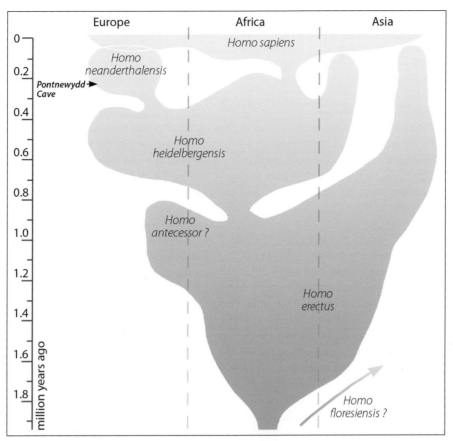

*Figure 1.1. A representation of the later stages of human evolution out of Africa and into Asia and Europe. We now know there was an additional Asian descendant population of* Homo heidelbergensis, *known as the 'Denisovans'.*

more primitive human or even pre-human species emerged from Africa before 2 million years ago, and evolved in Asia to give rise to the Dmanisi people, the *Homo erectus* populations of the Far East, and the Flores hominins. Some groups then re-entered Africa and evolved into the later forms of humans known from that continent.

The East Asian populations are best known from the finds of 'Java Man' in the 1890s and 'Peking Man' in the 1930s, although many additional finds have since been made in both Indonesia and China. The Javanese finds are generally earlier in date, and more robust, with relatively small brain volumes, although there is also an enigmatic sample of shin bones and skulls, lacking faces, from Ngandong (Solo) in Java, which may represent a late-surviving descendant form. The East Asian finds show general differences from the African fossils of *Homo erectus*; the skulls are often more strongly reinforced with ridges of bone, and the walls of the skulls are generally thicker. The fragmentary bones of the rest of the skeleton known from Zhoukoudian (the 'Peking Man' cave site) are strongly built, like their equivalents from Africa. One of the thigh bones found in the Javanese excavations in the 1890s looks rather more modern and research suggests that it may be geologically younger than the *Homo erectus* skulls.

Information about the way of life of *Homo erectus* has been gathered from both caves and open sites. The early African and the Asian representatives used flake tools

manufactured from local materials such as lava, flint, and quartz, but from about 1.5 million years ago African groups produced larger, bifacially worked tools, such as handaxes and cleavers. These were also used by post-*Homo erectus* peoples in Europe and western Asia from at least 500,000 years ago. The *Homo erectus* peoples were nomadic hunters and gatherers, although living more simply and opportunistically than any hunter-gatherers alive today. Their teeth were similar to our own, albeit larger, and indicate a mixed diet of meat and plant foods.

### *Homo antecessor* **and** *Homo heidelbergensis*

We now know from archaeological evidence that southern Europe was populated around 1.5 million years ago, not long after the time of the Dmanisi site in Georgia. Fossil human remains that may represent these early Europeans are known from Sima del Elefante and Gran Dolina, part of the Atapuerca complex of sites in northern Spain. The oldest material, from Elefante, consists of the front part of a jawbone and a hand bone, dated at about 1.2 million years old. The somewhat more complete material from Gran Dolina dated to about 800,000 years, has been assigned to a new human species called *Homo antecessor* ('Pioneer Man'), characterized by a combination of primitive features found in early *Homo* fossils from Africa and Dmanisi, and some more derived features also found in Chinese *Homo erectus* (Bermúdez de Castro *et al.* 2008; Carbonell *et al.* 2008). The earliest occupation of northern Europe, recorded archaeologically at East Anglian sites such as Pakefield and Happisburgh (Parfitt *et al.* 2005; 2010; Stringer 2007; 2010), overlaps the time-frame of *Homo antecessor*, and it may well have been this species which undertook the first colonizations of Europe at higher latitudes.

By about 600,000 years ago, another human species had appeared: *Homo heidelbergensis*. The applicable fossil remains have sometimes been known by the unsatisfactory term 'archaic *Homo sapiens*' (implying that they belong to the same species as modern humans), but it seems more appropriate to regard them as a distinct species, one which has been named after the 1907 discovery of a lower jaw at Mauer, near Heidelberg, Germany (Stringer 2002). This species had a larger average brain size (around 1,100–1,300 millilitres in volume) than *Homo erectus*, with a taller, parallel-sided braincase. There were also reductions in the reinforcements of the skull and in the projection of the face in front of the braincase, an increase in the prominence of the face around the nose, and changes in the base of the skull that might indicate the presence of a vocal apparatus of more modern type. The rest of the skeleton is not so well represented in the fossil record (*e.g.* there are disparate bones from Broken Hill in Zambia, and a partial tibia from Boxgrove in Sussex, England), but what evidence there is suggests that *Homo heidelbergensis* was at least as strongly built in the body as was *Homo erectus*.

It is not generally agreed which particular fossils from 250,000 to 600,000 years ago actually represent *Homo heidelbergensis*, although African specimens such as the material from Broken Hill or Kabwe (Zambia), Elandsfontein (South Africa) and Bodo (Ethiopia) are usually included by those who accept that *Homo heidelbergensis* extended outside of Europe. Similarly, in Europe, there has been dispute about whether the fossils from Mauer (Germany), Vértesszöllös (Hungary), Petralona (Greece), Bilzingsleben (Germany), and Boxgrove (England) represent 'advanced' *Homo erectus, Homo heidelbergensis,* or ancestral Neanderthals. It appears that *Homo erectus* persisted in the Far East until at least 400,000 years ago, and the Ngandong (Solo) remains from Java may be as young as 50,000 years. However, in China there is evidence that after 400,000 years *Homo erectus* was succeeded by more derived populations exemplified by the skull from Dali, and the partial skeleton from Jinniushan, which might represent a new species, or even local examples of *Homo heidelbergensis*. There is a comparable partial skull from deposits of the Narmada River in western India, which is similarly difficult to classify. These Asian specimens may eventually turn out to be examples of the population known as 'Denisovans', identified from distinctive ancient DNA in fragmentary fossils from Denisova Cave, Siberia (Stringer 2011).

## Neanderthals and Modern Humans

By about 400,000 years ago, further evolutionary changes in *Homo heidelbergensis* led to the differentiation of a distinct lineage in Europe: that of the Neanderthals (*Homo neanderthalensis*). Early examples are recognized from sites such as Swanscombe (England), Atapuerca Sima de los Huesos (Spain), and Ehringsdorf (Germany), and indeed evolutionary continuity is such that there are disputes about whether the Sima material might alternatively represent a late form of *Homo heidelbergensis* (some dating of the Sima material would place the fossils at more than 530,000 years old (Bischoff *et al.* 2007)). By 130,000 years ago, the late Neanderthals had evolved, characterized by large brains housed in a long and low braincase, with their distinctive faces, dominated by an enormous and projecting nose. The most characteristic Neanderthals were European, but closely related peoples lived in Asia, as far east as Uzbekistan and even (using DNA evidence from fragmentary fossils) southern Siberia, and in Iraq, Syria and Israel. The physique of the Neanderthals seems to have been suited to the conditions of Ice Age Europe, yet by about 30,000 years ago they had apparently become physically extinct over their whole range. However, genomic reconstructions of their DNA suggest that this still survives in Eurasian populations today, as a result of at least isolated occurrences of ancient interbreeding (Stringer 2011).

The disappearance of the Neanderthals from Europe and Asia may have had much to do with the arrival of early modern people (*Homo sapiens*), who potentially competed with them for the available resources, and growing climatic instability between 30,000–50,000 years ago may have exacerbated the situation. These first modern humans were anatomically distinct from Neanderthals, with less prominent brow ridges; higher, shorter, and more rounded skulls; shorter lower jaws with a bony chin (at best only slightly developed in some Neanderthals); and a taller, relatively narrower, and less robust skeleton.

The first modern people known in Asia, from the Israeli sites of Qafzeh and Skhul, had a way of life superficially little different from that of the Neanderthals, although there is some evidence from the structure of their skeletons that they may have exploited their environment more efficiently. In addition, there are signs of greater behavioural complexity in burial patterns and the apparent symbolic use of shell beads and red ochre. However, thermoluminescence and electron spin resonance dating tests suggest that they are between 90,000–120,000 years old, and therefore the same age or even older than many Neanderthal fossils. If this is so, there was potentially a long period of coexistence, or alternating occupation of the region, by early *Homo sapiens* and Neanderthals. By 45,000 years ago, however, modern people seem to have been the sole occupants left in the Middle East.

The dispersal of early modern people (the Cro-Magnons) into Europe probably occurred about 45,000 years ago, and there is evidence of behavioural differences between Neanderthals and early modern people by this time. Although most Neanderthals are associated with Middle Palaeolithic (Middle Old Stone Age) or Mousterian tool industries, the Cro-Magnons are associated with Upper

Palaeolithic industries. These contain narrow blade tools of stone, which could be used to work bone, antler, and ivory, and even to produce engravings and sculptures. However, some of the last Neanderthals in Europe also developed tool industries with Upper Palaeolithic characteristics, suggesting possible contact and even intermixing with the contemporaneous Cro-Magnons.

The ancestors of present-day Europeans, Asians, and the native populations of the American and Australian continents probably shared common ancestors within the past 60,000 years (Endicott *et al.* 2009). The early modern people who reached Australia by at least 40,000 years ago must have used boats or rafts, because even when sea level was at its lowest (with water locked up in the expanded ice caps of the last Ice Age), there were numerous channels still separating the chains of islands leading to Australia and New Guinea. On their way, they evidently encountered surviving archaic humans such as the Denisovans and perhaps also the small and small-brained humanoid form called *Homo floresiensis*, known only from the island of Flores, which may have survived until as recently as 17,000 years ago (Morwood and Jungers 2009). For people to reach the Americas, it would then have been possible to walk from Asia across the land bridge between Siberia and Alaska, or to travel along a more southerly coastal route by island hopping. However, it is still uncertain whether this had happened only by about 14,000 years ago, or several millennia earlier, and there is disputed evidence that distinct populations may have been involved in these early migrations.

So if early modern people did not evolve from the Neanderthals of Europe and Asia, where did they originate? Modern people had appeared in China at least 40,000 years ago, and as we have seen, they had also arrived in Australia by that time. However, there are no fossils that show a convincing local evolution from more archaic predecessors, although this has been claimed by proponents of 'Multiregional Evolution' for China and Australia. In my view, only Africa has credible transitional fossils between pre-modern and modern humans, and it is here that *Homo heidelbergensis* was apparently transformed into *Homo sapiens*. Fossil remains of modern affinities have been discovered at sites such as Border Cave and Klasies River Mouth Caves (South Africa), Guomde (Kenya) and Omo-Kibish and Herto (Ethiopia). The South African remains are between 60,000 and 120,000 years old, while the Guomde skull and femur, and the Omo and Herto fossils, are probably all more than 150,000 years old. Although they can be classified as predominantly modern in anatomy, these people still retained some primitive features and were apparently not yet fully modern in behaviour. The transition from *Homo heidelbergensis* to these early *Homo sapiens* may be represented by fossils of even greater antiquity, such as the Florisbad skull from South Africa, a cranium from Eliye Springs (Kenya), and several fossils from Jebel Irhoud (Morocco).

How the evolution of modern people proceeded in Africa, and what lay behind the transition, is still uncertain.

There is some evidence of an increasing sophistication in African Middle Stone Age industries, which could have promoted evolutionary change, including the beginning of symbolism and even art. Alternatively, following severe climatic changes, geographical isolation and changes in population density may also have been responsible for this. Genetic evidence indicates that all living people are closely related and share common ancestors who lived in Africa during the last 200,000 years (the time range of the first known *Homo sapiens* fossils of modern aspect (Endicott *et al.* 2009)).

## The significance of the Pontnewydd Cave fossils

Amongst the bones and stones in the mudflows at Pontnewydd Cave excavated by Stephen Aldhouse-Green and his team were human teeth and jaw fragments, which I have been studying with Tim Compton, a colleague at the Natural History Museum. The teeth are from at least five people, and it seems likely that the human tooth found and then lost after 1874 was part of this series. They were almost certainly much more complete fossils before they were transported from their original location, and only two of the Middle Pleistocene teeth are now in their original sockets. Judging by dental attrition, three of the individuals were children, one was a young adult, and the last was a mature adult. In chronological terms, the human fossils from Pontnewydd represent an interesting time period in European human evolution, one which is still poorly represented, and for which they are the only record in Britain. At this time, human presence in Britain was apparently in decline, even during interglacial periods, and this has been the subject of much debate (Stringer 2007). However, it is believed that the English Channel had begun at least the earliest stages in its formation, and that the British peninsula was becoming increasingly isolated by the sea during high water stands, and by the development of a major river system flowing south-westwards in the Channel floor during times of lower sea level. Thus the free transit of fauna, including humans, between the continent and Britain was increasingly constrained through the later Middle Pleistocene, as is evidenced by the idiosyncratic composition of British mammal faunas compared with those of mainland Europe (Bridgland and Schreve 2004).

It is assumed that from the time of the Hoxnian Interglacial equivalent to Marine Isotope Stage 11 (around 400,000 years ago) onwards, until MIS 3 (around 40,000 years ago), the humans who episodically colonized Britain were members of an evolving Neanderthal lineage, and the Pontnewydd fossils allow us to test, and support, this assumption. Given the relative rarity of European fossil humans between the rich samples known from Atapuerca Sima de los Huesos (probably around 400,000 years old) and those known from the Croatian site of Krapina (predominantly dated to around 130,000 years ago), they thus provide an important record of Neanderthal evolution. Many of the molars had lost their roots, but where these were preserved, several show the condition of taurodontism, in which the roots merge for much of their length. This unusual conformation is uncommon in most recent human populations, but is present in many Neanderthal fossils, where about half of their molar teeth show it to one degree or another. If this feature had a function, it may have been to confer some advantage where the teeth were suffering heavy wear. While a molar would normally cease to function as a chewing unit when the crown has worn down to root level, the roots of a taurodont tooth can fill with secondary dentine and remain functional for longer.

There are also features on the Pontnewydd tooth crowns, such as crests and cusps, that are typical of Neanderthal teeth, and their size and shape is not dissimilar to the earlier samples from the Sima de los Huesos at Atapuerca, and to the later Neanderthal teeth from Krapina. Overall they fit a European pattern of 'neanderthalization' between about 400,000 and 150,000 years ago. Given the re-deposited nature of the Pontnewydd finds, it is difficult to reconstruct much about the human occupation there. We have no real clues about how these early Neanderthals died and became fossilized, or whether their bodies were left by the occupants or worked over by scavengers. Sites like Krapina show cut-marks on the human bones suggestive (to some) of ancient cannibalism, but no evidence of this survives on the Pontnewydd fossils, although as described here, the teeth do show some evidence of marks inflicted during life. But the very existence of the Pontnewydd fossils is significant, since through their date and their location, the Pontnewydd humans represent the furthest north-westward extent of people prior to the Upper Palaeolithic. They are thus a valuable indication of both Neanderthal biogeography and evolution during the late Middle Pleistocene, and provide valuable comparisons with the larger samples known from mainland Europe.

# 2. The History of the Caves

## Elizabeth A. Walker and Tristan Gray Hulse

*The parish of Cefn Meiriadog, Denbighshire, lies in what is today a tranquil, largely agricultural and most beautiful area of North Wales. The boundary is delineated on its southern and eastern edges by the River Elwy, today flowing eastward from the foothills of Snowdonia to join into the broad valley of the River Clwyd just north of the cathedral city of Llanelwy, St Asaph. At its eastern edge the Elwy has cut its valley through Carboniferous Limestone to leave a dramatic landscape of south facing craggy cliffs peppered with caves above the river below.*

*Anyone familiar with the area will not be surprised to learn that Cefn Meiriadog has the most extended chronological story of any parish in Wales, with a long and dramatic history from its early Neanderthal occupants, mysterious saints, seventeenth century romantic tourists and Victorian scientists trying to make sense of the world. The main locations that reveal this long prehistory are the limestone rocks and caves today known as Cefn Caves and Pontnewydd Cave. This chapter will concern itself with the more recent past, looking at the origins of the names and the myths, legends and history associated with the area and with the discovery and development of knowledge about its caves.*

### Carreg y Tyllfaen: the rocks of Cefn Meiriadog in early history and tradition

*Tristan Gray Hulse*

During the late nineteenth century the Cefn Caves were a landmark on the local tourist trail, and regularly appeared in local travel literature. To cite a single example: Joseph Henry Austen, in his *Companion to St Asaph*, in the section *the neighbourhood of St Asaph*, has the following, illustrated with photographs of the rocks, cave, and natural archway:

> The Narrow Stairs and the celebrated Caves are situated not very far from [Cefn] church. The view as you look across from the Caves is glorious. In summer time there is a guide who will provide you with candles if you care to enter the Caves. Many fossil remains were found here during the explorations that took place when the Caves were discovered.
>
> If you should happen, by mistake, to take the road below that leading to the Caves, you will pass through a natural arch, through which the old road from Abergele to Denbigh used to run in days gone by. The view from the *top* of the Caves is very grand.
>
> Austen 1898, 173–175.

Knowledge about Cefn Caves was for long limited to the above, but we now know the history of the caves was vastly more detailed, curious and interesting. Some time in the 1530s, the Tudor antiquary John Leland noted the following in his Itineraries:

> On the farther ripe of Elwy a 3. or 4. miles above S. Asaphes is a stony rok caullid Kereg thetylluaine [Carreg y tyllfaen], *i.e.* the rok with hole stones, wher a great cave is, having divers romes in it hewid out of the mayne rok.
>
> Toulmin Smith 1906, 99.

This is usually accepted as the earliest mention of Cefn Cave located within the parish of Cefn Meiriadog, but in fact there may be a much earlier plausible, if not certain, reference to the site, in a medieval Latin romance called the *Historia Meriadoci, Regis Cambrie*, the Story of Meriadoc, King of Wales (text and translation, Day 1988).

Cefn Meiriadog came into being only in 1865, when the name was coined for the new parish created by merging two of the townships of the huge medieval Llanelwy/St Asaph parish, Wigfair and Meiriadog. Each township was named for its principal house. Meiriadog, now just a site in the corner of a field overlooking the River Elwy, midway between Bont Newydd and Pont y Ddol, was still a 'house of note' in Edward Lhuyd's time, in the late seventeenth century (Thomas 1883, passim; Morris 1909, 48). The township name is attested from 1256, when it appears as a donation to the monastery/see of Llanelwy in the text of the, at least partially fabricated, foundation charter given in the *Llyfr coch Asaph* (Anon. 1868, 336–338). The personal name Meiriadog was in use in the immediate locality in the medieval period, as the 1334 *Survey of Denbigh* reveals (Vinogradoff and Morgan 1914, 212), but is met with nowhere else in Wales. In fact, outside Cefn Meiriadog, the name is apparently known only in Cornwall, at Camborne, and in Brittany; in the former place exclusively, and in Brittany, mostly, as the name of an obscure early medieval Welsh saint (Doble 1960).

In the central middle ages, and for reasons unknown, the name also came to be used in Brittany as the cognomen (third name) of the fourth century semi-legendary Cynan (Breton, Conan), the brother of Elen of the Hosts, born in Caernarfon, who – according to the Mabinogion tale *The Dream of Macsen* – participated in the military campaign of Elen's husband Magnus Maximus (Macsen Wledig) in Europe, eventually settling in Brittany (Bromwich 1978, 316–318, 341–343, 451–454; G. Jones and T. Jones 2000). Basing himself in part presumably on Breton sources, Geoffrey of Monmouth gave the story of Conanus Meriadocus in his *Historia Regum Britanniae* (V. 9–16; Wright 1985, 52–58; Bartrum 1993, 165–166). The medieval Breton Latin *Vita* of St Mériadec made the Saint a descendant of Conan Mériadec. The person of 'Cynan Meiriadog', it is said, finds no place in authentic medieval Welsh tradition; but the name 'Meiriadog' was eventually given as the cognomen of Cynan in the late sixteenth century, when it was suggested, because of the unique St Asaph place name, that the Caernarfon hero Cynan must have had Denbighshire connections (Bartrum 1993, 166). Because of the extreme rarity of the name, Canon Doble suggested that the Welsh Meiriadog, the Cornish St Meriasek, and the Breton St Mériadec must have been the same person.

The author of the Breton *Vita Mercadoci* (Doble 1960, 124–126, 135–139) knew little about his Saint beyond the liturgical cultus and a number of place names and landscape features bearing his name, which he worked up into an itinerary, and then fleshed out with the legends attached to these, plus a large amount of guesswork. The similarity of name-forms was presumably responsible for making the Saint a descendant of the hero Conan Mériadec. In Camborne (*Ecclesiam ... Sancti Mereadoci* in 1426 – (Orme 1996, 72); in Cornish, *Meriasek* certainly by 1500) the Saint's story is witnessed principally in the late-medieval Cornish vernacular play *Beunans Meriasek* (Doble 1960, 112–116; Thomas 1967, 21–39; translated in Combellack 1988), which used the *Vita Mercadoci*, but embellished it with traditions then adhering to numbers of landscape features in and around Camborne. (In one of these Meriasek hides from a pursuing tyrant under a rock, which he prophesies will afterwards be known as

Carrek Veryasek.) Thomas suggested that 'far and away the most likely candidate' for the site is Reens Rock, opposite the ruined medieval chapel and holy well of St Ia (Thomas 1967, 63). Apart from the place-name, and the survival of the personal name in the middle ages, both in Llanelwy parish, he was completely forgotten in Wales, until sixteenth century antiquarians linked him, via the Conanus Meriadocus of Geoffrey of Monmouth, with the semi-legendary Cynan ab Eudaf Hen, of Caernarfon. Writing *c.*1136, Geoffrey of Monmouth (who, curiously enough, was to be consecrated as the second bishop of Llanelwy in 1152, though he apparently never set foot in his diocese; Anon. 1959, 274–275) further complicated the story of Conan Mériadoc by adding to it a version of the legend of St Ursula and the 11,000 virgins (Bartrum 1993, 635); prompting Baring-Gould to suggest – doubtless, tongue-in-cheek – that the 11,000 virgins must have come, if not specifically from Cefn Meiriadog, then at least from North Wales (Baring-Gould 1903, 149–150).

While it certainly owes something (though perhaps only a little) to the legend of the Welsh Cynan/Breton Conan Mériadec, the *Historia Meriadoci* is actually an Arthurian romance. It appears to have been composed in the late twelfth century (Day 1988, xiv, xvi), is sometimes attributed to Robert of Torigni (ibid. xvii, xxii), and may have been composed in Normandy, though by someone with a considerable knowledge of Welsh traditions – one scholar has even argued that the author must have been Welsh (ibid. xx). The text survives in just two manuscripts, BL Cotton Faustina Bvi (early fourteenth century), and Bodleian Rawlinson B149 (late fourteenth or early fifteenth century). Day thought that 'the Rawlinson is a transcription of the Cotton Faustina', though not everyone has agreed (ibid. xlvi–xlviii). Though the manuscripts are thus 'quite close', they are clearly at least one remove from the original text.

One thing however is not in doubt. The *Historia*, as we know it, is obviously a composite, fusing together a North Welsh account of the childhood of Meriadoc, which has relatively few obvious characteristics of medieval romance literature, and which appears to exhibit a detailed knowledge of the topography of North Wales; with a typical amalgam of romance motifs which serve to incorporate the adult Meriadoc into the Arthurian corpus, and makes of him an Arthurian knight fighting in Europe, but lacks any precise locational information, at least in Britain. Not until he has grown up does Meriadoc first come in contact with the world of Arthur, in the person of Sir Kay.

Meriadoc and his sister Orwen are the twin children of Caradoc, ruler of the kingdom of Cambria (*regnum Kambrie*), whose principal seat 'was under the snowcapped mountain the Cambrians called Snowdon' (*Kambrice Snavdone resonat* Day 1988, 4–5).

In the medieval Welsh tradition represented by *The Dream of Macsen*, Cynan is the son of Eudaf Hen; but, writing in 1604, the Pembrokeshire antiquary George Owen Harry (Anon. 1959, 343) knew that 'Kynan Meriadock' was 'the son of Karadawc, Lord of Meriadock or Denbighland'

(Bartrum 1993, 166). However, in *The Dream* Caradawg is made the father of Eudaf, and, thus, grandfather, rather than father, of Cynan (Bartrum 1993, 101; G. Jones and T. Jones 2000, 76). Thus it would appear that the author of the *Historia* knew, if not *The Dream of Macsen* itself, then at least the body of (pseudo-) genealogical material that went into the make-up of *The Dream*; thus strengthening the connections of the source(s) of the first part of the *Historia* with North Wales.

Orwen is mentioned nowhere else, the only Orwen known to genuine Welsh tradition being the witch of that name in *Culhwch ac Olwen* (G. Jones and T. Jones 2000, 513). Later in the *Historia*, Orwen is abducted and married by Urien Rheged (Day 1988, 45–51) and thus becomes Queen of Scotland; but in Welsh tradition Urien's wife was Modron (Bromwich 1978, 185, 188, 458–463).

The location of Caradoc's 'capital city' (Day's translation of the *Historia's sedes vero regni Caradoci*) is curiously precise (Day 1988, 4–5). A casual reading might suggest Caernarfon/Segontium, the major, and widely-known, civil settlement in north-west Wales at the time of composition; but if so, why is it not named? However, 'under the snowcapped mountain … called Snowdon' is not really an accurate description of the location of Caernarfon, but it would be an accurate description of the location of Dolbadarn Castle; and recent research by Smith strongly suggests that at precisely the time of the composition of the *Historia*, the Welsh Princes had adopted Dolbadarn as their principal court (S. Smith pers. comm. 2004). The first half of the *Historia* has thus an impressively exact knowledge of contemporary North Welsh topography and tradition.

Caradoc is murdered by his brother Griffin, who wants the throne for himself. To prevent his nephew rightfully inheriting as *Rex Cambrie*, Griffin orders that Meriadoc and his sister be 'taken to the forest called Arglud' (*ad silvam que Arglud nuncupatur*), and there killed (Day 1988, 28–29). Arglud is not too far away from *Snavdone*, being still 'within the kingdom' (*in patria* ibid. 39).

Arglud/Alclud has regularly been assumed by modern scholars to be somewhere in Scotland (following the consensus, Day suggests Dumbarton (Day 1988, xxviii)), on or around the Clyde, on the assumption that 'Clud' represents Clyde, and that Clyde and Clwyd cannot be the same word. But Humphrey Lhuyd (or at least his translator – in *The Breviary of Britaine*) knew the Vale of Clwyd as Strathclyde; and Egerton Phillimore suggested that Geoffrey of Monmouth (*Hist. Regum Britanniae* IX.15) must have derived his Bishop Eledenius of Alclud (*pontificalis insula Alsclud Eledemio*; Wright 1985, 112) from St Elidan, of Llanelidan, in the Vale of Clwyd (Bartrum 1993, 234, 240); so that, potentially, a medieval or late medieval/early modern audience would not necessarily have assumed a Scottish location for Arglud. And anyway, since it became clear that the Anglo-Saxon *Cledemutha*, 'Clyde- or Clwyd-mouth', is to be securely identified as Rhuddlan (Edwards 1991, 139), 'Arglud' can easily be accepted as the Vale of Clwyd – which is exactly the location the *Historia* seems to imply.

Meriadoc and his sister are rescued by their guardian Ivor and his wife Morwen, who take the children into hiding in 'the forest of Fleventan' (*ad silvam Fleventanam*: Day 1988, 38–39). While not overstressing the point, it is worth noticing that while the earlier of the two surviving manuscripts of the *Historia* (Cotton Faustina) reads *Fleventana*, the other (Rawlinson) has *Eleventana* (Day 1988, xxviii, 38, f.n. 5). Could Rawlinson have preserved the better reading? When Giraldus Cambrensis, in his *Welsh Itinerary* of 1188, mentions the cathedral of Llanelwy (*Itin. Camb.* ii. 10) – he was writing just at the suggested time of the composition of the *Historia* – he has *sedis Lanelvensis* (Dimock 1868, 137). This conventional Latinization of Llanelwy might suggest that *Eleventana* is in fact a not very corrupted reference to the River Elwy, meaning nothing more than, perhaps, '[the land] along the Elwy'? If so, the passage in the *Historia*, describing the hide-out of Meriadoc and his companions, becomes especially fascinating, because it is so precisely located.

Morwen is otherwise unknown. Ivor cannot be linked to any of the other Ifors mentioned in Welsh tradition (Bartrum 1993, 384–385), but there are possible echoes of the name in the toponomy of the old Llanelwy parish. One of the former townships of St Asaph is Maen Efa, where there is a well named Ffynnon Efa. The named stone and holy well, and the nearby place-name Croes Efa, in Llangwyfan (Davies 1959, 62, 104), are all suggestive of a long-forgotten saint; and as Canon Doble often pointed out with regard to the early 'Celtic' Saints, who have so frequently left behind them no more than a place-name to perpetuate their memories, such forgotten Saints regularly changed their gender (most commonly, male to female) in the records of the high middle ages. Thus, 'Efa' (Latin, *Eva*) could easily have been a man. (For an exactly similar problem with regard to Ivy/Eva place-names in Brittany – here, affecting an interpretation of the Breton cultus of St Divy/David – see Tanguy 1999.) In this respect it is instructive to notice that the Cornish parish of St Mereadoc/Meriasek, Camborne, had a holy well and chapel of St Ia (like Efa, commonly regarded as a form of Eva), while in Brittany St Mériadec's principal foundation at Stival, in the Morbihan, is adjacent to the major parish of Pontivy, whose patron is the (male) Saint Ivy – that is, place-names incorporating the name-forms Efa/Ia/Ivy are found in close proximity to place-names having the name-forms Meiriadog/Mereadoc/Mériadec, in North Wales, Cornwall, and Brittany.

The *Historia* goes on to describe the hiding-place near Arglud found by Ivor:

> In that forest, however, an extremely steep cliff rises called the 'cliff of the eagles' [*rupe aquilarum nuncupata*] where at all time four eagles build their nests high on it, turning their faces always into the four directions of the winds. And in this very cliff are a great cavern, a very beautiful chamber, and various other hollowed-out rooms, with marvellous structures hanging from what is the roof of the cave [*Et ipsa vero et in ipsa rupe aula perampla, perpulcri thalami, diversaque miri operis*

*ad insta testudinis erant incisa edificia* – the *perpulcri thalami* is surely in apposition to the *aula perampla*, rather than indicating a further section of the cave complex?]. It is believed to have been at one time the dwelling place of the Cyclopes, but since that age it has scarcely been seen by anyone, concealed as it is in the depths of that hidden and extremely dense forest.

Day 1988, 38–39.

Here they lived for five years, until Orwen was abducted by Urien, and Meriadoc was captured by Sir Kay. The account of Orwen's abduction further demonstrates that for the *Historia*'s author Arglud was not in Scotland, for we are told that Urien, the King of Scotland (*rex Scocie*), had been visiting the court of Arthur, and that at the time they came upon Orwen Kay 'was escorting him on his return to his own country' (Day 1988, 45); that is, they had not yet reached Scotland. After two years, Morwen followed Orwen to Scotland, while Ivor sought Meriadoc at Arthur's court (nowhere identified), before being reunited with Morwen at Urien's court (ibid. 57).

The name Eagles' Cliff is inexplicable; unless it represents a knowledge of, and then confusion with, the Welsh name for *Snavdone* (later – ibid. 60 – *Snawdown*), Eryri, the Place of Eagles, on the part of the author? The reference to the Cyclopes is similarly puzzling. However, the *Historia* is full of pseudo-Classical references, and the Cyclops Polyphemus lived in a cave (Homer, *Odyssey*), so that here it may be simply an allusion to the hoary antiquity and cave-ness of the cave? However, it is perhaps worth noticing that, well into the twentieth century, a large mound on Bryn Meiriadog was known as Bedd-y-Gawr (Giant's Grave), while Meiriadog himself was identified as a giant who lived in Cefn Cave, near to which is a large boulder identified as a 'pebble' which he once removed from his shoe (Fisher 1915; Rees Jones 2007, 188).

It seems a remarkable coincidence, but the *Historia*'s 'great cavern ... [with] various other hollowed-out rooms' is uncannily like Leland's 'great cave ... having divers romes in it hewid out of the mayne rok'. This is the more surprising in that neither can be considered an exact description of the great natural arch and the higher choked cave mouths in the Cefn Rocks. Indeed, it more plausibly describes the cave system rather than the rock arch. It is unlikely that Leland saw the rocks himself. In the same way that George Owen Harry knew – against the mainstream of Welsh tradition, but with the *Historia* – that Karadawc was the father of Kynan Meriadock, and was moreover the Lord of Meriadock or Denbighland', could Leland have known the *Historia Meriadoci*? If so, it might suggest that lingering local tradition and/or antiquarian speculation had by the mid-sixteenth century identified the cave *ad silvum Eleventanam* of the *Historia* with the Cefn Cave; which in turn would reinforce any impression that this was exactly the force of the North Welsh tradition known to and reworked by the *Historia*'s twelfth century author.

Leland's *Kereg thetylluaine* can definitely be identified with the Cefn Rocks. In an article on local place-names, Fisher wrote:

The old name for what are known as the Cefn Rocks and Caves was *Carreg y Tyllfaen*, where *carreg* has the old meaning of rock or crag. [Fisher then quotes Leland] In an indenture of 1666 among the Plas-yn-Cefn papers it is called *Carreg y twll vaen*.

Fisher 1914, 237.

Edward Lhuyd, *c*. 1698, precisely located the 'great cave' in Wigfair: *Mae Ogo Vawr yn y Wicwer a gelwir Karreg y Tylhvaen* (Morris 1909, 49). In a letter to *Archaeologia Cambrensis* Archdeacon D. R. Thomas quoted Leland before going on to say:

The cave here alluded to is, I have little doubt, the natural opening in the rock through which the old highway from Cefn to Denbigh at one time passed; a little distance below the more famous Pontnewydd Cave, which even as late as 1830, when the late Bishop Stanley of Norwich wrote his interesting notice in the Edinburgh New Philosophical Journal, had not been opened for more than a few feet from its mouth.

Thomas 1872, 160.

Perversely, perhaps, considering that he has just described the 'natural opening ... through which the old highway ... at one time passed', and surely wrongly, the Archdeacon differed from Leland, from E. S. D., whose letter on the subject immediately followed his own in *Archaeologia Cambrensis*, and from Canon Fisher, as to the correct translation of the place-name.

I rather suspect that *thetylluaine* has not so much to do with *tyllau*, 'holes', as with *dylluan*, the 'owl'; and that in less public times it may have been a favourite home for such birds. And in corroboration I may add that I have myself, when exploring the rocks, been saved from falling headlong into one of the *tyllau* by the sudden rise of the *dylluan* close below me.

Thomas 1872, 160.

Anything further is – and can only be – guesswork. But the point about Cefn as a haunt of owls is well made for rodent remains recovered by the recent excavations almost certainly arrived in the cave in the form of pellets of bone regurgitated by owls (Price 2003, 28).

It is at least curious that in two apparently unconnected medieval texts (*Historia Meriadoci* and *Beunans Meriasek*) two persons of the first half of the sixth century having the same exceptionally rare name are said to have hidden from pursuing tyrants in caves in the rock. In tentative outline, my conclusion is that underlying the North Welsh hero and the Cornish Saint is a single early medieval personage called, variously, Meiriadog (Wales), Mereadoc/Meriasek (Cornwall) and Mériadec (Brittany).

## The caves of Cefn Meiriadog, their discovery and exploration

*Elizabeth A. Walker*

The history of work at the caves in north-east Wales is

closely related to developments in the history of geology, the understanding of the origins of the earth and the antiquity of the humans who inhabit it. The knowledge different people gleaned by visiting, looking and digging in the caves at times in the past has contributed to the picture the rest of this volume is able to paint of the caves and their human and animal occupants during the more distant past. This twenty-first century picture is influenced by the development and application of scientific techniques that were not available to the earlier researchers. So, it is important for us to recognize that by looking back in time we are reading the past with our modern eyes. On occasion we may find the early work in the caves frustrating. We might ask why dig so much of the cave deposit away and not leave more for future study? Yet in time, future scientists may well raise the same complaints about the late twentieth or early twenty-first century archaeologists. Today we may feel we are justified in removing the deposits we have from the caves and in taking decisions about what should, and what should not, be retained long-term in museum collections. Yet our decisions are taken in the same spirit as those made by the earlier investigators who grasped the opportunities the caves provided to satisfy their curiosity about the World. We therefore need to be mindful, rather than critical, of the times in which these researchers were working and to remember it was they who broke the ground and laid the foundations from which we have been able to develop our techniques and build our interpretations today.

This chapter will not look in detail at the complete history of geology or cave investigation; as such work has been done amply in other forms (*e.g.* Davies 1969; O'Connor 2007). Instead it will offer a history of some caves, where applicable explaining the specific roles they played in the development of scientific knowledge and the contributions they made to contemporary debates. It will look at the interpretations in an historical way, offering less in the way of modern interpretation, and more on how, why and what was done and found; and the meanings of these findings in the context of the contemporary understanding of the World.

The Cefn Estate is now owned by Sir Watkin Williams Wynn of Plas-yn-Cefn. The connection of the Williams Wynn family with Cefn does not, however, extend back beyond the latter half of the nineteenth century. During the earlier part of that century, the estate was owned by Edward Lloyd. It entered the Williams Wynn family through the marriage on 26th July 1855 of Anna, the daughter and heiress of Edward Lloyd, to Herbert Watkin Williams Wynn (born 29th April 1822; died 22nd June 1862), younger brother of the sixth baronet Sir Watkin Williams Wynn and great-grandfather of the present owner (Aldhouse-Green pers. comm; Owen 2007). Edward Lloyd and members of the Williams Wynn family were involved with some of the exploration of deposits in the caves. They entertained some of the many visiting geologists and played their own parts in the discoveries made on their land.

*Figure 2.1. The rock arch beside the River Elwy at the foot of Cefn Rocks.*

*Figure 2.2. The Old Cefn Cave located within the rock arch.*

## The caves

The old road from Denbigh to Kinmel passed along the Elwy valley through the magnificent natural limestone arch (Figure 2.1) at the bottom of the valley just downstream of the village of Bont Newydd. The first cave to be recorded is located within this arch (Figure 2.2). The cave was originally referred to as Cefn Cave (Stanley 1833, 40) and this appears to have caused some confusion in the literature when, during the early 1830s, two further caves were identified in the rock face above, which also became known as Cefn Caves (ibid. 42). The cave directly above that in the rock arch is still known as Cefn Cave, whilst the second, located a little further to the west, entered the literature as Pontnewydd Cave following its investigation by Thomas McKenny Hughes in 1874 (Hughes and Thomas 1874). This name is used throughout this volume, although it has occasionally also been referred to as Bont Newydd Cave or Bontnewydd Cave (Green 1984, 9). In the absence of two separate names for the caves known as Cefn Caves, and for clarity, the cave within the arch will be referred to here as the Old Cefn Cave and the one above simply as Cefn Cave in part using the terminology Old and New Caves adopted by Davies (1929, 63). A small untouched cave entrance was recorded by A. E. Valdemar in 1970 directly above the entrance to Pontnewydd Cave (Valdemar and Jones 1970). This cave, Cae Gronw, was known about by workers on the Cefn estate for some time, but only underwent formal excavation in 1979, 1980 and 1985, by Stephen Aldhouse-Green, as part of the research described by the rest of this volume.

### The Cefn Caves

With the route of the original road passing through the natural arch at the bottom of the valley it is no surprise to learn that the caves are mentioned historically. Leland's travels took him through the valley in the 1530s and the rocks he mentions have variously been interpreted as the Old Cefn Cave within the natural arch and the main Cefn Cave above (see Gray Hulse above). Thomas Pennant undertook a tour of North Wales 1778–1783 and also would have travelled along the road through the arch. He was clearly aware of the significance of the Elwy valley which he described as travelling 'along most romantic dingles, varied with meadows, woods and cavernous rocks. Neither is [it] destitute of antiquities' (Pennant (reprint) 1991). The first description of an antiquarian investigation of the Old Cefn Cave is supplied by Richard Fenton who recorded having undertaken some investigations in the cave some seven or so years before the day he described in his diary.

> Monday, Sep^r 5th [1808].
> This day opened most propitiously, bringing the glorious news of our defeat of the French in Portugal and the surrender of Junot, not without a considerable loss of several brave officers, and several hundred men [the Battle of Vimiero, 21st August 1808, during the Peninsular Wars]. After breakfast we mounted our horses, Sir John Williams our Cicerone, to visit the natural arch in the rocks of Cefn *etc*. The day began

> to lower. We arrived at the cave. Of which Sir Richard [Colt] Hoare made a drawing below it. This archway opens through a projecting point of the lime stone ridge at the back of Cefn. The entrance on the west side is lofty, but narrow, to that on the other. The interior, expanding into another chamber to the left, shews a most stupendous and picturesque roof. The excavations on each side, within 5 feet of the bottom, still filled with a deposit of gravel and sand, evidently the deposit of waters, and with which the cave to that height once appeared to have been filled. On each side of the entrance, I, about 7 years ago, discovered strata in the earth and gravel of 4 or 5 inches deep, of small bones, such as those of rats, squirrels, or some small animals; and, from their form, some that must have belonged to animals now unknown; and quantities of stags horns of a great age, with marks of their having been sawed and hacked with an edged tool, and some half burned, with quantities of charcoal. But in this visit I found the strata had been plundered, and the earth washed away; but still here and there were traces of charcoal, so that I conceive this to have been a place of sacrifice, perhaps a rude temple to some British Deity that presided o'er the chace.

> Fisher 1917, 146–147.

At the time Fenton was writing, the Romantic Movement of antiquarianism had firmly taken hold. An element of this entailed presenting graphic images to convey ideas about the monuments in the landscape. Whilst this movement had the benefit of making the past visible to more people, it also began to influence and shape people's perceptions about British antiquities. Several of the ideas were fabricated by the antiquarians in order to present more dramatic images (Smiles 2003, 180). Fenton was certainly writing in this way, linking sites to fanciful events in much the same way as William Stukeley did with his theories about Druids and their connection with prehistoric burial places (Piggott 1985, 79). Other writers were more matter-of-fact; Edward Pugh, writing in 1816, visited Cefn and was the first writer identified to have commented upon the picturesque nature of the Elwy valley (Pugh 1816, 382). Pugh was engaged in creating an artistic diary, sketching the landscape of North Wales to accompany his observations and thoughts on what he saw. He described the rock arch after he had travelled through it to get upstream along the banks of the Elwy. He then returned and, '… came to the caves, one of which has a walk through it, lately made by – Lloyd Esq., of Cefn' (ibid.). This provides us with a first description of some major landscaping work that had been undertaken by the landowner Edward Lloyd and which was to be described by the Reverend Edward Stanley some years later (Stanley 1833, 41). From these two descriptions we can establish that Edward Lloyd had created an extensive series of walks through the valley which involved cutting away projecting areas of the cliff and smoothing the irregular surfaces of the rock ledges (ibid.). He opened up the cave and created a series of gentle steps and staircases through it connecting its two entrances. Outside on the hillside today the remnants

*Figure 2.3. An Edwardian seat cut into the limestone in Cefn Rocks to provide a view across the valley.*

of steps can be seen leading up the valley side from the rock arch to Cefn Cave and continuing up onto the top of the plateau above. Seats have been cut into the limestone at strategic places along this path to offer views across the Elwy valley and possibly to provide some shelter from the elements (Figure 2.3).

Stanley's visit, however, post-dates that of a rather more famous personage; for a young Charles Darwin, aged 22 and fresh from university, visited the caves at Cefn during August 1831 on the geological tour of North Wales he made in the company of Professor Adam Sedgwick of Cambridge University. The tour was set up for Darwin by John Henslow, Professor of Botany at Cambridge (Barrett 1974, 148; Secord 1991). It seems Darwin had an opportunity to gain first-hand experience of geology in the company of one of the most outstanding and respected geologists in England, whilst Sedgwick had an energetic, enthusiastic and knowledgeable young companion. The purpose of the trip was for Sedgwick to undertake research into the older rocks of Wales, as part of his continuing project to produce a treatise on all the rocks in Great Britain lying below the Old Red Sandstone.

Sedgwick and Darwin left Shrewsbury together on Friday 5th August 1831 for Llangollen. The next day they went north towards St Asaph and Abergele. It seems they went their separate ways after about one week (Barrett 1974, 148). The differences between the two men's records have been noted; Darwin's notes describe the limestone at Cefn: 'at Cefn grand escarpement, rock with caverns, wooded, river winding at bottom giving very much the same character to scenery as in Derbyshire the strata dip N25°E – for about 3 miles before St. Asaph'. A later addition inserted between lines of this entry reads 'Sedgwick saw that [—] in the mud in a cavern rhinoceros bones' (Wyhe 2009 CUL–DAR5.B5–B16). Sedgwick, however, mentions

a 'rhinoceros tooth' having been found (Barrett 1974, 150). Unfortunately for us today, neither Sedgwick nor Darwin commented upon the palaeontological significance of their find in their notebooks. After the visit, on his return home to Shrewsbury, it is clear that the tour was an influencing factor in Darwin deciding to accept passage on the *Beagle* later that same year. It also appears that the tour of North Wales had a longer-term influence upon Darwin. In a letter he wrote to Sedgwick shortly before the latter's death in 1873, Darwin wrote:

> 'I am pleased that you remember my attending you in your excursions in 1831. To me, it was a memorable event in my life: I felt it a great honour, and it stimulated me to work, and made me appreciate the noble science of geology.'
> Letter quoted in Clark and Hughes 1890, 380.

Yet which of the caves did Darwin and Sedgwick visit? Secord has linked Stanley's report published the following year to Darwin and Sedgwick's notes and has suggested that it was probably Cefn Cave (Secord 1991, 146). Sedgwick's correspondence was published in 1890 and the first volume covers the tour of North Wales with Darwin. In a letter he wrote to Murchison, Sedgwick described the geology around Denbigh, St Asaph and the Vale of Clwyd, but made no specific mention of Cefn (Clark and Hughes 1890). It seems most likely that it was Cefn Cave that they visited. Lloyd's excavations at the cave had led to bones remaining 'in the mud for the taking'. The discovery of rhinoceros remains would also indicate this, particularly as we know that this cave had recently been discovered and extended (see below). Stanley's report suggests that most of the animal bones were dismissed and used as fertilizer on the meadows, but he recorded seeing a rhinoceros tooth in Lloyd's private collection. Could this be the find made by Sedgwick and Darwin (letter in National Museum of Wales accession file 68.88 from Edward Stanley to Edward Lloyd dated 6th April 1832; Stanley 1833, 41–42)? This tooth is preserved in the National Museum of Wales' collection but does not hold any useful markings on it to enable us to answer this question.

A detailed early record of discoveries at Cefn Cave was published by the Reverend Edward Stanley, a geologist, who later became Bishop of Norwich. Stanley observed that he was not the first to see the cave and recalled a tale of a mysterious hermit who lived in its porch 70 or 80 years previously, when the cave entrance only extended back 20 feet (ibid. 43). Stanley's own visit in February 1832 was recommended to him by some friends who encouraged him to visit the local beauty-spot, the perforated rock called Cefn Cave, through which the road passed.

During his visit he learnt that the landowner, Edward Lloyd, had found some bones in the rocks higher up the valley. Stanley investigated these and his published report provides a very detailed description of the discovery of Cefn Cave. He tells us that whilst Edward Lloyd was engaged in creating the extensive series of walks through the valley he also extended the cave and found it to be a cavern of about

*Figure 2.4. The four flint artefacts found in the Lower Cefn Cave.*

eighty feet in depth, varying in height from six to ten feet (ibid. 42). The soil removed from the cave was reportedly used to manure the meadows below so, on learning that bones could be found on these fields, Stanley returned the following day and collected a number of bones from the surface of the field (ibid. 41). He sent these to Professor William Buckland at Oxford for identification. In a letter he wrote to Lloyd he explained Buckland's interest in the scientific potential of the cave and Stanley also sought permission to return to Cefn in early April to undertake a further investigation there (letter in National Museum of Wales accession file 68.88 from Edward Stanley to Edward Lloyd dated 10th March 1832). He spent one further day there; 4th April 1832 with four men whom he employed to dig, remove and sieve the soil in an attempt to find the cave floor (letter in National Museum of Wales accession file 68.88 from Edward Stanley to Edward Lloyd dated 6th April 1832; Stanley 1833, 41). During this visit Stanley recorded the stratigraphy he found at the cave as a sequence with an upper deposit comprising a fine loam or clay of an ochreous colour and calcareous nature, deposited in horizontal laminae containing pieces of limestone and with animal bone scattered throughout it. The lower layer contained pebbles and animal bones. Stanley also learnt of earlier finds which he saw at Edward Lloyd's house. It appears these were all kept by the family until 1968 when Sir Watkin Williams Wynn donated human remains, cut stags' horns and four stone tools to the National Museum of Wales (National Museum of Wales accession file 68.88). It is very probable that the four stone tools are the same ancient implements mentioned by Stanley as originating from the Old Cefn Cave (Figure 2.4). In 1836 Edward Lloyd invited Buckland to visit the cave with him and letters in the National Museum of Wales' archive show that Buckland was keen to be present, but was prevented from doing so by delays caused by his work on his *Bridgewater Treatise* and the imminent birth of a child (letters in National Museum of Wales accession file 68.88 from William Buckland to Edward Lloyd dated Sunday 14th 1836 and 3rd August 1836).

Many subsequent writers cited Stanley's paper about Cefn Caves as they recorded their own attempts to interpret the cave deposits. William Bowman visited the cave sometime between August and November 1836. He arrived just a few days after William Buckland had visited. He observed marine shells and features in the rocks of the cave and Buckland asked Lloyd to send him samples of these for him to study too (letter in National Museum of Wales accession file 68.88 from William Buckland to Edward Lloyd dated 24th November 1836). William Bowman referred to Stanley's ground plan and described finding a series of beds within the cave. The descriptions he provided of the cave demonstrate that extensive excavation had taken place at the cave by this date (Bowman 1837, 88–91). Joshua Trimmer recorded a visit to Cefn to investigate the occurrence of the marine remains he observed overlying land mammal bones in Cefn Cave. He was particularly interested in the relative positions of bones and stalagmite. He noted that the bones in lower deposits were associated with rounded pebbles of graywacke, slate and limestone, whereas the surface of the upper deposits contained angular pieces of limestone and bones exactly as Stanley himself had earlier recorded. Overlying this he recorded a deposit of sand, containing marine shells, divided by a layer of finely laminated marl (Trimmer 1838, 87). Trimmer was one of the earliest people interested in the sequencing of sediments overlying the hard rock geology. He was an early participant in debates about the origins of, and the emplacement of, 'diluvial' deposits across North Wales (O'Connor 2007, 8–10). He supported theories of a marine inundation, as he found marine shells at 1392 feet in the diluvial deposits on Moel Tryfan (Davies 1969, 248–249). At this time Moel Tryfan was considered to be the minimum height of the flood water. Trimmer used the findings from his visit to Cefn to commence a debate about the age of the deposits in the cave and whether or not they were linked to marine events, or to the submergence of the land, a topic that became key to the later interpretations and debates concerning the ice ages (Trimmer 1839; O'Connor 2007, 10).

The caves at Cefn thus began to play a part in the contemporary debates being waged at the Geological Society of London and in publications about theories of the origins of deposits on the Earth. The Ice Age debate was opened up in Britain by Buckland who was challenged by the Swiss scientist Louis Agassiz, who observed that the deposits within the caves he was studying were the result of glacial action and not flood (Lewis 2005, 2). Agassiz suggested that it was the melting of the glaciers that had formerly covered large areas of the globe that was responsible for rises in sea levels and the inundation of large areas of land (Davies 1969, 267). This concept gradually became widely accepted. Many of the scientists visiting North Wales were incorporating the evidence they saw there of shell-bearing deposits as evidence for this submergence (Trimmer 1839, 873). Sir A. C. Ramsay was to emerge from the debates as a notable supporter of the land-ice theory and in 1852 he described how a second glacial period had followed the first submergence (Ramsay 1852, 373). Ramsay suggested a three-stage division for the glacial period in Wales starting with the advance of the valley glaciers from the mountains; a marine submergence as the glaciers melted back into the uplands and sea levels rose with occasional icebergs floating into the Welsh valleys; then a later re-advance of the valley glaciers. In the 1860s he reconsidered his idea that floating icebergs had contributed to the carving out of the depressions that subsequently became lakes and within which he observed glacial striations (Lewis 2005, 4). Geike also suggested that land-ice and not glacial submergence had been responsible for the landforms and sediments of Wales and other regions of Britain. In 1870 when James Croll suggested that shelly till was material dredged from the floor of the North Sea by glacier ice flowing from Scandinavia the problem of the shelly drifts in North Wales' caves was resolved (ibid.). Ramsay became the first person to suggest that the present-day landscape is a consequence of glacial erosion and that North Wales was covered by ice at times during the past (Davies 1969, 303). The three-stage theory suggested by Ramsay dominated thinking in Britain until the early twentieth century when attention moved away from North Wales to the Alps with Albrecht Penck and Eduard Brückner suggesting that the glacial sequence might well have been rather more complicated than had previously been thought (Lewis 2005, 3). It is in this geological context that the later nineteenth century studies of Cefn Cave fitted and held their place in the contemporary debates taking place at this time.

Yet this was not the only debate underway; discussions about human antiquity and the relationship of humans to extinct animals had also been ignited in Britain by William Pengelly's discoveries at Windmill Hill Cave at Brixham, Devon (Walker 2009, 30) and in France by Jacques Boucher de Perthes at Abbeville (Gowlett 2009). In 1859 Joseph Prestwich and John Evans visited Abbeville to meet Boucher de Perthes. They returned set upon convincing doubters in Britain that humans and extinct animals were contemporary by delivering presentations to the Society of Antiquaries of London (Evans 1860) and to the Royal Society of London (Prestwich 1860). The importance of good recording and accurate observation therefore became important to those researchers investigating deposits in caves (Gamble and Kruszynski 2009, 463).

Hugh Falconer visited Cefn Cave on 27th August 1859 and spent some time studying the bones collected from earlier work that were housed at Plas-yn-Cefn (de Rance 1888a). Falconer observed that there was yellow cave-earth in crevices in Cefn Cave and that the bones were found in 'an insular irregular cylinder', around which the cave passage turns. He listed all the species he identified; *Elaphus antiquus*, *Rhinoceros hemitoechus*, *Rhinoceros tichorhinus*, *Hippopotamus major*, *Equus* (species undetermined), *Strongyloceros spelaeus*, *Cervus guettardi*, *Cervus eurycerus*, *Bos*, *Felis spelaea*, *Hyaena spelaea*, *Ursus spelaea* and *Canis lupus* (Falconer 1868). The collection of bones from Plas-yn-Cefn, now preserved

in the National Museum of Wales, contains a number of notes and identifications glued onto specimens. Amongst these are labels in Falconer's handwriting, some of which are also labelled with his name as the source of the identifications. Falconer was already convinced that Quaternary mammals could be divided into two groups; pre-glacial – *Hippopotamus major* and *Elaphus antiquus*, and post-glacial – *Rhinoceros tichorhinus* and *Elaphus primigenius*. The latter he believed indicated land recently emerged from the sea (O'Connor 2007, 32). He returned to the cave with Ramsay of the Geological Survey of Great Britain in July 1861 (letter from Sir Roderick Murchison to Colonel Wynn in National Museum of Wales accession file 68.88 dated 4th July 1861).

An unnamed author published a note on Cefn Cave in 1863, in which he claimed most of the bones had been dragged into the cave by carnivores for which it had served as a den. He thought that other bones may have dropped in through cracks in the roof. He listed all the species identified by Falconer and noted that human remains were not found within the deposits in Cefn Cave, despite some having been found at the Old Cefn Cave. He also offered Ramsay's observations that the cave was submerged during the glacial or drift period as he and Falconer had found fragments of cockles and other marine shells in the clay and amongst the gravel and stones with which the cave is filled (Anon. 1863, 114).

In 1866 T. J. Moore, then Curator of the Liverpool City Museum, excavated at Cefn Cave for a short period of time (Neaverson 1942, 72). The specimens found were described as a 'collection of teeth and bones of the cave bear and other animals excavated by the Curator'. These were donated by Mrs Williams Wynn to the Liverpool Museum collection (letter of acknowledgement from the Mayor of the town of Liverpool to Mrs Williams Wynn in National Museum of Wales accession file 68.88 dated 16th July 1866). These were never fully described and were destroyed in the incendiary fire that engulfed the Museum on 3rd May 1941 (A. Bowden pers. comm. 2009). Further explorations were undertaken in the cave by Mr Williams Wynn in 1869–1870, with some of the bones retained at Plas-yn-Cefn and a representative series was also presented by Mrs Williams Wynn to the Grosvenor Museum, Chester (Neaverson 1942, 72).

It was during this turbulent time, with debates about the origin of deposits in caves, the understanding of ice ages and human antiquity raging, that an article appeared in *The Times* on 20th October 1870 claiming the existence of a strange amphibian living in Cefn Cave. It called upon naturalists to investigate the survival of such an ancient creature in North Wales. The *Flintshire Observer* for 4th November 1870 told a tale of a living lizard, four feet seven in length and 'very like a crocodile' which had emerged from the depths of the celebrated repository of prehistoric relics in Cefn Cave near Rhyl. This lizard reportedly had emerged and been slain by a valiant Welshman, a Mr Thomas Hughes, a sweep from Rhyl. The tale retold suggests the crocodile did not reach Cefn Cave at all, unless it was taken there after its death, which apparently had occurred whilst it was part of a travelling menagerie visiting Rhyl. Upon learning of the death of the crocodile Mr Hughes ingeniously devised the tale of its capture in the cave, and having purchased it, proceeded to show it as the marvellous lizard of Cefn (tale retold in Owen 2007, 29). Whether Mr Hughes was in fact aware of the debates underway in scientific circles at this time is unknown; however he entered the limelight at a fortuitous time in the story of the age of investigation of caves and the discovery of mysterious animals within them, just one year before publication of Darwin's *On the Descent of Man* in 1871.

Tales such as this could only enhance the popularity of the caves and it is interesting that Paxton quotes from the 1879 guidebook to Wales that mentions their popularity, and the many visiting sightseers who travelled from Rhyl and other holiday resorts to see them. Indeed guides were even provided to take tourists through the caves (Paxton 1952). Visitors were frequent enough for a guidebook to be published. The *Illustrated Handbook for Visitors to St Asaph (Cathedral and Parish Church), Bodelwyddan and Cefn* published in 1894, gave a short description of the caves (Thomas 1894, 22).

William Boyd Dawkins visited the caves at Cefn in 1872. At Cefn Cave he recorded finding a deposit of comminuted bone that rose in clouds of dust as it was disturbed (Boyd Dawkins 1874, 286). Boyd Dawkins had the opportunity to study the human remains and the artefacts kept at Plas-yn-Cefn (ibid. 159–160). Specimens in the original Plas-yn-Cefn collection have labels glued to them with his identifications and initials. His diaries are preserved in the Manchester University Museum; transcripts made by Stephen Aldhouse-Green show that Boyd Dawkins visited Cefn several times, often staying at Plas-yn-Cefn with the Williams Wynns over Easter. He visited on 18th April 1870; 23rd–24th April 1870; 22nd September 1870; 10th–19th April 1871; 13th January 1872; 1st–3rd July 1872; 5th–6th July 1872; 18th–24th September 1874; 29th March–5th April 1877. It should be noted that he also spent some time digging in the Neolithic tombs on the estate, including that of Tyddyn Bleiddyn (ibid. 161–164). Unfortunately there is nothing further in his diaries or notebooks which might shed light on his understanding and interpretation of the caves at this time. In fact in his book *Cave Hunting* he confused the story by claiming that Neolithic remains were found amongst the collection of fossil bones in the possession of Mrs Williams Wynn, discovered in 1833 in a cave at Cefn by Mr Edward Lloyd. These comprise a human skull and mandible along with limb-bones. He described these as found mingled with the bones of goat, pig, fox and badger and cut red deer antlers inside the lower entrance of the cave in which the extinct Pleistocene animals were found in the valley of the Elwy. Four flint flakes were also discovered with them (ibid. 159). This account differs from that given by Stanley who, as the first recorder of the discoveries at Cefn, is clear that the human remains, animal bones, stags' horns (cut antlers) and stone tools were found in the Old Cefn Cave within

the rock arch. The Pleistocene bones originated from Cefn Cave above (Stanley 1833, 41). So one wonders on what basis Boyd Dawkins made this statement. Subsequent literature tends to cite Boyd Dawkins' references and the confusion of the attribution of bones to specific caves has been perpetuated.

The next person to describe the caves at Cefn was W. S. Symonds (Symonds 1872, 313). He visited with Sir Charles and Lady Mary Lyell on 4th August 1863. Sir Charles being particularly interested in the formation of the caves. They investigated the cave deposits in order to study the fragments of marine shells and corals recorded within them. Symonds noted how much of the original cave deposit had been removed by the time of his visit, observing that whilst the bone-rich cave earth had once almost filled the cave, little survived for study (ibid.). A thank you letter sent from Mary Lyell to Mrs Wynn a few days later also survives (letter from Mary Lyell to Mrs Wynn in National Museum of Wales accession file 68.88 dated 7th August 1863).

G. H. Morton also visited in 1887 to investigate the deposits within the caves and he saw similarities between the animal species recorded by Hicks at the Tremeirchion Caves of Ffynnon Beuno and Cae Gwyn and those found at Cefn. He was particularly interested in the presence of elephant and hippopotamus at all the sites (Morton 1897, 187). His collection, now in the World Museum Liverpool, comprises five hyaena teeth from Cefn Cave (A. Bowden pers. comm. 2009).

During the late nineteenth century the caves continued to be popular with visitors and tourists; but the scientists turned their attention away from Cefn towards the investigation of the glacial sequences of the Alps and few further mentions are made to it. Cefn Cave was designated a Scheduled Ancient Monument on 27th October 1923 and has been legally protected ever since (Cadw Scheduled Ancient Monument archive De–115).

There are no further records of work at Cefn Cave until members of the Shepton Mallet Caving Club undertook a survey there during Easter 1966 (Ellis 1973). Later correspondence between Ellis and Aldhouse-Green indicates that this was purely for the means of testing out some new surveying equipment rather than for any scientific purpose (letter dated 2nd September 1981, National Museum of Wales Cefn Cave Archive). In 1967 the Birkenhead Y.M.C.A. Speleology Club illegally placed a trench of approximately 15 inches wide and 18 inches deep along the cave passage in an attempt to 'finish' it (Kelly 1967). A. E. Valdemar investigated this and found they had uncovered a deposit he described as charcoal and stratified glacial deposits, but he observed that the trench had not done much damage (letter from A. E. Valdemar to Mr J. K. Knight dated 21st April 1968 in Cadw archive files). In May 1968 Valdemar himself sought permission from the Ministry to dig in both Cefn Cave and Pontnewydd Cave during the last two weeks of August 1968. He proposed to dig trenches across the main passages in both caves, with a view to determining their stratigraphic sequences. In Cefn Cave he aimed to find out whether or not there is a lower cave system, and if so, to attempt to enter it. He was also keen to try to locate the 'chimney' figured in Trimmer's section plan of the cave (letter from A. E. Valdemar to Mr J. K. Knight dated 11th May 1968 in Cadw archive files). Permission was granted in June 1968, but, a later note in the file suggests that the excavations did not take place and he made no mention of such excavations in his published reports (Valdemar 1970; Valdemar and Jones 1970). Indeed Valdemar participated in the first two seasons of the National Museum of Wales' excavations as he hoped that his questions would be answered then (S. Aldhouse-Green pers. comm. 2010). The next excavations at the cave were those undertaken by Stephen Aldhouse-Green for the National Museum of Wales in 1982 and 1983. The results of this investigation form a part of the rest of this volume.

*Pontnewydd Cave*
Pontnewydd Cave was first recorded in 1832 by Stanley who described visiting it when the road that runs downhill from Cefn Meiriadog to Bont Newydd in the valley bottom was being constructed (Stanley 1833, 42). Stanley described the cave as having great potential,

> I found [it] to be entirely blocked up with soil, and [it] has clearly never been open to human observation. But I have no doubt, from its appearance and character, that

it will … exhibit as rich a prospect [as Cefn], whenever its recesses may be explored, in search of those organic remains now unknown in the temperate zones.

Stanley 1833, 53.

William Boyd Dawkins, Mrs Williams Wynn and the Reverend D. R. Thomas, Vicar of Cefn, are the first people recorded to have investigated Pontnewydd Cave at a date sometime prior to 1874. The exact dates and the extent of their excavations are not recorded, but, it seems these were extensive as Thomas McKenny Hughes and the Reverend Thomas, who published a note of their investigations of the cave in 1874, noted that the deposits had already been removed from the first 25 yards into the cave from the entrance (Hughes and Thomas 1874, 388). In his 1874 book Boyd Dawkins mentioned Hughes and Thomas' excavations of the cave but did not mention anyone else working at the cave between his and their visits (Boyd Dawkins 1874, 287). This suggests Boyd Dawkins was responsible for the excavation of the quantities of 'material thrown out of the cave' noted by Hughes and Thomas on their profile drawing (Figure 2.5; Hughes and Thomas 1874). Boyd Dawkins recorded that his excavations uncovered animal bones found embedded in stiff re-arranged boulder clay, in the condition of water-worn pebbles. Amongst these he identified the brown, grizzly and cave bears (Boyd Dawkins 1874, 286–287).

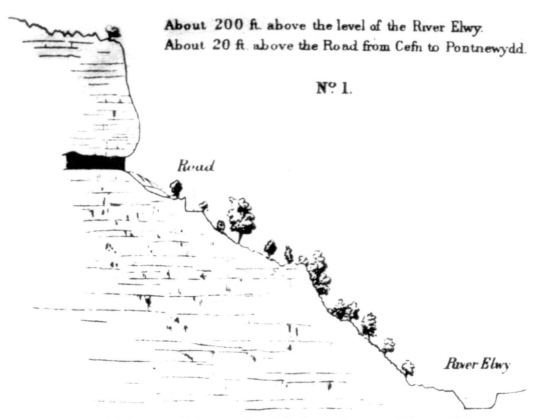

POSITION OF PONTNEWYDD CAVE, CEFN, S⸏ ASAPH.

About 200 ft. above the level of the River Elwy.
About 20 ft. above the Road from Cefn to Pontnewydd.

N° 1.

Road

River Elwy

*Figure 2.5. Pontnewydd Cave: profile of hillside from Hughes and Thomas 1874.*

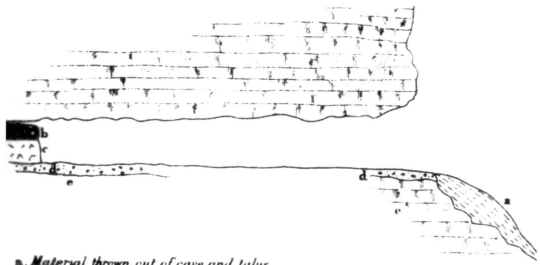

PONTNEWYDD CAVE. CEFN, S! ASAPH.

Scale 20 Feet to 1 Inch.

Nº 2.

a. *Material thrown out of cave and talus.*

b. *Yellow cave earth, about 5 ft. seen in section at the end, evidence that it was near roof all along, lines of black oxide of iron at base.*

c. *Breccia of clay with angular fragments of limestone, few Silurian &c. washed in.*

d. *Gravel almost all rolled Silurian, felstone &c such as might be derived from Boulder Clay*

e. *Mountain limestone*

Figure 2.6. Pontnewydd Cave: section through the cave from Hughes and Thomas 1874.

Hughes and Thomas published their findings in some detail. The section drawing (Figure 2.6) shows a sequence of deposits which they described in their publication. They recorded seeing a yellow clay loam, overlying a breccia deposit, over a gravel layer that overlay the limestone bedrock (Hughes and Thomas 1874, 387–388). They investigated the debris that had been thrown out of the cave as well as undisturbed deposits inside it. They found felstone and flint artefacts in the dump and also in the breccia. These artefacts interested them as they noted their similarities to those at Le Moustier in France. They also discovered a number of bones which they referred to Professor Busk for identification and from whose letter they quoted in their publication:

I have looked over the collection of bones and teeth from Pontnewydd Cave, and find they belong to *Hyaena spelaea, Ursus spelaeus, Ursus ferox, Equus caballus, Rhinoceros hemithoechus, Cervus elaphus, Capreolus capreolus, Canis lupus, Canis vulpes, Meles taxus, Homo sapiens*, besides indeterminable or not easily determinable splinters, many of which appear to be gnawed by hyaena or wolf. Some are rather less infiltrated with manganese than the others, but all appear to be pretty nearly of the same antiquity not excepting the human molar tooth, which looks quite as ancient as the rest. It is of very large size, and in this respect

exceeds any with which I have compared it, except one or two from Australia and Tasmania.

Hughes and Thomas 1874, 390.

The tooth referred to remains unlocated today. That it was human is not in doubt, for Professor George Busk was at this time an anatomist and former naval surgeon with ample experience of the identification of human remains (O'Connor 2007, 126).

Hughes applied the findings from Pontnewydd Cave to his theories about the direction of the movement of the ice from the higher mountains of North Wales. He was particularly interested in the origin of the felstone (felsite) and other rock types used for the artefacts he found in the cave and he was also concerned with the transportation of them to the cave. He and Williams Wynn studied the drift deposits in the valley of the River Clwyd, in which they found granites, flints and marine shells. They concluded that the deposits in Pontnewydd Cave mainly overlay the mass of fossiliferous cave-earth. From this they inferred that all the known remains in the cave must be later than both the period of extension of the Snowdonian ice into that area and to the submergence that marked the end of the great glaciation (Hughes and Thomas 1874, 390; Hughes and Williams Wynn 1882, 700; Hughes 1885, 33; Hughes 1887).

Debate about the relative ages of stone tools and cave

deposits in England and Wales continued throughout the 1870s. Hughes was one of the earliest to observe the importance of separating questions as to how the cave itself was formed from the method of emplacement of the deposits within it. He noted that cave formation required water to pass through it in considerable quantities. Such water would have removed any deposits that might once have been within the caves so that the deposits contained within them must have been formed later, when local conditions permitted deposits to be laid down, rather than washed out of the cave (Hughes 1887). However, a few years earlier, in August 1883, Henry Hicks reported investigating a previously unexplored cave with Mr E. Bouverie Luxmoore (Hicks 1884, 12). This cave, Ffynnon Beuno, is located on the limestone escarpment on the eastern side of the Vale of Clwyd near Tremeirchion. Above it they found a second cave, Cae Gwyn which they also explored. Hicks uncovered a stalagmite floor sealing the underlying deposits at Ffynnon Beuno. On breaking through this he found a deposit containing rhinoceros and mammoth bones. This cave earth deposit overlay loose gravel (Hicks 1884, 13–14). A tool, a leaf-point now known to be of early Upper Palaeolithic date, was found with the mammoth remains in the cave-earth (Hicks 1886a, 8). Cae Gwyn was mainly undisturbed, although the entrance was almost closed up by a heap of debris (ibid. 15). A portion of the cave had been quarried away at some time and Hicks thought that the original entrance must have been at least 25 feet further forward, although later this was shown not to have been the case (Davies 1949). On excavating he obtained a sequence of deposits comprising the topsoil, below which was stiff boulder clay containing ice-scratched boulders amongst which were narrow bands and pockets of sand. Beneath this he found seven feet of gravel and sand with occasional bands of red clay. Then laminated brown clay that overlay a bone-earth containing angular fragments of limestone, stalagmite, stalactite and amongst which were hyaena and reindeer teeth as well as a worked flint flake and bones (Hicks 1886b, 220–221).

Hicks used this work to inform his understanding of the relationships between deposits in caves and their dates of formation. He presented his results in a series of lectures and publications. These sparked off a debate about the origin of deposits within the North Wales caves with Hughes, Boyd Dawkins, John Evans and the Reverend Thomas (Hicks 1884, 18; 1886b, 221–222; 1886c). Hicks' view was that the caves were occupied by an early Pleistocene fauna and humans before the submergence of the land beneath the waters that laid down the marine sands and boulder clays. He claimed that the animal bones and flint implements pre-dated the glacial deposits found in North Wales (Hicks 1886b, 220). However, after he expressed his views at a meeting of the Geological Society of London, Evans and Boyd Dawkins raised their objections to his interpretation. They believed that the boulder clays and pressure of water after the re-emergence of land after the glacial period could have caused the breaking up and mixing of the contents of the caves (Hicks 1886a, 19). Boyd Dawkins cited evidence

he observed at Pontnewydd Cave from the artefacts, which he said were made of felstone derived from the glacial deposits available locally. This, he claimed, proved the human presence was after, rather than before, the glacial period (ibid.). He had previously published a discussion about the finds made in Pontnewydd Cave, being especially interested in the association of the tools with the mammal remains. He observed the human molar tooth found by Hughes had been found with a quartzite implement and 'rude splinters and chips of quartzite'. He concurred with Hughes, concluding that as the pebbles on which the tools were made were obtained from the glacial deposits in the neighbourhood, the Palaeolithic hunter was present after the glaciers in post-glacial times (Boyd Dawkins 1880, 192). Hicks replied and cited Ramsay, Mackintosh and Trimmer as supporters of his interpretation. De Rance also entered the debate in support of Hicks, presenting evidence from the North Wales caves including Cefn Cave. He believed that the bones discovered at Cefn belonged to mammals that lived before the filling up of the Vale of Clwyd and the sealing of its caverns by the glacial drift (de Rance 1888b, 303).

Hughes, however, continued to question the interpretation of the faunal evidence from Ffynnon Beuno, claiming that the species were those he believed to have been recorded on the newer post-glacial gravels of the south and east of England and he argued that therefore the drift deposits had to be post-glacial in date (Hughes 1887). Similarly at Cae Gwyn, Hughes made his own observations and disagreed with Hicks' interpretation (ibid.). Here he noted the Limestone Breccia contained few bones and a flint flake, found just within the upper mouth of the cave, under a projecting mass of rock which was removed with a view to making steps up to the surface of the ground outside. This was found under a mass of rock which nearly touched the floor and had to be removed. Hughes described the place where it lay as more like a side crevice in the limestone into which it had been washed or worked down, than part of the regular cave-deposits. The flake and bones occurred just where the swallow-hole must have descended which fed the upper entrance to the upper cave before it was filled up with deposit. He believed that these drift deposits must therefore be of an age subsequent to the post-glacial emergence, there having been no glacial action in the Vale since then. He believed that if the drift closed the cave mouth then the bones outside must have been emplaced by run-off from rain-wash and the fact that the limestone talus contained the remains of Palaeolithic man and other animals was not unremarkable (ibid.). Hicks objected to this view, stating that the quantity of bones in the boulder clays indicated that they must have accumulated within the caves and not washed in from deposits at higher levels (Hicks 1887).

Mackintosh also visited Pontnewydd Cave with the aim of interpreting the sequence of deposits within it. He entered the debate, concluding that the great glacial submergence commenced before the ice sheet or ice sheets disappeared from the country. He believed that the lower boulder clay

*Figure 2.7. Pontnewydd Cave in the 1920s. By permission of Derbyshire County Council: Buxton Museum and Art Gallery (Jackson Collection).*

was accumulated while the land was sinking; and the sand and gravel formation was deposited while the land was rising. He saw evidence for an interglacial period, during the first part of which the land was still submerging, but with dry land prevailing during the second part. He recorded a second submergence during which the upper boulder clay was deposited in Pontnewydd Cave. He attributed the lower pebble bed in Pontnewydd Cave to the time when the land was rising and linked these gravels to those at Cefn Cave. But, as he believed that land animals could not have existed here until after the land emergence, he thought that the bones and teeth found in the lowest deposit at Cefn Cave had been washed in by rain through fissures in the roof. The stalagmite layer developed on top of this after which more bones must have been introduced and the cave may have been inhabited temporarily by hyaenas. It was, he believed, a later submergence of the cave beneath the waters of the upper boulder clay sea that filled the cave almost to the roof (Mackintosh 1876, 94).

Morton also appears to have visited Pontnewydd Cave around 1887 (Morton 1897, 184). He disagreed with Boyd Dawkins' interpretation of the cave as not being pre-glacial, rather believing it to be older. He observed that people could have obtained the stone they used to make their tools from its original locality, or from local glacial moraines dating to the early period before the submergence (ibid. 188–189). Boyd Dawkins' interpretations of Pontnewydd Cave were also commented upon by Shone, who argued in favour of Morton's observations (Shone 1894, 79).

The debate about the antiquity of deposits within the caves continued. Ultimately Hicks was to be proved correct; when the matter was referred to James Geikie, who studied the shaft at Cae Gwyn, he found no evidence for slippage through a cavity. He concluded that the cave had been more extensive over the bone-earth and that the

roof had collapsed before the deposition of the glacial deposits (Garrod 1926). Geikie's examination of deposits in the south-east of England caused him to agree with Hicks' findings and was ultimately confirmed (O'Connor 2007, 137–140).

Pontnewydd Cave, like Cefn Cave, was largely left as the nineteenth century drew to a close. Attention began to move to the continent and the caves played a lesser part in the discussions that ensued. On 27th October 1923 Pontnewydd Cave was designated a Scheduled Ancient Monument, thus affording it legal protection (Cadw Scheduled Ancient Monument archive De–116). Photographs taken around this time by J. Wilfrid Jackson and preserved in the Buxton Museum (Figure 2.7) shows that the extent of the deposits within the cave were much as Hughes and Thomas had recorded on their section drawing of 1874 (Hughes and Thomas 1874).

In 1940 the cave was requisitioned for wartime use and the floor was levelled and covered with gravel over which duck-boards were placed. Spoil from this work was placed outside the cave entrance. The entrance was faced with limestone blocks to camouflage it against possible enemy attack. Beyond the wall a concrete floored guard-chamber complete with a coke stove was constructed with an inner brick wall separating the guard from his charge. The cave was then used as a store for land mines and depth charges (Green 1984, 19). The extent of the removal of deposit from the cave was not too great, as the later record of the extent of the main cave passage was the same as in Jackson's photograph (ibid. 16).

The next disturbance in the cave took place in 1966 or 1967 when members of the Birkenhead Y.M.C.A. Speleological Club dug a 20 ft (*c*. 6.1 m) horizontal trench at the rear of the cave. They recorded finding some undisturbed narrow side passages off the main cave and a wolf skull (Kelly 1967). In May 1968 Valdemar sought permission to dig in both Pontnewydd Cave and Cefn Cave during the last two weeks in August 1968. Permission to undertake this work was granted, but it did not take place (Valdemar and Jones 1970). An application made in January 1978 by Stephen Aldhouse-Green (Cadw archive files) led to the current research project, the results of which are detailed in the chapters that follow in this volume.

## Conclusion

The parish of Cefn Meiriadog and its caves have had a long and important part to play in both local legend and national and international science. The people who have contributed to the history above have included many notable names. No doubt many others whose names are now unrecorded were also inspired by the caves in different ways as also by the beauty of the area and the fascinating facts that were gleaned by the scientists' discoveries in the caves.

The next episode in the interpretation of the caves concerns the excavations directed by Stephen Aldhouse-Green between 1978 and 1995, to which the rest of this monograph is devoted. During these years many new scientists have visited the caves and have used them and their finds to develop, or to refine, scientific techniques. Several dating techniques have been trialled at Pontnewydd Cave. Many researchers study the artefacts to seek comparisons between these and those found at other U.K. and world-wide sites. Pontnewydd Cave has also acted as an international comparator for discoveries of early Neanderthal teeth elsewhere in Europe. The main researchers responsible for the recent work have offered their formal contributions in the writing of the reports that follow. However, excavations themselves can leave their own mark. The recent work at the caves in Cefn Meiriadog has had the benefit of being a research excavation, rather than rescue work or mitigation ahead of a time-defined commercial development project. As such the doors and

*Figure 2.8. Pontnewydd Cave 1988: the team's campsite beside Neuadd Owen, Cefn Village Hall.*

walls of the Guard Chamber were a welcome feature for the excavation trenches could be left open and the infrastructure for the complex lighting system left in place at the end of each excavation season simply by locking the doors. The excavations have also left their mark on the social history of the area. Excavations normally took place for four weeks at a time. Those at Cefn Cave were undertaken during 1982 and 1983, at Cae Gronw 1979, 1980 and 1985, whilst the main focus of work at Pontnewydd Cave saw fourteen excavation seasons in 1978–1985, 1987–1989, and 1993–1995. The trenches were backfilled in 2003. Stephen Aldhouse-Green recruited teams of volunteers, mostly students from universities across the U.K. but with some from across the world; many of whom would return year after year. Participation meant taking up residence in a canvas make-shift campsite amongst the sheep in the field beside Cefn village hall (Figure 2.8). The hall itself became the kitchen, recreation area and place to dry out, or even to sleep in, after strong gales or after a day working beneath a persistent drip from the cave roof. The *Dolben Arms*, then at the bottom of the valley beside the bridge over the River Elwy in Bont Newydd, was also the place where many of the team would find themselves later in the evenings. It was here that villagers and diggers – or scratchers, as the villagers preferred to call the archaeologists – would meet up and events such as post-work football or darts matches were arranged. Rumour had it that the village pub was once sold on the basis of its September profits from 25 people annually descending on the village. Other evening events

*Figure 2.9. Pontnewydd Cave open evening 1995.*

would include shopping expeditions to Kinmel Bay and a couple of times a week to use the showers at Eryl Hall Caravan Park in St Asaph, the only alternative being a cold hosepipe and little privacy. Notable too was the annual climb up Moel Arthur led by the Deputy Project Director Kenneth Brassil, followed by a visit to one of the pubs at Tremeirchion; all these evening trips usually ended in a visit to the fish and chip shop at Trefnant.

The excavations themselves attracted interest from the local and national press. Any new discovery of a hominin fossil would immediately draw attention. 'Found – the oldest Welshman's tooth' (*New Scientist* 7th January 1982) and 'Caveman's cavity' (*Doctor* 21st January 1982) are amongst the more notable headlines that appeared at different times. By 1989 the hand-made posters placed on the three village notice-boards were alone responsible for an attendance of well over two hundred visitors to an open evening (Figure 2.9). With a rare chance afforded to see within the locked steel doors, the cave once again became the attraction it had been over a century before.

The villagers themselves have observed and noted their recollections of the annual invasion of student archaeologists, the humming of the generators echoing across the valley, the annual camp fire in the village hall field and the beer consumed in the *Dolben Arms*. All those who joined the excavation, for however long, will hold a special memory of Cefn and the friendliness and generosity of the villagers who live in a beautiful and peaceful area of North Wales, safely just beyond earshot of the A55 expressway, the seaside town of Rhyl and the cathedral city of St Asaph. The noisy early morning walk of the hounds, the delight in finding a tiny rodent tooth in a wet sieve, the excitement of the discovery of a quarter-of-a-million year old handaxe, the buzz around the cave as work stopped when a new hominin tooth was found, to the sun setting over the valley at the end of the day all feature in memories of the place. Many solid friendships were made between members of the excavation team and diggers will turn up in unexpected places from time to time recollecting their experiences of working at Pontnewydd Cave. All this is a by-product generated by Stephen Aldhouse-Green's research excavations that threw a random selection of people together to live in a field beside the village hall near the Cefn Caves for a few weeks each year and which themselves have created their own place in the social history of the parish and the science the rest of this volume will present.

# 3. The Geomorphology of the Country Around Pontnewydd Cave

## David Q. Bowen and Helen J. Livingston

*While the main elements of the geomorphology have altered only in degree and not in kind since the times of the Pontnewydd people almost a quarter of a million years ago, interpretation has changed and old concepts have been revised. It was once held that the geomorphology evolved under conditions of tectonic stability. It is now clear that landscape and stream evolution have been influenced by deep weathering and tectonics throughout the Cenozoic (Tertiary and Quaternary time). The interpretation of Quaternary events on orbital timescales ('marine isotope stages') has been enhanced by the recognition of rapid millennial and sub-millennial changes in climate, sea levels and, notably, the pace of glaciation, especially in and around the Elwy valley and the Vale of Clwyd. An interpretive key for the timing of events comes from the interaction of Welsh and Irish Sea ice streams in north-east Wales, adjacent parts of England and the Irish Sea Basin. Much, however, is indeterminate, and the concept of multiple working hypotheses is followed (Chamberlin 1897).*

What was the landscape of the Pontnewydd people like? And what were its antecedents? Any evolutionary narrative of the country around Pontnewydd Cave must journey far in space and time. Despite the vicissitudes of glaciation much of the present physical landscape and especially the skyline horizons were familiar to Pontnewydd people. Svensson *et al.* (2010) have called millennial pulsing ice sheets in Europe 'pacemakers' for the expansion and contraction of hominins, a notion consistent with a new paradigm of climate pulsing on millennial and sub-millennial timescales throughout the ice ages and interglacials (Jouzel *et al.* 2007). Much, however, remains indeterminate, not least because of a scarcity of geochronological age estimates.

### Rocks and relief

North-east Wales consists of five landform regions (Brown 1960) on which the general control of rocks on relief is evident (Figures 3.1; 3.2):

1) The Denbighshire Moors and Mynydd Hiraethog consist of Ludlow (Silurian) mudstones, siltstones and sandstones (Warren *et al.* 1984). Summit elevations range from 300 m in the north to over 500 m in the south. On its eastern margin lies the outcrop of Carboniferous Limestone where Pontnewydd Cave is located (Figure 3.3).

2) The Clwydian Range also consists of Ludlovian rocks and culminates in Moel Fama (554 m).

3) Between the Ludlovian rocks of the Denbigh Moors and Clwydian Range, the rift structure of the Vale of Clwyd is floored by Permo-Triassic red sandstones and Coal Measures.

4) The dissected plateaux of Halkyn Mountain consists of Coal Measures, Namurian Sandstone and Carboniferous Limestone which is host to probable Tertiary sediments preserved in solution subsidence hollows (below).

5) The coastal plain is bounded landwards by a degraded coastal slope modified by interglacial high sea levels, the 'preglacial cliff' of Steers (1956).

An even greater correspondence exists between rocks and relief on smaller scales: for example, on the Denbigh Moors grits correspond with higher and shales with lower topographic features respectively. Warren *et al.* (1984) describe many such examples and remark on 10 m high scarps along fault lines that bring harder and softer rocks into juxtaposition (see plate 4 in Warren *et al.* 1984). Indeed, despite the survival of older elements in the landform, it is difficult to resist an impression that the area has been subject to long-continued weathering and erosion. But when did this long-continued denudation commence?

### Upland plains and drainage evolution

Ever since 1902 (cf. Brown 1960) a traditional parental

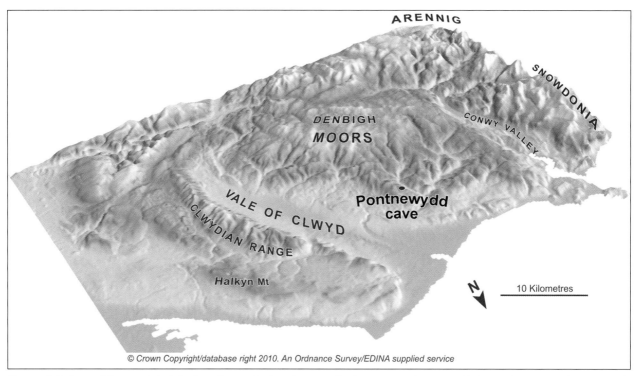

*Figure 3.1. Digital Terrain Model of north-east Wales showing the location and geomorphological context of Pontnewydd Cave.*

surface has been that of an uplifted Chalk cover, long since vanished, on which an original drainage system came into existence. Streams were deemed to have run away from Snowdonia in a radial pattern. In north-east Wales the master stream was a west-to-east flowing proto-Elwy. It ran sub-parallel to a proto-upper Conway-Dee-Trent, a relic of which may be the great wind-gap at Cerrigydrudion (Linton 1951; Brown 1960). Since then a younger parental surface has been recognized from Tertiary outliers of Oligocene (Palaeogene) and Miocene (Neogene) sediments in western Britain and Ireland (Walsh *et al.* 1999; Walsh 2001). Several occur no great distance from Pontnewydd at Llandudno (Maw 1865) and on Halkyn Mountain (Strahan and de Rance 1890). No diagnostic fossil flora was found in the latter but Walsh and Brown (1971) commented on the similarity of the Halkyn Mountain deposits to others in Wales and, especially, to the sands and clays of the Brassington Formation, in the southern Pennines, where the palaeobotanical evidence shows a late Miocene age (Walsh *et al.* 1972).

The Palaeogene-Neogene surface was deformed by earth movements throughout Britain and, despite its palimpsest faintness in Wales, it composes the level or gently sloped skyline vistas seen from many a vantage point. These too were the distant horizons of Pontnewydd people. The 'upland plains' ('peneplains') of Brown (1960) are much modified, not least by deep chemical weathering, and lowered remnants of that parental and ancestral plain (Walsh and Brown 1971).

Throughout and after the plate tectonics revolution it was assumed that 'passive margins' such as western Europe were relatively stable. But recent developments

in apatite fission track dating allow geologically recent surface uplift and denudation to be proposed (Hillis *et al.* 2008). Some of this may be induced by ice sheet loading and unloading associated with offshore sedimentary basins (Blundell and Waltham 2009). Thus, Britain has undergone considerable uplift in late Tertiary (Neogene) and even Pleistocene time which has influenced geomorphology: for example, the faults in the Denbighshire Moors and especially faulting in the Vale of Clwyd on the Denbigh and Vale of Clwyd faults. It is remarkable to note that the influence of faulting and prolonged deep weathering in the present landscape was anticipated by Yvonne Battiau-Queney (1984) over a quarter of a century ago. Despite such uplift and depression of the Palaeogene-Neogene land-surface that was accompanied by great denudation, Walsh (2001) was able to draw contours on the deformed landsurface throughout Britain and Ireland. In north-east Wales they resemble generalized contours on the present landsurface.

The reconstructed Palaeogene-Neogene landsurface may be the means of understanding how the drainage system evolved. Boswell (1949) believed that the Elwy was dip-stream (which he also called a consequent-stream) that was controlled by the east or north-east dip of the Silurian rocks that formerly extended west into Snowdonia. He further suggested that the River Aled (as between Llansannan and Bryn-Rhyd-yr-Arian) also represented the original drainage direction; farther south Afon Ystrad follows the same direction before it joins the Vale of Clwyd at Denbigh. He noted that after its north-south course as a strike-stream it resumed its dip-stream status near Cefn Rocks where it joined the Meirchion stream, which also

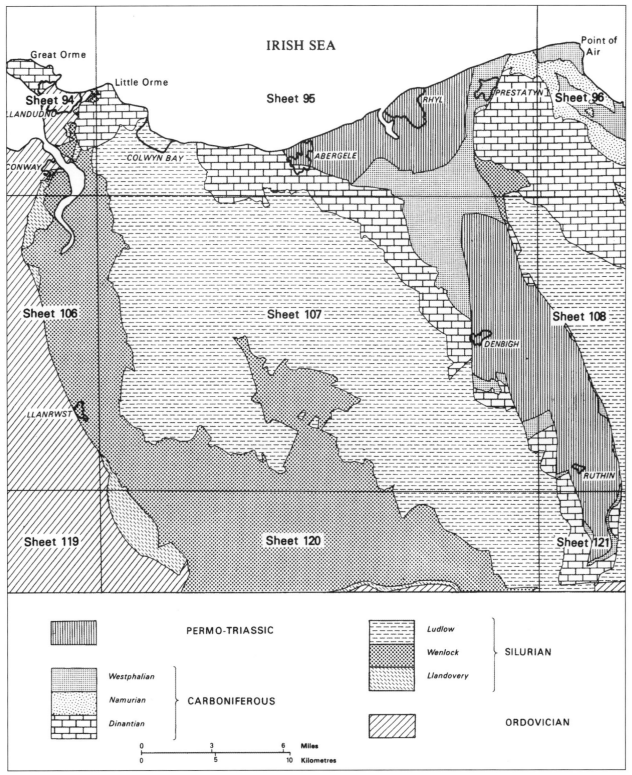

*Figure 3.2. The solid geology of the Rhyl (95) and Denbigh (107) British Geological Survey Sheets, described in detail in Warren et al. 1984. Crown copyright reserved and published by permission of the Director of the British Geological Survey.*

follows a 'consequent' direction, to cross the Carboniferous Limestone outcrop. The reconstruction of Brown (1957; 1960) showed a proto-Elwy, superimposed from a Chalk cover, flowing from west to east. Embleton (1960; 1984) did not refer to the views of Boswell (1949), but disagreed with Brown by suggesting that the original drainage consisted of

northward flowing sub-parallel streams such as the Aled and Cledwen. These, he suggested, were subsequently subject to river capture by the Elwy which developed by headward erosion from east to west along an 'Elwy valley Fault'. The former courses of the north-flowing streams are indicated by wind-gaps north of the Elwy at Pwll-y-Cibau and west

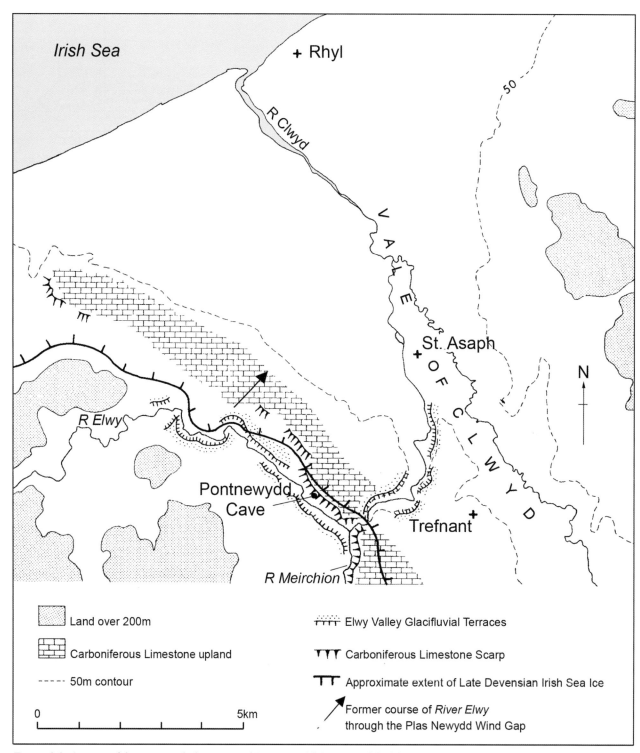

*Figure 3.3. Aspects of the geomorphology around Pontnewydd Cave. Modified from Embleton (1984). Note that the approximate line of separation of Welsh and Irish Sea deposits differs from Warren* et al. *(1984) in the vicinity of Pontnewydd Cave.*

of Moelfre Uchaf (Embleton 1960). But not all cols are wind-gaps and those identified by Embleton (1960; 1984) coincide with major faults that run from south to north, thus might merely be depressions exploited by weathering and erosion along fault-lines.

The Denbigh Sheet of the British Geological Survey (B.G.S.) (1973) superseded the mapping of Jones (1937), and Boswell (1949) but neither the B.G.S. map nor its memoir, *Geology of the Country around Rhyl and Denbigh*

(Warren *et al.* 1984), showed an east to west Elwy valley fault. Instead the Elwy crosses numerous faults on its west to east course (B.G.S. 1973; Warren *et al.* 1984). Embleton (1960), however, did observe that the Elwy's course below Llangernyw is 'characteristic of a stream picking its way among faults crossing mainly at right angles – a series of straight east-west portions linked by shorter north-south reaches'. But the reconstruction of Brown (1960) rests entirely on a notional Chalk cover on which the original

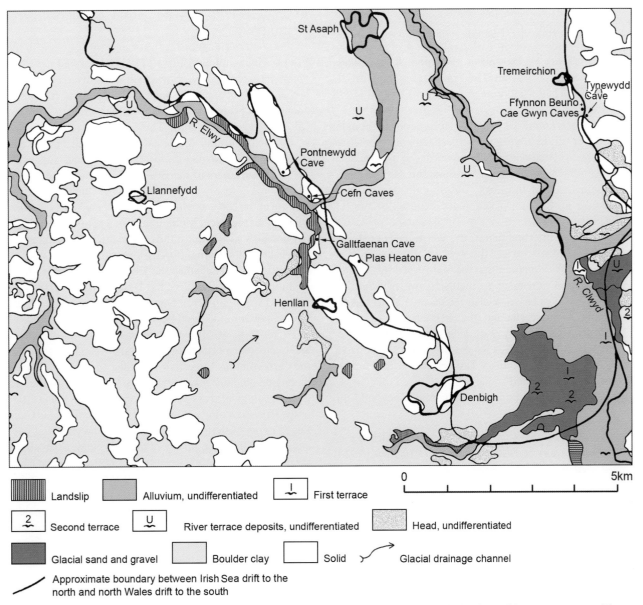

*Figure 3.4. Quaternary deposits of the Rhyl and Denbigh districts redrawn from the British Geological Survey mapping of figure 27, Warren* et al. *(1984). Note that the approximate line of separation of Welsh and Irish Sea deposits differ from Embleton (1984). Crown copyright reserved and published by permission of the Director of the British Geological Survey.*

River Elwy came into existence. Others, however, (George 1974a; 1974b; Walsh 2001) believed that a Chalk cover 'for so long a central hypothesis of geomorphological evolution, can be discounted' (George 1974a, 347).

Based on an analysis of drainage systems in southern Scotland and northern England (Sissons 1960), the parental Welsh drainage system may have been centrifugal and deployed away from existing uplands (Bowen 1989). This is consistent with the contoured Palaeogene-Neogene surface of Walsh (2001), especially in Ceredigion (Cardiganshire) (Bowen 1994). Part of that pattern is a River Elwy that ran from south-west to north-east. Of the three hypotheses, it is that of Boswell (1949) which is most consistent with that inferred from the Palaeogene-Neogene surface. Subsequent adjustment by the river to the complex structures of folds and minor faults mapped during 1963–1967 by officers

of the British Geological Survey resulted in the detailed integration of the present drainage pattern.

Two explanations may be adduced for the change in course of the west to east River Elwy to one of north to south near Ddôl: is it the result of glacial diversion or river capture? Boswell (1949) suggested that it was caused by glacial diversion when the course of the Elwy was blocked by an Irish Sea ice stream that diverted the river along its ice margin from north to south parallel to the ridge of Cefn Meiriadog which overlooks Pontnewydd Cave. He did, however, write that further investigation was needed. At least five major questions arise:

1) When did it occur? Embleton (1960; 1970; 1984) realized that it must have been pre-Devensian in age because Welsh deposits of that glaciation infill the valley. He was followed by Livingston (1984; 1990)

and Jones (chapter 4, this volume). There is, however, a serious risk of confusing time and space because the hypothesis of an earlier glacial diversion relies on evidence of Devensian glaciation. It is unlikely that pre-Devensian and Devensian ice-margins would have reached a more or less identical limit (Figures 3.3; 3.4).

2) There are no pre-Devensian glacial deposits (boulder clay or till) or any stratigraphical actuality of such an event. Any ice-dam would have caused a pro-glacial lake which over-spilled to fashion the earliest north-south reach of the Elwy; but no evidence for such a lake in the form of laminated deposits occurs (cf. Gibbard 1976).

3) What was the condition of the Welsh ice coeval with that of the Irish Sea ice? Boswell (1949) concurred with Wills (1937): namely, that the more powerful Arennig ice stream prevented an incursion by Irish Sea ice. Such pre-Devensian Welsh ice reached almost as far south as Gloucester and glaciated the west Midlands (Wills 1937; Maddy *et al.* 1995) (see below).

4) If Welsh and Irish Sea ice masses were co-extensive, how could a River Elwy have existed at that time to have been diverted?

5) Why did the diverted river not continue beyond Cefn Rocks?

The pre-225 ka (MIS 7) Upper Sands and Gravels of Pontnewydd Cave consist of debris flows (Collcutt 1984) transported into the cave: they consist of gravels from Silurian mudstones (Mourne and Case chapter 5, this volume) together with some erratics of northern (Irish Sea) provenance (Bevins 1984). Collcutt (1984) interpreted the unit as glacifluvial. Since then further samples have been analysed (Jackson and Bevins chapter 10, this volume) and confirmed their northern (Lake District) origin. Their occurrence in the debris flows, however, shows they are not in primary position and have been re-worked from earlier glacial deposits. It is likely that this would have been from the west because the unit does not contain Carboniferous Limestone pebbles, the outcrop of which lies to the north and east, and which would have been traversed by a northern ice stream. Thus an absence of Carboniferous Limestone fragments is unsurprising. The Upper Sands and Gravels were derived from the west as its Silurian constituents show. Where, then, might the northern erratics have come from? Unlike north-east Wales, where pre-Devensian Irish Sea ice was held offshore by powerful Welsh ice (Wills 1937; 1952; Boswell 1949), ice of Irish Sea origin did invade the north-eastern Snowdonian foothills (Embleton 1961) up to elevations of approximately 350 m (Billinghurst 1929).

Boswell (1949) noted that the erratics in the eastern Denbighshire Moors were 'local' in origin, but that Welsh glacial deposits in the west contained Ordovician volcanic rocks, namely tuffs, andesites and felsites, with one tuff measuring some '15 ft in diameter'. He thought their source was Snowdonia or Arennig. While these occur in glacial deposits now known to be Devensian in age (Fishwick

1977; Warren *et al.* 1984) they provide a mode of delivery for earlier events.

A second explanation for the change in the course of the Elwy is river capture. Boswell (1949) described the Elwy before its change in direction as a discordant stream, before it changed direction to become a strike-stream. Its former course is represented by the wind-gap at Plas Newydd (SH998731) (Figure 3.3). These are classic indications of river capture and it is clear that Boswell (1949) had considered such a possibility, just as he had suggested that the headwaters of the Elwy had formerly flowed into Snowdonia before its river capture by the Conwy. The river capture of the Elwy would have been affected by a left-bank tributary of the River Meirchion, also a consequent stream in Boswell's terminology, through headward erosion along the strike of the Carboniferous Limestone beds.

Regardless of whether the Elwy was subject to river capture or glacial diversion, the degraded nature of the Plas Newydd wind-gap not only points to its antiquity but may be an indication of the time when the Elwy valley caves were initiated. An alternative hypothesis is that the caves are much older and developed at a time when the outcrop of the Carboniferous Limestone extended an unknown but not inconsiderable distance to the west, as is clearly indicated by the geological cross-section on the Denbigh Sheet (107) of the British Geological Survey (1973). Pontnewydd Cave lies 35 m below the elevation of the Plas Newydd wind-gap; and, according to the survey of the cave, some 50 m above the present valley floor (Green 1984, 13). Pontnewydd Cave some 225,000 years ago was above the water table but if it is assumed it was still close to it, some 50 m of incision of the Elwy has occurred since that time at approximately 0.22 m a thousand years (0.22 m/ka). Using that estimate, the 35 m incision from the elevation of the wind-gap to the cave would have taken about 159,000 years placing the abandonment of that former course of the Elwy at about 384,000 years ago, a time close to the MIS 11/10 boundary at 360,000 years ago (Bassinot *et al.* 1994). This would place the initial infill of the cave close to estimates based on an age greater than MIS 8. Such numbers are, of course, speculative and conceal the numerous rejuvenation pulses forced by sea level which fluctuated on millennial and orbital timescales but most of all on tectonic uplift. Interestingly, not entirely dissimilar estimates from the Mendips show the water table of MIS 7 caves there to have been at about 66 m before further incision took place in response to local uplift (Westaway 2010). A map of British Isles gravity anomalies (Al-Kindi *et al.* 2003) suggests that similar local uplift cannot be discounted for the country around Pontnewydd. As much can be inferred from the river base-levels calculated from the analysis of river profiles. Harris (1947) found evidence for these at 1,046; 844; 637; 436 and 240 feet in polycyclic river profiles. Embleton's (1960) figures from the Aled-Elwy were 800; 680; 620; 510 and 430 feet; while Brown (1957) mapped a marine platform between 650 and 700 feet, which influenced the course of the River Dulas. Whereas at one time these were considered against a background of tectonic stability, the plate tectonics revolution influenced a new paradigm for sea level (base-level) changes (Bowen 1978).

Is there a solution to the uncertainties rehearsed above? The stratigraphical, geological and geochronological constraints are considerable: how can evidence for Late Devensian glaciation (*c.* 28–20 cal. ka) be used to elucidate what happened during a considerably earlier event? Confusion of time and space may occasion mis-interpretation. Given the uncertainties is it possible to reconcile the data? A vital clue may be the overwhelming evidence for the western provenance of the Upper Sands and Gravel as is shown by their lithostratigraphical mode of Silurian gravels and also the absence of Carboniferous Limestone pebbles. Their subordinate erratics of northern provenance lie in a secondary rather than primary position and are derived. Happily, Boswell (1949) inadvertently provided a mechanism for the similar but earlier emplacement of these erratics when he discovered that some of the Denbighshire Moorland Welsh boulder clays of Devensian age (Fishwick 1977; Warren *et al.* 1984) contained Ordovician igneous erratics. Thus an ice stream of Welsh and western provenance carried such erratics across the Conwy valley, which presumably carried an ice flow from south to north, a 'basal ice-shed' phenomenon first described in Edenside and the Lake District (Hollingworth 1931) and also described in South Wales (Bowen 2005).

An older Welsh ice stream covered Denbighshire and, critically, as with pre-Devensian glaciations, was sufficiently powerful to exclude Irish Sea ice. During Welsh ice deglaciation, ice thinning revealed the Cefn Meiriadog ridge against which supraglacial streams carried and deposited their sediment load, either carried directly into Pontewydd Cave when the ice filled the Elwy valley close to that elevation, or soon afterwards by paraglacial fluvial means to deposit the debris flows of the Upper Sands and Gravels.

Two corollaries arise: first, when the Upper Sands and Gravels were deposited the Elwy valley was already deeply incised and filled with Welsh ice. Second, the entrance to Pontnewydd Cave was close to its present position.

## Glaciation

Over the 2,600,000 years of Quaternary time many glaciations varied greatly in both space and time. The country around Pontnewydd was glaciated on several occasions and while it lacks the spectacular effects of upland glaciation, modification of the 'pre-glacial' landform was not inconsiderable. Topographic features were moulded and streamlined, while hill slopes were over-steepened. Glaciation was effected by Welsh and Irish Sea ice streams. Indicator erratics show that the former grew in the Arennig and Migneint districts of Merioneth and Snowdonia; and the latter in southern Scotland and north-west England, notably the Lake District. But how many glaciations have there been? Rocks from Arennig occur in the gravels at Happisburgh, East Anglia, (probably delivered by glaciers

for an unknown distance and then re-worked by streams), a hominin site more than 780,000 years old (Parfitt *et al.* 2010). While it has been argued that there were only four major glaciations during the Brunhes Chron of the last 780,000 years (Bowen 1999a), many lesser ones may have impacted either directly or indirectly on the country around Pontnewydd.

Glacial and other Quaternary deposits have been systematically mapped by officers of the British Geological Survey and appear on the 1973 Denbigh Sheet (107) on a scale of 1:50,000. They are comprehensively described in the sheet memoir (Warren *et al.* 1984). More detailed field slips on a scale of 1:10,560 (six-inches to a mile) are also available. Quaternary deposits (Figure 3.4) consist of:

1) A ubiquitous mantle of glacigenic (boulder clay/till) covering upland and lowland alike. Welsh boulder clays (Meirion Formation; Bowen 1999b) are typically stiff, steel-grey to blue black in colour and contain far-travelled erratics from Arennig and Snowdonia. Irish Sea boulder clays (St Asaph Formation; Bowen 1999b) are typically stiff red-brown to chocolate-brown in colour and contain far-travelled erratics from Scotland and the Lake District (Warren *et al.* 1984). Occasionally Welsh boulder clay is red in colour and includes lenses of Irish Sea material (Embleton 1970; Warren *et al.* 1984). Figures 3.3 and 3.4 show the approximate boundary between the two boulder clays, detailed descriptions of which are provided by Warren *et al.* (1984). Drumlins, some of which are rock-cored, occur in extensive areas of boulder clay and are comprehensively described in Warren *et al.* (1984) who mapped over 500 in the Denbighshire Moors (Figure 3.5); (see also Bowen 1982).

2) 'Undifferentiated' glacifluvial sands and gravels occur on valley bottoms: in the lower Elwy valley Livingston (1986; 1990) mapped glacifluvial outwash, solifluction terraces, and landslides. East of the Vale of Clwyd, the glacial deposits and landforms of the Wheeler valley (Brown and Cooke 1977) and the Alun valley (Thomas 2005) are important for elucidating Pleistocene chronology (see below).

3) River terraces are composed of both re-worked outwash deposits and cold climate fluvial gravels. During their accumulation they consisted of wide valley gravel floors occupied by braided streams, fed in some instances by alluvial fans on valley sides. Near Denbigh three terrace levels were mapped (Warren *et al.* 1984), which had earlier been interpreted as glacial lake levels (Rowlands 1955).

4) 'Head' is a heterogeneous mixture of clay or loam with small angular frost-shattered fragments of local rocks. It is widespread and sometimes admixed with boulder clay or landslip sediments. The Hiraethog Formation (Bowen 1999b) consists of head overlying bedrock which pre-dates the last glacial cycle.

5) Landslips are found on steep slopes with Welsh boulder clay mostly involved. On valley slopes they

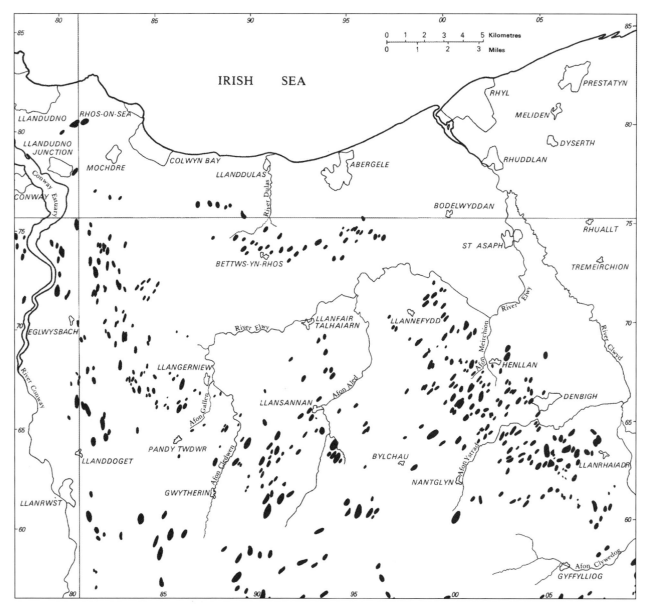

*Figure 3.5. The drumlins of the Rhyl and Denbigh district (Warren* et al. *1984). Crown copyright reserved and published by permission of the Director of the British Geological Survey.*

probably represent slope failure once the support of ice in the valleys disappeared. Those in the Elwy valley (Livingston 1986; 1990) are described below.

6)  Alluvium on valley floors and marine alluvium along the coastal plain.

7)  Peat is widespread on the uplands.

## The Elwy valley landslips

Close to Pontnewydd Cave the geomorphology of the Elwy valley is dominated by landslips in superficial materials (Figure 3.3). Three episodes of mass movement have been identified (Livingston 1986; 1990). First, massive late glacial landslides which exposed the limestone scarp; second, large rotational slides at a lower level; and third, smaller-scale movements (slumped blocks) a process which may still be continuing. Between Pen-y-Gribin and Ddôl,

where the material is glacifluvial sand and gravel of Welsh provenance, the valley sides consist of large pronounced concave scars below which slumped material lies adjacent to the modern floodplain. By contrast, below Ddôl, where the valley fill consists of clay tills and silts, the slump blocks are far less broken up and there is a complex zone of landslides. On the limestone, downstream of Ddôl, the south-west-facing slope of the valley, beneath the exposed limestone scarp, is dominated by a wide and extensive terrace feature approximately between 90 m and 125 m O.D. It is some 300–500 m wide and slopes south-west at an angle between 0.5° and 7.0°. The down-slope edge of the terrace lies some 35 m above the River Elwy and 70 m below the crest of Cefn-Meiriadog. Its surface is composed of Irish Sea till, the uppermost 1–2 m of which has undergone down-slope movement, as the preferred long-axis orientation of its individual pebbles lie parallel to the direction of maximum slope show. The terrace is composed of a number of distinct units running parallel to the ridge crest. These consist of treads between 100 m and 300 m in width separated by short, steep convexo-concave risers. Thus the terrace is a complex zone of older landslips which have been degraded by solifluction and other slope processes, and have been eroded by younger landslides. The treads are interpreted as displaced masses and the risers as degraded scars. The limestone cliff which backs the treads is regarded as the main scar of these old landslips. Laminated silts near Tan-y-Graig represent ancient ponds in the hollows formed between slump blocks and scars. A zone of landslide scars and conspicuous slump blocks runs along valley sides at a lower elevation than the older landslides. This zone of landslips formed as the River Elwy continued to excavate the valley fill when it undercut the older ones (Livingston 1986; 1990). The landslips developed between the start of deglaciation of late Devensian ice and the Holocene. But movement continued into the Holocene. This sequence of landslips is an analogue for many earlier events in the Pleistocene. In a complex but indeterminate earlier Pleistocene history the Elwy valley was subject to repeated incision caused by rejuvenation; and repeated infilling and excavation of earlier valley fills. Debris flows in Pontnewydd Cave are related to such earlier events but it is difficult to relate them with identifiable features in the present-day landscape.

## The sequence of events

Traditionally, British ice sheets were believed to be essentially 'static', but it is now evident that they were dynamic and pulsed on millennial and sub-millennial timescales. The interpretive key to the geochronological evolution of Welsh and Irish Sea ice sheets comes from 'a probably complex zone of interaction between the two ice sheets and their deposits' (Warren *et al.* 1984) which also accounts for variability in the colour of Welsh deposits (Embleton 1970; Warren *et al.* 1984). The earliest known Welsh glaciation from the Arennig region was correlated with the Anglian and marine (oxygen) isotope stage 12 (MIS 12) by Maddy *et al.* (1995), and reached Woolridge, north of Gloucester (Wills 1937; 1938) where it met ice from eastern England. In north-east Wales it was sufficiently powerful to hold off Irish Sea ice in Denbighshire (Wills 1937; Boswell 1949). A second Arennig ice stream was not so extensive but it reached south of the Clent Hills (Ridgacre Glaciation) and is correlated with MIS 6 by cosmogenic ages of 150±9 and 170±13 ka on glacial boulders (Maddy *et al.* 1995), the earliest application of cosmogenic rock exposure dating in Britain (Phillips *et al.* 1994). Downstream, glacifluvial outwash merges with the gravels of the Kidderminster Station Member of the Severn valley Formation (Maddy *et al.* 1995; Maddy 1999), which overlie the MIS 7 hominin site at Upper Strensham (de Rouffignac *et al.* 1995). Evidence for pre-Devensian glaciation in north-east Wales is provided by bore-holes along the coast showing Irish Sea deposits separated from underlying Welsh deposits

in the Oval borehole by interglacial deposits of presumed Ipswichian (MIS 5.5) age (Warren *et al.* 1984).

## Interglacials

The occupation of Pontnewydd Cave during MIS 7 is detailed elsewhere in this book. Of the major subdivisions of MIS 7, a relatively high sea level would have obtained along the north coast during MIS 7c and MIS 7a (Rowlands 1955; Wood unpublished maps). Global sea level on both occasions is estimated at 18 m below present-day sea level (Dutton *et al.* 2009) which points to considerable uplift of north-east Wales since that time. During MIS 7 millennial fluctuations in climate and sea level would have occurred and it is possible that a periodically enlarged coastal plain might have been a migration route? While there continues to be much debate about the last interglacial (MIS 5e) sea level there is agreement that it was higher than present (Bowen 2010) and further uplift would have occurred since.

## The Last Glacial cycle (Devensian)

The variability of glacially abraded quartz grains in the Barra Fan over some 40,000 years (Knutz 2000; Knutz *et al.* 2007) and cosmogenic rock exposure ages in Ireland over the same period (Bowen *et al.* 2002) shows that British and Irish ice sheets (BIIS) were probably periodically present throughout the Devensian and pulsed on millennial timescales (McCabe and Clark 1998). This brings the BIIS into phase with Scandinavian glacial variability (Svensson *et al.* 2010), evidence from North Atlantic marine cores (Bond and Lotti 1995; Hodell *et al.* 2010), Greenland ice cores (Wolff *et al.* 2009), and thus into phase with hemispheric climate variability. Sea level also fluctuated on millennial time-scales (Siddall *et al.* 2003). Shortly after 34 cal. ka Irish Sea ice, coeval with Welsh ice entered the Cheshire-Shropshire-Staffordshire Lowland. Its maximum extent, when it reached the 'Wolverhampton Line' (Morgan 1973) is generally taken as around 28 cal. ka (McCabe 2008), as it is throughout Europe (*e.g.* Svensson *et al.* 2010). Coeval Welsh ice was over 600 m thick (Embleton 1970; Thomas 2005), estimates supported by ice-profile reconstructions from Snowdon across Mynydd Hiraethog to Wrexham (Jansson and Glasser 2005). Welsh ice from Snowdonia and Arennig, crossed the Denbigh Moors, Vale of Clwyd and the Clwydian Range to impinge on the Cheshire Plain (the Ruabon Formation of Thomas 2005) somewhat before the arrival of the Irish Sea ice stream, a conclusion reached earlier by Hughes (1887), Embleton (1970) and Warren *et al.* (1984) on the North Wales coast. The Irish Sea ice sheet in the Irish Sea Basin was over 800 m thick and it caused considerable isostatic depression (McCabe 2008). Attempts at modelling the interplay between ice, glacio-isostatic depression and sea level fail to take such early timing into account not least because their data base generally starts about 10 cal. ka (Lambeck and Purcell 2001; Shennan *et al.* 2006).

The Irish Sea Basin was ice free by at least 20 cal. ka

(McCabe *et al.* 2005). Thus, the 'last' glaciation of the area, from maximum extent after 34.8±453 cal. ka (Morgan, 1973), probably about 28 cal. ka (McCabe 2008), to complete deglaciation about 20 cal. ka, a time which also included a major ice re-advance, lasted probably less than 14,000 years. The re-advance of the Irish Sea ice stream to the Wrexham-Ellesmere-Whitchurch-Macclesfield Moraine was probably the same age as that into the Vale of Clwyd almost as far as Rhuthun (Ruthin) and to Cefn Meiriadog (Warren *et al.* 1984). Another may be represented by the low hills composed of glacial deposits between Trefnant and Bodfari (Warren *et al.* 1984), interpreted as a terminal moraine (Rowlands 1955; Embleton 1970; 1984), but as supraglacial deposits let down from the ice surface as it melted (Livingston 1990). These are continued into the western end of the Wheeler valley (Livingston 1990) where their red colour diminishes eastwards (Brown and Cooke 1977). The complex landform-sediment associations of the Alun valley and eastwards to the Wrexham 'delta-terrace' are discussed by Thomas (1985; 1989; 2005), and are probably the same age as those of the Elwy valley (Livingston 1990).

The penetration of Irish Sea ice into the Vale of Clwyd beyond Denbigh, and partly into the Elwy valley at Ddôl and west of Trefnant (Figures 3.3 and 3.4), was only possible after the area had become free of Welsh ice. During that deglaciation the drumlins of the area were formed under conditions of fast flowing ice streams (Eyles and McCabe 1989; McCabe 2008). The timing of the re-advance may be indicated by the radiocarbon age from Ffynnon Beuno Cave of 18,000+1200/−1400 years (Rowlands 1971). This age estimate was determined many years ago in the Birmingham University Laboratory (BM-146) and Professor F. W. Shotton observed that 'a reputably-sized sample of collagen from the mammoth carpal bone, particularly after treatment to remove any possible contamination' was obtained, and that the 'large standard deviation is unavoidable because the sample was so small – only about half a litre of methane' (Rowlands, 1970). Any calibrated age must be older and averaging that standard deviation provides a calibrated age of 21,556±1,535 (CalPal 2007_HULU). This is close to the end of glaciation and is compatible with the geochronology of glacial events as currently understood. Somewhat earlier climate and vegetation pulsed to millennial timescales throughout Europe (Sanchez Goñi and Harrison 2010) and corresponding variability in glaciation may have allowed access for people and animals to the Clwyd bone caves, perhaps during Dansgaard-Oeschger (D-O) warming Event 2 (23.34 cal. ka, Wolff *et al.* 2009), that falls into the Trofers interstadial, (OSL: 25–20 cal. ka) known at several sites in central Norway (Johnsen *et al.* in press). Earlier, access to the caves may have been available during the Ålesund interstadial (*c.* 38–34 cal. ka) of coastal Norway (Svensson *et al.* 2010) which included D-O events 8 (38.22 cal. ka) and 7 (35.49 cal. ka) (Wolff *et al.* 2009). On this evidence, calibrated radiocarbon ages from Pontnewydd (CalPal 2007_HULU) are not incompatible with the times when access to the cave by animals was possible.

Deglaciation was catastrophic (Eyles and McCabe 1989). The Irish Sea was ice free by at least 20 cal. ka, perhaps earlier if the oldest Harwell radiocarbon ages of 20,040±210 and 19,210±690 from a stratigraphical sequence of muddy sediments (31 radiocarbon ages) in the north Irish Sea are indicative (Kershaw 1986); as well as an ice-free coast at Kilkeel, Ulster at 19 cal. ka (Clark *et al.* 2004). On the sea-floor north of Anglesey drumlins and 'cross-valley moraines terminated into a water-mass where there was extensive iceberg calving' (van Landeghem *et al.* 2008). This is consistent with the catastrophic disappearance of a marine-based Irish Sea ice (Eyles and McCabe 1989). On land, this pattern is supported by cosmogenic ages on glacial boulders in north-west England (Vincent *et al.* 2010). Probable re-advances of ice from Arennig may be marked by the Llanelidan drumlins, products of a 'Bala ice stream' (Jansson and Glasser 2005); and moraines at Bryneglwys and Pwll Glas as well as in the upper Arennig valleys (Rowlands 1970; 1977), followed by Younger Dryas glaciation in the Arennig and Aran Mountains (Hughes 2002). This sequence of re-advances probably correlate with similar radiocarbon dated events in Ireland at 18.2 cal. ka (Clogher Head), 16.5 cal. ka (Killard Point) (McCabe and Clark 1998; J. Clark *et al.* 2009) and 14.7 cal. ka (Antrim) (M. McCabe pers. comm. 2010). The Killard Point event is correlated with the Heinrich 1 event when ice streams around the North Atlantic surged into the ocean (Bond and Lotti 1995).

Between the start of deglaciation and the commencement of the Holocene, some nine thousand years remained for the operation of slope processes under mostly cold periglacial conditions when rapid environmental changes occurred. The late-glacial Younger Dryas (12.9–11.6 cal. ka) was a time of major changes on hill slopes and braided flood plains. Many landslips occurred and: for example, drumlins were modified by this process (Warren *et al.* 1984). Soon afterwards climate improved although still subject to millennial pulses of greater cold (Bond *et al.* 1997) when sea-ice extended farther south. Sea level rose to the Bryn-Carrog shoreline along the north coast Rowlands (1955). Some of the later stages of this marine transgression were documented by a combination of pollen analysis and radiocarbon dating by Tooley (1974).

*End-note: 'cal. ka'*

> The conversion of radiocarbon years into calendar or sidereal years is a technique subject to continuing refinement as it has been for the past forty or so years (*e.g.* Taylor 2009). It is desirable to use calibrated ages in *the Geomorphology of the country around Pontnewydd* in order to relate events in north-east Wales to Pleistocene timescales used in the scientific literature that are calculated from annual counts in ice sheet cores and speleothems (Wolff *et al.* 2009) as well as OSL dating (Berger 2009) and cosmogenic rock exposure dating (Gosse and Phillips 2001). Thus 'cal. ka' is used to distinguish such ages from radiocarbon ages which are given in full: *e.g.* 20,040±210. Some papers such as Clark *et al.* 2009, which used 5,704 calibrated radiocarbon and cosmogenic rock-exposure ages, present calibrated radiocarbon ages as, for example, simply 26.5 ka.

# 4. The Geology of Pontnewydd Cave

## William B. Jones

*Pontnewydd Cave is one of a series of caves in the Carboniferous Limestone outcrop along the middle Elwy valley that also includes the Cefn Caves. Modern springs indicate that an active cave system persists along the valley. Pontnewydd Cave itself is a phreatic tube about 4 m wide intersected by side passages of probably vadose origin. The walls are partially covered with remnants of flowstone and corroded stumps of stalactites. The cave mouth appears to open out into a now vanished large chamber.*

*Joint orientation measurements show two dominant directions, north–south and west-north-west–east-south-east, which are much the same as the orientations of the cave and side passages. Bedding plane attitudes on an exposed limestone surface around the New Entrance show an anticline plunging gently to the east. It is proposed that the Elwy valley caves are remnants of a larger system with a trunk cave along the line of the present middle Elwy River.*

## Regional setting

### Limestone geology

Pontnewydd Cave is situated in the Carboniferous Limestone which forms a discontinuous outcrop along the northern and eastern margins of the uplands of North Wales (Figure 4.1). At the cave the limestone outcrop is about 2 km wide. It dips to the north-east and overlies thin Carboniferous Basement Beds resting on the Silurian shales of the Denbigh Moors. To the north-east of the limestone ridge the low ground of the Vale of Clwyd is occupied by the poorly exposed Coal Measures. The limestones along the Elwy valley are part of the Dyserth Limestone Group which belongs to the Asbian stage of the Visean Series (Warren *et al.* 1984).

The Dyserth Limestone in the Pontnewydd area is generally a grey bioclastic wackestone. Macrofossils are usually uncommon but small and large brachiopods, solitary corals and occasional crinoid ossicles may be seen. There is a horizon of small coral logs exposed by the path along the cliff leading to Cefn Cave. The lower part of the limestone sometimes has a purple-grey colour as can be seen at Pontnewydd Bridge.

Outcrops of the limestone are usually massive, clear bedding planes occurring at intervals of between 100 mm and 1 m. The bedding planes tend to be undulose with a wavelength of 100–200 mm. Sedimentary structures on a smaller scale than this cannot usually be made out. However the beds can occasionally be seen to be made up of millimetre scale laminae, the beds in this case being low angle cross lamination sets.

Examination of 15 thin sections of Dyserth Limestone from the Pontnewydd area showed them to be mostly of a similar lithology. They consist predominantly of bioclasts (broken fragments of fossils) and peloids (pellets of calcite mud which in this case are mostly broken down bioclasts) set in a matrix of sparry (crystalline) calcite and micrite (calcite mud, possibly crushed peloids). The commonest fossils are foraminifera, often unbroken, and fragments of brachiopods. There are also algae, ostracods and crinoid ossicles. Corals and rhizoliths (root casts) occur in samples from Cefn Cave. One sample from near the base of the succession in the Brasgyll Gorge consists mostly of dolomite, a common occurrence at the base of the Carboniferous Limestone in North Wales (Warren *et al.* 1984).

### Formation of cave systems

Caves form as a result of dissolution of limestone by groundwater which has a high concentration of carbon dioxide derived from biological activity in the soil profile (Waltham *et al.* 1997, 5). Limestone dissolution is most intense just below the water table where the water still has its high $CO_2$ charge. The resulting 'phreatic' cave has a

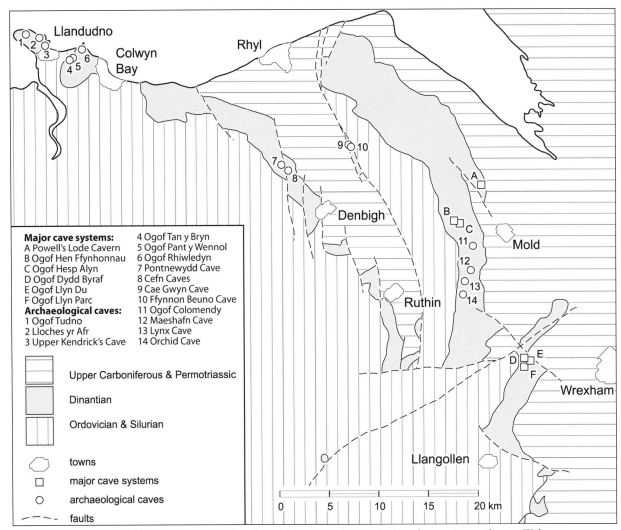

*Figure 4.1. Distribution of Carboniferous Limestone (Dinantian) and caves in north-east Wales.*

rounded cross-section with scalloped walls and runs sub-horizontally (Moore and Sullivan 1997). At deeper levels the water has lost most of its $CO_2$ and is saturated with calcite. If the water table drops the cave becomes 'vadose' with an air space above the water surface. It is in effect a roofed over river valley characterised by a 'V'-shaped cross-section produced by downward erosion of the floor. Caves may be abandoned by flowing water and so become 'fossil' or 'inactive'. This can happen if water finds a deeper path through the rock in response to a deepening of its base level, the level at which the water reaches the surface in an adjacent valley.

Calcium carbonate dissolved out of the limestone by downward moving groundwater may be re-precipitated within the open spaces in caves as speleothem, a term which includes stalagmite, stalactite and flowstone. Sediment transported by a surface stream can be swept into a cave when the stream flows underground resulting in substantial deposits of externally derived material accumulating in and even choking underground passages.

The formation of caves and precipitation of speleothem are strongly affected by climate change. During inter-glacials and interstadials the limestone surface may be covered by vegetation producing soil pore water that is acid and rich in carbon dioxide. The ground water seeping into the bedrock is corrosive and can dissolve out passages in the limestone and re-deposit the dissolved material elsewhere as speleothem. On the other hand during ice age stadials there is no vegetation cover and the soil may be removed by glaciers and periglacial processes. Cave entrances may be blocked by glacial and/or periglacial debris. Thus cave formation takes place predominantly during interglacials and interstadials.

Major cave systems are known in the limestones of North Wales (Appleton 1989) (Figure 4.1). The largest are in the area from Holywell in the north to the Eglwyseg Escarpment in the south. The underground drainage which originally fed the spring at Holywell includes Powell's Lode Cavern, a chamber 70 m long and 22 m wide extending over a vertical range of 110 m. Two major caves adjacent to the Alyn Gorge are the 2 km long Ogof Hesp Alyn and the 800 m long Ogof Hen Ffynhonau. A complex of cave systems in the Minera lead mining district includes Ogof Dydd Byraf, Ogof Llyn Du and Ogof Llyn Parc which, with over 4 km of passages, is the largest in North Wales. There are numerous small caves in the limestone, some

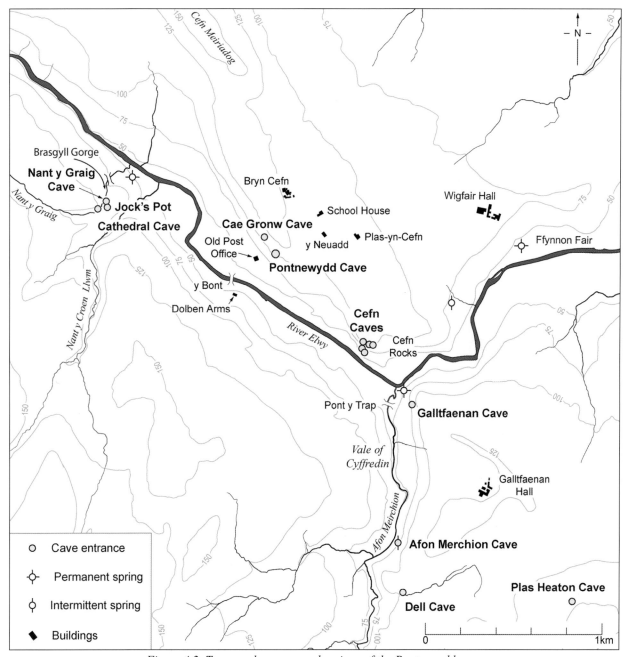

*Figure 4.2. Topography, caves and springs of the Pontnewydd area.*

of which, including Pontnewydd Cave, contain deposits of archaeological importance (Davies 1989).

### Elwy valley caves

Pontnewydd is one of several caves along the Elwy valley and its tributaries, the Nant y Graig and Afon Meirchion valleys (Figure 4.2). These include both inactive fossil and presently active caves (Appleton 1989). Nant y Graig runs eastwards along the Silurian/Carboniferous contact with a limestone escarpment on its left bank before turning northwards onto the limestone where it runs through the Brasgyll Gorge and finally debouches onto the floor of the Elwy valley. Several caves open onto the gorge, the largest being Nant y Graig Cave which is 4 m wide and

3 m high at its entrance (Meeson 1966). Other caves which can be entered from the gorge include Cathedral Cave, which contains a vertical pitch of 11 m, and Jock's Pot, terminating in a straight passage 11 m long. Plans of the caves by the Moldywarps Speleological Group (1987) are reproduced here as Figure 4.3.

The Cefn Caves are situated in a prominent limestone escarpment forming the north side of the Elwy valley at the point where the river turns from its south-easterly course and cuts through the limestone escarpment to the north-east. There are two sets of caves: a rock arch near the base of the escarpment and a separate set of interconnected passages about halfway up the slope (Figure 4.4). The Rock Arch is a passage about 20 m long in a north-west–south-east direction. It has a roughly rectangular cross-section 10 m

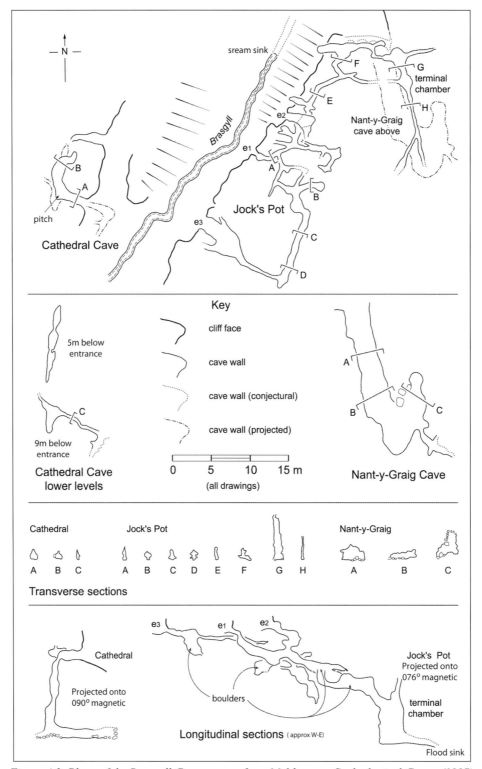

*Figure 4.3. Plans of the Brasgyll Gorge caves, from Moldywarps Speleological Group (1987).*

high by 2.5 m wide (Figure 2.1). The cave cuts through the end of the limestone spur about 20 m above the level of the river. The main Cefn Cave itself forms a network with three entrances about 20 m higher up the same ridge as the arch (Figure 4.5).

Dell Cave lies in a gulley on the east side of the Afon Meirchion valley. The entrance is 4 m wide and 3 m high. The stream that enters Dell Cave emerges at Afon Meirchion Cave in the valley below (Appleton 1989). Galltfaenan Cave is situated opposite Cefn Caves in the angle between the Meirchion and Elwy valleys. It is a solution-widened joint which may be followed for about 15 m (Davies and Ellis 1960). Cae Gronw Cave is a rock shelter on the south-west side of Bryn Cefn about 150 m north-west of Pontnewydd Cave.

There are several springs along the Elwy valley. Pont y

*Figure 4.4. Cefn Rock from across the Elwy River. The upper arrow marks the western entrance to Cefn Cave. The lower arrow marks the north-western entrance to the Cefn Rock Arch.*

Trap spring lies on the south side of the Elwy about 50 m downstream from the confluence with the Afon Meirchion. The flow is very variable from 1 litre/second in dry weather to 125 litres/second after wet weather. Ffynnon Fair is situated at the edge of the floodplain on the north-west side of the Elwy about 1 km downstream from Cefn Caves. Another spring, at the edge of the Elwy floodplain by the entrance to the Brasgyll Gorge, marks the re-appearance of the water from the Nant y Graig which has largely drained into the limestone along the gorge. These springs serve to demonstrate that there is still an active cave system below the fossil caves of the Elwy valley.

## Geological features of Pontnewydd Cave

### Main Passage

The rounded cross section of Pontnewydd Cave (see Figure 6.1 for nomenclature) is characteristic of caves produced under phreatic conditions, *i.e.* by dissolution below the water table. Water working its way along joints and bedding planes gradually dissolves away the limestone along its path until a round tube is produced. A characteristic feature of phreatic caves is scalloping, scallops being asymmetric concave depressions in the limestone surface with the steepest surface indicating the direction from which turbulent water flowed (Ford 1976). There are scallops about 300 mm across in the roof of Pontnewydd Cave just outside the inner door of the guard chamber (Figure 4.6). These are poorly preserved and do not give a clear current direction but their size indicates a

*Figure 4.5. Cefn Cave west entrance. On the right are two prominent bedding planes parallel with the roof and joint planes parellel with the passage axis.*

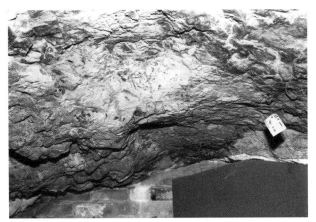

*Figure 4.6. Scallops in the roof of Pontnewydd Cave just outside the inner door.*

*Figure 4.7. View along the Main Passage looking east. The roof is composed of segments belonging to two parallel planes, one dipping to the north and the other to the south. The former corresponds to the bedding in the limestone.*

water flow rate of the order of 50 mm/second (Moore and Sullivan 1997, 12). Scallops may also be seen at the foot of the cliff immediately to the east of the entrance in the small recess known as the South Entrance.

The eastern end of Pontnewydd Cave, at the back wall of the Cross Rift, is an unexcavated cave fill. It is unlikely that the cave originally ended abruptly here. If the cave were formed by phreatic processes then it would at that stage have been filled with flowing water. This water must have had a continuous underground path from the point where it sank into the limestone as far as the spring at which it re-emerged. The cave therefore probably continues with much the same dimensions eastwards beyond the limit of the excavation. Indeed there is a gap of up to 200 mm between the clay and the roof at the eastern limit of the excavation along which the cave can be seen to continue for a metre or so. This is probably similar to the prospect confronting members of the Birkenhead Y.M.C.A. Spelaeology Club when they excavated the cavers' trench during the 1960s, starting from about the beginning of the East Passage.

One clear bedding plane is visible in the wall of the cave. It appears high in the South Passage and continues halfway

across the Main Passage as an area of planar roof over the Deep Sounding. Its strike direction of 116° is about 15° away from the 100° orientation of the cave in this zone. The dip at 8° is gently downwards to the north.

Areas of the roof of the cave at the entrance to the East Passage, between the South-East Fissure and South Passage and on the low arch at 194 m on the site grid, define a set of approximately parallel planes. This set dips approximately southwards at about 18° and is quite distinct from the northward dipping bedding. Competition between these two sets of planes could account for the highest point in the roof of the Main Passage alternating between the north and south sides of the cave along its length (Figure 4.7).

### Side passages

Several minor branches oriented about north-south lead off the south side of the Main Passage of Pontnewydd Cave. They thin away from the axis of the cave and taper upwards into recognizable joints (Figure 4.8). Most of these joints can be traced across the roof of the Main Passage as recesses up to a metre deep but corresponding passages on the north side of the cave are small or absent. Corrosion along these joints has produced recesses in the ceiling with gothic arch shaped profiles. Their tapering profile away from the Main Passage implies that the latter was already there when the side passages were formed. Also the nucleation along joint planes indicates that they were dissolved out by water flowing along these planes rather than along the axis of the Main Cave. The side passages probably belong to a period of dissolution under vadose conditions and so post-date the phreatic phase during which the Main Passage was formed.

### Speleothem

Over most of the cave roof where the host limestone is visible, the surface shows boxwork solution. The limestone has been corroded to produce a pattern of polygons separated by channels a centimetre or so deep. Overlying this corroded surface much of the roof is encrusted with speleothem, particularly in the area of the South Fissure and Deep Sounding (Figure 4.9). Figure 4.8 shows the area with speleothem west of the north-east and south-east fissures. Speleothem does also exist east of there, particularly at the Cross Rift.

The speleothem has itself been eroded. The margins of encrusted areas show the truncated edges of successive layers of calcite which add up to an original characteristic speleothem thickness of the order of 50 mm. Adjacent areas of boxwork textured limestone still have remnant infills of calcite in the channels. Some parts of the speleothem crust have clusters of stalactite stumps with their radial and concentric structures clearly etched out.

It would appear that the speleothem once covered a greater proportion and perhaps most of the roof. It has undergone a subsequent phase of dissolution. Speleothem forms by deposition of calcite as carbonate-saturated

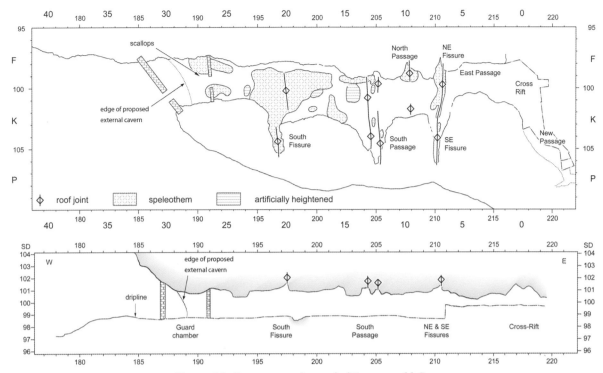

*Figure 4.8. Features on the roof of Pontnewydd Cave.*

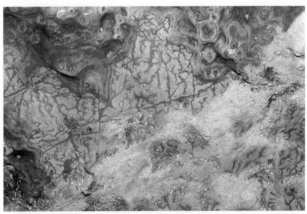

*Figure 4.9. View of part of Pontnewydd Cave roof showing boxwork solution of the limestone and the corroded edge of a speleothem covering. Remnants of speleothem infill channels in the limestone. The white material coating both types of surface is soft calcite growing at the present-day ['moon rock'].*

*Figure 4.10. View of the north side of the Main Passage between the inner door and the Deep Sounding. The wall shows an abrupt change from sloping outwards to sloping inwards about a metre above the floor. On the left of the picture speleothem coats both parts of the wall.*

water evaporates into an air space. The speleothem must therefore have grown in the vadose zone above the water table. Roof flowstone may be seen merging with the edge of stalagmite floors at several places in Pontnewydd Cave, *e.g.* 1.7 m above the floor at 207 m east and high on the wall at 196 m east on the site grid, both on the north wall. The range of dates obtained for stalagmite fragments within the sediments therefore probably also applies to the roof speleothem. Dissolution of the latter may have taken place as erosion at the surface reduced the thickness of limestone above the cave so that water seeping into the open space was still undersaturated with carbonate.

## Blocky cave wall

The upper part of the cave wall slopes steeply downwards and outwards away from the centre and shows the corroded and speleothem encrusted surface texture. However this ends at a distinct notch about one metre above the floor below which the slope is steeply inwards (Figure 4.10). The wall may also be set backwards by a distance of up to half a metre, producing a marked overhang. Below this discontinuity the wall has a blocky appearance, more like the freshly exposed surface around the New Entrance than the rest of the cave surface. Parts of this blocky cave wall are faced with remnants of cave sediments.

The blocky texture of the lower cave wall may have been produced by periglacial frost shattering. The restriction of this texture to the lower part of the wall could be because the cave was filled with water saturated sediment only up to this level. The lower cave wall was affected by freeze-thaw activity as a result of water penetration but the upper wall was dry.

The notch seems to correspond roughly with the top of the calcareous breccias. The fragments of limestone generated in those areas where the wall has receded may have become incorporated in the adjacent breccia deposits, from whose clasts it might subsequently be impossible to distinguish them. The blocky textured wall is in places faced with speleothem, indicating that the periglacial erosion event pre-dates at least one phase of speleothem precipitation.

### Recent changes

A few patches of soft framboidal or fluffy crystal growth a few mm thick can be seen in various places on the walls and ceilings. It has a distinctive milky-white colour, sometimes with an iron red stain. This is probably 'moonmilk' which is finely crystalline calcite deposited from a bacterial film (Moore and Sullivan 1997, 85).

Four areas were identified and are shown on Figure 4.8 where the roof has been artificially chipped away to raise the height of particularly low points. They are recognizable by their blocky appearance which is quite distinct from the corroded texture of adjacent areas. These artificial changes are probably a relic of the army's occupation of the cave during World War II.

### External Cavern

The main entrance to Pontnewydd Cave lies in a recess in the cliff face with the wall of the guard chamber being set back about a metre from the plane of the cliff (see Green 1984, illustration on the front cover). The walls of the recess have the shape of an arch opening outwards to the south-west. This can be interpreted as the edge of a larger chamber from which the present cave branched off. This chamber is here referred to as the 'External Cavern'. A similar feature may be seen outside the western entrance to Cefn Cave.

The lower part of the slope below the cave mouth and above the road is an outcrop of limestone. This can be followed continuously behind the undergrowth from a small steep path south-south-west of the door around to the massive cliff north of the entrance. The top surface of the limestone is a bedding plane lying 2–3 m below the floor of the entrance chamber, *i.e.* at 86–87 m O.D. or about 96 m on the site datum. This presumably represents the floor of the External Cavern. It is also approximately at the same elevation as the floor of the Deep Sounding. This correlation supports the contention that the latter is close to the deepest part of the sub-sediment floor of the cave.

The recess in the cliff face begins about 6 m above the floor of the Guard Chamber. Adding this height to the 2–3 m depth of the chamber floor below the entrance gives a minimum height for the External Cavern of 8–9 m. This is not an unusual size since the Cefn Cave and Afon Meirchion Cave both reach 11 m high.

A few metres west from the entrance, the platform in front of the cave pinches out and the limestone cliff extends down to the road. Two small openings, the larger half a metre across, may be seen in this cliff about 5 m above the road. At the south-west end of the cliff there is a recess in the limestone, perhaps an old quarry. In the back of this recess, 7 m above the road, there is a pattern of interconnected horizontal and vertical tubes in the limestone. The tubes are of the order of 100 mm in diameter, have smooth rounded outlines and are filled with clayey gravel which seems to have entered the system from the top. These miniature passages thus show the principal features of Pontnewydd Cave in microcosm. These small caves and also the openings on the adjacent cliff seem to be at roughly the same elevation as the floor of the External Cavern.

### New Passage and New Entrance

A joint in the roof of the Cross Rift continues into the beginning of the New Passage, giving the latter a gothic vaulted form. The New Passage then offsets eastwards by about 3–4 m from this joint before resuming a southwards course along a straight passage 10 m long. This long passage usually has a semicircular cross-section above the clay fill, indicating a phreatic origin. It is mostly encrusted with speleothem but at intervals a north-south joint may be seen in the roof. About halfway along it, the roof is wet and has been corroded into a very rough surface. This is probably a site where ground water is actively dissolving the limestone at the present-day.

The New Passage connects with a cave mouth, the New Entrance, uncovered by removal of the scree on the hillside. On the principle that cave passages are generally continuously connected because they were formed by flowing water, we may expect the South Fissure, South Passage and South-East Fissure also to emerge on the hillside behind the scree.

The New Entrance, as seen from the outside, has a semicircular arched roof with a diameter of about 2 m. This is consistent with the New Passage and indicates a phreatic origin. On the other hand the floor has a 'V'-shaped cross section which would result from vadose erosion, *i.e.* scouring by a stream running through a passage with air above it. The segment of cave floor revealed by excavation slopes southward at roughly 45°. Since vadose currents must flow downhill, this shows that the water in the passage was flowing from north to south. This passage would have been formed originally by solution under the water table. Subsequently the water table fell and the passage was then modified by a stream running along its bottom on its way down to the new base level.

Although the roof is no longer present south of the New

*Figure 4.11. Exposed bedrock surface on the west side of the New Entrance. The hammer lies between the traces of Bedding Planes 3 and 4 on the steep surface above and Bedding Plane 5 forming the broad surface below.*

Entrance, the walls of this cave can be followed as a trench in the limestone for another 6–7 m. The floor and lower part of the passage may well continue southwards beyond the limit of the excavation as a feature in the surface of the limestone.

### *Exposed bedrock surface*

Removal of the scree from around the New Entrance during the course of the excavation has exposed an extensive area of limestone bedrock surface. This surface presumably represents the hillside as it was just before burial by periglacial scree in late Devensian time. It provides an opportunity to examine the structural features in the limestone on a relatively fresh surface.

Bedding planes are well displayed on this limestone exposure (Figure 4.11). They have been numbered from 1, the youngest and highest in the section, to 8 at the bottom. The distribution of the bedding planes is shown on the plan (Figure 4.12).

The attitudes of the bedding planes around the New Entrance depart from the normal north-easterly dip displayed by the limestone elsewhere along the Elwy valley (Figure 4.13). The dips are less than the usual 16° or so and vary in direction from north-easterly at the north-west end of Plane 2, through easterly to south-easterly at the southern end of Plane 7. The variation of dip direction may be explained by postulating an anticlinal fold with its axis running approximately west–east through the cave mouth and plunging at about 5° to the east. This would also explain the pattern of what appear to be west–east tensional fractures on the surface of Bedding Plane 5 (Figure 4.14) and the zone of strongly fractured and brecciated limestone

on the opposite side of the New Entrance. An anticline with a similar orientation can be deduced from bedding plane measurements in the upper Meirchion valley (Figure 4.13).

### *Comparison with other local caves*

Pontnewydd has a crudely rounded cross section above the artificial flat floor cut in the sediment infill during World War II. Its width of about 4 m is wider than the Cefn Caves but comparable with Nant y Graig Cave. The accessible length at 30 m is about one and a half times greater than the Cefn Arch passage, but the latter has been truncated at both ends by surface erosion. The length of the passage between the west and east entrances of Cefn Cave is about 35 m and this is also an erosional remnant. Afon Meirchion Cave at 300 m is an order of magnitude longer. The height of the roof of Pontnewydd Cave is generally of the order of 2 m above the present floor. The Deep Sounding adds another 2 m or so. This compares with a height of 3 m at the entrance to Nant y Graig Cave and a range of 1 m to 5 m for the Cefn Cave system. The dimensions of Pontnewydd Cave are within the range shown by the other caves in the Elwy valley although its width and height are at the larger end of the scale. It appears to be merely one among many similar cave remnants now truncated by the present land surface.

## Formation of Pontnewydd Cave

### *Joint patterns and cave orientations*

Four joint zones may be seen in the higher part of the

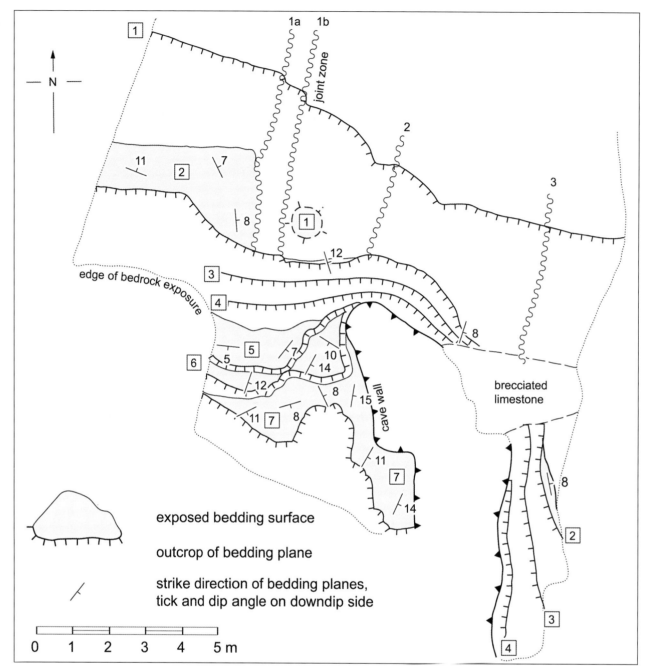

*Figure 4.12. Structural features of the exposed bedrock surface around the New Entrance. The numbers indicate the Bedding Planes and Joints referred to in the text.*

exposed bedrock surface (Figure 4.15). They run slightly east of north, approximately parallel with each other and roughly perpendicular to the cliff face. In detail they are formed by the joining up of a succession of short joint surfaces showing a range of orientations. The steep slopes between the bedding planes lower in the outcrop are made up of similar intersecting subplanar joint surfaces. The orientations of 71 of these surfaces were measured and the results are presented as a rose diagram in Figure 4.16. This shows the dominant direction of jointing as being north–south, with a subsidiary west-north-west to east-south-east trend. The relative importance of these two trends on the rose diagram may not reflect their true relationship in the

field, as joint surfaces at a high angle to the cliff face are more obvious than those parallel with it.

There is a striking congruity between the chief joint directions recorded at the exposed bedrock surface and the orientations of the main and side passages inside Pontnewydd Cave (Figure 4.17). This makes it clear that joints are the main control on the orientation of cave passages. The same conclusion can be drawn from other caves in the region. For example Cefn Cave has passages in two directions about 60° apart (Figure 4.18), the two directions corresponding with joint trends visible on the cliff face outside. There is also a prominent set of joints on the south-east side of the west entrance to Cefn Cave

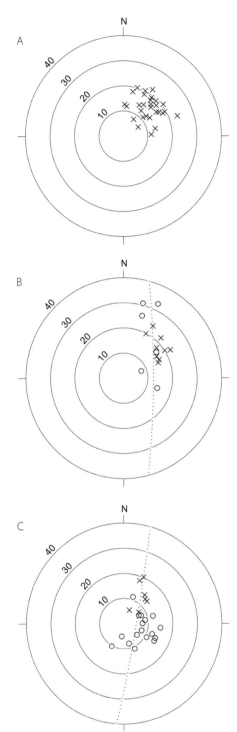

*Figure 4.14. The surface of Bedding Plane 5 next to the New Entrance. The east-west fractures may represent tension over the crest of an anticline.*

*Figure 4.15. Joint zones (numbered) in the upper part of the exposed bedrock surface by the New Entrance. Two zones are visible in the back wall, the one which rests on Bedding Plane 1, being double. The double zone projects into the foreground, between Bedding Planes 1 and 2.*

*Figure 4.13. Orientations of bedding planes in the Carboniferous rocks of the Pontnewydd area. The diagrams are stereograms of the poles to bedding planes (northern hemisphere equal area projection). A) Bedding plane measurements along the Elwy valley except for the vicinity of Pontnewydd Cave and the southern Afon Meirchion valley; B) Measurements in the upper Afon Meirchion valley. Circles – the monclinal fold, crosses – other measurements. The dotted line is the trace of a fold with vertical axial plane striking at 090° and hinge plunging east at 12°; C) Measurements around Pontnewydd Cave: circles – New Entrance exposure; crosses – inside the cave, around the mouth and by the road below. Dotted line is the trace of a fold with vertical axial plane striking at 100° and hinge plunging at 5° east.*

which parallels the adjacent passage wall. The anticlinal folds at the New Entrance and in the Meirchion valley also parallel the long axis of Pontnewydd Cave.

The approximately linear form of Pontnewydd Cave suggests that its shape is controlled by a linear feature such as a fault or joint. In fact there is no continuous joint to be seen running along the crest of the ceiling, such as may be seen in parts of Cefn Cave. Two sets of joints are however exposed in the floor of the Deep Sounding. One has an average azimuth of 074° with a range of 072°–086° whereas the other has an average of 170° and a range of 140°–180°. The former set do not correlate well with the

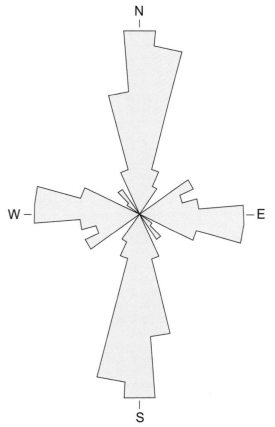

*Figure 4.16. Rose diagram of the azimuths of 71 joint surfaces measured on the exposed bedrock surface around the New Entrance.*

100°–110° orientation of the Main Passage but the latter set do fit well with the cross passages.

Seven joint directions measured within Pontnewydd Cave show a limited range of 159°–175°, the mean being 168° (Figure 4.8). The orientation of this set of joints is rotated slightly anticlockwise from the dominant fracture direction at the exposed bedrock surface around the New Entrance by about 15° (Figure 4.16). This minor nonequivalence is exemplified by the offset between the South Fissure and the joint in the roof of the adjacent part of the Main Passage (Figure 4.8).

The one instance where a passage can be followed from inside the cave as far as the hillside is the connection between the New Passage and the New Entrance (Figure 4.17). The New Passage begins within the cave at the Cross Rift but leads off in a south-eastwards direction so as to end up 3–4 m east of the line of the rift. It then runs in a north–south direction for about 10 m. This straight section shows signs of a joint in its roof. From the outside it looks as though this joint may correspond to Joints 1A and 1B on the back wall of the exposed bedrock surface. Joint 2 runs down into the roof of the New Entrance but the half eroded passage in front of the cave mouth moves diagonally away from it and then turns so that its eastern side runs along Joint 3. The passage thus steps from one joint to another, so that between the Cross Rift and the truncated passage

outside the New Entrance, a distance of approximately 25 m, it has migrated by about 8 m eastwards from the line of the Cross Rift. The end result is a passage which follows segments of joints but has an overall orientation which is largely independent of the joint pattern.

On exposed rock outcrops such as the south-west face of Cefn Rocks and the lower part of the exposed bedrock around the New Entrance the whole surface is a patchwork of small joint segments. It seems that the limestone has particular directions along which it is prone to fracture. Underground such fractures are few and confined to narrow zones producing joints. At the ground surface the whole rock mass breaks up along these preferred directions producing the faceted appearance of the outcrops. While it is not certain that all the Elwy valley caves originate as joints, the close similarity between joint and passage orientations does indicate that these preferred fracturing directions were the major determinant of passage orientation. However the minor discrepancies at Pontnewydd Cave suggest that other factors do also play a part.

The form of a cave system is largely governed by the frequency of fissures in the host rock (Ford and Ewers 1978). When there are few fissures the water is forced to follow a tortuous path including loops deep under the water table. On the other hand a high fissure frequency allows the water to generate a cave system which follows the water table. The Elwy valley caves are largely subhorizontal along their long axes suggesting that they belong near the high fissure frequency end of the spectrum. Certainly joints do seem to be common in the limestone. However cavers have reported vertical pitches in some of the caves (Appleton 1989).

## Origin of the Elwy valley caves and cave sediments

The caves in the Elwy valley would have been formed at some time when the Dyserth Limestone was within reach of meteoric water circulating down from a contemporary ground surface. The area around the eastern Irish Sea has been uplifted by about 3 km since late Cretaceous time (Lewis *et al.* 1992) and it is probable that a 1–2 km thickness of Mesozoic strata has been removed from this area during the Cenozoic (Holliday 1993). The formation of the caves could have been before the burial of the limestone by Mesozoic strata or after the removal of these overlying strata during the Cenozoic. In the former case any caves produced would have become filled with younger sediments, probably of Permian or Triassic age. No such occurrences have been demonstrated in North Wales. On the other hand Cenozoic solution is indicated by pockets of sediments of poorly constrained Cenozoic age infilling solutional hollows in the limestone (Walsh and Brown 1971).

There is considerable evidence that the presently accessible caves along the Elwy valley are remnants of larger systems. The entrance to Pontnewydd Cave originally led off from a larger chamber and the New Entrance passage seems to continue out into the valley as

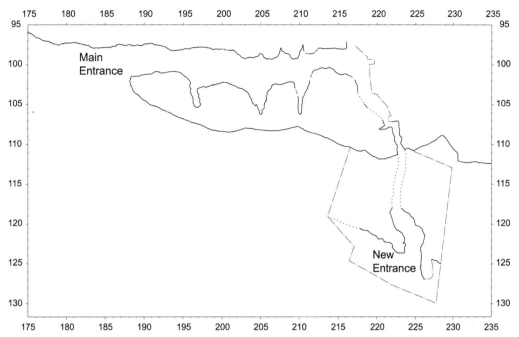

*Figure 4.17. Plan of Pontnewydd Cave. The orientations of the passages approximately coincide with the joint pattern.*

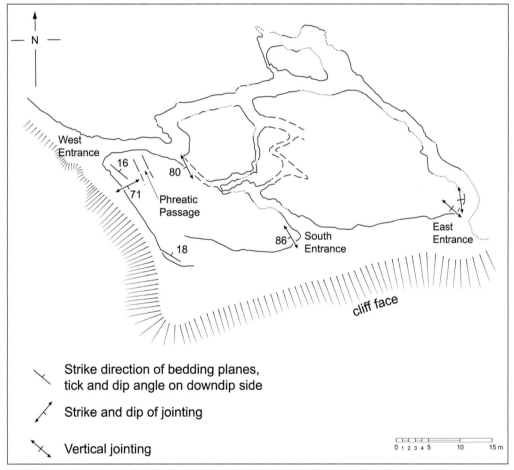

*Figure 4.18. Structural features of Cefn Cave. Passage orientations are near parallel to two prominent joint directions.*

though the hillside were not there. The west entrance to Cefn Cave also appears to have joined onto a now vanished large chamber. The series of caves along the valley at present may be merely the peripheral remnants of an originally much more extensive system, the axial part of which lay along the centre of the Elwy valley.

However the middle Elwy came to run along its north-west to south-east course, one consequence was that this

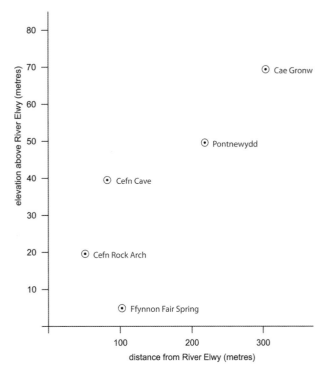

*Figure 4.19. Distances of some cave mouths from the River Elwy compared with their height above the river.*

section of the river valley flowed across a continuous outcrop of limestone approximately along its strike direction. This allowed ample opportunity for some of the water to be diverted underground during interglacial or interstadial cave forming episodes.

The sediments inside Pontnewydd Cave consist of a lower 'Siliceous member' and a higher 'Calcareous member' (Collcutt 1984; Mourne and Case chapter 5, this volume). The siliceous unit consists of gravels with rounded clasts of siltstone, mudstone and subordinate igneous rocks. The thinner calcareous member is dominated by breccias of angular limestone clasts. Collcutt suggested that the siliceous unit consists of material from a fluvioglacial source outside the cave but was surprised at its lack of limestone clasts since they are common in the modern Elwy River gravels. Limestone clasts of local derivation become increasingly common and finally dominant upwards through the calcareous unit.

The gravels of the siliceous unit may have originated as fluvioglacial sediments derived ultimately from the Ordovician and Silurian bedrock of North Wales. The lack of limestone clasts in the siliceous unit could be because there had been little physical erosion of the limestone at the time of their formation or that the source of the sediments lay to the west (see Bowen and Livingston chapter 3, this volume). The ground underlain by limestone may initially not have shown much topography, so that there were no limestone outcrops to be eroded. Chemical dissolution of the underground limestone would have allowed rivers running off the country south of the outcrop to drop into the evolving phreatic cave system through sink holes. Gravels could then

have accumulated within the caves without containing a carbonate component. Periodic surges of water through the caves would have picked up and transported pockets of sediment far from their initial entry point. Pontnewydd Cave lies about 2 km downstream of the wind-gap where the Elwy originally crossed the limestone outcrop. The siliceous sediments in the cave may have travelled underground by anything up to this distance.

Progressive lowering of the base level would have led to abandonment of earlier phreatic tubes and their replacement by deeper passages. The higher caves would become vadose with water running only along their floors. During periods of deglaciation, there would be much more water in the river than at present and it would be carrying a considerable load of rock debris freed from the ice. The limestone would have been weakened by the complex of passages within it. Frost shattering of the exposed limestone faces would have supplemented the erosive effect of the river and generated banks of scree. This destruction of the limestone enclosing the caves would have generated accumulations of angular limestone breccia, both as scree on the surface and as secondary deposits within the cave, including the calcareous unit in Pontnewydd Cave.

### Age of the caves

Caves are not confined to any one elevation in the Elwy valley and actually seem to occur throughout the height of the limestone outcrop (Figure 4.19). In several places they are stacked one above another. The most obvious example of this is the Cefn Caves where Cefn Cave itself is 20 m above the Cefn Arch. Caves can also be seen throughout the 10–15 m height of the Nant y Graig rock gorge. Stacking of caves like this can be interpreted as recording an episodic fall in base level, probably related to a fall in relative sea level.

Gascoyne *et al.* (1983) have shown on the basis of uranium series dating that the higher levels of limestone caves in the Craven district of Yorkshire are more than 350 ka old. Their data indicates that the floors of the Dales have fallen at a rate of 50–200 mm per 1,000 years. This approach may be applied to Pontnewydd Cave by assuming that the date of 225 ka for the *in situ* stalagmite (Ivanovich *et al.* 1984) is soon after the abandonment of the cave as a water table passage. The rate of incision for the water table to fall the 50 m to its present elevation at Pontnewydd Bridge is 220 mm per 1,000 years which is at the high end of the range of the Yorkshire data. It is however a maximum value because the cave could be considerably older than the stalagmite.

Taking an erosion rate of 220 mm per 1,000 years and applying it to the height difference between the col at Plas Newydd through which the river originally flowed (125 m) and the present river level nearby (55 m) gives a date of 320 ka for the diversion of the River Elwy onto its present course. This should be regarded as a minimum age since the erosion rate is itself a maximum figure. The erosion rate will also not have been uniform as limestone dissolution is more intense during interglacial than during glacial episodes (Gascoyne *et al.* 1983). Furthermore base level will not have dropped continuously since relative sea level rises and falls during glacial/interglacial cycles must also be taken into account. The glacial cycle corresponding to Marine Isotope Stage 10 began at 400 and climaxed at 320 ka (Huybers 2007, figure 1) but this episode has not been identified in the British Isles (Bowen 1999a). However the previous cold period, MIS 12 which began at 500 ka and reached its maximum ice volume at 440 ka, is well known in England as the Anglian Glaciation. It might be that at this time an ice front diverted the River Elwy onto its present course near parallel with the limestone ridge.

### Relationship of the archaeological deposits to the contemporary cave mouth

The archaeological materials are found within the Calcareous member and largely within the Lower Breccia. This places them after deposition of the fluvioglacial sediments ended, perhaps as a result of diversion of the main river flow to a lower level in the limestone. On the other hand they belong before any significant quantity of limestone breccia reached this part of the cave system. This implies that the source of breccia, the zone outside and within the entrance which was susceptible to diurnal or annual temperature fluctuations leading to frost shattering, was still some distance away.

The cliff face outside the present cave mouth shows signs of having been once part of a chamber, the External Cavern, rising above the roof of the existing cave and probably having a larger diameter. The roof and southern side of this chamber have been eroded away. This implies that before the destruction of this larger chamber the cave mouth was some distance from its present position. The modern River Elwy runs 50 m below the cave mouth, so the river has cut down to this lower position since the sediments were deposited within the cave. Downcutting of the river bed implies a simultaneous wearing back of the valley side, again indicating removal of large amounts of limestone from outside the present cave mouth. The evidence for cave formation at progressively deeper levels on both sides of the Elwy valley suggests that the cave system was controlled by a master cave running along the axis of the valley. This has been eroded away to leave the subsidiary caves opening onto the modern valley sides.

Diversion of the Elwy to the south-east along the limestone outcrop and the subsequent onset of dissolution would have generated a cave system along the line of the future middle Elwy valley. The river would have found its way underground through an entrance into the cave system somewhere between the diversion point at Ddôl and the present day Elwy valley cave remnants. The cave mouth may have been initially anything up to 2 km upstream of Pontnewydd Cave.

It has been suggested above that the diversion of the Elwy may have occurred at 320 ka or 440 ka which would place the 225 ka old cave sediments at some 50–70% of the time since the onset of cave formation. The cave system

would be less mature than at present and the limestone would have undergone only part of the erosion that is visible today. Continuing deposition of sediments in Pontnewydd Cave indicates that water was still flowing over the floor of the cave but the subsequent onset of flowstone growth shows that the upper part of the cave at least was above the water table by that time. For water to flow over the floor of Pontnewydd Cave it must have entered the cave system from an entrance at a higher elevation. This implies that the Elwy, whether running within a trunk cave or in an open river valley, was at an elevation about 50 m higher than it is at Pontnewydd Bridge now. There is no trunk cave at present as the Elwy is open to the sky along its whole course. However the evidence for Pontnewydd Cave being a fragment of a much larger cave system argues for a trunk cave existing along the Elwy valley at the time of the emplacement of the archaeological layers, with its entrance farther upstream to the north-west. A cave extending the whole distance from Ddôl to Pontnewydd would have been about 2 km long, which is the length of Ogof Hesp Alyn, another North Wales cave (Appleton 1989). However it is likely that a significant fraction of the cave would already have been unroofed at the time of the archaeological deposits.

There is no definitive evidence for how far the archaeological deposits in Pontnewydd are from the contemporary cave mouth. The human remains, and much of the fauna probably always belonged to the darkness zone (see chapters 10 and 13, this volume), but the artefacts must have been made and lost in the light. The evidence for the wearing back of the hillside around the cave entrance, the inferences from the position of the deposits within the cave sediments, and the evidence of external caverns at both the Main Cave and the New Entrance (see chapter 6, this volume), indicate a minimum of ten – possibly several tens – of metres. However, more contentiously – the discussion of the length of the trunk cave between Ddôl and Pontnewydd Cave suggests a significant fraction of 2 km, perhaps as much as several hundred metres.

### Conclusions

Pontnewydd Cave is one of a set of caves along the Elwy valley which are remnants of a once much more extensive system. The orientation of the cave passages is governed by the joint pattern in the limestone. It is proposed that the cave system was initiated at a time when the Elwy was prevented by an ice front from crossing the limestone outcrop at Ddôl, possibly during MIS 12. Subsequent development involved the creation of caves at lower levels in response to falling base levels and the abandonment and destruction of earlier passages.

The siliceous sediments in Pontnewydd Cave would have originated as fluvioglacial material which had been washed into the cave and may have come to rest far from the contemporary cave entrance. The overlying limestone breccias are the debris from physical erosion of the host limestone by frost shattering.

# 5. The Sedimentary Sequence

*Richard W. Mourne, David J. Case, Heather A. Viles and Peter A. Bull*

*The Pontnewydd Cave sedimentary sequence (Mourne and Case) is dominated by in-fill from debris flows. Such flows are generally associated with cold environments where an ample supply of glacial and periglacial sediments may become mobile through high pore-water pressures generated by the melting of interstitial ice. These flows may run for considerable distances within caves as de-watering opportunities are limited. They incorporate both from outside and from within the mouth of the cave, hominin, faunal and artefactual material which, as part of the flows, become largely protected from subsequent geomorphic and sedimentary activity. Fabric analyses show the direction of the flows in the Main Cave to have been from west to east. Scanning Electron Microscopy (SEM) (Bull) supports the evolving provenance of succeeding debris flows. They demonstrate the generally non-destructive nature of such flows, which show little evidence of erosion and mixing between units, accounting thereby for the preservation of contained fauna and artefacts.*

*The sequence within the cave comprises a basal Siliceous member of Lower Sands and Gravels overlain by Upper Sands and Gravels. The debris flows which make up these gravels reflect, through a lack of incorporated limestone, a cave system with an entrance at least at the very edge of the Carboniferous Limestone outcrop. The debris flows would have originated within catchments upon Silurian mudstones beyond the limestone. Overlying fines (Grey Silts) indicate a cessation in debris flow activity, and a period of ponding within the cave. This ponding event was followed by a second episode of debris flows, laying down the overlying Intermediate complex and Lower Breccia. The former incorporates soil material and exhibits evidence for post-depositional alteration through translocation of colloids. The Intermediate complex and overlying Lower Breccia are mixtures of mudstone and limestone gravel, the latter showing that the cave system was opening up by this stage. Nearly all hominin remains were retrieved from the Lower Breccia, with single finds from the Intermediate of the Main Cave and Layer 38 of the New Entrance sequence.*

*The Lower Breccia bed seems to have plugged the cave entrance for some time. It is covered locally by a stalagmitic floor, the dating of which indicates that there was no clastic deposition within the cave from 224,000+41,000/–31,000 BP (grand average) to 83,000±9,000 BP. During this period the only event seems to have been the episodic formation of stalagmite focused on temperate episodes around 225,000, 175,000, 120,000 and 85,000 years ago. The re-opening of the cave mouth – at or after 80,000 BP – is marked by the deposition of the Silt beds, followed by another debris flow event forming the Upper Breccia, characterized by a dominance of fresh limestone clasts indicating extensive excavation and exposure of the cave system. This sequence, from the Intermediate complex to the Upper Breccia, has been identified as the Calcareous member.*

*The New Entrance, to the south of the Main Cave, exposes a sequence of mudstone-rich layers (34–41) overlain by limestone rich debris flows (Layers 23–33), the whole dated as younger than 85,000 BP on the basis of a U-series determination on the basal in situ flowstone (Layer 43) on bedrock. The contained fauna of the mudstone-rich layers comprises wolf, fox, bear, duck, jackdaw and* Homo. *This very limited fauna is consistent with that of the much older Lower Breccia, suggesting erosion, and mixing with that deposit. The presence of a tooth of* Homo *in this layer, indeed, lends weight to this interpretation as, also, do TL determinations on burnt flint artefacts centred on 175,000 BP and plausibly 'stored' within the cave system before their eventual emplacement. SEM studies (Bull) have identified similarities between the New Entrance mudstone-rich sediments and the Lower Breccia supporting erosion and mixing, but the SEM evidence is not conclusive. Fabric analysis (Mourne and Case) indicates flow into the New Entrance from its original entrance to the south. The exception to this is Layer 20, which is interpreted as a spread of tufaceous carbonate and corroded stalagmite generated as part of the Upper Breccia emplacement process and washed through the system from the Main Cave. The debris flows are overlain by a sequence of solifluction, scree and possibly aeolian deposits which apron the lower valley slope. The boundary between the youngest debris flow and oldest slope deposit marks the final opening up of the New Entrance cave at this site, although the increasing limestone content of preceding units, and the SEM analysis of stalagmites from both the limestone and mudstone units (Viles), indicates a proximal cave entrance during the emplacement of these flows.*

## The sedimentary sequence of Pontnewydd Cave

*Richard W. Mourne and David J. Case*

### Introduction

Detailed description of each section exposed during excavations from 1978 to 1981 enabled the establishment of an initial cave lithostratigraphy through correlation of deposits based upon data reflecting ten major sediment characteristics (Collcutt 1984). Subsequent excavation within the cave, from 1982, has resulted in the development and extension of Collcutt's lithostratigraphy, with a separate lithostratigraphy being established for new excavations outside of the cave at the 'New Entrance' (*e.g.* Green *et al.* 1989).

The opening of the New Entrance (Area H) raised questions of correlation with the cave sequence, of flow directions for the debris flows, and of the location of the original cave entrance(s), particularly with respect to the Lower Breccia from which most of the hominin finds had been recovered. Establishing location of the cave entrances at the time of the emplacement of hominin fossils, fauna and artefacts is fundamental to palaeogeographical reconstruction. Thus, Collcutt (1984) states that '... *it is most probable that future qualification of spatial trends in shape, size, orientation and damage of sediment particles, bones and artefacts could be related to local details of flow regime and cave morphology*'.

In 1987 a programme of work was initiated to address these sedimentological questions. The work had three main aims. First, to augment the field descriptions of geometry, thickness, structure and colour of the identified sedimentological units within and without the cave with data on clast size, shape, lithology, surface condition and fracturing, matrix/fines particle size and carbonate content. As well as characterizing the sedimentological units according to criteria largely identifiable in the field, this work was also aimed at extending correlations within the cave, and between the cave and the New Entrance.

Second, the work aimed to establish flow directions of the main debris flows, namely the Lower and Upper Breccia within the cave, and the possible correlation of the sequence of Layers 23, 24, 26, 28, 29, 34 and 38 at the New Entrance.

Third, to develop a geomorphological, sedimentological and post-depositional history for the cave and its fill, thereby establishing a context for the artefactual and faunal inclusions. The lithostratigraphic and sedimentological interpretations of Collcutt (1984) provide the framework for this history which is extended within and without the cave.

### Sediment characteristics, methods of investigation

Ninety bulk samples from within (Areas B, D, F and G) and without the cave (Area H) (Figure 6.1) have been analysed in the laboratory at the University of the West of England, Bristol. The following characteristics were measured and investigated; clast and matrix particle size, clast roundness, clast lithology, degree of limestone alteration, and degree to which exotics are fractured.

#### Particle size

Each sample was subdivided into the following size ranges by sieving; >-1 phi (<2 mm), -1 phi to -2.7 phi (4–6.3 mm), -2.7 phi to -3.8 phi (6.3–14 mm), -3.8 phi to -5.0 phi (14–32 mm), <-5.0 phi (>32 mm). Fines particle size analysis was determined from a sub-sample of 10–100 g of material smaller than -1 phi which was gently disaggregated with a rubber pestle prior to the addition of 100 ml of 4% calgon solution to deflocculate the clay/silt fraction. The sample was occasionally stirred and left overnight before being wet-sieved using a 4 phi (0.063 mm) mesh into a 500 ml glass tube and topped up with distilled water. The residual sand fraction was dried and then passed through a nest of sieves giving a breakdown from -1 phi to 4 phi at 0.5 phi intervals. The suspension in the tube was thoroughly shaken and allowed to settle. Pipette samples were taken at fixed time intervals (in accordance with Stokes's Law) to give a breakdown from 4 phi to >9 phi (0.002 mm) at 1 phi intervals.

The particle size data were plotted on a sand-silt-clay triangular graph to give an overall descriptor for the fines (Hodgson 1974) which is presented in brackets for each unit. A clasts to fines ratio by weight (c:f = $^{2\text{-}32 \text{ mm}}/_{<2 \text{ mm}}$) has been calculated to quantify the relative proportions of clasts and matrix. For selected samples the matrix particle size distributions are presented as histograms.

*Clast lithology*

Each clast <-2.7 phi was examined, its lithology noted and assigned to one of three classes: Carboniferous Limestone, siliceous clasts, and secondary carbonate clasts. The siliceous category is subdivided into: mud/siltstone, sandstone, igneous, vein quartz, quartzite, and flint/chert. The secondary carbonate class is subdivided into stalagmite and calcite. The stalagmite category contains clasts of hard, compact, crystalline, sometimes laminated well-developed travertine, which became incorporated within the sediment unit during transport and emplacement. The calcite category contains clear and milky calcite and also amorphous carbonate nodules, which may constitute post-depositional formation within the sediment unit.

*Clast shape*

The Powers (1953) visual comparison chart has been used in describing clast shape. Six classes of roundness/angularity are represented in this chart, with an associated roundness index number which ranges from 0 (totally angular) to 1 (perfect roundness), the grades are (geometric mean values in brackets): very angular (0.14), angular (0.21), subangular (0.30), subrounded (0.41), rounded (0.59), well-rounded (0.84). Each clast in the size range -2.7 to -5.0 phi was assigned to a roundness/angularity class; a mean roundness value for the particular sediment unit was then calculated.

*Fracturing of pebbles*

For the exotic sedimentary clasts, the proportion of whole (or virtually whole) pebbles was noted. If the pebble had lost just a chip then it was counted as a whole pebble. Angular clasts or clearly split pebbles were not counted as whole pebbles.

*Limestone alteration – condition of the clasts*

A scheme for describing the weathering of limestone clasts has been used which identifies 5 indices of alteration/corrosion (AI 1 to 5). These are shown in Table 5.1.

*Carbonate content*

This measurement was carried out on 1 g of material from the >-1 phi fraction for each sample. A gasometric technique was employed which involved measuring the volume of carbon dioxide produced during the reaction of the material with hydrochloric acid. The procedure followed was that given in Hodgson (1974).

*Fabric analysis*

Fabric data was collected through long axis azimuth and dip measurement of up to 50 clasts in samples from Areas D, F and H. Small exposures and limited clast availability, and the nature of the archaeological excavation preventing excessive digging of exposures, has resulted in some samples having data sets comprising fewer than 40 measurements. Also, for the same reasons, it was not possible to carry out more than one set of fabric measurements in some layers. The significance of the orientation data has been tested by means of eigenvalue analysis according to the method of Woodcock and Naylor (1983), a development of that of Anderson and Stephens (1972). The analysis tests whether the distribution is one of random chance or determined organization. A graphical summary of the fabric data is presented in the sections below arranged by area as appropriate. An overall discussion of the data is presented at the end of the report.

### The Main Cave geography: description and interpretation of the sediments

As part of the excavation process, the cave and its environs were divided into eight areas labelled A to H (see Figure 6.1). Sediments have been sampled and analysed from areas B, D, F, G and H. In the following sections each layer is described, the descriptions in many cases encompassing results from a number of samples. Where there is significant variation between the characteristics of samples from the same unit, this is noted in the descriptions. The percentage figures in the brackets associated with clast lithologies refer to the proportion of that lithology in each clast size fraction examined. Therefore limestone (44% and 8%) means that 44% of the -3.8 to -5 phi fraction and 8% of the -2.7 to -3.8 phi fraction is limestone (the figure for the larger size fraction is always given first). Layer descriptions are followed by a discussion of possible sources, depositional mechanisms and sedimentological environments.

*Area B*

Area B is delimited by the outer Guard Chamber Wall to the west, and the eastern face of the Deep Sounding to the east, and includes the South Fissure. In the 1984 report, the wall sediments in the Guard Chamber were simply referred to as 'GC' (Collcutt 1984, 34 and figure III.2), but these are now incorporated within B. The Deep Sounding presents the only significant exposure in the cave of a sequence of gravels referred to by Collcutt (1984, 49–50) as the 'Siliceous member', comprising the Lower Sands

| *AI 1* | Weak | Little or no alteration, fresh |
|---|---|---|
| *AI 2* | Weak-moderate | Lightly corroded, discoloured |
| *AI 3* | Moderate | Tiny perforations, whitish surface |
| *AI 4* | Moderate-extreme | Very perforated, 'powdery' surface |
| *AI 5* | Extreme | Highly rotted, broken shell, core exposed, friable |

*Table 5.1. A scheme for describing the weathering of limestone clasts which identifies five indices of alteration/corrosion (AI 1 to 5).*

and Gravel sub-member (LSG), Upper Sands and Gravel sub-member (USG) (units 5–1), and the Grey Silts (GS). Overlying the Siliceous member is a pedo-sedimentary complex labelled the Intermediate complex (Ic). Field descriptions show the LSG to comprise clast supported exotic gravel deposits free of limestone, but no samples were collected for this study. The USG and Ic have been examined in more detail:

**Upper Sands and Gravel sub-member unit 5**
Mudstone gravel (c:f = 2.7 to 3.5). Mudstone (87% and 96%) and other exotics (13% and 4%), no limestone. Exotics are rounded (0.53) and 52% are whole pebbles. Matrix well represented in coarse sand and fine silt, very high clay content (clay). Dull orange-brown colour.

**Upper Sands and Gravel sub-member unit 4**
Not sampled for sedimentological description.

**Upper Sands and Gravel sub-member unit 3**
Matrix rich mudstone gravel (c:f = 0.41). Mudstone (100% and 90%) with some other exotics (0% and 10%), no limestone. Exotics are rounded (0.51) and 49% are whole pebbles. Matrix

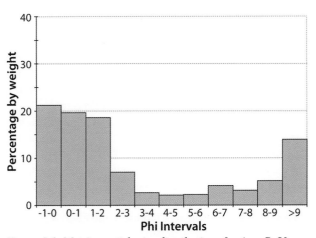

*Figure 5.1. Matrix particle size distributions for Area B, Upper Sands and Gravel sub-member unit 1.*

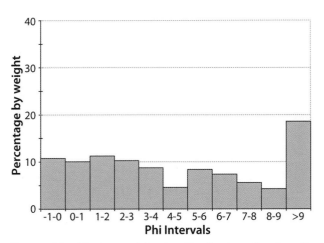

*Figure 5.2. Matrix particle size distributions for Area B, Intermediate complex.*

is well-sorted and shows a strong medium sand peak, quite low clay content (sandy loam).

**Upper Sands and Gravel sub-member unit 2**
Mudstone gravel (c:f = 2.2). Mudstone (94% and 96%) with some other exotics (6% and 4%), no limestone. Exotics are rounded (0.55) and 60% are whole pebbles. Matrix poorly sorted, with a peak in coarse sand (clay loam/sandy silt loam).

**Upper Sands and Gravel sub-member unit 1**
Mudstone gravel (c:f = 2.0). Mudstone (90% and 97%) with some other exotics (10% and 3%), no limestone. Exotics are rounded (0.55) and 59% are whole pebbles. Matrix dominated by coarse and medium sand, moderate clay content (sandy loam) (Figure 5.1).

**Grey Silts**
Fine deposit, poorly sorted. Bulk of this deposit >4 phi in size. Fine sand and coarse silt are best represented, moderate clay content (sandy silt loam).

**Intermediate complex**
Mudstone gravel (c:f = 1.4). Mudstone dominates (56% and 91%) some limestone (38% and 6%) and other exotics (6% and 3%). Exotics are subrounded (0.39) and 14% are whole pebbles. Limestone is subangular (0.33) and moderately corroded (AI = 3). Matrix is very poorly sorted, dominated by sand, with moderate silt and clay content (clay loam/sandy silt loam) (Figure 5.2).

*Interpretation of Area B sediments*
The USG are characterized by: the absence of limestone clasts; high proportion of mudstone (generally >87%); high degree of clast roundness; high percentage of whole pebbles; low carbonate content (<1%); c:f ratio >2; low clay and silt content, with locally intercalated sand and silt lenses. Plotted on a triangular graph the units all cluster strongly at the gravel peak, with the exception of USG unit 3 which has a higher sand matrix component. USG 3 is also distinctive in that it has no sandstone exotics. The geometry, bedding and gravel composition, with well-rounded clasts and a lack of sorting and structures, coupled with the exotic nature of the clasts all indicate a series of debris flows with a glacial or more likely fluvio-glacial source. In particular, the sorted sand component evident in USG 3 suggests fluvial re-working. The lack of any limestone clasts in the LSG and USG has been explained by Collcutt (1984) as a derivation from 'more or less pure exotic sediment' filling the valley or spread on the plateau surface entering the cave *via* a nearby entrance or *via* vertical chimneys. However, William Jones (chapter 4, this volume) argues the cave system sediment provenance to be Silurian rocks at the margin of the Carboniferous Limestone outcrop. These would have supported a surface water drainage system feeding into the karst landforms of the limestone. The Grey Silts represent a hiatus in debris flow activity when standing water enabled fines to decant, whether washed through the cave system from a source underground or washed into the system through bedrock fissures from the surface. The

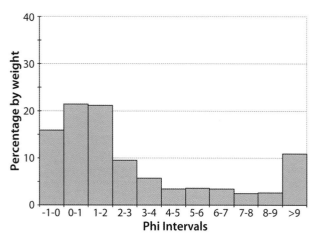

*Figure 5.3. Matrix particle size distributions for Area D, Upper Sands and Gravel sub-member.*

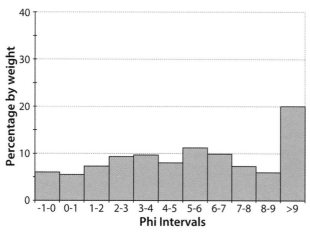

*Figure 5.6. Matrix particle size distributions for Area D, Lower Breccia.*

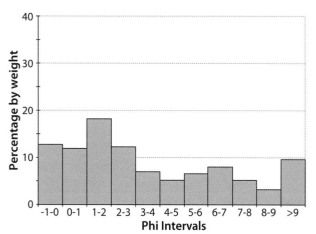

*Figure 5.4. Matrix particle size distributions for Area D, Intermediate complex – orange.*

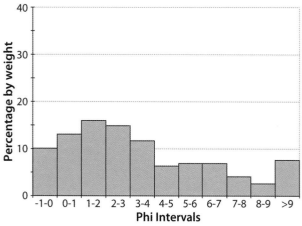

*Figure 5.5. Matrix particle size distributions for Area D, Intermediate complex – buff.*

presence of silt in varying proportions throughout the USG may indicate a series of similar episodes, the products of which have been integrated into the matrix by subsequent flow re-working. It is also possible for silt to have been translocated through the USG interstices.

The Intermediate complex in this area is characterized by a mudstone gravel with moderately corroded subangular limestone clasts, a subrounded exotic fraction of which only a small proportion are unbroken, and a poorly sorted matrix. As such the deposit is significantly different from the LSG and USG, but has similarities to the Lower Breccia beds (LB) as described below in Areas D and F. The subangular limestone clasts suggest an initial exposure of the cave system, of which Pontnewydd is a relict, through erosion and roof collapse. Such exposure would create new catchments for sediment solely in the limestone terrain, providing a significant source and ingress conduit for sub-aerially (physically) weathered limestone. Debris flow is the main mode of emplacement for the Intermediate complex, but with some evidence in the form of rounding and sorting, of fluvial re-working. This has stratigraphic equivalence, and to an extent sedimentological equivalence, to the Intermediate complex recorded at Areas D and F. Applying the interpretation of the latter units at Area D (below), this complex may represent the altered remnant base of the Lower Breccia beds.

### Area D

Area D runs east from the North Passage to the central north-south section on grid line 213, and includes the North-East Fissure and South-East Fissure. A sequence of 6 units is exposed: Upper Sands and Gravel sub-member (USG); Intermediate complex (Ic), subdivided on the basis of colour into Orange Intermediate (OI) and Buff Intermediate (BI); Lower Breccia bed (LB); Stalagmitic lithozone (Sl); Silt beds (Sb); and Upper Breccia bed (UB).

**Upper Sands and Gravel sub-member**
Mudstone gravel with little matrix (c:f = 2.8). Mudstone (100% and 99%), very rare other exotics (0% and 1%), no limestone. Exotics (mudstone) are rounded (0.56) and 70% are whole pebbles. Matrix is sorted and dominated by coarse and medium sand with a low clay content (sandy loam) (Figure 5.3).

**Intermediate complex – orange**
Mudstone gravel (c:f = 1.4). Mudstone (100% and 98%), rare

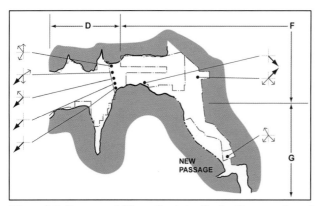

*Figure 5.7. Pontnewydd Cave. Statistically significant preferred clast orientations (bold arrows) and secondary orientations (small arrows) within the Lower Breccia bed.*

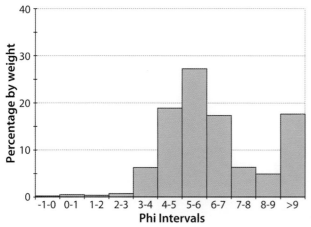

*Figure 5.8. Matrix particle size distributions for Area D, Silt beds.*

other exotics (0% and 2%), no limestone. Exotics (mudstone) are subrounded (0.42) and between 19% and 35% are whole pebbles. Matrix is poorly sorted sand low in silt and very low in clay (sandy loam) (Figure 5.4).

### Intermediate complex – buff

Mudstone gravel (c:f = 1.5). Mudstone dominates (74% and 92%) with some limestone (22% and 6%) and rare other exotics (4% and 2%). Exotics are subrounded (0.38) and 13% are whole pebbles. Limestone is subrounded (0.37) and is strongly corroded (AI = 4). Matrix is poorly sorted sand with low silt and clay (sandy loam/sandy silt loam) (Figure 5.5).

### Lower Breccia bed

The sedimentology of the Lower Breccia beds is variable. In the centre of the central baulk it is matrix rich mudstone gravel (c:f = 0.84). Mudstone (100% and 97%), very rare other exotics (0% and 2%) and very rare limestone (0% and 1%). Exotics are subrounded (0.37) and 9% are whole pebbles. Limestone is rounded (0.50) and is strongly corroded (AI = 4). Matrix poorly sorted with slight clay peak (clay loam) (Figure 5.6). Fabrics were recorded at five points along the exposure. Four show a statistically significant preferred clast orientation as illustrated in Figure 5.7.

On the north side of the cave and in the North-East Fissure

limestone presence increases to 58% and 9% at the expense of mudstone with a very small amount of broken stalagmite.

### Stalagmite lithozone

The Lower Breccia bed is locally covered by a stalagmitic floor. Radiometric dates indicate stalagmite accumulation from 262,000+69,000/–44,000 BP to 83,000±9,000 BP (see Debenham *et al.* chapter 11, this volume). Collcutt (1984) has suggested that in order for there to be such a long period of accumulation uninterrupted by any significant clastic deposition the cave entrance must have been blocked by a plug of Lower Breccia. The depositional history of the cave during this period also includes the formation of stalagmites with ages of 116,800+10,600/–9,700 BP and 137,400+8,600/–7,900 BP on the cave walls at 100.50 m S.D., around one metre higher than the adjacent portions of the Lower Breccia bed (see Aldhouse-Green and Peterson chapter 6, this volume for a further discussion of these problematic stalagmites).

### Silt beds

A fine deposit, silt dominated, well-sorted with a strong coarse to medium silt peak and a moderate clay content (silty clay loam) (Figure 5.8). Locally there is a slight coarsening with fine sand to coarse silt peak. Clasts are very rare, generally fractured stalagmite (50%), subangular/angular limestone (25%) of variable alteration (AI = 1–3), and subrounded mudstone (25%). The boundary between the Silt beds and the overlying Upper Breccia beds is generally sharp; however in places it is diffuse and indicates mixing between the two units (Figure 6.14, for example).

### Upper Breccia bed

No samples of Upper Breccia bed were collected from Area D exposures. Samples were collected from the immediately adjacent exposure at the west end of Area F. Six fabrics were recorded from Area D five of which show a statistically significant clast orientation as shown in Figure 5.14.

### *Interpretation of Area D sediments*

The Upper Sands and Gravel sub-member in Area D and the Upper Sands and Gravel sub-member unit 1 in Area B exhibit very similar values for c:f ratios (2.8 and 2.0), mudstone content (80% and 95% compared with 90% and 97%), exotic roundness values (0.56 and 0.55), percentage of whole pebbles (70% and 59%), and matrix textures of sandy loam. Limestone is absent from both deposits. These common characteristics coupled with stratigraphic and altitudinal position enable their correlation.

The Intermediate complex is characterized, here, by a subangular to subrounded mudstone gravel in which most of the clasts are broken, set within a poorly sorted matrix. Subdivided on the basis of colour the Intermediate complex comprises an upper buff horizon passing downwards into a lower orange horizon. The orange horizon contains no limestone clasts, whereas the upper buff horizon contains strongly corroded limestone clasts. Sedimentologically, this unit is an extension of the Intermediate complex debris flow in Area B. In detail the orange horizon is similar to the Upper Sands and Gravel sub-member, the buff to the overlying Lower Breccia beds, and particularly to the

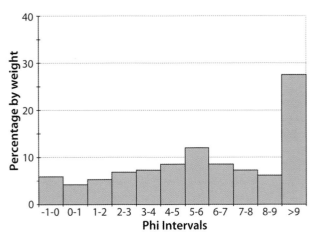

*Figure 5.9. Matrix particle size distributions for Area F, Lower Breccia beds c/d.*

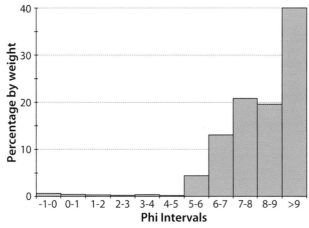

*Figure 5.11. Matrix particle size distributions for Area F, Silt beds.*

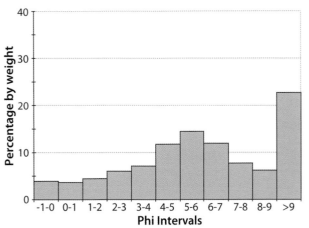

*Figure 5.10. Matrix particle size distributions for Area F, Lower Breccia beds a/b.*

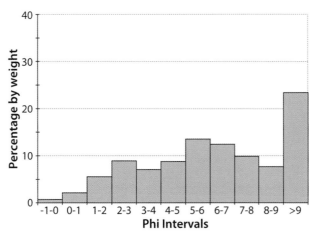

*Figure 5.12. Matrix particle size distributions for Area F, Silt beds sandier facies.*

Lower Breccia beds samples from the north side of the cave which are mudstone gravels with strongly corroded limestone. Jenkins (1984) has described the Intermediate complex as an eroded soil that moved into the cave as part of a debris flow, with subsequent alteration through translocation of colloids following the deposition of the Lower Breccia beds. The preservation of soil characteristics within the deposit suggests the cave mouth was nearby, this supporting an argument for the opening up of the Elwy valley and the exposure of the current cave entrance at this time. Accepting this, the sedimentology would suggest that in Area D the Intermediate complex debris flow initially re-activated the top of the USG, before subsequently introducing limestone material from the newly exposed cave entrance. It is possible that the Intermediate complex is the initial phase of Lower Breccia beds deposition with mobilization being effected by environmental change as postulated by Currant (1984) from the included fauna.

The Lower Breccia beds have the characteristics of a debris flow, the source material of which was a combination of glacial deposits and angular limestone. The presence of the latter indicates that the cave system has been excavated to a degree where there was a significant input of sub-aerial

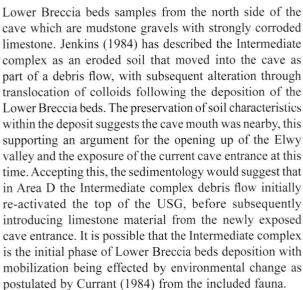

*Figure 5.13. Matrix particle size distributions for Area F, Upper Breccia bed.*

physically weathered limestone. As stated above, stalagmite accumulation on the surface of the Lower Breccia beds from 262,000+69,000/–44,000 BP to 83,000±9,000 BP without any significant clastic deposition suggests that the Lower Breccia beds had completely plugged the cave.

The Silt beds may have been translocated into the cave by water percolating through the limestone, or could have been washed into or concentrated within the cave by low energy streams with ponding, the local variation to fine sand suggesting the latter. The sediment is very similar to the matrix of the Lower Breccia beds and it is conceivable that the Silt beds represent the re-opening of the cave mouth through erosion, with an ingress of water eroding the Lower Breccia beds matrix and re-depositing it further within the cave system. As stated by Collcutt (1984, 72), the Silt beds contain no sedimentological climatic fingerprint, but he noted that they do contain a cold fauna (Currant 1984); a new quartz grain suite, characterized by angularity and a lack of chemical alteration (Bull 1984, 82–84); and a degree of mineral alteration reflecting the influence of a period of cold climate (Jenkins 1984). The Silt beds are overlain by the Upper Breccia bed described in detail in the next section. The latter is representative of another and much later debris flow event which accumulated on top of the Silt beds. Laminated Silt beds survive close to the cave walls. In the centre of the cave, the UBb not only locally 'bulldozed' the surface layers of the Silt beds producing a mixed/diffuse boundary, but also channelled deep into the underlying Lower Breccia in those areas of the cave where the absence of side-fissures – through which the UBb could be 'vented' – concentrated the erosive force of the flow (Green 1984, 201 and figure IX.2).

*Area F*
Area F runs from the eastern face of the central baulk to the Cross Rift. A sequence of five units is exposed: Intermediate complex (Ic), subdivided into Orange Intermediate (OI) and Buff Intermediate (BI); Lower Breccia beds (LB), subdivided on the basis of matrix colour into LB c/d and LB a/b; Stalagmitic lithozone (Sl); Silt beds (Sb); and Upper Breccia beds (UB) (Figure 6.13).

**Intermediate complex – orange**
Matrix rich gravel (c:f = 0.82). Mudstone dominates (74% and 92%) with some limestone (16% and 5%) and other exotics (11% and 2%). Exotics are subrounded (0.45) and 35% are whole pebbles. Limestone is subangular (0.27) and is extremely corroded (AI = 5). The matrix is a poorly sorted sand/silt with a slight peak in the medium silt, and a high clay content (clay loam).

**Intermediate complex – buff**
Mudstone gravel, locally matrix rich (c:f = 1.2 varying to 0.9 locally). Mudstone (67% and 97%) with some limestone (22% and 2%) and other exotics (11% and 1%). Exotics are subrounded (0.41) and 23% are whole pebbles. Limestone is subangular (0.32) and is strongly corroded (AI = 4). The matrix is a poorly sorted sand/silt with a slight peak in the medium silt, and a high clay content (clay loam).

**Lower Breccia beds sub-layers c/d**
Gravel (c:f = variable between 1.7 and 1.3). Mudstone dominates (73% and 93%) with some limestone (18% and 2%) and other exotics (9% and 5%). Exotics are subrounded

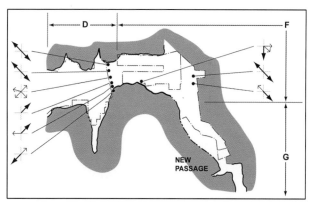

*Figure 5.14. Pontnewydd Cave. Statistically significant preferred clast orientations (bold arrows) and secondary orientations (small arrows) within the Upper Breccia beds.*

(0.38) and 12% are whole pebbles. Limestone is subangular (0.32) and is strongly corroded (AI = 4). The matrix is a poorly sorted sand/silt with a very slight coarse silt peak, and a high clay content (clay loam) (Figure 5.9). The identification of sub-layers a–f in the LBb is discussed by Aldhouse-Green and Peterson (chapter 6, this volume).

**Lower Breccia beds sub-layers a/b**
Matrix rich gravel (c:f = variable between 0.4 and 0.8). Generally very few clasts in the -3.8 phi to -5 phi range, in the -2.7 phi to -3.8 phi range clasts of mudstone (94%), limestone (3%) and other exotics (2%) are found. Exotics are subrounded (0.40) and 14% are whole pebbles. Limestone is subangular (0.30) and is moderately corroded (AI = 3). The matrix has a peak in the coarse silt fraction, and a high clay content (silty clay loam) (Figure 5.10). The identification of sub-layers a–f in the LBb is discussed by Aldhouse-Green and Peterson (chapter 6, this volume). Fabrics were recorded at two points along the exposure. Both show a statistically significant preferred clast orientation as illustrated on Figure 5.7.

**Stalagmite lithozone**
In the Cross-Rift the Lower Breccia beds are locally covered by a stalagmite floor as described for Area D.

**Silt beds**
Fine deposit (c:f = variable between 0.01 and 0.08). Well-sorted with a strong peak in the coarse silt fraction, moderate clay content (silt loam) (Figure 5.11). As for Area D, the Silt beds locally exhibit a sandier facies (Figure 5.12).

**Upper Breccia bed**
Gravel (c:f = variable between 1.0 and 1.8). Limestone dominates (95% and 87%) with some mudstone (1% and 10%), stalagmite (3% and 2%) and occasional other exotics (1% and 1%). The limestone is angular (0.24) and fresh (AI = 1) with an occasional lightly corroded clast (AI = 2). Exotics are subangular/subrounded (0.34/0.35) and 10% are whole pebbles. The matrix shows some sorting with a broad peak centred on the medium silt (silty clay loam) (Figure 5.13). Three fabrics were recorded from Area F, all of which show a statistically significant clast orientation as shown in Figure 5.14.

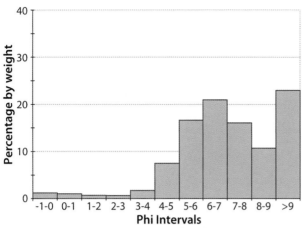

*Figure 5.15. Matrix particle size distributions for Area G, Yellow Silt.*

## Interpretation of Area F sediments

The Intermediate complex can again be differentiated on the basis of colour into the upper buff and lower orange horizons, but are otherwise similar, notwithstanding local variations in matrix richness. This sedimentological similarity can be extended upwards into the sub-layers (c/d) of the Lower Breccia bed. The mode of emplacement and alteration of the Intermediate complex is comparable to that of Area D, described above. The Stalagmitic lithozone and Silt beds have also been discussed above.

The Upper Breccia bed represents a further phase of debris flow, characterized by gravels dominated by angular, fresh limestone clasts with only small amounts of exotics. There is also a clast contribution from stalagmitic sources, which, as postulated above, would have developed

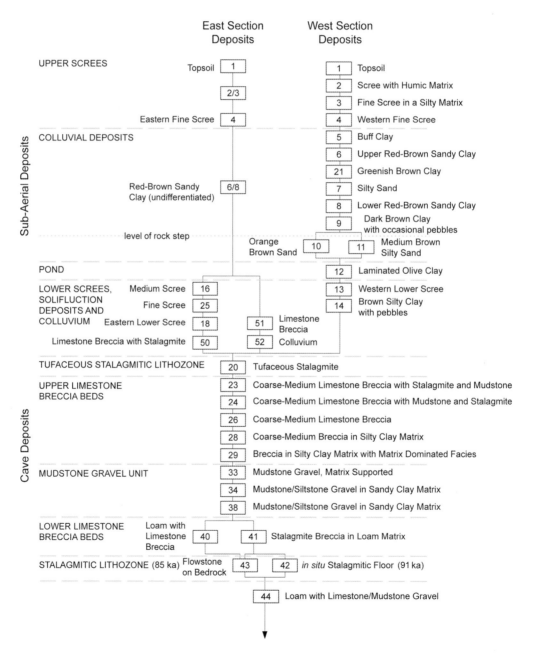

*Figure 5.16. Pontnewydd Cave. New Entrance (Area H): stratigraphic sequence revealed by excavation.*

during a warm episode. The limestone content indicates that the cave system was being excavated through the erosion of the limestone landscape, with frost shattered talus accumulations in gorges and cymoedd (coombes) providing an ample source of angular material for the Upper Breccia bed.

### Area G

Area G extends south-east from the Cross Rift along the New Passage. This passage runs through to Area H (see below). The passage as currently exposed is extremely narrow with small exposures of Yellow Silt (YS) overlying a gravel deposit interpreted as Lower Breccia on the basis of sedimentological characteristics.

**Lower Breccia**
Mixed gravel (c:f = 1.3). Comprises limestone (64% and 20%) and mudstone (27% and 75%) with some other exotics (9% and 5%). Limestone is subangular (0.31) and is moderately corroded (AI = 3). Exotics are subrounded (0.39) and 21% are whole pebbles. Matrix shows a small peak centred on the coarse silt, some sand and a very high clay content (silty clay). One fabric was recorded, presenting a pattern of clast orientation that is not statistically significant, the fabric being random at the 90% confidence limit.

**Yellow Silt**
Fine deposit with variable but very small amounts of included gravel (c:f = 0.18 to 0.07). The fines are moderately sorted with a medium silt peak, and have a moderate clay content. Very little material coarser than 3 phi. Very few clasts found, the general representation being limestone (60%), stalagmite (20%) and mudstone (20%). The limestone is angular (0.21) and varies from fresh to moderately corroded (AI = 1 to 3), the exotics are subrounded (0.37) and 29% are whole pebbles (Figure 5.15).

### Interpretation of Area G sediments

Sedimentologically the Yellow Silt is very similar to the Upper Breccia beds matrix. The contained clasts, although sparse, are also similar to those found in the Upper Breccia beds in terms of size, shape, lithology and alteration. The Upper Breccia beds do not extend into the New Passage. It is suggested that they plugged the New Passage in Area F, the Yellow Silts representing a wash of matrix from this plug into the passage during de-watering.

## The New Entrance (Area H): geology, description and interpretation of the sediments

Area H is located outside of the Main Cave to the south and east of the cave entrance. Sediments preserved in a rock cleft and cave entrance (this cave becomes the New Passage – Area G) are buried beneath a sequence of colluvial, solifluction and scree deposits. The full stratigraphy is outlined in Figure 5.16. The following descriptions and interpretations are presented in two parts. Firstly the layers associated with the cave fill (Layers 44–20) are examined, and then the overlying slope deposits, Layers 14–1 are

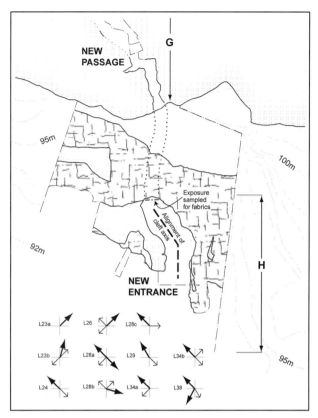

*Figure 5.17. Pontnewydd Cave. New Entrance (Area H), statistically significant preferred clast orientations (bold arrows) and secondary orientations (small arrows) within the cave deposits.*

considered (including Layers 21, 25, 50, 51 and 52 which are out of numerical sequence – Figure 5.16). Not all layers have been sampled and so not all are described in detail. Fabric data was recorded for Layers 23, 24, 26, 28, 29, 34 and 38. All samples show a statistically significant preferred clast orientation as illustrated in Figure 5.17.

### Area H cave fill deposits, Layers 44 to 20 (Figure 5.16)
**Layer 44**
Matrix rich mixed gravel (c:f = 0.6). Limestone (50% and 18%), mudstone (33% and 43%), stalagmite (17% and 38%), and rare other exotics (0% and 2%). Limestone is subangular (0.29) and fresh. Exotics are subrounded (0.43) and 29% are whole pebbles. The matrix is poorly sorted with slight peaks in coarse sand and medium silt, moderate clay content (sandy silt loam) (Figure 5.18).

**Layer 43**
Flowstone on bedrock dated at 85,000±9,000 BP.

**Layer 42**
*In situ* stalagmite floor dated at 91,000±7,000 BP.

**Layer 41**
Stalagmite gravel (c:f = 1.8). Stalagmite dominates (100% and 85%), some mudstone (0% and 8%) and limestone (0% and 6%), very rare other exotics (0% and <1%). Limestone is

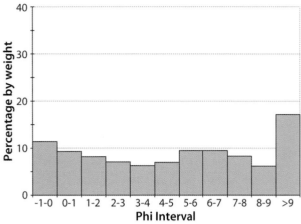

*Figure 5.18. Matrix particle size distributions for Area H, Layer 44.*

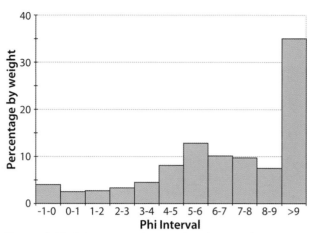

*Figure 5.21. Matrix particle size distributions for Area H, Layer 29.*

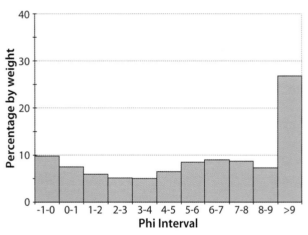

*Figure 5.19. Matrix particle size distributions for Area H, Layer 41.*

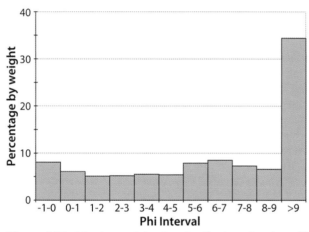

*Figure 5.22. Matrix particle size distributions for Area H, Layer 28.*

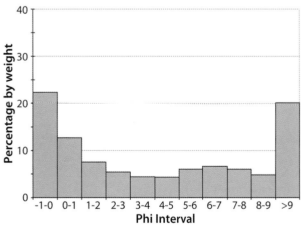

*Figure 5.20. Matrix particle size distributions for Area H, Layer 34.*

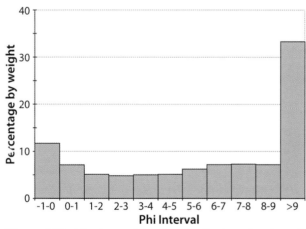

*Figure 5.23. Matrix particle size distributions for Area H, Layer 26.*

angular (0.20) with weak to moderate surface corrosion (AI = 2). Exotics are subrounded (0.40) and 5% are whole pebbles. The matrix is poorly sorted with slight peaks in coarse sand and medium silt, high clay content (clay loam) (Figure 5.19).

**Layer 40**

Sand with gravel (c:f = 0.37). Clast fraction dominated by limestone (80% and 59%) and stalagmite (20% and 23%) with some mudstone (0% and 15%) and rare other exotics (5% and 3%). Limestone is subangular (0.29) with weak to moderate

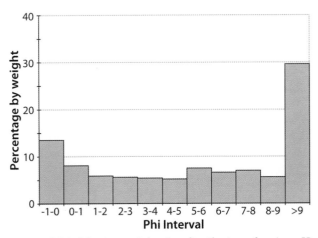

*Figure 5.24. Matrix particle size distributions for Area H, Layer 24.*

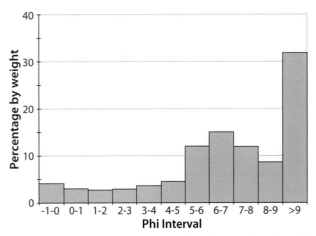

*Figure 5.25. Matrix particle size distributions for Area H, Layer 23.*

surface corrosion (AI = 1 to 2). Exotics are subrounded (0.43) and 28% are whole pebbles. The matrix shows a strong fine sand peak and moderately high clay content (clay loam).

**Layer 38**

Mudstone gravel (c:f = 2.0). Mudstone (89% and 93%) with some limestone (7% and 3%) and some other exotics (4% and 3%). Exotics are rounded (0.50) and 36% are whole pebbles. Limestone is angular/subangular (0.25) with weak to moderate surface corrosion (AI = 1 to 2). The matrix is high in coarse/medium sand with moderate clay content (sandy loam).

**Layer 34**

Mudstone gravel (too much cementation to calculate an accurate c:f). Mudstone (70% and 95%), limestone (26% and 3%), some other exotics (4% and 1%). Exotics are subrounded (0.42) and 27% are whole pebbles. Limestone is subangular (0.28) with weak to moderate surface corrosion (AI = 1 to 2). The matrix is high in coarse sand with a moderate to high clay content (sandy clay loam) (Figure 5.20).

**Layer 33**

Matrix supported mudstone gravel – not sampled.

**Layer 29**

Matrix rich gravel (c:f = variable between 0.63 and 1.1). Limestone (80% and 60%), mudstone (18% and 39%), other exotics (2% and 1%). Limestone is angular (0.23) with weak to moderate surface corrosion (AI = 1 to 2). Exotics are subangular (0.33) and 11% are whole pebbles. The matrix is moderately well-sorted, high in medium silt and high in clay (silt clay/silty clay loam) (Figure 5.21).

**Layer 28**

Gravel (c:f = 1.9). Limestone (84% and 59%), mudstone (13% and 40%), some other exotics (3% and 1%). Limestone is subangular (0.26) with weak to moderate surface corrosion (AI = 1 to 2). Exotics are subangular (0.34) and 11% are whole pebbles. The matrix is poorly sorted sand/silt, very high clay content (clay loam/clay) (Figure 5.22). The top of this unit is marked by a thin horizon of black manganese staining.

**Layer 26**

Limestone gravel (c:f = 3.4). Limestone (93% and 77%), mudstone (7% and 22%), some other exotics (1% and 1%). Limestone is angular (0.24) with very little surface alteration (AI = 1). Exotics are subangular (0.32) and 12% are whole pebbles. The matrix shows a small peak in the coarse sand, but otherwise has a uniform sand/silt distribution with a very high clay content (clay loam) (Figure 5.23).

**Layer 24**

Limestone gravel (c:f = 2.6). Limestone (94% and 52%), mudstone (3% and 21%), stalagmite (3% and 26%), very rare other exotics (0% and <1%). Limestone is angular (0.24) with very little surface alteration (AI = 1). Exotics are subangular (0.33) and 19% are whole pebbles. The matrix shows a small peak in coarse sand, otherwise a uniform sand/silt distribution, high to very high clay content (clay loam) (Figure 5.24).

**Layer 23**

The base of this layer comprises a matrix rich limestone gravel (c:f = 0.73). Limestone (68% and 57%), stalagmite (25% and 25%), mudstone (6% and 17%), very rare other exotics (0% and <1%). Limestone is subangular (0.27) with very little surface corrosion (AI = 1). Exotics are subangular (0.32) and 14% are whole pebbles. The matrix is high in medium silt, very high clay content (silty clay loam) (Figure 5.25).

The layer changes upwards into a matrix rich limestone gravel (c:f = 0.62). Limestone (81% and 59%), stalagmite (17% and 13%), mudstone (2% and 28%), very rare other exotics (0% and <1%). Limestone is subangular (0.28) with weak to moderate surface corrosion (AI = 1 to 2). Exotics are subangular (0.32) and 16% are whole pebbles. The matrix is high in medium/coarse silt, high clay content (clay loam).

**Layer 20**

Matrix rich deposit of tufa and corroded stalagmite. Tufa/stalagmite (88% and 87%), limestone (12% and 2%), very rare mudstone (0% and <1%). Limestone is angular (0.19) with weak to moderate surface corrosion (AI = 1 to 2). The matrix was not analysed due to the presence of large amounts of friable tufa and stalagmite.

*Interpretation of the external New Entrance (Area H) cave deposits*

The cave passage deposits at Area H comprise a sequence of debris flows of varying character. Layer 44 is a lithologically mixed layer which sits beneath the *in situ* discontinuous stalagmite floor (Layer 42) which is dated to 91,000±7,000 BP (although there is the possibility that Layer 44 may have been pushed up underneath a 'shelf' of pre-existing stalagmitic floor). Layer 41 is a stalagmite-rich debris flow overlain by a mudstone-rich debris flow (Layers 38 and 34). Layer 42 gives a *terminus post quem* for the mudstone gravels of Layers 38 and 34 of *c.* 91,000 BP. Within the cave the mudstone gravels constitute the Lower Breccia bed and older deposits, all capped by the Stalagmitic lithozone which gives a *terminus ante quem* of 225,000 BP. The overlying Upper Breccia bed is limestone-rich, associated with the exposure of the cave system, the Stalagmitic lithozone giving this a *terminus post quem* of 83,000 BP. The Upper Breccia bed and Area H mudstone gravels therefore occupy similar chronostratigraphic positions in that they are both Devensian in age. It is suggested that the Layers 38 and 34 represent a debris flow into the cave which eroded the exposed surface of the Lower Breccia beds where the stalagmite floor was missing or had been eroded in the emplacement of Layer 41, this accounting for the mudstone component. It would also account for the inclusion of a hominin fossil within Layer 34, all other *in situ* hominin remains within the cave system being derived from the Lower Breccia beds or the Intermediate complex. This would infer that the Lower Breccia bed extended through the Main Cave and the New Passage to the New Entrance.

The succeeding debris flows represented by Layers 29, 28, 26, 24, and 23, are all dominated by limestone clasts. The corrosion of the limestone in Layer 28 and at the surface of 23 may represent an hiatus in debris flow emplacement. These layers are regarded as part of an overall debris flow episode which started with Layer 41, and are also regarded as equivalents to the Upper Breccia bed episode. Fabric analysis suggest these layers were deposited by flows into the New Passage from the south, the interpretation of the Yellow Silts above indicating that the passage would be open to ingress as the Upper Breccia did not flow into it (Figure 5.17).

The spread of tufaceous carbonate and corroded stalagmite (Layer 20) thins with distance from the cave mouth indicating flow from within the cave system. It also flows over the bedding plane exposed at the level of the cave mouth. This indicates that any more extensive cave roof in Area H had already collapsed and had been removed by the time of the Layer 20 event.

*The New Entrance (Area H) sub-aerial deposits: east sections, Layers 50, 18, 25, 16, 51, 52 (Figure 5.16)*

**Layer 50**

Matrix rich limestone gravel (c:f = 0.8). Limestone (60% and 87%), stalagmite (40% and 10%) rare calcite (0% and 3%). Limestone is angular (0.22) with weak to moderate surface alteration (AI = 2). No exotics. The matrix is poorly sorted, with a small coarse silt peak (sandy silt loam).

**Layer 18**

Limestone gravel (c:f = 1.1). Limestone (75% and 77%), stalagmite (25% and 23%). Limestone is angular (0.18) with very little surface alteration (AI = 1). No exotics. The matrix is high in sand, slight coarse silt peak, moderate clay content (sandy loam).

**Layer 25**

Matrix rich limestone gravel (c:f = 0.73). Limestone (100% and 79%), some mudstone (0% and 19%) rare other exotics (0% and 2%). Limestone is angular (0.20) with very little surface alteration (AI = 2). Exotics are subangular (0.33) with no whole pebbles. The matrix shows a small coarse silt peak otherwise a uniform silt/sand distribution, high clay content (clay loam).

**Layer 16**

Limestone gravel (c:f = 1.8). Limestone (100% and 81%), some mudstone (0% and 18%) rare other exotics (0% and 1%) and very rare calcite (0% and <1%). Limestone is angular (0.21) with weak to moderate surface alteration (AI = 2). Exotics are subangular (0.28) with no whole pebbles. The matrix is poorly sorted with a high clay content (clay loam).

**Layer 52**

Fine deposit (c:f = 0.19). Only limestone clasts are present, weak to moderate surface alteration (AI = 2). The matrix has a small coarse silt peak, high in sand, moderate to low clay content (sandy silt loam).

**Layer 51**

Limestone gravel (c:f = 1.3). Limestone (100% and 99%), very rare mudstone (0% and 1%). Limestone is angular (0.21) with weak to moderate surface alteration (AI = 2). The matrix is very poorly sorted, with a high clay content (clay loam).

*The New Entrance (Area H) sub-aerial deposits: west section, Layers 14 to 1 (Figure 5.16)*

**Layer 14**

Matrix rich limestone gravel (c:f = 0.46). Limestone (96% and 93%), some mudstone (4% and 7%), very rare other exotics (0% and <1%). Limestone is angular (0.19) with weak to moderate surface corrosion (AI = 1 to 2). Exotics are subangular (0.31) and 8% are whole pebbles. The matrix is poorly sorted, with a high clay content (clay loam).

**Layer 13**

Limestone gravel (c:f = 1.04). Limestone (100% and 96%), rare mudstone (0% and 2%), very rare other exotics (0% and 2%). Limestone is angular (0.19) with very little surface corrosion (AI = 1). Exotics are angular (0.24). The matrix is dominated by clay and fine silt, with some sand present (clay).

**Layer 12**

Fine deposit (c:f = 0.08). Limestone (0% and 87%), some mudstone (0% and 13%), one other exotic clast present. Limestone is angular (0.20) with weak to moderate surface corrosion (AI = 1 to 2). The matrix is clay and fine silt, very little sand present (silty clay/clay).

**Layer 11**

Limestone gravel (c:f = 2.5). Limestone (100% and 98%), very rare mudstone (0% and 1%), very rare other exotics (0% and 1%). Limestone is angular (0.21) with very little surface alteration (AI = 1). Exotics are subrounded (0.37) and 10% are whole pebbles. The matrix is poorly sorted with a high clay content (sandy clay loam).

**Layer 10**

Matrix rich limestone gravel (c:f = 0.29). Limestone (100% and 68%), some mudstone (0% and 19%), very rare other exotics (0% and 12%) and very rare calcite (0% and 1%). Limestone is angular (0.24) with moderate surface corrosion (AI = 3). Exotics are subrounded (0.40) and 9% are whole pebbles. The matrix shows some sorting, strong (medium) sand peak, moderate clay content (sandy loam).

**Layer 9**

Matrix rich gravel (c:f = 0.45). Limestone (88% and 79%), some mudstone (8% and 13%), and some other exotics (4% and 8%). Limestone is angular (0.23) with weak to moderate surface alteration (AI = 2). Exotics are subangular (0.33) and 10% are whole pebbles. The matrix shows a peak in the medium sand, low in silt, moderate clay content (sandy clay loam).

**Layer 8**

Matrix rich limestone gravel (c:f = 0.54). Limestone (95% and 83%), some other exotics (5% and 5%) and some mudstone (0% and 8%), rare calcite (0% and 4%). Limestone is subangular (0.27) with weak to moderate surface alteration (AI = 2). Exotics are subangular (0.30) none are whole pebbles. The matrix (similar to Layer 11) is poorly sorted with a moderate to high clay content (clay loam/sandy clay loam).

**Layer 7**

Sand with few clasts (c:f = 0.25). Limestone (100% and 82%), some other exotics (0% and 11%), rare mudstone (0% and 5%), very rare calcite (0% and 2%). Limestone is angular/subangular (0.25) with weak to moderate surface alteration (AI = 1 to 2). Exotics are subangular (0.35). The matrix is well-sorted sand, medium sand peak, low clay content (sandy loam).

**Layer 6**

Matrix rich gravel (c:f = 0.42). Limestone (70% and 76%), some other exotics (19% and 13%) some mudstone (11% and 10%). Limestone is subangular (0.29) with close to moderate surface alteration (AI = 2). Exotics are subrounded (0.37) and 10% are whole pebbles. The matrix shows a peak in the medium sand, moderate to high clay content (clay loam).

**Layer 5**

Matrix rich limestone gravel (c:f = 0.34). Limestone (100% and 66%), some other exotics (0% and 18%) and some mudstone (0% and 16%). Limestone is subangular (0.26) with weak to moderate surface alteration (AI = 2). Exotics are subrounded (0.39) and 4% are whole pebbles. The matrix is poorly sorted with a high to very high clay content (clay loam).

**Layer 4**

Limestone gravel (c:f = 2.9). Limestone (97% and 95%), rare mudstone (1% and 5%) very rare other exotics (1% and <1%) and very rare calcite (0% and <1%). Limestone is angular (0.21) with weak to moderate surface alteration (AI = 2). Exotics are subangular (0.28) with no whole pebbles. The matrix shows a slight peak in the medium silt, otherwise a uniform sand/silt distribution, with a high clay content (clay loam).

**Layer 3**

Limestone gravel (c:f = 1.8). Limestone (100% and 93%), some mudstone (0% and 6%) very rare other exotics (0% and <1%) and very rare calcite (0% and <1%). Limestone is angular (0.19) with weak to moderate surface alteration (AI = 2). Exotics are subangular (0.33) with no whole pebbles. The matrix shows a broad silt peak, high clay content (clay loam).

**Layer 2**

Limestone gravel (c:f = 1.9). Limestone (100% and 94%), some mudstone (0% and 5%) very rare calcite (0% and 1%). Limestone is angular (0.23) with weak to moderate surface alteration (AI = 2). Exotics are subangular (0.33) with no whole pebbles. The matrix shows a uniform sand/silt distribution, slight medium silt peak, high clay content (clay loam).

**Layer 1**

Organo-mineral soil horizon developed into the top of Layer 2.

*Interpretation of the New Entrance sub-aerial deposits*

The three sections sampled at Area H reveal a sequence of colluvial, solifluction and scree deposits. Layers 50 and 18 sit immediately on top of Layer 20. The contained thin stalagmite fragments have probably been derived from the erosion of a flowstone upslope, slope erosion being initiated by the continued development of the Elwy valley, the erosion and opening up of the Area H entrance to the New Passage recorded in the Layer 23 to Layer 20 transition, and the subsequent regrading of the limestone hillslope above. Layers 14 and 52 are fines-rich, rest on bedrock, and are here interpreted as colluvial wash deposits. The overlying limestone dominated clast supported Layers 13, 18, 25, 16, and 51 represent the physical weathering of the subsequently exposed limestone. These layers are classed as the 'Lower Screes'. Layers 10, 11, 9, 8, 7, and 6, are matrix-supported with an overall lithology comparable to the Late Devensian drift deposits lying in and above the Elwy valley (Livingston 1986). These layers are interpreted as solifluction deposits although Layer 11 may be a local scree deposit being clast rich and almost exclusively limestone. Layer 7 is a well-sorted sand possibly representing a cover-sand deposit. Layers 5, 4, 3 and 2 comprise the Holocene, clast rich, limestone dominated 'Upper Screes'.

***The debris flows: fabric data***

Blatt, Middleton and Murray (1980) describe a debris flow as a sediment gravity flow '*... in which the larger grains are* *supported by a "matrix"– that is, by a mixture of interstitial fluid and fine sediment that has enough strength (cohesion) to prevent the larger grains from settling but not so much that the mass itself cannot flow'*. They go on to state that '... *in a single flow, different mechanisms of grain support may be dominant at different stages of the "life history" of the flow'*. Life history can include laminar and turbulent flow under varying viscous states (Pierson 1981), snowploughing at the snout, matrix supported flow (with varying sand, silt and clay matrices), and muddy water flow. Flow can be erosive; thus, a number of authors describe the erosive power of flows particularly when confined to channels (*e.g.* Pierson 1980; Wood and Campbell 1995), whereas others describe major flows with little or no associated erosion. Sharp and Nobles (1953) for example, state that '... *a house and shed near the margin of the flow at Wrightwood were buried to the eaves and filled to approximately the same level without other apparent damage...'*.

Debris flows, therefore, are complex sedimentary mechanisms which comprise a series of processes from flow initiation on a gradient, through to flow cessation, stabilization and de-watering. The pattern and behaviour of flow is complicated further when confined to a channel or cave, and the de-watering phase may be prolonged compared to a sub-aerial deposit. These mechanisms were reviewed thoroughly by Collcutt (1984, 54–59) and, accordingly, our purpose here is to focus specifically on the dynamics of clast motion and alignment, and to attempt to draw some conclusions regarding fabric with respect either to flow direction or flow mechanism.

Davies and Walker (1974) identify important clast orientation principles from their work on the Cap Enrage Formation, Quebec. This formation represents a conglomerate re-sedimented under sub-aqueous conditions, and as such is not a direct analogue of the Pontnewydd debris flows. However the internal organization of the deposits suggests that, in the final stages of flow, turbulence may give way to laminar flow in a viscous fluid, similar to that described by various authors for debris flows. The fabric of clasts >3 cm on the *a* axis showed this to be aligned with the direction of flow and dipping upstream. As clasts are dispersed above the bed due to the viscosity of flow there has been clast contact during flow. Rees (1968) models this form of contact and describes a state where the long axes of clasts are aligned with the direction of flow as the most stable.

Lindsay (1968) examines flow dynamics in his consideration of mudflow fabrics. Through an extensive review of other work Lindsay has been able to establish that elongated clasts in a mudflow sediment are likely to undergo rotational movement. This motion is elliptical in plan, with a conical shape in three dimensions. The speed of rotation is greatest at the point where the long axis is normal to flow, and least when it is aligned with flow. This means that statistically there will be, at any one point in time, a majority of clasts aligned with or close to the direction of flow. The direction of dip relative to flow direction is more problematic. Modelling the elliptical/conical motion produced a cyclical pattern of fabrics through time with

episodes of strong dip downstream, and upstream. The actual fabric which develops therefore may vary; indeed, it '... *can dip in either direction depending on the instant at which the mudflow is arrested'*. This means that some samples may show weak fabrics. The weight of published evidence since 1968 indicates that most flows show an alignment dipping with flow. Mills (1991), for example, presents and analyses data on a wide range of debris flows where the majority show a fabric with long axis aligned with flow and dipping downstream. However, the data mostly relates to flows on open slopes. When studying the Pontnewydd flows, consideration has to be given to channel confinement, and to the virtual absence of gradient (although the nature of the source-material, and the gradient that it may have presented outside the cave, remains a matter for speculation). This means that alignments will be controlled by the dynamics of flow, but also by the channel wall configuration.

The thesis presented here is that debris flowed into the cave through both of the known entrances. Bed geometry accommodates a flow from west to east for the Lower Breccia, but indicates a more irregular surface for the Upper Breccia. The exposure of the beds at the New Entrance is too limited spatially for meaningful interpretation. The fabrics obtained are all, with the exception of one from Layer 26 (not included in this report), statistically significant and therefore the product of a process of organization.

The fabrics from the Lower Breccia at Area D (Figure 5.7) show a pattern of alignment with the fluting of the cave wall as it constricts eastwards towards Area F, the clasts dipping westwards towards the Main Entrance. Sedimentologically the Lower Breccia is matrix supported with in excess of 60% fines, the clast content decreasing upwards through the unit. This 'graded bedding' and the absence of bedding structures, indicates that emplacement was not through turbulent, but rather through laminar flow. The orientation of the clasts, the lack of gradient, and cave confinement with associated de-watering restrictions would suggest laminar flow under low viscosity, hydrostatic conditions. This environment could have resembled that described by Davies and Walker (1974) for the Cap Enrage Formation, Quebec. The environment may not have been entirely sub-aqueous, but sufficient fluid would have been present to enable a muddy water flow as described by Pierson (1981) in which an imbricate structure could have developed, with clasts dipping upstream. The Lower Breccia is, therefore, interpreted as a muddy water or possibly sub-aqueous flow, which ran eastward through the cave.

The Upper Breccia Area F (Figure 5.14) fabrics exhibit a pattern of alignment with the cave walls and a dominant eastwards dip vector. The Upper Breccia has a high clast content, containing <50% fines compared with >60% in the Lower Breccia. The uniform distribution of clasts throughout the unit with no evidence of bedding, suggests emplacement under turbulent flow conditions. The organization of clasts would seem, therefore, to have been the product of processes similar to those described by Lindsay (1968) and Pierson (1981) for viscous matrix supported flows. The dominant alignment associated with such environments is one with

| Find no. | Context | Area | Description | SEM no. |
|----------|---------|------|-------------|---------|
| *H2979* | 39 (Mudstone Gravel Unit) | New Entrance | Derived stalagmite in external cave deposits | 1–2 |
| *F5957* | Silt beds | Main Cave (F) | In darkness zone, 25 metres from current entrance | 3 |
| *H3095* | 31 (Stalagmitic clast within layer 29, originally regarded as *in situ* and therefore numbered as a layer) | New Entrance | Derived stalagmite in external cave deposits | 4–5 |
| *H3090* | 26 (Upper Limestone Breccia Bed) | New Entrance | Interstitial cement in external cave deposits | 6 |

*Table 5.2. SEM samples showing context, area of the site and a description.*

| Transect no. and length (mm) | No. of depressions 10μm diameter | No. of depressions 10-19μm diameter | No. of depressions 20 + μm diameter | No. of depressions per transect | No. of depressions per mm of transect |
|---|---|---|---|---|---|
| *1* 8 | 0 | 3 | 4 | 7 | 0.87 |
| *2* 6 | 2 | 1 | 0 | 3 | 0.5 |
| *3* 5 | 1 | 2 | 0 | 3 | 0.6 |
| *4* 3 | 0 | 3 | 0 | 3 | 1 |
| *5* 3.5 | 3 | 2 | 0 | 5 | 1.4 |
| *6* 7 | 4 | 2 | 0 | 6 | 0.85 |

*Table 5.3. Details of transects scanned across the surface of samples showing the densities of possible micro-organisms within the sample.*

clasts orientated with the flow (Mills 1991), suggesting a predominance of long axes dipping downstream. It is likely, therefore, that the Upper Breccia was laid down by a debris flow running eastwards through the cave.

At Area H, in the external cave deposits of the New Entrance, fabrics were recorded from Layers 23 to 38 (excepting Layer 33) at an exposure cut across the entrance to the New Passage at the north end of a south-east to north-west cleft in the limestone (Figure 5.17). These layers, with the exception of Layer 23, are generally clast rich suggesting a mode of emplacement comparable to the Upper Breccia, interpreted here as their stratigraphic equivalent within the Main Cave. The dipping of clasts into the cave therefore indicates a flow to the north-east through the cleft, or the cave passage that preceded the cleft, and into the New Passage. Layer 23 is matrix supported and so could be the product of a muddy water flow. Its strongest fabrics are generally normal to those of the other layers at this site. This could be due both to muddy water conditions and also due to proximity to the cave roof with its influence on flow.

## Pontnewydd cemented cave deposits: speleothem or travertine?

*Heather A. Viles*

### Background and research questions

Four samples of cemented cave deposits from Pontnewydd were investigated using a Scanning Electron Microscope (SEM) to see whether there was evidence of micro-organic influences on the formation of the deposits. Such evidence

might help resolve the issue of whether the deposits were formed within the daylight zone of the cave or not. Characteristically, speleothems produced in parts of a cave not receiving daylight are largely inorganically produced features, consisting of pure calcium carbonate. Some records have been made of non-photosynthetic bacteria colonizing such speleothems, but most appear to lack significant organic influence. Some authors, however, have discovered evidence of micro-organisms within laminated cave deposits including speleothems (Jones and Motyka 1987; Jones and McDonald 1989) which seem to suggest that even in dark environments micro-organisms can influence calcite deposits.

On the other hand, travertines formed in terrestrial freshwater environments, and at cave entrances where daylight penetrates, are in most cases highly populated by a range of micro-organisms (bacteria, cyanobacteria, algae *etc.*) which have been found to play a range of active and passive roles in the formation of the travertine deposits (Chafetz and Folk 1984; Pedley 1992). Many cyanobacterial travertines, for example, contain seasonal banding with light-coloured winter layers (characterized by sparite and little organic remains) interspersed with darker-coloured summer layers (characterized by many encrusted cyanobacterial filaments and cells). Under the SEM these travertine deposits can be seen to contain clear evidence of micro-organisms, usually in the form of filaments and circular cells (or traces of filaments and cells) encrusted with microcrystalline calcite. In some cases, boreholes produced by micro-organisms such as cyanobacteria may be found within sparite crystals.

The aims of this study were to examine whether there were any traces of micro-organisms in the Pontnewydd Cave deposits and to use micro-organic remains to infer whether the deposits were formed within terrestrial environments or the lit zone of the cave entrance (and were travertines), or within true cave environments (and were speleothems of some sort).

## Sample details and dissecting microscope observations

Four separate stalagmite samples were examined, as shown in Table 5.2.

### SEM samples 1 and 2. (H2979, AB 994 SE, Layer 39, derived stalagmite from the New Entrance)

This deposit, some 2 cm thick and clearly banded, is hard, densely crystalline with occasional pore spaces. Under the dissecting microscope, the banding appears quite complex, with light and dark coarsely crystalline layers interbedded with medium hued finely banded layers. At high magnifications some black dots are evident, which may be micro-organic communities.

### SEM samples 4 and 5. (H3095, 97.99 m S.D. Layer 31, derived stalagmite from the New Entrance)

This deposit now covered in cave mud, is hard, densely crystalline and clearly banded. The portion sampled for SEM analysis was 0.8 mm thick. Under the dissecting microscope the banding is not very clear, but light and slightly darker layers are visible. There are no obvious black dots at high magnification.

### SEM sample 6. (H3090, AE 993 NE, 99.20–99.10 m S.D. Layer 26 in the New Entrance, interstitial cement)

This sample appears to be some kind of cave breccia, with chunks of a brown crystalline material embedded in a clayey deposit.

### SEM sample 3. (F5957, I1NW, 99.74 m S.D. calcite from Silt beds of the Main Cave)

This sample is a relatively fine-grained clearly banded deposit, varying in thickness from 1–2 cm thick, and showing four clear bands:

1) A thin (*c.* 1 mm) surface dark brown layer, capped with paler material;
2) a reddish-brown, somewhat contorted layer 3–5 mm in thickness;
3) a beige layer some 5 mm in thickness;
4) a darker brown layer 3–5 mm in thickness, capped with paler material.

The sample banding is somewhat contorted, with pore spaces mostly in the reddish-brown layer.

## Scanning Electron Microscope observations

### Sample preparation

Small samples for SEM observations were taken from the hand specimens by fracturing using a hammer and cold chisel. Fractured SEM samples which provided a cross-section across any banding were selected, glued onto standard SEM stubs with Araldite and sputter-coated with a thin layer of gold prior to observation with a Cambridge SEM.

### SEM sample 1

Coarsely crystalline, dense calcite material, with interlocking crystals. Circular depressions, from 5–50 µm in diameter were patchily present, which may be the traces of micro-organisms which have become embedded in the crystalline matrix. Sometimes, there was clearer evidence of micro-organisms, with hollow tubules and spheres (*c.* 20 µm in diameter) fashioned out of microcrystalline calcite. Six transects scanned across the sample at *c.* × 350 magnification revealed the following results on the presence of circular, presumed organic, depressions shown in Table 5.3.

Each transect had a width of around 200 µm. These results show that, throughout the SEM sample depressions, presumed to be of organic origin, are present but do not dominate the sample. One corner of the sample, however, possessed many more organically-produced remains, especially concentrated within one 1 mm thick band.

### SEM sample 2

This sample contained similar depressions presumed to be produced by micro-organisms as sample 1.

### SEM sample 3

This fine-grained, mainly microcrystalline calcite sample contained no obvious evidence of micro-organisms (no circular depressions, boreholes or encrusted filaments).

### SEM sample 4

This sample was coarsely crystalline like samples 1 and 2 and contained some interesting evidence of micro-organic influence. Patchily very common were 1–2 µm diameter rounded or dumbell shaped microcrystalline calcite forms, often found on or between sparite crystals, in groups or clumps. Such features look remarkably like colonies of bacteria which have become encrusted with calcite. Within the sample, a band of 4–5 mm thickness contained virtually no organic traces, whereas a band of around 2 mm thickness contained many of these possible encrusted bacterial communities.

### SEM sample 5

This sample was very similar to sample 4 discussed above, containing a band some 1–2 mm thick with many traces of encrusted bacterial communities, sandwiched between two layers *c.* 2 mm thick with no such traces. This layering of organic traces is found very commonly in travertines formed in conjunction with seasonal growth of cyanobacterial communities in freshwater environments.

### SEM sample 6

This sample contained a complex arrangement of cemented,

often platey, debris within a matrix of microcrystalline material, but there were no obvious traces of micro-organisms.

## Discussion and conclusions

The brief microscopic observations reported above show evidence that micro-organic communities have become encrusted by microcrystalline calcite and form an integral part of two samples (H2979 and H3095). Both are stalagmites from the New Entrance and would have formed within or close to, the daylight zone. A third example (H3090), with no evidence of micro-organic communities was an interstitial cement. This, coupled with the clear laminations in these coarsely crystalline deposits, suggests that they were formed in freshwater within the daylight zone (either within a cave entrance or on the surface). The banding may represent seasonal growth of micro-organisms (probably bacteria, such as cyanobacteria) in summer interspersed with winter layers dominated by inorganically precipitated sparite. Although the evidence for micro-organisms is sparse in some parts of these samples, work from other similar laminated deposits has shown their importance (Love and Chafetz 1988). However, the fact that similar laminated deposits with some micro-organic influences have been ascribed to cave environments by Jones and Motyka (1987) means that this interpretation must be regarded with some caution. Additional evidence to prove that the micro-organisms encrusted within the deposits were photosynthetic is required before one can confidently say they are surficial forms. Study of other cave deposits from Pontnewydd might also indicate whether micro-organic remains are widely present within the cave deposits or not. It may however be significant that micro-organisms were wholly absent from a sample (F5957) from the darkness zone of the Main Cave.

## A scanning electron microscope study of sediments from the Main Cave sequence and the New Entrance sequence of Pontnewydd Cave

*Peter A. Bull*

## Introduction

Sediments were collected from the main sequence of deposits in the Main Cave (Areas D and F) and from a vertical sequence throughout the deposits in the New Entrance (Area H). Quartz sand grains were separated from the samples by washing in distilled water, boiling in dilute hydrochloric acid, drying and mounting on aluminium stubs for analysis of their surface textures by scanning electron microscopy (SEM). All samples were coded prior to analysis in order to avoid subconscious operator bias during the examination procedure.

## Sediment sequence from the Main Cave

The sediments analysed in the study are shown in Table 5.4

and consist of the majority of the upper layers previously identified (Collcutt 1984).

*Intermediate complex-orange*
Samples analysed from this layer include PN1 and PN13. They both show quartz sand grains with diagenetically smoothed surfaces, with contemporary hertzian fractures and precipitation. The grains show no evidence of late grain indentors which would be indicative of fluvial transportation.

*Intermediate complex-buff*
This horizon is represented by PN19, PN27 and PN51. PN19 shows angular grains with strong evidence for fluvial alteration (late grain indentors and edge abrasion). The other samples (PN27 and PN51) portray grains well-rounded and diagenetically smoothed (as found in the Intermediate complex-orange layer below). These samples differentiate themselves, however, from the underlying beds as they contain late grain indentors which are suggestive of some element of late phase, fluvial transportation.

*Lower Breccia bed*
As Table 5.4 shows, the Lower Breccia bed is an undifferentiated sediment body with six horizons recorded in the field. SEM analyses are only able here to identify three main groups. The first group, designated LBc in Table 5.4, comprises only samples PN3 and PN14. These samples are made up of two different types of quartz. One component is very angular, edge fresh with a great deal of comminution debris and crushed fragments. The other component of this sample comprises very well-rounded, diagenetic smooth grains with fluvial late grain indentors together, significantly, with euhedral growths exhibited on quartz grains.

The second group identified in the Lower Breccia beds comprise of all those collected in LBa, LBb and LBd. Scanning electron microscopy cannot differentiate these different layers as all grains from all layers exhibited quartz grains which contain the same surface texture suites as each other. All of these samples show rounded grains with diagenetic smoothing and late grain indentors of fluvial origin. Significantly, an angular element is also present throughout showing edge abrasion, again by fluvial transportation and subsequent modification.

The third main group within the Lower Breccia bed, identified by SEM, is designated LB/Blm and is represented by PN20, PN21 and PN50. On-site interpretation suggested that this deposit is the transition (a zone of mixing) between the Lower Breccia beds and the Intermediate-buff layer immediately below. Samples PN20 and PN21 contain grains which are very angular and, in turn, exhibit no edge abrasion whatsoever. Euhedral overgrowths, found on some grains, are clearly diagenetic, and do not exhibit any late grain indentors characteristic of fluvial transportation. Sample PN50 by contrast is very different: it contains grains which are rounded and diagenetically altered, exhibiting late grain indentors of fluvial origin. It also contains grains

| Upper Clays and Sands | UCS | |
|---|---|---|
| divided into | UCS/sm | PN11 |
| | upper most | |
| | UCS/rcm | PN10, 42, 43 |
| | lower most | |
| **Upper Breccia** | Upper Breccia | PN18, 44 |
| divided into | (undifferentiated) | |
| | UB/rcm | PN9, 17, 23 |
| | UB/Sbm | PN8, 22, 45 |
| **Silt beds** | sSb | PN15 |
| divided into lateral facies | uSb | PN7 |
| sSb is further divided in stratigraphic order | sSb upper | PN6, 16 |
| | stal 1 | |
| | middle | PN5 |
| | stal 2 | PN12 |
| | lower | PN4 |
| **Lower Breccia** | Lower Breccia | |
| divided in stratigraphic order | (undifferentiated) | PN2, 24, 46 |
| | LBa | |
| | | PN25, 47 |
| | LBb | PN3, 14, 26, 48 |
| | LBc | PN49 |
| | LBd | PN20, 21, 50 |
| | Lower Breccia/Blm | |
| **Buff Intermediate** | BI | PN19, 27, 51 |
| **Orange Intermediate** | OI | PN1, 13 |
| **Upper/Lower Sands and Gravels** | | ------------ |

*Table 5.4. The sediment sequence in the Main Cave.*

which are angular and have edge abrasion quite evident on the grain surfaces. SEM analysis suggests that PN50 belongs to the second group of Lower Breccia bed deposits rather than this third group as displayed in Table 5.4.

*Silt beds*
Overlying the Lower Breccia bed are the Silt beds which are divided into two lateral facies (uSb unstructured, and sSb which has a clear laminated structure). Layer sSb is further divided into upper, middle and lower horizons which are intercalated with 'proto-stalagmite' layers.

Samples from the undifferentiated Silt beds (Sb) contain very angular silt grains which have suffered no obvious fluvial transportation, but which show evidence of some chemical rounding to the grain surface. It is possible that this rounding has been caused by the small nature of the quartz particles, which are themselves more prone to chemical alteration as silt-sized rather than sand-sized particles. The structured Silt beds (sSb) contains in its uppermost layer, edge abraded silt and angular grains (PN15). It is likely that the modification seen here is caused by very low energy, local, fluvial modification. The lower stalagmite layer (Stal 2 in Table 5.4) contains quartz grains which are very well-rounded in a diagenetic phase prior to

deposition or edge abrasion but which have suffered heavily from chemical precipitation and deposition, probably due to the close proximity of the stalagmite layer. The lowermost layer within sSb contains grains which are very angular, exhibit no edge abrasion and contain much comminution debris (PN4). They are very similar to samples from the Lower Breccia beds, as described above, and are distinctly different from the overlying beds within this sub-section or indeed, within the Silt beds as a whole.

*Upper Breccia beds*
The Upper Breccia divides into three groups as shown in Table 5.4. The undifferentiated groups (UB) contains grains which exhibit both diagenetically smooth, well-rounded grains with obvious late grain indentors (fluvial modification) together with extensive angular grains. These latter suites of angular grains are really complete grain breakage expressions of the well-rounded diagentic suite. This complete grain breakage shows extensive fracturing and crushing with no mechanical edge abrasion. The only modification is chemical edge-rounding. This suite of grains may well represent the source of the fine, angular silts found in PN18.

The second group (the UB/rcm) contains remarkably

| Layer | Sample no. |
|-------|-----------|
| 20 | PN28 |
| 22 | PN33 |
| 23 | PN29 |
| 24 | PN30 |
| 26 | PN31 |
| 28 | PN32 |
| 29 | PN34 |
| 33 | PN38 |
| 34 | PN39 |
| 38 | PN36, PN37, PN40 |
| 40 | PN41 |
| 41 | PN35 |
| 42 | *In situ* stalagmite |
| 44 | ----------- |

*Table 5.5. The sediment sequence in the New Entrance.*

similar grains in all three samples analysed (PN9, PN17 and PN23). The grains from these samples are very angular and contain fresh fractured faces and exhibit low energy, fluvial edge abrasion. These samples contrast with grains found in the lower unit (UB/Sbm) of the Upper Breccia (PN8, PN22 and PN45) which are very well-rounded and have heavy chemical post-depositional sedimentation. Equally, there are no angular grains to be found in these samples. This unit is very different from the underlying unit (Sb), although PN45 may well be a mixture of the two units.

*Upper Clays and Sands*

The Upper Clays and Sands are divided into two main units (Table 5.4) the lowermost unit (UCS/rcm) contains grains which exhibit, in PN42, fluvial grains with late grain breakage (and complete grain breakage) of well-rounded low relief grains. In contrast sample PN10 and PN43 contains only about 5% of grains similar to PN42. The rest of the grains are very angular of high relief and contain no edge abrasion, but only chemical rounding and precipitation. The uppermost layer UCS/sm contains sands with obvious fluvial edge abrasion which have suffered heavy, post-depositional chemical alteration. The silt component in this sample shows only chemical alteration to the grain surfaces.

### Sediment sequence from the New Entrance

The samples taken from this sediment sequence (Aldhouse-Green 1995 and chapter 6, this volume) are shown in Table 5.5. Perhaps the most striking feature of this sediment sequence is that they group into five layers which can be differentiated by SEM analysis alone. The lowermost unit identified comprises Layers 40 and 41 (PN41 and PN35 respectively). The grains from these layers are rounded and very diagenetically affected and exhibit no fluvial

modification or edge abrasion whatsoever. There appears to be no subsequent chemical alteration to the grains – the only alteration is during the diagenetic phase of sandstone alteration prior to this cycle of erosion.

The next major unit identified by the SEM analysis comprises those samples taken from Layers 33, 34 and 38 (PN39; PN39 and PN3, PN37, PN40). The uppermost Layer 33, contains sand grains which have three main types of sediment suite. There are angular grains with no abrasion, rounded diagenetic grains with no edge abrasion (similar to Layers 40 and 41 below) and the third set of grains which are rounded but show extensive late grain abrasion caused during fluvial transportation. Layers 34 and 38 contain the same suites of grains as Layer 33 above but do not contain the angular element as described in this unit.

Immediately above this designated unit is a third, identified by SEM analysis alone, these represent Layers 26, 28 and 29 in Table 5.5. All three layers are similar to each other and show rounded diagenetic grains with chemical, post-depositional modification. The lowermost unit, Layer 29, also contains grains with euhedral crystal faces.

The next stratigraphic unit identified only by SEM analysis, comprises Layers 23 and 24 (PN29 and PN30). These grains from this unit show evidence of strong fluvial modification in high energy river conditions.

The last unit identified by SEM analysis comprises of Layers 20 and 22 (PN28 and PN33 respectively). The grains from this unit are very mixed, rounded to angular in outline and contain a mixture of fluvial modification grains similar to the unit below (Layers 23 and 24). These also contain a different suite of samples which show major diagenetic alteration. These samples do not appear to be similar to the Upper Breccia beds found in the Main Cave, although an element of the Upper Breccia beds may be found in the mixed rounded to angular grains of this unit. There is no obvious correlation.

### Conclusion

What is striking from the analysis of these sediments is the broad groupings of particular types of quartz grains within discrete stratigraphic units or groups of units. Many of the samples designated as groupings by SEM pre-exist this analysis. There are only a few exceptions or contradictions to the proven story. Even so, the marked differences between layers as identified by SEM analysis suggests that materials from previously deposited events were not, on the whole, picked up by fluvial erosion and transported as a mixture into the cave. Thus, each layer appears to contain discrete provenances and does not represent admixtures. It is also possible to infer from these results that there are significant time gaps between layers and that the sharp differences between units reflects these gaps since in only a few places are there gradations between units indicative of the mixing of layers.

# 6. The Excavations at Pontnewydd Cave

## Stephen Aldhouse-Green and Rick Peterson

*The three caves which are the subject of this report lie at different levels in the Elwy valley – Cae Gronw at 113 m, Pontnewydd at 90 m and Cefn at 75 m above mean sea level – but display comparable depositional patterns of sedimentation and faunal accumulation. Their histories of Palaeolithic human presence are, however, quite different with Neanderthals represented only at Pontnewydd, whilst Holocene humans were present at all three caves.*

*Excavation began in the Main Cave at Pontnewydd in 1978. The sequence – beginning with the lowermost deposits – consists of limestone bedrock, the Lower and Upper Sands and Gravels, the Intermediate complex, and the Lower Breccia (the layer containing the bulk of the hominin remains). Above the Lower Breccia are stalagmitic formations (the Stalagmite lithozone), which grew episodically over the period from 225,000 BP or earlier until at least 80,000 BP, perhaps even until c. 35,000 BP. This spatially and chronologically discontinuous layer of speleothem is in turn overlain successively by the Silt beds, the Upper Breccia and, above that by the Upper Clays and Sands. The overall sequence is capped by a Holocene travertine. Both the Upper and Lower Breccias appear to have eroded channels into the layers beneath as they were deposited. At these points there were notable zones of alteration and mixing where, for example, the very distinctive laminar structure of the Silt beds has been totally destroyed by pressure or, again, where the normally highly clast-rich Upper Breccia has acquired a considerable quantity of Silt beds matrix and, so, has become clast-poor.*

*The position of the New Entrance was first identified by tunnelling from inside the cave, but was eventually fully exposed externally by deep trenching in 1987. The excavated sequence was located in a length of cave where it had lost its roof. This collapse had taken place by 20,000 BP. At the lowest point so far reached were flowstone deposits of post-Last Interglacial age. These were covered by a layer of Mudstone Gravel – thought to be correlative with the Lower Breccia of the Main Cave – which included a hominin tooth, the only one from the New Entrance. U-series dates on derived stalagmites in the mudstone gravel suggest primary emplacement before 230,000 BP at youngest. This deposit was capped by the Yellow Stony layer, a debris flow with fauna but only rare artefacts. This was in turn succeeded by two limestone-rich breccias, themselves sealed by a spread of stalagmite, correlative with the Upper Breccia of the Main Cave. Finally, this 'cave-sequence' was in turn covered with a sub-aerial sequence of screes, solifluction and hillslope deposits.*

## Pontnewydd Cave

### Introduction

Excavation within and around Pontnewydd Cave took place at eight separate areas, each given a letter code from A to H (Figure 6.1). Area A lay in part outside the Main Entrance to the cave, taking in dumped deposits both from 19th century excavations and disturbance connected with the use of the cave during the Second World War, and extended to the inner wall of the Guard Chamber. Area B took in the western portion of the Main Passage (191.00 to 201.00 m E), including the South Fissure and the site of the Deep Sounding. Area C was the central portion of the Main Passage (between 201.00 m and 206.00 m E), including the South Passage. Area D covered the western part of the Main Chamber (between 206.00 and 212.00 m E), which included the North Passage and the North-East and South-East Fissures. Area E was opened in 1981 as

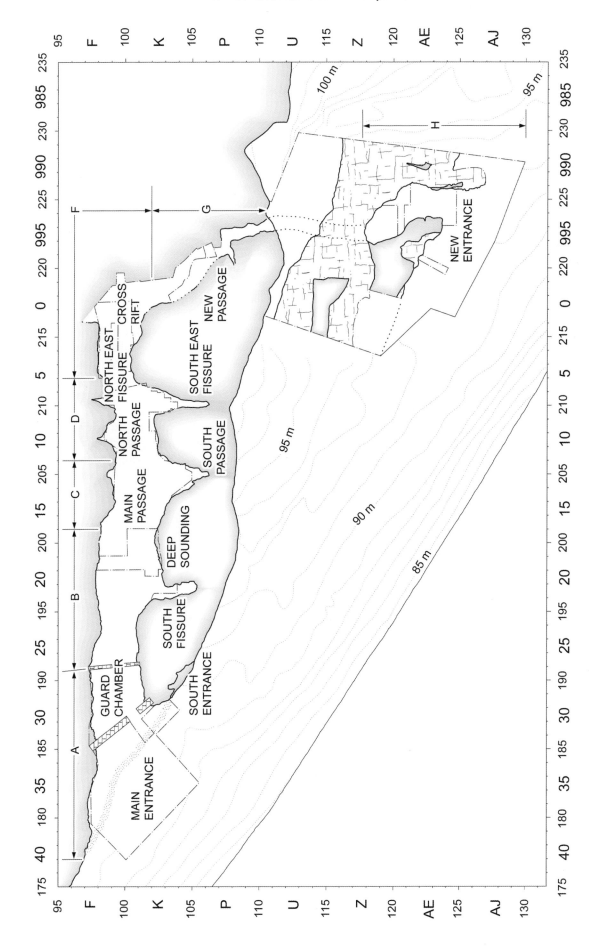

*Figure 6.1. Pontnewydd Cave. Areas excavated 1978–1995.*

an attempt to locate a second entrance to the cave. It was positioned on the hillslope above the cave to investigate a resistivity anomaly identified by Arnold Aspinall, but revealed only a highly cemented periglacial scree. Work at all of these sites was initiated before the publication of the first report on the cave (Green 1984).

Further work subsequently took place at areas A, B and D, together with the opening of three new areas. Area F included the East Passage and the Cross-Rift (between 212.00 and around 220.00 m E, but not extending south of 102.00 m N). Area G covered the New Passage (between

*Figure 6.2. Area A,* in situ *stalagmite (A517) on the north wall (99.78 m S.D.) above limestone deposit with numerous small mudstones.*

102.00 and 110.00 m N). Area H took in all the excavations outside the New Entrance.

### *Area A, re-deposited material outside the Main Entrance*

Excavations between 1978 and 1982 established that the dumped material outside the cave was the result of two episodes of clearance, separated by a thin turf line (Green 1984, 12–20). The first of these was recorded by Hughes and Thomas (1874) but its age is uncertain. It may date from Boyd Dawkins' presence at the site just before (see Walker chapter 2, this volume). The upper layers of the dump were formed during the 1940s when the cave was converted into a munitions store. All these layers contained re-deposited prehistoric material, including worked stone tools and human remains. Both dated human bone finds from this area have yielded Holocene radiocarbon results: PN2, a mandible fragment from the Second World War dump, dating to 7,420±90 BP (OxA-5819); and PN14, a metatarsal from the earlier layer, dating to 4,495±70 BP (OxA-5820; Aldhouse-Green *et al.* 1996 and see Compton and Stringer chapter 9, this volume). Chamberlain (1996) and Blockley (2005) review dates of comparable human remains from other British sites.

Additional areas of the external dumps were excavated in 1985 and 1995 and yielded Pleistocene artefacts and fauna. One artefact (A532) was deeply retouched through patina and showed thereby clear evidence of two discrete

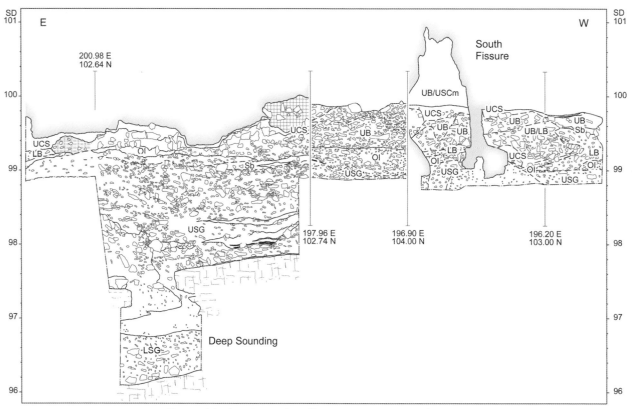

*Figure 6.3. Area B, south wall section, entrance to the right.*

*Figure 6.4. Areas C and D under excavation in 1985, looking into the cave towards the main east section.*

phases of use and, in consequence, of occupation. Also located were two postholes – one still containing a post – of a fence across the cave-mouth. A photograph taken by J. Wilfred Jackson in the 1920s (see Figure 2.7) shows the fence still in place and about 1.20 m in height. It was apparently erected in 1903 or earlier and was faced with wire netting (information from the late Hughie Jones born 1898 in the Old Post Office, Bont Newydd).

An *in situ* stalagmite (A517) was found to survive on the north wall, where it sat on a limestone deposit with numerous small mudstones at a height of 99.78 m (Figure 6.2). This deposit might be equivalent to the Lower Breccia of the Main Cave sequence. The stalagmite was sampled for Uranium series dating and gave results of 36,000±8,500 BP and 66,600±6,600 BP (UEA-772). The sample proved to have been contaminated with Thorium and all that can be said is that the stalagmite probably formed during MIS 3 (Debenham *et al.* chapter 11, this volume). As speleothem does not normally form in open-air conditions, this date implies that the 'external cavern' discussed by Jones (chapter 4, this volume) was still in existence in the Middle Devensian. Accordingly, it would seem that the scale of that recession has been of the order of at least ten metres.

### Area B, Deep Sounding

The Deep Sounding was excavated between 1978 and 1983 to provide a section through the full depth of the basal deposits in the cave (Collcutt 1984, 36–38 and see Figure 6.3). The excavations at Area B were used to establish the suggested sequence for the main chamber. This comprises two major elements: a lower siliceous member and an overlying calcareous member. These are in turn sub-divided into named sub-members. The siliceous member is divided into the Lower Sands and Gravels 1 (LSG1); Lower Sands and Gravels 2 (LSG2); Lower Sands and Gravels 3 (LSG3) and the Upper Sands and Gravels (USG). The important faunal and archaeological deposits are all contained within the eight calcareous sub-members. The lowest of these is the Intermediate complex, above which lies the Lower Breccia (LB), Stalagmitic lithozone (Sl), Silt beds (Sb), Upper Breccia (UB), Red Cave Earth (RCE) and the Upper Clays and Sands (UCS): all of which are sealed by a deposit of laminated Holocene travertine.

It is important to note that key layers, of the calcareous member in particular, were not well represented in Area B; the overall sequence depends on correlation between the Deep Sounding and other excavated areas in the main chamber. Excavated evidence up to the end of the 1983 season established the following probable mechanisms for the emplacement of the various sub-members (Collcutt 1984; Green 1984, 202–205). The Lower Sands and Gravels are best interpreted as a series of debris flows (LSG1 and LSG3) and fluvial events (LSG2). The succeeding Upper Sands and Gravels contain layers deposited by a variety of processes including both debris flows, running and still

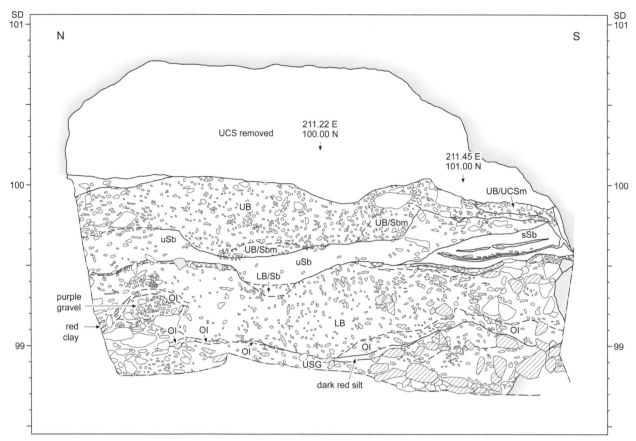

*Figure 6.5. Area D, east section.*

water. The Intermediate complex was interpreted in 1984 as the remains of a debris flow (Green 1984, 204). This interpretation has since been substantially modified by new work at Area D (see below and Mourne and Case chapter 5, this volume). Both the Lower and Upper Breccias represent substantial debris flow events divided by silt formation in standing water, which gave rise to the Silt beds, and the speleothem formation of the Stalagmitic Lithozone. The Upper Clays and Sands are water-laid deposits introduced from higher up within the cave system.

In 1993 and 1994 grid squares J20SE and K20SE were excavated by hand and wet-sieved in order to ascertain whether microfauna was present in the Upper Sands and Gravels (but none was recovered). In 1995, an additional column (grid square J20NE) through the Upper Sands and Gravels was excavated by hand and dry-sieved to examine clast content. Some natural flint and a number of well-stratified small limestone chips were recovered.

### Area D, the Main Passage

Further work in Area D was carried out in 1984, 1985 and from 1987 to 1995 (Figure 6.4). The sequence within this part of the cave has been described previously (Collcutt 1984) but there is a major change in the interpretation of the sediment sequence concerning the Intermediate complex. Thus, these layers are now considered to be (more probably) the result of *in situ* alteration of the base of the Lower

Breccia after its emplacement (Mourne and Case chapter 5, this volume). The layers of the Intermediate complex were, however, excavated and recorded as separate stratigraphic units and the nomenclature will be maintained in the text below. In summary, the sequence in Area D consists of basal Sands and Gravels (a term used in areas D and F where the full USG/LSG sequence was not present), overlain by the Intermediate complex and the Lower Breccia. The latter is locally sealed by the remains of stalagmitic formations, which grew episodically from *c.* 225,000 to 80,000 BP – or perhaps, on the evidence of Area A until 36,000 BP – and which is in turn overlain by structured and unstructured Silt beds. It may be significant that speleothem formation ceases with the onset of glaciation in North Wales (see Bowen and Livingston chapter 3, this volume). Above the Silt beds is the Upper Breccia and above that the Upper Clays and Sands. In Area D both the Upper and Lower Breccias appear to have eroded channels into the layers beneath as they were deposited (Figure 6.5 and 6.7).

### Upper and Lower Sands and Gravels

Of these layers, only the Upper Sands and Gravels has been exposed in Area D. The emplacement of the Sands and Gravels as a whole cannot be dated with any more certainty than to during or before MIS 8. The deposits had probably become cemented before the MIS 7 interglacial, which may indicate an origin in MIS 10, with cementation taking place during MIS 9. However, it is equally possible

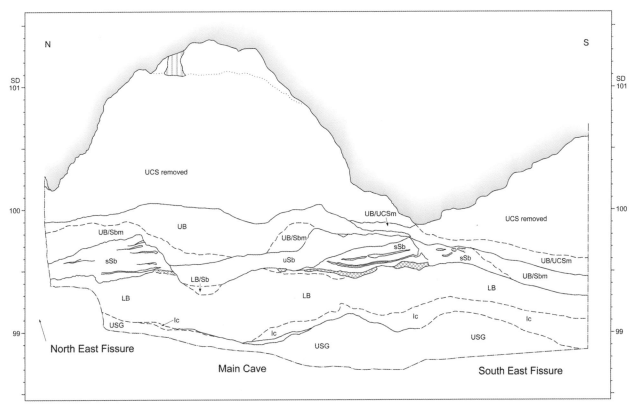

*Figure 6.6. Area D, composite section through North East and South East Fissures, projected on 210.00 m E.*

| **South Fissure area** | B279 | Floor on Lower Breccia cemented to wall | 217+24/-20 ka |
|---|---|---|---|
| **North Passage** | D534 | Boss | 227±13 ka (upper middle) 300+54/-37 ka (lower middle) |
| **East Passage** | D1288C HAR-5612 | Floor on Lower Breccia | 224±41/-31 ka |
| | F2996 UEA-646 | Stalagmite A (cemented to wall) | 197.5+25.1/-20.6 ka (middle) |

*Table 6.1. Uranium series ages on the stalagmitic floor sealing the Lower Breccia.*

that the Sands and Gravels were emplaced during MIS 8, with cementation taking place during a milder phase within that cold stage (Campbell and Bowen 1989, 83).

*Intermediate complex*
Both Orange and Buff Intermediate layers are present in Area D, identified by their conspicuous colouration. The distribution of the Intermediate complex is intermittent and, in several places, patches of orange occur relatively high within the main body of the Lower Breccia. The sediment colours also are now seen as the result of chemical weathering taking place in warm climate conditions when iron was released from the deposits to form hydrous ferric oxides. As discussed above (Mourne and Case chapter 5, this volume), this process probably took place *in situ* within the lower-most deposits of the Lower Breccia. The fauna from within the basal deposit of the Lower Breccia is, in part, interglacial in character, and so is consistent with an MIS 7 (or even MIS 9) age for its incorporation.

*Lower Breccia*
The Lower Breccia in Area D (Figure 6.7) is a thick deposit, over 0.5 m deep in the centre of the cave, and internally undifferentiated except for the patches of coloured sediment discussed above. The dating evidence for the remnant stalagmitic floor above this layer (Table 6.1) suggests that the debris flow event which moved the Lower Breccia into this part of the cave took place before 220,000 BP. The faunal evidence for the Lower Breccia (Currant 1984 and chapter 8, this volume) includes both temperate and cold climate species. This fauna is likely to represent material of different dates, transported into the cave together during MIS 7, perhaps with cold climate species belonging to the stadial sub-stage 7b (Lowe and Walker 1997, 284–285) or MIS 8 (Currant chapter 8, this volume). It may be, as Currant suggests, that temperate elements of the fauna are of MIS 9 age. The Lower Breccia faunal assemblage yielded additional fragments of hominin remains from Areas D and F (Stringer 1984; Compton and Stringer chapter 9, this volume). There is some evidence

*Figure 6.7. Area D, looking into the cave towards the main east section in 1985.*

that the Lower Breccia deposits eroded a channel through the existing Upper Sands and Gravels in Area D, although this is not as marked in the transverse section (Figure 6.6) as it is in similar sections in Area F. This may relate to the energy of the flow decreasing at this point as it spread out into the North-East and South-East Fissures.

In situ *stalagmite*

Substantial fragments of *in situ* stalagmite survive on the surface of the Lower Breccia in Area D (Figure 6.8). Based on six samples, the average height of the surface of the Lower Breccia is *c.* 99.62 in Area F, with a range from 99.53–99.75 S.D. A *terminus ante quem* is indicated for the Lower Breccia by a series of dates on this stalagmite and, by inference also, by stalagmites cemented to the cave-wall and left 'hanging' by later disturbance. Their determinations (Table 6.1) clearly demonstrate the former existence of a stalagmitic floor, *in situ* on the Lower Breccia, distributed widely in the Main Cave. The earliest dates tend to focus around 220,000 BP and are consistent with thermoluminescence dates on burnt flint (Debenham *et al.* chapter 11, this volume) of 200,000±25,000 BP (OX TL 226d1) from the Buff Intermediate and 269,000±37,000 BP (PND-25) from the Lower Breccia. Later determinations on speleothems (in Green 1984 and Debenham *et al.* chapter 11, this volume) show that episodes of stalagmite formation continued down to at least 83,000±9,000 BP, if not to 36,000±8,500 BP the latter based on flowstone from the original cave-wall of the entrance chamber now surviving in the open-air on the north side of Area A.

Two stalagmites in Area D (Figures 6.9 and 6.10; D4698 and D5901), cemented to the cave-wall at heights of 100.50 S.D. (a comparable elevation to the Holocene Laminated Travertine) have produced ages respectively of 116,800+10,600/–9,700 BP (UEA-644) and 137,400+8,600/–7,900 BP (UEA-775). These stalagmites, positioned four to five metres apart on the north and south sides of the cave, appear to represent an early floor level, with a hard crystalline structure which was clearly very different from the Laminated Travertine. Formation at such a height would appear, at first sight, to be incompatible with the height of MIS 5 stalagmite in the East Passage and Cross Rift. It would seem that there were once wall-deposits higher than, but not necessarily directly overlying the Lower Breccia, which were later totally removed from the sequence. Such a formation is likely to have been relict and perhaps very localized, emplaced before *c.* 120,000 BP, but substantially removed before the beginning of the Early Devensian.

*Silt beds and the Upper Breccia*

Above the Lower Breccia and the stalagmite floor *in situ* on it are deposits of structured and unstructured Silt beds. In Area D the unstructured Silt beds overlie more extensive structured deposits (Figure 6.5). The deposition of these layers is discussed in more detail above (Mourne and Case chapter 5, this volume). They are low energy events which probably took place during very cold conditions. They cannot be more precisely dated than <83,000 BP. The Silt beds were heavily channelled and modified during

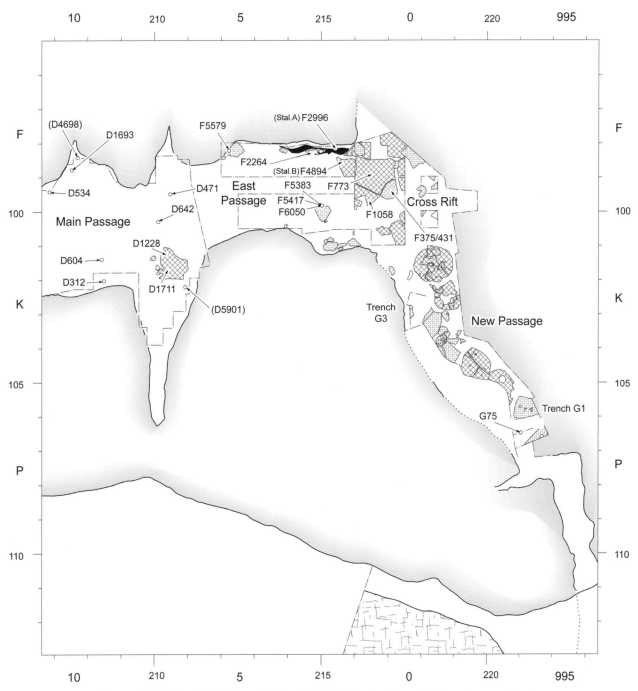

*Figure 6.8. Stalagmite in Areas D, F and G. High level stalagmite shown in parenthesis.*

the emplacement of the succeeding Upper Breccia, even in those areas of the cave where channelling had been less marked in the Lower Breccia (Figure 6.6). It seems likely that the Silt beds were formerly much thicker than the present surviving deposit and that large parts of the lower layers of the Upper Breccia have incorporated Silt beds material as matrix. The 'scooping up' by the Upper Breccia of artefacts and bones, together with substantial fragments of stalagmite, indicates that the Upper Breccia was emplaced with exceptional force. The Upper Breccia appears to consist of source material of Middle Devensian age but emplaced towards or after 20,000 BP on the basis of [14]C determinations (see Area F discussion below).

## Area F, the East Passage

The excavation of Area F took place within two trenches – F north and F south – located in the east passage parallel to the long axis of the cave, divided by a central east-west baulk of undisturbed sediment (Figure 6.11). Trench F south extended eastwards into the Cross Rift. The stratigraphic sequence in Area F displays the following Middle Pleistocene layers. The Basal Sands and Gravels are overlain by the Lower Breccia; which incorporates the Intermediate complex at its base. The Lower Breccia is itself sealed by the Stalagmite lithozone. There is evidence of channelling, to a limited extent by the Lower Breccia but especially by the Upper Breccia (Figures 6.12–6.13).

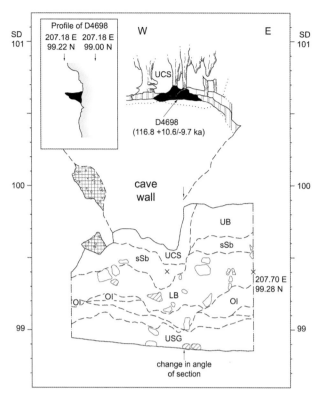

*Figure 6.9. Area D, section of deposits on the wall of the North Passage showing high level stalagmite D4698.*

*Figure 6.10. Area D, detail of high level stalagmite D4698 after sampling.*

*Figure 6.11. Area F, looking out of the cave showing the central baulk and Area F south.*

*The Intermediate complex*

Additional substantial excavation of this level produced fauna but no artefacts. The rare discoveries of artefacts and the hominin tooth (PN1 from Site D) from this level from earlier excavations strengthen the case that the Intermediate complex is part of the Lower Breccia debris flow. The frequency of limestone clasts in the Buff Intermediate of the South-East Fissure is also suggestive of a link with the Lower Breccia, unless they derive from locally shattered bedrock.

*The Lower Breccia*

In Area F, three distinct matrices have been observed in the Lower Breccia (Figures 6.12–6.15). Lower Breccia (a) has a white matrix of what is possibly calcareous mud associated with stalagmite formation at this level. Lower Breccia (b) has a pink matrix. Lower Breccia (c) has a grey matrix. In 1993 the Lower Breccia was dug in 50 mm spits in order to evaluate whether the differences between these layers were of chrono-stratigraphic or other significance. Micro-excavation, however, yielded no helpful results in this regard.

*In situ stalagmite*

Stalagmite of MIS 7 age is present on the north-east wall of the East Passage (Figures 6.12; 6.15 and 6.16). Here stalagmite is cemented to the wall (Stalagmite A) and stands 0.20 m higher than conjoining areas of the same floor (Stalagmite B). Various models may be suggested for this phenomenon (see also chapter 13, this volume) and include solutional lowering of the bedrock floor of the cave; post-emplacement compaction of sediments; and undercutting of stalagmite by fluvial action leading to collapse of a perched floor. There is no evidence for the latter hypothesis. By contrast, post-emplacement compaction would seem to have much to commend it, particularly given the weight of the stalagmite (up to 0.6 m thick in places). A clay-filled vertical crack, exposed in 1994, running north to south through the Lower Breccia in the south side of the East Passage is judged most likely to have been tensional in origin, possibly related to the force of emplacement of the Upper Breccia, although the precise cause is unclear. The crack is, in appearance, a typical periglacial feature but it stands alone in the cave where periglacial action would be implausible in such a protected environment. Again, a crack caused by dessication is unlikely because of the isolation of the feature (D. A. Jenkins pers. comm.). There is likely also to have been differential consolidation of the deposits according to the varying depth of bedrock. This factor would itself have erected variable stresses within the sediment. What is important about the above is that it is clear that the *in situ* stalagmite had become cracked and broken before the deposition of the Silt beds and the overlying sequence (Figure 6.17). Such stalagmite could then have been more easily disturbed and rafted by the later Upper Breccia debris flow.

Within the time-span of calcite deposition in the cave (220,000–83,000 BP), thick stalagmite formation of MIS 5

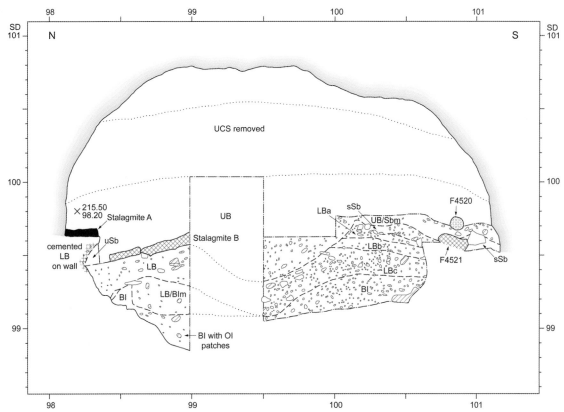

*Figure 6.12. Area F, east section on 215.50 m E, showing* in situ *and slumped stalagmite.*

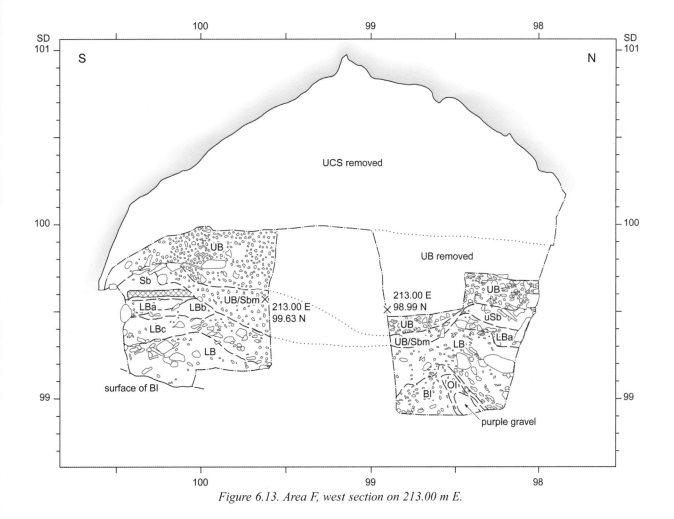

*Figure 6.13. Area F, west section on 213.00 m E.*

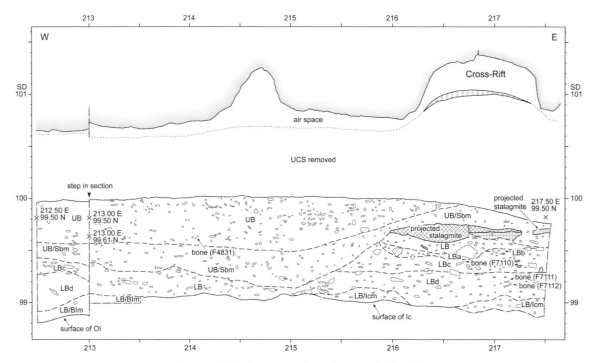

*Figure 6.14. Area F, north section on 99.50 m N.*

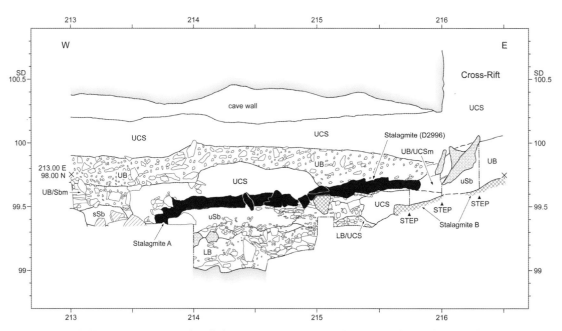

*Figure 6.15. Area F, section of wall deposits on 98.00 m N, showing* in situ *and slumped stalagmite.*

age took place in the Cross Rift (Figure 6.8; Table 6.2). The stalagmitic boss represented by sample F375/F431 (Figure 6.18) was of massive size and had clearly not been moved far by the action of the Upper Breccia debris flow. It lay tilted at an angle of 20° with a total thickness of 420 mm; it was cored *in situ* in 1983. Because of its size this sample provides a history of this phase of stalagmite formation. The process evidently began with the formation of isolated bosses later spreading out to form areas of more continuous but thinner floor. It appeared from field observation that the Cross Rift Stalagmite B had once joined the Wall

Stalagmite A, but later slumped through consolidation or some other mechanism. Stalagmite A is divided into four layers (as described by Peter Rowe):

1) Upper       A hard creamy white calcite;
2)             probable hiatus;
3) Middle      a hard creamy white laminated calcite, dated 197,500+25,100/−20,600 BP (UEA–646), a range at 2σ of 247.7 to 156.3;
4) Base        irregularly shaped hard crystals.

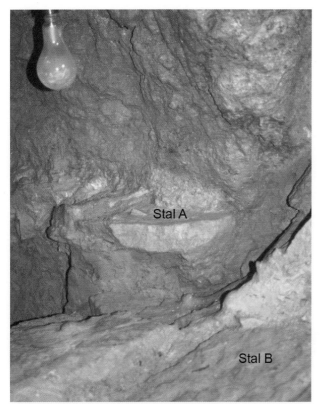

*Figure 6.16. Area F north, looking north-west at the* in situ *wall stalagmite A and the slumped stalagmite B at the east end of the area.*

The 2σ range of the determination on the middle of the Stalagmite A shows that the layer must be of MIS 7 or early MIS 6 age. It may be that the upper layer of Stalagmite A is of MIS 5e age and represents a re-growth of this stalagmite. If so, the vertical slumping of Stalagmite B could not have occurred until after the cessation of the formation of this floor (post *c.* 100,000 BP). There is evidence for massive disruption, including faulting, of the MIS 5 stalagmite

*Figure 6.17. An inverted stalagmitic boss sealed by the structured Silt beds, showing how the stalagmitic floor had become disrupted before the deposition of the Silt beds.*

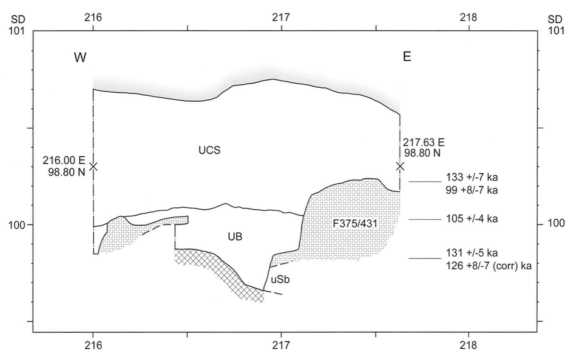

*Figure 6.18. Area F, stratigraphy of dated stalagmite F375/F431.*

| | | |
|---|---|---|
| *F1058* | 100.4+4.4/4.2 ka | Thin *in situ* floor (Stalagmite B) |
| *F375/431* | 99+8/-7 ka (top) | Rafted boss (42 cm thick) in |
| | 126+8/-7 ka (base) | Upper Breccia |

*Table 6.2. Uranium series ages on stalagmite in the Cross-Rift.*

*Figure 6.19. Area F, cracked flowstone on the south-eastern Cross-Rift roof.*

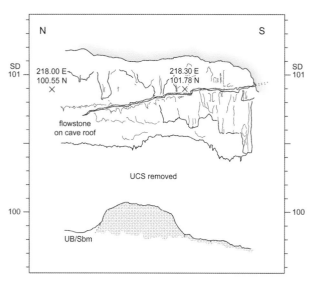

*Figure 6.20. Area F, elevation drawing of crack in flowstone on the eastern Cross-Rift roof.*

*Figure 6.21. Area G, Trench 3, looking south towards the New Passage from the Cross-Rift.*

floor in the East Passage. The flowstone formations on the eastern roof of the Cross Rift are also cracked (Figures 6.19 and 6.20) and it is possible that these features relate to the massive sub-surface vibration associated either with a landslip or an earthquake. Trevor Ford (1997) has identified possible Pleistocene seismic activity over a wide area of Britain from Devon to Derbyshire. In particular there is evidence from Kent's Cavern, Devon, in the form

of widespread disruption and destruction of the Crystalline Stalagmite layer, of a severe earthquake event falling within the time-span 115,000–74,000 BP (Straw 1995, 202; 1996, 23). Another possible example dated after 85,000±10,000

| Pontnewydd (>40–20 ka) | Coygan (>38–24 ka) | Long Hole (Breccia) |
|---|---|---|
| arctic hare | hyaena | hyaena |
| *Arvicola* | wolf | mammoth |
| *Microtus* | red fox | woolly rhino |
| collared lemming | arctic fox | horse |
| pika | polecat | giant deer |
| Norway lemming | brown bear | reindeer |
| wolf | mammoth | mountain hare |
| red fox | woolly rhino | |
| brown bear | horse | |
| horse | red deer | |
| narrow-nosed rhinoceros | reindeer | |
| red deer | giant deer | |
| reindeer | bison or aurochs | |
| musk ox | | |

*Table 6.3. Pontnewydd Upper Breccia fauna compared with other Middle Devensian faunas from Wales.*

BP comes from Hound's Hole, located on the south coast of Gower (Aldhouse-Green 2000, 10); here, stalagmite was also badly shattered and disrupted.

*The Silt beds*
Unmodified Silt beds layers in Area F, largely confined to areas close to the cave walls, were protected from destruction by the surviving Wall Stalagmite A (Figure 6.15). The more constricted shape of the cave in the East Passage may have served to increase the erosive power of the debris flow which transported the Upper Breccia, with a consequential re-working of much of the Silt beds.

*Upper Breccia*
The Upper Breccia lies above the Silt beds. In the Main Cave, this debris flow is characterized by a clast-rich deposit of sub-angular limestone likely to have been derived from an external cryoclastic scree. In Area F, however, where it has deeply eroded or even removed the Silt beds, its basal layer is a matrix-rich 'Silt beds' silt and it is clast-poor (Figure 6.14). Excavations in the New Passage suggest that the classic Upper Breccia ends at the entrance to the Cross Rift, continuing only as a matrix-rich flow into the Cross Rift and through the New Passage to the New Entrance. This spatial evidence leaves no reasonable doubt that its origin lies outside the Main Entrance.

A series of accelerator radiocarbon determinations available from the Upper Breccia, indicates that this fauna is not Late Glacial as originally suggested (Currant 1984), but is actually of Middle Devensian age and falls within the range *c.* 50,000–20,000 BP (see Pettitt *et al.* chapter 11, this volume). A single determination of 27,070±360 BP (OxA-4373) from the Upper Breccia correlative layer (20) in the New Entrance lends substance to that correlation. There is no reason to believe that any elements of the Upper Breccia fauna belong outside this chronological range. The Upper Breccia fauna may be compared with the Middle Devensian faunal assemblages in Wales (Table 6.3). Unlike the material from Coygan Cave, Carmarthenshire and Long

Hole, Gower, Swansea, the fauna from Pontnewydd does not correspond to the Middle Devensian Pin Hole mammal assemblage zone defined by Currant and Jacobi (2001, 1711–1712) dominated by horse, hyaena, mammoth and woolly rhinoceros. The Upper Breccia fauna was evidently accumulated, for the most part, by cub-raising female wolves (see Scott chapter 8, this volume) and it may be that the absence of mammoth and woolly rhinoceros relate both to the composition of the local environment and to the agents of accumulation. Thus, the locally rocky and upland terrain may have led, as has been suggested in the specific case of mammoth (Singer *et al.* 1993), to avoidance of the locality by the larger herbivores. However, such an interpretation would seem to conflict with the presence of rhinoceros at all levels of the site and with the occurrence of woolly rhinoceros and mammoth, at the nearby Cefn Cave (Valdemar 1970).

### Area G, the New Passage

Excavation in the New Passage deposits below the Upper Clays and Sands was confined to two small areas named G1 and G3 (Figures 6.8, 6.21 and 6.22). Trench G1 extended down into the Intermediate complex, whilst in Trench G3 only the upper portion of the Lower Breccia was exposed.

*Intermediate complex*
The Buff Intermediate was revealed in the base of Trench G1. No artefacts were found in that level, but the layer yielded eight fragments of animal bone, including one bear tooth (G216).

*Lower Breccia*
In Trench G1, as in Area F, three different matrices could be distinguished within the Lower Breccia. These correspond to the Lower Breccias (a), (b) and (c) described above, and overlay the Intermediate complex. There were patches of heavily cemented material, particularly within LB(c).

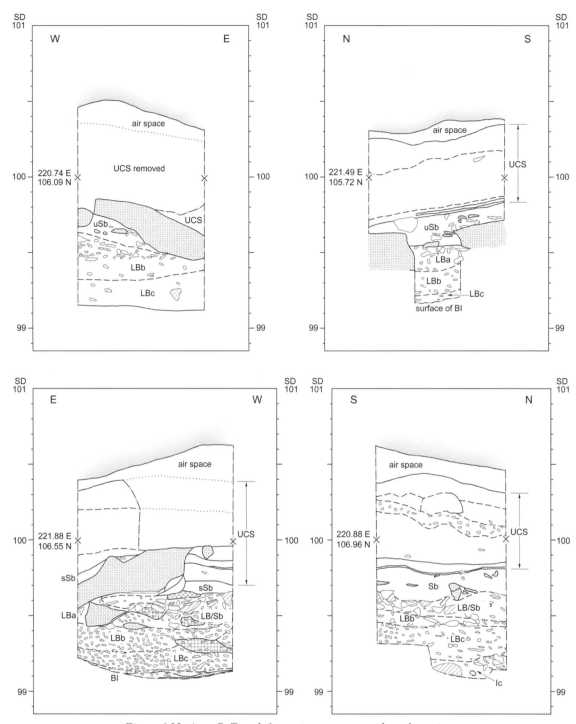

*Figure 6.22. Area G, Trench 1, north, east, west and south sections.*

Two flint flakes, two chunks of flint and eight animal bone fragments, including two vole teeth and a cervid tooth, were found in the Lower Breccia.

*The Silt beds, and Upper Breccia with Silt beds matrix*
The nature of the layers immediately above the Lower Breccia changes distinctly between the site examined in Trench G3 and Trench G1. At the northern end of the New Passage channelling by the later debris flow has produced a

deposit of Upper Breccia with Silt beds matrix containing numerous and substantial fragments of rafted stalagmite floor. To the south, in Trench G1, similar substantial portions of stalagmitic floor were contained within unstructured Silt beds. A yellow clay layer in Trench G3 represents a localized variation in the Silt beds matrix. More structured Silt beds, with much less stalagmite, were found in the south and west areas of Trench G1. The Silt beds matrix re-deposited in the Upper Breccia debris flow seems to

| North face (Trench 1) Grid line = 222.40 | Site O.D. North | South face (Trench 1) Grid line = 223.00 | Site O.D. South | Geological core (located to south) | Dates |
|---|---|---|---|---|---|
| Cave Roof | 100.45 | | - | - | |
| Silty Sand layer | 100.45 | | - | - | |
| Screes (18) | 100.39 | | - | - | 32±6 ka (PND-23)[1] |
| Cave wall collapse (50) | ? | | - | - | 130±29 ka (PND-43)[2] 154±36 ka (PND-44)[2] |
| Stalagmite Spread (20) | 100.17 | | - | - | 27,070±360 BP (OxA-4323)[3] |
| Limestone Breccia (23) | 99.82 | | - | - | |
| (24) | 99.48 | | - | - | |
| (26) | 99.16 | | - | - | 173±20 ka (PND-32)[4] 214±21 ka (PND-62)[4] |
| (28) | 98.82 | | - | - | 179±22 ka (PND-33)[4] |
| Yellow Stony layer (29) | 98.70 | YSL (29) | 98.75 | - | *132+8.2/-7.6 ka (top) *141.6+7.3/-6.8 ka (base) (H1713)[5] |
| Mudstone Gravel unit (MGU) (33) | 98.18 | MGU (33) | 97.88 | - | |
| (38) | - 98.05 | MGU (34) | 97.82 97.42 | (a) cemented Mudstone Gravel (down to 97.10) | |
| | - | Stal (39) within MGU (38/41) | 97.20-06 | (b) stalagmite 97.10-96.95 | *269.4=24/-19 ka (UEA-683)[6] |
| | - | MGU (41) | 97.06 | (c) 96.95-63 cemented limestone and mudstone | 226±21 ka (PND-66)[4] |
| | 97.50-96.60 | in situ flowstone (43) | | (d) no retrieval (96.63-95.84) | 85±9 ka (J5630)[5] |
| | - | in situ floor (42) | 96.56 | | 91±7 ka (J5627)[5] |
| | - | Silt with Limestone (44) | 96.52 | | |
| Bedrock | 97.27 - | limit of excavation in (44) | - 96.20 | | |
| | | | | (e) derived stal (96.63-95.74) | *218.3+23/-19 ka (UEA-684)[6] |
| | | | | (f) no retrieval (95.74-49) | |
| | | | | (g) stiff yellow clay (95.49-42) | |
| | | | | (h) bedrock (95.42) | |

Table 6.4. New Entrance (Trench 1) sedimentological sequence and comparison with the 1993 geological core. All Trench 1 heights at top of layer on grid-lines indicated for the north and south faces respectively. Notes: (1) TL on sediment (2) TL on calcite (3) [14]C determination on fauna (4) TL on burnt flint (5) U-series AEA (6) U-series UEA. * = derived stalagmite.

have become progressively more impregnated with flecks and clasts of stalagmite during transport through the New Passage, eventually emerging as a spread of corroded stalagmite (20/22) through the New Entrance.

## Area H, the New Entrance

The position of the New Entrance had been identified by tunnelling from the inside of the cave through the UCS along the line of the New Passage during the mid 1980s.

*Figure 6.23. Area H, view of excavations in 1988 looking north towards the Main Cave.*

It was fully exposed externally by deep trenching in 1987 (Figures 6.1 and 6.23). By the end of the 1992 season, excavation had reached the maximum depth that could easily and safely be accomplished within the size of trench opened. As a precursor to more substantive excavation, it seemed desirable to establish the main features of the underlying sequence by coring.

*The core and its re-interpretation in the light of excavation*

In 1993, coring revealed a sequence around 5 metres in depth from the roof of the New Entrance at 100.45 m S.D. to bedrock at 95.42 m S.D. or, translated into heights above mean sea-level, 90.92 and 85.89 m O.D. (100.000 Site Datum = 90.473 O.D. (Green 1984, 20)). In fact, as later excavation showed, the core proved to have been fortuitously located on the lower edge of a very steep 'pitch'. In consequence, bedrock was reached at *c*. 97.20 m on the north side of Trench 1 in the mouth of the entrance – an overall depth of only 3.25 m – whereas on the south edge of the trench the limit of the excavation achieved was 96.20 m (4.25 m long) with bedrock potentially still 0.78 m below at 95.42 m S.D. (Figures 6.24 and 6.25). The sequence eventually revealed by excavation is set out in Table 6.4 where the results from the coring are shown by way of contrast.

The 1993 coring sequence (Table 6.4) involved three one metre coring-tubes (lettered A–C, with A the uppermost) and drilling began at 97.50 m S.D., the lowest level

excavation had reached by 1993. In addition, 170 mm of a fourth coring tube (D) was drilled through limestone to support the hypothesis that bedrock had been reached. Core A yielded a full column of sediment; core B produced only a derived stalagmite (H2217), dated to 218,000+23,000/–19,000 BP (UEA-684), 30 mm above the base of the core, in an otherwise empty tube; core C recovered only a 70 mm thickness of yellow clay and the apparent bedrock-surface. Although three one metre cores were used, plus 170 mm of a fourth, the depth achieved (as recorded directly at the end of drilling by measuring down the bore-hole) was not 3.17 m but only 2.25 m (including 170 mm of bedrock). The individual column lengths, which had been achieved before drilling was discontinued and a replacement core-tube put in place, were A = 0.87 m; B = 1.06 m; C = 0.44 m; D = 0.17 m. These figures add up to a total of 2.54 m compared with 2.25 m actually cored. Thus, 290 mm was added through incremental error. Continuous sediments were not recovered by coring below 96.63 m. We had presumed, during the coring in 1993, this was because the water lubricant of the coring process had washed away unconsolidated sediments. Yet we were to find, in 1995, that the sediments were very strongly cemented down to 96.52 m and were only unconsolidated thereafter. Within the limits of accuracy of coring, we may regard these two levels (96.63 m and 96.52 m) as being in close agreement. It is possible that stalagmite H2217 may actually have been retrieved closer to 96.63 m and that it wedged in the base of the otherwise empty tube leading, thereby, to no

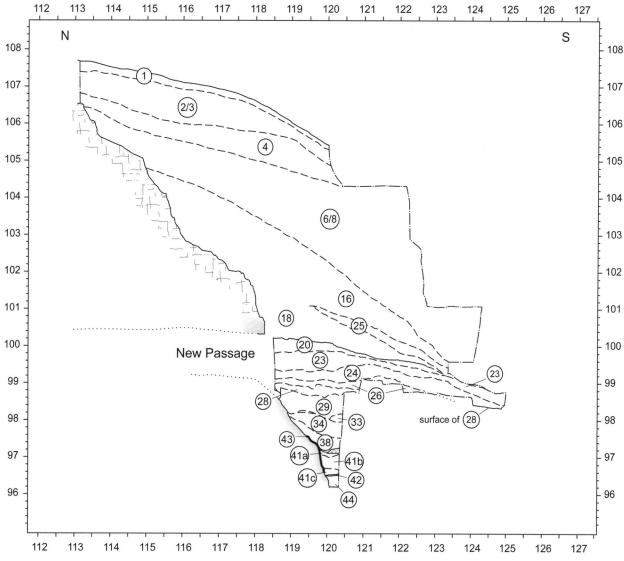

*Figure 6.24. Area H, composite east section through screes and cave deposits.*

recovery either of the *in situ* floor (42) or of any of the sediment underlying that floor. In any event, given the fact that stalagmite H2217 was not recovered as part of a continuous sediment column, its context must remain unresolved.

### The sedimentary sequence in the New Entrance (Tables 6.4–6.6)

In 1994, the New Entrance excavations were expanded with the aim of reaching the base of the sediments by the end of the 1995 season. The complex stratigraphic sequence that was revealed is described below from the base upwards (Table 6.5; Figures 6.26 and 6.27).

### In situ flowstone on bedrock (43), Stalagmite floor (42), and underlying Silt with Limestone (44)

The dating of the *in situ* flowstone (43), which had formed on the steeply sloping surface of the 'pitch', and the stalagmitic 'floor' (42) to 85,000 and 91,000 BP, provide important keys to our understanding of the chronology of

the New Entrance (Figure 6.26). The flowstone is present on bedrock from a top height of *c*. 97.85 m (S.D.), falling rapidly down the 'pitch' to 96.50 m. This flowstone wholly underlies the Mudstone Gravel unit described below and it is clear that the formation of that unit must provide a *terminus post quem* for the emplacement of the Mudstone Gravel. Layer (44), which was the very deepest layer reached by excavation, comprises a relatively uncemented deposit with silty/sandy matrix and some limestone. Only a very small sample could be excavated at the very base of Trench 1, but the fact that neither fauna nor artefacts were recovered may suggest that the layer was emplaced in a biologically hostile environment.

### Mudstone Gravel unit (33, 34, 38, 39, 41)

This unit contains only rare limestone and is composed largely of Mudstone Gravel (Figures 6.26 and 6.27). One layer is of fluvial deposition (33) but the remaining layers comprise one or more debris flows. A few artefacts are present plus one hominin tooth (PN20, H2942), a heavily

| **Subaerial Deposits** | | **Layers** |
|---|---|---|
| I | Topsoil and Colluvium | 1–4 |
| II | Solifluction | 5–11 |
| III | Loess | 12 |
| IV | Screes – including a TL age of 32±6 ka on loess | 13–19 |
| | | |
| **Cave Deposits** | | |
| V | Stalagmite spread (20) – Stal. undated but 27 ka fauna present and layer is overlain locally by cave wall collapse (50) with derived TL ages on stalagmite of 154 and 130 ka. | 20 |
| VI | Limestone Breccia | 23–28 |
| VII | Yellow Stony layer – contains derived stalagmite *c.*142–132 ka | 29 |
| VIII | Mudstone Gravel unit | 33–34,38–39,41 |
| IX | *In situ* Stalagmite floor (42) | 42 |
| | Flowstone on bedrock (43) | 43 |
| X | Silt and Limestone deposit | 44 |
| | -.-.-.-.-.- Limit of excavation .-.-.-.-.-.-.-.-. | |

*Table 6.5. New Entrance stratigraphic units.*

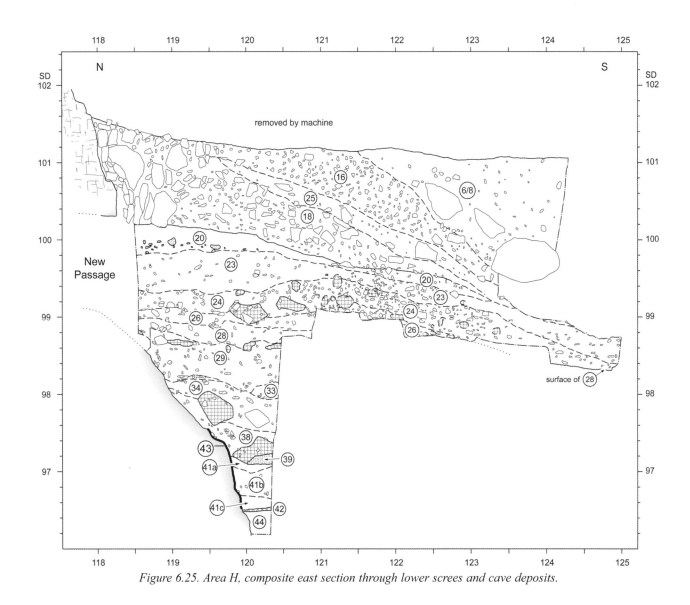

*Figure 6.25. Area H, composite east section through lower screes and cave deposits.*

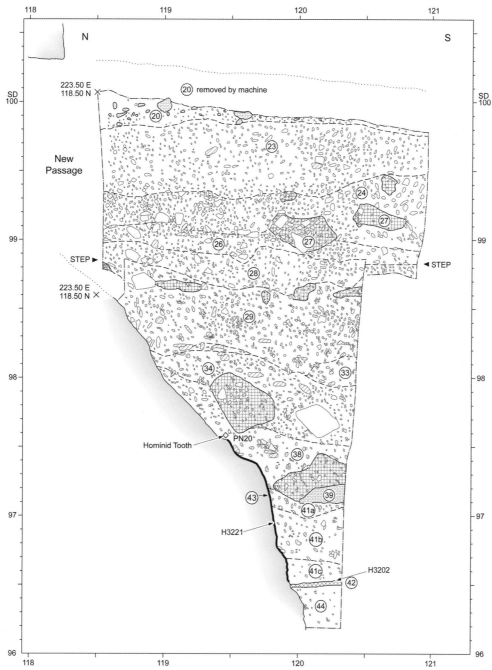

*Figure 6.26. Area H, east section on 223.50 m E. The sampling positions of* in situ *stalagmites H3221 and H3202 are shown.*

worn premolar. Fauna is limited to bird, bear, wolf and fox. The layer contains a substantial deposit of derived stalagmite (39), a sample of which has been U-series dated to 269,400+24,000/–19,000 BP (UEA-683) a range at 2σ, of 313,400–231,400. This derived stalagmite, originally of intra-cave origin, had spilled out through the mouth of the New Entrance, falling down the slope of the 'pitch' like a collapsed deck of cards. The matrix may be most simply interpreted as a slumped river-bank deposit, on account of it containing a substantial component of rounded mudstone pebbles. The presence of a hominin tooth plus artefacts suggests that it may have been on the surface of just such a river-bank that the Pontnewydd hominins were encamped.

The Lower Breccia of the Main Cave is likewise mudstone-rich but has acquired some limestone during its passage through the cave-system. The Mudstone Gravel unit may correlate with the Lower Breccia because it contains a derived stalagmite floor of similar age to that which formed on the Lower Breccia and, so, may have been part of the same sediment body which gave rise to both units.

*Yellow Stony layer (29, 31)*
The Yellow Stony layer (Figures 6.26 and 6.27) is a debris flow with fauna but only rare artefacts (less than half a dozen). These artefacts did, however, include two bifaces of which one was quite rolled. Given the rarity of bifaces

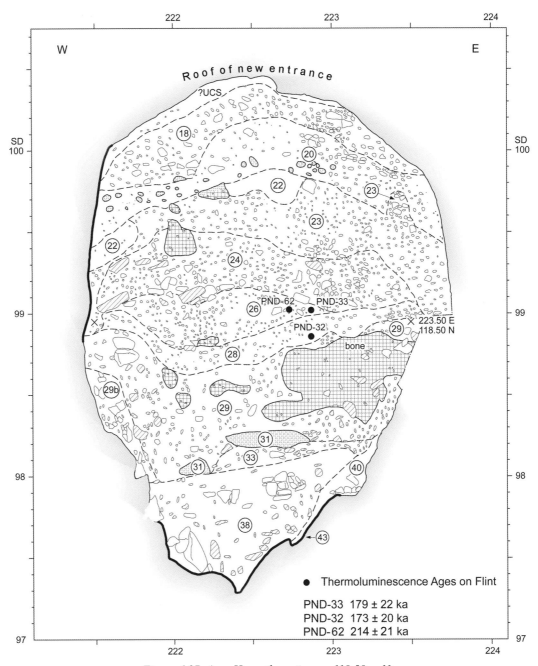

*Figure 6.27. Area H, north section on 118.50 m N.*

in the New Entrance deposits, these occurrences may be significant and, so, perhaps hint at the presence of different phases of occupation characterized by differing assemblages of artefacts (see Aldhouse-Green *et al.* chapter 10, this volume). Derived stalagmite in Layer 29 termed (31) has been dated to 142,000/132,000 BP (H1713). The Yellow Stony layer has no correlative inside the cave and, so, seems likely to have originated outside the cave-system.

*The Limestone Breccia unit (23–24, 26, 28)*
This unit comprises four layers (Figures 6.26 and 6.27), viz.:

| 23–24, 26 | upper Limestone Breccia |
|-----------|-------------------------|
| 28        | lower Limestone Breccia |

Excavation in the New Entrance demonstrated a sharp stratigraphic contact at the interface of layers (26) and (28). Accordingly the unit has been sub-divided into upper Limestone Breccia (23, 24, 26) and lower Limestone Breccia (28). Internal sedimentological differences within the upper Limestone Breccia are not significant and the contained layers are best regarded, therefore, as being no more than different facies of a single event. However, the surface of the lower Limestone Breccia is characterized by an area of intense black staining which is present to a

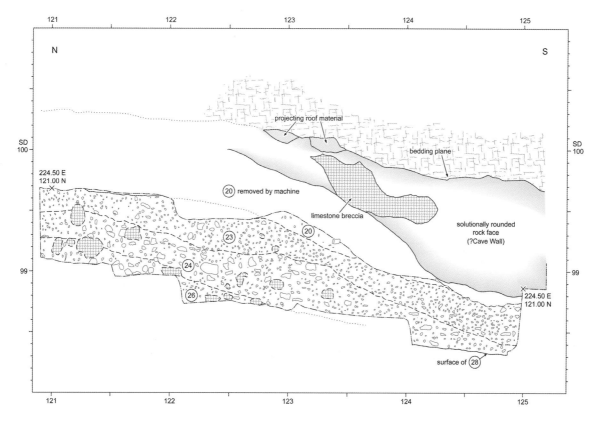

*Figure 6.28. Area H, east section of Trench 2 and elevation of adjacent rock face.*

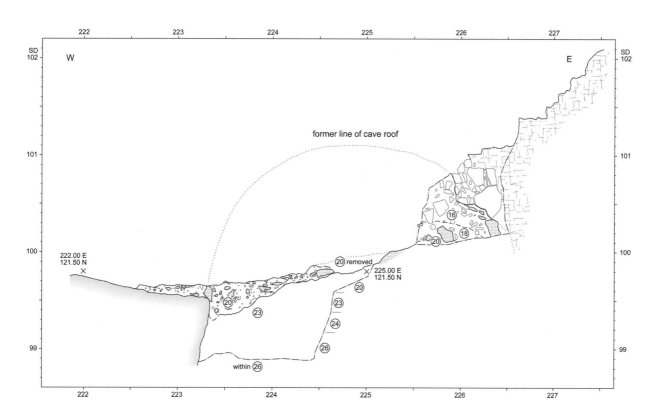

*Figure 6.29. Area H, Trench 2, north section on 121.50 m N showing Layer 20 overlying bedrock on the site of the collapsed cave wall.*

| Main Cave B–F | New Passage G | New Entrance H | External H | Age |
|---|---|---|---|---|
| Cave Roof | Cave Roof | Cave Roof | | |
| LT | LT | - | TC | Post Glacial |
| UCS | UCS | ?UCS | SL | UCS = LG+PG <br> SL = LG |
| | | Screes (18/19) | Screes (18/19) | Late Devensian |
| Upper Breccia | (20/22) | (20/22) | Stalagmite Spread (20/22) | Middle Devensian (35-25 ka) |
| | | Limestone Breccia (23–24, 26, 28) | | Middle Pleistocene (*c.* 200 ka) sediment deposited post 85 ka |
| | | Yellow Stony layer (29) | - | Middle Pleistocene (*c.* 200 ka) sediment deposited post 85 ka |
| | | Mudstone Gravel unit (33–34, 38–39, 41) Stalagmite floor (42) | | Middle Pleistocene (*c.* 200 ka) sediment deposited post 85 ka 85 ka |
| | | *In situ* flowstone (43) Silt with Limestone (44) .-.-.-.-.-.-. | - | |
| Silt Beds | Silt Beds | | - | MIS 2–5b |
| Stalagmite (MIS 7, 5) | Stalagmite (MIS 5) | | - | MIS 5–7 |
| Lower Breccia | Lower Breccia | | | *c.* 230 ka |
| Intermediate | Intermediate | - | - | *c.* 240 ka |
| Basal Sands and Gravels | .-.-.-.-.-. | | | MIS 8 or older |
| Bedrock | | | | |

*Table 6.6. The principal stratigraphic units: proposed correlation between the Main Cave and the New Entrance. Key: TC = topsoil and colluvium; SL = solifluction; LT = laminated travertine; MIS = Marine Isotope Stage; DEV = Devensian; LG = Late Glacial; PG = Post-Glacial; UCS = Upper Clays and Sands.*

lesser extent throughout the deposit. This colouration is likely to pre-date emplacement of the overlying layers. Such staining is also present on the surface of the Upper Breccia of the Main Cave (Collcutt 1984, 41 (DCE: 5 and 52)) where it has been identified as a zone of alteration composed of FeMnAl oxides and carbon. There named the Pan lithozone, it was interpreted by Collcutt (1984, 73) as arising from the onset of stream-flow which significantly altered underlying deposits. Our correlation (Table 6.6) of the Main Cave and the New Entrance deposits would seem to rule out a coeval event, but a similar context of alteration seems plausible.

The geometry of the upper and lower Limestone Breccia (Figures 6.26 and 6.28) would seem to indicate flow into the New Passage. The deposits are clearly composed of dense and relatively un-rounded limestone clasts which are unlikely to have been transported over a long distance and which must have originated as external screes. In addition, the contained artefacts are mostly in a sharp condition

compared with the Main Cave and so cannot have travelled far. As in the Main Cave, the fauna is dominated by bear remains and, accordingly, is here interpreted as a cave-fauna which might well have originated within the zone of permanent darkness and, quite possibly, deep within the cave-system. Dates on *in situ* stalagmite at the base of the New Entrance sequence confirm that the artefacts, as also certainly the fauna, are in a derived context. Burnt flint artefacts directly dated by thermoluminescence, have yielded ages of 173,000±20,000 BP (28), 179,000±22,000 BP (26) and 214,000±26,000 BP (26). Accordingly, it would seem that the Limestone Breccia was a very ancient deposit at the time of its final emplacement and, presumably, had been 'stored' in a part of the cave system which no longer exists. It is conceivable that it reached its present position via a now vanished chimney or aven. Indeed, the former existence of such a chimney may account, in part at least, for the fact that the cave-roof is absent south of the New Entrance. Given that recession of the order of 10 m can be

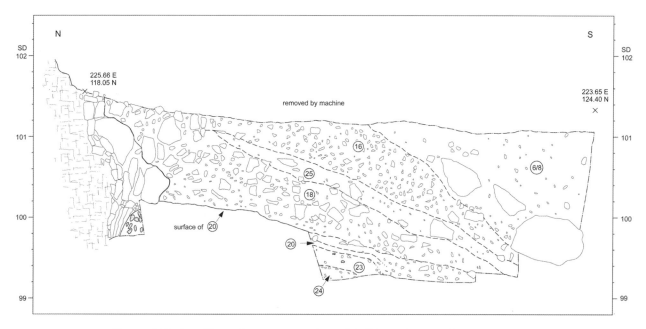

*Figure 6.30. Area H, north east section through hillslope deposits above cave mouth.*

demonstrated for the Main Entrance (see Area A discussed above) a loss of *c.* 9.0 m in the New Entrance seems wholly plausible. On the basis of artefacts, and indeed faunal frequencies and species, there is nothing to differentiate the upper and lower units of the Limestone Breccia.

As we have seen, the Limestone Breccia sequence (23, 24, 26, 28) in the New Entrance has no certain chronostratigraphic correlative in the Main Cave. Indeed fabric studies suggest that the flow has moved *into* the cave from the New Entrance and the fresh condition of the contained artefacts is consistent with such an interpretation (Mourne and Case chapter 5, this volume). The artefacts and fauna compare, however, with those from the Lower Breccia in the Main Cave and demonstrate the former existence of source material outside both entrances. The preservation of such source material – unless perhaps protected within a since collapsed entrance chamber – would seem to be inconsistent with any suggestion of MIS 6 glaciation in North Wales. The (23, 24, 26) sequence layers all possess the domed surfaces characteristic of the debris flows in the Main Cave. By contrast, the underlying layer (28) – a manganese-stained limestone breccia (field test 1993 by D. A. Jenkins) – is concave-surfaced and the implication is that it is a pre-existing layer which has been channelled by a fluvial event or by the (23, 24, 26) debris flow itself. In the latter case its manganese-staining would be a post-emplacement event, since the surface of (28) displays a marked zone of staining and alteration.

*The Stalagmite spread (20, 22)*
Layers (20/22) consist of a debris flow rich in stalagmite clasts, often very corroded, and with many tiny flecks of stalagmite (Figure 6.27). The context, as equally the geometry, of the Stalagmite Spread (SS) is indicative of an origin within the cave system. The layer is identifiable

in the New Passage (Area G, Trenches 1 and 3) where it 'replaces' the classic Upper Breccia. The Stalagmite Spread is regarded here as a continuation of the Upper Breccia event and the radiocarbon dates on fauna from both layers are consistent with this. Layer 20 clearly formed after the collapse of the New Entrance as it partially overlies the remains of the former western cave wall (Figure 6.29). Accordingly, the collapse is likely to have taken place by 20,000 BP.

*The Late Devensian/Post Glacial sequence*
The Upper Breccia analogue (20/22) in the New Entrance is overlain (Figures 3.25, 6.29 and 6.30) by an angular scree deposit (50, 18/19), with the lowest layer (50) full of thin pieces of derived stalagmite, perhaps flowstone in origin. Two of these pieces have given thermoluminescence ages of 154,000±36,000 BP (PND-43) and 130,000±29,000 BP (PND-44). These clasts may derive from the collapse of the New Entrance chamber (possibly from the wall or roof of an 'external' cavern). The structure of the bedrock at the entrance itself and the massive fragmentation of the overlying lower limestone cliff are all relevant to this interpretation. More telling, perhaps, is the massive post-depositional cementation of deposits, likely to have formed in an intra-cave situation but extending at least three metres outside the present entrance.

Livingston's work (1986) demonstrated that the geomorphological deposits of the Elwy valley were likely to be largely or entirely of Devensian or Holocene age. An aspect of this work involved a consideration of the significance of an enigmatic 'solifluction terrace' present locally at about 90 m O.D. (or about 99.50 m S.D.) In short, the terrace is at the level of the cave. Subsequent unpublished work (*in litt*, 26.10.93) has revealed that this terrace is:

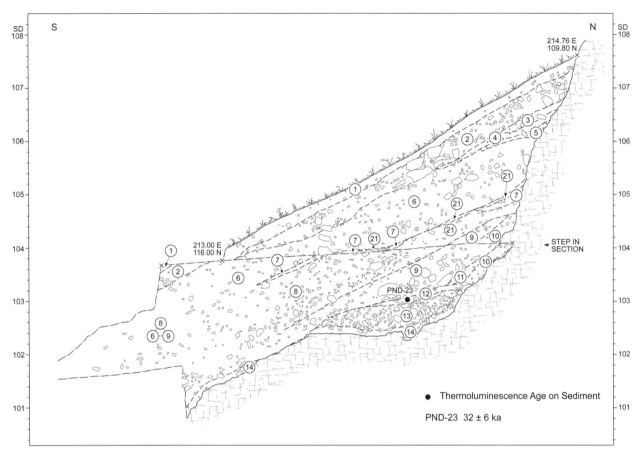

*Figure 6.31. Area H, main west section through hillslope deposits.*

a degraded ancient landslide block which has been truncated downslope by younger landslides. [Moreover] it is possible that the ponding events noted on the solifluction terrace relate to small ponds formed in irregularities in the bedrock. There seem to have been four distinct phases of landsliding [beginning, probably] in Late Glacial times when massive, mainly rotational, movement occurred in the glacial infill (and perhaps in the bedrock) on both sides of the valley, particularly on the limestone downstream from Ddôl. This massive landsliding probably created the limestone scars which run along the Bryn. It is probable that rock-falls also occurred and that screes were formed.

Livingston unpublished.

We see in this evidence, therefore, that the New Entrance collapse and scree-formation events were just part of a much more widespread process occurring along both sides of the valley and at roughly the height of the cave entrances. If the Upper Breccia and its equivalent New Entrance layers are to be related to this process then, on the basis of [14]C determinations on the contained fauna, the scree formation was probably occurring sometime within the period leading up to 20,000 BP. The collapse of the New Entrance (50) occurred before 20,000 BP when it was sealed by Upper Breccia outwash; local later scree formation is represented by layers 18/19. The emplacement of layers 18/19 may,

plausibly, be related to a Late Devensian or perhaps Late Glacial context.

### Loess (12)

Within the sequence of screes overlying the New Entrance (Figure 6.31), a localized band of fine-grained sediment interpreted as loess (layer 12) has been given a TL age of 32,000±6,000 BP (PND-23). It lay above a scree (the latter on bedrock) and beneath probable later Devensian screes and solifluction. On an age-range of two standard deviations (44,000–20,000 BP), it is stratigraphically consistent with the post 27,000 BP age evidenced by the [14]C determination of 27,070±360 BP (OxA-4373) on a cervid calcaneum from a sequentially earlier layer in the New Entrance (20) (Unit IV). Accordingly, it would seem reasonable to see this latter unit as an outflow event arising from the input of Upper Breccia. A [14]C determination of 21,330±140 BP (OxA-11565) on Upper Breccia fauna in the Main Cave has yielded a *terminus post quem* for the emplacement of the Upper Breccia which plausibly, may relate to the events leading up to or associated with the Devensian glacial maximum of *c.* 18,000 BP (in radiocarbon years) or after.

Above the screes lie massive deposits of solifluction (H. Livingston pers. comm. on site 1993). Landslip was rejected as a mechanism because of the absence of a smooth underlying surface (Figure 6.31). This solifluction is of Late Glacial age and probably coeval with the basal unit of the Upper Clays and Sands inside the cave (which seems also to be present in the very top of the New Entrance). It is clear that the New Entrance was effectively blocked when the UCS was laid down, thereby creating the 'ponding' conditions necessary for its emplacement. Finally, in Post Glacial times colluvium formed on the surface of the sub-aerial solifluction and, within the cave, a green silt unit (full of Holocene fauna) was added to the pre-existing UCS unit which was then itself capped with a locally massive *in situ* Laminated Travertine stalagmitic floor.

# 7.  The Excavations at Cefn and Cae Gronw

## Stephen Aldhouse-Green and Rick Peterson

### Cefn West Cave

*Excavations were carried out in the west entrance of Cefn Cave in 1982 and 1983. In Trench 1 (near the entrance and within the daylight zone), the sequence detected comprised an almost sterile basal silt overlain by an MIS 7 stalagmitic floor, a debris flow, and a massive layer of stalagmite, of MIS 5 age. Above this, a considerable thickness of deposit had been removed, with little doubt at some time during the nineteenth century. Trench 2 was situated further into the cave, around a right angle bend and within the darkness zone. But, in a distance of as little as 35 m, the strata were found to slope dramatically, such that the surface of the MIS 5 stalagmitic floor was found to lie fully two metres deeper. A thick sequence of fluvial Devensian layers overlay the stalagmite and, almost certainly as a consequence of this waterlogging, the stalagmite had become decayed and powdery. No Palaeolithic artefacts were found in the cave by these excavations, although Holocene human remains, Late Glacial lithic artefacts, and a Last Interglacial 'hippopotamus fauna' were recovered from the cave by earlier work.*

### Introduction

The Cefn Caves are situated on the north-east side of the Elwy valley, approximately 750 m south-west of Pontnewydd at around 70 m O.D. (Figures 4.2, 4.4 and 7.1). Investigations at Cefn began in the 1830s, following the removal of much of the upper fills of the cave during the construction of a landscaped walk through the cave (see Walker chapter 2, this volume). Excavations were carried out at Cefn West in 1982 and 1983 (Figure 7.2) together with a small exploratory excavation at Cefn East in 1982. Work initiated at Cefn East would have involved digging though large depths of unstable rubble deposits and was abandoned before any *in situ* Pleistocene deposits were exposed.

### Trench 1

The stratigraphy within Cefn West Trench 1 represents at least five main events below the level of the 'cave earth' removed in the early nineteenth century (Figures 7.2 and 7.3). The earliest of these was an almost sterile silt; above which were the remains of a stalagmitic floor; this latter was sealed by two silt layers with limestone rubble, overlain in turn by a layer of stalagmite.

### *Grey Silt (8)*

This basal cave fill, Layer 8, was almost completely sterile. It contained angular limestone fragments, including portions of cave-wall showing ripple marks, within a clean grey silty matrix. There was some local reddish-brown mottling of the matrix around the clasts. A derived stalagmite fragment from within Layer 8 was dated to around 284,000 BP (Table 7.1).

### *Lower Stalagmitic Floor*

A thin band, around 150 mm thick, of *in situ* stalagmitic floor covered Layer 8 at the southernmost edge of the trench. This floor did not survive – or perhaps had not been present – over the whole area of the trench and was very rotted at its edges. A single Uranium series result on this Lower Stalagmitic floor gave an age of around 240,000 BP (Table 7.1).

### *Silt and rubble complex (7, 6)*

Above Layer 8 was orange silt, Layer 7. At its upper boundary this layer merged into a mixture of mudstone and limestone rubble within the silty matrix. This mixture

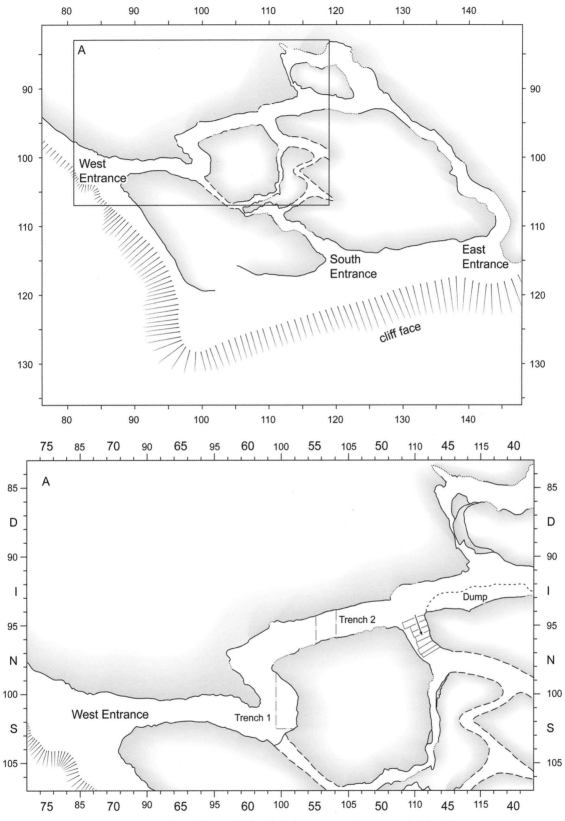

*Figure 7.1. General plan and detail of the excavated portion of Cefn West.*

formed the lowest portion of Layer 6; a green silt containing rolled limestone rubble. It is likely that these silts represent two separate events.

### Upper Stalagmitic Floor (5, 4)

The speleothem above Layer 6 can be subdivided into three layers, which probably represent episodes of formation.

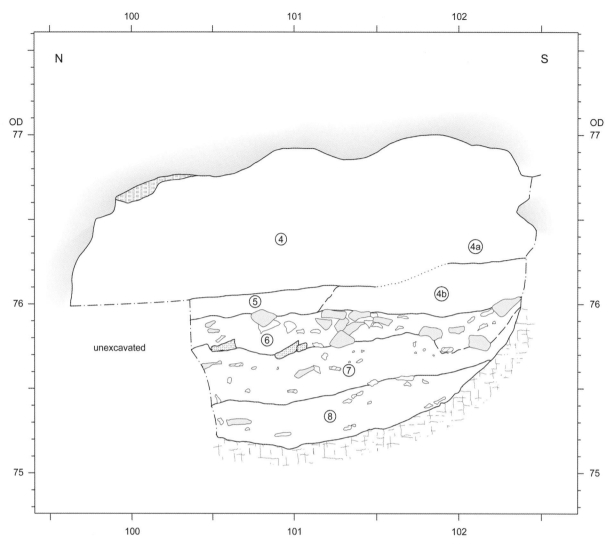

*Figure 7.2. Cefn. West Entrance. East section of Trench 1 on grid line 100.00 m E.*

Layer 5, which occurred locally in the northern part of Trench 1, consisted of laminated layers of green silt and stalagmite. Above Layer 5 was a more extensive deposit of stalagmite, Layer 4, which extended over the whole of Trench 1. Layer 4 varied considerably in texture, hard and laminated in places but considerably softer and more friable in others. In the southern part of the trench these distinctions could be observed vertically; the softer Layer 4a overlying the harder Layer 4b. Two Uranium Series ages on stalagmite from Layer 4 gave results of 105,000 and 181,000 BP (Table 7.1). However, a thermoluminescence result on stalagmite from the same layer gave an age of around 264,000 BP (Table 7.2).

## Trench 2

Trench 2 was excavated in the hope of finding a better preserved section of the Upper Stalagmitic Floor but, in the event this layer was more heavily decomposed in Trench 2 than it had been in Trench 1. Layer 4 was the deepest point reached by excavations in Trench 2 and is the equivalent of Layer 6 in Trench 1. The green silt matrix contained

plentiful well-preserved bone, mudstone pebbles, limestone fragments and some pieces of derived speleothem.

### *Upper Stalagmitic Floor (3)*

Sealing Layer 4 was Layer 3, the highly decomposed remains of a stalagmite floor. Together with the crystalline remains of *in situ* stalagmite this layer also contained some silt lenses together with occasional fragments of angular limestone and bone. It seems likely that this stalagmite was the remains of a floor which would correlate with the Upper Stalagmitic Floor in Trench 1.

### *Laminated complex*

Above the stalagmitic floor was Layer 2, made up of an extremely complex sequence of laminated sands silts and clays. This layer was extensively disturbed by animal burrowing and was entirely devoid of finds except for intrusive modern material.

Two human femur fragments from the historic collections held by the Williams Wynn family have been dated to

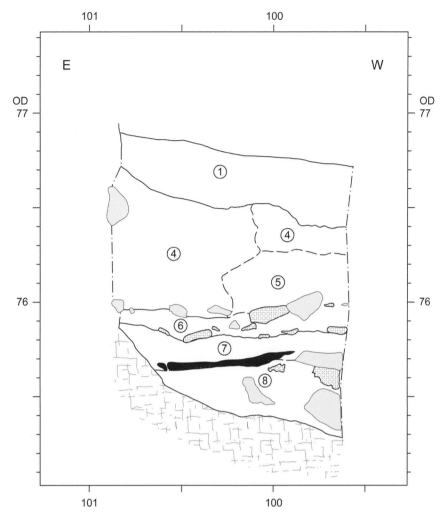

*Figure 7.3. Cefn. West Entrance. South section of Trench 1 on grid line 102.55 m N.*

| Find no. | Layer | In situ/ derived | Age (ka, corrected unless stated) | Description |
|----------|-------|------------------|-----------------------------------|-------------|
| *CW00* | 4 | i/s | 105+10/-9 (uncorr) | Upper Stalagmitic floor |
| *CW356* | 4 | i/s | 181+44/-30 | Upper Stalagmitic floor (note TL age is 264±104) |
| *CW632* | 8 | d | 284+38/-28 | Stalactite (derived) |
| *CW805* | Lower Stalagmite | i/s | 240±32/-23 | Lower Stalagmitic floor (between orange and grey silts) |

*Table 7.1. Cefn Cave uranium series dates on calcite.*

| Find no. | Context | Determination | Sample |
|----------|---------|---------------|--------|
| CW356 | Layer 4 (Upper Stalagmite) | 264+38/-28 ka | *in situ* floor |

*Table 7.2. Cefn Cave thermoluminescence date on calcite.*

| Sample | Species | Determination | Lab. ref. | $\delta^{13}C$ |
|--------|---------|---------------|-----------|----------------|
| femoral fragment | *Homo* | 2835 ± 60 | OxA-6233 | 21.4 per mil |
| femoral fragment | *Homo* | 1445 ± 60 | OxA-6234 | 20.3 per mil |
| bone | *C. crocuta* | 34700 ± 1100 | OxA-9697 | -18.8‰ |
| tooth | *C. crocuta* | 31900 ± 450 | OxA-9698 | -18.0‰ |

*Table 7.3. Cefn Cave dates on human and hyaena remains from historic excavations and their backfill.*

2,835±60 BP and 1,445±60 BP (OxA-6233 and OxA-6234) (Table 7.3). This adds to the evidence that the cave had limited use after the Pleistocene period.

## Cae Gronw Cave

Work carried out at Cae Gronw during 1979, 1980 and 1985, revealed two Middle Pleistocene levels: a basal fluvial clay unit, resting on limestone, contained large stalagmitic clasts and an overlying fluvial mudstone gravel unit with many smaller pieces of stalagmite. Angular limestone scree overlying the fluvial unit was probably emplaced within the Late Devensian and may be analogous with the Pontnewydd Upper Breccia. The sequence was capped by colluvium.

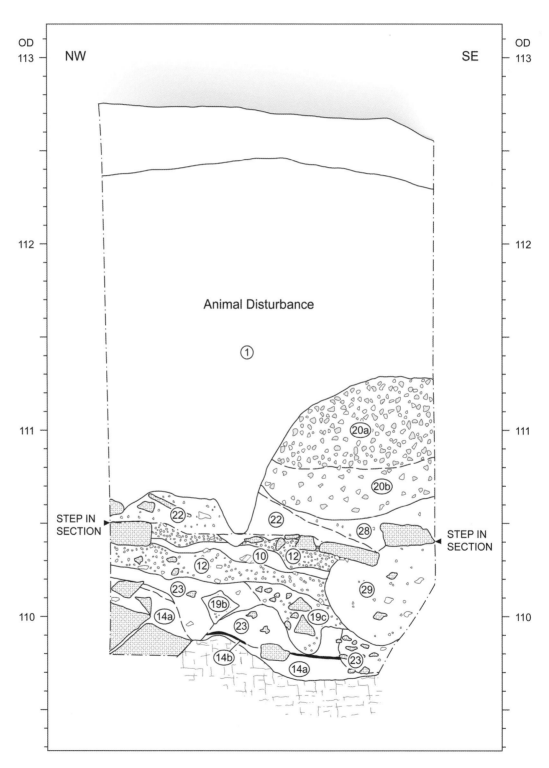

*Figure 7.4. Cae Gronw Cave. North-east section through deposits in cave mouth.*

## Introduction

Like Pontnewydd and Cefn, the site is on the north-east side of the Elwy valley. It is around 300 m north of Pontnewydd and 21 m higher at around 111.00 m O.D. (Figure 4.2). Cae Gronw was completely filled with sediment at the beginning of the excavations with the cave entrance visible as a small overhanging rock-shelter. An area 2.50 m by 2.40 m was opened in the centre of the cave entrance and excavated down to the bedrock.

## Stratigraphic sequence

The deposits revealed by this limited exploration seem to relate to four different events (Figure 7.4). The first and deepest of these was a unit dominated by clays, which appeared to be of fluvial origin, and which contained large, well preserved pieces of stalagmite. This was succeeded by a mudstone gravel unit, also probably of fluvial origin, with many smaller pieces of stalagmite, which included some very comminuted and decayed fragments. In turn this unit was succeeded by a unit made up of angular limestone breccia with no stalagmite fragments. Above this were modern hillwash deposits.

### *Clay Unit (14, 23)*

There were two sub-units within the clay unit. Layer 14, which was greenish-brown clay, was sealed by Layer 23, yellow clay, both of which contained stalagmite clasts but no mudstone or limestone. A stalagmite clast from Layer 14 provided a Uranium Series age of around 130,000 BP (Table 7.4).

| CG5 | Layer 14 stalagmite | 130,000 BP |
|-----|---------------------|------------|

*Table 7.4. Cae Gronw uranium series date on calcite.*

| PND 1 | Layer 12 | 139±15 ka | Stalagmite |
|-------|----------|-----------|------------|
| PND 2.1 | Layer 12 | 217±34 ka | Stalagmite |
| PND 2.2 | Layer 12 | 208±30 ka | Stalagmite |

*Table 7.5. Cae Gronw thermoluminescence dates on calcite. PND 2.1 and 2.2 are different portions of the same stalagmite.*

### *Mudstone Gravel Unit (19, 12, 10)*

This unit was also sub-divided. Immediately above Layer 23 was Layer 19, mudstone gravel, containing both stalagmite clasts and comminuted fragments of stalagmite. The boundary between this layer and Layer 23 was not distinct. Above Layer 19 were Layers 12 and 10. Layer 12 was mudstone gravel with lenses of small rolled mudstone pebbles and comminuted stalagmite fragments. It was interleaved with the green laminated silt of Layer 10. Two stalagmite clasts from Layer 12 have thermoluminescence ages, respectively of *c.* 212,000 BP and of 139,000 BP (Table 7.5). This suggests that both the clay unit and the mudstone gravel unit were emplaced after the beginning of the Last Interglacial.

### *Breccia Unit (20a, 20b)*

Two differing breccias could be distinguished. The lower of these, Layer 20b, consisted of scattered angular limestone fragments within a red silty matrix, which also contained frequent small mudstone pebbles. The upper breccia, Layer 20a, was made up of plentiful angular limestone fragments (up to 95% of the volume) in a red silty matrix with occasional small mudstone pebbles. Faunal material from the breccias included the remains of bear, collared lemming and reindeer, consonant with a later Devensian date for the emplacement of the breccias (Currant and Jacobi 2001, 1713–1714). A radiocarbon date on a bear canine from Layer 20 (Table 7.6) has given an age of 35,100±1,500 BP (OxA-6335), and would be compatible with an interpretation that the Cae Gronw Breccia and the Pontnewydd Upper Breccia are coeval in date and may be related events.

### *Hillwash deposits (1)*

This unit was heavily disturbed by burrowing animals and roots. It consisted of loose grey loam with plentiful large angular and sub-angular limestone blocks. Some of the fauna from these layers was clearly of relatively recent origin. Two radiocarbon dates were obtained on bones from Layer 1: a human radius gave an age of 3,955±60 BP (OxA-5731) and a reindeer phalange of 20,200±460 BP (OxA-5990) (Table 7.6). The first of these dates would fall within the well documented tradition of Neolithic burial in caves (Barnatt and Edmonds 2002).

| Find no. | Sample | Species | Context | Determination BP | Lab. ref. | $\delta^{13}C$ |
|----------|--------|---------|---------|------------------|-----------|----------------|
| CG38 | Radius | *Homo* | 1 | 3,955±60 | OxA-5731 | |
| CG62 | Phalange | *Rangifer tarandus* | 1 | 20,200±460 | OxA-5990 | -19.4% |
| CG86 | Permanent canine | *Ursus sp.* | 20 | 35,100 | OxA-6335 | -20.1% |

*Table 7.6. Cae Gronw radiometric dating on bone. Note: Layer 1 is a recent context and CG62 should be regarded as derived.*

# 8. The Fauna

*Andrew P. Currant and Anne Eastham with notes by Kate Scott and Bryony Coles*

*Excavations at Pontnewydd Cave have uncovered 4,822 identifiable bones and bone fragments and many thousands of indeterminate fragments. The mammal assemblage has been reconstructed from contextual information as well as by using preservation types observed on the bones originating from within the Main Cave. An understanding of the different periods represented, the different local environmental conditions and climate can be pieced together from their study. This chapter brings the work on preservation types up to date, in the context of a fuller understanding of the mammal assemblage. It also focuses on the environment and climate indicators as represented by the avian faunal assemblage.*

## The Pleistocene mammalian fauna of Pontnewydd Cave

*Andrew P. Currant*

In the 1984 interim report on the mammalian fauna of Pontnewydd Cave the author identified three distinct faunal assemblages based primarily on the preservation characteristics of individual specimens – types I, II and III, oldest to youngest (Currant 1984). Type I included species broadly indicative of a late Middle Pleistocene temperate environment and was first met with in deposits of the Intermediate complex. It also occurred as a major derived component in the overlying Lower Breccia, a debris flow deposit of considerable extent within the cave. Type II was interpreted as a slightly later faunal input containing several cooler climate indicators which came in with the Lower Breccia debris flow. Type III included elements of a Late Pleistocene cold stage fauna and was restricted to units above the Stalagmite lithozone marking the top of the Lower Breccia.

Since publication of that account, the Pontnewydd collection has grown considerably as excavations have progressed, the Intermediate complex being notably better represented than it was prior to the 1984 account. The distinction between preservation type I and type II as originally understood is now regarded as being so blurred as to become meaningless for all practical purposes. In view of the reinterpretation of the Intermediate complex as a modified component of the Lower Breccia (see Mourne and Case chapter 5, this volume) there is now no need to

see the type I material in this layer as derived. It is therefore proposed to use types I and III in more or less their original sense, but now much more rigorously defined. Type II still survives in a rather modified form on the basis of a very small number of specimens.

### *Definitions of the Pontnewydd types*

Quoted colours are based on the Munsell Soil Color Charts (2009 edition).

*Preservation type I*

D205, the distal end of metacarpal of a roe deer, *Capreolus capreolus*, from the Intermediate complex is designated as the reference specimen for preservation type I in its typical form. It has a base colour approaching 7.5YR 6/6 (reddish yellow) with highlights on the articular surfaces approaching 7.5YR 5/8 (strong brown). Whatever the technicalities, one gets the impression of a distinctly 'orange' hue to this and similar specimens. The surface is irregularly mottled with dark brown to black staining (manganese?). Surface detail is well preserved and sharp, but there are signs of pressure chipping. The broken surfaces are irregular, with similar colouring and mottling to the natural surfaces.

Type Ia is a variant in which the darker mottling has spread to become the dominant surface colour over all or much of the specimen. The normal base colour often shows on freshly broken surfaces. This is just an extreme form of type I and is only distinguished in case it is found to have limited spatial occurrence. No reference specimen is designated. Type Ib is a more significant variant, and in part the origin of the largely spurious type II material in its derived form in the Lower Breccia. This type is also found in the Intermediate complex, notably in the so-called 'Buff Intermediate'. D3693, a left calcaneum of red deer, *Cervus elaphus*, from the Intermediate complex is chosen as the reference specimen for preservation type Ib. This type lacks the distinctive 'orange' hue of type I but retains all of the other characteristics. The base colour approaches 7.5YR 7/4 (pink), in this case with quite strong darker mottling and staining. This bone shows crisp surface detail, but again has been chipped and slightly abraded.

The distinction between I and Ib only really becomes significant when trying to assess the origins of material in the Lower Breccia, where the absence of the distinctive 'orange' look to derived Ib specimens can cause confusion. Some specimens in the Lower Breccia have a rather paler base colour and generally more 'washed out' appearance than their Intermediate deposit counterparts, but many retain their colouration.

*Preservation type II*

A very small number of specimens from the Lower Breccia appear to be distinct from type I material. F2035, the distal end of a cervid metacarpal is designated as the reference specimen for preservation type II. It has a base colour approaching 2.5Y 8/2 (white), locally 2.5Y 8/4 (pale yellow) with localized faint dark mottling. The bone feels like fine china; it is light and delicate. This specimen is edge-rounded, but still has fine surface detail. Freshly broken surfaces are pure white.

Also from the Lower Breccia comes a very fragmented right astralagus of a horse. *Equus* sp. D4781. This specimen has a base colour approaching 10YR 8/3 to 8/4 (very pale brown). Again the specimen has a brittle, chalky feel and old broken surfaces are dull white. It has been extensively smashed and abraded. Surviving surface detail appears to be very good. The only specimen referable to giant deer, *Megaloceros giganteus* is of almost identical preservation – a left unciform D4648 with a base colour approaching 10YR 8/3 to 8/4 (very pale brown). Although much chipped and abraded, this specimen also shows the remains of fine, crisp surface detail. There are faint local patches of fine, dark grey speckling. This specimen is perhaps the closest to the dividing line between types I and II and is foremost in making one doubt the validity of the distinction, but my subjective impression is that it remains in type II.

A remarkable specimen which falls into this group is F955 a complete narrow-nosed rhinoceros metapodial from the Silt beds. This is one of the most beautifully preserved bones to have come from Pontnewydd Cave. Its colour characteristics are the same as for the previous specimen – base colour 10YR 8/3 to 8/4 (very pale brown), but the surface is very crisp with very fine surface detail. There are some minor chips and abrasions, but otherwise this specimen could come from a recent osteological collection.

It has the characteristic 'fine china' quality – the bone 'whispers' to the touch, rather like very dry plaster of Paris. It is unlike anything else from the Silt beds and its occurrence there is a little difficult to account for.

This small group in many ways forms a bridge between preservation types I and III. The base colour lacks the red and yellow (= 'orange') component of typical type I specimens, yet has a base colour overlapping with the paler end of the range found in type III, but lacking the deeply penetrating greyness of the later material. They are the least modified specimens in the entire assemblage.

*Preservation type III*

F1010, the almost complete right maxilla and right and left pre-maxilla with RI3, RC, RP4 to M2 of a brown bear *Ursus arctos,* is designated as the reference specimen for preservation type III. The base colour is a complex patchwork of colours ranging from 10YR 8/2 (white) through value ranges 7, 6 and 5 and chroma ranges 1 and 2 (greys and browns), with highlights ranging to 10YR 8/3 to 8/4 (very pale brown). The staining is complete, freshly broken surfaces showing a fairly uniform 10YR 6/2 (light brownish grey) colouration. The teeth have white enamel with yellow roots and dentine areas, the latter stained very dark brown to black in places. There is local yellow-brown to bluish-grey streaking of the tooth enamel associated with cracks and fissures. Naturally broken surfaces are rounded off to a fine polish and the bone surface is noticeably glossy as if finely abraded, but still retaining excellent surface detail. Recently broken surfaces are very irregular.

The localized bluish-grey staining of tooth enamel is a very noticeable feature of type III. There is considerable variation in the balance of colours represented in any one specimen, but yellow to dark grey with the 'blue' look to the teeth characterize the type. Type III is very distinctive and represents very little problem in interpretation.

### Discussion of the preservation types

The natural colour of bone is ivory white. Many fossil bones retain their original colour, even though they may be buried in quite strongly coloured sediments – the beautifully preserved mammalian remains from the deep red cave earths of Kent's Cavern, Torquay, Devon serve as a good example. Bones do not just 'take up' colour. If they have become deeply and permanently stained in a particular way, then they have become subjected to alteration as a result of diagenetic processes within an enclosing sediment matrix.

Mourne and Case (chapter 5, this volume) have established that the Intermediate complex was created through heavy chemical alteration of the existing Lower Breccia sediments. Jenkins (1984), in his examination of sand and clay mineralogy observed that 'the severity of weathering … was most pronounced in example 3' [= 'Orange Intermediate']; and Collcutt (1984) notes that the carbonate particles in the Intermediate complex are heavily altered with extensive and deeply penetrating

| | Intermediate complex | Lower Breccia |
|---|:---:|:---:|
| *Homo* sp. | X | |
| *Canis lupus* | X | |
| *Ursus* sp. | X | |
| *Felis sylvestris* | | X |
| *Panthera pardus* | X | |
| *Panthera leo* | | X |
| *Equus* sp. | X | |
| *Stephanorhinus kirchbergensis* | | X |
| *Stephanorhinus hemitoechus* | | X |
| *Capreolus capreolus* | X | |
| *Cervus elaphus* | X | |
| *Lepus timidus* | X | |
| *Castor fiber* | X | |
| *Apodemus sylvaticus* | X | |
| *Dicrostonyx torquatus* | X | |
| *Lemmus lemmus* | | X |
| *Arvicola cantiana* | X | |
| *Microtus* cf. *agrestis* | X | |
| *Microtus gregalis* | X | |
| *Microtus oeconomus* | | X |

*Table 8.1. The first stratigraphic occurrence of preservation type I material.*

| |
|---|
| *Canis lupus* |
| *Vulpes vulpes* |
| *Ursus arctos* |
| *Equus ferus* |
| *Rangifer tarandus* |
| *Bison priscus* |
| *Ovibos moschatus* |
| *Dicrostonyx torquatus* |
| *Lemmus lemmus* |
| *Microtus oeconomus* |
| *Lepus timidus* |

*Table 8.2. Species represented by preservation type III, either in the Silt beds, or as a derived component in the Upper Breccia.*

corrosion of limestone and stalagmite clasts, while those in the overlying units are progressively less altered. The creation of preservation type I appears to be related to this period of very active diagenesis, which has in turn been linked to the existence of temperate climatic conditions and soil formation. Given the temperate indicators present among the fauna representing this preservation type, one might reasonably infer that the staining of many of the bones took place early in their history of burial. It seems likely that preservation type I fauna was emplaced as part of the Lower Breccia debris flow and altered as part of the wider processes which led to the formation of the Intermediate complex.

The strong 'orange' colouration of the fine matrix of major parts of the Intermediate complex suggests that the contained bones and their present matrix material have been closely associated since that temperate phase. The interpretation of the Intermediate complex as Lower Breccia debris flow deposits altered *in situ* would not be

inconsistent with the rounded and battered nature of some of the finds, most notably the horse remains.

The linking of the staining of the type I material to the phase of sediment diagenesis under temperate conditions has important implications. There is no internal evidence for there having been a subsequent stage of similar activity affecting the cave deposits, so any material with type I preservation must necessarily be as old, or older than, that diagenetic event.

The type I assemblage now includes the species listed in Table 8.1. The table shows whether remains have been found in the Intermediate complex itself or only within the Lower Breccia, as is the case for a number of the rarer taxa. Those species represented in this list which are only known from derived fossils in the Lower Breccia are in each case based on specimens which can be confidently assigned to preservation type I.

The Silt beds are the least altered of the Pontnewydd deposits, so the origin of the distinctive preservation characteristics of the type III material must be sought elsewhere. The small-scale edge-rounding and surface polish exhibited by nearly all specimens of this preservation type suggest that they lay in, and possibly moved along in, sediment-charged water for some time prior to burial, and may not even be in primary context. It is possible that the grey base-colour is a degraded form of the heavy black staining found in some modern river environments and caused by bacterial colonization. The teeth, which would have been affected by identical processes, where stained, have remained comparatively dark in colour, while the relatively porous bone appears to have been partly leached of its dark pigmentation.

It would appear that almost all of the material in the Upper Breccia is directly derived from the underlying Silt beds, with the exception of a small but significant component derived from the Lower Breccia (Table 8.2).

## Discussion

Given the potentially derived, derived, and multiply derived condition of virtually all elements of the Pontnewydd Cave fauna, there is no reason for assuming that the detailed histories of the individual faunal elements should be simple, and there can be no guarantee that there is enough surviving evidence to unravel them one from another. The 'preservation types' approach is an attempt to gain an understanding of the diagenetic history of the sediments and their contained fauna, but it is necessarily rather subjective and at best an inspired guess at the original structure of the faunal assemblages.

Within the type I assemblage as listed in Table 8.1 it is possible to see elements of an interglacial assemblage which appears to date to MIS 7 or earlier. The rhinoceros *Stephanorhinus kirchbergensis* is not known after this stage in Britain and the presence of a relatively large horse, *Equus ferus*, also effectively precludes a significantly later date. The leopard, *Panthera pardus* is an extremely rare and unusual occurrence in Britain. The only other known

| Species | Main Cave | | | | | New Entrance | | | |
|---|---|---|---|---|---|---|---|---|---|
| | Ic | LB | Sb | UB | UCS | 29 | 28 | 23–26 | 20–22 |
| **Primates** | | | | | | | | | |
| *Homo neanderthalensis* | + | + | | | | | | | |
| **Lagomorpha** | | | | | | | | | |
| *Lepus timidus* | + | + | | + | | | | | |
| *Lepus* sp. | | | + | + | | + | + | + | |
| **Rodentia** | | | | | | | | | |
| *Castor fiber* | + | + | | | | | | | |
| *Arvicola* sp. | + | + | | + | | | | + | |
| *Microtus* sp. | | + | | + | | | | + | |
| *Microtus gregalis* | + | + | | | | | | | |
| *Microtus oeconomus* | | + | | | | | | + | |
| *Microtus* cf. *agrestis* | + | | | | | | | | |
| *Microtus/pitymys* sp. | | + | | + | | | | + | |
| *Microtus arvalis/agrestis* group | + | | | | | | | | |
| *Dicrostonyx torquatus* | | + | + | + | | | | | |
| *Lemmus lemmus* | + | + | + | + | | | | | |
| *Ochotona* sp. | | | | + | | | | | |
| *Apodemus sylvaticus* | + | | | | + | | | | |
| **Carnivora** | | | | | | | | | |
| *Canid* | | + | | | | + | + | | |
| *Canis lupus* | + | + | | + | | | | + | |
| *Vulpes vulpes* | | + | | + | | + | + | + | |
| *Ursus* | + | + | + | + | | | + | + | + |
| *Ursus arctos* | | | | + | | +cf. | | | |
| cf. *Crocuta crocuta* | | + | | | | | | | |
| *Felis sylvestris* | | + | | | | | | | |
| *Panthera leo* | | + | | | | + | | | |
| *Panthera pardus* | + | + | | | | | | | |
| **Perissodactyla** | | | | | | | | | |
| *Equus* | + | + | + | + | + | | + | + | |
| *Equus ferus* | | | | + | | | | | |
| *Stephanorhinus* sp. | | + | | + | | | | + | |
| *Stephanorhinus hemitoechus* | | + | + | + | | | | | |
| *Stephanorhinus kirchbergensis* | | + | | | | | | | |
| *Coelodonta antiquitatis* | | | | + | | | | | |
| **Artiodactyla** | | | | | | | | | |
| *Cervus elephus* | + | + | | + | | | + | + | |
| *Rangifer tarandus* | | + | + | + | | | | | + |
| *Capreolus capreolus* | + | + | | | | | + | | |
| cf. *Megaloceros* | | + | | | | | | | |
| Bos or Bison | | + | | | | | | | |
| *Bison priscus* | | | | + | | | | | |
| *Ovibos moschatus* | | | | + | | | | | |

Table 8.3. Pontnewydd Cave mammalian fauna identifications by Andrew Currant.

records come from Bleadon Cave in Somerset, from an assemblage which is interpreted as being of MIS 7 age. It has to be noted here that cave assemblages representing MIS 9 and 11 have not been identified in the U.K. and an earlier date for the interglacial elements in the type I assemblage cannot be ruled out.

However, preservation type I does *not* represent a unitary interglacial faunal assemblage. It represents a collection of derived material, only part of which can be confidently identified, which comes from heavily disturbed and altered sediments of apparently heterogeneous origin but which appear to share a common diagenetic history. Out of that material one can subjectively extract a plausible late Middle Pleistocene interglacial assemblage which appears to fit into our growing model of Quaternary faunal evolution (Table 8.3). One can equally well extract a rather fine suite of cold stage micro-mammals including *Dicrostonyx*, *Lemmus* and *Microtus gregalis*. If the origins of the distinctive type I preservation are to be sought in the phase of temperate diagenesis identified in the Intermediate complex, then this cold fauna must pre-date the interglacial assemblage. There is circumstantial evidence that this might be so in the relative abundance of cold stage microfauna in the Lower Breccia.

Given that the Intermediate complex and its parent material the Lower Breccia are interpreted as debris flows, they may well have come from mobilization of different parts of the same original sediment body, the upper units being represented by the Intermediate complex and successively lower units by the Lower Breccia, creating a rather crude inverted stratigraphy. The mixture of TL dates from burnt flint in these two units is interesting in this context. Horse is notably more abundant in the Lower Breccia than one might expect from its limited occurrence in the Intermediate complex, while *Lemmus*, though found at the interface of the two deposits, is apparently absent from the Intermediate complex yet common as a derived type I fossil in the Lower Breccia.

A critical element of the fauna – indeed the commonest identifiable faunal component – are remains of bear, most of which show quite clearly spelaeoid (cave bear-like) dental characters, with low crowned cheek teeth and considerable dental cusp complexity. Danielle Schreve has observed that spelaeoid bears (*Ursus spelaeus*) appear to be replaced by brown bears (*Ursus arctos*) at some time between MIS 11 and MIS 9 in lowland Britain (Schreve 2001, 1698). Perhaps cave bears survived in upland Wales longer than elsewhere. Alternatively the spelaeoid bears at Pontnewydd may represent a much-derived, earlier faunal component representing a significantly older phase in the cave's history. Given the fact that cave bears are known to have hibernated and raised their young in caves, and that juvenile bears form a large component of the recorded finds at Pontnewydd, perhaps this interpretation has some weight behind it. At nearby Cefn Caves, in levels underlying the Last Interglacial (MIS 5) deposits for which the caves were historically famous, spelaeoid bear remains have been found. Interestingly a macaque tooth was also found during the excavations at Cefn; this species is known to have a fossil history in Britain which is not known to extend beyond MIS 9 (although its provenance in nineteenth century backfill is not secure). There is therefore circumstantial evidence (if these species were associated) for a large local population of cave bears during MIS 9 or earlier. It is highly unlikely that humans and cave bears could have coexisted at the same site at the same time. Although cave bears are believed to have been primarily vegetarian, they were still very large members of the order Carnivora which were well equipped to defend themselves and the sites on which they relied for year-round survival.

The occurrence of distinctly boreal elements such as the lemmings, *Lemmus lemmus* and *Dicrostonyx torquatus*, in the Intermediate complex and overlying Lower Breccia show that a simple interpretation of the Pontnewydd sequence is not possible. These may represent the passage into cooler conditions during MIS 6, but could just as easily represent one or more faunal inputs during any other cooler stage during the Middle Pleistocene. The most important point, in view of the hominin remains and the archaeology

in Pontnewydd Cave, is that the derived faunal remains in the Intermediate complex and Lower Breccia do not necessarily constrain the age of human activity at the site. The only way in which this would be demonstrable would be if unequivocal butchery marks were to be found on some biostratigraphically significant element of the fauna. Given the highly fragmented and abraded state of almost all of the faunal material concerned, such a discovery is extremely unlikely.

The author makes no apologies for reshuffling the faunal groupings and changing his views on the preservation types. Some years on from the original study, we have a much better understanding of what one might expect to find in Stage 7 and earlier faunas (Currant 1989) and a more conservative approach to the preservation types problem based on a growing understanding of how bones acquire distinctive preservations in the first place. To some extent the problems we have been trying to tackle at Pontnewydd sparked off both those interests, so this is good positive feedback.

## Short note on the Pontnewydd reindeer remains examined for gnawing
### Kate Scott

The Pontnewydd reindeer remains from the Upper Breccia and specimens from other contexts with a preservation type III (see Currant above) were examined for evidence of gnawing and other taphonomic processes. The results of the observations made are presented in Table 8.4. The conclusion drawn from this examination is that the remains are mostly likely to have been accumulated by wolves. Both males and females provision their young at the point of weaning and males bring food to the den for the females. Many of the bones look exactly like modern wolf den material the author has examined in the United States. They also resemble the material from Picken's Hole, on the southern edge of Mendip, which is interpreted as a wolf den (ApSimon 1986; Scott in preparation). Some of the very slight damage (small pitting, tiny scratches) might equally have been caused by smaller animals scrounging around at the den (foxes or rodents) but no literature has been identified to suggest that these other animals bring meat bones to dens. Bears, which form a very large percentage of the Carnivora, do not habitually transport bones into their dens and are unlikely to have contributed to the cave's assemblage other than in the addition of their own remains (Currant pers. comm.). This review accords well with Currant's interpretation of the faunal assemblage (1984) and confirms that hyaenas were not involved in accumulating bones at Pontnewydd Cave in the Upper Pleistocene.

## Beavers at Pontnewydd
### Bryony Coles

Beavers (here the European beaver, *Castor fiber*) live in family groups consisting of an adult pair and their offspring

| Find No. | Skeletal element | Comment | ¹⁴C |
|---|---|---|---|
| A43 | Metapodial, distal | Very damaged and possibly gnawed | |
| A60 | Humerus, distal | Gnawed | |
| B1 | Astragalus | Gnawed | |
| B2 | 1st phalange | Distinct gnawing distal end | |
| D1 | 1st phalange | Very slight 'scoring' | |
| D156 | Astragalus | Some gnawing | |
| D334 | Scapula fragment | Slightly gnawed | |
| D431 | Cuneiform | ?Acid damage: regurgitated? | |
| D959 | 1st phalange | Gnawed diaphysis and distal | |
| D1131 | 1st phalange | Gnawed proximal end | |
| D1154 | 1st phalange | Distinctive gnawing | 25,210 ± 120 (OxA-13984) |
| D1786 | Humerus, distal | Gnawed | |
| D5270 | 1st phalange | Gnawed proximal and distal | |
| D5285 | Astragalus | Some gnawing | |
| D5296 | Antler tine | Gnawing not evident but size and shape typical in wolf accumulations | |
| D5819 | Mandible fragment | Possible gnawing | |
| D5960 | Tibia | Some gnawing | |
| F13 | Naviculo-cuboid | Slight gnawing but not on articular surface (as in F556) | |
| F308 | Calcaneum | Gnawed (as in F556) | |
| F556 | Calcaneum | Bone strongly gnawed except articular surfaces, indicating ankle joint still intact when gnawed | |
| F916 | Astragalus | Some gnawing | |
| F970 | Tibia, distal | Gnawed | |
| F1122 | Metapodial, distal | Some pitting on distal end | |
| F1186 | Humerus, diaphysis and distal | Gnawing of distal without damage to articular surface suggesting humerus was still articulated with radius when gnawed | |
| F1217 | Metatarsal | Small 'pitting' on distal end | |
| F1329 | Humerus | Possible, very slight | |
| F1390 | Calcaneum fragment | Heavily gnawed | |
| F1362 | Metacarpal shaft | Heavily gnawed | |
| F1418 | Calcaneum | Gnawed (as in F556) | |
| F1462 | Metacarpal | Slight 'pitting' and 'scoring' | |
| F1472 | 1st phalange | Gnawed | |
| F1678 | Metapodial diaphysis | Some gnawing | |
| F1780 | Antler | Pitting but also weathered | |
| F1819 | 2nd phalange | Distinctive gnawing | |
| F1828 | Left metacarpal | Very distinctive gnawing both ends and shaft | 30,240 ± 230 (OxA-13993) |
| F1898 | Mandible | Possible tooth-marks | 39,600 ± 900 (OxA-14052) |
| F2205 | Tibia | Scoring on prox. shaft | |
| F2238 | 2nd phalange | Damage, no clear tooth-marks | |
| F2549 | Astragalus | Some gnawing | 41,400 ± 1,400 (OxA-14055) |
| F2997 | Antler | Some gnawing | |
| F4876 | Rib | Possible gnawing | |
| F5543 | Lumbar vertebra | Very gnawed | |

*Table 8.4. Reindeer remains showing gnawing and taphonomic processes.*

| Find no. | Tooth | Context, grid square and height in relation to S.D. |
|----------|-------|------------------------------------------------------|
| D4538 | Cheek tooth | Lower Breccia K8NE, 99.48–99.38 |
| F5425 | Cheek tooth | Lower Breccia (d), H5SE, 99.22–99.12 |
| D5501 | Cheek tooth | Lower Breccia, L7NW, 99.10–99.05 |
| D3815 | Cheek tooth | Lower Breccia (e), H8SE, 99.07 |
| D5091 | Lower left incisor | Lower Breccia, K8SE, 99.03 |
| D403 | Cheek tooth | Lower Breccia/Buff Intermediate, H9S, 99.07 |
| F5859 | Lower left incisor | Buff Intermediate  H5SE, 99.02–99.00 |
| D2024 | Cheek tooth | Buff Intermediate, J7NW, 99.07–98.97 |
| D46400 | Cheek tooth | Orange Intermediate, I6NW, 99.01 |
| H2053 | Cheek tooth | Layer 26, AB993NW, 99.30–99.10 |
| H2543 | Cheek tooth | Layer 26, AB993NW, 99.30–99.10 |

*Table 8.5. Beaver teeth and their contexts.*

of the current and previous year, usually about five to eight individuals all told. They are semi-aquatic vegetarians, living beside freshwater and feeding on the twigs and bark of trees such as willow, aspen, poplar, ash and hazel; in summer they add a variety of herbaceous plants to their diet. They make underground dens in river banks, reached by a burrow with an underwater entrance, which gives them protection from most predators. If there is not enough depth of water to protect the burrow entrances, they build a dam to raise the water level, thereby often creating a pond behind the dam and side-channels around it. Where river banks are low, they may build a heap of wood and mud and stone, a lodge, to ensure a safe, dry den which is still reached by a burrow dug from below water.

One beaver family may occupy 500–1,500 m or more of water's edge, depending on local conditions especially food supply, and within their territory they will have a number of burrows and dens, and perhaps six to ten dams on a small, shallow watercourse. Each complex of dam and pond acts as a nutrient and silt trap, leading to an increase in plant and animal life, both in terms of biomass and in the range of species present. A number of early hominin sites are located by water where beavers were present, the omnivorous hominins no doubt attracted by the enriched local environment (*e.g.* Boxgrove and Hoxne). Many of the birds identified at Pontnewydd (see Eastham below) would also have been attracted to beaver territories, particularly where the topography allowed the development of reed beds and marshland, and variable water depths.

Most of the Pontnewydd beaver remains are contemporary with the hominin evidence found at the site. The other associated mammals are predominantly wolf and bear and the overall assemblage is indicative of open woodland, a habitat well-suited to beavers. The recent investigations have suggested that the bears were using the cave system for hibernation and as a den (E. Walker pers. comm.), and it is possible that the beavers too were cave-dwellers. They sometimes use these ready-made natural shelters rather than digging out an underground den or building a lodge. Beavers will swim along flooded underground tunnels, and den in small dry cavities (Érome 1982; Coles 2006), so they would not necessarily have been in direct competition with

the bears for space, nor prey to the much larger omnivores. However, the identified beaver remains are from debris flow deposits and the part of the cave where they were found is unlikely to have been where they lived.

The beaver remains are all teeth. In life, beavers have two upper incisors and two lower incisors, together with one premolar and three molars on each side of both upper and lower jaw; beavers use their incisors to cut through wood, whether severing a small branch or biting into and eventually through a larger branch or trunk and then severing the topwood from the fallen stem. In addition, incisors are an effective weapon in fights with other beavers, or in defence against predators. The cheek teeth are used to grind up leaves, twigs, bark and other woody matter into small and relatively digestible fragments. There is evidence from Holocene contexts that humans made use of beaver teeth singly or still in the mandible as wood-working tools, incisors as chisels or gouges and molars as rasps or planes.

Beaver teeth grow in length and width throughout the individual's life, and they are continually being worn down and the incisors re-sharpened. In general, the bigger the teeth the older the beaver. Clara Stefen (2009) has carried out an analysis of the variability in size of beaver teeth across species and through time, and concluded that beavers cannot be precisely aged by tooth size, but she does provide a general guide for *Castor fiber*. Incisors increase in width from 4–6 mm in juveniles (0–12 months) to 8–9 mm at 50 months or 4 years, and from 4 to 18 years the width ranges from just under 8 to 10 mm with the majority (8 out of 11) in the 9 to 10 mm range. Cheek teeth (one premolar and three molars per row) range from 4–10 mm depending on position as well as age, and should probably not be used for more than distinguishing juveniles from adults.

The Pontnewydd teeth include two quite large fragments of incisor (Table 8.5; Figure 8.1). Both are 9 mm wide across the external enamel face, indicating that they probably come from one or two adult beavers, rather than from juveniles or sub-adults. One of the incisors (D5091) survives as a fragment 39 mm long, creamy ivory in colour with blue-grey streaks and slight orange mottling. The inner or back part has been lost, but the front face

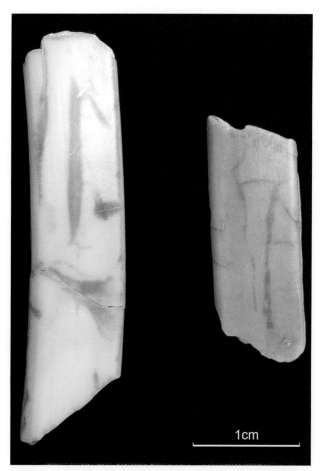

*Figure 8.1. The two incomplete beaver incisors from Pontnewydd. D5091 left and F5859 right.*

and edges survive in good condition, and the right-angled inner edge which once lay adjacent to its fellow incisor can be easily distinguished from the more rounded outer edge which in life was separated by a gap from the first of the cheek teeth. The gentle curve of the fragment suggests it most probably (but not certainly) came from the lower jaw, and was therefore a left lower incisor. The other incisor (F5859) survives as a fragment 14 mm long with front face and edges in good condition, and it too is likely to be a lower left incisor, but in this case bright orange in colour. Although many of the associated mammalian remains have an orange mottling and sometimes what looks like a patchy surface film of orange, in this instance the colouring has every appearance of being the original bright orange of beaver incisors in life. Of the beaver incisors from Holocene archaeological contexts examined for *Beavers in Britain's Past* (Coles 2006) relatively few retained their original orange colour, and no obvious correlation could be identified between time elapsed since death and preservation of colour. The orange colouration has been preserved on many Pleistocene specimens (A. Currant pers. comm.) and its survival is not in itself unusual, but the contrast between the two incisors must indicate some difference in conditions either prior to burial or within the burial environment itself. At Pontnewydd it was perhaps

a difference in conditions prior to the debris flow into the cave that caused the loss of colour for one incisor and its preservation for the other.

Five of the nine cheek teeth are preserved to their full width, which ranges from 7–10.5 mm measured across the enamel folds. This is similar to the range obtained by Stefen, apart from her smallest examples (Stefen 2009, table 1), which suggests the Pontnewydd cheek teeth are from well-grown individuals, though not necessarily all fully adult. Length from crown towards root ranges from 14–25 mm, with those between 18 mm and 25 mm possibly at or close to their original length, but the root ends are damaged or worn and it is difficult to be certain how much has been lost. What is clear is that several of the cheek teeth retain their original very smooth, worn grinding surface.

As a group, the teeth from the cave carry some remarkably well-preserved detail. Although a beaver skeleton in general and the skull and teeth in particular are very dense and strong and often survive in good condition, the high degree of preservation at Pontnewydd suggests that the teeth were not exposed to weathering for any length of time. Nor were they subject to lengthy or severe mechanical action during the debris flow which carried them to where they were found, which suggests this process moved them only a short distance. The probability of two lower left incisors points to the remains of at least two adults. In all likelihood, the beavers came from a nearby territory on the banks of the Elwy, that could have been established, abandoned and re-occupied over the beaver generations, and maybe at times there was a beaver den in the cave system and other times a beaver carcass was carried in by one of their several predators, such as a wolf.

## The bird bones of Pontnewydd Cave

*Anne Eastham*

The avian faunal material from the recent excavations at Pontnewydd Cave totals 36 bones. It would appear that earlier explorations did not recover any bird material – the Ruthin Museum collection has been examined, as has the Boyd Dawkins collection at Buxton – and a single bird bone at Buxton Museum was the only exception and that appears to be of more recent date. A further collection, unexamined so far, lies in obscurity in the geography storerooms at Stoneyhurst College in Lancashire. This appears to have been a gift to the college by Boyd Dawkins and is therefore more likely to contain fragments of large mammals rather than birds or microfauna.

Many of the bird bones from the recent excavations were originally identified by C. J. O. Harrison of the Natural History Museum. The present study is in accord with most of those determinations but has also considered some of the more fragmentary material and bones from the limb extremities in order to extract as much information as possible from the collection.

The condition of the bird bones is not excessively fragile; they have not been heavily leached by organic acids and the fragments are fairly robust. However, as with the rest of the faunal assemblage, the bones are much broken and in many cases damage to the surface made identification of fragments relatively difficult. As far as the material allowed, diagnostic measurements were recorded.

Table 8.6 gives a summary of the distribution of bird bones throughout the different areas of the cave. The detail for each separate level is shown below. There were no birds recorded in the Intermediate complex but bird remains were recovered from the Lower Breccia, from within the Upper Breccia and from layers in the New Entrance. In the Main Cave it has been possible in many instances to distinguish the preservation types by colour, and this is noted against the bones in the separate tables using the criteria defined by Currant in this chapter.

### Main Cave

#### Lower Breccia (Table 8.7)

In these levels the species diversity is limited. All the bones for which definition was possible were of preservation type I. Of the eight bones recovered from the Lower Breccia, six belong to aquatic species. Of these only the Goosander breeds in northern Britain at the present-day and in the light of other evidence concerning the local environment during mid- to late MIS 7, these wildfowl were most probably wintering on the shores and waters of Liverpool Bay. In this sequence the distal epiphysis of left ulna, attributed by Harrison to Brent Goose, appears rather more robust than the average for recent specimens of *Branta bernicla*, so it could be a large male or it is possible that it might belong to Barnacle Goose, *Branta leucopsis*. The difficulty of making a precise identification of this bone is considered in the systematic study below. By contrast, the Wheatear, *Oenanthe oenanthe*, was likely to have been a summer migrant to Britain, that could have been present in the locality between March and August or September and would have been well suited by the increasingly open conditions around the site. Both the coracoid and humerus are large by comparison with recent reference material and are studied in more detail below.

#### Upper Breccia (Table 8.8)

The Upper Breccia deposits contained a greater diversity of avifaunal remains than the Lower Breccia. Even so, during this later stage the pattern remains dominated by aquatic

| Species | | LB | UB | UCS | BD Dump | 36–34 | 28–23 | 20 | Total |
|---|---|---|---|---|---|---|---|---|---|
| *Cygnus columbianus bewickii* | Bewick's swan | | | | 1 | | | | 1 |
| *Anser anser* | Greylag goose | | 3 | 1 | | | | | 4 |
| *Anser brachyrhyncos/albifrons* | Pink footed/White fronted goose | | 1 | | | | | | 1 |
| *Branta leucopsis/bernicla* | Barnacle/Brent goose | | 1 | | | | | | 1 |
| *Branta bernicla* | Brent goose | 2 | 2 | | | | 1 | | 5 |
| *Anas platyrhyncos* | Mallard | 1 | 2 | | 1cf. | 1cf. | 1cf. | 1cf. | 7 |
| cf. *Aythya fuligula* | Tufted duck | | | 1 | | | | | 1 |
| *Melanitta nigra* | Common Scoter | 2 | | | | | | | 2 |
| *Mergus albellus* | Smew | | 1 | | | | | | 1 |
| *Mergus merganser* | Goosander | 1 | | | | | | | 1 |
| cf. *Buteo* sp. | Buzzard/medium-sized raptor | | | | 1 | | | | 1 |
| cf. *Aquila* sp. | Eagle/large raptor | | | | | 1 | 1 | | 2 |
| *Falco tinnunculus* | Kestrel | | 1 | | | | | | 1 |
| cf. *Tetrao urogallus* | cf. Capercaillie | | | | 1 | | | | 1 |
| *Pavo cristatus* | Peafowl | | | | 1 | | | | 1 |
| *Oenanthe oenanthe* | Wheatear | 2 | 1 | | | | | | 3 |
| cf. *Corvid* sp. | Jackdaw/Magpie | | | | | 1 | | | 1 |
| *Carduelis chloris/cannabina* | Greenfinch/Linnet | | 1 | | | | | | 1 |
| *Coccothraustes coccothraustes* | Hawfinch | | 1 | | | | | | 1 |
| **Total** | | **8** | **14** | **2** | **5** | **3** | **3** | **1** | **36** |

*Table 8.6. The stratigraphic distribution of bird bones in Pontnewydd Cave.*

| Species | Find no. | Context | Bone | Preservation type |
|---|---|---|---|---|
| *Branta bernicla* | F4423 | LB | L. humerus, proximal, frag. caput humeri | I |
| *B. bernicla/B. leucopsis* | D2591 | LB | L. ulna, proximal epiphysis | I |
| | F2788 | Sb | R. coracoids, distal | I |
| *Anas platyrhyncos* | D2635 | LB | R. Humerus, proximal frag. caput humeri | I |
| | D5962 | UB-Sb | R. humerus, distal female | I |
| *Melanitta nigra* | D1367 | LB | R. humerus, distal epiphysis | I |
| | D4576 | LB | R. radius | I |
| *Mergus merganser* | D2089 | LB | L. coracoids, distal | I |
| *Oenanthe oenanthe* | D3089 | LB | R. coracoids, distal | I |
| | D3091 | LB | R. humerus, distal epiphysis | I |
| | F1931 | UB/Sb | L. tibiotarsus, distal | I |
| *Anas sp.* | H2909 | 34 | Pes phalange | |
| *Corvid sp. cf. Pica pica/* | H3379 | 36 | Terminal pes phalange | |
| *Corvus monedula* | | | | |
| No identification | H1646 | 36 | Terminal pes phalange, fragment | |

*Table 8.7. Main Cave, Lower Breccia specimens of preservation type I and correlative layers in the New Entrance 34–36 (Mudstone Gravels).*

| Species | Find no. | 14C Age | Context | Bone | Preservation type |
|---|---|---|---|---|---|
| *Anser anser* | F1394 | 28,230±170 BP | UB | R. femur, proximal | III |
| *Branta bernicla* | F5528 | | UB/RCm | L. carpometcarpus, proximal | III |
| *Anas platyrhyncos* | F835 | 28,210±150 BP | UB | L. humerus, distal | III |
| *Coccothraustes coccothraustes* | S210 | | UB | R. humerus, distal | III |
| *Anser brachyrhyncos/albifrons* | D3115 | | Silt beds | R. coracoid | III |
| *Anser anser* | F1967 | | UB/Sb | L. phalange, digit ala majoris, distal | III |
| *Branta bernicla* | F2232 | 25,950±220 BP | UB/Sb | R. femur, proximal facies artic. acetabularis | III |
| *Mergus albellus* | D3140 | | UB/Sb | R. metacarpus | III |
| *Falco tinnunculus* | D497 | | Silt beds | L. tarsometatarsus, distal | III |
| *Carduelis chloris/cannabina* | S220 | | UB/Sb | L. humerus, proximal | III |
| *Branta bernicla/B. leucopsis* | H2486 | | 23 | R. tibiotarsus, frag. epicondylus lateralis | III |
| *Anas sp.* | H2472 | | 23 | Pes phalange | |
| cf. *Aquila chrysaetos* | H1001 | | 27 | Pes phalange, proximal | |
| cf. *Falco tinnunculus* | H2554 | | 24 | Pes phalange, digit4 distal | |
| No identification | H2533 | | 28 | Pes phalange | |

*Table 8.8. Main Cave specimens of preservation type III from the Upper Breccia and correlative layers from the New Entrance (Limestone Gravels).*

| Species | | Find no. | Bone | Preservation type |
|---|---|---|---|---|
| cf. *Cygnus columbianus bewickii/A.anser* | cf. Bewick's swan/Greylag goose | F453 | R. tarsometatarsus, distal | III |
| *Anser anser* | Greylag goose | F25 | R. femur, proximal | III |
| cf. *Aythya fuligula* | Tufted duck | F4227 | R. ulna, distal | III |

Table 8.9. *Main Cave, Upper Clays and Sands, Late Glacial and Holocene deposits.*

species. Most of the bones are of preservation type III and so must be middle Pleistocene, with just three specimens of Brent or Barnacle Goose, Mallard and Wheatear derived from lower layers and displaying a preservation of type I. In the Upper Breccia five, possibly seven, species of wildfowl may be represented. A femur of Brent Goose from these levels, F2232 gave a date of 25,950±220 BP (OxA-12381). Other dates from the Upper Breccia were: Greylag femur F1394, 28,230±170 BP (OxA-12381) and Mallard humerus F835, 28,210±150 BP (OxA-12363). On the basis of present-day distribution and niche preference patterns, it would appear that these were winter residents of the marshes, arriving in stages from the Arctic between late October and December and moving back north between March and May.

### Bird bone from late Last Glacial and Holocene deposits (Table 8.9)

The deposits of Upper Clays and Sands with unstratified trample material contained few fragments of avian material and these few were all from aquatic species.

#### Boyd Dawkins Dump

Three terminal pes phalanges came from the remaining dump material. A217 is probably from a member of the Duck family, *Anatidae*, a medium-sized raptor similar to a Buzzard (A544) and a Capercaillie (A780). This last seems to indicate a level of available forest cover with open spreads of low-growing shrubs like heather and bilberry. A tarsometatarsal bone of Peacock, *Pavo cristatus*, undoubtedly of recent date, is held in Buxton Museum and is discussed further below.

### New Entrance (Tables 8.7 and 8.8)

Although bird bones were recovered from both the lower and upper levels of the deposits in the New Entrance, they pose considerable identification problems. With a single exception, all are foot bones, either broken segments of pes phalanges or claws – terminal phalanges. Such are difficult to determine as to genus and more difficult to identify with any certainty as to species. Nevertheless, the attempt has been made and the probable results are presented. In a number of cases determination did not seem possible. Where comparisons became awkward, a photographic record of possible comparative material was made.

The recoveries derived from Middle Pleistocene deposits began with a number of phalanges from layers 36–34.

Following this initial stage, there is a gap in the avian record between layers 34–28 and subsequent finds belong to levels 28–23. These include fragments of phalanges belonging to aquatic and raptorial species.

Layer 20 in the New Entrance is believed to be of the same age as the Upper Breccia in the Main Cave but only a single fragment of avian bone, a phalange from a species of duck was recovered (H2373).

### Systematic study

For many of the details relating to the western Palaearctic distribution and ethology of the birds in this sequence, reference has been made to Cramp (1988), Cramp and Perrins (1994), Cramp and Simmons (1977 and 1980) and Voous (1960). Figure 8.2 shows the present-day habitats of the birds in the landscape around Pontnewydd.

#### Wildfowl

Throughout the sequence of levels in the Main Cave bones of wildfowl are more numerous than those of any other group, though the available sample from any level is extremely small. The fragmentary nature of much of the material also makes an absolute determination of species within a particular genus quite difficult in some instances. The wildfowl include species with varied niche and dietary requirements that give some guidance as clues from which a reconstruction of the contemporary environment may be attempted. Tables 8.10 and 8.11 explore the feeding behaviour of the geese, ducks and Mergansers found at Pontnewydd.

The geese have an almost exclusively vegetarian diet, while the diving ducks and Mergansers take mainly molluscs, crustaceans and fish. The very long time sequence which these cave deposits represent means that their relationship to the alternating climates provides a further factor to be taken into account when considering the behaviour patterns and seasonal migration of individual species. The present-day niche requirements and habitats during the breeding season of the different species found at Pontnewydd are precise and extremely diverse and are briefly described when considering individual species. The indications are that the lower reaches of the Rivers Elwy and Clwyd and the coastal marshes were resting places for wildfowl mainly on autumn and spring passage and during the winter.

#### Bewick's Swan, Cygnus columbianus bewickii

It is difficult to determine whether the fragment of

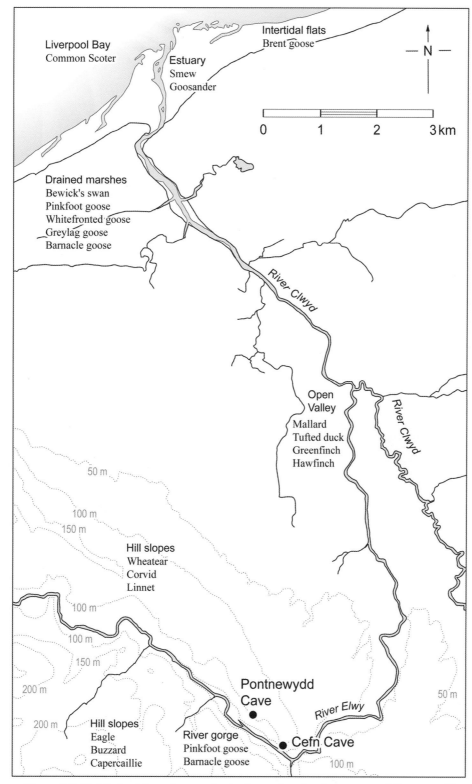

*Figure 8.2. Habitats of the avian species in the modern landscape around Pontnewydd.*

tarsometatarsus from the unstratified sample belongs to Bewick's Swan or is a large male Greylag Goose. The fragment is from the distal end and only the trochlea of the third metatarsal remains. This means that standard measurements, as used by Bacher (1967) to distinguish the different species of geese and swans can not be applied.

Table 8.12 gives measurements of F453 compared with specimens in the British Museum collection. These are not standard measurements but taken as the width/diameter of the base of the shaft, the length of the trochlea and the width of the articular surface of the trochlea. The measurements indicate some compatibility between the specimen and

| | | *Anser anser* | *Anser brachyr-hynchus* | *Anser albi-frons* | *Branta leucopsis* | *Branta bernicla* | *Aythya fuligula* | *Mell-anitta nigra* | *Mergus albellus* |
|---|---|---|---|---|---|---|---|---|---|
| *Salix glauca* | Bluish willow | | S | S | | | | | |
| *S. trianda* | Almond willow | A | | | | | | | |
| *S.herbacea* | dwarf willow | | | | S | Sp | | | |
| *Equisetum* | Horsetail | S | S/A | S/A | A/W | | | | |
| *Selaginella* sp. | Club moss | | S | S | | | | | |
| *Oxyria digna* | Mountain sorrel | | S | S | S | S | | | |
| *Polygonum viviparum* | Bistort | S | S/W | S/W | S/W | | S | | |
| *Chenopodiae* | Goosefoot | S | | | | | | | |
| *Stellaria* sp. | Chickweed | S | W | W | | | | | |
| *Salicomia* | Marsh samphire | | | | Sp | W/Sp | | | |
| *Cerastium* sp. | Mouse ear | | S/A | S/A | S | S | | | |
| *Ranunculus* sp. | Buttercup family | | | | S/W | S/W | | | |
| *Capsella bursa pastoris* | Sheps. Purse | S | | | | | | | |
| *S.saxifraga* | Saxifrage | S | S/A | S/A | S | S | | | |
| *Apium nodiflora* | Fool's watercress | | | | W | | | | |
| *Potentifla palustris* | Cinquefoil | S | | | | | | | |
| *Dryas octopetala* | Mountain avens | | | | S | | | | |
| *Trifolium* sp. | Clover family | S | | | A/W ~ | | | | |
| *Vaccinium* sp. | Cowberry | | | | | | | | |
| *Empetrum nigrum* | Crowberry | | | | | | | | |
| *Veronica* sp. | Speedwell | S | | | | | | | |
| *Plantago maritima* | Sea plantain | | | | W | | | | |
| *Triglochin maritima* | Sea arrow grass | | | | A/Sp | W | | | |
| *Armeria maritima* | Thrift | | | | A/W | | | | |
| *Aster trifolium* | Sea aster | | | | W/Sp | W | | | |
| *Sonchus* sp. | Sow thistle family | S | | | | | | | |
| *Taxacum* sp. | Dandelion family | S | | | | | | | |
| *Potamogatonaceae* | Pondweeds | S | | | | | W/S | S | W/Oc |
| *Zostera* sp. | Eel grass family | | | | W | W/Sp | | | W/Oc |
| *Ruppia maritima* | Tassel weed | | | | | | W/S | | W/Oc |
| *Lemnaceae* | Duckweeds | S | | | | | | | W/Oc |
| *Sparganaceae* | Burr reed | S/A | | S | | | | | |
| *Bolboschoenus maritimus* | Sedge | S/W | | | | | | | |
| *Cyperaceae: Eriophorum* | Cottongrass | | S | A | | S | | | |
| *Rhychospora alba* | Beak sedge | | | | | | | | |
| *Carex* | Sedges | W | A | | | | | | |
| *Scirpus* | Club rush | S/W | | | | | W | | |
| *Eleocharis palustris* | Spike rush | | | | | | W | | |
| *Phalaris* sp. | Reed grass | S/W | | S | | | | | |
| *Leersia* | Cut grass | S | | | | | | | |
| *Festuca* sp. | Fescue | S | S | | W | W | | | |
| *Phragmites communis* | Reed | S | | | | | | | |
| *Pulchinella maritima* | Sea poa | | | W | W/Sp | Sp | | | |
| *Glyceria* sp. | Water grasses | S | | W | | | | | |
| *Poa* sp. | Poa | S | W | W | W | | | | |
| *Triticum* sp. | Wheat | W | W | | | | | | |
| *Hordeum seccanum* | Barley | W | W | W | | | | | |
| *Agropyron repens* | Couch grass | W | | W | | | | | |
| *Avena* | Oats | W | W | W | | | | | |
| *Phleum* sp. | Cat's tail grass | S | W | | | | | | |
| *Lollium* sp. | Rye grass | S | W | | A/W | | | | |
| *Agrostis stolonifera* | Fiorin | | | | | | | | |
| *Juncus gerardii* | Mud rush | | | | A/W | | | | |
| *Algae:* | *Fucus* | | | | S | S | | | |
| | *Cladophora, VIva, Enteromorpha* | | | | W | W | | | |

Table 8.10. Plants recorded as food items for the wildfowl species present at Pontnewydd. Sp = taken in spring; S = taken in summer; A = taken in autumn; W = taken in winter; All = exploited at all seasons; Oc = taken occasionally.

| | | *Aythya fuligula* | *Melanitta nigra* | *Mergus albellus* | *Mergus merganser* |
|---|---|---|---|---|---|
| **Mollusca** Freshwater: | | | | | |
| *Dreissena polymorpha* | | W | | | |
| *Hydrobia jenkinsi* | | W | | | |
| *Pisidium* sp. | | W/S | | | |
| *Anodonta* sp. | | W | All | | |
| *Lymnea* sp. | | W/S | All | | |
| *Unio* sp. | | S | | | |
| *Valvata* sp. | | S | | | |
| *Viviparus duboisiana* | | S | | | |
| Marine: | | | | | |
| *Mytilis edulis* | | W | All | | |
| *Cardium* sp. | | W | All | | |
| *Littorina* sp. | | W | All | | |
| *Hydrobia* sp. | | W | All | | |
| *Mya* sp. | | | All | | |
| *Spisula* sp. | | | All | | |
| *Nassa* sp. | | | All | | |
| **Crustacea** Freshwater: | | | | | |
| *Gammarus* sp. | | S/All | | | S |
| *Asellus* sp. | | S/All | | | |
| Marine: | | | | | |
| *Idonta* sp. | | | All | | |
| *Isopodiae* | | | All | | |
| *Carcinus* sp. | | | All | | |
| **Invertebrate** Insect: | | | | | |
| *Phrygmea sp.* | | S | S | | |
| *Hydropsyche angustiponis* | | S | | | |
| *Chironimidae* | | | S | | |
| **Invertebrate**: Annelidae | | | All | | |
| **Fish** | | | | | |
| *Anguilla anguilla* | Eel | | | All | All |
| *Clypea harengus* | Herring | | | All | All |
| *Salmo salar* | Salmon | | | All | All |
| *Salmo trutta* | Trout | | | All | All |
| *Thyamalis thyamalis* | Grayling | | | | All |
| *Esox lucius* | Pike | | | All | All |
| *Abramis brama* | Bream | | | | All |
| *Alburnus alburnus* | Bleak | | | All | |
| *Barbus barbus* | Barbel | | | | All |
| *Gobio gobio* | Gudgeon | | | All | |
| *Leuciscus leuciscus* | Dace | | | | All |
| *Phoxinus phoxinus* | Minnow | | W/S | All | All |
| *Rutilus rutilus* | Roach | | | All | All |
| *Scardinus erythrophthalmus* | Rudd | | | | All |
| *Cobitidae* | Loach | | | | All |
| *Gadus morhua* | Cod | | | | All |
| *Lota Iota* | Burbot | | | All | |
| *Zoarces viviparus* | Blenny | | | All | All |
| *Gasterostidae* | Stickleback | | W/S | All | |
| *Spinachia spinachia* | 15 spine Stickleback | | | All | |
| *Perca fluviatilis* | Perch | | | | All |
| *Cottus gobbio* | Bullhead | | | | All |
| *Ammoditidae* | Sand eel | | | All | |
| *Pleuronectes platessa* | Plaice | | | All | All |

Table 8.11. Mollusca, Crustacea, invertebrates and fish recorded in the diet of wildfowl at Pontnewydd. S = taken in summer; W = taken in winter; All = taken at all seasons.

| Level and species | Tarsometatarsus | W. base shaft | L. trochlea | W. dist. artic. |
|---|---|---|---|---|
| **Unstrat.** | **F453** | **10.4** | **15.5** | **9.1** |
| cf. Bewick | BM. s/1972.1.44 | 10.6 | 17.1 | 11.5 |
| *A. anser* | BM. 1930.3.24.208 | 7.9 | 12.25 | 7.45 |
| *A. anser* | BM. s/1999.43.139 | 7.85 | 11.8 | 7 |
| *A. anser* | BM. s/1972.1.51 | 10.55 | 16 | 8.45 |

*Table 8.12. Comparative measurements* Cygnus columbianus bewickii/Anser anser *in mm.*

BM.1972.1.51 and BM.1972.1.44, a male Greylag Goose and Bewick's Swan respectively. In structure the bones are difficult to distinguish. Were this a tarsometatarsus of Bewick's Swan, its location in a level of probable Holocene date suggests that it was a winter migrant to the locality feeding in rivers, estuaries and pools below 100 m O.D., on marsh and water plants and winter pasture. Because there is some degree of doubt in the identification, Bewick's Swan has not been included in the tables of wildfowl diet (Tables 8.10 and 8.11).

*Greylag Goose,* Anser anser

Three bones of Greylag Goose were recovered from different layers in the Upper Breccia and a fourth from the late Last Glacial Upper Clays and Sands. Unlike the other *Anseridae* at Pontnewydd, the Greylag breeds mainly in boreal and temperate habitats in wetland swamps and reedbeds. They prefer stretches of open, eutrophic fresh water with dense emergent vegetation. Table 8.10 shows the wide range of aquatic and flowering plants that are exploited as food by this species. In winter it feeds mainly on grassland and will take all types of available cereals and agricultural root crops. At the present-day, they breed in a number of locations throughout central and eastern Britain. In addition, from October onwards, Icelandic breeders move south-westerly towards Britain, while the migration of the Fennoscandian and German breeding populations, beginning in late September/October, follows the west coast of France to arrive at wintering areas in Portugal and the Guadalquivir, Spain. The situation at Pontnewydd relative to this species is equivocal and it is questionable whether the occurrence of Greylag bones in these levels represents a partially migrant or a wintering population.

*Pink Footed/White Fronted Goose,* Anser brachyrhyncos/albifrons

The single coracoid, D3115, from the Upper Breccia is heavily abraded and it was not in consequence possible to take definitive measurements as the morphology of the coracoids of both species are very similar. In recent times, the Pink Foot breed on high ground and inaccessible gorges in Iceland, Spitsbergen and Greenland; while the White Fronted Geese summer in the tundra zone of North Russia, Novaya Zemla and in Greenland. Both species move south during the autumn, remaining in their wintering grounds from December until March. At the present-day, many of the Greenland breeding population spend the winter months in Ireland, western Scotland and Wales.

*Barnacle Goose,* Branta leucopsis *and Brent Goose,* Branta bernicla

One distal fragment of a coracoid (F2788) from the lower layers of the Upper Breccia appears to be larger than average specimens of Brent Goose of either sex. Standard measurements were not possible but a reading was taken of the distance between the cotyla scapularis and the process acrocoracoideus and comparison made with specimens of Barnacle and Brent Geese from the British Museum. The Pontnewydd specimen gave a reading over 2 mm larger than that of recent bones of the Brent Geese in those collections.

This difference in the measurement of a small section of the coracoid may perhaps be within the range of biological variation for Brent Goose, the species most frequently recovered from the site, but it is worth noting because conversely, it could indicate that both species were present in the locality of the Clwyd marshes during the winter months. Other bones from the Upper Breccia and the Middle Pleistocene levels of the New Entrance may be attributed unequivocally to Brent Goose.

These two species have divergent habitat requirements during the breeding season. The Barnacle Goose prefers precipices or slopes overlooking fjords mainly in Greenland, Spitzbergen and Novaya Zemla, while Brent Goose also breeds in northern Greenland and Spitzbergen but in low-lying tundra with pools, often close to coastal waters. The autumn migration patterns of recent times show that Barnacle Geese tend to spend the winter on the western seaboard of the Continent of Europe as well as of Ireland and Scotland. They feed in grassland, marsh, floodplain and even on stubble fields but are not normally found within the inter-tidal zones. Brent Geese move to more southerly locations as far south as the Loire, Gironde and Thames, frequenting the habitats of the estuaries and inter-tidal zones. Despite the difference in habitat, there is some overlap in their feeding behaviour during most seasons of the year as seen in Table 8.10. Both are wholly dependent on plant material.

*Mallard,* Anas platyrhyncos

The Mallard breeds throughout the west Palaearctic region in habitats from Arctic tundra to sub-tropical. In winter the populations of northern Fennoscandia and eastern Europe move south and west, some wintering south of the Mediterranean, wherever there are pools or flowing fresh water. Their diet is entirely omnivorous and opportunistic but much of it gained by dabbling in shallow water.

After careful comparison, a fragment of the caput humeri (D2635) from the Upper Breccia, originally identified by Harrison as Brent Goose, appears to be Mallard. It is a very small fragment but the fossa pneumotricipitalis is more rounded than in goose and the form of the incisura capitis and tuberculum dorsale compares well with Mallard. A number of pes phalanges recovered in the series of Pleistocene levels of the New Entrance appear to have the characteristics of *Anatidae* and are compatible in size with Mallard.

### Tufted Duck, Aythya fuligula

The identification of F4227 from the Upper Clays and Sands is not without doubt. The specimen is seriously abraded but is closely comparable with Tufted Duck. A member of the Pochard family, the Tufted Duck currently breeds in Britain and northern and eastern Europe yet only sporadically in France and the Low Countries. In winter, movement is towards western Europe and the Mediterranean. The preferred habitat is in deep, open fresh water river, lake or inshore waters, where they may congregate in flocks from October to March. Table 8.11 shows that molluscs form the basis of their diet at all times of the year.

### Common Scoter, Melanitta nigra

During the breeding season the Scoter occupies inland sites within the limits of the boreal and low Arctic region. Outside the breeding season, it is almost exclusively a marine species preferring open shallow seas just off the coast to rough waters and rugged coastlines. Currently they may be seen gathering in rafts on Liverpool Bay and off the Welsh coast in winter and occasionally during the moult migration of late summer. Like the Tufted Duck, it feeds largely on molluscs and some crustaceans (Table 8.11). Bones of the Common Scoter were found in the Lower Breccia and therefore may date to the later part of MIS 7, during a relatively temperate climatic phase.

### Smew, Mergus albellus

The single carpometacarpus from the Upper Breccia probably indicates that the Smew was also a winter visitor to the locality of Pontnewydd. At the present-day, the Smew has a much more continental distribution than other Sawbills, preferring nest sites in old hollow trees in wooded tundra and coniferous forest and moving south in autumn to central and eastern Europe and some to countries bordering the North Sea. Its food is mainly fish obtained by surface diving in sheltered fresh and salt waters (Table 8.11).

### Goosander, Mergus merganser

At the present-day, the Goosander breeds in the highland areas of Scotland, north-west England and at one site in mid-Wales, though its main breeding area is in Fennoscandia and Russia. Like the Smew it nests in holes in trees, situated near water. In winter, it is widely distributed over Western Europe and Britain and lives primarily on fish, including both fresh water and marine species, depending on location.

### The raptors

The evidence for raptorial bird species at Pontnewydd is slight. A buzzard terminal phalange is unstratified, found within the Boyd Dawkins dump, whilst two terminal phalanges from the recent levels of the New Entrance sequence, comparable respectively in size with Eagle and Falcon or small Hawk. A tarsometatarsus of Kestrel, *Falco tinnunculus*, was found in the Upper Breccia. This species is not a particularly good ecological indicator, being found today both throughout the Palaearctic region as well as in Africa, south of the Sahara. The eastern European and Fennoscandian populations migrate in a south-westerly direction in autumn but elsewhere they tend to be dispersive or partial migrants, living throughout the year on small mammals.

### The galliforms

The evidence for the presence of galliforms comes from two bones, both of relatively recent origin. The terminal pes digit from the Boyd Dawkins dump seems to belong to a member of the family *Tetraonidae*. Examination showed that although the claw is worn, it compares most closely with Capercaillie, *Tetrao urogallus*. The presence of Capercaillie on the site during the late Last Glacial or the early Holocene could provide significant indications as to the local ecology at that time. If the determination is correct, it is predominantly a woodland species of the temperate and boreal forest zones. It favours areas of either coniferous or broad-leafed woodland alternating with glades opening onto dwarf heathland with berried plants like Bilberry, *Vaccinium myrtilis*. In winter its main food is pine needles taken from a variety of coniferous trees, while at other times of year a variety of plant material is taken, including leaves, stems and fruits.

The second bone in this group was probably deposited in the cave much later during the late 18th or early 19th centuries. It belongs to the J. Wilfrid Jackson collection in Buxton Museum. It is a male tarsometarsus and was classified in the collections as Common Fowl with spur, *Gallus*. Examination showed that it was not Domestic Fowl but was in fact Peafowl, *Pavo cristatus*. Comparative measurements of other specimens from archaeological contexts and recent collections confirmed the determination. How a Peacock arrived in the cave deposits and was recovered during the 19th century excavations is a matter for conjecture. It seems likely that it is the inedible remains from a fox kill. The tarsometatarsus shows no visible signs of tooth marks except in the damage to the crista hypotarsi at the proximal end, such as might have occurred when the tendons were severed at the distal end of the tibiotarsus. The most likely source of this vulpine meal would have been the Williams Wynn property Plas-yn-Cefn on the hill above the cave. As a gentry house, a family of Peacocks might have ornamented its walks and shrubberies during the eighteenth or nineteenth century. However, no confirmation has been forthcoming from the Estate records.

| Level | Find/specimen no. | Greatest length | Proximal width | Proximal depth | Distal width | Distal depth | Minimum diameter of shaft |
|---|---|---|---|---|---|---|---|
| **LB** | **D3091** | | | | 5.45 | 2.8 | 1.9 |
| BMNH | S/1983.32.2. | 20.45 | 6.95 | 3.1 | 5.1 | 2.65 | 1.8 |
| | S/1985.101.4. fem. | 19.9 | 6.2 | 2.65 | 4.85 | 2.5 | 1.7 |
| | 1915.10.11.1 | 19.55 | 6.05 | 2.5 | 4.8 | 2.4 | 1.65 |
| | S/1980.29.1 | 19.25 | 6 | 2.75 | 4.25 | 2.4 | 1.7 |
| | S/1968.4.6. male | 19.5 | 6.05 | 2.65 | 4.7 | 2.45 | 1.7 |
| | S/1952.105.1 | 20 | 6.7 | 3 | 5 | 2.8 | 1.75 |

*Table 8.13. Wheatear,* Oenanthe oenanthe, *humerus distal measurements in mm.*

Turdidae
*Wheatear,* Oenanthe oenanthe
There is evidence for the presence of Wheatears in the Lower Breccia and in the Upper Breccia. It is a summer migrant to Palaearctic regions. In recent times, the Wheatear, in its nominate form has bred over large parts of Europe, arriving in Britain from Africa south of the Sahara in early March, beginning the passage south again in July, August and September. As a summer visitor to all parts of Britain, it may be regarded as a good seasonal indicator but by contrast it has been recorded on other sites of Devensian age during periods of glacial advance and maxima. It seems that summer visitors arrived and bred at the same northern latitudes as at present, even though the season may have been shorter (Eastham 1988). Since the diet of the Wheatear is mainly insect, especially grasshoppers, *Orthoptera* and beetles, *Coleoptera*, seasonally supplemented by berries, its presence suggests that these items would have been readily available in the vicinity of the cave.

Examination of the Wheatear bones from the Lower Breccia showed that distal sections of coracoid and humerus are larger than recent specimens of the southern race. It was possible to compare the humerus distal end with a series of specimens from a number of locations in Britain and the Mediterranean (Table 8.13). These Wheatear bones may belong to the Iceland, Greenland race, *Oenanthe oenanthe leucorhoa*, that is measurably more robust than the nominate form. These tend to travel south later in the year than the British birds but stop off in passage on these islands. A tibiotarsus of Wheatear was recovered from the Upper Breccia but this was not noticeably larger than recent specimens.

Corvidae
The crow family are unusually absent from the Main Cave. A single terminal pes digit, claw, in the lower levels of the New Entrance sequence is characteristically corvid and may be tentatively ascribed to either Jackdaw or Magpie. Both are resident throughout most of the western Palaearctic region and are eclectic feeders.

Fringillidae
*Linnet,* Carduelis cannabina
A proximal fragment of humerus, S220 from the Upper Breccia (wet-sieve sample) was identified by Harrison as

Linnet, *Carduelis cannabina*. On further examination, this bone appeared rather more robust than recent specimens (Eastham collection). Anatomically it is equally comparable with Greenfinch, *Carduelis chloris*. The distal width of the bone is 6.0 mm and the same measurement gives a reading of 5.7 mm for Linnet and 6.5 mm for Greenfinch, that places the Pontnewydd specimen somewhere between the two.

The behaviour and ecological requirements of the two species are not entirely dissimilar. The distribution of both covers almost the whole Palaearctic region including Africa north of the Sahara but excluding the extreme north of Russia and Fennoscandia. Both are only partial migrants, all populations moving south-west to winter within the breeding range of the species. The Greenfinch tends to be a lowland species of the woodland edge or tall hedgerows where there is an abundance of hard seeds, while the Linnet favours more scrub vegetation, and open ground with low trees and easy access to food plants. Both are predominantly seed and fruit eaters, but also take a variety of insect prey with other invertebrates.

*Hawfinch,* Coccothraustes coccothraustes
The Hawfinch was found as a single humerus in the Upper Breccia. It has fairly specific niche requirements. It is an inhabitant of the canopy in broadleaved and mixed woodland but is especially characteristic of Oak, *Quercus,* and Hornbeam, *Carpinus,* forest and also inhabits the trees lining the valley bottoms along river banks. It takes all types of fruit and seeds in its diet as well as leaves, buds and catkins. Fruits from the *Prunus* family especially Bird cherry, *Prunus avium,* are an important component in some areas, as are larval invertebrates, caterpillars and other pupae in the feeding of the young chicks. Even in winter it will collect dropped nuts and seeds from the trees from the ground.

### The avian environment
The pattern of bird environments in the locality of Pontnewydd Cave is richer and more complex than a cursory glance at the species list might imply. It was an environment which appears to have undergone a number of changes over time related to climatic fluctuations. The structure of the landfall is an important influence on avian habitats. There are no strictly montane species from the

site but, to the south-west, between the Rivers Elwy and Aled, a range of hills, dominated by Moel Fodiar, over 350 m above present sea level, would provide a hunting out-post for large raptors and may have been partially covered with the forest to heathland habitat favoured by the Capercaillie. This environment may also have existed on the 120 m plateau to the north of the River Elwy above the escarpment of the cave, providing a niche for species like the Linnet.

The Elwy valley itself would have not only provided a rich habitat for both aquatic and passerine species but also a passage between the coast and the hinterland for people and animals. The diversity of wildfowl on the site indicates extensive stretches of water and the existence of marsh habitats in the vicinity of the cave at different periods in its history, at times enhanced by beaver activity. Of the nine, or possibly up to eleven, species of waterfowl recovered from the site, three favour fresh water locations exclusively, two prefer it but are also found in brackish water and coastal inlets; a further three species will tolerate both fresh water and coastal water habitats and one species is almost exclusively coastal and marine except during the breeding season.

In considering these factors, two questions emerge; the first is how far glacial advance and retreat affected eustatic and isostatic change in the land/sea levels and the second is the degree to which this altered the seasonal habits of these migratory bird species. Little confirmed detail about sea levels or raised beaches is available for the North Wales coast for the period of the late Middle Pleistocene of the Lower Breccia. The climatic indications for the Lower Breccia are that it was cool but with no extremes of cold, suggesting that avian migratory movements might not vary greatly from the present-day and that the geese and other wildfowl could be winter visitors. At the same time, the presence of Wheatear, a summer migrant, may be accidental but indicates that the cave was open at all times of year. Recent work on the effects of glaciations in the Irish Sea has involved the plotting the sequence of marine and terrestrial deposits in different sectors of the eastern margins of the Irish Sea basin and the consequent isostatic and eustatic changes (Lambeck 1996; Knight 2001). In the circumstances of ice plugging the river mouths water would have been held back and covered much of the flood plain, considerably affecting the avian environment.

## Sites with comparable patterns of bird fauna

The closest comparisons with the Pontnewydd material in terms of avifauna may be found at La Cotte de Saint Brelade, Jersey (Andrews 1920; Callow and Cornford 1986) and in some of the long sequence of Mousterian levels at Pinhole Cave, Creswell Crags, Derbyshire (Bramwell 1960; Jenkinson 1984). Pink Footed, Brent and Barnacle Geese were identified at La Cotte, and were found with bones of both Scoter and Goosander in levels 8–12 at Pinhole Cave. Two open sites in Essex in the gravel deposits at Gray's Thurrock and Ilford may possibly belong to the period of MIS 7. They were found to have bones of a number of species of swans and geese but do not appear to have had any hominin remains in association and are therefore not strictly comparable with the Pontnewydd material (Harrison and Walker 1977). There are few parallel sites in continental Europe, although from cave sites in Basilicata and Lazio, Italy a similar diversity of swans and geese were recovered in layers dated to before 200,000 BP (Cassoli 1978; 1980).

# 9. The Human Remains

## Tim Compton and Chris Stringer

*The 17 hominin teeth (plus a tooth fragment) discovered in stratified Middle Pleistocene deposits between 1980 and 1995 represent a minimum of five individuals with age estimates, based on late Neanderthal development criteria, as follows – an 8.5 year old, a nine year old, an 11–11.5 year old, a young adult (14–16 years) and a mature adult. Based on tooth sizes, the individual with an estimated age of nine years (with two teeth) is possibly female and the remaining individuals possibly male. The maximum possible number of individuals represented is sixteen; nine juveniles/adolescents and seven adults. Two teeth were found in position in a maxillary fragment, the remainder being isolated finds. The crowns are mostly complete but the roots generally broken or absent.*

*The crown areas of the two smaller (possibly female) teeth are small compared with the mean crown areas of teeth from the major early Neanderthal site of Krapina in Croatia, and one of these, PN12, is also small compared with most European later Middle Pleistocene teeth, but similar in size to 'female' teeth from the Sima de los Huesos (SH) site at Atapuerca in northern Spain. The crown areas of the remaining teeth are large compared with most other European later Middle Pleistocene teeth and similar to the mean values of Krapina. In most cases, the sizes of individual later Middle Pleistocene finds are within the range of values reported for the large collection from Atapuerca-SH but, in the case of lower second molars, the individual finds, including Pontnewydd, are larger than any of those from this site. A Penrose size and shape coefficient calculated using length and breadth measurements shows a greater affinity of the shape of the Pontnewydd teeth to the Atapuerca-SH and Krapina samples than to a later European Neanderthal sample. Root measurements are comparable to those of Atapuerca-SH but the Pontnewydd roots are more robust.*

*The form of occlusal wear on molars suggests a diet with a large shearing component, probably indicative of an important element of tough fibrous vegetable foods. A similar form of wear is found in other European later Middle Pleistocene teeth but generally it is not so pronounced. There is a distinct difference between this and the form of wear described for the Krapina teeth. The rate of wear is relatively high in comparison with Krapina and some other later Middle Pleistocene teeth, and the frequency of occlusal chipping is high compared with other reference groups. There is some evidence of non-masticatory use of the teeth, in the form of unusual wear, and a lower lateral incisor and a lower fourth premolar exhibit faint 'cut-marks'.*

*Subvertical grooves (possibly caused by heavy chewing) occur on eleven interproximal facets. Only one tooth (the deciduous premolar) has a deposit of dental calculus. Hypoplasia – probably indicative of disease or starvation at a time when the teeth were still forming – occurs on four teeth, a higher frequency than that found at Atapuerca-SH. Anomalies of alignment and eruption are prevalent amongst the upper and lower premolars.*

*The morphology of the teeth is compatible with that of other European later Middle Pleistocene hominins, particularly where trends can be seen between earlier and later material. Traits that are characteristic of both European Middle Pleistocene hominins and Krapina Neanderthals, such as supraradicular taurodontism, mid trigonid crest and large hypocones on upper first molars, are present. Other traits that only occur on eastern Asian and north-west African Middle Pleistocene hominins, such as buccal cinguli on molars, are absent.*

*Later (Mesolithic and Neolithic) material discovered in unstratified deposits consists of two lower molars, one in a mandibular fragment, a thoracic vertebra and a metatarsal. The two molars may come from the same individual, an adolescent (about 14–15 years based on dental development). The teeth are similar in size to the means of samples of European late Upper Palaeolithic and Mesolithic teeth. The morphology of these teeth is described but not compared with other samples.*

## Introduction

The hominin remains from the excavations at Pontnewydd fall into two groups; the first comprises 17 teeth plus a tooth fragment, and a possible nasal bone fragment, discovered in stratified Middle Pleistocene deposits. With the exception of one tooth (PN20), which was found at the New Entrance, these were all in a small area at the end of the cave, at the entrance to, and within, the East Passage (Figure 9.1). Two teeth were in place in a fragment of maxilla (PN4) but the remainder were isolated and without any associated bone.

The second group comprises two teeth (one in place in an immature mandibular fragment), a fragment of adult thoracic vertebra and a left third metatarsal, all discovered in unstratified deposits mainly associated with the mouth of the cave. The two teeth (PN2 and PN8) came from the spoil heap produced when the cave was converted into an ammunition store in World War II. The mandible has been dated at 7,420±90 BP (OxA-5819; Aldhouse-Green *et al.* 1996). A thoracic vertebra (PN3) was found in a dump of modern spoil in the South Passage (Figure 9.2). This has not been dated but is also assumed to be of Holocene age (ibid.). However, Green *et al.* (1989) have pointed out that the morphology and dimensions are equally comparable to finds from Neanderthal sites such as Kébara and Shanidar as to material that is more recent. The metatarsal (PN14) was found in the spoil heap created by excavations in the nineteenth century and has been dated at 4,495±70 BP (OxA-5820; Figure 9.2; Aldhouse-Green *et al.* 1996). These excavations removed most of the upper deposits for 25 m into the cave some time before 1870 (Hughes and Thomas 1874).

The early excavations produced one hominin molar, described by George Busk as being of very large size 'and in this respect exceeds any with which I have compared it, except one or two from Australia or Tasmania' (ibid.). This was unearthed with bones and teeth of Pleistocene mammals, and felstone artefacts representing a 'Mousterian industry' (Hughes and Thomas 1874; Oakley *et al.* 1971). The whereabouts of this tooth today is unknown.

Most of the Middle Pleistocene permanent molars exhibit a marked degree of taurodontism. This is the name given to a trait in which the pulp chamber of the tooth is considerably enlarged (see below for a fuller description). The presence of taurodontism at this early date, showing an affinity with Krapina and later classic Neanderthals, has been commented on as being of considerable interest by, for example, Green *et al.* (1981), Stringer (1984; 1986) and Day (1986). It is noted that Pontnewydd is one of the earliest sites at which this degree of taurodontism has been found and that it is a condition readily matched in

fossil hominins only amongst the Neanderthals. The fact that this appears to be a population characteristic has also been noted (Green 1983; Stringer 1984; Green *et al.* 1989). In this connection Stringer observes that taurodontism is not a trait found in all Neanderthals, nor is it exclusive to them. The degree of taurodontism observed in Pontnewydd molars does not match those of the more extreme examples from some later sites (*e.g.* Krapina and La Cotte de St Brelade), and some Middle/Late Pleistocene sites (*e.g.* Bourgeois-Delaunay) do not exhibit this trait (Green *et al.* 1981; Stringer 1984).

Attention has also been drawn to the close match of size and overall morphology of the Pontnewydd Middle Pleistocene teeth with those of Krapina (Green *et al.* 1981; Cook *et al.* 1982; Stringer 1984; Stringer *et al.* 1984; Green *et al.* 1989). Stringer *et al.* (1984) considered that the level of taurodontism at Pontnewydd could be used tentatively to reinforce the model of an early European emergence of characters later found in Neanderthals, and Stringer (1986) further considered that this, together with the specifically Neanderthal-like characteristics of the Swanscombe occipital bone, suggested that Britain was probably peopled by Neanderthal precursors during the later Middle Pleistocene. Green *et al.* (1989) and Aldhouse-Green (1995) also noted the parallels in the degree of taurodontism to that encountered at the later Middle Pleistocene site of Atapuerca-SH. Day (1986) noted that there were no features suggesting a strong affinity with *Homo erectus*.

Estimates of the number of Middle Pleistocene individuals represented have varied as more teeth have been discovered:

- Stringer (1986), PN1–7, minimum three individuals – adult, sub-adult/adolescent and child (9 years);
- Green *et al.* (1989), PN1–8, minimum one adult and two juveniles (possibly 11 years plus and 8/9 years), maximum two adults and five juveniles;
- Aldhouse-Green (1995), PN1–14, minimum two adults and two juveniles, maximum two adults and five juveniles.

PN2 and PN8 were originally considered to be of the same date as the teeth coming from the Pleistocene deposits, from both relative dating and the lack of any later archaeological material (Green *et al.* 1981; Green *et al.* 1989). In contrast, it was noted that the simple crown morphology and small size of PN2 were at variance with Early/Middle Pleistocene teeth (Green *et al.* 1981; Stringer 1984). The minimum breadth of the ascending ramus of the mandible is within the range of a recent British sample of 11–13 year olds but can also be matched by Krapina C (11–12 years) (Stringer

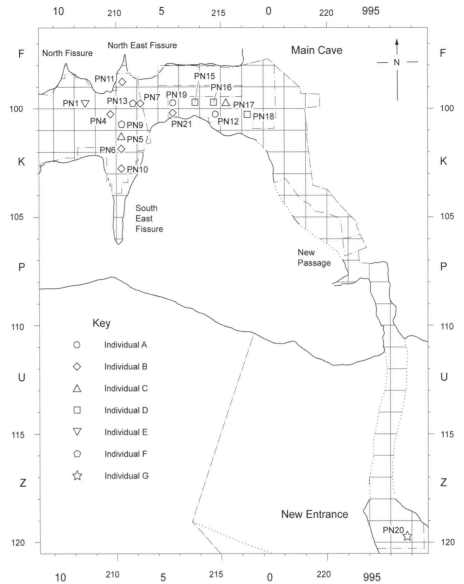

*Figure 9.1. Locations at which teeth were discovered within Pontnewydd Cave.*

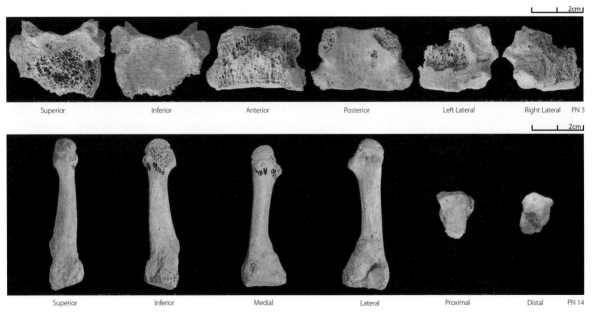

*Figure 9.2. PN3 vertebra and PN14 metatarsal.*

1984). Stringer *et al.* (1984), Stringer (1984), Day (1986) and Aldhouse-Green (1995) also stated that the unstratified finds in general could not be excluded from representing anatomically modern *Homo sapiens*. As stated above, PN2 and PN14 were subsequently dated and found to be younger in age. The recent date of these finds unearthed in the mouth of the cave must now throw doubt on the Pleistocene attribution for the lost tooth (Aldhouse-Green *et al.* 1996).

The possible identity of PN2 has also been discussed (Green *et al.* 1981; Green *et al.* 1989). If it was a lower second permanent molar, the size of the ascending ramus indicated that it was a non anatomically modern human aged 8/9 years (comparable with earlier Upper Pleistocene hominins *e.g.* Teshik-Tash 1 and Irhoud 3) otherwise, if it was a third molar, it was more likely to be anatomically modern and of an age greater than 11 years. Stringer considered that the degree of posterior narrowing of the tooth favoured identification as a third molar and that the morphology of the mandible was more consistent with an age of 11 years plus (Stringer 1984). The discovery of PN8 (a lower second permanent molar), which has been associated with PN2 (Day 1986; Stringer 1986), helped to confirm this identification (Green *et al.* 1989).

Finds PN1–8 have all been previously described in detail by Stringer (1984; Stringer in Green *et al.* 1981; 1989).

- **PN1** – the crown diameters (length and breadth) were noted as being close to the mean values of a *Homo erectus* sample and the Krapina hominins but below those of earlier Middle Pleistocene European hominins. The lack of any Carabelli's trait was noted and also the lack of a cingulum. The roots were described as being robust and prismatic, with marked enlargement of the pulp chamber, which displays an hourglass shape. It was considered that the tooth derived from a young adult individual in view of the moderate level of occlusal wear, and at least an adolescent in view of the completeness of the root and the presence of a distal interstitial wear facet (Stringer in Green *et al.* 1981). Stringer later noted that the morphology and size of the crown, but not the root, could be closely matched with certain French middle and early Upper Pleistocene sites (Stringer 1984);
- **PN2** – the morphology and measurements of the mandible fragment and the molar were discussed, and the molar was noted as being of small size and simple crown morphology (Stringer in Green *et al.* 1981; Day 1986);
- **PN3** – the fragment of thoracic vertebra was noted as being large but that its size could be matched by recent large adult specimens (Stringer in Green *et al.* 1981; Stringer 1984);
- **PN4** – the crown length and breadth measurements of the first permanent molar were noted as being a little below the mean for Krapina, but slightly above that for a European late Neanderthal sample; whereas the fourth deciduous premolar was relatively smaller, at the lower end of the Krapina range and close to the mean value for Neanderthals generally. The anomalous lingual position of the crypt for the fourth permanent premolar, leading to non-resorption of the roots of the fourth deciduous premolar, was commented on, and also the robust prismatic but waisted root of the first permanent molar, which had an unusual lobed apex buccally and a degree of taurodontism as marked as in PN1. However, the roots of the fourth deciduous premolar were not prismatic.

The age was estimated to be 8/9 years on developmental grounds (Stringer 1984). The find was first announced in Green (1983);

- **PN5, PN6 and PN7** – these teeth were noted as being large compared with modern human teeth but similar in size to Neanderthal specimens. PN7 was probably the homologue of PN6. PN6 and PN7 were considered to come from a child of 8–12 years and PN5 from a somewhat older individual (possibly adolescent) (Stringer 1984; Stringer in Green *et al.* 1989);
- **PN8** – the level of wear was noted as being compatible with the tooth being associated with PN2. The small amount of root present suggested a certain degree of taurodontism (Stringer in Green *et al.* 1989).

In addition to the references given above, descriptions of the teeth are also given in Green (1981) (PN1), Green and Currant (1982) (PN1–3), and Orban (1990) (PN1–11). Day (1986) lists measurements for PN1–4.

This chapter provides a detailed description of the measurements, wear, dental anomalies and morphology of the Pontnewydd hominin teeth and, where possible, will compare these characteristics with those of other European Pleistocene teeth to find similarities and differences, and any secular trends.

### Basic terms and abbreviations

The upper and lower permanent dental arcades are illustrated in Figure 9.3 (based on diagrams in Hillson 1996 and Scott and Turner 1997). Figure 9.4 illustrates how molars have evolved from single-cusped teeth to their present form in hominins (taken from *Gray's Anatomy*, Williams *et al.* 1989).

In the following sections, permanent teeth are being referred to unless otherwise stated. These are: first and second incisors (or central and lateral), canine, third and fourth premolars (in line with the convention that the original first and second premolars of primitive mammals have been lost in hominoid evolution), first to third molars.

Abbreviations used for tooth types in tables are:

- Prefix: L/R for left/right, d – deciduous
- Type: I – incisor, P – premolar, M – molar
- Tooth number: superscript for upper teeth, subscript for lower teeth.

Abbreviations for positions and measurements on a tooth are:

- M – mesial; D – distal; B – buccal; L – lingual (buccal is also referred to as labial for anterior teeth (incisors and canines) and vestibular for posterior teeth (premolars and molars)
- MB – mesiobuccal; DB – distobuccal; ML – mesiolingual; DL – distolingual; MD – mesiodistal (length); BL – buccolingual (breadth).

(See Appendix A for an explanation of cusp names.)

Middle Pleistocene teeth are referred to in this chapter unless stated otherwise. Middle Pleistocene material

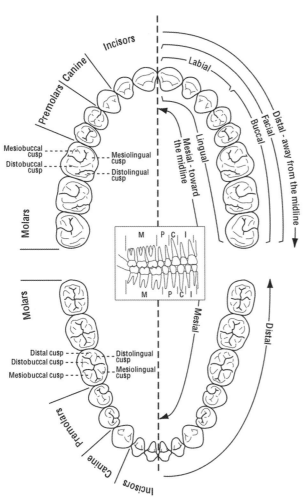

*Figure 9.3. Maxillary and mandibular permanent dental arcades.*

used for comparison is split between 'earlier' (*Homo heidelbergensis*) and 'later' (including Atapuerca-SH) (early or pre-Neanderthal). The classification of the site of Bilzingsleben is uncertain, but it has been placed with the later group on chronological grounds. 'Neanderthal' in the text refers to later 'classic' Neanderthals from the Late (Upper) Pleistocene and includes the site of Krapina unless it is being discussed as a separate sample.

Ages at death given for comparative material are generally based on recent human standards of development. Recent work has indicated that late Neanderthals had a reduced period of dental development compared with anatomically modern humans. The Pontnewydd teeth are aged using both criteria.

## Catalogue of Pontnewydd teeth

The hominin finds from Pontnewydd are listed by their location on the site. Information given is also summarized in Table 9.1. The reference number is the hominin reference number followed by the site find number in brackets. The reasons for identifying a tooth as a particular type are only given where the type is not clear from the morphology of the crown. Most of the tooth crowns are complete but the roots are in general absent or damaged. The majority of teeth have little wear. The condition of the teeth is Type 1 (indicating good preservation) as defined by Currant (1984; and chapter 8, this volume) for the Pontnewydd mammalian remains. They are dense and solid, and breaks are clean and secondary. There is usually brown staining, often with black spots. Frequently there is black staining under the enamel and in the pulp chamber. The crowns have fine vertical cracking of the enamel, which tends to be greatest at the cervix, with one or more lines of horizontal cracking round the crown and also on the occlusal surface.

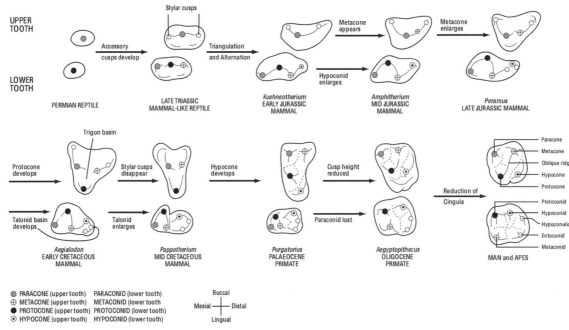

*Figure 9.4. Evolution of hominin molars.*

| Hominin ref. no. | Excavation season | Site find no. | Context | Grid square (depth) & co-ordinates | Description |
|---|---|---|---|---|---|
| **PN1** | 1980 | D415 | Intermediate complex | H9SW/SE (98.92) | Left $M^2$ (moderate wear) |
| **PN2*** | 1980 | A80 | World War II Dump | - | Immature right mandible fragment with crown of unerupted $M_3$ in place, roots initiated. |
| **PN3*** | 1978 | C5 | Dump of modern spoil in South Passage | - | Fragment of adult thoracic vertebra |
| **PN4** | 1982 | D1740-1 | Lower Breccia | I8NE (98.95) 100.19/209.56 | Fragment of right maxilla with lightly worn $M^1$ and heavily worn $dp^4$ in place |
| **PN5** | 1983 | D2212 | Lower Breccia | J7NW (99.18-08) | Left $P_4$ (slight wear). Root does not survive |
| **PN6** | 1983 | D2261 | Lower Breccia | J7SW (99.66-33) | Right $P_3$ (unworn). Root incompletely formed |
| **PN7** | 1985 | D3970 | Lower Breccia | H6SW (99.26) 99.57/211.10 | Left $P_3$ (unworn). Root incompletely formed (antimere of PN6?) |
| **PN8*** | 1984 | A354 | World War II Dump | - | Right $M_2$ (very slight wear). Roots do not survive. Probably part of specimen PN2 |
| **PN9** | 1983 | D2069 | Lower Breccia | I7SW (99.20-10) | Fragment of very heavily worn molar, possibly upper |
| **PN10** | 1988 | D4852 | Lower Breccia – Silt Beds | K7SW (99.48-38) | Right $I_2$ (moderate wear). Root does not survive |
| **PN11** | 1988 | D4843 | Lower Breccia | G7SW (99.21) 98.95/210.19 | Left $M_1$ (light wear) |
| **PN12** | 1989 | F2859 | Lower Breccia | I3NE (99.40-30) | Left $M^1$ (light wear) |
| **PN13** | 1985 | D4029 | Lower Breccia (f) | H7SE (99.10-00) | Right $M_2$ (or $M_1$) (very heavily worn) |
| **PN14*** | 1980 | A114 | Bottom of Boyd Dawkins Dump | - | Left third metatarsal from small individual (not robust) |
| **PN15** | 1993 | F3346 F3597 | Lower Breccia (c) | Found in two fragments: H4SE (99.35-33) & (99.33-31) | Right $M_2$ (light wear). Roots do not survive |
| **PN16** | 1993 | F3576 | Lower Breccia (b/c) | H3SE (99.21-16) | Right $M_3$ (slight wear). Roots do not survive |
| **PN17** | 1993 | F3577 | Lower Breccia (c) | H2SW (99.23-18) | Unerupted right $M^3$. Roots initiated |
| **PN18** | 1994 | F4753 | Lower Breccia (a) | I1NW (99.73-68) | Left $P^4$ (light wear). Root(s) does not survive |
| **PN19** | 1995 | F5523 | Lower Breccia (d) / BI | H5SE (99.10-05) | Unerupted right $M^3$. Roots initiated |
| **PN20** | 1995 | H2942 | Mudstone Gravel Unit (38) | AB994SE (97.60-50) | Left $P_3$ (heavy wear). Root does not survive |
| **PN21** | 1995 | F6095 | Lower Breccia (c) | I5NE (99.17-12) | Unerupted right $M_3$. Roots initiated |
|  | 1995 | F5387 | Lower Breccia (d) | I1NW (99.25-22) | ? nasal bone fragment (dubious) |

\* Actual or probable Holocene context.

*Table 9.1. Pontnewydd Cave, list of hominin finds.*

Pitting, chipping, scratches and polish principally occur on erupted crowns and are consistent with *ante mortem* wear. Detailing is good on both crowns and roots, with no signs of erosion, crushing or rounding other than that resulting from *ante mortem* wear. Cracking of the enamel, which is likely to be due to *post mortem* factors, is only described for individual teeth where it deviates from the above. The locations at which all the stratified teeth were discovered are shown in Figure 9.1.

### Lower Breccia – Silt beds matrix

*PN10 (D4852) Figure 9.5*

TYPE: lower right lateral permanent incisor. This tooth has been identified as a lower lateral incisor, rather than an upper lateral, because of its symmetry, its relatively small mesiodistal dimension and the presence of a buccally facing occlusal facet. The shape of the interproximal wear facets suggests a lateral incisor, not a central incisor.

DEVELOPMENT STAGE: in occlusion.

COMPLETENESS:

  Crown – most of the cingulum is missing and also the mesial base of the crown.

  Root – only a fragment of the cervical part of the root on the distal and buccal sides is present.

CONDITION:

  Crown – there is a black deposit under the enamel, particularly around the cracks. Horizontal cracking is only found on the lingual surface.

  Root – stained dark brown externally.

SEASON: 1988.

LOCATION: K7SW (99.48–99.38).

### Lower Breccia

*PN18 (F4753) Figure 9.5*

TYPE: upper left fourth permanent premolar. The mesial and distal interproximal wear facets on this tooth are both large for the level of wear (in particular the distal facet) and horizontally elongate, and for this reason it has been identified as a fourth premolar rather than as a third. This identification is consistent with the morphology of the tooth.

DEVELOPMENT STAGE: in occlusion.

COMPLETENESS:

  Crown – complete.

  Root – only a narrow rim of root is present.

CONDITION:

  Crown – spots of black deposit are present, especially around the cervix.

  Root – there are black spots on the outside of the root, and a black deposit on the broken edges and in the pulp chamber.

SEASON: 1994.

LOCATION: I1NW (99.73–99.68).

*PN6 (D2261) Figure 9.5*

TYPE: lower right third permanent premolar.

DEVELOPMENT STAGE: not in occlusion. Root at least half developed.

COMPLETENESS:

  Crown – complete.

  Root – only the upper part of the root is present (7.7 mm).

CONDITION:

  Crown – patches of brown stain are present and a few black spots. There is a horizontal orange line in the centre of the buccal surface. The vertical cracks are stained black at the cervix.

  Root – stained brown with black spots.

SEASON: 1983.

LOCATION: J7SW (99.66–99.33).

*PN7 (D3970) Figure 9.5*

TYPE: lower left third permanent premolar (possible antimere of PN6).

DEVELOPMENT STAGE: erupted but not in occlusion. Root three-quarters developed (12.7 mm).

COMPLETENESS:

  Crown – complete.

  Root – the apical half of the mesial side is missing. The root has been damaged *post mortem* (tooth reconstructed by A. P. Currant).

CONDITION:

  Crown – there is black staining under the enamel at the cervix.

  Root – stained brown, with darker brown and black patches.

SEASON: 1985.

LOCATION: H6SW (99.26).

*PN5 (D2212) Figure 9.5*

TYPE: lower left fourth permanent premolar. The mesial interproximal wear facet is small and vertically elongate, which might suggest contact with a canine. However, the crown morphology has greater similarities to Middle Pleistocene fourth premolars than to third premolars, in particular the similar height of the buccal and mesiolingual cusps.

DEVELOPMENT STAGE: in occlusion.

COMPLETENESS:

  Crown – complete apart from missing fragments of enamel on the mesiobuccal and distobuccal corners at the cervix.

  Root – absent.

CONDITION:

  Crown – the buccal surface is stained light brown and there is black staining under the enamel at the cervix. The pulp chamber is stained black.

SEASON: 1983.

LOCATION: J7NW (99.18–99.08).

*PN4 (D1740) Figure 9.6*

TYPE: upper right first permanent molar. Found in position in a maxillary fragment that extends from the distal side of the third permanent premolar crypt to the mesial side of the second permanent molar root socket; present in conjunction with an upper right fourth deciduous premolar. Maxilla reconstructed by A. P. Currant.

DEVELOPMENT STAGE: in occlusion and fully developed.

COMPLETENESS:

  Crown – complete.

  Root – the apex of the lingual root is missing and the apex of the distobuccal root is chipped.

CONDITION:

  Crown – not stained.

  Root – not stained.

SEASON: 1982.

LOCATION: I8NE (98.95).

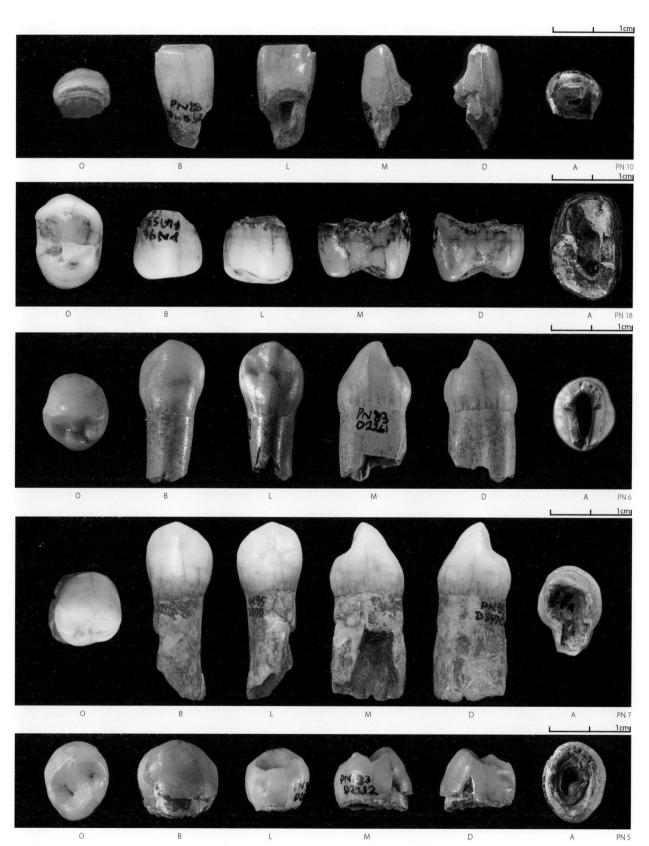

*Figure 9.5. The hominin teeth from Pontnewydd Cave.*

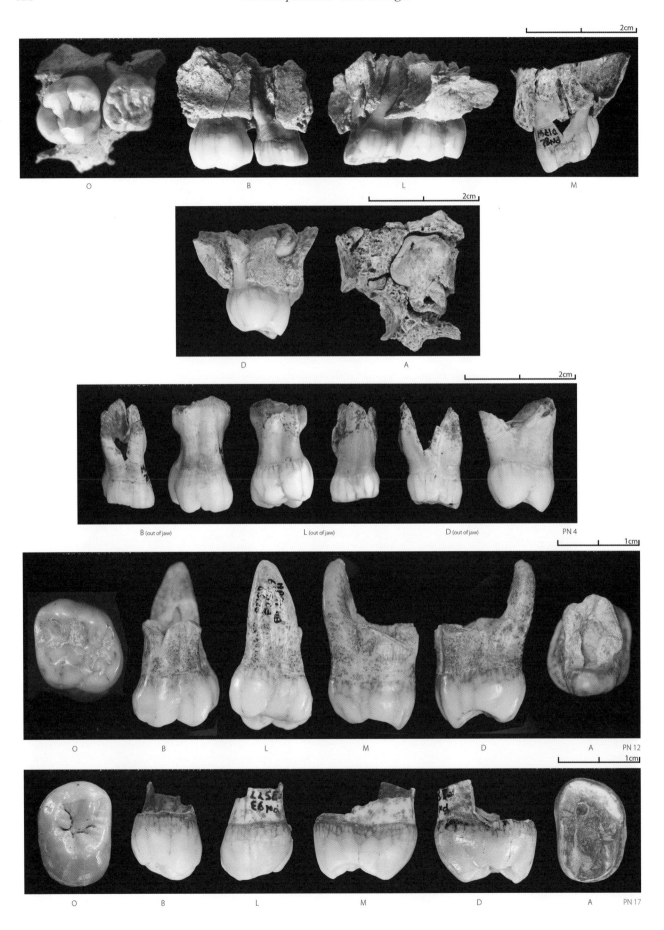

*Figure 9.6. The hominin teeth from Pontnewydd Cave.*

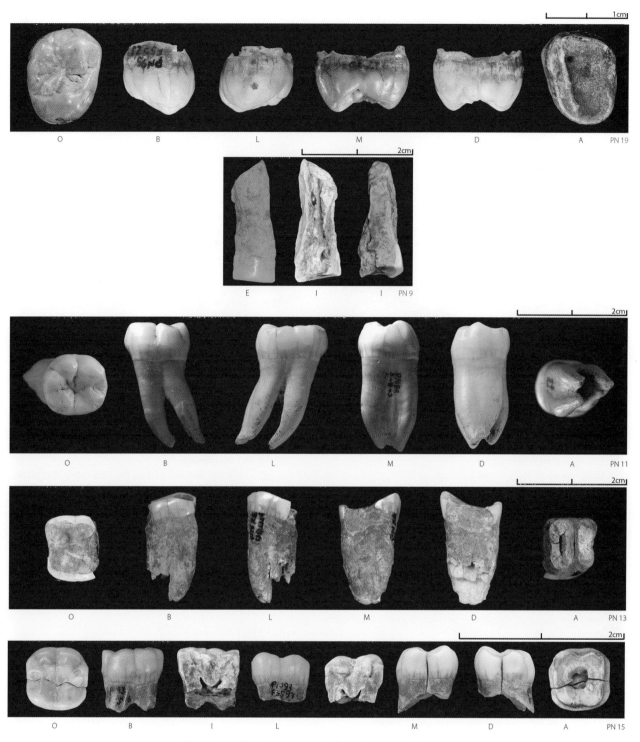

*Figure 9.7. The hominin teeth from Pontnewydd Cave.*

*PN12 (F2859) Figure 9.6*

TYPE: upper left first permanent molar. Smaller than PN4 but of similar shape and morphology.

DEVELOPMENT STAGE: in occlusion and fully developed.

COMPLETENESS:

Crown – complete.

Root – the buccal roots are missing beyond the root trunk.

CONDITION:

Crown – there is black staining under the enamel at the cervix and also on the occlusal surface.

Root – some brown staining with black spots.

SEASON: 1989.

LOCATION: I3NE (99.40–99.30).

*PN17 (F3577) Figure 9.6*

TYPE: upper right third permanent molar.

DEVELOPMENT STAGE: not in occlusion. Root initiated, grown to 3.9 mm.

COMPLETENESS:

Crown – complete. Slight, and irregular, *post mortem* facet present on tip of mesiolingual cusp.

Root – only the lingual side of the root trunk is present.

CONDITION:

Crown – there is dark brown staining around the cervix and light brown staining on the lingual side.

Root – there are brown spots on the outside of the root. The pulp chamber is stained black.

SEASON: 1993.

LOCATION: H2SW (99.23–99.18).

*PN19 (F5523) Figure 9.7*

TYPE: upper right third permanent molar.

DEVELOPMENT STAGE: not in occlusion. Root initiated, grown to 1.3 mm.

COMPLETENESS:

Crown – complete apart from the tip of the metaconule, which has been broken off *post mortem*.

Root – mesial and distal sides absent.

CONDITION:

Crown – there is brown staining of the crown, which is darker around the cervix.

Root – the root is stained dark brown and the pulp chamber is stained black.

SEASON: 1995.

LOCATION: H5SE (99.10–99.05).

*PN4 (D1741) Figure 9.6*

TYPE: upper right fourth deciduous premolar (sometimes known as a second deciduous molar). Found in position.

DEVELOPMENT STAGE: in occlusion and fully developed.

COMPLETENESS:

Crown – complete.

Root – apex of lingual root missing.

CONDITION:

Crown – there is black staining in the enamel cracks. Exposed dentine is stained brown.

Root – stained brown.

SEASON: 1982.

LOCATION: I8NE (98.95).

*PN9 (D2069) Figure 9.7*

TYPE: fragment of a permanent molar, possibly an upper molar from the shape of the root, which has a convex outward curve.

DEVELOPMENT STAGE: in occlusion.

COMPLETENESS:

Crown and root – this fragment consists of a small segment of very worn crown and part of the upper portion of a root, with the root canal exposed, measuring 14.6 mm from top to base. The occlusal surface consists of an enamel rim and exposed dentine.

CONDITION:

Crown – some black staining on exposed dentine and under the enamel.

Root – stained brown, with black staining in the pulp cavity.

SEASON: 1983.

LOCATION: I7SW (99.20–99.10).

*PN11 (D4843) Figure 9.7*

TYPE: lower left first permanent molar.

DEVELOPMENT STAGE: in occlusion and fully developed.

COMPLETENESS:

Crown – complete.

Root – complete.

CONDITION:

Crown – not stained.

Root – there are patches of dark brown staining.

SEASON: 1988.

LOCATION: G7SW (99.21).

*PN13 (D4029) Figure 9.7*

TYPE: lower right second permanent molar (identified as a first molar in Aldhouse-Green 1995). The shape of the roots and the size of the mesial interproximal facet suggest that this is a second molar rather than a first.

DEVELOPMENT STAGE: in occlusion and fully developed.

COMPLETENESS:

Crown – complete but most enamel on the mesial and distal sides of the tooth is missing because of wear.

Root – the distal root is missing below the point of fusion and the apex of the mesial root is damaged.

CONDITION:

Crown – the exposed dentine has light and dark brown staining.

Root – there is light and dark brown staining.

SEASON: 1985.

LOCATION: H7SE (99.10–99.00).

*PN15 (F3346 and F3597) Figure 9.7*

TYPE: lower right second permanent molar.

DEVELOPMENT STAGE: in occlusion.

COMPLETENESS:

Crown – complete but has been split into two mesiodistally along the mesiodistal occlusal groove. The two pieces were unearthed separately and fit exactly, the broken edges being sharp and unrounded.

Root – only the cervical part of the root trunk is present.

CONDITION:

Crown – there is light brown staining around the cervix and patches on the occlusal surface. The broken sides of the crown are stained dark brown/black. There is no horizontal cracking on the sides of the crown.

Root – stained dark brown externally and dark brown/black in the pulp chamber.

SEASON: 1993.

LOCATION: H4SE (99.35–99.33 and 99.33–99.31).

*PN16 (F3576) Figure 9.8*

TYPE: lower right third permanent molar.

DEVELOPMENT STAGE: in occlusion.

COMPLETENESS:

Crown – the mesiolingual corner of the enamel of the crown has been broken off *post mortem*.

Root – only 1.9 mm of the root trunk is present, on the distal half of the tooth.

CONDITION:

Crown – there is black staining under the enamel and black/dark brown stain in the pulp chamber.

SEASON: 1993.

LOCATION: H3SE (99.21–99.16).

*PN21 (F6095) Figure 9.8*

TYPE: lower right third permanent molar.

DEVELOPMENT STAGE: not in occlusion. Root initiated, grown to 1.3 mm.

COMPLETENESS:

Crown – complete. *Post mortem* chip on tip of distobuccal cusp.

Root – only mesial and lingual parts are present.

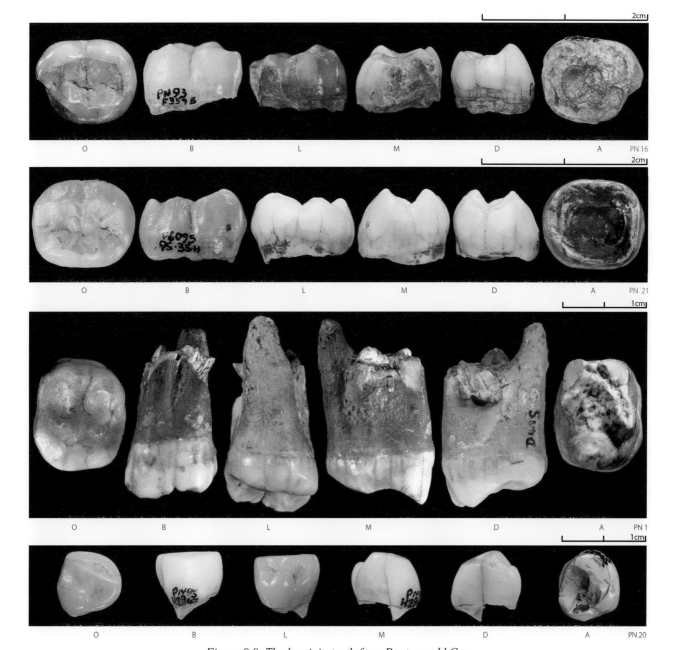

*Figure 9.8. The hominin teeth from Pontnewydd Cave.*

CONDITION:
> Crown – there is some light brown staining, with dark brown patches around the cervix, and black in the pulp chamber.

SEASON: 1995.
LOCATION: I5NE (99.17–99.12).

## Intermediate complex

*PN1 (D415) Figure 9.8*
TYPE: upper left second permanent molar.
DEVELOPMENT STAGE: in occlusion and fully developed.
COMPLETENESS:
> Crown – complete.
> Root – buccal roots missing beyond the root trunk.

CONDITION:
> Crown – there is some black staining under the enamel, and

traces of brown, and brown spots, on the buccal surface along the gingival line.
> Root – the root is an orange-brown colour.

SEASON: 1980.
LOCATION: H9SW/SE (98.92).

## Mudstone Gravel Unit (38) New Entrance

*PN20 (H2942) Figure 9.8*
TYPE: lower left third permanent premolar.
DEVELOPMENT STAGE: in occlusion.
COMPLETENESS:
> Crown – complete.
> Roots – absent apart from a very small mesiobuccal fragment.

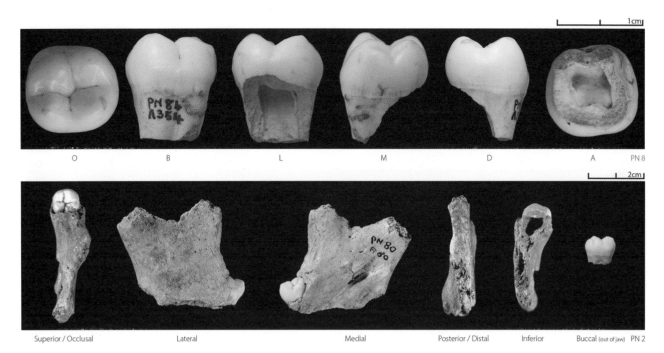

*Figure 9.9. The Mesolithic teeth from Pontnewydd Cave.*

CONDITION:
> Crown – no staining and no horizontal cracking.

SEASON: 1995.
LOCATION: AB994SE (97.60–99.50).

### World War II Dump, Mesolithic teeth

(PN2 has been dated at 7,420 BP±90 BP (OxA-5819; Aldhouse-Green *et al.* 1996). PN8 is assumed to be Mesolithic on account of its likely association with PN2.)

*PN8 (A354) Figure 9.9*
TYPE: lower right second permanent molar.
DEVELOPMENT STAGE: in occlusion.
COMPLETENESS:
> Crown – the cervical part of the lingual surface is missing.
> Root – only the cervical part of the root trunk on the buccal side is present (5.4 mm) with lesser amounts mesially and distally.

CONDITION:
> Crown – no staining and no horizontal cracking.
> Root – not stained. An irregular horizontal groove curves round the mesiobuccal corner of the buccal root (5 mm long).

SEASON: 1984.

*PN2 (A80) Figure 9.9*
TYPE: lower right third permanent molar. For a recent human the presence of a protostylid pit at the mesial end of the buccal surface, and a reduced distobuccal cusp, would suggest that this is a third molar. Found in position in a fragment of mandible.
DEVELOPMENT STAGE: not in occlusion. Grooves between mesial and distal roots distinct, a quarter of root formed overall (4.0 mm).
COMPLETENESS:

Crown – complete.
Root – part formed root complete apart from a fragment at the mesiolingual corner.
CONDITION:
> Crown – there is a slight horizontal band of brown stain at the cervix. There is no horizontal cracking of the enamel.
> Root – not stained.

SEASON: 1980.

### Note on identification of lower molars

It is difficult to differentiate between Middle Pleistocene lower molars on purely morphological grounds, particularly first and second molars:

*PN11 and PN15*
These teeth have the same level of occlusal wear. The distal interproximal wear facet on PN11 is very faint, whereas that on PN15 is large and well defined. If the Pontnewydd individuals were a cohesive group, it would be expected that the times of eruption of teeth would be approximately the same in different individuals. On this basis, PN11 and PN15 have to be identified as different teeth. PN11 has an 'X' groove pattern and so would normally be identified as a second molar, rather than as a first molar, although first molars with an 'X' pattern are not unknown (*e.g.* Arago 13). Nevertheless, there are aspects of the wear that would suggest otherwise.

MESIAL INTERPROXIMAL WEAR FACET
The mesial interproximal facet is small (3.3 × 3.3 mm). This is the same width as the mesial interproximal facets on the Ehringsdorf juvenile and Atapuerca-SH AT2 first molars (3.2 and 3.5 mm respectively). On both these teeth,

the level of wear is similar to that of PN11 and the adjacent permanent fourth premolar is erupting or has just erupted. In addition, the mesial interproximal facet on PN11 is on the buccal side of the tooth and slanted buccally (it is also placed slightly buccally on the Ehringsdorf juvenile first molar). A displacement of this nature is less likely to occur between first and second molars than between second and third molars or between fourth premolars and first molars (although the second molar of the Ehringsdorf juvenile is slightly rotated in an anticlockwise direction). (However, see comments by Legoux (1961) relating to the way in which the Ehringsdorf juvenile mandible was reconstructed by Virchow). The mesial interproximal facet on PN15, conversely, is centrally placed, horizontally elongated and much wider (5.3 mm), of similar size to the distal interproximal facet. For a tooth with similar wear to that of PN11, this suggests that it was in contact with a permanent molar mesially as well as distally.

Distal interproximal wear facet
There is some evidence (discussed below) that, in Middle Pleistocene and Neanderthal teeth, the time between eruption of second and third molars could be less than that between first and second molars. The tooth with the larger distal interproximal facet would therefore be expected to be a second molar. In support of this it has been noted that in six Middle Pleistocene specimens there is a third molar in occlusion and no dentine exposure on the second molars. On PN11 there is dentine exposure, whilst the tooth distal to it is newly erupted.

Buccal phase 1 facets
On PN11 there are large buccal phase 1 facets on the distobuccal cusp (distally) and cusp 5 (mesially) but they are very faint on the mesiobuccal cusp. The same situation, of large phase 1 facets on the distobuccal cusp but not on the mesiobuccal cusp, is encountered on the first molars of the Ehringsdorf juvenile and Atapuerca-SH AT2 specimens, and suggests contact mesially with a tooth with worn down buccal cusps, as seen on the PN4 upper fourth deciduous premolar. Conversely, the buccal phase 1 facets on PN15 are distinct and of the same size on both mesial and distal cusps (two on each). This pattern is found on the Atapuerca-SH AT1 second molar and AT75 second and third molars.

If PN11 is identified as a first molar and PN15 as a second molar, as is indicated by the above, then the distal interproximal facets on the two teeth are similar in size and development to those on the corresponding upper molars with similar levels of wear. A contrary argument to the above is the level of taurodontism in PN11. This would be more typical of a European Middle Pleistocene lower second or third molar (see below). In this paper, PN11 is taken to be, on balance, a lower first molar and PN15 more certainly a lower second molar.

*PN21*
On morphological grounds this tooth is most likely to be a third molar because of the absence of both a mesial marginal ridge and a mid trigonid crest, the rounded distal end (viewed occlusally) and the reduced size of the distolingual cusp compared with those of PN11 and PN15.

*PN16*
This tooth has almost identical crown measurements to PN21, and the same rounded distal end and reduced distolingual cusp. It seems likely therefore that it is also a third molar. The central placement of cusp five would anyway make it unlikely that it was a first molar.

### The identification of the premolars
*PN6 and PN7*
These two teeth have nearly identical measurements and are at the same stage of development. As described below there are specific minor differences in root and crown morphology. However, asymmetry in the degree of development of certain morphological traits between antimeres is not uncommon (Scott and Turner 1997). Notwithstanding this, the overall shape of the crowns of the two teeth is very similar and it seems reasonable to assume that they are antimeres, as suggested in Green *et al.* (1989). The similar levels and position of hypoplasia on the two teeth supports this assumption.

### Tooth measurements
### Method
Measurements taken on each tooth are:
- Mesiodistal crown diameter (length)
- Buccolingual crown diameter (breadth)
- Crown height
- Root length (each root measured)
- Root robusticity
- Root trunk length (measured between each root).

Different sliding callipers were used for each measurement:
- Length – callipers with needle-points
- Breadth and root robusticity – bull-nosed callipers with flat surfaces
- Crown height, root length and root trunk length – callipers with the upper arm longer than the lower to allow measurements to be taken along a line parallel to the long axis of the tooth.

Each measurement is recorded to the nearest 0.1 mm.

Definitions used for mesiodistal crown diameter, buccolingual crown diameter, crown height and root length are those of Moorrees (1957).

### Mesiodistal crown diameter
'The greatest mesiodistal dimension of the tooth crown, measured parallel to the (original) occlusal and labial surfaces' (Moorrees 1957). This definition is interpreted as being the greatest dimension between two points ('Length 1' in Table 9.2) rather than the distance between two parallel planes touching the mesial and distal surfaces (as is the case in the methods of Korenhof 1960 and Tobias 1967).

| Tooth type | Tooth identity | Length 1 (MD) mm | Length 2 (see text) mm | Length 3 (see text) mm | Breadth (BL) mm | Crown height mm | Wear Grade |
|---|---|---|---|---|---|---|---|
| Left P⁴ | PN18 | 8.4 | | | 11.4 | 7.7 | 3 |
| Right M¹ | PN4 | 12.2 | 12.8 | 12.0 | 12.4 | 6.8 | 3 |
| Left M¹ | PN12 | 11.2 | 12.2 | 10.9 | 11.1 | 5.4 | 3 |
| Left M² | PN1 | 10.9 | 11.5 | 10.8 | 13.3 | 4.4 | 3/4 |
| Right M³ | PN17 | 9.4 | 10.0 | 9.0 | 12.3 | 6.6 | 0 |
| Right M³ | PN19 | 9.5 | 9.9 | 9.0 | 11.4 | 6.3 | 0 |
| Rt dm²/dp⁴ | PN4 | 9.2 | 9.9 | 9.0 | 10.3 | 5.4 | 5 |
| Right I₂ | PN10 | 7.1 | | | (6.8) | 9.6 | 4 |
| Right P₃ | PN6 | 8.1 | | | 9.3 | 8.8 | 0 |
| Left P₃ | PN7 | 8.3 | | | 9.3 | 9.0 | 0 |
| Left P₃ | PN20 | 8.2 | | | 9.0 | 6.8 | 4 |
| Left P₄ | PN5 | 8.0 | | | 9.5 | 7.6 | 2 |
| Left M₁ | PN11 | 12.4 | | | 11.2 | 7.1 | 3 |
| Right M₂ | PN13 | (10.0) | | | 11.6 | 3.9 | 6 |
| Right M₂ | PN15 | 11.7 | | | 11.4 | 6.0 | 3 |
| Right M₃ | PN16 | 12.6 | | | 10.6 | 6.6 | 2 |
| Right M₃ | PN21 | 12.8 | | | 10.9 | 7.6 | 0 |
| Right M₂ | PN8 | 11.3 | | | 10.7 | 6.6 | 2 |
| Right M₃ | PN2 | 11.0 | | | 10.5 | 6.9 | 0 |

*Table 9.2. Crown measurements of Pontnewydd teeth.*

The latter interpretation can give a considerably larger figure for upper molars. The dimensions found for the upper molars using this second interpretation are given as 'Length 2' in Table 9.2. 'Length 1' is the length used to compute crown area and crown index, and when making comparisons with other specimens.

The interpretation of Moorrees' method (1957) used is the same as that applied by Frayer (1978) when measuring Neanderthal and early Upper Palaeolithic teeth. He describes the mesiodistal diameter as being the sagittal-horizontal distance measured wherever the greatest distance occurs. This contrasts with the method used by Wolpoff (1971) (measuring Krapina and later Neanderthal teeth) who measures between the mid-points of the inter-tooth contact surfaces. Frayer (1978) compared his method with that of Wolpoff and observed, on unworn or slightly worn teeth, that the differences were no greater than, and in most cases less than, 0.5 mm or 1–3 %. The difference was more pronounced on moderate to heavily worn teeth, with Frayer's method generally giving higher lengths than Wolpoff's method. Measuring the Pontnewydd teeth using both methods either gives identical results or Frayer's

method gives lengths up to 0.3 mm greater. Bermúdez de Castro (1986) uses the method of Lefèvre (1973) to measure the Atapuerca-SH teeth. In this method the mesiodistal diameter of molars is defined as the maximum measurement at right angles to the mesial surface. Again, this can make a considerable difference when measuring upper molars, and the lengths of the Pontnewydd upper molars measured using this method are given as 'Length 3' in Table 9.2. Lefèvre (1973) calculated correspondence coefficients for the difference between his method and what he refers to as the classical geometric method (*i.e.* that used by Frayer 1978) which generally gives higher figures. These ratios were 1.04 for upper molars and 1.015 for lower molars.

The direction of the buccal and mesial surfaces is taken as being the direction at the occlusal margin, not at the cervix. Where a tooth is rotated, the inferred mesial, distal and buccal surfaces are used.

### Buccolingual crown diameter

'The greatest distance between the labial and lingual surfaces of the tooth crown in a plane perpendicular to that in which the mesiodistal diameter was measured'

| Tooth identity | Measured length mm | Mesial adjustment mm | Distal adjustment mm | Estimated original length mm |
|---|---|---|---|---|
| PN1* | 10.9 | 0.35 | 0.35 | 11.6 |
| PN4 (dec)* | 9.2 | 0.3 | 0.3 | 9.8 |
| PN12 | 11.2 | 0.1 | 0.0 | 11.3 |
| PN15* | 11.7 | 0.5 | 0.5 | 12.7 |
| PN16 | 12.6 | 0.2 | 0.0 | 12.8 |
| PN18 | 8.4 | 0.2 | 0.0 | 8.6 |
| PN20* | 8.2 | 0.4 | 0.0 | 8.6 |

*Table 9.3. Estimated original tooth lengths.*

(Moorrees 1957). Unlike the mesiodistal crown diameter, this measurement is taken as being the maximum between two planes, not between two points, as described by Tobias (1967). For incisors and canines, the buccolingual crown diameter is measured as the maximum in a buccolingual direction, which may not be exactly at right angles to the labial surface. This slightly amended definition makes it easier to replicate measurements. In the method of Lefèvre (1973), used by Bermúdez de Castro (1986), the buccolingual dimension of upper molars is measured at right angles to the buccal surface and of lower molars at right angles to the lingual surface.

### Crown height

'The distance between the tip of the mesiobuccal (or only buccal) cusp and the deepest point of the cemento-enamel junction on the vestibular side (of the cusp) measured along a line parallel to the long axis of the tooth' (Moorrees 1957). In the case of upper molars the mesiolingual cusp is measured on the lingual side.

### Root length

'The distance between the apex of the mesiobuccal root and the deepest point of the cemento-enamel junction on the vestibular side (of the root) measured along a line parallel to the long axis of the tooth' (Moorrees 1957). All roots are measured in this study, on the buccal side for roots with a buccal surface, otherwise on the lingual side.

### Root robusticity

'The robustness of the root is expressed by the product of the length and breadth measurements immediately below the neck of the tooth' (Weidenreich 1937). The length is measured in a direction perpendicular to the mesial side of the root at the cervix, and the breadth perpendicular to the buccal side. Both measurements are made in a direction parallel to the cervix.

### Root trunk length

The distance between the deepest part of the cemento-enamel junction (ignoring any enamel extensions) and the point at which the individual roots become clearly defined (though not necessarily separated), measured along a line parallel to the long axis of the tooth. The measurement is made between each pair of roots on each side of the tooth.

Where there is dental calculus on a tooth, a measurement is only used when the thickness of the dental calculus can be estimated and an adjustment made.

On worn teeth, length/breadth measurements are not used if the sides of the tooth at the occlusal edge are not either vertical or curving inwards towards the occlusal surface and crown height measurements are made to the highest remaining point of the relevant cusp.

### Occlusal dimensions

The interproximal wear on most of the Pontnewydd teeth is minor but, on certain teeth, it can be clearly seen that the occlusal outline has been truncated. On these teeth it is possible to infer the original occlusal outline from the shape of the remaining parts of the occlusal edge adjacent to the interproximal wear facet, and so to estimate the reduction in the mesiodistal dimension resulting from wear. This has been done with the aid of enlarged photographs of the occlusal surface (method used by Wood and Abbott 1983). Where possible, relatively unworn teeth have been studied to provide guidance, PN6 for PN20 and PN11 for PN15. The results are listed in Table 9.3. Where the estimated original length is within 0.2 mm of the measured length, it is considered that this is within measurement error and the measured length is still used. However, for the four most worn teeth (marked by an asterisk in Table 9.3) the estimated original length is used in place of the measured length for calculation of crown area and crown index, and for comparison with other specimens, and is the length shown in Tables 9.4–9.6, and 9.18. It is not possible to make any estimate of the original length of the very worn PN13.

The occlusal dimensions (given in millimetres) for the Pontnewydd teeth, the Gran Dolina teeth and individual European Middle Pleistocene teeth are listed in Tables 9.4–9.6. Because of the level of asymmetry in some Middle Pleistocene teeth (*e.g.* the Ehringsdorf adult, possibly due to the level of wear), the right and left measurements are averaged where both measurements for both antimeres are reported. The average (mean) dimensions for teeth from the sites of Atapuerca-SH (Spain) and Krapina (Croatia), a European later Neanderthal sample and a European early Upper Palaeolithic sample are also shown. The sources for the dimensions are listed in Table 9.7. The sites included in the later Neanderthal and early Upper Palaeolithic samples are listed in Table 9.8.

Table 9.4. Comparative occlusal measurements for $P^4$, $M^{1-3}$ (mm).

| Tooth ID/sample | UPPER FOURTH PREMOLAR | | | | | UPPER FIRST MOLAR | | | | | UPPER SECOND MOLAR | | | | | UPPER THIRD MOLAR | | | | |
|---|---|---|---|---|---|---|---|---|---|---|---|---|---|---|---|---|---|---|---|---|
| | 'n' | Length (MD) | Breadth (BL) | Crown area | Crown index | 'n' | Length (MD) | Breadth (BL) | Crown area | Crown index | 'n' | Length (MD) | Breadth (BL) | Crown area | Crown index | 'n' | Length (MD) | Breadth (BL) | Crown area | Crown index |
| **GRAN DOLINA** | | | | | | | | | | | | | | | | | | | | |
| Hominid 1 | | 8.1 | 11.7 | 94 | 145 | | 12.1 | 13.0 | 157 | 107 | | 12.1 | 13.7 | 166 | 113 | | | | | |
| Hominid 3 | | | 11.6 | | | | 12.0 | 12.1 | 144 | 101 | | | | | | | | | | |
| **EARLIER MID PLEISTOCENE** | | | | | | | | | | | | | | | | | | | | |
| Arago Individual 7 | | 7.0 | 10.1 | 71 | 144 | | | | | | | | | | | | | | | |
| Arago XIV | | | | | | | 11.7 | 12.3 | 144 | 105 | | 12.4 | 16.0 | 198 | 129 | | | | | |
| Arago XXI | | | | | | | | | | | | 11.7 | 13.1 | 153 | 112 | | 9.0 | 11.4 | 103 | 127 |
| Arago XXXI | | | | | | | | | | | | 12.6 | 14.6 | 184 | 116 | | | | | |
| Petralona | | 8.0 | 11.9 | 95 | 149 | | 12.2 | 13.0 | 159 | 107 | | 11.6 | 13.7 | 159 | 118 | | 10.3 | 13.0 | 134 | 126 |
| Visogliano 5/6/3/1 | | 7.7 | 10.9 | 84 | 142 | | 12.0 | 12.9 | 155 | 108 | | 10.4 | 12.7 | 132 | 122 | | 10.7 | 12.3 | 132 | 115 |
| **ATAPUERCA-SH X̄** | 12 | 7.6 | 10.4 | 79 | 137 | 16 | 11.1 | 11.5 | 128 | 104 | 17 | 9.9 | 12.1 | 120 | 122 | 19 | 8.6 | 11.5 | 99 | 134 |
| Range | | (7.1-8.4) | (9.5-11.3) | (72-94) | (130-144) | | (9.9-12.3) | (10.3-13.0) | (120-150) | (99-111) | | (8.1-11.6) | (11.0-13.8) | (110-160) | (117-127) | | (7.4-9.3) | (10.1-13.0) | (81-121) | (126-140) |
| SD | | 0.5 | 0.6 | 8 | 6 | | 0.6 | 0.7 | 12 | 5 | | 0.9 | 0.8 | 20 | 4 | | 0.6 | 0.9 | 14 | 5 |
| **LATER MID PLEISTOCENE** | | | | | | | | | | | | | | | | | | | | |
| Bilzingsleben C1 | | 8.0 | 10.9 | 87 | 136 | | 12.0 | 13.0 | 156 | 108 | | | | | | | | | | |
| Montmaurin CG14 | | | | | | | | | | | | | | | | | | | | |
| Steinheim | | 7.1 | 9.3 | 66 | 131 | | 11.7 | 12.4 | 145 | 106 | | 10.8* | 12.5* | 135 | 116 | | 8.8 | 10.2 | 90 | 116 |
| Biache | | 8.3 | 10.7 | 89 | 129 | | 11.9 | 11.9 | 142 | 100 | | 11.6 | 12.0 | 139 | 103 | | 10.3 | 11.8 | 122 | 115 |
| Pesada 2 | | | | | | | | | | | | | | | | | 9.8 | 13.2 | 129 | 135 |
| **PONTNEWYDD** | | | | | | | | | | | | | | | | | | | | |
| PN18 | | 8.4 | 11.4 | 96 | 136 | | | | | | | | | | | | | | | |
| PN4 | | | | | | | | | | | | | | | | | | | | |
| PN12 | | | | | | | | | | | | | | | | | | | | |
| PN1 | | | | | | | 12.2 | 12.4 | 151 | 102 | | 11.6 | 13.3 | 154 | 115 | | | | | |
| PN17 | | | | | | | 11.2 | 11.1 | 124 | 99 | | | | | | | 9.4 | 12.3 | 116 | 131 |
| PN19 | | | | | | | | | | | | | | | | | 9.5 | 11.4 | 108 | 120 |
| **KRAPINA X̄** | 12 | 8.1 | 10.9 | 89 | 135 | 9 | 12.4 | 12.6 | 157 | 101 | 10 | 11.1 | 12.8 | 142 | 116 | 9 | 10.4 | 12.5 | 130 | 120 |
| Range | | (6.8-8.8) | (10.4-11.7) | (70-103) | (121-152) | | (11.3-13.6) | (11.3-14.2) | (128-185) | (95-109) | | (10.0-13.1) | (11.7-14.2) | (118-175) | (100-130) | | (9.8-11.4) | (11.7-13.5) | (114-149) | (110-129) |
| SD | | 0.6 | 0.4 | 10 | 8 | | 0.8 | 1.0 | 21 | 3 | | 1.2 | 0.7 | 22 | 9 | | 0.6 | 0.6 | 12 | 6 |
| **NEANDERTHAL X̄** | 9 | 7.2 | 10.7 | 76 | 150 | 18 | 11.2 | 12.1 | 137 | 109 | 11 | 10.4 | 12.9 | 135 | 124 | 9 | 9.8 | 12.3 | 121 | 126 |
| Range | | (6.5-8.0) | (9.8-12.0) | (63-88) | (131-185) | | (10.0-12.6) | (11.2-13.0) | (112-158) | (99-130) | | (9.6-11.5) | (10.7-14.5) | (105-160) | (109-142) | | (8.8-11.0) | (11.3-13.9) | (102-133) | (109-145) |
| SD | | 0.6 | 0.7 | 8 | 18 | | 0.9 | 0.6 | 12 | 10 | | 0.7 | 1.2 | 17 | 12 | | 0.8 | 0.8 | 11 | 14 |
| **EARLY UPPER PALAEOLITHIC X̄** | 15 | 7.1 | 9.7 | 70 | 138 | 23 | 10.7 | 12.3 | 133 | 115 | 19 | 10.6 | 12.3 | 131 | 117 | 12 | 9.5 | 11.5 | 110 | 119 |
| Range | | (6.2-7.9) | (8.5-11.2) | (55-88) | (123-145) | | (9.1-12.0) | (11.0-14.0) | (102-165) | (107-133) | | (8.9-11.8) | (10.8-13.8) | (96-159) | (103-130) | | (7.7-11.1) | (9.2-13.2) | (78-145) | (107-145) |
| SD | | 0.5 | 0.7 | 10 | 6 | | 0.8 | 0.7 | 16 | 6 | | 0.8 | 1.0 | 19 | 7 | | 1.0 | 1.2 | 21 | 11 |

*left tooth. The sources for the dimensions are listed in table 9.7 and the sites included in the Neanderthal and Early Upper Palaeolithic samples are listed in table 9.8.

| Tooth ID/sample | LOWER SECOND INCISOR | | | | | LOWER THIRD PREMOLAR | | | | | LOWER FOURTH PREMOLAR | | | | |
|---|---|---|---|---|---|---|---|---|---|---|---|---|---|---|---|
| | 'n' | Length (MD) | Breadth (BL) | Crown area | Crown index | 'n' | Length (MD) | Breadth (BL) | Crown area | Crown index | 'n' | Length (MD) | Breadth (BL) | Crown area | Crown index |
| **GRAN DOLINA** | | | | | | | | | | | | | | | |
| **Hominid 1** | | 7.0 | 7.8 | 55 | 111 | | 8.8 | 10.6 | 93 | 120 | | 8.2 | 10.2 | 84 | 124 |
| **Hominid 4** | | 7.6 | 7.7 | 59 | 101 | | | | | | | | | | |
| **Hominid 7** | | | | | | | 8.0 | 9.7 | 78 | 121 | | 7.6 | 9.4 | 71 | 124 |
| **EARLIER MID PLEISTOCENE** | | | | | | | | | | | | | | | |
| **Mauer** | | 6.0 | 7.8 | 47 | 130 | | 8.1 | 9.0 | 73 | 111 | | 7.5 | 9.2 | 69 | 123 |
| **Arago II** | | | | | | | | | | | | 7.3 | 9.2 | 67 | 126 |
| **Arago XIII** | | | | | | | | | | | | 8.7 | 11.6 | 101 | 133 |
| **Arago XXV** | | 7.9 | 8.6 | 68 | 109 | | 8.9 | 11.5 | 102 | 129 | | | | | |
| **Arago XXVIII** | | | | | | | | | | | | 8.8 | 10.2 | 90 | 116 |
| **Boxgrove 2/3** | | | 7.4 | | | | | | | | | | | | |
| **ATAPUERCA-SH** X̄ | 11 | 6.6 | 7.3 | 48 | 111 | 19 | 7.9 | 8.9 | 71 | 113 | 23 | 7.2 | 8.6 | 62 | 119 |
| Range | | (6.2-7.5) | (6.7-8.1) | (42-56) | (97-117) | | (7.2-9.0) | (7.9-10.0) | (57-90) | (106-119) | | (6.0-8.0) | (7.2-10.1) | (49-79) | (106-143) |
| SD | | 0.3 | 0.4 | 4 | 6 | | 0.4 | 0.6 | 10 | 4 | | 0.5 | 0.6 | 10 | 10 |
| **LATER MID PLEISTOCENE** | | | | | | | | | | | | | | | |
| **Ehringsdorf - Adult** | | 6.5 | 8.1 | 53 | 125 | | 7.9 | 8.5 | 67 | 108 | | 7.7 | 9.6 | 74 | 125 |
| **Juvenile** | | 7.2 | 7.5 | 54 | 104 | | 8.2 | 8.5 | 70 | 104 | | 8.0 | 9.0 | 72 | 113 |
| **PONTNEWYDD** | | | | | | | | | | | | | | | |
| **PN10** | | 7.1 | (6.8) | | | | | | | | | | | | |
| **PN6** | | | | | | | 8.1 | 9.3 | 75 | 115 | | | | | |
| **PN7** | | | | | | | 8.3 | 9.3 | 77 | 112 | | | | | |
| **PN20** | | | | | | | 8.6 | 9.0 | 77 | 105 | | | | | |
| **PN5** | | | | | | | | | | | | 8.0 | 9.5 | 76 | 119 |
| **KRAPINA** X̄ | 9 | 6.8 | 8.0 | 55 | 118 | 11 | 8.3 | 9.4 | 78 | 112 | 13 | 8.1 | 9.6 | 78 | 119 |
| Range | | (6.1-7.5) | (7.3-8.8) | (47-66) | (108-144) | | (7.8-9.2) | (8.7-10.3) | (68-94) | (105-116) | | (6.9-9.4) | (8.8-10.5) | (65-87) | (98-137) |
| SD | | 0.5 | 0.5 | 6 | 10 | | 0.4 | 0.5 | 8 | 3 | | 0.6 | 0.5 | 7 | 11 |
| **NEANDERTHAL** X̄ | 12 | 6.9 | 7.9 | 53 | 117 | 16 | 8.0 | 9.3 | 75 | 117 | 19 | 7.7 | 9.2 | 72 | 121 |
| Range | | (6.0-7.8) | (7.2-8.2) | (48-62) | (103-133) | | (6.8-10.0) | (7.8-11.3) | (61-113) | (95-133) | | (6.0-10.5) | (7.5-11.4) | (51-119) | (103-142) |
| SD | | 0.6 | 0.5 | 6 | 11 | | 0.7 | 1.0 | 14 | 12 | | 0.9 | 1.1 | 16 | 12 |
| **EARLY UPPER PALAEOLITHIC** X̄ | 17 | 6.4 | 7.0 | 44 | 109 | 12 | 7.4 | 8.5 | 64 | 117 | 10 | 7.5 | 8.8 | 66 | 118 |
| Range | | (5.0-7.3) | (6.0-8.5) | (34-54) | (95-140) | | (6.2-8.1) | (7.8-9.3) | (48-74) | (103-126) | | (6.6-8.5) | (8.0-10.1) | (53-86) | (112-124) |
| SD | | 0.7 | 0.5 | 12 | 12 | | 0.5 | 0.5 | 7 | 7 | | 0.5 | 0.6 | 9 | 4 |

The sources for the dimensions are listed in Table 9.7 and the sites included in the Neanderthal and Early Upper Palaeolithic samples are listed in Table 9.8.

Table 9.5. Comparative occlusal measurements for $I_2$, $P_{3-4}$ (mm).

| Tooth id/sample | *'n'* | *Length (MD) mm* | *Breadth (BL) mm* | *Crown area* | *Crown index* | *'n'* | *Length (MD) mm* | *Breadth (BL) mm* | *Crown area* | *Crown index* | *'n'* | *Length (MD) mm* | *Breadth (BL) mm* | *Crown area* | *Crown index* |
|---|---|---|---|---|---|---|---|---|---|---|---|---|---|---|---|
| | | *LOWER FIRST MOLAR* | | | | | *LOWER SECOND MOLAR* | | | | | *LOWER THIRD MOLAR* | | | |
| **GRAN DOLINA** | | | | | | | | | | | | | | | |
| Hominid 1 | | 12.2 | 11.8 | 144 | 97 | | 13.5 | 12.0 | 162 | 89 | | | | | |
| Hominid 7 | | 11.5 | 11.0 | 127 | 96 | | 12.3 | 11.0 | 135 | 89 | | 9.2 | 8.8 | 81 | 96 |
| **EARLIER MID PLEISTOCENE** | | | | | | | | | | | | | | | |
| Mauer | | 11.6 | 11.2 | 130 | 97 | | 12.7 | 12.0 | 152 | 94 | | 11.9 | 11.1 | 132 | 93 |
| Arago II | | 11.2 | 10.8 | 121 | 96 | | 11.9 | 10.9 | 130 | 92 | | 10.4 | 9.5 | 99 | 91 |
| Arago XIII | | 13.5 | 13.0 | 176 | 96 | | 14.4 | 13.8 | 199 | 96 | | 13.2 | 12.5 | 165 | 95 |
| Arago XXXII | | | | | | | 14.8 | 12.4 | 184 | 84 | | | | | |
| **ATAPUERCA-SH** $\overline{X}$ | 23 | 11.2 | 10.4 | 116 | 93 | 26 | 11.0 | 10.2 | 112 | 93 | 26 | 11.3 | 9.8 | 111 | 87 |
| Range | | (10.3–12.1) | (9.6–11.6) | (100–137) | (89–101) | | (9.9–12.1) | (9.3–11.5) | (89–123) | (89–100) | | (10.0–12.9) | (8.6–11.3) | (82–144) | (81–98) |
| SD | | 0.5 | 0.5 | 10 | 4 | | 0.5 | 0.5 | 10 | 3 | | 0.7 | 0.7 | 17 | 4 |
| **LATER MID PLEISTOCENE** | | | | | | | | | | | | | | | |
| Bilzingsleben E2/E1 | | (14.0)# | 11.1 | (155) | (79) | | 12.5 | 10.5 | 131 | 84 | | 12.8 | 10.5 | 134 | 82 |
| Montmaurin | | 11.7 | 10.5 | 122 | 90 | | 11.7 | 10.9 | 126 | 93 | | 12.6 | 11.0 | 139 | 87 |
| Montmaurin CG 2D3 | | | | | | | | | | | | 11.4* | 9.5* | 108 | 83 |
| Ehringsdorf – Adult | | 12.2 | 10.9 | 133 | 89 | | 12.8 | 11.0 | 141 | 86 | | 12.0 | 11.0 | 132 | 92 |
| Juvenile | | 12.0 | 10.4 | 125 | 87 | | 12.8 | 10.7 | 137 | 84 | | | | | |
| **PONTNEWYDD** | | | | | | | | | | | | | | | |
| PN11 | | 12.4 | 11.2 | 139 | 90 | | | | | | | | | | |
| PN13 | | | | | | | (10.0) | 11.6 | | | | | | | |
| PN15 | | | | | | | 12.7 | 11.4 | 145 | 90 | | | | | |
| PN16 | | | | | | | | | | | | 12.6 | 10.6 | 134 | 84 |
| PN21 | | | | | | | | | | | | 12.8 | 10.9 | 140 | 85 |
| **KRAPINA** $\overline{X}$ | 14 | 12.5 | 11.5 | 143 | 92 | 12 | 12.7 | 11.5 | 147 | 90 | 11 | 12.2 | 10.8 | 132 | 89 |
| Range | | (11.4–13.6) | (10.2–12.9) | (116–175) | (84–97) | | (11.5–14.0) | (9.8–12.4) | (113–172) | (85–96) | | (11.2–13.9) | (9.8–11.4) | (117–156) | (76–96) |
| SD | | 0.8 | 0.8 | 18 | 3 | | 0.8 | 0.7 | 16 | 4 | | 0.7 | 0.5 | 11 | 6 |
| **NEANDERTHAL** $\overline{X}$ | 21 | 11.8 | 11.1 | 131 | 94 | 18 | 11.8 | 11.3 | 134 | 96 | 15 | 11.9 | 11.4 | 137 | 96 |
| Range | | (10.7–14.0) | (9.6–12.6) | (103–176) | (84–102) | | (10.8–13.7) | (10.0–12.6) | (115–170) | (84–105) | | (10.8–13.0) | (10.5–12.7) | (114–160) | (87–106) |
| SD | | 0.8 | 0.7 | 16 | 4 | | 0.7 | 0.7 | 15 | 6 | | 0.7 | 0.7 | 15 | 5 |
| **EARLY UPPER PALAEOLITHIC** $\overline{X}$ | 26 | 11.6 | 10.9 | 127 | 95 | 21 | 11.3 | 10.8 | 122 | 97 | 11 | 11.2 | 10.7 | 121 | 96 |
| Range | | (10.0–13.0) | (10.0–12.0) | (101–150) | (85–109) | | (9.5–12.8) | (9.8–12.0) | (95–154) | (89–107) | | (9.5–13.0) | (9.3–12.5) | (88–153) | (85–102) |
| SD | | 0.9 | 0.6 | 15 | 6 | | 1.0 | 0.8 | 19 | 5 | | 1.3 | 1.0 | 24 | 5 |

# estimate  * right tooth, left reduced  The sources for the dimensions are listed in Table 9.7 and the sites included in the Neanderthal and Early Upper Palaeolithic samples are listed in Table 9.8.

*Table 9.6. Comparative occlusal measurements for* $M_{1–3}$ *mm.*

| Site/sample | Source |
|---|---|
| **Arago** | Genet-Varcin (1976) (Individual 7, $P^4$) |
| | Bermúdez de Castro & Aguirre (1987) (remainder) |
| **Biache** | Measured by C. B. Stringer |
| **Bilzingsleben** | Vlček & Mania (1987) (Lower Molars) |
| | Vlček (1978) (Upper Molar) |
| **Boxgrove** | Hillson *et al.* (2006) |
| **Ehringsdorf** | Vlček (1993) (juvenile $M_3$) |
| | Remainder measured by C. B. Stringer |
| **Gran Dolina** | Carbonell *et al.* (2005) and J. M. Bermúdez de Castro (personal communication) (Hominid 7) |
| | Bermúdez de Castro *et al.* (1999b) (remainder) |
| **Mauer** | Twiesselmann (1973) ($I_2$) |
| | Howell (1960) (remainder) |
| **Montmaurin** | Billy & Vallois (1977) (Mandible) |
| | Billy (1982) (Isolated) |
| **Pesada** | Trinkaus *et al.* (2003) |
| **Petralona** | Stringer *et al.* (1979) |
| **Steinheim** | Wolpoff (1971) |
| **Visogliano** | Mallegni *et al.* (2002) |
| **Atapuerca-SH** | Bermúdez de Castro *et al.* (2004a) except for: |
| |   1.  Third molars – M. Martinón-Torres (pers. comm.) |
| |   2.  Ranges and SDs for crown areas and crown indices: |
| |       a.  Bermúdez de Castro (1986; 1988; 1993) (upper teeth) |
| |       b.  Bermúdez de Castro & Nicolás (1995) (lower teeth) |
| **Krapina** | Wolpoff (1979) |
| **Neanderthal** | Frayer (1978) and Wolpoff (1971) |
| **Early Upper Palaeolithic** | Frayer (1978) |

*Table 9.7. Sources for comparative occlusal measurements.*

Crown area (the buccolingual dimension multiplied by the mesiodistal dimension) is given for each entry in the tables, as also is crown index (buccolingual dimension divided by mesiodistal dimension, stated as a percentage). These are rounded to the nearest whole number. For each sample, each mean figure is followed by the range of values reported and the standard deviation. The number of teeth in each sample is given against each tooth. The most recent measurements available for Atapuerca-SH teeth do not include figures for the range of values, or standard deviation, for crown areas or crown indices. The figures quoted for these, based on smaller sample sizes, come from the earlier sources quoted in Table 9.7.

The buccolingual dimension of PN10 and the mesiodistal dimension of PN13 are shown in brackets as minima since PN10 is broken and PN13 is very worn (enamel margins missing). The teeth of Arago 2 and the Ehringsdorf adult are also very worn. This will have reduced the mesiodistal dimension quite considerably, thus reducing the figure for crown area and increasing the figure for crown index.

In some cases, measurements given by different authors vary. For instance, the mesiodistal dimensions quoted by Howell (1960) for the Montmaurin first and second molars are higher than those given by Billy and Vallois (1977) or Bermúdez de Castro (1986). In this case the measurements given by Billy and Vallois (1977) are used.

### Chronological considerations

Grouping the individual comparative sites from the European Middle Pleistocene into 'earlier' and 'later' presents a number of problems (see *e.g.* Klein 2009). Many of the sites do not have accurate dates assigned to them although, on biostratigraphic grounds, Mauer (Germany) is likely to date from at least Marine Isotope Stage (MIS) 13 (*c.* 500,000 BP). On morphological grounds, Arago (France) and Petralona (Greece) can be grouped with Mauer (= *Homo heidelbergensis*). Recent dating of mammal teeth (ESR/uranium series) and sand grains (infrared radiofluorescence) from the site of Mauer (Wagner *et al.* 2010) give a date of 609,000 BP and uranium series dates for Arago (Falguères *et al.* 2004) give a minimum age of 350,000 BP. Visogliano (Italy) can also be grouped with Mauer on biostratigraphic grounds, belonging to MIS 11 or 13 (Abbazzi *et al.* 2000). Pontnewydd and Ehringsdorf (Germany) can be assigned to MIS 7 (*c.* 220,000 BP) through absolute dating. Sites like Montmaurin (France), Steinheim (Germany), Bilzingsleben (Germany) and Biache (France) are assumed here to post-date the Mauer, Arago and Petralona group. Bau de l'Aubesier (France) has been dated as later Middle Pleistocene but over 169,000 BP (MIS 6/7) (Lebel and Trinkaus 2002), and Pesada (Portugal) as middle to late Middle Pleistocene, with a minimum age of 241,000 BP (Trinkaus *et al.* 2003).

The Gran Dolina (Atapuerca, Spain) material has been dated as greater than 780,000 BP (Bermúdez de Castro

| **A. Sites grouped in European Neanderthal (Late Mousterian) sample** (mainly following Frayer (1978) and Wolpoff (1971)) | **B. Sites grouped in European Early Upper Palaeolithic sample** (mainly following Frayer (1978)) |
|---|---|
| Akhystyr | Arcy-sur-Cure |
| Arcy-sur-Cure | Brno |
| Bombarral | Castelmerle |
| La Chapelle-aux-Saints | Castanet |
| Combe Grenal | Cro-Magnon |
| La Croze de Dua | Fontéchevade |
| Dzhruchula | Grotte des Enfants |
| La Ferrassie | Isturitz |
| Forbes' Quarry / Devil's Tower | Kent's Cavern |
| Guattari | Miesslingtal |
| Hortus | Mladeč |
| Jersey | Předmostí |
| Kůlna | Les Roches |
| Leuca | La Rochette |
| Marina-de-Camerota | Le Rois |
| Macassargues | Silická Brezová |
| Meridionale | Stetten |
| Monsempron | Les Vachons |
| Le Moustier | Zlatý Kůň |
| Ochoz | |
| Pech de l'Azé | |
| Petit Puymoyen | |
| La Placard | |
| La Quina | |
| Régourdou | |
| Šipka | |
| Spy | |
| Subalyuk | |
| Teshik Tash | |
| Vergisson | |
| Vindija | |

*Table 9.8. Sites included in European Neanderthal and Early Upper Palaeolithic samples.*

*et al.* 1999a), probably MIS 21 (865,000–810,000 BP) (Antoñanzas and Bescós 2002), and therefore falls in the Early Pleistocene. Several attempts have been made to date the Atapuerca-SH (Sima de los Huesos) site. Aguirre *et al.* (1990) gave uranium series and ESR dates ranging from 105,000–360,000 BP, and ruled out a Late Pleistocene date from the presence of the bear species *Ursus deningeri*. Bischoff *et al.* (1997) tested both human bones and bear bones, using the same methods, and concluded that there was a minimum age of about 200,000 BP for human entry and suggestive evidence of entry prior to 320,000 BP. Parés *et al.* (2000) have dated the site as being between 205,000 and 325,000 BP, MIS 7/8, based on palaeomagnetic evidence. A more recent determination is that of Bischoff *et al.* (2003) giving a minimum age of 350,000 BP. Hominin bones were found under an *in situ* speleothem (SRA-3) at the top of the ramp leading down to the Sima de los Huesos ('the pit of bones'), where the other hominin remains have principally been discovered, and this was dated using uranium series dating. The speleothem thickness represented by this date is the lower 10 cm out

of a total of 14 cm, and these authors suggest that, if the growth rate of the speleothem is the same overall as it is in its upper 4 cm (1 cm in 32,000 years), the date of the site could be as great as 600,000 BP. Rates of growth do, though, vary considerably over time, depending on such factors as rainfall, temperature, soil carbon dioxide level, calcium concentration in the feed water and the type of water flow (Dreybrodt 1996). Field measurements of recent flowstone growth rates at two English cave sites by Baker and Smart (1995) gave figures between 0.009 and 0.261 mm per year. These would equate to times between 11,111 years and 383 years to form 10 cm of speleothem. Bischoff *et al.* (2003) note that rodent fauna at Atapuerca-SH correlates with levels TD10 and TD11 at Gran Dolina that have been dated at 308,000–418,000 BP. A further paper by Bischoff *et al.* (2007), using a revised high-resolution uranium series dating method to date six samples from the lower part of the same speleothem, suggests a much earlier minimum age of 530,000 BP, and faunal evidence from the site is put forward to support this. Nevertheless, the SRA-3 speleothem is only found at the top of the ramp and not

| Tooth | Gran Dolina % | Earlier Mid Pleistocene | Later Mid Pleistocene | Atapuerca-SH | Krapina | Neanderthal | EUP |
|---|---|---|---|---|---|---|---|
| $P^4$ | +4 | AR | AR | + | 0 | +, AR | ++, AR |
| $M^1$-PN4 | +1 | IR | AR | + | 0 | + | +, AR |
| -PN12 | -7 | BR | BR | 0 | -, BR | 0 | 0 |
| $M^2$ | -4 | IR | IR | + | 0 | +, AR | + |
| $M^3$-PN17 | | IR | IR | +, AR | -, BR | 0 | 0 |
| -PN19 | | IR | IR | +, AR | -, BR | 0 | 0 |
| $I_2$ | +1 | IR | IR | + | 0 | 0 | 0 |
| $P_3$-PN6/7 | -7 | IR | IR | 0 | 0 | 0 | +, AR |
| -PN20 | -2 | IR | AR | + | 0 | 0 | ++, AR |
| $P_4$ | -2 | IR | IR | + | 0 | 0 | 0 |
| $M_1$ | +2 | IR | AR | ++, AR | 0 | 0 | 0 |
| $M_2$ | -6 | IR | IR | +++, AR | 0 | + | + |
| $M_3$-PN16 | | IR | IR | + | 0 | 0 | + |
| -PN21 | | IR | IR | ++ | 0 | + | + |

% = Percentage difference from Gran Dolina Hominid 1; AR = Above range; IR = In range; BR = Below range; 0 = Within one standard deviation of mean; +/- = Over one standard deviation above/below mean; ++/-- = Over two standard deviations above/below mean; +++/--- = Over three standard deviations above/below mean.

*Table 9.9. Lengths of Pontnewydd teeth compared with other European Pleistocene teeth.*

over 'the pit of bones'. Whilst these dates apply, therefore, to material found under SRA-3, they are not necessarily applicable to the Sima de los Huesos proper. These authors state that material from Atapuerca-SH Individual VI has been found at the top and bottom of the ramp as well as in the Sima but, from their diagram, it can be seen that the SRA-3 speleothem does not extend over the area excavated at the base of the ramp, and the only item found at the top of the ramp that may have been from Individual VI was a lower third premolar with similar wear and cusp morphology to its supposed antimere found in the Sima. It is true that lower third premolars found at the nearby earlier site of Gran Dolina have a different morphology to those found in the Sima (Bermúdez de Castro *et al.* 1999b; Carbonell *et al.* 2005) but the differences are less marked in the more recently reported Hominid 7 (Carbonell *et al.* 2005) and it cannot as yet be known at what time (assuming continuity) their morphology became similar to those discovered at Atapuerca-SH. It is contended that there is room for uncertainty and that, in view of the ramifications of this most recent date, further evidence is needed to link the finds under the SRA-3 speleothem with those in the Sima. In contrast to the above, Aguirre (2007) considers that there has possibly been stratigraphic inversion through broken stalagmitic crusts in the Sima and that the likelihood of this, and subsequent movement of the deposits, is supported by the post mortem breaks in the bones in the Sima noted by Andrews and Fernandez-Jalvo (1997). Aguirre (2007) identifies the faunal complex of the Sima as Atapuerca III, similar to those of other later (not latest) Middle Pleistocene European sites, and puts the date of the Atapuerca-SH hominin bones as being *c.* 320,000 BP (MIS 9). Endicott *et al.* (2010) have determined that genetic divergence of Neanderthals and modern humans commenced at approximately 410,000–440,000 BP, and no earlier than 538,000 BP, based on mitochondrial

genomes. These authors consider that the present early date for Atapuerca-SH is incompatible with these findings in view of the many Neanderthal characteristics seen in this collection. They also comment that the Atapuerca-SH fossils have a higher level of Neanderthal characteristics than is seen in apparently later fossils such as Arago and Ceprano. It may well be that further direct dating of the faunal and human material is required in order to resolve these issues. In view of the debate over the dating of this site, Atapuerca-SH is still considered as later Middle Pleistocene in the following sections but differences in conclusions that would result if it were referred to the earlier Middle Pleistocene are noted. Krapina is dated as being close to the MIS 6/5 transition, *c.* 130,000 BP (Rink *et al.* 1995), on the boundary between the Middle Pleistocene and the Late Pleistocene.

### Comparison of individual Pontnewydd teeth with other European Pleistocene teeth

As well as comparing Pontnewydd teeth with other teeth, it is necessary to explore how different teeth vary in size and shape over time and between sites. Generally, the sizes of hominin teeth have reduced over time but the picture in the European Pleistocene is more confused. The two major sites are Atapuerca-SH, which is still being dug and for which the current minimum number of individuals is 28 (Bermúdez de Castro *et al.* 2004b) and Krapina, with a minimum number of 35 individuals (Radovčić *et al.* 1988) (based on the dental remains, estimates from other authors vary considerably). Hominins at the earlier site of Atapuerca-SH have very small teeth, similar in size to those of some modern humans, but teeth from the later site of Krapina are large, larger than many earlier teeth from the Middle Pleistocene. Again, the largest teeth being compared occur at the earlier Middle Pleistocene site of Arago and some from this site are larger than any discovered to

| Tooth | Gran Dolina % | Earlier Mid Pleistocene | Later Mid Pleistocene | Atapuerca-SH | Krapina | Neand-erthal | EUP |
|---|---|---|---|---|---|---|---|
| P⁴ | -3 | IR | AR | +, AR | + | 0 | ++, AR |
| M¹-PN4 | -5 | IR | IR | + | 0 | 0 | 0 |
| -PN12 | -15 | BR | BR | 0 | -, BR | -, BR | - |
| M² | -3 | IR | AR | + | 0 | 0 | 0 |
| M³-PN17 | | IR | IR | 0 | 0 | 0 | 0 |
| -PN19 | | IR | IR | 0 | -, BR | - | 0 |
| P₃ | -13 | IR | AR | 0 | 0 | 0 | + |
| P₄ | -7 | IR | IR | + | 0 | 0 | + |
| M₁ | -5 | IR | AR | + | 0 | 0 | 0 |
| M₂ | -4 | IR | AR | ++, PN13,AR | 0 | 0 | 0 |
| M₃-PN16 | | IR | IR | + | 0 | - | 0 |
| -PN21 | | IR | IR | + | 0 | 0 | 0 |

*Table 9.10. Breadths of Pontnewydd teeth compared with other European Pleistocene teeth. Key as Table 9.9.*

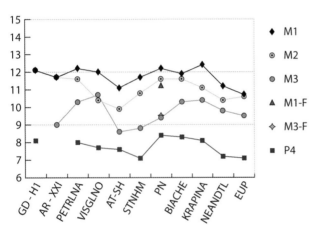

*Figure 9.10. Lengths of upper teeth (mm).*

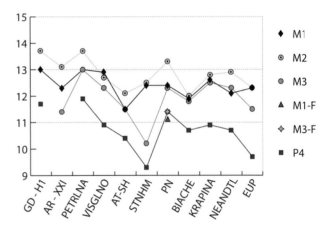

*Figure 9.12. Breadths of upper teeth (mm).*

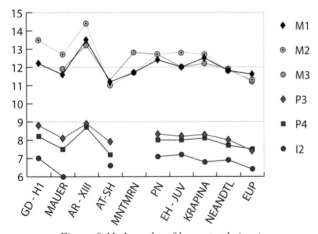

*Figure 9.11. Lengths of lower teeth (mm).*

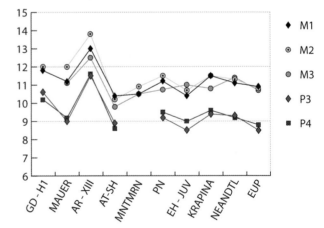

*Figure 9.13. Breadths of lower teeth (mm).*

date at the much earlier site of Gran Dolina. A further confusing factor is the considerable variation in size of the teeth from some sites, possibly due to sexual dimorphism. Despite this, it is possible to see trends in the relative sizes of teeth and in the shape of teeth, for instance a relative decrease in the size of lower third premolars during the Pleistocene. Comparisons made between other groups in the following relate to tooth types present at Pontnewydd unless otherwise stated.

LENGTH AND BREADTH

The relationships between the lengths and breadths of Pontnewydd teeth and those of other European Pleistocene teeth are summarized in Tables 9.9 and 9.10 and Figures

9.10–9.13. Comparing Pontnewydd teeth against each group:

Gran Dolina – it is clear, since the discovery of the mandible of Hominid 7, that there is a fair degree of variation in the size of the Gran Dolina teeth. Hominid 1 is the most complete specimen dentally and has the largest teeth. Percentage variations of Pontnewydd teeth from Hominid 1 are shown in Tables 9.9–9.12 to demonstrate the relative differences in size of the different teeth. Generally, both the lengths and the breadths of the Pontnewydd teeth are lower than in the corresponding Gran Dolina (Hominid 1) teeth but the lengths of the upper fourth premolar (PN18), the lower lateral incisor (PN10) and two first molars (PN4 and PN11), are greater. The lengths and breadths of most of the teeth are within 7.5% of the Gran Dolina values. The greatest differences (over 10% lower) are seen in the breadths of the lower third premolars (PN6, PN7 and PN20) and the smaller of the upper first molars (PN12). A similar pattern occurs at Atapuerca-SH, but with distinctly lower measurements, in terms of number of standard deviations difference, in the lower second molar. The differences between the Atapuerca-SH mean values and the higher Gran Dolina Hominid 1 values is two standard deviations or more for the lengths and breadths of all the posterior teeth, with the exception of upper third premolar length and breadth, upper fourth premolar length and upper first molar length. However, for lower second molars, the differences are five standard deviations for the length and greater than three standard deviations for the breadth. The smallest differences (at or under one standard deviation) are in the lengths of the upper premolars. At Krapina the difference is most marked in the lower breadth of lower third premolars, paralleling Pontnewydd. The dimensions of the smaller teeth of the Hominid 7 mandible are below those of the corresponding Pontnewydd teeth, with the exception of the breadth of the lower third premolar. The Hominid 7 lower third molar is remarkably small, below the range of values, in both dimensions, of all other groups with the exception of Atapuerca-SH breadth. Likewise, the Hominid 3 upper first molar is smaller than PN4 in both dimensions.

Earlier Middle Pleistocene (Mauer, Arago, Petralona, Visogliano) – the lengths and breadths of the Pontnewydd teeth are mostly within the range of values found in the earlier Middle Pleistocene teeth but the length of upper fourth premolar PN18 is above range. Both the length and breadth of upper first molar PN12 are below range. By comparison, at Atapuerca-SH, the ranges of length and breadth mainly overlap the lower end of the ranges for earlier Middle Pleistocene, the least overlap being in the upper and lower second molars. There is near complete overlap in upper third premolar (length and breadth), upper fourth premolar (length), upper first molar (length and breadth), upper third molar (breadth) and lower third premolars (length). Similar, therefore, to comparisons with Gran Dolina Hominid 1.

Later Middle Pleistocene (Bilzingsleben, Montmaurin, Steinheim, Ehringsdorf, Biache, Pesada) – several of the Pontnewydd teeth are above the ranges of values found for later Middle Pleistocene teeth in one or both dimensions, principally breadth:

- Length – upper fourth premolar, lower third premolar PN20, and upper and lower first molars PN4 and PN11.
- Breadth – upper fourth premolar, lower third premolars, lower first molar, and upper and lower second molars.

PN12 is below range in both length and breadth.

Atapuerca-SH – the dimensions of the Pontnewydd teeth are, in most cases, over one standard deviation above the mean values of the Atapuerca-SH teeth. This difference is particularly marked in the lower first and second molars. The lower first molar is over two standard deviations above the Atapuerca-SH mean in length, and the lower second molar(s) over three standard deviations above in length and over two in breadth. Both lengths are above the Atapuerca-SH ranges of values, as also are the lengths of the upper third molars. The greatest similarity in measurements is seen in PN12, the lower third premolars and the breadth of the upper third molars.

The Pontnewydd lower first and second molars are, therefore, proportionally larger in length and breadth than the upper first and second molars when compared with those of Atapuerca-SH. The mean values of Atapuerca-SH upper and lower first and second molar lengths are considerably lower than those of Krapina, below the range of values found there. The lengths of the Atapuerca-SH lower second molars are also particularly low compared with individual later Middle Pleistocene teeth, there being little overlap in the ranges of values.

Krapina – the lengths and breadths of the Pontnewydd teeth are mostly similar to the mean values for Krapina teeth. In contrast to the comparisons with Atapuerca-SH, the lengths of the upper third molars, and the breadth of upper third molar PN19, are each over one standard deviation below the Krapina mean and below the Krapina range of values. Both the length and breadth of PN12 are also over one standard deviation below the Krapina mean and below range. However, the breadth of the upper fourth premolar is over one standard deviation above the Krapina mean.

Neanderthals – the lengths and breadths of the Pontnewydd teeth are, in most cases, above the mean values of Neanderthal teeth. The lengths of five Pontnewydd teeth are over one standard deviation above the relevant Neanderthal mean, and those of the upper fourth premolar and upper second molar are above the Neanderthal value ranges. In contrast, the breadths of PN12 and two of the third molars (PN19 – upper and PN16 – lower) are over one standard deviation below the Neanderthal means, and that of PN12 is below the Neanderthal range.

Early Upper Palaeolithic (EUP) – the smaller size of the premolars compared with those from Pontnewydd is noticeable. The lengths and breadths of the Pontnewydd lower third premolars, and the breadth of the lower fourth premolar, are over one standard deviation above the mean values for EUP; and the length and breadth of the upper fourth premolar, and the length of one lower third premolar

| Tooth | Gran Dolina% | Earlier Mid Pleistocene | Later Mid Pleistocene | Atapuerca-SH | Krapina | Neand-erthal | EUP |
|---|---|---|---|---|---|---|---|
| $P^4$ | +2 | AR | AR | ++, AR | 0 | ++, AR | ++, AR |
| $M^1$-PN4 | -4 | IR | IR | +, AR | 0 | + | + |
| -PN12 | -21 | BR | BR | 0 | -, BR | - | 0 |
| $M^2$ | -7 | IR | AR | + | 0 | + | + |
| $M^3$-PN17 | | IR | IR | + | - | 0 | 0 |
| -PN19 | | IR | IR | 0 | -, BR | - | 0 |
| $P_3$ | -18 | IR | AR | 0 | 0 | 0 | +, AR |
| $P_4$ | -10 | IR | AR | + | 0 | 0 | + |
| $M_1$ | -4 | IR | AR | ++, AR | 0 | 0 | 0 |
| $M_2$ | -10 | IR | AR | +++, AR | 0 | 0 | + |
| $M_3$-PN16 | | IR | IR | + | 0 | 0 | 0 |
| -PN21 | | IR | AR | + | 0 | 0 | 0 |

*Table 9.11. Crown areas of Pontnewydd teeth compared with other European Pleistocene teeth. Key as Table 9.9.*

(PN20), are over two standard deviations above, and above the EUP value ranges. The lengths of the upper first molar PN4, upper and lower second molars, and both lower third molars, are also over one standard deviation above the EUP means and that of PN4 is above the EUP range, but the breadth of PN12 is over one standard deviation below the EUP mean.

Generalizations that can be made are:

1) upper first molar PN12 is small compared with most other upper first molars, in both dimensions, other than the lengths of Atapuerca-SH, Neanderthals and EUP. Against this, the length of upper first molar PN4 is high compared with these and the later Middle Pleistocene specimens, as also is the length of the upper second molar PN1;

2) the lengths and breadths of the Pontnewydd lower first and second molars are high compared with those of individual later Middle Pleistocene teeth and Atapuerca-SH. The length of the lower second molar PN15 is particularly high compared with Atapuerca-SH;

3) upper and lower Pontnewydd second molars both show the same pattern of: the lengths being 4–6% below those of the Gran Dolina Hominid 1 teeth but within the ranges of values found for both earlier and later Middle Pleistocene teeth; the breadths being above the ranges found for later Middle Pleistocene teeth; and the lengths being within one standard deviation of the Krapina means, and over one standard deviation above the Neanderthal and EUP means. The breadths are within one standard deviation of the means for all three samples;

4) there is considerable variation in the dimensions of third molars. Taking the *upper* third molars, it can be seen that the ranges of values for *length* for Atapuerca-SH and Krapina do not overlap. The values for Pontnewydd upper third molars lie between the two, being similar to the mean for Neanderthals. The ranges of values for *breadth* partly overlap, with the range for Krapina being higher and similar to

Neanderthals. The breadths of the two Pontnewydd teeth are very different, the breadth of PN17 being similar to the Krapina mean and that of PN19 being similar to the Atapuerca-SH mean. In the *lower* third molars, both the *length and breadth* of Pontnewydd teeth are more similar to Krapina lower third molars than to the smaller Atapuerca-SH teeth. They are also very similar to the Montmaurin lower third molars. The Neanderthal lower third molars have a higher crown index, with the mean length being below that of Krapina and the mean breadth being greater than that of Krapina. The lengths of the Pontnewydd teeth are at the top of the Neanderthal range, whilst the breadths are at the bottom;

5) where the lengths of the Pontnewydd teeth are very similar to, or above, those of Gran Dolina Hominid 1 (*i.e.* lower lateral incisor, upper and lower fourth premolars, and upper and lower first molars other than PN12), the ranges of values for earlier and later individual Middle Pleistocene teeth are also very similar, with none of the later Middle Pleistocene teeth having values below the range for earlier Middle Pleistocene. The same applies for upper second molar lengths (because of the low length of the Visogliano tooth) and lower third molar lengths and breadths. The individual later Middle Pleistocene values are almost entirely below the earlier Middle Pleistocene ranges for upper and lower second molar breadths, and lower third premolar lengths and breadths.

CROWN AREA (the buccolingual dimension multiplied by the mesiodistal dimension)

The relationships between the crown areas of Pontnewydd teeth and other European Pleistocene teeth are summarized in Table 9.11 and Figures 9.14–9.15. In comparing Pontnewydd teeth with the other teeth studied, it can be seen that:

- the upper fourth premolar PN18 is relatively large, with a crown area above range compared with all other groups apart from Krapina;
- the upper first molar PN4 and the upper second

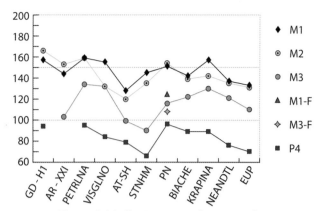

*Figure 9.14. Crown areas of upper teeth.*

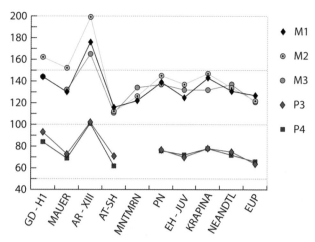

*Figure 9.15. Crown areas of lower teeth.*

molar PN1 are relatively larger than the upper third molars. Similarly, the lower first and second molars are relatively larger than the lower third molars;

- the upper first molar PN12 and the upper third molar PN19 are relatively small compared with other teeth, in particular PN12, which has a crown area below range, or over one standard deviation below the mean, for all groups excepting Atapuerca-SH and EUP. The difference in size between PN4 and PN12 is in both dimensions equally, but that between PN17 and PN19 is in the buccolingual dimension only;

- the upper third molars are small compared with the Krapina mean, and intermediate in size between the Neanderthal and Atapuerca-SH means. The reverse is true for lower third molars, which are similar in size to Krapina and Neanderthal means, but larger than the Atapuerca-SH mean.

Comparing Pontnewydd teeth against each group:

Gran Dolina – the crown areas of Pontnewydd teeth are, in the main, lower than those of Gran Dolina Hominid 1, but the crown areas of PN18, PN4 and lower first molar PN11 are very similar. The greatest differences are in the lower third premolars (average 18% lower) and upper first molar PN12 (21% lower). The lower fourth premolar and upper and lower second molars are 7–10% lower.

Earlier Middle Pleistocene (Mauer, Arago, Petralona, Visogliano) – the crown area of PN18 is just above the range of values found in the earlier Middle Pleistocene teeth and that of PN12 below range. The remaining Pontnewydd teeth are within range. Of these, the lower premolars, upper and lower second molars and upper third molar PN19 are at the bottom of the ranges of values found, and other teeth (first molars and third molars) are mid-range. The pattern is therefore similar to that observed in comparison with Gran Dolina Hominid 1.

Later Middle Pleistocene (Bilzingsleben, Montmaurin, Steinheim, Ehringsdorf, Biache, Pesada) – the Pontnewydd teeth mostly have crown areas above the ranges of values found in later Middle Pleistocene teeth or, in the case of the lower third molar PN16, at the top end of the range. PN4, and both upper third molars, have mid-range values and, as with earlier Middle Pleistocene, the value of PN12 is below range.

Atapuerca-SH – all the Pontnewydd teeth have crown areas above the mean values for Atapuerca-SH teeth, with the exception of PN12. Apart from upper third molar PN19 and the lower third premolars, they have values over one standard deviation from the Atapuerca-SH means. The upper fourth premolar and lower first molar have values over two standard deviations from the Atapuerca-SH mean, and the lower second molar in excess of three. The values for all these teeth, and also PN4, are above the Atapuerca-SH ranges.

Krapina – the majority of the Pontnewydd teeth have mid range crown areas compared with the Krapina sample. Upper first molar PN12, and both upper third molars, have crown areas over one standard deviation below the Krapina means and the values for PN12 and PN19 are below the Krapina ranges of values.

Neanderthals – as with the Krapina sample, the majority of the Pontnewydd teeth have mid-range crown areas compared with the Neanderthal sample, and PN12 and PN19 have crown areas over one standard deviation below the Neanderthal mean values. Upper molars PN4 and PN1 have crown areas over one standard deviation above the Neanderthal means, and that of the upper fourth premolar PN18 is over two standard deviations above, and above the Neanderthal range of values. The Pontnewydd lower teeth therefore have a greater similarity in size to the Neanderthal teeth than do the upper teeth, and the smaller size of the upper fourth premolar is very evident in the Neanderthal sample.

Early Upper Palaeolithic – the smaller size of EUP premolars is apparent, the crown area of PN18 being over two standard deviations above the EUP mean and above the EUP range of values, and the Pontnewydd lower premolars being over one standard deviation above the EUP means, with the lower third premolars being above the EUP range. Additionally, upper first molar PN4, and both upper and lower second molars, are over one standard deviation above the EUP means.

With the exception of PN12, the Pontnewydd teeth sizes are very consistent within themselves, particularly in view of the wide range of crown areas found in the groups studied.

| Tooth | Gran Dolina% | Earlier Mid Pleistocene | Later Mid Pleistocene | Atapuerca-SH | Krapina | Neand-erthal | EUP |
|-------|--------------|-------------------------|-----------------------|--------------|---------|--------------|-----|
| P$^4$ | -6 | BR | IR | 0 | 0 | 0 | 0 |
| M$^1$-PN4 | -5 | BR | IR | 0 | 0 | 0 | --, BR |
| -PN12 | -8 | BR | BR | 0 | 0 | 0 | --, BR |
| M$^2$ | +2 | IR | IR | -, BR | 0 | 0 | 0 |
| M$^3$-PN17 | | AR | IR | 0 | +, AR | 0 | + |
| -PN19 | | IR | IR | --, BR | 0 | 0 | 0 |
| P$_3$-PN6/7 | -6 | IR | AR | 0 | 0 | 0 | 0 |
| -PN20 | -13 | BR | IR | -, BR | -- | 0 | - |
| P$_4$ | -4 | IR | IR | 0 | 0 | 0 | 0 |
| M$_1$ | -7 | BR | IR | 0 | 0 | 0 | 0 |
| M$_2$ | +1 | IR | IR | 0 | 0 | 0 | - |
| M$_3$-PN16 | | BR | IR | 0 | 0 | --, BR | --, BR |
| -PN21 | | BR | IR | 0 | 0 | --, BR | -- |

*Table 9.12. Crown indices of Pontnewydd teeth compared with other European Pleistocene teeth. Key as Table 9.9.*

For instance, the range of values for lower first molar crown areas at Atapuerca-SH and Krapina is 100–137 mm$^2$ for Atapuerca-SH and 116–175 mm$^2$ for Krapina. The fact that patterns can be discerned in relationships with other sites suggests a very cohesive group.

The smaller crown areas seen in the Pontnewydd teeth compared with those from Gran Dolina Hominid 1 are also found in the means of the Atapuerca-SH, Krapina and Neanderthal samples. Compared with Gran Dolina Hominid 1, the teeth at Atapuerca-SH that are most different (over 23% smaller) are the lower third and fourth premolars and the upper and lower second molars. The least difference is 16% in the upper fourth premolar. The Atapuerca-SH differences for upper and lower molars are very similar – first molar; upper: 18%, lower: 19%; second molar; upper: 28%, lower: 31%. At Krapina, the greatest differences (14–16%) are in the lower third premolar and upper second molar, and least (0–1%) in the upper and lower first molars. The Neanderthal teeth are more consistently smaller, in the range 9–19%, the greatest differences being in premolars and second molars, and the least in first molars. In each group, the second molar is proportionally smaller than the first compared to Gran Dolina Hominid 1, and the lower third premolar proportionally smaller than the lower fourth premolar. (At Atapuerca-SH the percentage decreases in size of the two lower premolars, and also of the two upper premolars, are very similar). The difference in size in the upper fourth premolar is very variable, from none at Pontnewydd to 19% in Neanderthals.

In comparing the Atapuerca-SH, Krapina and Neanderthal samples with the earlier Middle Pleistocene specimens, the same pattern emerges, with the smaller size particularly evident in the upper and lower second molars. There is little difference compared with these in the size of the upper fourth premolar in the Atapuerca-SH and Krapina samples. The large upper and lower third molars of the Krapina and Neanderthal samples have a similar range of values to the earlier Middle Pleistocene specimens, but those of Atapuerca-SH only overlap at the lower end.

The range of values of the individual later Middle Pleistocene specimens are lower than those found in the earlier Middle Pleistocene specimens for lower third premolar, and for upper and lower second molars there is little overlap. They are similar for lower fourth premolars, and lower first and third molars, with values found in the later Middle Pleistocene specimens no lower than the range of values seen in earlier Middle Pleistocene specimens. For upper fourth premolars, and upper first and third molars, the ranges of values in the two groups also mostly overlap. The smaller size of second molars is as described by Bermúdez de Castro and Nicolás (1995).

The crown areas of the individual later Middle Pleistocene specimens are generally higher than the Atapuerca-SH means but within the Atapuerca-SH ranges of values. The principal exceptions are lower third premolars, with values below the Atapuerca-SH mean, and upper third and lower second molars, which (with the exception of Steinheim) all have crown areas above the Atapuerca-SH range. The Steinheim upper fourth premolar and upper third molar are exceptionally small, with the crown area of the upper fourth premolar being below the range of values found at Atapuerca-SH.

In relation to the apparent rapid change in the size of the lower third premolar during the Middle Pleistocene, Bermúdez de Castro and Nicolás (1996) point out that the crown area of lower third premolars in European Middle Pleistocene hominins is greater than that of lower fourth premolars, unlike the relationship seen in African fossil hominins and recent humans, and that this is greatest at Atapuerca-SH. At Atapuerca-SH, and in the Gran Dolina hominins, the lower third premolar is larger than the lower fourth premolar by 10% or more. In other specimens, and in the means of the Krapina and Neanderthal samples, the difference is under 6%. In both Ehringsdorf specimens the size relationship is reversed. Although from different individuals, the Pontnewydd lower third and fourth premolars are very similar in size. In comparison with the earlier Middle Pleistocene specimens, the smaller size of lower third premolars in later Middle Pleistocene specimens, and in the Krapina sample, is more evident

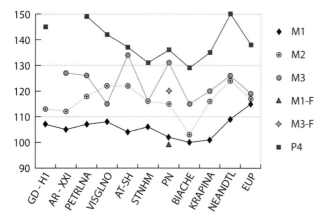

*Figure 9.16. Crown indices of upper teeth.*

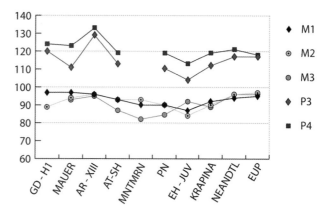

*Figure 9.17. Crown indices of lower teeth.*

than that observed in lower fourth premolars, but the difference is not as pronounced as it is in comparison with Gran Dolina.

The size relationship between upper first and second molars varies. At Gran Dolina, and in one of the earlier Middle Pleistocene specimens (Arago), the *upper second molar* is larger than the first but at Petralona they are the same size and at Visogliano the second molar is considerably smaller. In the later teeth the second molar is always smaller than the first. Of these, the biggest drops in crown area between upper first and second molars are in the Steinheim specimen and at Krapina. The *lower second molar* is larger than the first in all the individual specimens, and in the means of groups other than those of Atapuerca-SH and EUP in which the reverse is the case. (Trinkaus notes that the relative size of all three molars, in both upper and lower dentitions, is not constant between individuals in either Neanderthals or recent humans (Trinkaus 1983)).

The upper fourth premolars used for comparison at Gran Dolina come from Hominid 1 (none complete in Hominid 3). If the upper third premolars from Hominid 1 are compared with the four sample groups, a similar pattern as for the fourth premolars is encountered. The mean crown areas of the Krapina teeth are almost identical, whilst those of Atapuerca-SH, Neanderthals and EUP are distinctly lower (by 13%, 16% and 28% respectively). However, the upper third premolars of Hominid 3 have crown areas that are, on average, 7 mm² larger than those of Hominid 1.

CROWN INDEX (buccolingual dimension divided by mesiodistal dimension stated as a percentage).
This ratio measures the relative width of a tooth compared with the length. The higher the figure, the relatively broader is the tooth. The relationships between the crown indices of teeth from Pontnewydd and other European Pleistocene teeth are summarized in Table 9.12 and Figures 9.16–9.17. Comparing teeth from Pontnewydd against each group:
Gran Dolina – the crown indices of Pontnewydd teeth are 4–13% lower than those of Gran Dolina Hominid 1, with the exception of the upper and lower second molars,

which have higher indices by 1–2%. This reflects the proportionally lower breadth of the Pontnewydd teeth compared with the Gran Dolina teeth, apart from second molars, where the length is proportionally smaller. The same situation is seen in comparing the mean values of Atapuerca-SH and Krapina with Gran Dolina Hominid 1 – the crown indices are lower apart from second molars. In the Neanderthal sample the upper third and fourth premolars, and upper first molar, also have higher crown indices. The crown indices of Gran Dolina Hominid 7 are almost identical to those of Hominid 1.
Earlier Middle Pleistocene (Mauer, Arago, Petralona, Visogliano) – the pattern is similar to that observed in comparing Pontnewydd teeth with those of Gran Dolina. Half of the Pontnewydd teeth have crown indices below the range of values found in earlier Middle Pleistocene teeth, but upper second molar PN1 and lower premolars (other than PN20) are bottom of range, and lower second molar PN15 mid-range. Upper third molars PN19 and PN17 are mid range and above range respectively.
Later Middle Pleistocene (Bilzingsleben, Montmaurin, Steinheim, Ehringsdorf, Biache, Pesada) – The Pontnewydd teeth have a spread of crown indices similar to the ranges of values found in later Middle Pleistocene teeth – *Premolars*: upper fourth premolar top of range, lower third premolars above range (PN6 and PN7) or bottom of range (PN20), and lower fourth premolar mid range. *Molars*: upper first molars bottom of range (PN4) or below range (PN12), lower first molar and both upper and lower second molars top of range, upper third molars top of range (PN17) or bottom of range (PN19), and lower third molars bottom of range.

A number of the later Middle Pleistocene teeth studied are distinctive in having low crown indices (*i.e.* narrow teeth) (discussed more fully below). This is because of a relatively smaller breadth measurement compared with Gran Dolina and earlier Middle Pleistocene teeth. The difference in breadth is greater than the difference in length in the second molars of the Bilzingsleben, Biache and Ehringsdorf specimens, unlike Pontnewydd (and Montmaurin and Steinheim) and unlike the means of the

Atapuerca-SH, Krapina and Neanderthal samples.

Atapuerca-SH – The Pontnewydd teeth are mostly within one standard deviation of the Atapuerca-SH mean values. The upper second molar PN1 and lower third premolar PN20 are over one standard deviation below (*i.e.* narrower) and below the Atapuerca-SH ranges of values, and upper third molar PN19 is over two standard deviations below, and also below range.

Krapina – the Pontnewydd teeth have a slightly higher crown index compared with Krapina mean values than they have compared with Atapuerca-SH mean values. One upper third molar (PN17) is more than one standard deviation above the Krapina mean (unlike Atapuerca-SH) and also above the Krapina range of values, but lower third premolar PN20 is over two standard deviations below the Krapina mean.

Neanderthals – the crown indices for Pontnewydd teeth are, with one exception (upper third molar PN17), similar to or below the mean values of Neanderthal teeth. Both lower third molars are considerably narrower, over two standard deviations below the Neanderthal mean, and are also below the Neanderthal range of values (see comments below).

Early Upper Palaeolithic – as with the Neanderthal group, both Pontnewydd lower third molars are over two standard deviations below the EUP mean value and one is below the EUP range of values. As with Krapina, PN17 is over one standard deviation above the EUP mean. The lower second molar, and the lower third premolar PN20, are over one standard deviation below the EUP means, and both upper first molars are over two standard deviations below and below the EUP range.

General comments:

1) In comparing the individual earlier and later Middle Pleistocene specimens, there is a very evident decrease over time in crown index between early and late for upper fourth premolars, lower third premolars and lower first molars, with no overlap in the ranges of values, and also in lower third molars. The decrease is evident at Atapuerca-SH in the upper fourth premolar and the lower third premolar;

2) the mean crown index of Neanderthal upper fourth premolars (and upper third premolars) is higher than the other later material, including Pontnewydd, and similar to the Gran Dolina and earlier Middle Pleistocene specimens;

3) there is a distinct increase in the crown index of the upper first molar between the later Middle Pleistocene /Krapina material and EUP. Unlike the other sample groups and the individual specimens (with the exception of Biache), the EUP upper first molars have similar crown indices to upper second and third molars. They have a more rectangular shape than the earlier nearly square upper first molars;

4) the range of values for Atapuerca-SH upper third molars is very high, above the values for Biache, Steinheim, Visogliano and PN19, and all but one of those for Krapina. It is within the wide ranges of values reported for Neanderthals and EUP. The crown index

| Molar | 1st | 2nd | 3rd |
|-------|-----|-----|-------|
| **Pontnewydd** | 90 | 90 | 84/85 |
| **Montmaurin** | 90 | 93 | 82/87 |

*Table 9.13. Comparison between crown indices of lower molars from Pontnewydd and Montmaurin. (If the measurements given by Bermúdez de Castro (1986) are used, the crown index of the Montmaurin second molar is 99).*

for PN19 is the same as the mean for Krapina, but that for PN17 is within the range for Atapuerca-SH. Both teeth are within range for Neanderthals;

5) Bermúdez de Castro and Nicolás (1995) comment on the crown indices of Atapuerca-SH lower second and third molars being considerably smaller (*i.e.* narrower) than those of modern human and Neanderthal samples, lower third molars in particular, the difference for these between Atapuerca-SH and the sample of European and Near Eastern Neanderthals they used being statistically significant. The same comment applies, in general, to the individual later Middle Pleistocene specimens. As regards Pontnewydd teeth the crown index for the lower second molar PN15 is in the middle of the range for individual Middle Pleistocene specimens and equal to the mean for Krapina. It is near the bottom of the range for Atapuerca-SH, Neanderthals and EUP. The crown indices for the two Pontnewydd lower third molars are also low, towards the bottom of the range for Atapuerca-SH and other later Middle Pleistocene material, below the range for Neanderthals and below/ bottom of range for EUP. Again, the same comments therefore apply;

6) although it must be borne in mind that the Pontnewydd lower molars are probably from at least two different individuals, it is worth noting the similarity of the crown indices of these teeth to those of Montmaurin (Table 9.13).

SUMMARY OF RESULTS FROM THE COMPARISON OF PONTNEWYDD WITH OTHER SITES

Apart from upper first molar PN12, the Pontnewydd teeth form a very cohesive group.

Gran Dolina – The crown areas of Pontnewydd (and other later Middle Pleistocene) second molars and lower third and fourth premolars are markedly smaller than those of Hominid 1 from the much earlier Gran Dolina site, particularly lower third premolars. Pontnewydd teeth are generally narrower than Gran Dolina teeth, with the exception of second molars, which are a little broader. A similar pattern is seen in the means of Atapuerca-SH and Krapina teeth.

Earlier Middle Pleistocene – The sizes of Pontnewydd teeth are mainly within the range of values found in earlier Middle Pleistocene teeth, with the upper fourth premolar being a little larger. As observed in comparison with the Gran Dolina teeth, the Pontnewydd teeth tend to be narrower than the earlier Middle Pleistocene teeth.

Later Middle Pleistocene – Individual later Middle

| Tooth | PN no. | PN value | AT-SH Individual VII | AT-SH male discriminant* | AT-SH male individuals* | AT-SH female discriminant* | AT-SH female individuals* |
|---|---|---|---|---|---|---|---|
| P⁴ | 18 | 96 | 92 | | 90 (3, 86-94) | | |
| P₃ | 6,7,20 | 75-77 | | 87 (2, 84-90) | 81 (3, 69-90) | 65 (6, 57-69) | 63 (3, 57-68) |
| P₄ | 5 | 76 | 79 | 75 (3, 71-79) | 73 (4, 65-79) | 58 (7, 49-67) | 56 (5, 49-67) |
| M¹ | 4 | 151 | 145 | | 148 (2, 145-150) | | |
| M¹ | 12 | 124 | | | | | 126 (4, 120-128) |
| M² | 1 | 154 | 143 | | 147 (3, 137-160) | | 116 (2, 110-123) |
| M³ | 17 | 116 | 121 | | 121 (1) | | |
| M³ | 19 | 108 | | | | | 97 (4, 81-105) |
| M₁ | 11 | 139 | 137 | 130 (3, 124-137) | 127 (3, 120-137) | 113 (7, 104-120) | 118 (3, 110-131) |
| M₂ | 15 | 145 | | | 121 (2, 120-122) | | 106 (5, 89-123) |
| M₃ | 16,21 | 134-140 | 144 | | 135 (2, 127-144) | | 98 (4, 82-109) |

*Mean, with number in sample, and range, in brackets underneath.

*Table 9.14. Sexual dimorphism, crown areas.*

Pleistocene premolars, second molars and lower first molars are all smaller than the corresponding Pontnewydd teeth. Two of the Pontnewydd lower third premolars are distinctly broader in shape.

Atapuerca-SH – The mean crown areas of the Atapuerca-SH teeth are small compared with those of Pontnewydd teeth, in particular the lower first and second molars. The Atapuerca-SH lower second molars are also notably small in comparison with individual later Middle Pleistocene specimens and the Krapina sample.

Krapina and Neanderthals – With certain exceptions, the Pontnewydd teeth are similar in size to the means of both the Krapina and Neanderthal samples, more so in the lower teeth than in the upper teeth. They are also similar in shape to the means of these (and to the means of the Atapuerca-SH sample), with a few exceptions that are significantly narrower. A smaller size of upper premolars compared with Pontnewydd is seen in the Neanderthal sample.

Third molars – Third molars are varied in size and shape, the Pontnewydd lower third molars being relatively larger than the upper third molars in relation to other later Middle Pleistocene specimens and to the Krapina and Neanderthal samples. Pontnewydd and other later Middle Pleistocene lower third molars are relatively narrower than earlier and later teeth. Amongst upper third molars; PN17, Pesada 2 and the Atapuerca-SH teeth are notably broader than PN19, the other later Middle Pleistocene teeth and the Krapina sample.

PN12 – PN12 is small in breadth compared with all the individual teeth, and sample means other than Atapuerca-SH, and small in length compared with most.

Early Upper Palaeolithic – In comparison with Pontnewydd teeth, a smaller size of premolars and a difference in the shape of upper first molars is evident in the EUP sample.

*Sexual dimorphism*

Details of individual Atapuerca-SH tooth dimensions in the following are taken from Bermúdez de Castro (1986, 1988 and 1993). The allocation of teeth to individuals, and the sex of individuals, come from Bermúdez de Castro and Nicolás (1997).

The difference in size between the upper first molars, PN4 and PN12, could be because of sexual dimorphism. Bermúdez de Castro *et al.* (1993) note that, in the Atapuerca-SH teeth, specimens of the same tooth class tend to cluster in two sets of very different size. This pattern is particularly evident in the upper canines, lower premolars, and upper first and second molars. The crown areas of PN4 and PN12 are 151 and 124 mm² respectively, at the top and bottom of the range for Atapuerca-SH of 120–150 mm². The individual Atapuerca-SH values are: 120, 127, 128, 128, 145, 150.

Using a discriminant analysis, Bermúdez de Castro *et al.* (1993) determined that Atapuerca-SH teeth show a size sexual dimorphism significantly greater than that of a modern human sample in each of the teeth tested (lower lateral incisor, canine, third and fourth premolars and first molar). The differences in mean crown area figures determined for male and female were: lateral incisor: 8, canine: 16, third premolar: 22, fourth premolar: 17, first molar: 17.

A similar analysis on Krapina teeth showed significant differences for both lower premolars, and for the lower first molar, but not for the lower lateral incisor or canine.

Bermúdez de Castro et al. (1993) also cite the enormous difference in crown area of 73 mm² between the Arago 2 and Arago 13 lower second molars, far more than would be expected in a small group. In a further study, Bermúdez de Castro et al. (2001) calculated the index of sexual dimorphism for the Atapuerca-SH mandibular teeth, and a modern human sample, and found its value to be greater in all the Atapuerca-SH teeth studied (lateral incisor, canine, third and fourth premolars, and first and second molars). The difference was marked for the canines but small for other teeth.

If the small size of PN12 (and to a lesser extent PN19) is because of sexual dimorphism, and most of the other Pontnewydd teeth are from males, this could explain, in part, their relatively large size compared with Atapuerca-SH and other individual later Middle Pleistocene specimens. (Bermúdez de Castro and Nicolás (1997) identify ten individuals in the Atapuerca-SH sample as being female and eight as male). Nevertheless, this still leaves the fact that four Pontnewydd teeth are above the size ranges reported for Atapuerca-SH.

In Table 9.14 the crown areas of Pontnewydd teeth are compared with those of Atapuerca-SH, showing:

- means for male and female for lower third and fourth premolars, and lower first molars, generated by the discriminant function;
- means for teeth from individuals definitely identified as male or female. There are no female individuals identified that have upper posterior teeth. However, for upper molars, all the teeth not allocated to individuals are notably smaller than those allocated and these have been grouped to give the 'female' means;
- the mean crown areas of the most complete individual (VII), which is identified as male.

The number in the sample, and the range of values, is given below each mean.

The crown areas of the Pontnewydd lower fourth premolar and lower first molar are both above the Atapuerca-SH discriminant function male means. The values for Pontnewydd lower third premolars (75–77 mm²) are mid-way between the discriminant function means for male and female, and between the discriminant function male and female ranges.

Comparing Pontnewydd crown areas with Atapuerca-SH male and female means and ranges:

- PN18 is above the male range, as are PN4, PN11 and PN15;
- PN5, PN1, PN16 and PN21 are all near to, or above, the male means and well above the female ranges;
- lower third premolars PN6, PN7 and PN20 are between the male and female means but in the male range;
- upper third molars PN17 and PN19 are similarly intermediate, with PN17 nearer the male mean, and PN19 nearer the female mean but above the female range;
- upper first molar PN12 is below the female mean and well below the male range.

Two of the Pontnewydd teeth have only one dimension that is usable:

- PN10 has a mesiodistal dimension of 7.1 mm. The two Atapuerca-SH lower lateral incisors put in the male group by the discriminant function have mesiodistal dimensions of 6.7 and 7.5 mm, and the remainder are in the range 6.3–6.6 mm;
- PN13 has a buccolingual dimension of 11.6 mm, which is above the range of 9.3–11.5 mm reported for Atapuerca-SH lower second molars and similar to the value of 11.4 mm for PN15.

The crown area values for individual Pontnewydd teeth (excluding PN12 and PN19 and the relatively very large lower first and second molars) are not far from the Atapuerca-SH male means (maximum difference seven) and, in particular, there is a similarity between Pontnewydd 'male' teeth and Individual VII. The summary tooth sizes of all available teeth grouped together, as defined by Brace (1980), do not show a great deal of difference:

- Pontnewydd teeth (excluding PN12 and PN19) compared with Individual VII: 869 against 861;
- Pontnewydd teeth (excluding PN12 and PN19) compared with Atapuerca-SH male means: 1090 against 1043.

The Atapuerca-SH male and female means for crown area can be compared with teeth from three later Middle Pleistocene sites which have been identified as female:

- The Montmaurin mandible, sexed as female by de Lumley (1975) on account of the small size of the teeth. Stringer et al. (1984), however, note the mandible's massiveness and robusticity;
- the Biache and Steinheim skulls, sexed as female by Wolpoff (1980) on metric and morphological grounds. In particular, Wolpoff suggested that differences between Petralona (male) and Steinheim crania could be explained by sexual dimorphism. Opposing this, Stringer (1981) considered that the metrical contrasts between Petralona and Steinheim are such that they must reflect real evolutionary differences.

The Montmaurin lower first molar crown area of 123 mm² is close to the Atapuerca-SH male mean (130 mm²), and only just below the male range, generated by the discriminant analysis. Additionally, the lower first to third molar crown areas of 123, 126 and 134 mm² are close to the means of male individuals. Nonetheless, the first molar lies in both the male and female ranges of values. The third molar is in the male range only and the second molar above both ranges.

The crown areas of the Biache upper fourth premolar and upper first to third molars (89, 142, 139 and 122 mm²) are very similar to the crown areas of Atapuerca-SH Individual VII (male). The fourth premolar and third molar are also similar to the means of male individuals, but the first and second molars are a little below, in particular the second molar. The first molar is between the male and female ranges, but the second molar is still in the male range.

| | Atapuerca-SH | Atapuerca-SH male | Krapina | Neanderthal | EUP |
|---|---|---|---|---|---|
| **Crown area** | | | | | |
| Size | +378 | +28 | -7 | +38 | +208 |
| Shape | 89 | 70 | 97 | 77 | 64 |
| **Crown index** | | | | | |
| Size | -11 | -19 | 0 | -47 | -20 |
| Shape | 6 | 7 | 6 | 18 | 36 |
| **Length** | | | | | |
| Size | +108 | +20 | 0 | +39 | +89 |
| Shape | 12 | 7 | 22 | 26 | 22 |
| **Breadth** | | | | | |
| Size | +53 | 0 | -1 | 0 | +28 |
| Shape | 12 | 16 | 13 | 15 | 30 |
| **Length & breadth** | | | | | |
| Size | +78 | +6 | -1 | +10 | +55 |
| Shape | 14 | 15 | 18 | 29 | 31 |

*Table 9.15. Penrose size and shape differences. Pontnewydd to other groups.*

The Steinheim upper first molar has a crown area of 145 mm$^2$, which is similar to the mean of male Atapuerca-SH individuals of 148 mm$^2$, and is in the male range. The upper second molar (crown area 135 mm$^2$) is rather below the male mean, and between the male and female ranges, and the upper third molar (crown area 90 mm$^2$) is below the female mean. The upper fourth premolar (crown area 66 mm$^2$) is below the Atapuerca-SH range of 72–94 mm$^2$.

Using the same teeth as are present in the Pontnewydd sample, if the Montmaurin and Biache specimens were from the same population, they would both be tentatively identified as male. With the Steinheim specimen, unlike Montmaurin and Biache, there is a distinct lack of fit but female would seem to be the more likely.

The fact that the Montmaurin and Biache teeth look male, combined with the fact that four Pontnewydd teeth are above the corresponding Atapuerca-SH size ranges, could imply that Atapuerca-SH teeth are small compared with other European later Middle Pleistocene teeth, even after taking sexual dimorphism into account. The use of Atapuerca-SH male and female means to sex other teeth therefore needs to be treated with caution. Although there appear to be clear evolutionary trends in the sizes of hominin teeth, the size ranges within populations for which there are few finds cannot be known and may have differed significantly.

Bearing this in mind, it is suggested that the larger Pontnewydd teeth in relation to Atapuerca-SH identified above – PN18, PN4, PN11, PN15 and also PN5, PN1, PN16, PN21, PN10 and PN13 – can be tentatively classified as male, and that the smaller PN12 can be tentatively classified as female. This leaves two tooth classes – lower third premolars and upper third molars – that are intermediate in size. Of these, PN6, PN7 and PN20, together with PN17, are nearer the Atapuerca-SH male means and PN19 nearer the female mean.

If the crown areas of Pontnewydd teeth are compared with those of the individual later Middle Pleistocene teeth it can be seen that:

- the 'male' Pontnewydd teeth (first and second molars and upper fourth premolar) are larger than the female Biache, Steinheim and Montmaurin teeth; by 7–30 mm$^2$ on upper fourth premolar, 15–19 mm$^2$ on lower first molar, and upper and lower second molars, and 6–9 mm$^2$ on the upper first molar;
- the 'female' PN12 is much smaller than the Steinheim and Biache upper first molars; by 18–21 mm$^2$;
- the third molars are mixed, with both Pontnewydd 'male' and 'female' upper third molars being intermediate between those of Biache and Steinheim, and 'male' lower third molars being the same and a little larger than those from Montmaurin.

The sizes of lower first molars, and upper and lower second molars, at Biache, Steinheim and Montmaurin are very consistent in comparison with those from Pontnewydd.

*Penrose size and shape coefficient*
In order to further clarify the affinities of the Pontnewydd teeth, the Penrose size and shape coefficient is used to compare the Pontnewydd posterior teeth (upper and lower premolars and molars) with the corresponding posterior teeth of the four samples – Atapuerca-SH, Krapina, Neanderthals and EUP. In addition, the 'male' Pontnewydd teeth (*i.e.* excluding PN12 and PN19) are compared with the mean values for Atapuerca-SH male individuals (nos. II, VII, VIII, XII, XIII, XVII, XX). Sources are as described above and in Table 9.7. Comparisons made are of crown area, crown index, and length and breadth (both separately and together). To compensate for differences in tooth size, the length and breadth figures for each tooth type have first been divided by the mean of Atapuerca-SH, Krapina, Neanderthals and EUP combined, and then quoted as a percentage. For instance, for upper fourth premolar, the mean length of the four populations is (7.6 + 8.1 + 7.2 + 7.1)/4 = 7.5 mm. The mean length for Neanderthals is 7.2 mm so, when divided by 7.5, this gives a percentage figure of 96%. This correction has not been applied to

|  | Example 1 | | | Example 2 | | |
|---|---|---|---|---|---|---|
|  | *Object A* | *Object B* | *Difference* | *Object A* | *Object B* | *Difference* |
| **Length** | 10.5 mm | 11.0 mm | +0.5 | 10.5 mm | 11.0 mm | +0.5 |
| **Breadth** | 9.0 mm | 8.5 mm | -0.5 | 9.0 mm | 9.5 mm | +0.5 |

*Table 9.16. Penrose size and shape coefficients, examples.*

the figures for crown area and crown index. The results are given in Table 9.15. The formula for the Penrose size and shape coefficient, taken from Groeneveld and Kieser (1988), is:

$$P_{(A, B)} = \frac{1}{n} \sum_{i=1}^{n} (XA_i - XB_i)^2 - \frac{1}{n^2} \left[ \sum_{i=1}^{n} (XA_i - XB_i) \right]^2$$

Shape                Total                                Size

where 'n' is the number of measurements used, and A and B are the two groups being compared. Kieser (1990) quotes work done by Groeneveld and Kieser (1987) in evaluating the statistical accuracy of a battery of different metrics; paying particular attention to stability in the face of reduced sample size, and to statistical bias resulting from over or under estimation. Penrose's shape coefficient was clearly shown by the results to be the most reliable metric examined. In comparing two objects, there is a difference in size and a difference in shape. In the two simple examples given above, the difference in the first is entirely in shape, with no overall difference in size, and the difference in the second is entirely in size, since the two difference figures are the same. The Penrose size and shape coefficient differentiates between these two aspects (Table 9.16).

SIZE

- The overall crown area size of the Pontnewydd teeth is distant from Atapuerca-SH and, to a lesser extent, EUP but very close to Krapina. It is a similar distance from, and close to, Atapuerca-SH male and Neanderthals.
- Crown index distances are smaller than crown area distances, that to Krapina being the smallest and that to Neanderthals the largest. This is an indicator of the degree of similarity in shape of the teeth, showing that the Pontnewydd teeth are, on average, nearly identical in shape to the Krapina teeth and have lower indices than other samples (*i.e.* narrower teeth), especially Neanderthals.
- In most cases, a decrease in length contributes more than any decrease in breadth to the smaller size of Atapuerca-SH, Neanderthal and EUP teeth. This is reflected in the negative direction of crown index size differences. For Atapuerca-SH male and Neanderthals, there is scarcely any difference in breadth and, for Krapina, little difference in length or breadth.
- Length and breadth combined show a similar pattern to crown area, with small distances to Atapuerca-SH male, Krapina and Neanderthals (least to Krapina) and greater distances to Atapuerca-SH and EUP.

| Length & breadth | Krapina | Neanderthal | EUP |
|---|---|---|---|
| **Size** |  |  |  |
| Atapuerca-SH | -94 | -32 | -2 |
| Krapina |  | +17 | +68 |
| Neanderthal |  |  | +17 |
| **Shape** |  |  |  |
| Atapuerca-SH | 12 | 19 | 26 |
| Krapina |  | 16 | 13 |
| Neanderthal |  |  | 10 |
| **Size with P³** |  |  |  |
| Atapuerca-SH | -86 | -23 | 0 |
| Krapina |  | +20 | +81 |
| Neanderthal |  |  | +20 |
| **Shape with P³** |  |  |  |
| Atapuerca-SH | 13 | 24 | 36 |
| Krapina |  | 17 | 17 |
| Neanderthal |  |  | 10 |

*Table 9.17. Penrose size and shape differences between groups.*

SHAPE

The shape statistic is a measure of the variance of the mean differences. It thus identifies differences in proportion (*i.e.* differential size) having removed the size element, and is seen as the more important statistic in studying taxonomic distances (Corruccini 1973; Kieser 1990). Corruccini (1973) found that Penrose's shape statistic was one of only two methods that produced good results in separating hominins and pongids based on odontometric data. The crown area shape distances from Pontnewydd are high for all groups, the highest being to Krapina and the lowest to EUP. Krapina is therefore the group in which changes in absolute crown area are the least consistent compared with Pontnewydd, and EUP the most consistent. Crown index shape distances are lower than those for crown area, and this reflects the considerably smaller variation observed for crown index in most tooth classes in the samples studied. The distances increase from Atapuerca-SH/Krapina to EUP *via* Neanderthals, that to EUP being twice that to Neanderthals. This indicates that crown index differences between corresponding teeth are most consistent when comparing Pontnewydd with Atapuerca-SH and Krapina, and least with EUP. Breadth shape distances to Atapuerca-SH male and EUP are higher than those for length, the reverse of the situation with the corresponding size distances. However, for Krapina and Neanderthals, the length shape distance is the higher. The highest distances (*i.e.* where there is the least consistency of differences between teeth) are those for Krapina (length), Neanderthals (length) and EUP (length and breadth). The figure for Atapuerca-SH male length

| Sample/tooth id. | Length mm | Breadth mm | Crown area | Crown index |
|---|---|---|---|---|
| *Homo erectus* (n = 5) | | | 123 | |
| | | | (112-132) | |
| **Arago (n = 2)** | | | 96 | |
| | | | (94-98) | |
| **PN4 - as measured** | 9.2 | 10.3 | 95 | 112 |
| **PN4 - adjusted for wear** | 9.8 | 10.3 | 101 | 105 |
| **Ehringsdorf 1038/69** | 9.2 | 10.2 | 94 | 111 |
| **European Late Middle - Early** | | | 107 | |
| **Late Pleistocene (n = 5)** | | | (94-124) | |
| **Krapina (n = 6)** | 10.4 | 10.8 | 113 | 105 |
| | (9.1-11.1) | (9.9-11.5) | (90 & 97-126) | (95-110) |
| **European Late Neanderthal** | 9.6 | 10.4 | 99 | 109 |
| **(n = 8)** | (8.6-11.0) | (9.3-11.1) | (86-122) | (101-123) |

Mean figures, with range in brackets, given for samples.

*Homo erectus*: subset from Lake Turkana, Olduvai Gorge, Omo, Baringo, Laetoli, Ternifine, Thomas, Swartkrans, Jian Shi, Badong, Sangiran, Trinil, Lantian, Longgudong, Zhoukoudian, Mauer, Vergranne, Vértesszőllős.

European Late Middle - Early Late Pleistocene: subset from Biache, La Chaise, Lazaret, Orgnac L'Aven, Atapuerca, Bañolas, Malarnaud, Ehringsdorf, Taubach, Krapina.

European Late Neanderthal: Chateauneuf 2, Pech de L'Azé, Roc de Marsal, Gibraltar II, La Quina H18, Teshik-Tash, Subalyuk, Staroselye.

*Table 9.18. Deciduous upper fourth premolar, comparative occlusal measurements.*

is particularly low. The shape distances for length and breadth combined fall into two groups with similar values: 1) Atapuerca-SH, Atapuerca-SH male and Krapina; 2) Neanderthals and EUP. Determinations of size and shape normally use basic dimensions rather than derived figures (*e.g.* Corruccini 1973, Groeneveld and Kieser 1988), and length and breadth combined would be expected to give the best indication of taxonomic distance. The shape distances reflect the differences in the dates of the different groups, the values of the second group being approximately double those of the first.

The size and shape distances for length and breadth combined between the four samples – Atapuerca-SH, Krapina, Neanderthals and EUP – are shown in Table 9.17. It can be seen that the shape distances for length and breadth together, between Atapuerca-SH and other groups, are a little less than those from Pontnewydd – Krapina 12 against 18, Neanderthals 19 against 29, EUP 26 against 31 – and increase in the same sequence. The shape distances between Krapina, Neanderthals and EUP are not consistent in this way with those from Pontnewydd. This implies a similarity between Pontnewydd and Atapuerca-SH in their relationship towards the other groups. The shape distances overall show a definite secular trend. The table also shows the distances if the upper third premolar is included. The principal differences are:

- Size – smaller distances from Atapuerca-SH to Krapina and Neanderthals, and a greater distance from Krapina to EUP;
- Shape – greater distances from Atapuerca-SH to Neanderthals and EUP and, to a lesser extent, between Krapina and EUP.

The near identical sizes of Atapuerca-SH and EUP bear out Bermúdez de Castro and Nicolás' (1995) assertion that

the decrease in tooth size of Atapuerca-SH is the same as that of recent humans. Neanderthal size is equidistant from Krapina and EUP, and is a similar distance from Atapuerca-SH.

To summarize; for length and breadth combined:

- the 'best fit' in terms of size and shape is Krapina for size, and Atapuerca-SH and, to a slightly lesser extent, Krapina for shape;
- beyond this, size distances are least to Atapuerca-SH male and Neanderthals, and shape distances similar to Neanderthals and EUP;
- the shape distances to Krapina, Neanderthals and EUP from Pontnewydd and from Atapuerca-SH are consistent and show a secular trend.

*Deciduous tooth*

The single deciduous tooth PN4, an upper fourth premolar (also known as a second molar), is compared in Table 9.18 with:

- crown area data for *Homo erectus*, Arago, and European late Middle to early Late Pleistocene teeth, from Wolpoff (1982);
- the Ehringsdorf juvenile upper fourth deciduous premolar (Vlček 1993). The wear on this tooth, at grade 4, is similar to that on PN4 (photograph in Vlček 1993);
- a European late Neanderthal sample from Tillier (1979);
- a sample of upper fourth deciduous premolars from Krapina (6 KDPs), from Wolpoff (1979).

The length (as measured) and breadth measurements are similar to the mean values of the European late Neanderthal sample and near identical to the measurements of the Ehringsdorf tooth, but small compared with Krapina,

| Tooth | Sample | Length mm | Breadth mm | Crown area | Crown index |
|-------|--------|-----------|------------|------------|-------------|
| **M₂** | Late Upper Palaeolithic | 10.9 | 10.7 | 116 | 98 |
| | | (29, 0.7) | (29, 0.7) | (29, 13.5) | |
| | Mesolithic (Male) | 11.0 | 10.9 | 120 | 99 |
| | | (32, 0.65) | (33. 0.49) | (32, 11.6) | |
| | | (9.9-12.1) | (9.9-11.7) | (99-138) | |
| | Mesolithic (Female) | 10.3 | 10.3 | 106 | 100 |
| | | (28, 0.50) | (27, 0.52) | (27, 9.5) | |
| | | (9.3-11.5) | (8.8-11.2) | (82-127) | |
| | PN8 | 11.3 | 10.7 | 121 | 95 |
| | Recent | 10.7 | 10.1 | 108 | 94 |
| | | (10.0-11.0) | (9.5-10.5) | | |
| | | | | | |
| **M₃** | Late Upper Palaeolithic | 10.5 | 10.3 | 109 | 98 |
| | | (20, 0.8) | (19, 0.8) | (19, 16.0) | |
| | Mesolithic (Male) | 10.7 | 10.6 | 113 | 99 |
| | | (31, 0.68) | (31, 0.54) | (31, 11.4) | |
| | | (9.5-12.0) | (9.8-11.9) | (95-136) | |
| | Mesolithic (Female) | 10.4 | 10.0 | 103 | 96 |
| | | (23, 0.53) | (23, 0.60) | (22, 10.3) | |
| | | (9.3-11.4) | (8.8-11.5) | (82-117) | |
| | PN2 | 11.0 | 10.5 | 116 | 95 |
| | Recent | 10.7 | 9.8 | 105 | 92 |
| | | (8.0-12.0) | (9.0-10.5) | | |

Mean figures given for samples; number, SD and range of values in brackets as appropriate.
Late Upper Palaeolithic: Arcy-sur-Cure, Aurensan, Aveline's Hole, Barma Grande, Bédeilhac, Brassempouy, Bruniquel, Cap Blanc, Cheddar, Duruthy, Farincourt, Isturitz, Kent's Cavern, Kostenki, Lachaud, Laugerie-Basse, Lussac-les-Châteaux, La Madeleine, Le Morin, Oberkassel, Oetrange, Le Placard, Le Peyrat, La Pique, St Germain, St Vincent, Šandalja, Veyrier, Vindija.
Mesolithic Male: Arene Candide, Frankthi, Hohlenstein, Ofnet, Parabita, Le Peyrat, Rochereil, San Teodoro, Kaufertsberg, Fat'ma Koba, Korsør Nor, McArthur Cave, Muge (Moita & Arruda), Melby, Le Rastel, Stora Bjers, Téviec, Vedbaek, Gramat.
Mesolithic Female: Cheix, Frankthi, Hohlenstein, Ofnet, Bäckaskog, McArthur Cave, Muge (Moita & Arruda), Téviec, Birsmatten, Culoz.

*Table 9.19. Mesolithic teeth, comparative occlusal measurements.*

the length being near the bottom of the Krapina range of values. Stringer (1984) suggested that 0.6 mm should be added to the length measurement of the Pontnewydd tooth to allow for interstitial wear. The crown area and crown index that result from using the adjusted length are shown in Table 9.18.

The crown area calculated using the length as measured is similar to both the Arago and the European late Neanderthal means, and to the Ehringsdorf specimen, but small compared to *Homo erectus*, European late Middle to early Late Pleistocene and Krapina. If the length adjusted for interstitial wear is used, the crown area becomes intermediate between the European late Neanderthal and European late Middle to early Late Pleistocene means. Comparing crown areas of PN4 deciduous and permanent teeth against Krapina and Neanderthal samples, the deciduous tooth can be seen to be relatively smaller than the permanent, the permanent tooth being near the mean for Krapina and well above the mean for Neanderthals. The ratio of the crown areas of PN4 fourth deciduous premolar and first permanent molar is 0.63 (0.67 correcting for wear). This compares with a mean value of 0.71 for Krapina maxillae B and C, and mean values of 0.65 (Black 1902) and 0.72 (van Beek 1983) for recent human teeth.

The crown index calculated using the length as measured is a little above the mean for European late Neanderthals,

and almost identical to that of the Ehringsdorf tooth, but very different to Krapina, being above the range of values reported. The reverse applies if the adjusted length is used. By comparison, the PN4 first permanent molar has a crown index near equal to the mean for Krapina and below that for Neanderthals.

*Mesolithic teeth*

In Table 9.19 the two Mesolithic teeth are compared with samples of European late Upper Palaeolithic and European Mesolithic teeth published by Frayer (1984 and 1978 respectively) and mean figures for recent teeth (White Americans) from Black (1902). The breadth measurements of both teeth are similar to the mean values for late Upper Palaeolithic and for Mesolithic male, whilst the length measurements are a little higher. Both measurements are higher than the means for recent teeth. Those of the lower second molar, PN8, are above the range of values given by Black (1902) but those of the lower third molar, PN2, are within range. The crown area of PN8 is similar to the mean crown area for Mesolithic male, as is that of PN2. The crown areas of both teeth are above the means for late Upper Palaeolithic, over one standard deviation above the means for Mesolithic female (but still within the reported female ranges) and well above the means for recent teeth. The crown indices of both teeth are higher

| Tooth | Identity | Crown height mm | Length mm | Length/height index |
|-------|----------|-----------------|-----------|---------------------|
| M³ | Atapuerca-SH AT10 | 5.4 | 8.6 | 159 |
| | Pontnewydd PN17 | 6.6 | 9.4 | 142 |
| | Pontnewydd PN19 | 6.3 | 9.5 | 151 |
| | Neanderthal mean | 7.9 | - | - |
| | Recent ranges of means | 5.4-6.4 | 8.2-10.0 | 137-172 |
| | | | | |
| P₃ | 'Sinanthropus' mean | 8.7 | 9.0 | 103 |
| | Atapuerca-SH AT2 | 8.3 | 7.8 | 94 |
| | Pontnewydd PN6 | 8.8 | 8.1 | 92 |
| | Pontnewydd PN7 | 9.0 | 8.3 | 92 |
| | Ehringsdorf juvenile | 9.7 | 8.2 | 85 |
| | Neanderthal mean | 10.3 | - | - |
| | Recent ranges of means | 6.2-9.3 | 6.9-7.6 | 82-121 |
| | | | | |
| P₄ | 'Sinanthropus' mean | 7.4 | 8.8 | 119 |
| | Atapuerca-SH AT2 | 7.7 | 7.7 | 100 |
| | Pontnewydd PN5 | 7.6 | 8.0 | 105 |
| | Ehringsdorf juvenile | 8.7 | 8.0 | 92 |
| | Neanderthal mean | 7.1 | - | - |
| | Recent ranges of means | 5.9-8.0 | 7.0-7.7 | 90-128 |
| | | | | |
| M₃ | 'Sinanthropus' mean | 6.9 | 12.4 | 179 |
| | Atapuerca-SH AT1 | 6.9 | 10.7 | 155 |
| | Pontnewydd PN21 | 7.6 | 12.8 | 168 |
| | Ehringsdorf juvenile | 8.3 | 12.0 | 145 |
| | Neanderthal mean | 8.5 | - | - |
| | Pontnewydd PN2 (Meso) | 6.9 | 11.0 | 159 |
| | Recent ranges of means | 5.0-6.7 | 9.9-11.9 | 157-238 |

Table 9.20. Crown heights.

than the means for recent teeth and lower than those for late Upper Palaeolithic and Mesolithic.

### Crown height

Only the crown heights of Pontnewydd teeth with minimal occlusal wear are compared with other specimens. The crown heights of the Pontnewydd teeth are listed in Table 9.2. The wear grade has been determined using Molnar's method (Molnar 1971). Table 9.20 has comparative data for comparison with those Pontnewydd teeth that are relatively unworn (wear grade up to 2, but no apparent reduction in crown height). Mean figures for 'Sinanthropus pekinensis' and Neanderthals are taken from Weidenreich (1937). The ranges of mean figures shown for recent humans come from groups of; Australian Aborigines (Campbell 1925), San Bushmen (Drennan 1929), Bantu (Middleton Shaw 1931), Japanese (Miyabara 1916), East Greenland Eskimos (Pederson 1949), Aleut (Moorrees 1957), Europeans (Black 1902) and New Mexico Pecos Pueblo Indians (Nelson 1938). Figures for unworn or slightly worn (wear grade up to 2) teeth from Atapuerca-SH are measurements made by T. Compton on casts in the collection of the Natural History Museum, London. Of these, there is no apparent reduction in crown height resulting from wear of the two AT2 lower premolars, and estimated reductions of 0.5 mm on lower third molar AT1 and 1.0 mm on upper third

molar AT10. Figures for the Ehringsdorf juvenile come from Vlček (1993). The length/height index proposed by Weidenreich (1937) is recorded against each tooth. This is calculated as 'the crown length divided by the crown height' and is shown as a percentage. (The layers of the Zhoukoudian Cave site in China from which the *Homo erectus* '*Sinanthropus pekinensis*' remains came were dated at 300,000–550,000 BP by Grün *et al.* (1997) but a more recent determination by Shen *et al.* (2009) gives a substantially earlier date of 770,000 BP).

The crown height figures show no clear trend, but those of the Ehringsdorf juvenile lower premolars and lower third molar, and the Neanderthal lower third premolar and upper and lower third molars, are clearly above the others. The lowest mean crown height figures in recent lower premolars, and upper and lower third molars, are found in Australian Aborigines and San Bushmen, and the highest in the Japanese and European groups (and in the East Greenland Eskimo lower third premolar). Weidenreich (1937) noted a downward trend in length/height indices from '*Sinanthropus*' to recent, particularly in lower premolars and molars. This is true, in the teeth considered, for groups other than the low crowned Australian Aborigines and San Bushmen (and Pecos Pueblo Indians for lower third molar). The mean length/height indices of Australian Aborigines and San Bushmen are higher than those of '*Sinanthropus*'.

| Tooth | Identity | | Root robusticity (a) | Crown area (b) | Ratio b/a x 100 |
|---|---|---|---|---|---|
| **M¹** | 'Sinanthropus' | mean (range) | 99 (93-118) | 134 (117-162) | 135 (123-143) |
| | Atapuerca-SH AT16, AT20 range | | 94-110 | 127-145 | 132-135 |
| | Pontnewydd PN4 | | 115 | 151 | 131 |
| | Pontnewydd PN12 | | 93 | 124 | 133 |
| | Recent | mean | 81 | 125 | 154 |
| | | | | | |
| **M²** | 'Sinanthropus' | mean (range) | 98 (83-114) | 135 (129-142) | 140 (115-172) |
| | Atapuerca-SH AT12, AT15 range | | 85-104 | 110-160 | 129-154 |
| | Pontnewydd PN1 | | 129 | 154 | 119 |
| | Recent | mean | 79 | 113 | 143 |
| | | | | | |
| **P₃** | 'Sinanthropus' | mean (range) | 56 (45-64) | 84 (74-100) | 151 (132-168) |
| | Pontnewydd PN6 | | 50 | 75 | 150 |
| | Pontnewydd PN7 | | 54 | 77 | 143 |
| | Ehringsdorf adult | | 42 | 67 | 160 |
| | Ehringsdorf juvenile | | 32 | 70 | 219 |
| | Recent | mean | 31 | 59 | 190 |
| | | | | | |
| **M₁** | 'Sinanthropus' | mean (range) | 108 (86-130) | 149 (100-181) | 138 (116-164) |
| | Atapuerca-SH AT1, 2, 14, 21 range | | 82-102 | 113-137 | 131-151 |
| | Pontnewydd PN11 | | 105 | 139 | 132 |
| | Ehringsdorf adult | | 97 | 133 | 138 |
| | Ehringsdorf juvenile | | 66 | 125 | 188 |
| | Recent | mean | 77 | 124 | 161 |
| | | | | | |
| **M₂** | 'Sinanthropus' | mean (range) | 101 (89-124) | 146 (130-159) | 147 (128-169) |
| | Atapuerca-SH AT11, AT75 range | | 79-87 | 107 | 123-135 |
| | Pontnewydd PN13 | | 104 | - | - |
| | Pontnewydd PN15 | | 103 | 145 | 141 |
| | Ehringsdorf adult | | 101 | 141 | 140 |
| | Ehringsdorf juvenile | | 90 | 137 | 152 |
| | Recent | mean | 76 | 117 | 154 |
| | | | | | |
| **M₃** | 'Sinanthropus' | mean (range) | 94 (70-122) | 129 (100-160) | 140 (131-163) |
| | Atapuerca-SH AT1, 13, 75 range | | 87-111 | 98-144 | 107-130 |
| | Ehringsdorf adult (right tooth) | | 75 | 108 | 144 |
| | Pontnewydd PN2 (Mesolithic) | | 77 | 116 | 151 |
| | Recent | mean | 75 | 116 | 155 |
| | | | | | |
| **dp⁴** | Pontnewydd PN4 | | 74 | 101 | 136 |
| | Recent | mean | 53 | 82 | 154 |

*Table 9.21. Root robusticity.*

The downward trend in length/height indices is apparent in the teeth from Atapuerca-SH, Pontnewydd and, particularly, Ehringsdorf. The Ehringsdorf juvenile length/height indices are all lower than those of Atapuerca-SH and Pontnewydd and below, or at the low end of, the ranges for recent teeth. The length/height index for the Mesolithic tooth, PN2, is nearly identical to the mean figure for recent Europeans (160). If the crown heights of the Atapuerca-SH third molars are adjusted for wear, as suggested above, their heights become very similar to those of the Pontnewydd teeth, and their length/height indices lower than the figures for recent teeth (134 for AT10 and 145 for AT1).

### Root measurements

Three types of measurement are taken for each tooth; robusticity (Table 9.21), root length (Table 9.22) and trunk length (Table 9.23).

Comparative data are taken from Weidenreich (1937) for 'Sinanthropus pekinensis' and for root robusticities and crown areas of recent humans, from Vlček (1993) for the Ehringsdorf adult and juvenile, and from Lebel and Trinkaus (2002) for the Bau de l'Aubesier upper first/second molar (Aubesier 10) (listed under upper second molar in Tables 9.22 and 9.23). The mean figures for recent upper fourth deciduous premolar are taken from Black (1902). The sources for the ranges of mean figures shown for root lengths of recent permanent teeth are as listed in the previous section

| Tooth | Identity | MB/mesial mm | DB/distal mm | Lingual mm |
|---|---|---|---|---|
| **M¹** | Gran Dolina Hominid 1 | | | 15.8/16.1 |
| | 'Sinanthropus'     range | | | 13.7–15.4 |
| | Atapuerca-SH AT16 | 15.2 | 15.4 | 15.5 |
| | Atapuerca-SH AT20 | - | 13.1 | 14.7 |
| | Pontnewydd PN4 | 13.7 | 13.7 | - |
| | Pontnewydd PN12 | - | - | 14.4 |
| | Neanderthal  mean & (range) | | | 15.5 (12.5–18.4) |
| | Recent   ranges of means | | | 11.6–13.5 |
| | | | | |
| **M²** | 'Sinanthropus'     range | | | 13.5–17.7 |
| | Atapuerca-SH AT12 | 12.5 | 13.0 | 13.5 |
| | Atapuerca-SH AT15 | 13.3 | 13.2 | 13.1 |
| | Pontnewydd PN1 | - | - | 15.5 |
| | Bau de l'Aubesier | | 15.4 | 14.9 |
| | Neanderthal  mean & (range) | | | 15.5 (13.6–17.9) |
| | Recent   ranges of means | | | 12.3–13.6 |
| | | | | |
| **M₁** | Gran Dolina Hominid 1 | 16.7 | | |
| | 'Sinanthropus'     range | 13.1–16.1 | 14.2–18.5 | |
| | Atapuerca-SH AT14 | 16.2 | 15.5 | |
| | Atapuerca-SH AT21 | 15.5 | 14.5 | |
| | Pontnewydd PN11 | 16.2 | 16.0 | |
| | Ehringsdorf adult | 15.0 | 15.0 | |
| | Ehringsdorf juvenile | 14.1 | | |
| | Neanderthal  mean & (range) | 14.3 (12.2–16.8) | | |
| | Recent   ranges of means | 12.1–14.2 | | |
| | | | | |
| **M₂** | 'Sinanthropus' Nos 45/138 | 15.5 | 16.0 | |
| | Pontnewydd PN13 | 15.0 | - | |
| | Ehringsdorf adult | 15.5 | 15.5 | |
| | Neanderthal  mean & (range) | 15.3 (14.3–16.5) | | |
| | Recent    ranges of means | 11.3–15.0 | | |
| | | | | |
| **dp⁴** | Pontnewydd PN4 | 13.8 | 11.9 | 13.3 |
| | Recent     mean | | | 11.7 |

Neanderthal: Arcy-sur-Cure, Ciota Ciara, L'Hortus, Krapina, La Fate, La Ferrassie, La Quina, Monsempron, Petit Puymoyen, Pontnewydd, Regourdou, Spy, St Césaire, Tabun, Vindija.

*Table 9.22. Root lengths.*

and the mean and range figures for Neanderthal root lengths come from Bailey (2005; these include Pontnewydd). The measurements given for Atapuerca-SH teeth were made by T. Compton on casts in the collection of the Natural History Museum, London. Length measurements are quoted for the lingual, or only, roots measured of 'Sinanthropus' upper molars. Where both buccal and lingual measurements are recorded, the measurements of 'Sinanthropus' buccal roots are all at least a millimetre shorter than the lingual. The root lengths for teeth from Gran Dolina are taken from Bermúdez de Castro *et al.* (1999b).

*Root robusticity*

Weidenreich (1937) describes a decrease in root robusticity between 'Sinanthropus' teeth and recent teeth and, additionally, a relative decrease compared to crown area because recent teeth have a more pronounced constriction at the cervix. Consequently, if the ratio of crown area divided by root robusticity is calculated (quoted as a percentage), the figure tends to be higher for recent teeth.

The root robusticities of the Pontnewydd teeth (excluding the Mesolithic tooth PN2) are, in the main, close to the mean values of 'Sinanthropus' and above the figures for recent teeth. However, that of upper second molar PN1 is considerably higher, well above the range found in 'Sinanthropus'. The few Atapuerca-SH teeth measured also have root robusticity figures above the means of recent teeth. For upper molars and lower third molars, the range of values is within those of 'Sinanthropus', but three of the lower first and second molars are below, as might be expected from the relatively small size of these teeth. The figures for the Ehringsdorf teeth are all below the corresponding Pontnewydd figures and, in particular, that of the juvenile lower first molar is well below the mean

| Tooth | Identity | Buccal mm | Mesial/lingual mm | Distal mm | % of root length |
|-------|----------|-----------|-------------------|-----------|------------------|
| **M¹** | Atapuerca-SH AT16 | - | 10.4 | 12.8 | 67 |
| | Atapuerca-SH AT20 | 6.8 | 6.2 | 7.3 | 42 |
| | Pontnewydd PN4 | 9.3 | 7.9 | 7.0 | 51 |
| | Pontnewydd PN12 | - | 6.9 | - | 48 |
| **M²** | Atapuerca-SH AT12 | - | 5.5 | 5.7 | 41 |
| | Atapuerca-SH AT15 | - | 9.5 | 5.5 | 41 |
| | Pontnewydd PN1 | - | 10.5 | 11.0 | 68 |
| | Bau de l'Aubesier | 12.2 | 11.2 | 11.6 | 73 |
| **M₁** | Atapuerca-SH AT14 | - | 5.1 | | 31 |
| | Atapuerca-SH AT21 | 3.2 | 3.0 | | 19 |
| | Pontnewydd PN11 | 7.5 | 7.5 | | 46 |
| **M₂** | Atapuerca-SH AT11 | 5.0 | 5.0 | | - |
| | Pontnewydd PN13 | 7.2 | 4.0 | | 27 |
| **dp⁴** | Pontnewydd PN4 | 5.0 | - | - | 36 |

Table 9.23. Root trunk lengths.

figures for recent. This, and both lower third premolars, are also below the 'Sinanthropus' range. The robusticity figure for PN2, the Mesolithic lower third molar, is very similar to the figure for recent teeth.

Looking at the figures for the ratio of crown area to root robusticity, the ranges of values seen in 'Sinanthropus' are very wide and include most other teeth apart from:

- below – one Atapuerca-SH lower second molar and all Atapuerca-SH lower third molars, indicating proportionally more robust roots;
- above – the figures for recent upper first molar and lower third premolar, and the Ehringsdorf juvenile lower third premolar and lower first molar.

The Pontnewydd Middle Pleistocene teeth are all below the 'Sinanthropus' means. This is particularly marked in the upper second molar. The figures for Atapuerca-SH and Pontnewydd are all lower than the figures for recent teeth, with the exception of one Atapuerca-SH upper second molar. The figures for Ehringsdorf are varied, those of the adult being similar to 'Sinanthropus' means, but those of the juvenile being higher; close to or considerably above recent. The figure for the Mesolithic lower third molar, PN2, is similar to recent.

*Root lengths*
Weidenreich (1937) describes a decrease in root length between 'Sinanthropus' teeth and recent teeth. The root lengths of teeth from the later Middle Pleistocene sites – Pontnewydd, Atapuerca-SH, Ehringsdorf and Bau de l'Aubesier – as well as the means for Neanderthal teeth, are generally within, or close to, the range of values found for 'Sinanthropus' teeth. However, the Atapuerca-SH upper second molar AT15 and Pontnewydd lower second molar PN13 are a little below, and the ranges of values found in

the Neanderthal teeth tend to be wider. The average values for recent teeth are mostly below the range of values for 'Sinanthropus' and, with the exception of some Australian Aborigine teeth, below the figures for teeth from the later Middle Pleistocene sites. Of the recent teeth considered, the roots of San Bushmen upper first molars are notably short and, in the lower teeth, the roots of Australian Aborigine teeth are the longest and those of Japanese teeth the shortest. The roots of the Gran Dolina first molars are longer than those from the later Middle Pleistocene sites and the Neanderthal means, and those of the upper first molars are longer than those of 'Sinanthropus', and so fit the expected trend. The root lengths of 'Sinanthropus' and Gran Dolina lower molars are in turn mostly lower than the mean root lengths (max PRH) for EAFROB (East African *Australopithecus (Paranthropus) boisei*) (first molar, 20.2 mm; second molar, 21.1 mm) and EAFHOM (East African *Homo habilis* and *Homo ergaster*) (first molar, 18.4 mm; second molar, 19.1 mm) given by Wood *et al.* (1988).

*Root trunk lengths*
The trunk lengths reported are varied. The proportionally larger trunk lengths are in the upper molars for both Pontnewydd and Atapuerca-SH, minimums of 41–68% of maximum root length against 19–46% for lower molars.

In summary, the root robusticities, ratio of crown area to root robusticity, and root lengths of Pontnewydd Middle Pleistocene teeth are similar to those of 'Sinanthropus' teeth and distinct from recent human teeth. The root robusticities are higher than those of the Ehringsdorf specimens and (with the exception of upper first molar PN12) of the few Atapuerca-SH teeth measured, and the ratios of crown area to root robusticity are all below the 'Sinanthropus' means. The Pontnewydd roots are therefore relatively robust.

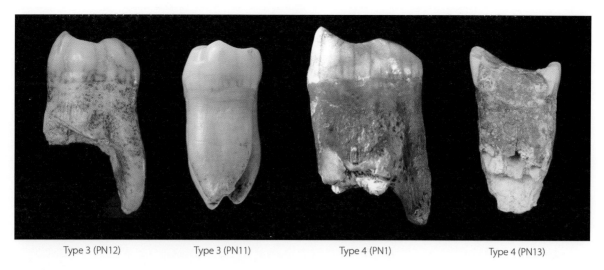

| Type 3 (PN12) | Type 3 (PN11) | Type 4 (PN1) | Type 4 (PN13) |

*Figure 9.18. Molnar cupped (concave) wear types.*

## Macroscopic wear

### *Method*

In studying the macroscopic wear of the Pontnewydd teeth, the following details are given for each tooth:

### *Category of wear*

Molnar's attrition scoring system is used to describe the wear on the teeth (Molnar 1971). This consists of three figures; defining the category of wear, the direction of wear and the form of wear. Category (grade) of wear identifies the degree of occlusal attrition. Wear on a tooth starts with wear facets appearing on one or more cusps. As wear progresses, the enamel is worn away and patches of dentine appear on individual cusps. Gradually these patches coalesce until the whole occlusal surface is dentine, with just an enamel rim. Eventually the entire crown is worn away, and the roots function as the occlusal surface. On Pontnewydd teeth, the coalescing of dentine exposure between cusps only occurs on the upper fourth deciduous premolar (PN4) and lower second molar PN13.

### *Direction of wear*

Horizontal, or in a mesiodistal or buccolingual direction, with the most worn side identified.

### *Form of wear*

Flat, cupped (*i.e.* concave) or rounded, as seen when viewed mesially or distally. Also notched wear, as seen when viewed buccally. There are two type grades of cupped wear; that which only involves half the tooth (mild, type 3), and that which involves most of the width of the tooth (type 4) (see Figure 9.18). In Molnar's system, 'cupped' wear is used to describe wear forms found on teeth that have considerable dentine exposure. Nonetheless, it can be used to describe wear shapes in enamel on less worn teeth, as it is here.

### *Dentine exposure*

On which cusps, and on which facets, and maximum width.

### *Dentine wear form*

Normally, because dentine wears faster than enamel, dentine is hollowed out in comparison with the surrounding enamel. However, it can be flat, in line with the surrounding enamel, or excavated out, such that there is a distinct step between the enamel and the dentine.

### *Description of occlusal wear*

Including the extent of pitting (fine, varied or coarse), and the presence of scratches (including their direction) or polish, as can be seen with a 10× magnifying glass. For molars, the wear facets produced by the two phases of the power stroke in the chewing cycle (Hiiemae 1978) are described separately. These are phase 1, the shearing action (the cusps of the upper and lower molars slide against each other as they come into contact) and phase 2, the grinding action (a lingual movement once the upper and lower molars have become fully in contact); see Hillson (1996). Upper molars overlap lower molars buccally. As a consequence, phase 1 facets are on the lingual surfaces of upper molar cusps and the buccal surfaces of lower molar cusps, and phase 2 facets are on the buccal surfaces of upper molar lingual cusps and the lingual surfaces of lower molar buccal cusps.

### *Occlusal edge chipping*

Any fractures or regular/isolated chips, and their position round the occlusal edge, again as seen with a 10× magnifying glass. Chips are defined as very mild (under 0.1 mm), mild (0.1–0.49 mm) or heavy (0.5–1 mm). Fractures (chips over 1 mm in breadth) are described and measured individually.

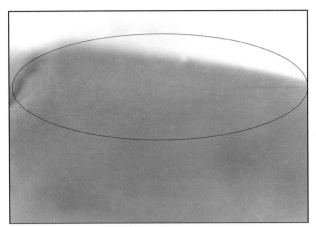

*Figure 9.19. PN10 showing cut-marks on buccal surface at occlusal edge.*

*Buccal/lingual face*
Scratches and any pitting or polish, as seen with a 10×
magnifying glass.

*Interproximal facets*
Shape, size (maximum height and width), position and type
of wear. As adjacent teeth move against each other, *e.g.*
during chewing, corresponding interproximal wear facets
having clearly defined edges are formed at the contact
points. These tend to be considerably larger on hominin
teeth of this date than those appearing on recent human
teeth. Commonly, where facets are not flat, they are concave
on the mesial sides of teeth and convex distally (Kaidonis
*et al.* 1992). Distinct near-vertical grooves can occur on
interproximal facets and these are described below.

No chipping of the occlusal edges, polish or pitting is
found on unerupted teeth, so it therefore can be assumed
to be *ante mortem*. A few isolated scratch-marks may be
seen on unerupted teeth but not in the concentration seen
on erupted teeth.

### Lower right lateral incisor PN10

The tooth has a clear line of exposed dentine along its length
(Molnar grade 4). This is 0.5 mm wide buccolingually and
worn normally and has mild chipping along the enamel
edges. The direction of wear is slightly mesial and the
form of wear is flat. There is a wear facet (without dentine
exposure), facing 60° from the buccal surface, on the buccal
edge of the occlusal surface. Well-defined buccolingually
directed scratch-marks (and some coarse pitting) can be
seen on this facet and on the occlusal surface. The distal
corner of the occlusal surface was broken off *ante mortem*,
leaving a 1.8 mm long jagged fracture that has been
rounded buccally and distally but not lingually. There are
severe vertical cracks in the enamel all around the tooth
(two buccal, two lingual, one mesial, one distal). At least
one on the buccal surface and one on the lingual may have
occurred before death, since in each case there is a chip
on the occlusal surface at the top of the crack. Vertical and
horizontal scratch-marks can be seen on the buccal surface

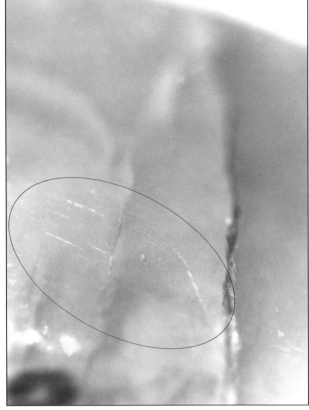

*Figure 9.20. PN10 showing cut-marks at centre of buccal
surface.*

but not on the lingual. Both the buccal and lingual surfaces
are polished, the buccal surface most.

There are a number of short, faint 'cut-marks', up to 2
mm long, on the occlusal two thirds of the buccal surface,
principally on the distal side (seen at 30× magnification).
Those on the distal side that are close to the occlusal edge
are generally horizontal, whilst below this they are near
horizontal, predominantly slanting superiorly distally (see
Figures 9.19 (occlusal edge) and 9.20 (centre of buccal
face)). Those on the mesial side are vertical, or near vertical
slanting both superiorly mesially and superiorly distally.

These marks are wider than most of the normal scratch-
marks (discussed below) that are caused by inorganic items
in the diet, such as phytoliths in vegetable matter, which
are generally less than 20 µm (Bermúdez de Castro *et al.*
1988; Lalueza Fox and Frayer 1997). They are also more
isolated. Lalueza Fox and Pérez-Pérez (1994) state that at
high magnification (*e.g.* ×400) it is possible to differentiate
*ante* and *post mortem* marks, the former being irregular
and eroded and the latter being sharper, with well-defined
margins. Although at lower magnification, the marks
near the occlusal edge appear possibly to be *post mortem*
whilst the remainder are more clearly *ante mortem*. The
mesial interproximal facet is vertically elongate. The
distal interproximal facet is circular and near the occlusal
edge. Both interproximal facets are finely pitted. They
are regularly set on the mesial and distal surfaces at right
angles to the mesiodistal axis of the tooth.

## Premolars

### Upper left fourth premolar PN18

Wear is grade 3, in line with the buccal and lingual cusps, and flat. Both cusps have small areas of exposed dentine that are normally worn – 1.5 mm wide on the top of the buccal cusp and 0.6 mm wide on the mesial side of the lingual cusp. The areas of wear on both cusps are coarsely pitted. There are wear facets on the lingual side of the buccal cusp (mesial and distal), on the mesial and distal margins, and on the distal side of the lingual cusp. They are also coarsely pitted (in particular the mesiobuccal facet). In addition, they have buccolingual scratches and some areas of polish. The positions of wear facets do not correspond with the areas of dentine exposure.

There is continuous mild chipping on the mesial and distal occlusal edges below the interproximal facets, and a single chip on the occlusal edge at the top of a severe vertical crack on the buccal surface. There are scratch-marks, mainly vertical, on both buccal and lingual surfaces, those on the buccal surface being quite heavy. There is also some lingual polish. The interproximal wear facets are both horizontally elongate, the distal being the larger, and centrally placed on the tooth at right angles to the mesiodistal occlusal groove. The distal facet is tilted up at 10° to the vertical. Both facets are finely pitted.

### Lower right third premolar PN6

There is no wear on this tooth.

### Lower left third premolar PN7

This tooth was not in occlusion. There are, though, some vertical scratches on the tip of the buccal surface of the buccal cusp. There is an interproximal wear facet on the distal margin, which is horizontally elongate and finely pitted. This is placed slightly lingually, and on the occlusal rim of the tooth, at 25° to the vertical.

### Lower left third premolar PN20

There is considerable wear and dentine exposure on the buccal cusp, to grade 4, but little wear on the lingual cusp (slight rounding). The occlusal wear facet on the buccal cusp is flat and inclined buccally and distally. The exposed dentine is 4.0 mm wide mesiodistally by 1.2 mm buccolingually, and worn normally. There is also a wear facet, without dentine exposure, on the distal margin. Both wear facets are finely pitted, and the wear facet on the buccal cusp has distinct buccolingual scratches. Unlike PN18, the buccal cusp wear facet covers the whole area of wear. It is slightly rounded on the lingual edge.

There is no chipping round the edge of the occlusal surface or round the buccal cusp wear facet, apart from very mild chipping over the distal interproximal facet. There are vertical scratches on the buccal and lingual faces, particularly strong buccally. The buccal and lingual faces are also polished (lingually just on the occlusal rim). The faint mesial interproximal facet is located slightly buccally and is vertically elongate. The distal interproximal facet is located slightly lingually and is horizontally elongate.

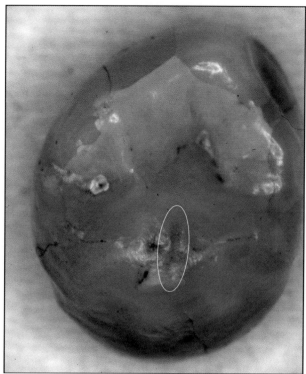

*Figure 9.21. PN5 showing buccolingual groove on tip of buccal cusp.*

Both interproximal facets are finely pitted. The occlusal wear pattern of this tooth is similar to the final stage for lower third premolars described by Wolpoff (1979) for the Krapina teeth, *i.e.* 'a single flattened wear plane on the buccal surface increasing in angulation until there is a sharp mesiodistal edge left on the occlusal surface'.

### Lower left fourth premolar PN5

Wear on this tooth is grade 2, with no dentine exposure. There are two wear facets on the buccal cusp, one on the mesial slope and one on the distal slope. The mesial facet is inclined 20° buccally and is coarsely pitted. The distal facet is inclined 45° buccally, is finely pitted and, in addition, has buccolingual scratches. This pattern of wear facets is the same as that described by Wolpoff (1979) for the second stage of wear for lower third premolar teeth from Krapina; 'formation of buccal mesial and buccal distal wear planes'.

The tip of the buccal cusp is severely chipped. In particular, there is a small 'groove' on the tip running buccolingually, 0.8 mm long, 0.2 mm wide and 0.1 mm deep (Figure 9.21). There is also continuous chipping along the mesial and distal slopes of the buccal cusp (mild distally and very mild mesially) and slight chipping on the tip of the mesiolingual cusp. There are scratches (mainly vertical) and some polish on the buccal surface, and on the occlusal rim of the lingual surface.

There are a number of straight, near-vertical 'cut-marks' on the buccal surface. The most distinct (visible to the naked eye) is at the tip of the buccal cusp, about 1 mm long

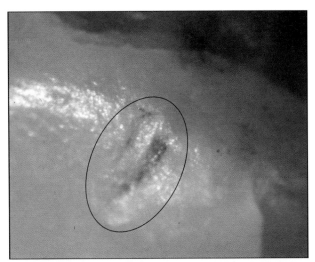

*Figure 9.22. PN5 showing cut-marks on buccal surface at occlusal edge.*

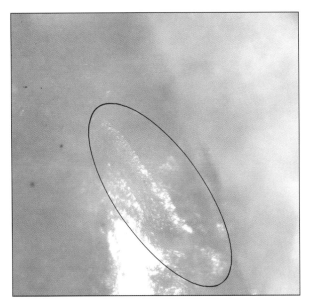

*Figure 9.23. PN5 showing cut-marks at centre of buccal surface.*

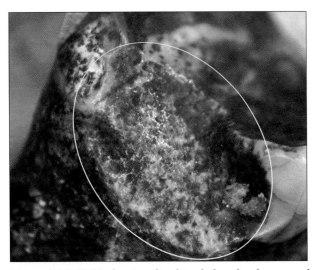

*Figure 9.24. PN13 showing distal angled occlusal wear and groove.*

and slanting superiorly distally. There is a shorter and less distinct mark just mesial to it (Figure 9.22). Milder marks can be seen (using a 10× magnifying glass) in the centre of the buccal face, running down from the most distinct cut-mark. These are 1–2 mm long and slanting superiorly mesially (Figure 9.23). They all have rounded edges and have the appearance of being *ante mortem*. The larger 'cut-mark' at the tip of the cusp is filled with a brown deposit; its shape cannot therefore be determined. The mark mesial to it has a 'V'-shaped outline and the other marks have a shallow rounded outline. The interproximal wear facets are located on the mesiobuccal and distolingual corners of the tooth. The mesial facet is small and vertically elongate, and the distal facet is oval in a horizontal direction. Both facets have fine pitting. The distal facet is tilted up at 20° to the vertical.

### Molars

Details of wear are given in Table 9.24 for upper molars and Table 9.25 for lower molars. The table for lower molars includes details of the Mesolithic tooth PN8.

#### Upper? molar fragment PN9
This small segment of a very worn tooth has an enamel rim 3.0 mm high, and normally worn exposed dentine. On one side, the top half of the fracture was *ante mortem* since there is slight horizontal and vertical rounding along its exposed edges. This is 3.7 mm high on the enamel and part of the root trunk, and 4.5 mm long on the exposed dentine on the occlusal surface (full width of fragment). The other side of the fracture is a clean break. Some vertical scratches and polish can be seen on the enamel, and areas of coarse pitting, but no occlusal edge chipping. This is likely therefore to be the buccal or lingual side of the tooth. There are no wear facets and there is no occlusal pitting or polish.

#### Upper right fourth deciduous premolar PN4
Dentine exposure has coalesced on all cusps except the hypocone. There are enamel margins on each side of the oblique ridge, with dentine exposure down the centre. There is also an area of enamel remaining between the buccal cusps.

#### Lower right second molar PN13
PN13 is very worn and in an unusual manner. All the occlusal enamel has been worn away, and the dentine has been scooped out over the width of the tooth to form a regular, smooth, mesiodistally-facing cylinder. The buccal and lingual enamel faces are of the same height, and the centre of the occlusal surface is approximately 2 mm below the buccal and lingual occlusal margins. The mesial end of the buccal margin is worn down at an angle, and the mesial and distal enamel faces have been worn/broken away. The exposed dentine is highly polished. The dentine at the distal end of the tooth has been worn down at an angle of 40° to the horizontal, below the level of the cylinder (see

| Identity / Tooth type | PN4 RM¹ | PN12 LM¹ | PN1 LM² | PN17 RM³ | PN19 RM³ | PN4 Rdm²/dp⁴ |
|---|---|---|---|---|---|---|
| **WEAR** Grade | 3 | 3 | 3/4 | 0 | 0 | 5 |
| Direction | 6, Horizontal | 6, Horizontal | 6, Horizontal | | | 6, Horizontal |
| Form | 3, Slight cupping (buccal cusps) | 3, Slight cupping (buccal cusps) | 4, Cupped (buccal to lingual) | | | 3, Slight cupping (buccal cusps) |
| **DENTINE** Exposure on cusps | MB 0.6 mm | MB 0.5 mm | MB (1.3 × 4.0 mm) & ML (Ph2) 1.6 mm | | | All |
| Wear form | Normal | Normal | Normal (MB nearly flat) | | | Normal |
| **WEAR FACETS** **PHASE 1 FACETS** Lingual cusps | ML: coarse pitting & buccolingual scratches / DL: coarse pitting | ML: coarse pitting & buccolingual scratches / DL: coarse pitting | ML: pitting / DL: pitting | | | Coarse pitting overall, some polish on hypocone & lingual rim mesiolingual cusp |
| Buccal cusps | MB: coarse pitting / DB: coarse pitting | MB: strong buccolingual scratches, polished area on mesial facet / DB: coarse pitting & buccolingual scratches | MB: coarse pitting / DB: coarse pitting | | | |
| **PHASE 2 FACETS** | ML: coarse pitting / DL: fine pitting | ML: coarse pitting / DL: fine pitting | ML: coarse pitting / DL: coarse pitting (& pitting on occlusal surface) | | | |
| **OCCLUSAL EDGE CHIPPING** | Two small mesial chips. Regular chipping; mild tip DL cusp & lingual side of ML cusp, very mild on buccal side | Single mesial chip & single chip tip mesiolingual cusp. Regular mild chipping on mesiobuccal corner | Regular chipping; mild on mesial & distal sides, heavy on buccal side | | | Regular chipping; mild on mesial side & buccal of DB cusp, very mild on distal side & buccal of MB cusp |
| **BUCCAL FACE** Scratches/Polish | A few, mainly vertical | A few, mainly vertical | Mainly horizontal | | | Vertical & horizontal, some heavy; polished |
| **LINGUAL FACE** Scratches/Polish | Mainly vertical, some horizontal; polished | Mainly vertical | Mainly horizontal; polished | | | Vertical & horizontal; very polished |
| **INTER-PROXIMAL FACETS** **MESIAL -** Shape | Square | Horizontal oval | Horizontal rectangle | None | None | Semicircle |
| Size | 3.2 × 2.7 mm | 4.3 × 2.4 mm | 6.5 × 2.8 mm | | | 4.5 × 2.2 mm |
| Position | Central | Central | Central | | | Central |
| Wear | Fine pitting | Fine pitting, vertical scratches | Fine pitting | | | Fine pitting |
| **DISTAL -** Shape | Trace, circular | Faint, circular | Horizontal rectangle | None | None | Square |
| Size | 1.3 × 1.3 mm | 1.5 × 1.5 mm | 5.8 × 2.8 mm | | | 3.2 × 2.7 mm |
| Position | Hypocone | Hypocone | Hypocone | | | Central |
| Wear | None | Fine pitting | Fine pitting | | | Fine pitting |

*Table 9.24. Wear on upper molars.*

| Identity / Tooth type | PN11 LM₁ | PN13 RM₂ | PN15 RM₂ | PN16 RM₃ | PN21 RM₃ | PN8 (Mesolithic) RM₂ |
|---|---|---|---|---|---|---|
| **WEAR** Grade | 3 | 6 | 3 | 2 | 0 | 2 |
| Direction | 6, Horizontal | 6, Horizontal | 6, Horizontal | 6, Horizontal | | 6, Horizontal |
| Form | 3, Slight cupping (D, & MB) | 4, Very cupped (whole tooth) | 4, Cupped (buccal to lingual) | 3, Slight cupping (DL & DB) | | 2, Flat |
| **DENTINE** Exposure on cusps | ML, DL, 0.3 mm | All, coalesced | DL, MB (Ph2), 0.4 mm | None | | None |
| Wear form | Normal | Normal | Normal | N/A | | N/A |
| **WEAR FACETS PHASE 1 FACETS** Lingual cusps | ML: coarse pitting  DL.: coarse pitting & polish | | ML: pitting & buccolingual scratches  DL: coarse pitting | ML: pitting  DL: pitting | | ML: –  DL.: fine pitting & mild buccolingual scratches |
| Buccal cusps | MB: buccolingual scratches  DB: pitting & buccolingual scratches | | MB: buccolingual scratches  DB: pitting & buccolingual scratches | MB: fine pitting  DB: fine pitting & polish | | MB: fine pitting & polish  DB: fine pitting |
| **PHASE 2 FACETS** | MB: pitting  DB: pitting | | MB: pitting  DB: pitting, coarse on cusp 5 | MB: fine pitting & polish  DB: fine pitting & buccolingual scratches; cusp 5 polished | | MB: –  DB: ML/DB scratches; polish on occlusal surface |
| **OCCLUSAL EDGE CHIPPING** | Single chip lingual side of ML cusp. Regular chipping; mild on mesial side, heavy on ML & DL corners & lingual side of DL cusp | 2 chips above DB facet. Regular chipping; mild on buccal side of MB cusp, very mild on ML corner | Regular chipping on mesial & distal sides (both very mild) | Regular chipping on distal side (heavy) | | Small distal chip |
| **BUCCAL FACE** Scratches/Polish | Vertical, & sup. distal to inf. mesial on DB cusp | Mild, all directions, mainly vertical; mild pitting, polished | Heavy, all directions; polished | Mainly vertical; polished on MB cusp | | Mild, vertical; very polished on occlusal rim |
| **LINGUAL FACE** Scratches/Polish | None, some roughening | Mild, all directions, mainly vertical; very polished | All directions; polished on occlusal rim | Mainly vertical; polished on occlusal rim | | Mild, vertical; polished on occlusal rim |
| **INTER-PROXIMAL FACETS** MESIAL - Shape | Square | Horizontal rectangle | Horizontal rectangle | Broken | None | Oval |
| Size | 3.3 × 3.3 mm | 8.0 × 4.3 mm | 5.3 × 3.4 mm | | | 4.0 × 3.0 mm |
| Position | MB cusp, tilted buccally | Central | Central | | | MB cusp |
| Wear | Fine pitting | Uneven (in dentine) | Fine pitting | Fine pitting | | Fine pitting, vertical step in centre |
| DISTAL - Shape | Horizontal, faint | Horizontal rectangle | Horizontal rectangle | None | None | None |
| Size | 2.9 × 1.5 mm | 7.0 × 2.7 mm | 5.5 × 3.8 mm | | | |
| Position | Central | Central | Central | | | |
| Wear | Fine pitting | Pitted (in dentine) | Fine pitting | | | |

*Table 9.25. Wear on lower molars.*

Figure 9.24). This area is 8 mm wide (most of the width of the tooth) buccolingually and 3 mm mesiodistally. It links to the distal edge of the buccal enamel face, upon which there is a vertical polished facet about 3 mm high and 0.8 mm deep, slightly concave and angled buccally (part of the original interproximal facet?). There is a buccolingual 'groove' on the vertical side of the enamel lingual to this, and in the dentine behind, 2.7 mm high, 0.5 mm deep and 2.3 mm long, joining to the worn down area. The dentine in the worn down area is very coarsely pitted and not polished. There are two occlusal chips above the vertical facet. The regular mild chipping on the mesiobuccal cusp is unusual in being on the lingual side of the enamel rim. The distal interproximal facet is apical to (below) the occlusal surface.

## Summary and discussion (excluding PN8)

The collection of casts of other European Middle Pleistocene teeth held by the Natural History Museum, London is used for comparison, as are photographs of the Biache and Steinheim specimens. Descriptions of the Visogliano specimens are taken from Abbazzi *et al.* (2000) and Mallegni *et al.* (2002) and of the Bau de l'Aubesier specimen from Lebel and Trinkaus (2002).

### Direction of wear

The inclination of wear on nearly all the Pontnewydd teeth is horizontal, including the very worn lower second molar PN13 and the upper fourth deciduous premolar PN4. The only exceptions are the lower lateral incisor PN10, worn in a slightly mesial direction, and the lower third premolar PN20, which is worn in a distobuccal direction. The distal component of this is because of the rotation of the tooth. The horizontal wear is in line with the findings of Smith (1984) for a sample of European Middle and Upper Palaeolithic lower first molars. These had the lowest angle of wear for any of the groups studied, lower than those for more recent hunter-gatherers.

### Form of wear

The general pattern of wear on Pontnewydd molars is slight cupping (*i.e.* concave wear) on one side of lightly worn teeth (Molnar type 3; PN4 (permanent molar), PN12, PN11, PN16) which then extends to the other side of the tooth (Molnar type 4; PN1 and PN15) and finally leads to the scooped out wear observed on PN13. In contrast, there is only mild Molnar type 3 wear on the upper fourth deciduous premolar (PN4) that has been worn to grade 5. On upper molars the Molnar type 3 wear is on the buccal cusp phase 1 facets. On lower molars, it is on the distal margin and mesiobuccal cusp of PN11, and on the distolingual and distobuccal cusps of PN16. The phase 1 facets are notably larger than the phase 2 facets on the upper permanent molars and on the lower first molar PN11.

A number of the Middle Pleistocene teeth have Molnar cupped wear:

- Two Arago teeth (a very worn lower first molar and

a moderately worn upper second molar) – both type 3;
- the Petralona upper second molars (both with slight dentine exposure) – type 3;
- the Visogliano upper first molar Vis 6 (type 3) and upper second molar Vis 3 (type 4) (both with slight dentine exposure);
- the Bau de l'Aubesier (Aubesier 10) upper first/second molar (with slight dentine exposure) – type 4;
- the lower first molars of the Ehringsdorf adult (very worn) – type 4 (in a mesiobuccal/distolingual direction).

Other teeth, though, have flat wear. Atapuerca-SH teeth exhibit cupped wear similar to Pontnewydd teeth, though with some variation:

- Two teeth (AT14 (lower first molar) and AT11 (lower second molar)), which have considerable dentine exposure, have flat wear;
- AT75 (lower second molar), with no dentine exposure, has Molnar type 4 wear.

The phase 1 facets are also larger than the phase 2 facets on a number of the Atapuerca-SH teeth, as with Pontnewydd.

Janis (1984) studied tooth wear on upper second molars of three species of Colobus monkeys with different diets, and found that the species with the highest proportion of leaves in its diet had extensive areas of buccal phase 1 shear facet reaching halfway across the tooth, whereas, in the species with a high proportion of seeds in its diet, these facets only reached one third of the way across the tooth at the same level of wear. Shearing wear was therefore associated with tough fibrous food such as leaf stems, petioles, twigs, *etc.* rather than soft or brittle food such as fruit, nuts, seeds, buds, *etc.* The high rate of wear on Pontnewydd phase 1 facets (see below) and their size, with the cupped wear progressing over the whole width of the tooth, therefore suggests a tough, fibrous vegetable diet. However, there is no evidence of the fern root planes described by Taylor (1963). The characteristic of this type of wear is that the buccal occlusal edges of both upper and lower posterior teeth are worn down such that they no longer occlude. It is caused by prolonged chewing of a lump of tough fibrous material (*e.g.* fern root) held between the cheek and the teeth.

Cupped wear also occurs on the La Ferrassie 1 upper and lower molars. Boule and Vallois (1957) considered that the great surface development and slight depth of the glenoid cavities, the barely projecting form of the temporal condyles, and the strength of the pterygoid muscles in this specimen indicated a dentition with great freedom of lateral movement, more employed for chewing than for biting, and implied a vegetarian rather than a carnivorous diet. Opposing this, isotope and trace element data (*e.g.* Bocherens *et al.* 1999 and Balter and Simon 2006; isotope data reviewed by Richards and Trinkaus 2009) suggest that later Neanderthals were, in fact, predominantly carnivorous. However, microwear analysis by El Zaatari (2007) detected a difference in Neanderthals and Pre-Neanderthals between those from steppe/tundra environments, who had signatures similar to known meat eaters (Fueguians), and those from forest environments, whose signatures indicated mixed diets. Hardy (2010) argues that Neanderthals would have needed energy from alternative sources to meat, particularly when animals were fat-depleted, and points out that 'native European wild edible plants with starchy underground storage organs would have been potentially available throughout the Neanderthal range, even during the coldest periods of the Late Pleistocene'. Henry *et al.* (2011) have studied microfossils in samples of calculus taken from Neanderthal teeth from the sites of Spy (Belgium) and Shanidar (Iraq). Starch granules in the Spy samples suggest a diversity of plant types in the diet but nearly half the starches recovered are considered to have come from underground storage organs, probably water lilies.

The wear on the lower lateral incisor, PN10, is flat. This is in contrast to the rounded wear seen on many Neanderthal teeth, *e.g.* Krapina, Shanidar I, La Ferrassie 1 (Brace 1975; Smith 1976a; Trinkaus 1978). The Middle Pleistocene teeth are varied. The Ehringsdorf adult and Atapuerca-SH AT5 lower lateral incisors have flat wear, whilst those of the Mauer specimen are slightly cupped, and those of the Ehringsdorf juvenile are mildly rounded.

*Pattern of dentine exposure*
For the Krapina dental remains, Wolpoff (1979) stated that the basic wear pattern on lower molars was normally more rapid wear on the buccal side, though the difference between the buccal and lingual sides varied from marked to minimal. Dentine exposure occurred on the mesial buccal cusp first, followed by the distal buccal cusp. Wear on the lingual side likewise proceeded from mesial to distal. The phase 2 buccal facets were therefore wearing at a faster rate than the phase 1 lingual facets. At Pontnewydd, the wear pattern is rather different:

LOWER MOLARS
Looking at the teeth with dentine exposure (excluding the very worn PN13); PN11 has dentine exposure on the two lingual cusps and PN15 has dentine exposure on the mesiobuccal and distolingual cusps. Wear on PN11 is therefore greater on the phase 1 facets, particularly on the lingual cusps, with little wear on the phase 2 facets. There is no phase 2 facet on the distobuccal cusp of this tooth, and the phase 1 facet on the distolingual cusp is near horizontal instead of running down the side of the cusp as would be expected. On PN15 the buccal (phase 2) and lingual (phase 1) wear is similar and in an oblique direction. There is very little wear on the mesiolingual cusp. The phase 2 facets on the three buccal cusps are of near equal size (the dentine exposure on the mesiobuccal cusp is not on the facet). The wear gradient on both teeth tends to be distal to mesial rather than mesial to distal. This is also the case on PN16, which has no dentine exposure. The greatest wear on this tooth is on the distolingual phase 1 facet, followed by the distobuccal phase 2 facet. There is little wear on the mesial cusps.

UPPER MOLARS
PN4 (permanent molar) and PN12 both have dentine exposure on the mesiobuccal cusp, and PN1 on both mesiobuccal and mesiolingual cusps at a similar level. The buccal and lingual phase 1 facets are larger than the phase 2 facets on all three teeth. Buccal and lingual phase 1 wear is therefore greater than lingual phase 2 wear, and the wear is going from mesial to distal. PN1 has an unusual exposure of dentine on the phase 1 mesiobuccal cusp facet, a line running buccolingually down the lingual side of the cusp.

Comparing this with other Middle Pleistocene molars and those from Gran Dolina:

LOWER MOLARS
With the exception of Bilzingsleben E1, all the lower molars that have exposed dentine have this on the mesiobuccal phase 2 facet. Casts of Atapuerca-SH teeth (excluding those that have dentine exposure on all cusps) also have exposed dentine on distolingual (phase 1) facets, and either cusp 5 or distobuccal (phase 2) facets. Bermúdez de Castro and Nicolás (1997) state that the mesiolingual cusp is the last to exhibit dentine in the Atapuerca-SH teeth. This appears to be the situation on the first molars of the Gran Dolina Hominid 7 specimen as well (picture in Carbonell *et al.* 2005), where there is dentine exposure on the remaining cusps, most evident on the mesiobuccal cusp. A similar pattern is found on the very worn Ehringsdorf adult first and second molars, where the wear is greatest on the mesiobuccal and distolingual cusps (particularly pronounced on the distolingual cusps on the right-hand side). Likewise, the Ehringsdorf juvenile first molar (with dentine exposure on the mesiobuccal cusp) has least wear on the mesiolingual cusp, and this is also the case on the teeth of the Arago 2 and 13 specimens. In the Arago 13 teeth, wear is similar on the remaining cusps. The wear on PN15 is consistent with all these. Greater lingual wear is seen on the Montmaurin first molars, with exposed dentine on the phase 1 facets of both lingual cusps as well as on the mesiobuccal cusp. One side also has dentine exposure on cusp 5. The degree of lingual wear seen on PN11 is most similar to that of the Bilzingsleben E1 second molar, on which just the two lingual cusps have exposed dentine (Vlček and Mania 1987). In contrast, the right second molar of the earlier Mauer specimen has dentine exposure on the mesiobuccal and mesiolingual cusps. Wear is therefore going from mesial to distal, unlike many of the other Middle Pleistocene teeth (the left second molar has dentine exposure on all five cusps). The Mauer right first molar has considerably greater wear buccally than lingually. There is also mostly greater wear buccally on Arago 2 but the third molar has most wear on the distolingual cusp.

UPPER MOLARS
The wear on many upper molars (Arago, Petralona, Atapuerca-SH, Steinheim, Biache) is heaviest on the mesial cusps, as with the Pontnewydd teeth. On the Petralona second and third molars, and the Steinheim first molars,

there is only dentine exposure on the mesiolingual phase 2 facet (and on one Petralona second molar distolingual cusp). Conversely, on one Biache first molar, and the Arago 21 second molars, there is only dentine exposure on the mesiobuccal phase 1 facet, as found on the PN4 and PN12 permanent molars. A similar pattern of dentine exposure to that seen on PN4 and PN12 is also found on the Gran Dolina Hominid 3 first molars, where the only dentine exposure is on the lingual slope of the paracone (Bermúdez de Castro *et al.* 1999b). The dentine exposure in Atapuerca-SH teeth, though, tends to be greatest on the mesiolingual phase 2 facet when it occurs on both mesial cusps, unlike PN1, and this is also the case in the Petralona first molars. In contrast to the above, on the Visogliano teeth the mesial and distal wear is more similar. Dentine exposure is greatest, or only present, on the phase 2 facets of the two lingual cusps on the first and second molars (Vis6 and Vis3). However, on the third molar (Vis1, from a different individual) the dentine exposure is greatest on the buccal cusp phase 1 facets. The same is the case on the Bau de l'Aubesier first/second molar (Aubesier 10), the two buccal cusps having a greater degree of dentine exposure than the two lingual cusps. Similarly, on the Bilzingsleben first molar (C1) the buccal cusps are more abraded than the lingual ones (Mania and Vlček 1981). The degree of buccal and lingual wear on the Arago teeth varies. None of the Middle Pleistocene teeth has the dentine wear pattern on the mesiobuccal cusp that occurs on PN1.

Wear on both upper and lower molars therefore tends to be similar to that observed at Pontnewydd, but with the degree of phase 1 facet wear found on Pontnewydd teeth being at the top end of the spectrum. The pattern of dentine exposure on the Pontnewydd teeth implies that there was a considerable shearing component to mastication, as opposed to crushing, causing a relatively greater level of wear on phase 1 facets (Hiiemae 1978; Janis 1984).

The difference in the form of wear between Middle Pleistocene samples and Krapina, with the Middle Pleistocene teeth tending to exhibit greater phase 1 wear, is in line with the findings of Pérez-Pérez *et al.* (2003) that a major shift in human dietary habits and food processing techniques may have taken place in Europe and the Near East at the end of the Middle Pleistocene. Studies of non-occlusal dental microwear indicate that Middle Pleistocene humans had more abrasive dietary habits, with possible inclusion of plant foods. Nevertheless, work by Fiorenza *et al.* (2008a) found that, for Neanderthals in general, phase 1 facets are better developed than phase 2 facets. This compares to early *Homo sapiens,* in which both phase 1 and 2 facets are prominent, indicating a greater level of grinding. In addition, wear areas on Neanderthal teeth have edges that are more clearly marked (seen at Pontnewydd) than is the case in early *Homo sapiens,* where the facet margins are rounded. These authors concluded that the Neanderthal diet was narrower and more specialized than that of early *Homo sapiens.* In a further paper, Fiorenza *et al.* (2008b) make comparisons with modern hunter-gatherers that largely rely on animal protein and conclude

that early *Homo sapiens* had a diet rich in meat but that in Neanderthals the proportions of the phase 1 facets indicate the processing of fibrous foodstuffs.

*Dentine wear form*
The dentine on the Pontnewydd teeth is normally worn, as it is on most of the teeth in the Middle Pleistocene sample. However, distinct excavation of the dentine is encountered in two of the earlier Middle Pleistocene specimens – Mauer (lower first molar) and Petralona (upper first molar) – both on phase 2 facets, suggesting a diet with a high crushing component. The Ehringsdorf adult lower second molars also have excavated out dentine, both on the distolingual cusp.

*Wear gradient*
Since the second molars relating to the first molars PN4, PN12 and PN11 were newly erupted, as determined from the small size of the distal interproximal facets, it can be safely assumed that they had wear at grades 1 or 2 (no dentine exposure). Using Lavelle's method (Lavelle 1970), the wear gradient between first and second molars is therefore '1' for the upper molars and '2' for the lower molars (the difference between first and second molar in the number of cusps with dentine exposure, excluding cusp 5 on lower molars). Lavelle found that the means for a variety of groups (modern British, Anglo-Saxon, Eskimo, West African, Australian Aborigine) varied between 1.7 and 2.4 for upper molars (with 14–32% at gradient 1), and 1.3–2.4 for lower molars (with 17–33% at gradient 2). The wear gradients observed on other Middle Pleistocene specimens using Lavelle's method are very varied; 0–4 on lower first to second molar and lower second to third molar, and 1–4 on upper first to second molar. However, if the width of dentine exposed is taken into account, the picture is more consistent.

WEAR GRADIENT, LOWER FIRST TO SECOND MOLAR
There are two mandibles that are of a similar developmental age to PN11; the Ehringsdorf juvenile and Atapuerca-SH AT2. The nearest in age is the Ehringsdorf juvenile, with the second molar just erupted (having very little wear) and the third molar unerupted. This has a similar level of dentine exposure on the first molar (0.4 mm wide) but only on one cusp, against two on PN11. Atapuerca-SH AT2 is possibly a little older, with a clear, but not deep, 3.0 mm wide distal interproximal facet on the first molar. The level of wear is a little greater than that on PN11, three cusps having exposed dentine with widths of 0.5–0.6 mm. If PN11 is correctly placed in Individual B, then the Ehringsdorf juvenile is at the same stage of development (lower third premolar erupting but not in occlusion), and Atapuerca-SH AT2, with third and fourth premolars in occlusion but having very little wear, about six months to one year older (aged at 14 by Bermúdez de Castro and Díez 1995).

There are three mandibles from older individuals; Montmaurin, Atapuerca-SH AT1 and Arago 13 (aged at 18 by Bermúdez de Castro and Díez 1995). In all of these there is no dentine exposure on the second molars, and the third molars are in occlusion. The degree of wear on the first molars is greater than that on PN11 on Montmaurin and Atapuerca-SH AT1, and distinctly greater on Arago 13:

- Montmaurin. Dentine exposure on three/four cusps and of greater width than on PN11, 0.3–1.6 mm.
- Atapuerca-SH AT1. Dentine exposure on five cusps, width 0.2–1.2 mm.
- Arago 13. Dentine exposure on five cusps, width 0.9–1.6 mm. The wear gradient between first and second molar is particularly high on this specimen.

The ages given by Bermúdez de Castro and Díez (1995) are based on the development stage of the third molar, using the method of Johansson, assuming eruption at a normal age of 18. As described below, the likely age of eruption of the third molar in these specimens is distinctly lower, so reducing these estimates. The rate of wear on PN11 appears to be higher than that on the Ehringsdorf juvenile and, in view of the small age difference, similar to that on Atapuerca-SH AT2.

##### Wear gradient, lower second to third molar

It is suggested that PN15 and PN16 could come from the same individual. PN15 has two cusps showing exposed dentine of up to 0.4 mm width and PN16 none. The wear gradient on the Mauer right second and third molars is similar (two cusps having exposed dentine on the second molar but none apparent on the third molar) but with the level of dentine exposure on the mesiobuccal cusp of the second molar being greater than that on PN15.

##### Wear gradient, upper first to second molar

The Biache specimen has slightly greater wear than PN4 and PN12, one/four cusps on the first molars having minimal dentine exposure. The second molars have moderate wear and the third molars appear to be newly erupted, which gives an age of 14–15 using the same bases of ageing as for the Pontnewydd teeth. The Steinheim specimen similarly has a small amount of dentine exposure on the mesiolingual cusps of the first molars, mild wear on the second molars, and very little wear on the third molars. The rate of wear on the Biache and Steinheim first molars is therefore probably less than on the Pontnewydd first molars in view of the three years plus age difference. The Visogliano first and second molars fit together, and the distal interproximal facet on the second molar is superficial, suggesting recent eruption of the third molar and a similar age. The level of wear is a little greater, with mild dentine exposure on all four cusps of the first molar and on the two lingual cusps of the second molar.

##### Level of wear on upper and lower first molars

The wear levels on the Pontnewydd first molars are high compared with Krapina first molars (Wolpoff 1979). Those of similar age have no dentine exposure, and those with similar levels of wear are aged 16–17 for upper first molars and 15–19 for lower first molars (wear grades determined from casts). Trinkaus (1995) found a uniform pattern of wear in a sample of Neanderthals, including Krapina, and noted that there was slight dentine exposure (Molnar stages 2–4) on first molars in the third decade of life. This again, therefore, is a lower rate of wear than appears at Pontnewydd, where Molnar level 3 wear occurs in the two individuals having estimated ages of eleven/8.5–9 years.

### Occlusal surfaces

The occlusal surfaces were examined at 10× magnification. This showed that almost all the facets and areas of occlusal wear on the molars are pitted, most of them coarsely. Exceptions are some of the upper and lower buccal phase 1 wear facets, and part of the occlusal surface of the very worn PN13. Of the buccal phase 1 facets that are pitted, those on upper molars are more coarsely pitted than those on lower molars.

Fine pitting is found on the buccal phase 1 facets, and mesial and distal phase 2 facets, of the lower third molar PN16. Fine pitting on the phase 1 facets is in place of the buccolingual scratches encountered on the lower first and second molars, PN11 and PN15. Fine pitting is also found on the distal phase 2 facets of the upper first molars, PN4 and PN12. The fine pitting on these facets contrasts with coarse pitting on the mesial phase 2 facets of these teeth.

Pitting on the occlusal surfaces of premolars is varied and not in proportion to wear. The least worn tooth, PN5, has both coarse and fine pitting, PN18 has coarse pitting, but the most worn, PN20, is only finely pitted. There is no pitting on the occlusal surface of the lower lateral incisor, PN10. The degree of pitting found on molars and premolars suggests the inclusion of hard objects in the diet.

Buccolingual scratches on molars are mainly confined to mesiolingual, mesiobuccal and distobuccal phase 1 facets on upper and lower first molars and on the lower second molar PN15. They do not occur on any phase 1 facets on PN1 or PN16. PN16, though, is the only tooth with buccolingual scratches on a phase two facet.

All the premolars, and the lower incisor, have buccolingual scratches on the occlusal surface. Those on PN10 are well defined. These could be the result of the 'stuff and cut' method of eating, described by Brace (1975), where the front teeth are used as a clamp to hold food while excess food is cut off with a knife, a method commonly used by hunter-gatherers. Alternatively, they could be the result of using the front teeth to strip off food, *e.g.* taking meat off a bone (Howells 1975). Lalueza Fox and Frayer (1997) differentiate between the scratches seen on PN10, and on incisors at Krapina, and the channelling or deep scratches caused by various types of manufacturing activity.

Some of the teeth have polished areas on the occlusal surface:

- PN12 (upper first molar) mesiobuccal cusp, mesial phase 1 facet.
- PN11 (lower first molar) distolingual phase 1 facet.
- PN16 (lower third molar) distobuccal phase 1 facets and mesial and distal phase 2 facets.
- PN4 (deciduous tooth) lingual cusps.

- PN18 (upper fourth premolar) occlusal facets.
- PN13 (lower second molar) exposed dentine at mesial end of tooth.

The presence/absence of occlusal polish does not appear to be related to the degree of wear.

*Trauma*

The chipping encountered is generally mild but occurs on all of the erupted teeth. PN11 has heavy chipping on the mesiolingual and distolingual corners, PN1 on the buccal occlusal edge and PN16 distally. The chipping on PN15 and PN20 is very mild. The only small fracture occurs on lower lateral incisor PN10. There is, though, evidence of major fractures. PN15 (lower second molar) is split mesiodistally along the mesiodistal groove. It is not possible to be certain that this occurred before death, but the direction of the split is typical of whole-tooth fractures (discussed below). There is no rounding or erosion of the broken edges and the two parts fit exactly, with no bits missing. On PN9, although only a fragment of the tooth is present, it appears to have been fractured before death, possibly in a buccolingual direction, along a length of at least 4.5 mm.

Several of the teeth have severe vertical cracks, as opposed to the normal post-depositional fine cracking of the enamel. Some appear on unerupted teeth, so must have occurred after death. However, on two teeth, lower lateral incisor PN10 and upper fourth premolar PN18, there are cracks with a chip at the top (buccal and lingual on PN10 and buccal on PN18). These could therefore possibly be *ante mortem* and, together with the distal fracture on PN10, indicate heavy use.

Although they are mostly not large chips, the frequency of occlusal edge chipping on the Pontnewydd teeth is higher than that found on some other fossil hominins and hunter-gatherers. Wallace (1973) studied three groups of australopithecines (Sterkfontein, Swartkrans and Makapansgat) and found rates of chipping (chip sizes 0.1–2.8 mm) of up to 7% on all teeth and 9% on cheek teeth, and a rate of multiple chipping on chipped teeth of up to 14%. The corresponding figures for Pontnewydd are 85%, 90% and 100%.

Turner and Cadien (1969) studied samples of Eskimo, Aleut and Native American and found percentages of dentitions with chipping of: Eskimo 72%, Aleut 23%, and Native American 18%. They concluded that part of the reason for the rate of chipping being higher in Eskimos was because they chewed the bones of their prey, unlike the Aleuts. They also pointed to the findings of Leigh (1925) of whole tooth fracture in Eskimos resulting from either external trauma or heavy masticatory stress. If the Pontnewydd teeth discovered in the Lower Breccia are grouped as proposed, all five individuals have teeth that are chipped.

The chips on the Pontnewydd teeth can be seen to be *ante mortem* from the degree of rounding, and the lack of any chipping on unerupted teeth. Of interest is the relative lack of fractures of intermediate size, such as removal of the whole or part of a cusp. The whole-tooth fractures would

be expected to be caused by large objects, *e.g.* a bone or a nut, and the smaller chips could be caused by grit, bone splinters, *etc*. This could also be the cause of the coarse pitting on the occlusal surfaces of many of the teeth, and the chips on the lingual cusp tips of upper first molars PN4 (permanent) and PN12.

In discussing the treatment of cracked and fractured teeth in modern dentistry, Walton (1996) states that craze lines (cracks in the enamel) and cusp or small fractures, as observed on PN10, can be the result of impact injuries. With split or cracked teeth:

- the teeth most frequently involved are mandibular molars followed by maxillary premolars followed by maxillary first molars;
- the split or crack is almost invariably mesiodistal;
- the more central the fracture the deeper it goes before shearing to one side;
- cracked and split teeth are often found in patients who chew hard, brittle substances, *e.g.* ice, unpopped popcorn kernels, hard candy;
- apart from impact injuries, cusp fractures occur when there is a lack of support, *e.g.* because of extensive caries.

All the erupted teeth, other than PN5, have chipping on the mesial and/or distal margins. The chipping is mesial only on the three first molars, mesial and distal on the two second molars (enamel margins missing on PN13) and distal on the only erupted third molar. Other chipping is more specific. The degree of chipping of the buccal and mesiolingual cusps of lower fourth premolar PN5, and the buccolingual 'groove' on the tip of the buccal cusp, is specific to this tooth and could be as a result of non-masticatory use. Barrett (1977), for instance, cites the use of the canines and premolars for sharpening spears or digging sticks, and the use of the teeth to sharpen stone tools by pressure flaking.

Specific to lower lateral incisor PN10 and lower fourth premolar PN5 are the presence of 'cut-marks' on the buccal surface. These could have been caused by hard, sharp objects being worked on, or by cutting implements. Similar 'cut-marks' have been found on anterior teeth (incisors and canines) at Atapuerca-SH (Bermúdez de Castro *et al.* 1988) and Krapina (Lalueza Fox and Frayer 1997) and on other fossil human teeth (Lalueza Fox and Pérez-Pérez 1994). As with PN10, these are on the buccal face near the occlusal surface, but not on the mesial or distal margins, nor in the area near the cervical margin. The 'cut-marks' at Atapuerca-SH (1–4 mm) and Krapina (up to 6 mm) are frequently longer than those on PN10 and PN5, and frequently deeper and more clearly visible to the naked eye. 'Cut-marks' have also been found on Krapina posterior teeth (Lalueza Fox and Frayer 1997). These are generally either vertical or horizontal and close to the occlusal edge. However, oblique 'cut-marks' were observed on a lower fourth premolar, though it was considered that these resulted from toothpicking probing. Several authors have suggested that 'cut-marks' on the anterior teeth could result from the 'stuff and cut' method of eating,

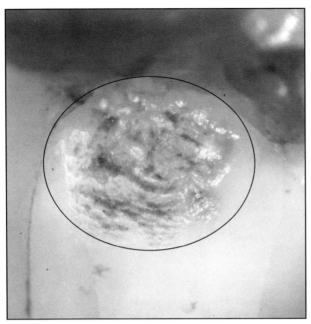

*Figure 9.25. PN11 showing wear on mesiolingual corner.*

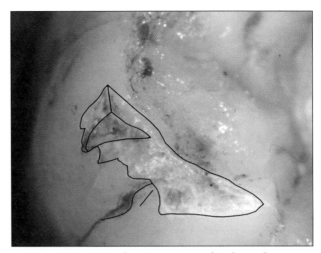

*Figure 9.26. PN11 showing wear on distolingual corner.*

where the cutting implement comes into contact with the teeth (reviewed by Lalueza Fox and Pérez-Pérez 1994). Bermúdez de Castro *et al.* (1988) further point out that the marks tend to be oblique, and predominantly sloping in the same direction, and suggest that this is evidence of handedness. The direction for the normal right-handedness on a lower right lateral incisor is distal-cervical to mesial-occlusal, which is the opposite direction to the majority of the marks on PN10, suggesting that this might have come from a left-handed individual. Marks going in the opposite direction are also found on Hortus VIII, and at Krapina (Lalueza Fox and Frayer 1997), though the same right-handed predominance occurs. Several Krapina incisors have oblique marks going in both directions, as seen on PN10. Against the above, Bax and Ungar (1999) studied four modern groups, including one (the Aleut) that used the 'stuff and cut' method of eating, and found no evidence of a relationship between striation orientation and handedness. There is a regular pattern to chipping of the buccal and lingual occlusal edges of the molars:

UPPER MOLARS
- PN4 buccal, and lingual on mesiolingual cusp;
- PN12 mesiobuccal corner;
- PN1 buccal;
- PN4 (deciduous tooth) buccal.

LOWER MOLARS
- PN11 mesiolingual and distolingual corners, also lingual side of distolingual cusp;
- PN13 buccal side of mesiobuccal cusp, distobuccal corner, mesiolingual corner.

PN15 and PN16 do not have any chipping on the buccal or lingual surfaces.

For those molars with buccal or lingual chipping, chipping occurs on the buccal side in all the upper molars and on the lingual side in all the lower molars. Barrett (1977) postulates similar chipping produced by the indigenous peoples of the Northern Territory of Australia by holding a spear-shaft between the teeth for straightening.

The chipping on the mesiolingual and distolingual corners of lower first molar PN11 is in the form of very heavily pitted/roughened areas on the lingual sides of the tips of the cusps, which contain deep mesiodistal scratches (especially mesially) and parts that have been excavated out (Figures 9.25–9.26). The distolingual area is triangular in shape, with a central pit and scratches running from this to the points of the triangle. These areas measure 2 × 2 mm on the mesiolingual cusp and 1.5 × 1.5 mm on the distolingual cusp. The ridges between these areas and the phase 1 facets on the buccal sides of these cusps are not themselves significantly chipped. On the distolingual cusp the roughening continues mesially, lingual to the phase 1 facet, and there are two deep vertical scratches in this area. It is not clear what could have caused this type of wear but the fact that it is so localized suggests that it results from non-masticatory use. Possibly it could have been caused by the end of a hard object (bone?) being held against this tooth from the right-hand side of the mouth whilst it was being worked on.

There are no chips around the occlusal edge of lower third premolar PN20, apart from very mild chipping over the distal interproximal facet. This is surprising for such a worn tooth, in view of the overall level of chipping. The occlusal surface of this tooth is only finely pitted, in contrast to the coarse pitting on many other teeth, and this, combined with the lack of chipping, could suggest a slightly different diet. The other worn tooth, with even greater wear, lower second molar PN13, has a mostly polished surface. It is only pitted in the distal worn down area. In addition, there is no occlusal pitting on the very worn tooth fragment, PN9. Could this be evidence of older individuals having a relatively more refined diet?

*Buccal and lingual surfaces*

The buccal and lingual surfaces were examined at 10×
magnification. This study showed fine scratch-marks on
buccal and/or lingual surfaces occur on all of the worn teeth,
and on most teeth (premolars and first and third molars)
are mainly vertical or near vertical. However, on the lower
lateral incisor, PN10, and on all second molars (PN1, PN4
(deciduous tooth), PN13, and PN15) they are both vertical
and horizontal, and in all directions on the lower second
molars. On PN1 they are mainly horizontal. The pattern
tends to be the same on both buccal and lingual surfaces.
Generally, the scratch-marks are stronger, or only present,
on the buccal surface. However, the reverse is true for PN4
(permanent tooth). The severity of the scratch-marks tends
to increase with wear, but the two most worn teeth, PN9
and PN13, only have mild scratch-marks. The scratch-
marks on the buccal surfaces of PN18, PN20, PN15 and
PN4 (deciduous) are noticeably heavy.

Buccal and lingual surfaces are in some cases polished,
the degree of polish tending to increase with wear, as with
the scratch-marks. Nevertheless, the relatively unworn
PN5 has both buccal and lingual polish, as also has PN16.
Unlike scratch-marks, the polish tends to be stronger, or
only present, on the lingual surface, apart from PN10, on
which the buccal surface is the most polished. On the lower
teeth, lingual polish is in most cases only on the occlusal
rim. There is no relationship between buccal/lingual polish
and occlusal polish. With the two most worn teeth there
is also pitting, PN9 has coarse pitting, and PN13 has mild
pitting on the buccal surface.

Lalueza-Fox and Pérez-Pérez (1993) and Lalueza *et
al.* (1993) have demonstrated that groups with a high
meat intake (Eskimos and Fueguians) have more vertical
vestibular striations than horizontal, whilst the reverse was
true for a vegetarian group of Hindu farmers. Groups with
a mixed diet are intermediate.

From the summary above it can be seen that the picture is
mixed at Pontnewydd but that the preponderance of vertical
striations suggests a fairly high meat intake. This is only
a qualitative assessment, unlike the Lalueza-Fox studies,
which were carried out using a higher magnification. It
may be of significance that the teeth with a high proportion
of horizontal striations are all second molars, whilst the
first molars all predominantly have vertical striations. This
could be seen as a split by age group, the older individuals
having a greater number of horizontal striations, but PN18,
PN20 and PN16 from older individuals mainly have vertical
striations, and PN4 (deciduous tooth) has both vertical
and horizontal striations. Alternatively, the direction of
the striations may be a function of the tooth's position in
the mouth. It is worth noting that one of the authors (T.
C.) has studied a collection of teeth from James Mellaart's
excavation of the Neolithic site of Çatal Hüyük in Turkey
(work in preparation) and found the vestibular striations
to be almost entirely vertical. The diet of this population
was undoubtedly mixed (Mellaart 1967).

*Interproximal facets*

All the interproximal facets are finely pitted. This type
of wear has been observed by Kaidonis *et al.* (1992) on
modern Australian teeth.

*Conclusions drawn from the study of the macroscopic
wear*

The principal conclusion to be drawn is that the shearing
component of mastication predominated over the crushing
component. This suggests the presence of tough, fibrous,
vegetable material as a major component of the diet. Similar
wear to that seen on the Pontnewydd molars can be found in
other Middle Pleistocene specimens, but in the lower molars
it is unlike the form of wear encountered at either the earlier
site of Mauer or the later site of Krapina. There is evidence
of a crushing diet in the Mauer and Petralona specimens,
in the form of excavated out dentine. The predominantly
vertical vestibular striations could indicate a high meat
content in the diet but the evidence is not conclusive. The
rate of wear is greater than that occurring at Krapina and
in certain Middle Pleistocene specimens. The frequency of
chipping is high compared with other reference groups and
this, together with the major trauma found, could result from
an activity such as chewing bones. In addition, the pattern
of chipping on some teeth suggests that it could be partly
as a consequence of non-masticatory use.

## Subvertical grooves on interproximal wear facets

This phenomenon is less frequently observed on recent
human teeth but has been quite commonly found on
the posterior teeth of Neanderthals. The grooves are not
randomly placed but generally radiate out from a point
beyond the occlusal surface. They are regular in form
and do not appear to be caused by grit caught between
the teeth.

Villa and Giacobini (1995a; 1995b) and Villa (1996)
have listed examples of these grooves that, whilst mainly
being associated with Neanderthals, are also encountered
on teeth of *Homo habilis*, archaic moderns and modern
humans. They have studied the morphology of these
grooves on Neanderthal teeth from Caverna Delle Fate and
Genay, and determined from scanning electron microscopic
examination that they were produced during the lifetime
of the individuals. They have observed a subvertical
disposition of Hunter-Schreger bands near interproximal
ridges on modern human molars, facilitating subvertical
microfractures that could lead to groove formation.
Possible correlations were found between complex crown
traits relating to the mesial and distal margins (and, in
particular, primitive 'Y' or '+' fissure patterns on lower
molars) and verticalization of Hunter-Schreger bands.
(Hunter-Schreger bands are lines of differently orientated
prisms in the enamel that can be seen when a section of
the tooth is studied under a microscope). They have also
noted that the grooves were strictly limited to the facet area
and that, from their contours, it could be seen that their

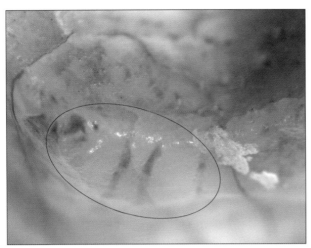

*Figure 9.27. PN1 showing subvertical grooves on mesial interproximal facet.*

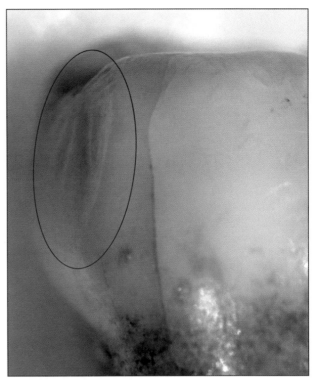

*Figure 9.28. PN11 showing subvertical grooves on mesial interproximal facet.*

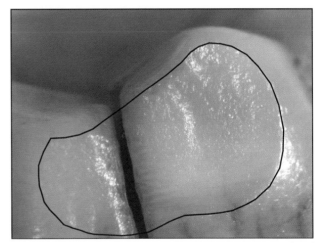

*Figure 9.29. PN15 showing subvertical grooves on distal interproximal facet.*

formation must have followed facet formation. The fan-shaped disposition of the grooves is in accordance with the probable distribution of occlusal forces within the tooth.

Egocheaga *et al.* (2004) have observed subvertical grooves on teeth from Atapuerca-SH, but state that they show a reduced number and are less profound. Kaidonis *et al.* (1992) studied modern Australian teeth and discovered subvertical grooves in 60% of Aboriginal teeth that exhibited interproximal wear but only in 30% of teeth from whites.

Poisson *et al.* (2002) have experimented on modern human teeth, and deduced that the first stage in the formation of subvertical grooves is a microfracture resulting from masticatory stress. This is enlarged into a subvertical groove by further masticatory action and the action of food particles (both mechanical and erosive). The formation of a groove on one interproximal facet facilitates the formation of a corresponding subvertical groove on the adjacent facet. The number and depth of grooves increases over time, and increases mesiodistally in line with the intensity of the forces of mastication.

Egocheaga *et al.* (2004) suggest that, since grooves on adjacent facets tend to interdigitate, this acts to lock the teeth together and so reduce vertical and horizontal movement during food mastication. This increases efficiency of chewing and reduces interproximal wear that could lead to dental caries, *etc.* They therefore consider that formation of these grooves provides a distinct advantage to groups that have highly abrasive diets or which employ high masticatory forces.

The grooves observed on the Pontnewydd teeth are described in Table 9.26 and examples are illustrated in Figures 9.27–9.29. The size and shape of the interproximal facets are also given. The morphology of the Pontnewydd grooves is very similar to those on teeth from Caverna Delle Fate and Genay (Villa and Giacobini 1995a). They are limited to the interproximal facet, and are semi-circular or 'U'-shaped in cross-section. They are subvertical and tend to be radial from a point above the occlusal edge.

The occlusal ends of grooves on the buccal side of a facet incline lingually, those on the lingual side of a facet incline buccally, and the degree of slant of the grooves increases from the centre. They only occur on molars and premolars (apart from a distal facet on an upper lateral incisor from Genay). The number of grooves on a facet varies 1–7 at Caverna Delle Fate/Genay and 1–8 at Pontnewydd.

A few grooves are curved but the majority are straight. In nearly all instances, the grooves on a facet run from the occlusal edge (one exception at Caverna Delle Fate, three at Genay and two at Pontnewydd, all but one of which are distal), but frequently one or more grooves on a facet do not reach the apical edge (four facets at Caverna Delle Fate out of eight with grooves, seven out of fifteen at Genay and six out of eleven at Pontnewydd).

The grooves vary in depth at both Caverna Delle Fate/ Genay and at Pontnewydd, sometimes within the one facet. At Pontnewydd the deeper grooves mainly occur on mesial facets. On PN1 (mesial), PN11 (mesial), PN12 (mesial) and PN20 (distal) the most buccal grooves are the deepest. The width of the grooves also varies, between 0.1 mm and 0.5 mm at Caverna Delle Fate/Genay, and between 0.1 mm and 0.4 mm at Pontnewydd. The grooves in the teeth from Caverna Delle Fate and Genay are described as being narrower than the spacing between them. At Pontnewydd this is the case on three facets, but on three facets the grooves are of similar width to the spacing between them, and on the remaining facets the spacing is varied. On two facets with multiple grooves (PN18 and PN20), the grooves are all on the lingual side of the facet, and on one (PN12), all on the buccal side of the facet.

A higher proportion of the interproximal facets at Pontnewydd have no grooves (6 out of 17, excluding trace distal facets on PN4 (permanent tooth) and PN12, the broken facet on PN16, the facets in dentine on PN13, and the lower incisor PN10) than at Caverna Delle Fate/Genay (8 out of 31). However, the interproximal facets with grooves at Pontnewydd have four grooves on average against three at Caverna Delle Fate/Genay. In all three collections, the number of grooves per facet tends to increase mesiodistally in the upper teeth. However, whereas at Genay the facets with seven grooves are on the upper second to third molar interface, the facet with eight grooves at Pontnewydd is mesial on an upper second molar.

There is no clear correlation between level of wear and presence/absence of grooves, or number of grooves, at Caverna Delle Fate/Genay, nor at Pontnewydd in that in most cases only either the mesial or distal facet has grooves. Nevertheless, none of the very faint distal facets (PN4 (permanent tooth), PN11, PN12) has grooves, nor the facets on the little worn PN5, nor the distal facet on the unworn PN7.

In all three collections, the width of the interproximal facet is not directly related to the number of grooves and there can be wide facets with no grooves (up to 5.8 mm at Caverna Delle Fate/Genay and 5.3 mm at Pontnewydd). There does appear, though, to be a minimum width for grooves to be present (4.4 mm against the smallest width of 2.3 mm at Caverna Delle Fate/Genay and 3.2 mm against 1.2 mm at Pontnewydd). In addition, it is the widest facets that have the largest number of grooves (8.5 mm with seven grooves at Genay and 6.5 mm with eight grooves at Pontnewydd). At Caverna Delle Fate/Genay, grooves are more frequently found on flat or 'S'-shaped facets. At Pontnewydd, 55% of facets with grooves are flat against 35% of facets without grooves. The vertical scratches on the mesial facet of PN12, and the two short scratches on the mesial facet of PN16, may represent the early stages of groove formation.

There are five instances at Genay where the facets of adjacent teeth may be studied. In three of these the grooves correspond reasonably with each other, though in one (right lower fourth premolar to first molar) the grooves on the lower fourth premolar run from the apical edge and those on the lower first molar run from the occlusal edge. In the other two instances, in one case one facet has no grooves and in the other the grooves do not correspond. Scanning electron microscope studies on Genay teeth show morphological differences between corresponding grooves. At Pontnewydd, the only two teeth that are definitely adjacent are those of PN4. The grooves on the adjacent facets correspond with each other but, as at Genay, the grooves on the upper fourth deciduous premolar distal facet run from the apical edge and those on the upper first molar mesial facet run from the occlusal edge. The grooves on the deciduous tooth are shallow, whereas those on the permanent tooth are deep.

A recent study of interproximal grooves on teeth from the Neanderthal site of El Sidrón in Spain found that they also occurred on incisors and canines (Rosas *et al.* 2007). Numbers of grooves found on individual facets varied between one and eight, in line with the other sites described. Further work by Estalrrich *et al.* (2011) relating to this site has determined that subvertical grooves on adjacent facets do not interdigitate but overlap each other, possibly forming channels. Statistical analysis shows that the number of grooves on a facet does not depend on age, occlusal wear or tooth position but is related to facet width. Two thirds of the teeth have subvertical grooves, including half of the anterior teeth.

## Oral health and anomalies

The incidences of traits in the Middle Pleistocene teeth at Pontnewydd are compared, where possible, with findings for Krapina and Atapuerca-SH. Details for Krapina are taken from Smith (1976b) and for Atapuerca-SH from Bermúdez de Castro (1988). Definitions are taken from Hillson (1996).

### *Dental calculus*

The term dental calculus refers to deposits of mineralized plaque sometimes found on teeth. No significant deposits of dental calculus are present at Pontnewydd, even on worn teeth. There is a trace (1 mm wide and 4.2 mm long horizontal line) on the mesial surface of the crown of the only deciduous tooth, PN4. However, dental calculus often fractures away in archaeological specimens and, in view of the fact that, with the possible exception of PN1, the Pontnewydd teeth have been carried some distance from their original point of deposition, this may well have happened here. Dental calculus is present on several Krapina specimens, especially mandible J. The only Atapuerca-SH tooth for which dental calculus is reported is AT74 (lower fourth premolar) (lingual). A low incidence of dental calculus is usual in hunter-gatherers (Lukacs 1989). Absence of dental calculus may suggest good oral

| TOOTH ID | WEAR STAGE | MAX WIDTH | MAX HEIGHT | FACET SHAPE | NO. OF GROOVES | MESIAL FACET DESCRIPTION (Spacing, position, length) | GROOVE WIDTH mm | X SECTION Shallow/ deep Shape |
|---|---|---|---|---|---|---|---|---|
| PN18 Left P⁴ | 3 | 4.0 | 2.6 | Flat | 2 | Spacing = width grooves; at lingual end of facet; from occlusal edge to halfway down facet | 0.25 | Shallow, rounded |
| PN4 Right M¹ | 3 | 3.2 | 2.7 | Concave | 4 | Spacing > groove width; evenly spaced over facet; from occlusal edge, the 2 most lingual grooves reach apical edge, others do not | 0.35 | Deep, squared, 2nd from lingual deepest |
| PN12 Left M¹ | 3 | 4.3 | 2.4 | Flat | 3 | Spacing > groove width; at buccal end of facet; at occlusal edge & v short; also vertical scratches | 0.1 | Shallow, rounded, buccal deepest |
| PN1 Left M² | 3/4 | 6.5 | 2.8 | Concave | 8 | Spacing varies over whole facet; from occlusal edge, buccal five grooves reach apical edge, lingual three do not & are v faint | 0.2 | 3rd to 5th grooves from buccal side deep & squared, others shallow & rounded/v-shaped |
| PN4 Right dm²/dp⁴ | 5 | 4.5 | 2.2 | Concave | 1 | Single, very deep; at buccal end of facet; from occlusal edge to apical edge | 0.4 | Deep, squared |
| PN10 Right I₂ | 4 | 1.8 | 3.2 | Flat | None | | | |
| PN7 Left P₃ | 0 | None | | | | | | |
| PN20 Left P₃ | 4 | 2.6 | 3.0 | Concave | None | | | |
| PN5 Left P₄ | 2 | 1.2 (Part missing) | 1.8 | Concave | None | | | |
| PN11 Left M₁ | 3 | 3.3 | 3.3 | Flat | 5 | Spacing varies over whole facet; from occlusal edge to two-thirds way down facet | 0.4 | 2nd groove from buccal side deep & squared, others shallow & rounded |
| PN13 Right M₂ | 6 | 8.0 | 4.3 | Irregular flat | None | Facet in dentine | | |
| PN15 Right M₂ | 3 | 5.3 | 3.4 | Concave | None | | | |
| PN16 Right M₃ | 2 | Broken, only fragment visible | | Flat | None | Two short scratches from apical edge to one quarter way up facet | | |

Table 9.26. Grooves on interproximal wear facets (continued opposite).

| MAX WIDTH | MAX HEIGHT | FACET SHAPE | NO. OF GROOVES | DESCRIPTION (Spacing, position, length) | GROOVE WIDTH mm | X SECTION Shallow/ deep Shape |
|---|---|---|---|---|---|---|
| | | | | **DISTAL FACET** | | |
| 5.9 | 3.1 | Flat | 1 | From sagittal sulcus to apical edge slanted inferiorly buccally | 0.3 | Deep, rounded |
| 1.3 | 1.3 | Flat, trace | None | | | |
| 1.5 | 1.5 | Flat, faint | None | | | |
| 5.8 | 2.8 | Slightly convex | 1 | Very faint; at lingual end of facet; from occlusal edge to apical edge | 0.2 | Shallow, rounded |
| 3.2 | 2.7 | Slightly convex | 4 | Spacing > groove width; evenly spaced over facet; from apical edge to halfway up facet | 0.3 | Shallow, rounded |
| 1.8 | 1.8 | Concave | None | | | |
| 2.8 | 1.0 | Concave | None | | | |
| 4.1 | 3.2 | Flat | 4 | Spacing = width grooves; at lingual end of facet; from occlusal edge to apical edge | 0.25 | Rounded,/ u-shaped, buccal deepest |
| 3.4 | 2.2 | Flat | None | | | |
| 2.9 | 1.5 | Flat, faint | None | | | |
| 7.0 | 2.7 | Irregular flat | None | Facet in dentine | | |
| 5.5 | 3.8 | Flat | 7 | Spacing = width grooves; 2 v faint at most lingual point, from occ edge to apical edge; 3 together lingually, from apical edge to quarter way up facet; 2 at buccal end convex buccally & from occlusal edge to halfway down facet | 0.3 | Shallow, rounded |
| None | | | | | | |

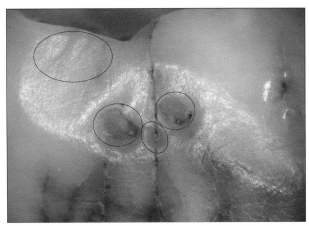

*Figure 9.30. PN12 showing pit hypoplasia and subvertical grooves on mesial surface.*

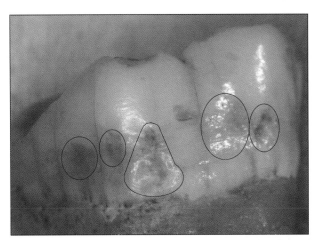

*Figure 9.31. PN1 showing pit hypoplasia on buccal and distal surfaces.*

hygiene and/or a lack of foods that are going to provide nutrients to assist in the development of plaque, such as starch, sugar and dairy products (Hillson 1996).

## *Hypoplasia*

Disruption of enamel formation may occur in localized horizontal bands running round the crown of a tooth. This is considered to relate to particular events that have happened in the life of an individual whilst the tooth crown was developing. These may be such things as disease, nutritional deficiencies, weaning, *etc.* Using the classification of Berten (1895), the three types of hypoplasia are furrow (one or more grooves), plane (*i.e.* missing enamel) and isolated pits. There is no evidence of plane hypoplasia at Pontnewydd but two teeth have pit hypoplasia, and two have furrow hypoplasia, that can be seen with the naked eye. (The two Mesolithic teeth have single mild grooves at the cervix, around the tooth on PN8 and on the lingual side on PN2).

### *PN12 (upper first molar)*

There is a horizontal line of small pits on the side of the crown, 2.5–3.2 mm below the cervix; three on the mesial

surface of the protocone (at 2.5 mm) (Figure 9.30) and two on its lingual surface (at 3.2 mm), one above the Carabelli's trait. Age of occurrence is about 18 months based on recent human tooth development (van Beek 1983) and also Neanderthal (Scladina) tooth development (Smith *et al.* 2007b).

### *PN1 (upper second molar)*

There is a horizontal line of five shallow irregular pits on the buccal surface and the buccal side of the distal surface (three buccal, one distobuccal and one distal; Figure 9.31). The lowest and highest points of these range between 0.5 mm and 3.4 mm below the cervix. Age of occurrence is about 5–7 years based on recent human tooth development (van Beek 1983) and 3.6–5.3 years based on Neanderthal (Scladina) tooth development (Smith *et al.* 2007b).

### *PN6 and PN7 (antimeres) (lower third premolars)*

Both teeth have an area of faint furrow hypoplasia on the buccal surface at 6–7 mm above the cervix. Age of occurrence is about 4 years based on recent human tooth development (van Beek 1983) and 2.2–2.5 years based on Neanderthal (Scladina) tooth development (Smith *et al.* 2007b).

No other instances of hypoplasia were found when the teeth were looked at using a 10× magnifying glass. The occurrence rate for Pontnewydd is therefore 19% of the permanent teeth (including PN9 and treating PN6/PN7 as one) or three of the minimum five individuals (see below). This is higher than that reported for Atapuerca-SH but lower than that found in a sample of Neanderthals:

### *Atapuerca-SH*

12.8% of Atapuerca-SH permanent teeth have linear (furrow) hypoplasia or multiple pits, mostly linear and the majority of instances only found by microscopic examination using a 14–20× microscope (Bermúdez de Castro and Pérez 1995). It is only seen clearly with the naked eye in three of 29 individuals. 37.9% of the individuals in total have hypoplasia. The age distribution peaks at 3–4 years (excluding third molars), with a range of 3 months to 6 years. A more recent study (Cunha *et al.* 2004) looking at linear and plane hypoplasia in a larger sample, using both 5× magnification and a scanning electron microscope, discovered an overall occurrence rate of 4.6%, mostly occurring in the third year of life (possibly because of weaning). Seven (28%) of the 25 individuals observed have at least one hypoplastic defect; three 2 year olds and others aged under 1 year and 4, 5 and 9 years. Two of the seven have plane form defects. Hypoplasia is most prevalent in the mandibular teeth (eleven of thirteen permanent teeth pairs having hypoplasia being lower teeth) and at its highest rate in lower incisors (18–19%).

### *Neanderthal sample*

European and Near East teeth, including Krapina but excluding Middle Pleistocene teeth, studied using a 20× microscope; 33.3% of permanent teeth have linear

| Tooth | Buccal cusps | | | Lingual cusps | |
| | Mesial | Distal | C5 | Mesial | Distal |
|---|---|---|---|---|---|
| PN4 (M¹) | 1 (central) | 1 (central) | - | 2 (mesial & distal) | 1 (mesial) |
| PN12 (M¹) | 2 (mesial & distal) | 1 (mesial) | - | 2 (mesial & distal) | 1 (distal) |
| PN1 (M²) | 1 (central) | 1 (central) | - | 2 (mesial) | 2 (mesial & distal)* |
| PN11 (M₁) | 2 (mesial & distal) | 1 (distal) | 1 (mesial) | 1 (central / distal) | 1 (central / distal) |
| PN15 (M₂) | 2 (mesial & distal) | 2 (mesial & distal) | 1 (mesial) | 1 (distal) | 2 (central & distal) |
| PN16 (M₃) | 2 (mesial & distal) | 2 (mesial & distal)+ | - | 1 (mesial) | 1 (central) |

Table 9.27. Positions of phase 1 facets on upper and lower molars. *Part of mesial facet is on mesiolingual cusp; +Both are double facets, one above the other.

hypoplasia or multiple pits, 50.9% of 165 individuals (Ogilvie *et al.* 1989). If the sample is restricted to individuals with three or more teeth, the incidence of individuals becomes 75.9% (at the upper end of recent human ranges of variation). The age distribution (excluding third molars) peaks at 2–5 years, with a mean of 3.9 years.

### Hypercementosis

The roots of teeth may become abnormally thickened, particularly at their tips, because of an excess deposition of cement. The cause of this is not fully understood but it can be associated with heavy tooth-wear and periapical inflammation, although it has been noted in unerupted impacted teeth. There is mild hypercementosis on the lingual root of upper second molar PN1, and on the mesial root of lower second molar PN13, especially towards their apices. The apices of the other roots of these two teeth are not present. These are two of the more worn teeth, but PN4 (deciduous) is also worn and has no hypercementosis. Hypercementosis is found on two Atapuerca-SH teeth (AT10, upper third molar, marked; Individual VII, lower fourth premolar, slight). There is no mention of hypercementosis being observed on Krapina teeth.

### Rotation/tilt

Positional irregularities of anterior teeth are common amongst more recent populations. These can be rotation of teeth, mesial or distal tilting, displacements buccally or lingually, or transposition of teeth. At Pontnewydd there is considerable evidence of rotation of lower premolars and other anomalies.

*PN5 (lower fourth premolar)*
The interproximal wear facets are located on the mesiobuccal and distolingual corners of the tooth, suggesting a rotation of the tooth by 35° in a clockwise direction when viewed occlusally. In addition, the distal facet is tilted upwards at

20° to the vertical. The shape of the interproximal wear facets on this tooth also suggests possible transposition with a third premolar, the mesial facet being vertically elongate, as would be expected from contact with a canine.

*PN7 (lower third premolar)*
There is an interproximal wear facet placed slightly lingually on the distal surface but tilted upwards at 25° to the vertical, indicating slight displacement. There is no mesial interproximal wear facet.

*PN20 (lower third premolar)*
The mesial interproximal wear facet is located slightly buccally and the distal interproximal wear facet slightly lingually, suggesting a clockwise rotation of the tooth by 25°.

*PN11 (lower first molar)*
The mesial interproximal wear facet located on the mesiobuccal cusp is tilted 10° buccally, suggesting an anticlockwise rotation or displacement of the adjacent lower fourth permanent or deciduous premolar. It is also tilted upwards at an angle of 10° to the vertical.

Since PN6 is unerupted and has no interproximal facets, all the lower premolars for which evidence exists are rotated or displaced. Both PN5 and PN7 would appear to have had a distinct distal tilt. The presence of a well-formed interproximal facet on PN7, formed when it was just erupting, suggests that it may have become impacted against the adjacent distal tooth. The distal interproximal facet of the upper fourth premolar (PN18) is tilted upwards at an angle of 10°, suggesting that this tooth also had a distal tilt. Rotation of premolars is unusual in European Middle Pleistocene specimens, though there is at least one instance in the Atapuerca-SH material – Mandible AT607 (Rosas 1995). At Krapina there is just the one instance of rotation recorded, a lower left fourth premolar in mandible H.

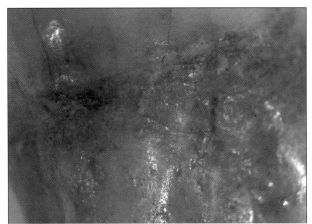

*Figure 9.32. PN11 showing grooves on mesial side of root trunk.*

### Retention of deciduous teeth

As described by Stringer (1984) the crypt for the unerupted upper fourth permanent premolar in specimen PN4 is lingual to the upper fourth deciduous premolar. This is the probable reason for the lack of resorption of the deciduous tooth's roots, particularly if recent human tooth development standards apply.

### Crossbite/anteroposterior molar relation/overbite

In normal occlusion, the upper cheek teeth overlap the lower cheek teeth (*i.e.* they are placed slightly buccally) such that the buccal cusps of the lower teeth fit into the central mesiodistal occlusal groove of the upper teeth. Deviations from this are known as posterior crossbite. Looking in a mesiodistal direction, it is normal for the upper cheek teeth to sit slightly distally to the lower teeth such that the buccal cusps of upper canines and premolars fit between the corresponding lower teeth and the teeth distal to them and the mesiobuccal cusp of the upper first molar fits into the buccal furrow of the lower first molar, and the distobuccal cusp of the lower first molar fits into the buccal furrow of the upper first molar. When referring to the mesiobuccal cusp of the upper first molar, this position is defined as the normal anteroposterior molar relationship. Nonetheless, minor deviations from this are common. In the normal position the upper and lower first molars would be expected to have two phase 1 facets on each buccal cusp. The positions and number of phase 1 facets on second and third molars will depend on tooth shape and the relative sizes of upper and lower molars. The normal relationship between upper and lower incisors is for the incisal edges of upper incisors to overlap mesially the incisal edges of lower incisors. This is known as overbite.

There is no evidence of crossbite. The positions of phase 1 facets on molars are shown in Table 9.27. The upper first molar PN4 would appear to be a little out of normal alignment, with only single centrally placed phase 1 facets on the buccal cusps. The same could be the case for lower first molar PN11, since there is no mesial phase 1 facet on

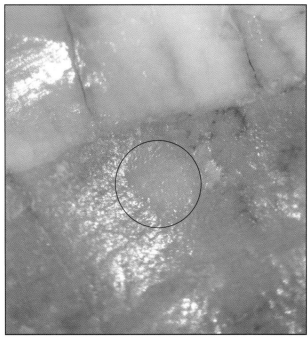

*Figure 9.33. PN1 showing polished area and facet on mesial side of root trunk.*

the distobuccal cusp. The buccal facing facet on the occlusal edge of PN10 suggests that there was slight overbite.

### Other features

There are a series of irregular grooves on the mesial and mesiobuccal sides of the root trunk of lower first molar PN11, that may be seen at 50× magnification (Figure 9.32). The cause of these, and whether they are *post mortem* or *ante mortem*, is not clear. There is an area of polish on the cervical half of the mesial side of the root trunk of upper second molar PN1 and, within this, a 1 mm wide polished facet on the raised ridge in the root trunk that leads to the lingual side of the mesiobuccal root (Figure 9.33).

### Estimates of age

There are two ways of approaching the investigation of dental development in fossil hominins – studying the microstructure and rates of growth of individual teeth, and looking at the overall 'best fit' of the relative development of teeth in a dentition to ape or recent human standards. (See overview by Skinner and Wood 2006).

Features seen in cross-sections of enamel and dentine represent two discrete biological rhythms, a short periodicity of 24 hours and a long periodicity of, in most cases, 6–10 days. For teeth whose crowns were developing at the time of birth, a clear neonatal line can be identified, resulting from a disturbance in enamel formation at this time. The horizontal development lines that may be seen in the enamel on the sides of the crown with the aid of a magnifying glass (perikymata) equate to the long periodicity. A differentiation has to be made between cuspal enamel, in which perikymata do not emerge, and lateral enamel, where perikymata are visible and can be counted. For a particular value of the long periodicity, the more widely the perikymata are spaced the greater will have been the speed of enamel formation and thus the extension rate of the crown. (See review by Dean 2006 and review of research in this area by Smith 2008).

There is evidence that age determination of earlier hominins using dental eruption times of recent humans gives figures that are too high. Bromage and Dean (1985) and Beynon and Dean (1988) determined the crown formation times of anterior teeth from African fossil hominins by counting the number of perikymata. They concluded that the growth periods of Plio-Pleistocene hominins were similar to the modern great apes. Ages at death of juveniles determined by this method were a half to three quarters of the ages found using recent human dental information criteria.

The original determination was based on a seven-day periodicity for perikymata formation, and onset of incisor calcification at three months after birth. In using this method to calculate the ages of children from the Spitalfields collection with known ages (Stringer *et al.* 1990), it was found that very good agreement between actual and calculated was obtained based on an eight-day period, instead of a seven-day period, and later calcification times (nine months in place of three months). Using the revised techniques to age the Devil's Tower Neanderthal child gave an age of 3.9 years, which was in good agreement with the mean age found by Smith (1986) of 4.1 years using conventional methods. Further work by Dean *et al.* (2001) on ground sections of teeth concluded that *Homo erectus* and earlier hominins had shorter crown formation times than are found in modern human teeth. Lacruz *et al.* (2006) came to the same conclusion in studying molars of South African fossil hominins.

Ramirez Rozzi and Bermúdez de Castro (2004) studied the perikymata packing pattern of anterior teeth in four groups – *Homo antecessor*, *Homo heidelbergensis*, *Homo neanderthalensis* and European Upper Palaeolithic/ Mesolithic *Homo sapiens* – and discovered that crown formation times for *Homo neanderthalensis* were 15% faster than for *Homo sapiens*, with *Homo antecessor* and *Homo heidelbergensis* intermediate.

Reid and Ferrell (2006) studied the relationship between the number of striae of Retzius in a tooth (analogous to perikymata) and their periodicity in a sample from medieval Denmark, and found them to be inversely related. Guatelli-Steinberg *et al.* (2005) used this result to study anterior tooth crown growth periods in Neanderthals, compared to three modern human groups (Inuit, South African and English; Inuit having the longest crown growth periods and South Africans the shortest), and concluded that Neanderthals fell within the recent human range. Similar studies on Neanderthal premolars (Reid *et al.* 2008) and Neanderthal molars (Guatelli-Steinberg and Reid 2008) found that their development times could also, in most cases, fall within the recent human range. However, Guatelli-Steinberg *et al.* (2007) and Guatelli-

Steinberg and Reid (2008) determined that the growth curves of Neanderthal crowns – anterior teeth and molars respectively – were different, more linear than are found in modern human teeth, perikymata in modern human teeth becoming more densely packed towards the cervix. In contrast, Smith *et al.* (2009) determined, using standard histological techniques (*i.e.* physical sectioning), that the crown formation time (hypoconid) of a lower third molar from the Neanderthal site of Lakonis was lower than is found in recent humans, at 2.6–2.7 years.

Some recent investigations have involved the use of high-resolution micro-computed tomography and preparation of longitudinal ground sections of fossil molar teeth. These have allowed detailed study of tooth microstructure and accurate determination of the long periodicity. Macchiarelli *et al.* (2006) studied a lower fourth deciduous premolar and a lower first permanent molar from the early Neanderthal site of La Chaise-de-Vouthon and concluded that the crown formation time of the permanent molar was a little over 70 days below the mean for recent humans of African origin (under two standard deviations), and that closure of the root apex occurred at 8.7 years, similar to the figure of about 9 years for recent humans. They estimated that gingival emergence of the permanent molar would have occurred at 6.7 years, again within the range for recent humans. The long periodicity was determined as being seven days.

Smith *et al.* (2007b) studied the nearly complete dentition of the Scladina (Belgium) Neanderthal juvenile, dated at 80,000–127,000 BP. The upper right first permanent molar was sectioned and, from the presence of developmental stress lines at 1.2, 2.4 and 4.9 years of age in this tooth, it was possible to line up the entire dentition and thus, from incomplete teeth, to determine the age of death as being about 8 years (the long periodicity having been determined as being eight days). Crown formation times of some of the anterior teeth are above recent human means but those of the lower canine and all post-canine teeth are below. Those of the upper first and second molars, and the lower third premolar, are over three standard deviations below the means for modern South African teeth. In addition, the age of crown completion of the lower second incisor was at a year less than that of a modern African tooth. The first molar root apices had closed before death and these authors consider that gingival eruption of this tooth would have occurred before the age of 6. Overall, compared with modern European standards, this individual is 2–3 years younger than expected. Calcification of the third molar was noted as being particularly advanced. The stage of development of the Scladina juvenile mandible is almost identical to that of PN4 – the fourth deciduous premolar is still in place and the second permanent molar is just coming into occlusion. Furthermore, as with PN4, there appears to be no resorption of the roots of the upper fourth deciduous premolar (photographs provided by T. M. Smith). In addition, the lower third premolar had started erupting, but was not in occlusion, and its root is two-thirds complete, similar to PN7 (T. M. Smith, pers. comm.). Smith *et al.* (2007b) also refer to an investigation

| Tooth id. | Population means: gingival eruption | | | Occlusal eruption lag | Estimated occlusal mean | Mean occlusal eruption[iii] |
|---|---|---|---|---|---|---|
| | Maximum | Minimum | Average | | | |
| $I^1$ | 7.7 | 6.2 | 6.8 | 0.4 | 7.2 | 7 |
| $I^2$ | 8.5 | 7.1 | 7.8 | 0.6 | 8.4 | 8 |
| $C^1$ | 11.3 | 9.3 | 10.5 | 0.6 | 11.1 | 11 |
| $P^3$ | 10.7 | 8.9 | 9.7 | 0.5 | 10.2 | 10 |
| $P^4$ | 11.3 | 10.0 | 10.7 | 0.4 | 11.1 | 11 |
| $M^1$ | 6.4 | 5.0 | 5.9 | 0.5 | 6.4 | 6 |
| $M^2$ | 12.3 | 10.1 | 11.6 | 0.7 | 12.3 | 12 |
| $M^3$ | 25.1 | 16.3 | 18.7 | | 19.4[i] | 19 |
| $I_1$ | 6.4 | 5.2 | 6.0 | 0.4 | 6.4 | 6 |
| $I_2$ | 7.5 | 6.1 | 6.9 | 0.5 | 7.4 | 7 |
| $C_2$ | 10.4 | 8.8 | 9.7 | 0.5 | 10.2 | 10 |
| $P_3$ | 11.0 | 9.3 | 10.1 | 0.7 | 10.8 | 11 |
| $P_4$ | 12.0 | 10.1 | 10.9 | 0.4 | 11.3 | 11 |
| $M_1$ | 6.2 | 4.7 | 5.7 | 0.6 | 6.3 | 6 |
| $M_2$ | 11.6 | 9.8 | 11.0 | 0.7 | 11.7 | 12 |
| $M_3$ | 24.8 | 16.3 | 18.4 | | 19.1[i] | 19 |
| $di^1$ | 0.8 | 0.7 | 0.8 | 0.3[ii] | 1.1 | 1 |
| $di^2$ | 1.1 | 0.9 | 1.0 | 0.3 | 1.3 | 1 |
| $dc^1$ | 1.5 | 1.4 | 1.5 | 0.4 | 1.9 | 2 |
| $dm^1$ | 1.4 | 1.2 | 1.3 | 0.5 | 1.8 | 2 |
| $dm^2$ | 2.3 | 1.8 | 2.0 | 0.5 | 2.5 | 3 |
| $di_1$ | 0.7 | 0.6 | 0.6 | 0.3 | 0.9 | 1 |
| $di_2$ | 1.2 | 1.0 | 1.1 | 0.3 | 1.4 | 1 |
| $dc_1$ | 1.6 | 1.4 | 1.5 | 0.4 | 1.9 | 2 |
| $dm_1$ | 1.4 | 1.2 | 1.3 | 0.5 | 1.8 | 2 |
| $dm_2$ | 2.3 | 1.8 | 2.0 | 0.5 | 2.5 | 3 |

i Uses second molar eruption lag; ii Deciduous eruption lags estimated; iii Rounded to nearest year, (after Wolpoff 1979).
Estimation of average occlusal eruption ages in years for fossil hominin samples. The data presented include maximum, minimum and average gingival eruption for comparable living human population means, the estimated difference between gingival eruption (emergence) and occlusal eruption, and the corresponding occlusal eruption schedule.

*Table 9.28. Estimation of eruption ages for fossil hominins.*

by Smith *et al.* (2011) of a Neanderthal juvenile from Obi-Rakhmat, Uzbekistan, in which the dental development is slightly less advanced than in the Scladina juvenile. In comparison, Smith *et al.* (2007a) studied the Jebel Irhoud 3 archaic *Homo sapiens* juvenile from Morocco dated at *c.* 160,000 BP, also using micro-computed tomography, and found that it displays an equivalent degree of dental development to modern European children of the same age. Smith *et al.* (2010) have extended this work to a study of a widely diverse sample of Middle Palaeolithic juveniles – eight Neanderthals and three fossil *Homo sapiens* – using synchrotron virtual histology. They found a faster dental development in Neanderthals than in recent humans but similar development to recent humans in Middle Palaeolithic *Homo sapiens*. A regression line of recent human predicted age against actual histological age gives Neanderthal ages of approximately nine years against a predicted age of 11 years, and 11.5 years against 15 years. The rapid development in Neanderthals was seen to primarily centre on the molars. First molar crown

completion was approximately six months earlier than is found in recent humans and occlusal eruption was in the faster half of recent human ranges. Mandibular second molar emergence and maxillary third molar initiation in the Scladina juvenile were 2–5 and 2–4 years respectively ahead of recent human mandibular means. The development in the Engis 2 and Scladina juveniles was seen as being particularly rapid.

Using the second approach referred to above, Smith (1986) aged individual teeth within developing dentitions of fossil hominins, using both recent human and ape standards, and determined which gave the best fit in terms of minimum dispersion of dental ages (*i.e.* lowest standard deviation). Within *Homo*, the Devil's Tower Neanderthal child fitted best to recent human standards, but both *erectus* and *habilis* fitted best to ape standards (*e.g.* within *erectus*; ER820, human range 5.5–7.5 years, ape 6.1–6.9 years; ER1507, human 4.0–6.1 years, ape 4.8–5.5 years. However, both lacked data for the contrast between the first molar and anterior teeth). This method was applied to a modern human

| Formation stage | Third premolar | | Third molar | |
|---|---|---|---|---|
| | Male | Female | Male | Female |
| Root initiated | 6.4 | 6.1 | 13.2 | 13.2 |
| Root one quarter formed | 7.8 | 7.4 | 14.8 | 15.2 |
| Root half formed | 9.3 | 8.7 | 15.6 | 16.2 |
| Root three quarters formed | 10.2 | 9.6 | 16.4 | 16.9 |
| Root complete | 11.2 | 10.5 | 17.5 | 17.7 |

(Extracts from table in Hillson 1996) (ages given in years).

*Table 9.29. Values for estimating age from permanent lower tooth formation stages.*

South African sample and samples of *Pan* and *Gorilla* by Smith (1994b) to determine the circumstances in which it is reliable. This was found to depend on the number and kind of teeth available in humans, and to be satisfactory for age classes other than 'infant' in apes. The method was then applied to fossil specimens satisfying these criteria. Gracile australopithecines and *Homo habilis* remained classified with African apes but *Homo erectus* was classified with recent humans, along with Neanderthals.

Bermúdez de Castro *et al.* (1999a) have used a similar approach to that of Smith (1986) in studying the pattern of development of the Gran Dolina hominins, and concluded that it was similar to *Homo sapiens*, but with earlier calcification of the lower third molar than that seen in recent Europeans. Nevertheless, this was still within the range of variation observed in modern populations overall. Bermúdez de Castro and Rosas (2001) also found that the pattern of dental development of Hominid XVIII at Atapuerca-SH was similar to recent humans, but with a notable delay in development of upper and lower canines and advanced development of upper and lower third molars. A further study by Bermúdez de Castro *et al.* (2010) of two sub-adults from Gran Dolina, using microcomputed tomography, concluded that they had a recent human pattern of dental development and that the gingival eruption time of first molars was within the range of variation of recent humans at 5.3–6.6 years.

Bayle *et al.* (2007; 2008; 2009) investigated dental development sequences of deciduous and permanent elements in three Neanderthal juveniles having mixed dentitions, using high resolution CT-scans. Those of the La Chaise and Krapina juveniles fell within the variation found in a modern human sample of African, European and Middle Eastern dentitions, but that of the juvenile mandible from the later site of Roc de Marsal was not compatible with recent human patterns.

Thompson and Nelson (2000) have studied dental maturation against femoral growth in some late Neanderthals and found that the pattern of Neanderthal ontogeny was not intermediate between *Homo erectus* and *Homo* sapiens. The Neanderthal growth trajectory was consistent with either slower linear growth or advanced dental development, and showed a difference at age 15 of approximately three years compared with the mean of samples of modern human males and females.

There is increasing evidence therefore that late Neanderthals had an accelerated rate of dental development compared with recent humans though, as with recent humans, there is variation. For Middle Pleistocene European teeth the picture is less certain. Two approaches are taken in estimating the ages of the individuals to whom the Pontnewydd teeth belonged; firstly using recent human standards but taking into account the early development of third molars, and secondly using late Neanderthal standards:

- For recent human standards the table prepared by Wolpoff (1979) is used, shown as Table 9.28. This gives minimum, maximum and mean gingival eruption times (*i.e.* time of tooth erupting through the gum) derived from samples of Europeans, Africans, Melanesians and Asiatics, and was used in estimating the ages of individuals in the Krapina dental remains. The ages given for occlusal eruption (tooth fully erupted) are for Europeans. The table produced by B. H. Smith (reproduced in Hillson 1996) is used for timings of tooth development, since it provides details of development of third molars. Extracts are shown in Table 9.29;

- for late Neanderthal standards, ageing is based on the determination of the age of the Scladina juvenile and the relative development of the teeth in this specimen (Smith *et al.* 2007b) augmented by information about this specimen and the Le Moustier juvenile in Smith *et al.* 2010.

### Lower lateral incisor
#### PN10 (right)
Since there are no molar or premolar teeth that can definitely be said to be from the same individual as the incisor, it is not possible to relate rates of wear between anterior and posterior teeth. Nonetheless, the low level of wear on PN10 suggests that it is from a juvenile or adolescent. The method developed by Bermúdez de Castro *et al.* (2003b) for determining the age of mandibular incisors at Atapuerca-SH, based on the height of tooth crown lost (in this case 1.5 mm), gives an age at death of just under 11 years (based on recent human standards).

### Upper fourth premolar
#### PN18 (left)
Recent human – the level of wear on PN18 is similar to the level of wear on the upper second molar PN1 (1.5 mm of dentine exposure on the buccal cusp against 1.6 mm on the mesiolingual cusp of PN1). If the rate of wear is the same, then this would be equivalent to about 8–9 years' wear, giving an age of 19–20 years.
Neanderthal – using the Neanderthal development regression line

(Smith *et al.* 2010, figure 3) gives an age of occlusal eruption of nine years. This is similar to the estimated occlusal eruption age of the upper second molar and, since the wear is similar to that of PN1, the likely age is 14.5 years if the wear rate is the same. Smith *et al.* (2010) state that the stage of development of the Scladina upper fourth premolar is the same as the lower second molar (root half complete) and one stage greater than the upper second molar. Occlusal eruption of the upper fourth premolar in this specimen may therefore have been earlier.

### Lower third premolars
#### PN6 (right)
Recent human – this tooth is not in occlusion but the crown is complete and the root initiated (at least half complete), giving an age of at least 8.7 years using Smith's table and less than 10.8 years using Wolpoff's table.

Neanderthal – the root of the Scladina lower third premolar has reached three-quarters of its length at age 8 in 3.7 years (Smith *et al.* 2007b, figure 2). This gives a minimum age of just under 7 years for root half complete.

#### PN7 (left)
Recent human – this tooth has commenced gingival eruption, as evidenced by the scratch-marks on the tip of the buccal cusp and the presence of a distal interproximal facet, but is not in occlusion. The root is three-quarters complete. This indicates an age of 9.6–10.2 years from Smith's table and 10.1 (9.3–11.0) years from Wolpoff's table. As stated above, this tooth is probably the antimere of PN6.

Neanderthal – this tooth is at a similar level of development to the Scladina lower third premolar, which has commenced gingival eruption at 8 years of age

#### PN20 (left)
The relatively high level of wear on this tooth indicates that it is likely to be from a young adult.

### Lower fourth premolar
#### PN5 (left)
Recent human – this tooth is in occlusion but there is no dentine exposure and the wear facets are small, which suggests recent eruption. If the wear is equivalent to 1–2 years' use, this gives an age of 12–13 years.

Neanderthal – from SI figure 6 in Smith *et al.* (2010) the length of the Scladina lower fourth premolar root is three-quarters of the length of that of the lower third premolar at 8 years of age. If the extension rates are the same, this is equivalent to a lag in development of at least 0.9 years. (The average length of Neanderthal lower fourth premolars is 2.1 mm longer than those of lower third premolars (Bailey 2005), making this a minimum). Using the recent human occlusal eruption lag of 0.4 years and assuming 1.5 years' wear gives an age of approximately 11 years.

### First molars
#### PN4 (upper right)
Recent human – this is the only specimen with teeth in position, an upper fourth deciduous premolar and a first permanent molar. Since the roots of the deciduous premolar are complete, the age on development grounds would be about 8 years. However, Stringer (1984) points out that the likely reason for the non-resorption of the roots of the deciduous premolar is that the crypt for the fourth permanent premolar is on the lingual side of this tooth. In view of this, the deciduous premolar could have been retained

beyond the normal age, meaning that PN4 could be as old as 10.7 years (range 10–11.3 years), the age at which the upper fourth permanent premolar would start erupting. The presence of a faint distal interproximal facet on the permanent molar indicates that the second molar has just, or nearly, reached occlusal eruption. This gives an age of 12 years (range 10.5–13 years). The likely age is therefore 10.5–11.5 years, which is higher than the age of 8–9 years originally reported (Stringer 1984). The eruption of the second molar before the fourth premolar is in keeping with Smith's (1994a) finding for early hominins. Bermúdez de Castro and Rosas (2001) likewise found that the upper fourth premolar in Hominid XVIII from Atapuerca-SH was retarded by 0.4 years compared with the first molar, and the upper second molar was advanced by 0.3 years.

Neanderthal – as stated above, in the Scladina juvenile the upper second deciduous premolar is still in place and no resorption of the roots has taken place. The upper second molar is not as developed as the lower second molar, which is just nearing occlusion. The developing roots of the upper second molar are approximately four-fifths of the length of those of the lower second molar (Smith *et al.* 2010, figure 6, SI). From figure 2 in Smith *et al.* 2007b this is equivalent to a development lag of 0.6 years if the extension rates are the same, giving a likely age of 8.6 years.

#### PN12 (upper left)
Recent human – this has a similar level of wear to that on PN4 and is likely to be from an individual of the same age. There is a nearly identical faint distal interproximal facet, indicating that the second molar has just erupted. This gives an age range of 10.5–13 years (average 12 years) with the lower end of the range being the more likely.

Neanderthal – as with PN4, the likely age is approximately 8.6 years. The slightly more definite distal interproximal facet indicates that the second molar has possibly been a little longer in occlusion.

#### PN11 (lower left)
Recent human – the level of wear on this tooth is similar to that observed on PN4 and PN12 in terms of width of dentine exposure (a little less) but with more cusps showing dentine. The distal interproximal facet is a little larger but still indicates recent eruption of the second molar, since it is still very faint, possibly within the previous year. The likely age is therefore 12–13 years (range 11–13.5 years). The level of wear on this tooth is equivalent to 7 years' use using the table prepared by Bermúdez de Castro and Nicolás (1997) for Atapuerca-SH lower first and second molars (rate of wear on both is very similar).

Neanderthal – in the Scladina juvenile the lower second molar is just reaching occlusal eruption giving a minimum age of 8 years. Allowing for the slightly larger distal interproximal facet than is found on PN4 and PN12, the probable age is 8.5 years.

### Second molars
#### PN1 (upper left)
Recent human – the average age of gingival eruption of second molars for recent humans is 11–11.5 years, with a minimum of about 10 years. Wolpoff (1979) found these figures satisfactory in ageing the Krapina hominins, though for mandible C he found the wear on the second molar argued for an older age than that shown by the other teeth, meaning a possible earlier eruption. The wear on PN11 is greater than the wear on the upper first molars (1.6 mm of dentine exposure on the mesiolingual cusp against 0.5/0.6 mm). The wear on the first molars relates to 5 or 6 years' use. If the rate of wear on the second molars is the same, the level of wear equates to an additional three years of use, 8–9 years in

all. The likely age is therefore 20–21 years, since the difference in occlusal eruption times is 6 years.

Neanderthal – first molar wear is equivalent to approximately three years use, so if wear on PN1 is half as much again at 4.5 years this gives an age of 13. The clear distal interproximal facet though suggests that the adjacent third molar had been in occlusion for at least a year, indicating an age of 15+ years (see below under *third molars*).

## PN13 (lower right)

The very high level of wear on this tooth indicates that it came from a mature adult.

## PN15 (lower right)

Recent human – this tooth has the same level of wear as the lower first molar, PN11, which relates to 6–7 years' use. Again, if the rate of wear on the second molars is the same, this gives a likely age of 18–19 years. The level of wear on this tooth is less than that on PN1.

Neanderthal – whilst the level of wear would indicate a younger age, the presence of a large distal interproximal facet shows that the third molar must have been in occlusion for some time, giving a minimum probable age of 14 years.

### Third molars

Recent human – as noted above, PN11 and PN15 have the same level of occlusal wear, but the size and development of the distal interproximal facets is very different. Wolpoff (1979) found that he needed to assume a shorter time interval between eruption of second and third molars than between first and second at Krapina, with an age of occlusal eruption of 15 for third molars, in order to fit in with the stages of development and levels of wear on other teeth. The age range suggested for the lower second molar PN15, of 18–19 years, fits in well with a third molar occlusal eruption age of 15 years. The earlier eruption of third molars is supported by the fact that six Middle Pleistocene specimens have the third molar in occlusion and no dentine exposure on the corresponding second molars – Arago 13, Montmaurin, Atapuerca-SH AT1 and AT75 (determined from casts) and Biache and Steinheim (determined from photographs). In contrast, the lower first molars of the Ehringsdorf juvenile and Atapuerca-SH AT2, in which the second molars are newly erupted, both have dentine exposure. In addition, Tompkins (1996) determined that calcification of third molars relative to second molars and fourth premolars was highly advanced in a sample of Neanderthals/archaic *Homo sapiens* compared with a sample of French Canadians, and advanced in comparison with a sample of Southern Africans. Furthermore, Bermúdez de Castro and Rosas (2001) have noted that, in Hominid XVIII from Atapuerca-SH, the upper and lower third molars are advanced by 2.8/2.7 years compared with the corresponding first molar, and in Bermúdez de Castro *et al.* (2004b) they note that Atapuerca-SH third molars are advanced relative to second molars by 1.5–3.4 years.

Neanderthal – the Le Moustier (France) upper third molars are shown in the present reconstruction of the specimen as having commenced gingival eruption. However, from micro CT evidence, and X-ray photographs taken at the time of discovery, Thompson and Illerhaus (2005) concluded that all four third molars were originally encased within the jaw. The roots of the upper and lower third molars are a quarter/half formed respectively at an age of 11.6–12.1 years (Smith *et al.* 2010). Using modern criteria (B. H. Smith's table), this suggests occlusal eruption between the ages of approximately 14–15 years for the upper third molar and 13–14 years for the lower third molar.

## PN17 (Upper right)

Recent human – the crown is fully formed and the root initiated to 3.9 mm, *i.e.* a quarter complete. If the age of occlusal eruption is 15 years, against the figures of 17.5–17.7 years given in Smith's table for 'lower third molar roots complete', and the rate of development is the same as in recent humans, then this gives a likely age of 12.3–12.5 years (assuming development of upper and lower third molars is the same).

Neanderthal – the level of root development is nearly identical to that of the Le Moustier upper third molar (3.8 mm of root; Smith *et al.* 2010), aged at 11.6–12.1 years by Smith *et al.* (2010). Age is therefore 11.7–12.2 years using the same criteria.

## PN19 (Upper right)

Recent human – the crown is fully formed and the root initiated to 1.3 mm. If the same assumptions are made as for PN17, the likely age is 10.5–10.7 years.

Neanderthal – using the same criteria of recent human third molar root extension rates, as used by Smith *et al.* (2010) to age the Le Moustier individual (no Neanderthal third molar extension rates being available), gives an approximate age of 9.6–9.8 years.

## PN16 (Lower right)

Recent human – the level of wear is less than on the lower first and second molars PN11 and PN15 (about half). If the rate of wear is the same, this suggests about 3 years' use, which, with an occlusal eruption age of 15 years, gives a likely age of 18 years. Using the table prepared by Bermúdez de Castro and Nicolás (1997) for Atapuerca-SH lower first and second molars gives a similar time of use of 2–3 years.

Neanderthal – the Le Moustier lower third molars are more developed than the upper third molars, roots half developed against a quarter developed (in Smith *et al.* 2010, figure 8, SI). Using recent human criteria would therefore suggest another 1.5–1.9 years until occlusal eruption, giving an occlusal eruption age range of approximately 13–14 years. At half the rate of wear on PN11 and PN15 this gives a probable age of approximately 15–16 years.

## PN21 (Lower right)

Recent human – as with PN19, the root is initiated to 1.3 mm, giving an age of 10.5–10.7 years.

Neanderthal – as stated above, the Le Moustier lower third molars are more developed than the upper, whereas the Scladina upper and lower third molars are at a similar stage of development (Smith *et al.* 2010). Using recent human criteria (Table 8.29) the difference between root one-quarter and one-half completed can be up to a year, which would give an age under nine (8.7–8.9 years), against approximately 9.6–9.8 years for PN19.

### Molar fragment
## PN9 (upper?)

If this fragment is from a permanent molar, the level of wear indicates that it is likely to have come from a mature adult.

### Mesolithic teeth

PN2 (lower right third molar) and PN8 (lower right second molar) have been linked to each other by Day (1986) and Stringer (1986).

## PN8

There are narrow wear facets on most cusps but no dentine exposure. This suggests recent eruption, with possibly one to two years use, giving an age of 13–14 years.

| Identity | Type | Age (years) (recent) | Age (years) (Neanderthal) |
|---|---|---|---|
| PN10 | $I_2$ | Juvenile/Adolescent (11) | Juvenile (9?) |
| PN18 | $P^4$ | 19/20 | 14.5 |
| PN6 | $P_3$ | Min. 8.5-11.0 | Min. 7 |
| PN7 | $P_3$ | 9.5-10.0 | 8 |
| PN20 | $P_3$ | Young adult | Young adult |
| PN5 | $P_4$ | 12/13 | 11 |
| PN4 | $M^1$&$dp^4$ | 10.5-11.5 | 8.5 |
| PN12 | $M^1$ | 12 (10.5-13) | 8.5-9 |
| PN11 | $M_1$ | 12/13 (11-13.5) | 8.5 |
| PN1 | $M^2$ | 20/21 | 15+ |
| PN13 | $M_2$ | Mature adult | Mature adult |
| PN15 | $M_2$ | 18/19 | 14+ |
| PN17 | $M^3$ | 12.5 | 11.5-12.0 |
| PN19 | $M^3$ | 10.5 | 9.5-10.0 |
| PN16 | $M_3$ | 18 | 15-16 |
| PN21 | $M_3$ | 10.5 | 8.5-9 |
| PN9 | Molar fragment | Mature adult | Mature adult |
| PN8 | $M_2$ | 13/14 | |
| PN2 | $M_3$ | 15 | |

*Table 9.30. Ages of Pontnewydd teeth.*

*PN2 is unerupted*
The root is a quarter formed, with a nearly complete trunk. Using Smith's chart, the average age for this stage of development in recent human teeth is 15 years.

### Discussion

The ageing of erupted teeth is very dependent on assumptions that teeth from different individuals, and different teeth within an individual, have the same rate of wear, and necessarily takes no account of asymmetric wear, sex differences, differences in diet between groups, *etc*. It is also the case that molar cuspal enamel on Neanderthal second and third molars is thicker than on first molars (Smith *et al.* 2007b), thus a greater level of wear will be required before there is any dentine exposure. In addition, in making any comparison between levels of wear on Neanderthal and modern human teeth, it needs to be borne in mind that Neanderthal teeth have thinner enamel (Olejniczak *et al.* 2008). The teeth ages (rounded to 0.5 years) are listed in Table 9.30. Eleven of the Middle Pleistocene teeth are from juveniles/adolescents (age range 9.5–13 years using recent human criteria, 8–12 years using Neanderthal criteria; excluding minimum ages for PN6), five from young adults and two from mature adults.

### Number of individuals

The Pontnewydd Middle Pleistocene teeth are grouped by size and context within approximate age categories (using both recent human and Neanderthal development criteria), which may represent individuals.

### Individual A, age 11 years (recent human) 9 years (Neanderthal), Lower Breccia, small

- PN12 upper left first molar
- PN19 upper right third molar

As noted above, PN12 is very small compared with the other Pontnewydd teeth. It cannot be the antimere of PN4. PN19 is also relatively small and can be put with PN12.

### Individual B, age 11 years (recent human) 8.5 years (Neanderthal), Lower Breccia, large

- PN10 lower right second incisor
- PN6 lower right third premolar
- PN7 lower left third premolar
- PN4 upper right first molar and fourth deciduous premolar

- PN11 lower left first molar
- PN21 lower right third molar

In order to age PN4 using recent human criteria, it was necessary to assume that gingival eruption of the upper fourth premolar was at a little above the average age, and occlusal eruption of the upper second molar at the start of the normal age range, both at 10.5–11.5 years. If the same applies to lower premolars and second molars, then these teeth can be grouped together. PN10 can be included in this group as the wear is consistent with this age. Weidenreich (1937) discusses the relative eruption times of lower second molars, and lower third and fourth premolars, and notes that in Krapina Mandible C the lower second molar has erupted while the lower fourth deciduous premolar is still in place, and that in the Ehringsdorf juvenile the lower second molar has erupted before either lower premolar. This order of eruption also occurs in '*Sinanthropus*' and in recent Bushmen. Smith (1994a) determined the sequence of gingival eruption in teeth in earlier hominins to be lower second molar followed by lower third premolar followed by fourth premolar. In the Gran Dolina hominins, calcification of the lower second molar in Hominid 1 is advanced compared with the lower third and fourth premolars, but in Hominid 3 the eruption sequence is the reverse – upper third premolar then upper fourth premolar followed by upper second molar (Bermúdez de Castro *et al.* 1999b). Tompkins (1996) determined that development of the third premolar relative to the first molar was delayed in a group of Neanderthals (including archaic *Homo sapiens* from Jebel Irhoud and Rabat) in comparison to recent human medians, and that development of the second molar was advanced. Moreover, Bermúdez de Castro and Rosas (2001) noted that the lower second molar of Atapuerca-SH Hominid XVIII was advanced by 0.5 years compared with the first molar. In Bermúdez de Castro *et al.* (2004b) they identify four individuals at Atapuerca-SH in which premolars (both upper and lower) are delayed relative to the second molar. In the Scladina mandible the third premolar and second molar appear to have been at a similar stage of eruption (picture in Schwartz and Tattersall 2002). In the Neanderthals studied by Smith *et al.* (2010) the third premolar is generally more advanced than the second molar but with the fourth premolar the situation is mixed.

### Individual C, age 12–13 years (recent human) 11–11.5 years (Neanderthal), Lower Breccia

- PN5 lower left fourth premolar
- PN17 upper right third molar

PN5 cannot be referred to Individual B since the eruption sequence would be incorrect, fourth premolar before third premolar. In addition, the interproximal facets on PN5 do not fit with PN7 or PN11. This still applies if PN5 has been transposed with the adjacent third premolar, as suggested above. PN17 is a little more developed than PN19 and PN21, and can be put with PN5.

### Individual D, age 18–19 years (recent human) 14–16 years (Neanderthal), Lower Breccia

- PN18 upper left fourth premolar
- PN15 lower right second molar
- PN16 lower right third molar

PN18 may appear relatively large to be put with PN15 and PN16, but the crown areas of PN18 and PN16 are in proportion if compared with the averages for the smaller Atapuerca-SH teeth, and PN15 is proportionally 10% larger than these compared to the very small Atapuerca-SH lower second molars. The mesial side of the mesiolingual cusp of PN16 is missing. It is difficult, therefore, to see if the interproximal facets on PN15 and PN16 match. The small amount of facet remaining on PN16 does not preclude this.

### Individual E, age 20–21 years (recent human) 15 years (Neanderthal), Intermediate complex

- PN1 upper left second molar

### Individual F, mature adult, Lower Breccia

- PN9 upper? molar fragment
- PN13 lower right second molar

### Individual G, young adult, Mudstone Gravel Unit (Layer 38) New Entrance

- PN20 lower left third premolar

This gives a minimum of seven individuals represented. If context is ignored, on the basis that all the teeth are likely to have come from the same source (Green 1984a), then D, E and G can possibly go together, giving five individuals. The position of PN1 being nearer the mouth of the cave in a lower layer is consistent with this. The proposition is supported by the close similarity of the crown measurements of the two second molars, PN1 and PN15, in comparison with other groups, described above.

If there are five individuals represented, the maximum number of permanent teeth expected would be 160. The sixteen permanent teeth recovered, plus a tooth fragment, represent a little over 10% of this figure. Even allowing for the fact that the deposits have not been fully excavated, this suggests either that the original remains were fragmentary before being incorporated into the Lower Breccia or that many teeth were destroyed whilst being incorporated. If the latter, this contrasts with the good condition of the crowns recovered. The proportion of molars is higher than the overall average (18%) and the proportion of incisors and canines lower (3% and 0%). The proportion of lower teeth is a little greater than that of upper teeth (13% against 9%).

Earlier it was shown that all the teeth in Individuals B to G were of similar size in relation to other groups. The teeth that were notably smaller in comparison to other groups were PN12 and, to a lesser extent, PN19. It was suggested that the large difference in crown area between the two upper first molars could possibly be because of sexual dimorphism. If this is so, and we have individuals from the same group at the same period of time, then Individual A may tentatively be put as being female and the other individuals as male. In summary, we therefore possibly have an 11/9-year-old female and four males aged 11/8.5, 12–13/11–11.5, 18–20/14–16 (depending on whether recent human or Neanderthal development criteria are used) and a mature adult. None of the Pontnewydd teeth definitely fit together (apart from PN4) and therefore could (excepting PN6 and PN7 as possible antimeres) alternatively come from different individuals. This would therefore give a maximum of 16 individuals; nine juveniles/adolescents, having a probable age range of 9.5/8–13/12 years, five young adults and two mature adults.

The range of ages of the individuals is consistent with other European Middle Pleistocene sites and with Krapina. Bermúdez de Castro and Díez (1995) quote figures for:

*Atapuerca-SH*
78% of individuals (25 out of 32) are in an age range of 12–27 years, with the total range being 3–36.

*Krapina*
88% of individuals (72 out of 82) are in an age range of 3–21 years, with a peak at 15–18 and a highest age of 30. (Trinkaus (1995), using a minimum number of individuals of 23, obtained figures of 26% children and juveniles, 44% adolescents and 30% young adults).

Bocquet-Appel and Arsuaga (1999) consider that the age distribution of both these groups suggests a demographic crisis caused by severe environmental fluctuation. Bermúdez de Castro and Díez (1995) also point out that most of the European Pleistocene fossil specimens are children, adolescents or young adults. In an updated study of Atapuerca-SH by Bermúdez de Castro *et al.* (2004b) using a larger sample, 64% of 28 individuals (number revised downwards and sexes approximately equally represented) are adolescents in the 11–20 year range, nine are older and only one is younger. (Employing their method of ageing teeth based on the level of wear, PN1 is aged at 26–30 years instead of 20–21/15+ years). These results were compared with modern forager groups and it was concluded that neither catastrophe nor attrition explained this age spread. For both scenarios there should be higher proportions of younger and older individuals. The ages of a sample of other European Middle Pleistocene specimens were studied, and this gave a similar picture but showing a greater spread – 38% adolescents, 35% in the 20–30 year range and 15% juveniles and infants, still not representing a stable population. Bermúdez de Castro *et al.* (2004b) considered that the relative lack of younger individuals in the European Middle Pleistocene sample could be because of poor preservation of their remains as against those of adolescents and adults. They did not think, though, that this was the case at Atapuerca-SH, where preservation is

very good. For Atapuerca-SH there are specific taphonomic considerations as to how the assemblage might have accumulated (Andrews and Fernandez-Jalvo 1997). These authors considered that the nature of the assemblage, and the tooth marks on the bones, were consistent with the cave being a lions' den, and human bodies being scavenged from elsewhere. Trinkaus (1995) studied a sample of Neanderthals, including Krapina, and discovered a similar pattern of 18% and 39% of adolescents and young adults respectively (10–19 and 20–39 years age ranges), and 33% younger than this. Comparisons with recent populations only saw parallels in those which were clearly under stress, and it was considered that the implication of the high level of adolescent and young adult mortality, and lack of older individuals, was that Neanderthals were under severe demographic stress, constantly on the brink of extinction. The high level of hypoplasia in Neanderthals was identified as a likely indicator of stress. Possible reasons given for the lack of older people were different burial practices or the problems of mobility in an older individual. Most specimens in the sample were discovered in natural shelters. A person no longer able to move with the group might be left, and so die away from the campsite, it being noted that no Neanderthal remains have been discovered of individuals clearly unable to walk. Trinkaus (1995) did point out that composite figures of many sites could be including sites that represent population collapses occurring as a result of ecological fluctuations, and so distort the figures. In contrast, Kennedy (2005) names several prehistoric anatomically modern human foraging populations having the same demography, a peak of deaths in the young adult category (aged 20–40 years) of 30% or more and 10–25% of adolescents, and considers that this was sustainable if alloparenting and adoption of orphans was practiced.

## Locations at which teeth were discovered

The locations at which the teeth were discovered are shown in Figure 9.1. Each tooth is plotted in the centre of its quadrant. The Mesolithic teeth (PN2 and PN8) are excluded. Teeth discovered in the Lower Breccia were located either in the East Passage, or in the area just west of the East Passage between the South-East and North-East Fissures. The overall area in which they were unearthed is in the form of a 'T', extending 6.5 m in an east–west direction and 4.0 m in a north–south direction. The teeth are in two distinct groups:

### *Group 1– East Passage*

Individuals A, D, part of B and part of C. The locations of the seven teeth are evenly spread over the passage but there are none above an east–west line from the north side of the central baulk.

### *Group 2 – area west of East Passage*

Individuals B, F and part of C. Most of the nine teeth lie

on a north–south line running across the entrance to the East Passage and away from the cave wall. The find spot of PN1 (Individual E), in the Intermediate complex, is 1.7 m west of this line.

The distances between teeth within an individual are very similar to each other:

- Individual A – 2.1 m
- Individual B – 1.6 m, 1.6 m, 1.6 m, 1.6 m, 1.0 m; 4.0 m overall N–S and 3.0 m E–W
- Individual C – 5.3 m
- Individual D – 1.0 m, 1.6 m
- Individual F – 1.2 m

All are in the range of 1.0–2.1 m apart from Individual C. Individuals B, C, D and F all contain both upper and lower teeth. Within Individual B the left and right teeth are separate. Both parts of PN15 (Individual D) were found in the same quadrant. PN6 and PN7 in Individual B, which are thought to be antimeres, were found 2.3 m apart.

The levels at which the teeth were discovered varies over a maximum of 0.78 m, which is most of the depth of the Lower Breccia at this point. The teeth found at the highest levels were PN18, the easternmost tooth in Group 1, and PN6 and PN10, the two southernmost teeth in Group 2. Without these three teeth the maximum variation in level would be 0.45 m. Within individuals, the maximum variations in level are A: 0.35 m, B: 0.71 m, C: 0.15 m, D: 0.57 m, F: 0.2 m.

Of the seven teeth with fairly complete roots discovered in the Lower Breccia, five are in Individual B and one each in Individuals A and F. There are four other teeth in these individuals; the unerupted PN19 and PN21, the molar fragment PN9, and PN10 for which the root is missing. In Individuals C and D, the roots are missing on all four erupted teeth. Looked at in terms of groups, six out of eight teeth erupted or erupting in Group 2 (excluding PN9) have fairly complete roots, but only one out of four in Group 1. A higher proportion of molars have nearly complete roots (five with, two without) than premolars and incisor (two with, three without).

## Conclusions

Whilst clearly all the teeth other than PN4 became separated from their jaws before final deposition, the closeness of teeth within individuals suggests that the teeth of individuals were in discrete locations, and possibly still in alveolar bone, when incorporated into the Lower Breccia. The difference in the proportion of nearly complete roots between individuals and groups might possibly suggest differences in the strength and preservation of the jaws from which they came, leading to either the jaw disintegrating round the tooth (or the tooth falling out), or the crown being snapped off, leaving the roots in the jaw. The good condition of the tooth crowns, together with the lack of mixing and the even spacing of the teeth, suggests that they may have been incorporated into the Lower Breccia within the cave. This is supported by the presence of PN1 in a lower layer,

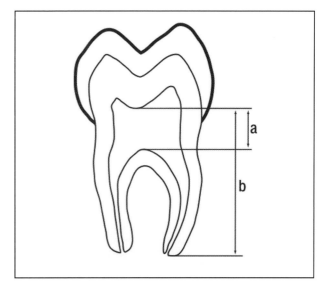

*Figure 9.34. Method of measurement for taurodontism.*

at the junction of the Buff and Orange Intermediate, to the west of Group 2. The small proportion of teeth found for the number of individuals (just over 10%), together with the almost complete lack of surviving bone, indicates that the remains were probably already fragmentary and degraded when incorporated into the Lower Breccia.

## Root morphology

The roots of Pontnewydd teeth are described and, where possible, compared with the roots of Atapuerca-SH teeth using descriptions in Bermúdez de Castro (1988) and casts of teeth held by the Natural History Museum, London for upper first molars AT16 and AT20; upper second molars AT12 and AT15; lower first molars AT14 and AT21 and lower second molar AT11.

AT15, 16 and 21 are identified as male by Bermúdez de Castro and Nicolás (1997) and AT14 as female. The roots of PN10 (lower lateral incisor), PN18 (upper fourth premolar), PN20 (lower third premolar), PN5 (lower fourth premolar), PN15 (lower second molar), and all upper and lower third molars, are not sufficiently complete to make any comparisons.

### *Taurodontism*

Taurodont teeth are those in which the pulp chamber is markedly enlarged and extends towards the tips of the roots. It is a characteristic particularly associated with Neanderthals (Day 1986). The level of taurodontism is measured using the definitions of Kallay (1970) and Shaw (1928):

*Kallay*

1: Supraradicular, where the pulp cavity is of normal shape above the bifurcation of the roots, but enlarged, and the root is partially prismatic. 2: Radicular, where the root is

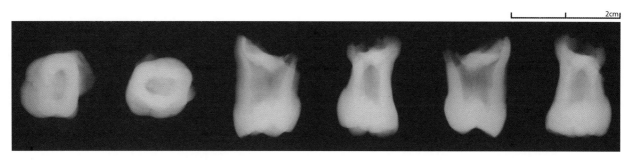

*Figure 9.35. PN4 upper right first permanent molar.*

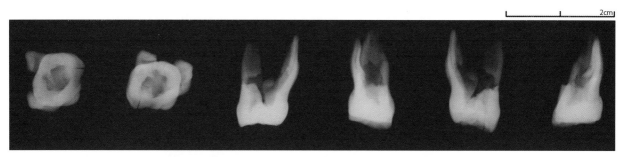

*Figure 9.36. PN4 upper right fourth deciduous premolar.*

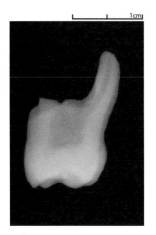

*Figure 9.37. PN12 upper left first permanent molar.*

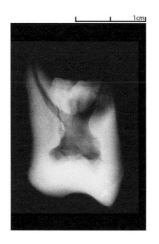

*Figure 9.38. PN1 upper left second permanent molar.*

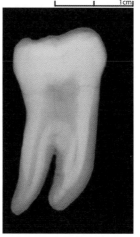

*Figure 9.39. PN11 lower left first permanent molar.*

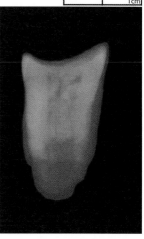

*Figure 9.40. PN13 lower right second permanent molar.*

fully prismatic and the pulp cavity hourglass shaped. 3: Total, where the root is fully prismatic and the pulp cavity barrel shaped. For both radicular and total taurodontism there is only the single root, with the pulp cavity extending to the apex.

*Shaw*

The Shaw definition has 'normal' and three grades of taurodontism, namely hypo, meso and hyper; which approximately equate to the height of the pulp chamber being a quarter, half or three quarters of the total length of the root. Keene (1966) further defines these in terms of a taurodontism index. This is ('a'×100)/'b' where 'a' is the minimum vertical height of the pulp chamber, and 'b' is the distance between the lowest point of the roof of the pulp chamber and the apex of the longest root (Figure 9.34). The value ranges for each grade are; hypo: 25–49.9%, meso: 50–74.9% and hyper: 75–100%. The taurodontism indices for the Pontnewydd teeth are: PN4 (upper first permanent molar), 46, (hypo); PN4 (upper fourth deciduous premolar), 22, (normal); PN12 (upper first permanent molar), 37, (hypo); PN1 (upper second permanent molar), 37, (hypo); PN11 (lower first permanent molar), 33, (hypo); PN13 (lower second permanent molar), 19, (normal). (see X-ray photographs Figures 9.35–9.40). Supraradicular taurodontism may be hypo, meso or hyper.

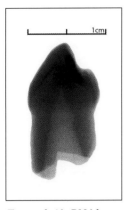

*Figure 9.41. PN6 lower right third permanent premolar.*

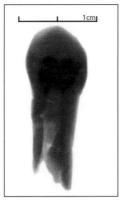

*Figure 9.42. PN7 lower left third permanent premolar.*

As with Atapuerca-SH, the upper molars from Pontnewydd are the most taurodont. Both the upper first permanent molars, PN4 and PN12, and the single upper second molar, PN1, exhibit supraradicular taurodontism, PN4 is meso-taurodont on the Shaw scale, and PN12 and PN1 are hypo-taurodont. The Atapuerca-SH first and second upper molars are similarly supraradicular, varying from hypo to meso. Hominid VII is reported as exhibiting radicular taurodontism in both first and second upper molars but the cast of the first molar, AT16, from this individual shows supraradicular taurodontism.

Of the two lower molars from Pontnewydd, the first molar, PN11, exhibits supraradicular hypo-taurodontism but the second molar, PN13, is not taurodont. At Atapuerca-SH, conversely, the lower first molars are not taurodont but the lower second molars mostly have some level of supraradicular taurodontism, though AT11 does not appear to. The pulp chambers of the taurodont Pontnewydd molars are barrel-shaped, with the exception of that of PN1 which is hourglass shaped.

Supraradicular taurodontism of the molars is found in many of the other Middle Pleistocene specimens: Mauer (meso), Montmaurin (moderate), Ehringsdorf juvenile (moderate) but not the adult, Steinheim (second molar moderate, first and third molars marked) (Howell 1960; Stringer *et al.* 1984). In addition, the two Bilzingsleben lower molars E2 and E12 (first and second) are described as being taurodont (Vlček and Mania 1987). The roots of the Bilzingsleben upper molar C1 are only preserved to 5.5 mm on the mesial side (measured from photograph) but show no sign of bifurcation, suggesting at least mild taurodontism in this tooth as well (Mania and Vlček 1981). Against this, the roots of the Biache teeth do not appear to be taurodont, being more divided than the Pontnewydd teeth (studied by C. B. S.), and there is an absence of taurodontism in the Pesada upper third molar (Trinkaus *et al.* 2003). This is also the case with the Visogliano upper teeth, in which the roots diverge at 3 mm beyond the cervix (Abbazzi *et al.* 2000; Mallegni *et al.* 2002). Similarly, the first molar in the mandibular fragment from this site does

not appear to have been taurodont (Cattani *et al.* 1991). X-ray photographs taken of the Petralona specimen show no evidence of taurodontism either (Marinos *et al.* 1965 translated in Murrill 1981). Of the casts available of Arago teeth (AR9 (upper first molar), AR14 (upper second molar), AR31 (upper second molar), AR32 (lower second molar) and mandibles AR2 and AR13) only the AR13 third molar has the appearance of being taurodont. (Bermúdez de Castro *et al.* (2003a) confirm that the second molar of AR13 is hypo-taurodont and the third molar meso-taurodont). Taurodontism indices calculated from X-ray photographs for the Mauer mandible (Schoetensack 1908), the Montmaurin mandible (Billy and Vallois 1977) and the Ehringsdorf juvenile mandible (Vlček 1993) are: Mauer – first molar approximately 20%, second molar approximately 15%, third molars approximately 35% (left 30%, right 40%); Montmaurin – first molar 13%, second molar 30%, third molar 25%; Ehringsdorf – first molar 20%, second molar approximately 26%, third molar similar to second molar. Taurodontism is therefore confined to the second and third molars. The most taurodont of the Middle Pleistocene teeth considered appears to be the Bau de l'Aubesier (Aubesier 10) upper first/second molar. Using external measurements (X-rays not giving any result), the minimum trunk size of this tooth as a percentage of root length is quoted as 71.4% (Lebel and Trinkaus 2002). This compares with 68% for PN1 but only 51% for the more taurodont PN4. However, the first molar in the mandible from this site (Aubesier 11) was not taurodont.

Supraradicular taurodontism is the most common form of taurodontism found at Krapina (Smith 1976b), accounting for 51% of the 90% of molars that exhibit taurodontism. 43% of cases had radicular taurodontism and 6% had total taurodontism. Dumančić *et al.* (2001) have studied 27 mandibular molars from Krapina. A little over a third of the first molars, but all the second and third molars, have taurodontism indices in excess of 20%. Just over half have a taurodontism index over 40%, the rate increasing from first to third molars.

The Krapina premolars are often taurodont (Smith 1976b). The developing root of the Pontnewydd lower third premolar PN6 gives no appearance of taurodontism in the X-ray photograph but that of its possible antimere, PN7, indicates a wider pulp chamber that continues to the apex of the root, and thinner walls (see X-ray photographs Figures 9.41–9.42). Taurodontism is not reported for the premolars from Atapuerca-SH (Bermúdez de Castro (1988). The pulp chambers of both PN6 and PN7 are egg-shaped, with the wide end buccal.

As noted by Stringer (1984); the degree of taurodontism at Pontnewydd is not as great as that found in Upper Pleistocene sites such as Krapina and La Cotte de St Brelade but the number of teeth at Pontnewydd exhibiting taurodontism suggests a population characteristic. In this last respect it can be noted that the only permanent tooth that does not exhibit taurodontism, PN13, is the molar from the mature adult. The other molars are all from young individuals. (It is not possible to determine if the fragment of very worn upper (?) molar, PN9, comes from a taurodont tooth). Also, PN1, which is hypo-taurodont, comes from the Intermediate complex, whereas the other molars with taurodontism come from the Lower Breccia.

The Mesolithic molars are not taurodont. Commencement of branching between the roots can be seen at about 3 mm below the cervix in both cases.

### Upper fourth premolar
Only the cervical rim of the root of PN18 is present. The mesial side is flat and the distal side is convex.

### Lower third premolars
PN7 has a single root (so far as it is developed), and this is the general case for Atapuerca-SH and Krapina lower premolars. One Krapina tooth has two roots (Smith 1976b). No lower third premolars with two roots are reported for Atapuerca-SH. From X-ray photographs, the Mauer premolars appear to have single roots (Schoetensack 1908) and similarly those of the Ehringsdorf adult (Vlček 1993). The Montmaurin premolars had single roots as well (Howell 1960). In contrast, the third and fourth premolars of the Arago 13 specimen both have two roots, that of the fourth premolar being similar in form to the Gran Dolina Hominid 1 fourth premolar (Bermúdez de Castro *et al.* 2003a).

Apart from the possible presence of taurodontism in PN7, there is little variation between Pontnewydd and Atapuerca-SH. The only difference noted is that the Atapuerca-SH teeth have both mesial and distal longitudinal grooves on the roots, but PN6 and PN7 only have distal grooves. The roots of PN6 and PN7 are mesiodistally compressed, as are those of the Atapuerca-SH teeth. Both are wider on the buccal side. The damaged root of PN7 continues at the same width to the apex and curves distally. The incomplete root of PN6 has a slight distal inclination. The distal curvature of the Atapuerca-SH roots is variable. Neither PN6 nor PN7 have a canine groove (*i.e.* a groove on the mesial surface supposedly formed by the tooth's eruption against a canine).

### Upper first and second molars
Comparing the roots of Pontnewydd and Atapuerca-SH upper molars (buccal roots of PN12 and PN1, and apex of lingual root of PN4, being missing):

#### Radicular plates
The radicular plate on the roots of PN4 (permanent tooth) fully links the buccal roots down to their apices, where it is convex buccally. A similar radicular plate occurs on AT12. Two of the Atapuerca-SH teeth (AT16 and AT15) have radicular plates linking the lingual root with either the mesiobuccal or the distobuccal root. This feature is not seen at Pontnewydd.

#### Buccal roots, upper first molars
The buccal roots on PN4 are close but clearly separate. They are also close or coalesce on the Atapuerca-SH teeth. The apices of the buccal roots of PN4 are straight but those of

AT16 and AT20 curve inwards. The mesiobuccal root of PN4 has a wide apex that is abbreviated on the lingual side. The buccal side inclines distally and is convex buccally. The distobuccal root has a greater distal inclination than the mesial (greatest on the lingual side) and is also inclined buccally. It has a greater distal inclination than the distobuccal roots of AT16 or AT20.

#### Buccal roots, upper second molars
The mesiobuccal root of PN1 is wider than that of AT12 buccolingually and has a slighter longitudinal groove. It is similar in width to that of AT15. The mesial face of the mesiobuccal root is very concave in AT12 but not in PN1.

#### Mesiobuccal root, upper first and second molars
The lingual side of the apex of the mesiobuccal root of PN4 inclines sharply mesially. This is also found in AT15 and AT16. In AT16 the apex of the root is bifurcated. In both Atapuerca-SH and Pontnewydd teeth, the mesiobuccal root is wider buccolingually than the distobuccal root. Both are mesiodistally flattened.

#### Lingual roots (shape)
In upper first molars the lingual roots of PN4 and PN12 extend more lingually than those of AT16 and AT20, but in upper second molars the lingual roots of AT12 and AT15 extend more lingually than that of PN1. The degree of buccal curvature of the apex of the lingual root varies; most on AT16, none on AT15, with PN12 and PN1 intermediate. All the lingual roots have a distal inclination.

#### Lingual roots (size)
The lingual root of AT20 is narrower mesiodistally than those of the other first molars, but that of AT16 is wider than that of PN12 and the same width as PN4. The lingual root of second molar PN1 is wider than that of AT15 and similar to that of AT12.

#### Radicals (segments of roots identified by vertical grooves)
Most of the upper molars have two radicals visible in the lingual root, but first molars PN4 and AT16 have three (grooves lingually and distally). The mesiobuccal roots ^f the Atapuerca-SH teeth have two radicals visible, as do PN12 and PN1. However, PN4 has three. The Atapuerca-SH first molars AT16 and AT20 also have two radicals visible in the distobuccal root, as does PN12, but PN4 only has one.

#### Root trunks
On first molars, the mesial longitudinal grooves on the root trunks of PN4 and PN12 (between the lingual and mesiobuccal roots), and the lingual groove on PN4, are deeper than those on AT16 and AT20. The buccal grooves on AT20 and PN12 are similar, and deeper than those on PN4 and AT16. On second molars, the mesial grooves on PN1 and AT15 are similar, and stronger than that on AT12.

*Miscellaneous*
There is an irregular pit on the distal surface of PN4, just beyond the cervix.

### Upper third molar
Only the cervical part of the root trunk of PN17 is present. This is inclined distally and has two slight longitudinal mesial grooves.

### Upper fourth deciduous premolar
There are no Atapuerca-SH upper fourth deciduous premolars with which to compare the morphology of PN4. The trunk is inclined distally and lingually. The buccal roots are round in cross-section. The mesiobuccal root is convex mesially, and inclined distally and lingually. The distobuccal root is convex distally and more inclined distally than the mesiobuccal root. The lingual root is wide and buccolingually compressed, with a lingual inclination and a vertical apex. The tip of the apex is on the mesial side. A prominent lingual groove runs from the trunk to the apex of the lingual root.

### Lower first and second molars
The principal points of comparison between the roots of the Pontnewydd and Atapuerca-SH first and second lower molars are:

*Shape, lower first molars*
The roots of AT14 and AT21 are closer and more parallel than those of PN11, and have the same distal inclination as PN11's mesial root. The distal root of PN11 extends more distally and has a slight buccal inclination. The apex of the mesial root of PN11 is curved more distally than those of AT14 and AT21. The apex of the distal root of PN11 has a slight distal curve but not those of AT14 or AT21.

*Shape, lower second molars*
The distally sloping fused roots of PN13 (fused for half their length) have the same distal inclination (greater than that of the mesial root of PN11) as the mesial root of AT11. The distal root of AT11 inclines sharply distally. However, on Atapuerca-SH first and second molars the degree of fusion/separation of buccal and lingual roots varies. The unfused part of the mesial root of PN13 curves distally (the unfused part of the distal root is missing).

*Shape, general*
In both Atapuerca-SH and Pontnewydd lower molars there is a distal inclination of the roots from the cervix, and the apices of the roots are on the buccal side. On PN11 the distal inclination of the trunk is only apparent on the mesial side.

*Rotation of distal root*
The slight mesiolingual/distobuccal rotation of the distal root of PN11 is seen in AT11 but not in AT14 or AT21.

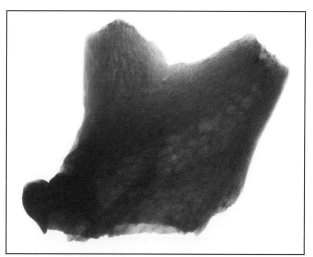

*Figure 9.43. PN2 right mandibular fragment.*

*Size*
The roots of PN11 are intermediate in buccolingual width between those of AT14 (the smaller) and AT21, and those of PN13 are wider than those of AT11. In all the teeth the mesial root is wider buccolingually than the distal root.

*Longitudinal periradicular bands (ridges along buccal and lingual margins of roots)*
FIRST MOLAR
On PN11 there are prominent rounded ridges running down the buccal and lingual margins of the roots. These occur on both the mesial and distal surfaces of the mesial root but on the mesial surface only of the distal root. On AT14 and AT21 the ridges only appear to occur on the mesial surface of the mesial root and are less prominent.

SECOND MOLAR
Both PN13 and AT11 have these ridges on the mesial face of the mesial root, and AT11 also on the distal face, but those on PN13 are more prominent.

*Horizontal ridges*
The second molar (PN13) has two irregular horizontal raised areas on the roots; one on the mesial side of the mesial root, connecting the ridges on the buccal and lingual margins, and one that is less distinct on the distal side of the distal root. Both are halfway down the root and go across its full width. These are not present on the Atapuerca-SH teeth studied, nor on PN11.

*Bifurcation*
The mesial root of the first molar (PN11) is bifurcated. This feature is not reported for Atapuerca-SH and is not seen on PN13.

*Root canals*
The distal roots of second molars PN13 and AT11 have a single wide root canal.

*Root trunks*

On PN11 and PN13 there are strong buccal and lingual vertical grooves between the roots, running from the cervix. These also occur on the Atapuerca-SH teeth.

The Ehringsdorf adult mandible first and second molar roots have the distal branch in a straight line, and the mesial root curved towards the tip of the distal (Weidenreich 1937), similarly to PN11, and described by Weidenreich as 'pithecoid'. This is also found in the juvenile (Vlček 1993). The roots of the Mauer mandible first and second molars are described by Weidenreich as nearly parallel, and weak compared with Neanderthal teeth. The roots of the Montmaurin lower molars are widely spaced and near parallel. The distal inclination of the roots increases from first (very little) to third, the distal inclination of the distal root being greater than that of the mesial root on the second and third molars (Billy and Vallois 1977).

### Mesolithic lower molars

*PN8, second molar*

Only part of the buccal side of the root trunk is present. This is vertical, in line with the crown, and has a longitudinal buccal groove.

*PN2, third molar*

The trunk of the part formed root is vertical, in line with the crown, and has buccal and lingual longitudinal grooves. The mesial end is wider than the distal end. Two distinct roots are forming (Figure 9.43).

### Interrelationships of Middle Pleistocene Pontnewydd teeth

Comparing the Pontnewydd permanent teeth with each other:

*Taurodontism*

All permanent molars with roots are taurodont, with the exception of PN13.

*Premolars*

Both lower third premolars, PN6 and PN7, have distal longitudinal grooves on the root but not mesial. However, the root shapes are slightly different, PN7 possibly being taurodont.

*Upper molars – radicular plates*

It is not possible to see if either PN1 or PN12 had the type of radicular plate present on PN4.

*Upper molars – buccal roots*

In so far as it is possible to tell, the buccal roots on upper molars are well separated. Those of PN1 are well separated lingually but broken on the buccal side. There is a deep buccal groove on PN12, suggesting that the roots were separated. The buccolingual widths of the mesiobuccal roots of PN4 and PN12 are similar, and both a little less than that of PN1.

*Upper molars – lingual roots*

The lingual roots of both the upper first molars (PN4 and PN12) have a buccolingually compressed rectangular cross-section, but that of PN1 is rounder in cross-section. (The lingual roots of the Atapuerca-SH teeth – AT12, 15, 16 and 20 – are square/rectangular in outline). The mesiodistal width and degree of lingual inclination of the lingual roots of the first molars are the same, and both greater than that of PN1. Both PN12 and PN1 have a buccal curvature of the apex of the lingual root, which is greatest in PN12.

*Upper molars – radicals*

All three upper molars, PN4, PN12 and PN1, have at least two radicals visible in the lingual root, most clearly on the first molars (three on PN4). PN1 and PN12 both have two radicals visible in the mesiobuccal root but PN4 has three. PN4 has a single radical visible in the distobuccal root and PN12 has two (site absent in PN1).

*Upper molars – root trunk*

In both PN12 and PN1 the root trunk has an overall distal inclination in relation to the crown. This is only seen on the lingual side of PN4. There are vertical grooves on the trunks between roots, and also on the lingual face which continue onto the lingual root. These are variable in depth and extent.

*Root trunks – upper and lower second molars*

The second molars have an inclination of the root trunk, lingually on PN1 (upper) and buccally on PN13 (lower), which is very slight or absent on the first molars. (There is no clear pattern between first and second molars in the Atapuerca-SH teeth).

*Lower molars*

The mesial roots of PN11 and PN13 are of similar width, both buccolingually and mesiodistally, where they connect to the root trunk, and the same applies to the distal roots. However, the mesial root of PN13 tapers more rapidly to the apex than that of PN11. The mesial root of PN13 has a greater distal inclination than that of PN11, but the apex of PN11 has a greater distal curvature. The roots of PN13 are part fused but those of PN11 are not. The ridges along the buccal and lingual margins of the roots of PN11 are more pronounced than those on PN13, but only PN13 has horizontal ridges linking these margins.

### Summary of root morphology

The roots of the Pontnewydd and Atapuerca-SH teeth are very similar and the few differences found are not significant in such a small sample. The lower molar roots have some characteristics not reported for Atapuerca-SH; namely the bifurcation of the mesial root of PN11 and horizontal ridges on the mesial and distal roots of PN13.

There are three characteristics not found at Pontnewydd that occur at Atapuerca-SH. These are: a radicular plate

| Trait | Pontnewydd PN10 | Mid Pleistocene Earlier* | Later* | Krapina* |
|---|---|---|---|---|
| Shovelling > 1 | Grade 1 mesial | 0/1 | 1/4 | 6/8 |
| | Grade 2 distal | 1 | 0-2 | 1-2 |
| Double shovelling – Mesial > 0 | Grade 0 | 0/1 | 1/1 | 3/6 |
| | | | 1 | 1 |
| Double shovelling – Distal > 0 | Grade 0 | 0/1 | 2/2 | 3/6 |
| | | | 1-2 | 1 |
| Labial convexity > 2 | Grade 3 | 1/1 | 3/4 | 4/6 |
| | | 3 | 0,3-4 | 2-3 |
| Lingual median ridge > 1 | Grade 1 | 1/1 | 0/4 | 5/7 |
| | | 2 | 0-1 | 0-2 |
| Flaring – Mesial | No | 0/1 | 0/2 | 7/8 |
| Flaring – Distal | Yes | 1/1 | 3/3 | 8/8 |
| Angle of buccal surface to vertical | 25° (App) | 15° | 15°-20° | 20°-35° Av. 28° |

*Number of specimens with trait over number of specimens scored. Range of grades found shown below.

*Table 9.31. Crown morphology, lower lateral incisors.*

linking lingual, and either mesiobuccal or distobuccal, roots (AT16 and AT15); bifurcation of the apex of the mesiobuccal root on an upper molar (AT16); and a vertical ridge in the centre of the buccal side of the root trunk of a lower molar, running from the cervix to the base of the root trunk (AT1 and AT2).

There are three specific aspects that the roots of the Pontnewydd and Atapuerca-SH teeth have in common. In the upper molars: the form of the radicular plate linking the buccal roots on PN4 and AT12; and the mesial inclination of the lingual side of the apex of the mesiobuccal root on PN4, AT15 and AT16. In the lower molars: rotation of the distal roots of PN11 and AT11.

## Crown morphology

### Method

The morphological traits of the Pontnewydd teeth are described by tooth type. In order to make comparisons with other European Middle and Late Pleistocene hominins, the same morphological traits have been studied on casts of teeth held by the Human Origins Group at the Natural History Museum, London. The sites covered (see earlier comments) are from the earlier European Middle Pleistocene (Mauer, Arago, Petralona, Visogliano); the later European Middle Pleistocene (Atapuerca-SH, Bilzingsleben, Montmaurin, Steinheim, Ehringsdorf, Biache, Pesada) and Krapina, *c.* 130,000 years BP (Rink *et al.* 1995; casts kindly donated by E. Trinkaus).

These observations have been augmented from morphological descriptions given by Weidenreich (1937), Howell (1960), Cattani *et al.* (1991), Abbazzi *et al.* (2000), Mallegni *et al.* (2002), Mania and Vlček (1981), Trinkaus *et al.* (2003), Billy (1982) and Billy and Vallois (1977). In addition, details of teeth from Atapuerca-SH for which casts are not available have been taken from published sources: Bermúdez de Castro (1988) and Bermúdez de Castro (1993). These do not cover all the traits scored

on casts. Traits not covered by Bermúdez de Castro are: double shovelling, additional buccal occlusal ridges on premolars, cusps on mesial marginal ridges of upper molars, parastyle, metaconule, anterior transverse ridge, deflecting wrinkle and distal trigonid crest. Photographs of original specimens taken by one of the authors (C. B. Stringer), from Delson (1985), and kindly donated by S. E. Bailey, along with photographs appearing in the references sited above and in the NESPOS Database (2010), have been used in conjunction with the casts. For Visogliano, Bilzingsleben, Steinheim and Biache, only photographs were available.

The intention is to indicate the affinities of Pontnewydd teeth with other European later Middle Pleistocene teeth and identify traits that could suggest affinities with earlier or later material. For each trait listed in the tables of comparative morphological data, an occurrence rate is given of the number of individuals with the trait against the number of individuals for which the trait could be scored. For traits involving a graded variation, rather than simple presence/absence, the range of grades for which 'present' is scored is indicated against the trait name. The grades observed are identified under each occurrence rate. Where both left and right antimeres are present, the highest expression of a trait encountered is the one used. This is the approach taken by Turner *et al.* (1991). 'KDP' in the text refers to Krapina Dental People and is based on the work of Radovčić *et al.* (1988) who grouped nearly all the isolated teeth, and jaws with teeth in place, at Krapina into individuals. For a fuller description, see Stringer *et al.* (1997).

The counts given for the incidence of cusp 5 and cusp 6 on lower molars are based on the method of Turner *et al.* (1991), which assumes that a single additional distal cusp on a lower molar is a cusp 5, and cusp 6 can only be scored as present if cusp 5 is also present. The published figures for Atapuerca-SH in Bermúdez de Castro (1993) have been adjusted to reflect this.

Descriptions of buccal, lingual, mesial and distal aspects of teeth are as viewed laterally. These traits are only described for Pontnewydd teeth. Angles and percentages* quoted

| Trait | Pontnewydd PN18 | Mid Pleistocene Earlier* | Later* | Krapina* |
|---|---|---|---|---|
| Buccal cusp medial | Medial | 1/3 | 1/4 | 7/9 |
| Multiple lingual cusps | Single | 0/3 | 0/5 | 4/9 |
| Principal lingual cusp mesial | Mesial | 3/3 | 5/5 | 8/9 |
| Buccal occlusal ridges: - | | | | |
|     Mesial | - | 2/3 | 0/3 | 5/9 |
|     Distal | - | 2/2 | 0/3 | 5/9 |
|     Median bifurcated | No | 1/3 | 1/3 | 8/9 |
| Sagittal sulcus interrupted | Yes | 3/3 | 3/5 | 7/9 |
| Mesial marginal ridge interrupted | No | 1/2 | 1/4 | 4/7 |
| Distal marginal ridge interrupted | Yes | 2/2 | 2/5 | 7/8 |
| Accessory marginal tubercles | None | 1/3 | 2/5 | 3/6 |
| Double shovelling – Mesial > 0 | Grade 2 | 2/3 (1,2) | 1/2 (2) | 7/9 (1-3) |
| Double shovelling – Distal > 0 | Grade 1 | 1/3 (1) | 0/2 | 5/9 (1) |

*Number of specimens with trait over number of specimens scored. Range of grades found shown in brackets.

*Table 9.32. Crown morphology, upper fourth premolars.*

are rounded to the nearest five. Definitions of individual traits, the way in which they are scored, and references, are given in Appendix A. The number for the trait description in Appendix A follows the trait name in the following sections. There is no entry in Appendix A where there is no specific scoring method and no reference. Most of the traits studied are in the ASU (Arizona State University) system (reference A in Appendix A) and the ASU scoring system is followed using their reference plaques. The ASU system has been widely used in studies investigating the relative distances between populations (*e.g.* Turner 1987; Irish 1993; Haydenblit 1996). There are a number of traits described by other authors, not included in the ASU system, in particular relating to premolars, which are also studied. The teeth showing the greatest morphological change between those of Gran Dolina and those of the later Middle Pleistocene are the lower premolars, and therefore particular attention has been paid to these. The intention of studying a wide range of traits is to see how many are present in early teeth, and therefore might be considered to be ancestral, and to maximize the chance of identifying trends in what is a small sample. (Morphological traits can either be ancestral (also referred to as primitive or plesiomorphic) or advanced (also referred to as derived or apomorphic)). In addition, there are a number of traits that are of greater interest in early teeth than in recent teeth. These include lingual median longitudinal ridge on lower incisors, metaconule and anterior transverse ridge on upper molars, and mid trigonid crest, posterior fovea and buccal surface vertical grooves on lower molars (see references in Appendix A). Also recorded are the traits identified by Bermúdez de Castro (1988), Bermúdez de Castro *et al.* (1999b) and Carbonell *et al.* (1995) as characterizing European Middle Pleistocene hominins.

### Lower lateral permanent incisor
#### PN10 (right)
This tooth is compared with earlier Middle Pleistocene: Mauer; later Middle Pleistocene: Ehringsdorf (adult and juvenile) and

Atapuerca-SH (cast: AT5; descriptions: AT55 and AT103); and Krapina (eight KDPs). Details of the morphology of PN10, and the teeth to which it is being compared, are given in Table 9.31.

Shovelling (1)
Of the teeth in the sample, only Atapuerca-SH AT55 is reported as having no shovelling. The shovelling on PN10 is not convergent at the cingulum.

Double shovelling (2)
Double shovelling is absent, or at trace level only, in the teeth studied, apart from the Ehringsdorf juvenile teeth on which it occurs at grade 2 distally.

Labial convexity (3)
This is marked on PN10, as it is on the other teeth in the sample, with the exception of one Atapuerca-SH tooth.

Lingual median longitudinal ridge (4)
PN10 has a faint grade 1 longitudinal ridge that does not reach the occlusal edge, similar to the one on Atapuerca-SH AT5. This trait is present on the Mauer and Ehringsdorf juvenile specimens (at grades 2 and 1 respectively) and all except one of the KDPs (70% at grade 2).

Mesial and distal flaring (5)
On PN10, and in all the casts studied, the distal margin is flared (*i.e.* leans distally) but mesial flaring is only found amongst KDPs. The mesial and distal borders of Atapuerca-SH AT55 and AT103 are described as being almost parallel.

Buccal aspect
All the teeth, including PN10, have a marked lingual inclination of the buccal surface. The buccal surface of PN10 is convex in the lower part and flat in the upper part, viewed laterally.

Lingual aspect
Viewed laterally, the lingual surface of PN10 is concave.

Cingulum
The lingual cingulum (a cingulum is an enamel shelf on the

| Trait | Pontnewydd | | | Mid Pleistocene | | |
|---|---|---|---|---|---|---|
| | PN6 | PN7 | PN20 | Earlier* | Later* | Krapina* |
| Mesiobuccal swelling | Yes | No | No | 2/2 | 5/7 | 3/10 |
| Buccal cusp medial | Med. | Mes. | Med. | 1/2 | 5/5 | 10/10 |
| Number of lingual cusps = 1 | 1 | 2 | 2? | 2/2 | 5/7 | 7/10 |
| Principal lingual cusp medial | Med. | Mes. | Med. | 1/2 | 2/7 | 7/10 |
| Angle between buccal and principal lingual cusps | 45° | 50° | Worn | 25°-35° | 35°-45° | 30°-45° Av. 38° |
| Buccal occlusal ridges: - | | | | | | |
| Mesial | No | No | No | 0/2 | 0/2 | 0/9 |
| Distal | No | Yes | Yes | 1/2 | 3/3 | 10/10 |
| Sagittal sulcus interrupted | No | Yes | Yes | 2/2 | 8/8 | 10/10 |
| Mes. marginal ridge interrupted | No | No | No | 0/2 | 0/5 | 0/9 |
| Dist. marginal ridge interrupted | No | No | No | 0/2 | 0/5 | 5/9 |
| Mesial occluso-lingual cleft | No | No | Yes | 1/2 | 3/8 | 4/10 |
| Distal occluso-lingual cleft | Yes | Yes | Yes | 1/2 | 7/8 | 0/10 |
| Double shovelling – Mesial > 0 | No | No | No | 1/2 (1) | 2/3 (1,2) | 2/9 (1,3) |
| Double shovelling – Distal > 0 | Gr. 2 | Gr. 2 | No | 1/2 (2) | 1/3 (1) | 7/9 (1-3) |

*Number of specimens with trait over number of specimens scored. Range of grades found shown in brackets.

*Table 9.33. Crown morphology, lower third premolars.*

side of a tooth) on PN10 is well-defined, although most of it is missing.

### Upper fourth premolar
*PN18 (left)*
This tooth is compared with earlier Middle Pleistocene: Arago 26, Petralona and Visogliano 5; later Middle Pleistocene: Montmaurin 14B3S and 6B3, Steinheim and Atapuerca-SH (descriptions: AT23 and AT68); and Krapina (nine KDPs). Details of the morphology of PN18, and the teeth to which it is being compared, are given in Table 9.32.

OCCLUSAL SHAPE
PN18 has an oval outline, with mesial and distal flattening, and the buccal mesiodistal dimension a little greater than the lingual mesiodistal dimension. Other teeth studied either have this shape or the outline of a rounded rectangle.

RELATIVE SIZES OF BUCCAL AND LINGUAL CUSPS
The buccal cusp of PN18 is slightly larger than the lingual cusp and this is generally the case in the teeth studied.

BUCCAL CUSP (6)
In the Middle Pleistocene and Krapina teeth the buccal cusp is either placed mesially or medially, mainly mesially in the Middle Pleistocene teeth and mainly medially in KDPs. That of PN18 is medial.

LINGUAL CUSPS (6 AND 13)
Just four KDPs have two or more lingual cusps. The (principal) lingual cusp of PN18 is mesial, as with other teeth in the sample, with the exception of one KDP (medial).

ADDITIONAL BUCCAL OCCLUSAL RIDGES (7)
The buccal cusp of PN18 is too worn to show mesial or distal accessory ridges. The median ridge is not bifurcated. Bifurcation of the median ridge is found in under half of Middle Pleistocene teeth but in nearly all KDPs.

SAGITTAL SULCUS INTERRUPTED (TRANSVERSE CREST) (8)
On PN18, and on most teeth in the sample, the sagittal sulcus (the mesiodistal developmental groove) is partly interrupted by a wide low ridge connecting the two cusps. The sagittal sulcus passes over this on PN18, as it generally does in the teeth studied. This trait is not found at Atapuerca-SH; on these teeth the sagittal sulcus is mildly convex lingually.

ANTERIOR AND POSTERIOR FOVEAE
PN18 has a distinct anterior fovea, which is narrow and fairly deep, with a groove running up the buccal cusp. The sagittal sulcus proceeds distally from this, as a groove of constant depth, to (and through) the distal margin. The posterior fovea is insignificant. Generally, in the teeth studied, both foveae are well defined, the posterior fovea being the widest. However, the occlusal morphology of the lingual part of Montmaurin 6B3 (buccal part missing) is nearly identical to that of PN18, with a deep anterior fovea but very shallow posterior fovea, and the sagittal sulcus, and the buccolingual ridge crossing it, of the same form. Visogliano Vis 5 also only has a well defined anterior fovea, similar in shape to that of PN18.

MARGINAL RIDGES INTERRUPTED (9)
Interruption of the distal margin is commoner in the teeth studied. On PN18 the sagittal sulcus bisects the distal margin.

ACCESSORY MARGINAL TUBERCLES (12)
Both mesial and distal tubercles are found in Middle Pleistocene and Krapina teeth, mesial tubercles being the more common, but none on PN18.

WRINKLING (15)
PN18 is too worn to show this trait. Wrinkling does not generally occur on the Middle Pleistocene teeth but is found in all KDPs.

DOUBLE SHOVELLING (2)
The distal double shovelling on PN18 only consists of two pits placed vertically. In both Middle Pleistocene and Krapina teeth there is stronger expression of this trait mesially than distally,

six out of nine KDPs having mesial double shovelling at grades 2 or 3.

## Buccal aspect

The buccal face of PN18 curves lingually, as viewed from a lateral aspect, and protrudes slightly beyond the line of the cervix. There is no basal bulge or cingulum.

## Lingual aspect (11)

The lingual surface of PN18 is mildly convex, viewed laterally, and not inclined buccally or lingually. The majority of KDPs have between one and four vertical grooves on the lingual surface. This trait is not seen on PN18 but is found on two of the Middle Pleistocene teeth.

## Lower third premolars
### PN6 (right), PN7 (left), PN20 (left)

These teeth are compared with earlier Middle Pleistocene: Arago 13 and Mauer; later Middle Pleistocene: Ehringsdorf (adult and juvenile) and Atapuerca-SH (cast: AT2; descriptions: AT47, AT64, AT102, AT148, AT149); and Krapina (ten KDPs). Details of the morphology of the Pontnewydd teeth, and the teeth to which they are being compared, are given in Table 9.33.

### General descriptions – cusps and marginal ridges

PN6 – The buccal cusp has prominent mesial and distal convex borders that curve downwards and coalesce with weak marginal ridges. These end in occluso-lingual grooves each side of the well-defined centrally placed lingual cusp. The occluso-lingual groove distal to the lingual cusp is a distinct cleft. There is no canine groove on the mesial surface.

PN7 – as for PN6 but there is an additional distolingual cusp on the lingual end of the distal marginal ridge (grade 3), with a mild occluso-lingual groove distal to it. PN6 has an enamel shelf in this position. The principal lingual cusp is narrower mesiodistally on PN7 than on PN6 and the mesial border of the buccal cusp is distinctly higher than the distal, more so than on PN6.

PN20 – The distal slope of the worn buccal cusp joins a strong distal marginal ridge. This ends in an occluso-lingual groove on the distal side of the prominent, and medially placed, lingual cusp. A weakly defined mesial marginal ridge passes down from the buccal cusp to an occluso-lingual groove on the mesial side of the medial-lingual cusp. Both mesial and distal occluso-lingual grooves are distinct clefts. There is a possible additional lingual cusp on the lingual end of the worn distal marginal ridge, defined by a horizontal groove on the side of the cleft.

## Occlusal shape

The occlusal shape of the Pontnewydd teeth, and other teeth studied, is near circular, with mesiolingual flattening, and the principal lingual cusp placed at the most lingual point. The mesiolingual flattening generally extends from the mid-point of the mesial surface to the principal lingual cusp. The Arago 13 tooth is distinctive in being deeper buccolingually, with very large foveae, and a longer buccolingual ridge crossing the sagittal sulcus. Viewed occlusally, PN6 has a pronounced mesiobuccal swelling on the lower part of the buccal surface, which is not found in PN7 or PN20. This feature occurs on both Ehringsdorf specimens, and on three of the Atapuerca-SH teeth, as well as on both of the earlier Middle Pleistocene specimens, but in just three KDPs. It appears on the right lower third premolar in the Ehringsdorf adult but not on the left. If, as suggested, PN6 and PN7 are antimeres, the same situation is found at Pontnewydd. The swelling on PN6 is not differentiated from the upper half

of the buccal surface when viewed laterally, as is described for Atapuerca-SH teeth.

## Buccal cusp (6)

The buccal cusps of PN6 and PN7 both have prominent mesial and distal borders, the mesial being the higher and more convex (site worn on PN20). This is also the case in the other teeth studied. The lingual faces of the buccal cusps of the Pontnewydd teeth are slightly rotated in a mesiobuccal/distolingual direction (PN20 very slight). This feature is encountered in other later Middle Pleistocene specimens, and in most KDPs, but not on the Arago 13 or Mauer teeth. The buccal cusps of PN6 and PN20 are medially placed but that of PN7 is slightly mesial. The buccal cusps of the other Middle Pleistocene teeth, and all KDPs, are likewise medially placed, with the exception of Arago 13, on which it is placed mesially.

## Marginal ridges

The mesial marginal ridges of all the Pontnewydd teeth are weakly defined (low and narrow). The distal marginal ridges are higher and wider, that of PN20 being the highest. The Middle Pleistocene teeth are similar to the Pontnewydd teeth, but the mesial and distal margins of the Mauer specimen and the Ehringsdorf juvenile are lower, and those of Arago 13 wider. The distal margins of Mauer and Atapuerca-SH AT2 are narrower. In the Krapina teeth the mesial and distal margins are generally wide and low.

## Lingual cusps (6 and 13)

Predominantly, the teeth in the sample have a single lingual cusp. PN20 has a faint possible additional cusp on the distal margin (grade 1 on the ASU scale, meaning one or two lingual cusps present) whilst that on PN7 is definite (grade 3 on the ASU scale, meaning two lingual cusps present, the mesial cusp being a little larger than the distal cusp). Two Atapuerca-SH teeth have extra smaller lingual cusps – AT2 on the distal margin, and AT102 on the mesial margin. Three KDPs have additional smaller distal cusps, one distinct and two very faint. In two KDPs the principal lingual cusp has a double tip. The principal lingual cusps on the Middle Pleistocene teeth are of a similar size to each other, apart from that on the Arago 13 tooth, which is very large and nearly equal in size to the buccal cusp. The principal lingual cusp is medially placed on PN6 and PN20 (the tip of the cusp on PN6 being mesial) and this is the case for the majority of KDPs and for Arago 13 and two Atapuerca-SH teeth. On PN7, and in one KDP, it is slightly mesially placed. It is placed distally on most of the Middle Pleistocene teeth and in two KDPs.

## Angle between buccal and lingual cusps

In all the teeth studied, with the exception of Arago 13, the buccal cusp is much larger than the lingual cusp. The angle to the horizontal between the tips of the buccal and lingual cusps varies between 25° and 50° (allowing for wear on mildly worn teeth). PN6 and PN7, at 45° and 50°, are at the top end of the range, along with Atapuerca-SH AT2 (45°), distinctly higher than Arago (25°), Mauer (35°) or the Ehringsdorf juvenile (35°). (See Bermúdez de Castro (1988) for comments on relative cusp sizes in Middle Pleistocene and Neanderthal teeth).

## Additional buccal occlusal ridges (7)

PN20 has a strongly formed additional distal ridge and PN7 a weakly defined one. There are no clear mesial ridges on the Pontnewydd teeth (PN6 has a trace mesial ridge, too fine to score). Additional mesial ridges are rare, only being found at trace level on the Ehringsdorf juvenile and in one KDP (not scored).

| Trait | Pontnewydd PN5 | Mid Pleistocene | | Krapina* |
|---|---|---|---|---|
| | | Earlier* | Later* | |
| Mesiolingual occlusal flattening | Yes | 1/4 | 3/7 | 6/12 |
| Buccal cusp medial | Medial | 1/3 | 0/6 | 2/12 |
| Number of lingual cusps    1 | | 1/3 | 2/6 | 0/12 |
|                            2 | Two | 0/3 | 2/6 | 3/12 |
|                            3+ | | 2/3 | 2/6 | 9/12 |
| Angle between buccal and | 20° | 10° | 15°-30° | 0°-20° |
| principal lingual cusps | | | | Av. 9° |
| Buccal occlusal ridges: | | | | |
|         Mesial | No | 1/3 | 0/3 | 3/6 |
|         Distal | Yes | 2/3 | 5/5 | 5/7 |
|         Median bifurcated | No | 2/3 | 2/3 | 7/10 |
| Sagittal sulcus interrupted | Yes | 2/3 | 5/7 | 10/11 |
| Mes. marginal ridge interrupted | Yes | 3/3 | 5/5 | 10/12 |
| Dist. marginal ridge interrupted | Yes | 1/3 | 2/3 | 5/7 |
| Mesial/Medial occluso-lingual grooves | 0 | 1/3 | 5/6 | 9/11 |
| Distal occluso-lingual grooves | 1 | 2/3 | 5/6 | 10/11 |
| Double shovelling – Mesial > 0 | Grade 2 | 2/3 (1,2) | 4/5 (1,2) | 11/12 (1-3) |
| Double shovelling – Distal > 0 | Grade 1 | 2/3 (1) | 2/5 (1) | 12/12 (1-3) |

*Number of specimens with trait over number of specimens scored. Range of grades found shown in brackets.

*Table 9.34. Crown morphology, lower fourth premolars.*

Additional distal ridges, conversely, are very common. None of the teeth studied have bifurcated median ridges.

SAGITTAL SULCUS INTERRUPTED (TRANSVERSE CREST) (8)
Of all the teeth in the sample, PN6 is the only one without a prominent buccolingual ridge crossing the sagittal sulcus. Normally, this ridge links to the largest lingual cusp, as it does on the other Pontnewydd teeth. On PN7 the ridge links to the tip of the lingual cusp but does not on PN20. The sagittal sulcus continues over the ridge on PN20 but not on PN7. The ridge is curved on both teeth, mesially on PN7 and distally on PN20, and in both cases links to the mesial side of the lingual cusp.

ANTERIOR AND POSTERIOR FOVEAE
In the Pontnewydd teeth the posterior fovea is the largest (wider on PN7 and PN20, and deeper on PN6 and PN7). The foveae on the Atapuerca-SH teeth are described as deep and variable, and this is also the case on the Krapina teeth and the other Middle Pleistocene teeth. The relative heights of the foveae on the teeth studied also vary. The posterior fovea is the higher on PN20 but on PN6 and PN7 the anterior fovea is the higher.

MARGINAL RIDGES INTERRUPTED (9)
The marginal ridges are not interrupted on the Pontnewydd teeth. None of the teeth studied have the mesial margin interrupted and just five KDPs have the distal margin interrupted.

OCCLUSO-LINGUAL GROOVES (14)
The general pattern is for there to be an occluso-lingual groove on each side of the principal lingual cusp. The distal grooves on the Pontnewydd teeth are distinct clefts and, on PN20, the mesial groove too. PN7 has an additional mild occluso-lingual groove distal to the distolingual cusp. The Arago 13 tooth has mesial and distal clefts but on the Mauer tooth they are little more than grooves, the mesial being the wider. The Ehringsdorf juvenile has a distal cleft and the Ehringsdorf adult has a mesial cleft. The

Atapuerca-SH teeth all have distal clefts, just two also having mesial clefts. In contrast, the situation is reversed in the KDPs, all of them having either mesial clefts, or the mesial groove more distinct than the distal, and none a distal cleft.

WRINKLING (15)
This is absent at Pontnewydd and in all the teeth studied apart from one KDP.

DOUBLE SHOVELLING (2)
The distal double shovelling groove on PN6 is slanted superiorly distally/inferiorly mesially. It is near vertical on PN7, as is normally the case. Double shovelling in the Middle Pleistocene sample is observed at a similar rate both mesially and distally. It is more prevalent distally than mesially amongst KDPs.

BUCCAL ASPECT
All three Pontnewydd teeth have a slight basal bulge on the lower third (most evident on PN7), and a strong lingual inclination to the upper two thirds, of the buccal surface. None have a cingulum. The whole surface is convex on PN20, whereas it is flat above the basal bulge on PN6 and PN7.

LINGUAL ASPECT (11)
The lingual aspect is convex and swollen on all the Pontnewydd teeth, with a definite protrusion beyond the line of the cervix, more so than on the buccal aspect. The lingual surfaces of PN6 and PN7 have mild lingual ridging (two in each case). This is not found on other Middle Pleistocene teeth, or on Krapina teeth.

*Lower fourth premolar*
*PN5 (left)*
This tooth is compared with earlier Middle Pleistocene: Arago 2, 13, 28 and Mauer; later Middle Pleistocene: Ehringsdorf (adult and juvenile) and Atapuerca-SH (casts: AT2, AT3, AT9; descriptions: AT28 (with AT3, Individual 111), AT74, AT147); and

Krapina (twelve KDPs). Details of the morphology of PN5, and the teeth to which it is being compared, are given in Table 9.34.

## GENERAL DESCRIPTION OF PN5 (CUSPS AND MARGINAL RIDGES)

The distal slope of the buccal cusp continues as a strong horizontal distal marginal ridge that passes round lingually through the distolingual cusp to the mesiolingual cusp. The mesial marginal ridge is very slight and cleft by a groove from the anterior fovea. There is a mild occluso-lingual groove on the distal side of the distolingual cusp. The mesiolingual cusp is larger than the distolingual cusp, which is less well defined. Both are smaller than the buccal cusp. A ridge crosses over the sagittal sulcus to the mesiolingual cusp.

## OCCLUSAL SHAPE

The occlusal outline of PN5 is near circular with partial mesiolingual flattening from the mid-point of the mesial surface, buccal to the mesiolingual cusp, to the distolingual cusp. There is also some distolingual and distal flattening. The outlines of the Atapuerca-SH AT2 and Ehringsdorf juvenile lower fourth premolars are similar, but AT2 is narrower distally. The Arago 13 and 28 lower fourth premolars are also similar but, as with the Arago 13 lower third premolar, are deeper buccolingually, with larger foveae. The Arago 28, Mauer and Atapuerca-SH AT3 teeth have no mesiolingual flattening, nor do the more worn Arago 2, Ehringsdorf adult and Atapuerca-SH AT9 teeth, which are more oval. The Krapina teeth are similarly varied, half of KDPs having mesiolingual flattening. Both the Arago 13 and Mauer lower fourth premolars have a mesiobuccal protrusion (mild on the Mauer tooth).

## BUCCAL CUSP (6)

The mesial slope of the buccal cusp of PN5 is convex, and higher than the straight distal slope, as is the case with the other teeth studied. The buccal cusps of Arago 13 and 28 and Atapuerca-SH AT9 are markedly larger than that of PN5, and that of Atapuerca-SH AT3 is smaller. The buccal cusp on PN5 is medially placed, as are those of Arago 13 and two KDPs. The buccal cusps of the other Middle Pleistocene teeth and KDPs are mesially placed.

## MARGINAL RIDGES

The slight (virtually absent) mesial marginal ridge and strong distal marginal ridge (both high and wide) of PN5 are similar to those seen on the teeth in the Middle Pleistocene sample. The mesial margins of Arago 13 and Atapuerca-SH AT3 are wider, and that of AT3 higher. The distal margins of other Middle Pleistocene teeth are generally wider and lower (not Mauer or Atapuerca-SH AT3). The Krapina teeth are variable, but with the distal margin always stronger than the mesial, which in most cases is very weak.

## LINGUAL CUSPS (6 AND 13)

The mesial of the two lingual cusps on PN5 is the larger and sits on the mesiolingually flattened side of the tooth. The smaller distal cusp is placed at the most lingual point of the tooth. The size difference is grade 2 on the ASU scale (meaning that two lingual cusps are present, the mesial cusp being much larger than the distal). The number of lingual cusps present is very mixed within each group. It varies between one and five in the Middle Pleistocene sample and between two and five at Krapina. The relationship between the lingual cusps of PN5 is typical of other teeth in the sample with more than one lingual cusp. Firstly, the most mesial of the lingual cusps is the largest (two KDPs have

additional, smaller, mesially placed cusps). In the Arago teeth, the Ehringsdorf juvenile, Atapuerca-SH AT9 and half the KDPs, the mesiolingual cusp is considerably larger than the other lingual cusps. Secondly, a single cusp is placed distinctly lingually to the remainder, at the most lingual point of the tooth. This is normally immediately distal to the largest cusp. Exceptions are; Atapuerca-SH AT3 and two KDPs, in which some/all of the lingual cusps are placed equally lingually, and Arago 13, on which there is a small cusp between the largest cusp and the most lingual cusp. A distinction can be made between lingual cusps that are bulbous and involve a considerable thickening of the marginal ridge, and those which are narrow and sit on the marginal ridge. Generally, the most mesial of the lingual cusps is bulbous (exceptions being found amongst Atapuerca-SH teeth and in a quarter of KDPs) and, occasionally, one or two cusps distal to this (usually adjacent) are also bulbous (*e.g.* Ehringsdorf juvenile, Atapuerca-SH AT74, and five out of 12 KDPs). Other cusps are narrow. Both lingual cusps on PN5 are of the smaller, narrow type. The single lingual cusp of the Mauer tooth is nearly equal in size to the buccal cusp.

## ANGLE BETWEEN BUCCAL AND MESIOLINGUAL CUSPS

In the teeth studied, the buccal cusp is always larger, and almost always higher, than the largest lingual cusp. The angle to the horizontal between the tips of the buccal and mesiolingual cusps on PN5 is 20°. This compares with 10° for the three earlier Middle Pleistocene teeth, 30° for the Ehringsdorf juvenile, 15° for Atapuerca-SH AT2 and AT3, and a range of 0° to 20° amongst KDPs. The difference in this angle between third and fourth premolars in the same jaw can vary from 5° for the Ehringsdorf juvenile to 45° for one KDP.

## ADDITIONAL BUCCAL OCCLUSAL RIDGES (7)

The additional distal ridge on PN5 is in the distal fovea. Unlike lower third premolars, both mesial ridges and bifurcated median ridges are encountered on lower fourth premolars in the sample. Nevertheless, distal ridges are still more common than mesial, though they are not found in all KDPs as is the case with lower third premolars.

## SAGITTAL SULCUS INTERRUPTED (TRANSVERSE CREST) (8)

This trait occurs on PN5 but, unlike the situation with lower third premolars, it is not found on all the teeth in the sample. In all the teeth with this trait, the ridge crossing the sagittal sulcus links to the largest lingual cusp and, in some cases, (*e.g.* four KDPs) to the cusp tip, as it does with PN5. As with PN7 and PN20, the ridge on PN5 is distinctly curved.

## ANTERIOR AND POSTERIOR FOVEAE

The posterior fovea is the wider in all the teeth studied, including PN5 (unlike the situation with lower third premolars). The posterior fovea of PN5 is buccolingually long but the anterior fovea is round. The posterior fovea of PN5 is at a lower level than the anterior fovea, and this is generally the case, with the exception of the Mauer tooth and two KDPs, where they are at the same height. This difference in level is particularly marked in Atapuerca-SH AT9.

## MARGINAL RIDGES INTERRUPTED (9)

The mesial marginal ridge of PN5 is interrupted, in common with all of the teeth in the Middle Pleistocene sample and most KDPs. On PN5, and in many of the teeth studied, this is in the form of a distinct cleft. Interruption of the distal marginal ridge is less common, occurring in a little over half the teeth studied. The distal interruption on PN5 is very mild.

| PN no.<br>Tooth type | PN4<br>Right, 1st | PN12<br>Left, 1st | PN1<br>Left, 2nd | PN17<br>Right, 3rd | PN19<br>Right, 3rd | PN4<br>Right dm²/dp⁴ |
|---|---|---|---|---|---|---|
| Metacone | 5 | 4 | 5 | 3 | 2 | 3.5 |
| Hypocone | 5+ | 5 | 5+ | 1 | 2 | 3.5 |
| Mesial marginal cusps | 0 | 0 | Worn | 0 | 0 | Worn |
| Cusp 5 | 0 | 2 | 0 (worn) | 2 | 3 | 0 |
| Carabelli's trait | 2 | 3 | Worn | 0 | 1 | 5 |
| Parastyle | 2 | 2 | 0 | 2 | 2 | 2 |
| Oblique ridge | 1 | 1 | 1 | 3 | 3 | 1 |
| Metaconule | 1 | 2 | 1 | 0 | 3 | 0 |
| Anterior transverse ridge | 2 & 4 | 5 & 4 | Worn | 2 | 3 | Worn |
| Wrinkling | Absent | Absent | Worn | Mild | Mild | Worn |
| Relative cusp sizes | ML>MB>DL>DB | ML>MB>DB>DL>C5 | ML>MB>DB>DL | ML>MB>DB>C5>DL | ML=MB>DB>MET>C5=DL | Sizes very Similar |

Table 9.35. Crown morphology, upper molars, Pontnewydd.

| Trait | M1<br>EMP | M1<br>LMP | M1<br>KR | M2<br>EMP | M2<br>LMP | M2<br>KR | M3<br>EMP | M3<br>LMP | M3<br>KR |
|---|---|---|---|---|---|---|---|---|---|
| Metacone >3.5 | 3/3 | 7/7 | 9/11 | 4/5 | 3/5 | 3/11 | 2/3 | 1/4 | 3/7 |
|  | 4,5+ | 4-5+ | 3.5-5 | 3.5,5 | 3,3.5,5 | 3-4 | 2,4 | 3,4 | 3-4 |
| Hypocone >2 | 3/3 | 7/7 | 11/11 | 5/5 | 4/5 | 9/10 | 3/3 | 2/5 | 3/5 |
|  | 5+ | 5+ | 4-5++ | 4-5+ | 1,3.5,5 | 1,3-5 | 3.5 | 1,2,3.5 | 2,3,4 |
| Mesial marginal cusps | 1/1 | 1/2 | 6/9 | 2/4 | 3/4 | 8/9 | 2/2 | 2/3 | 5/5 |
| Cusp 5 >0 | 1/2 | 3/5 | 6/9 | 4/5 | 2/4 | 7/7 | 2/3 | 2/2 | 3/4 |
|  | 4 | 3,4 | 1-3 | 4,5 | 2,4 | 1-3 | 4,5+ | 3,4 | 2-4 |
| Carabelli's trait >2 | 0/2 | 6/7 | 8/10 | 3/5 | 2/5 | 5/10 | 1/3 | 1/5 | 1/5 |
|  | 0,2 | 1,3,5,6 | 2-7 | 0,3,6,7 | 0,2,5 | 0-6 | 0,3 | 0,1,5 | 0-2,5 |
| Parastyle >1 | 2/3 | 4/4 | 10/10 | 1/5 | 2/4 | 3/11 | 1/3 | 1/4 | 4/7 |
|  | 0,2 | 2-3 | 2 | 0,2 | 0,2 | 0-2 | 0,2 | 0,2 | 0-3 |
| Oblique ridge <3 | 3/3 | 7/7 | 10/10 | 5/5 | 5/5 | 9/9 | 0/3 | 0/4 | 3/5 |
|  | 1 | 1 | 1 | 1-2 | 1-2 | 1-2 | 3 | 3 | 1-3 |
| Metaconule >1 | 1/3 | 1/6 | 0/10 | 2/5 | 2/4 | 1/9 | 1/3 | 1/4 | 0/4 |
|  | 0-2 | 0,2 | 0,1 | 1-2 | 0-3 | 0,1,3 | 0,3 | 0,3 | 0,1 |
| Anterior trans. ridge crest >0 | 1/2 | 5/6 | 6/10 | 4/5 | 0/4 | 3/9 | 2/3 | 3/4 | 0/5 |
| Wrinkling | - | 1/5 | 9/10 | 2/3 | 3/4 | 9/9 | 1/2 | 1/4 | 5/5 |

Number of specimens with trait over number of specimens scored. Range of grades found shown below.

Table 9.36. Crown morphology, upper molars, comparative data.

OCCLUSO-LINGUAL GROOVES (14)

The majority of the teeth studied have two grooves – mesial/medial and distal. The number of grooves is partly related to the number of lingual cusps. Teeth with more than two grooves (Arago 13 and five KDPs) all have more than two lingual cusps and, in two out of three cases where there are no grooves (Mauer, Atapuerca-SH AT2 and one KDP), there is a single lingual cusp. The occluso-lingual grooves do not generally appear as clefts, unlike lower third premolars. Of the Middle Pleistocene teeth, the Ehringsdorf juvenile has both mesial and distal clefts. Four KDPs have mesial clefts and one a distal cleft.

WRINKLING (15)

There is no wrinkling on PN5. It only occurs on one Middle Pleistocene tooth but occurs in eight out of eleven KDPs.

DOUBLE SHOVELLING (2)

The distal double shovelling on PN5 has two grooves instead of the normal single groove. The higher grades of double shovelling found in the Middle Pleistocene teeth are mesial. In addition, it is more prevalent mesially than it is with lower third premolars at Krapina, appearing at above grade 1 mesially and distally in nearly all KDPs. There are some irregularities in the Krapina double shovelling for third and fourth premolars – e.g. groove at an angle, as on PN6; double grooves, as on PN5; two vertical pits in place of a groove, as on PN18.

BUCCAL ASPECT

PN5 has a convexity and lingual inclination of the buccal surface. There is no basal bulge or cingulum.

LINGUAL ASPECT (11)

On PN5 the lingual face is mildly convex, protruding beyond the line of the cervix, and not inclined buccally or lingually. There is no lingual ridging and this is only seen in one tooth in the sample.

GROOVES IN POSTERIOR FOVEA

PN5 has four grooves emanating from the posterior fovea – buccal and lingual along the inside of the marginal ridge, the lingual being between the two lingual cusps; mesial up the enamel ridge connecting the buccal and mesiolingual cusps; and on the distal side of the distolingual cusp, passing over the margin. The distal occlusal ridge on the buccal cusp lies between the buccal and mesial grooves. There is a fainter groove within the posterior fovea, between the mesial and lingual grooves, which delineates two mild ridges. There is also a mild vertical groove below the distal occlusal edge, between the distal and buccal grooves. The pattern of grooves on PN5 contrasts with those described for Atapuerca-SH. On the Atapuerca-SH lower fourth premolars, two distal grooves from the posterior fovea separate out a posterior talonid from the buccal and lingual cusps. A third groove ascends the transverse ridge, as with PN5. There are also clearly defined talonids on the Arago 13 and 28 teeth.

MISCELLANEOUS

The enamel passes through the dentine into the pulp cavity on the mesial side of PN5 to form a 'pearl'.

## Upper permanent molars

*First – PN4 (right), PN12 (left); Second – PN1 (left) and Third – PN17 (right), PN19 (right)*

These teeth are compared with earlier Middle Pleistocene: Arago 9/21(Individual 4), 14, 31, Petralona and Visogliano 6, 3, 1; later Middle Pleistocene: Biache, Bilzingsleben C1, Steinheim, Pesada 2 and Atapuerca-SH (casts: AT10, AT12, AT15, AT16, AT20; descriptions: AT26, AT46/AT270 (Individual V11), AT138, AT139 (with AT16, Individual V11), AT140); and Krapina (14 KDPs). Details of the morphology of the Pontnewydd upper permanent molars and the deciduous premolar are given in Table 9.35. Trait frequencies and value ranges for teeth in the samples used for comparison are given in Table 9.36.

OCCLUSAL SHAPE

First Molars – PN4 and PN12 have a rounded rhomboid shape (PN12 being slanted and PN4 nearly square) with the rounded hypocone protruding distally. The other teeth studied are shaped similarly.

Second Molars – PN1 has a rounded rhomboid (near rectangular) shape, with a curved lingual protrusion of the mesiolingual cusp and a convex distal side, but no protrusion of the hypocone. Second molars at other sites have a varied irregular rounded rhomboid shape, with some sides curved. As with PN1, there is no protrusion of the hypocone.

Third Molars – Both teeth are oval in shape, in a mesiobuccal/distolingual direction, with the widest part buccally (the change in width is most pronounced on PN19). The distobuccal corner is abbreviated. The distal side of PN19 is very convex. The shape of other upper third molars is varied, but generally oval or a rounded triangle.

METACONE (16)

The size grades for metacones on Pontnewydd first molars are the same as those observed on other later Middle Pleistocene first molars, and the grade for second molar PN1 is at the top of the range for second molars. PN17 (grade 3) is the same as other later Middle Pleistocene third molars, and PN19 (grade 2) the same as the Arago 21 specimen.

HYPOCONE (17)

The difference in the size of Pontnewydd hypocones between first and second molars, and third molars, is even more pronounced than is the case for metacones. As with the metacone, the PN4 size grade is the same as for other later Middle Pleistocene first molars, but that for PN12 is a little lower. However, the 5+ grade of PN1 is only equalled in size by the Arago second molar AR31. It is distinctly higher than the Biache and Atapuerca-SH second molars (grades 3.5 and one grade 1). Bermúdez de Castro and Sarmiento (2001) state that on 47% of Atapuerca-SH second molars the hypocone is minimal or absent. This is not the case at Steinheim (grade 5) or Biache (grade 3.5). At grades 1/2 the Pontnewydd third molars are similar to the later Middle Pleistocene third molars from Atapuerca-SH and Steinheim. The later Middle Pleistocene third molar hypocones (with the exception of Biache and Pesada 2) are small compared with the three from the earlier Middle Pleistocene and most of those from Krapina.

MESIAL MARGINAL CUSPS (18)

Of the teeth that are sufficiently unworn to tell, a number have these mesial cusps, and in many cases more than one. All three cusp types are present and can be very large (equivalent to a grade 5 cusp 5). The proportion of KDPs with cusps on the mesial margin increases from first to third molars. None of the Pontnewydd teeth has these cusps.

CUSP 5 (19)

The Pontnewydd cusp 5s are medium in size and similar to the cusp 5s found on Steinheim and Atapuerca-SH teeth (smaller than those on the Biache teeth). The site is worn on PN1 but there is no clear differentiation to suggest the presence of a cusp 5. A cusp 5 is present on PN19 but it is not well differentiated from the metacone. The cusp 5s on earlier Middle Pleistocene teeth can be very large. The cusp 5s on two second molar KDPs, and all the third molar KDPs, are multiple (two to four present). This is also found on the Arago 21 second and third molars and the Biache third molar.

CARABELLI'S TRAIT (20)

Both Pontnewydd first molars, and one of the third molars (PN19), have mild expressions of Carabelli's trait. The instances of Carabelli's trait observed on Atapuerca-SH teeth are similarly mild, but higher grades are found on teeth from Arago, Biache, Steinheim and possibly Bilzingsleben. The Carabelli's traits encountered on Krapina teeth are variable and some of a different form. Most are of the normal form (*i.e.* as seen on more recent teeth), up to grade seven (the highest grade). However, a little over half the KDP first molars have a large vertical pit behind an enamel rim. This is normally mesiodistally elongate, between 1 and 2 mm long, and frequently has a cleft at the mesial end (one also distal). In a few there is a deep vertical groove below the pit. It has been questioned if this is a true Carabelli's cusp (Weidenreich 1937) but, in this study, it has been scored as a Carabelli cusp (grades 5–7). The frequency of Carabelli's traits of above grade 2 (*i.e.* a 'Y'-shaped depression or a distinct cusp) in Middle Pleistocene teeth and KDPs reduces from first to third molars and is similar in both. The frequency of Carabelli cusps (grades 5–7) is particularly high on KDP first molars, at 70%. They occur at between 20 and 40%, when present, on other Middle Pleistocene and Krapina teeth. All the later Middle Pleistocene first molars and almost all KDP molars (all first, 90% of second and 80% of third) have this trait at some level, but only half the earlier Middle Pleistocene molars, and a little over half the later Middle Pleistocene second and third molars.

PARASTYLE (21)

All the Pontnewydd teeth, other than PN1, have two parallel vertical grooves on the mesiobuccal cusp, with a bulge between them, but they are not convergent to form a cusp with a free apex (scored as grade 2). This feature is very mild on the two third molars. It is strongest on PN12, which also has a trace on the distobuccal cusp (single distal groove). PN1 has a single vertical groove on the distal side of the mesiobuccal cusp. Amongst the teeth studied, there are three instances of a parastyle above grade 2 – Biache first molar, Steinheim first molar, and one KDP third molar – all at grade 3 (small cusp with a free apex). In both Middle Pleistocene and Krapina teeth, the trait is commoner above grade 1 on first molars than it is on second or third molars. Most of the KDPs have this trait, at least at trace level, on all upper molars, and many have the trait on both mesial and distal buccal cusps. The four relatively unworn Pontnewydd molars have a small style on the distal slope of the mesiobuccal cusp that is associated with this trait.

OBLIQUE RIDGE (22)

The oblique ridge is continuous on the Pontnewydd first and second molars but absent on the third molars. The developmental groove passes over it on PN4 (the site is worn on the other teeth). On all but three of the first and second molars in the sample the oblique ridge is continuous, with or without the developmental groove crossing over it. The three exceptions, in which it is divided, are all second molars – Arago 21, Steinheim and one KDP. It also appears to be partly divided on the Visogliano Vis 3 second molar. On third molars, the oblique ridge is absent in all the Middle Pleistocene teeth and in two KDPs. It is divided in two KDPs and continuous in one KDP.

METACONULE (23)

The Pontnewydd first and second molars have a distal bulge in the centre of the oblique ridge. On PN12 this is a very prominent narrow extension. PN19 has a single pointed metaconule cusp sited at the lingual end position of the oblique ridge, within the distal slope of the mesiolingual cusp. Five Middle Pleistocene teeth have this trait at grade 2 (distinct swelling present). Metaconule cusps appear to be present on the Biache second and third molars and the Visogliano Vis 1 third molar. One KDP second molar has a possible metaconule cusp but none of the KDPs has the trait at grade two.

ANTERIOR TRANSVERSE RIDGE (24)

This is a highly variable trait, involving one or more enamel ridges running from the median ridge of the paracone (mesiobuccal cusp) and/or the mesial margin. Korenhof (1960) defines five types to describe the range of variation found in sub-recent teeth from Java, but these do not fully cover the variations observed in the Pontnewydd teeth and other teeth studied. Both first molars (PN4 and PN12) have two crests across the mesial occlusal groove – a crest at the mesial end delineating a deep anterior fovea, and a second lower crest distal to this towards the central fossa. On PN4 there is a transverse ridge running between the mesial margin and the median paracone ridge, which only connects to the mesial margin. An offshoot lingually from this forms the mesial crest. On PN12 (site worn) the ridge forming the mesial crest runs directly from the mesial margin to the mesiolingual cusp. In both cases the median ridge of the paracone forms the lower distal crest.

PN17 has a transverse ridge between the mesial margin and the median paracone ridge, as with PN4, but this is only attached to the median paracone ridge and is in the form of a tubercle.

The median paracone ridge of PN19 is bulbous and forms a crest over the mesial end of the occlusal groove, with a pit-like anterior fovea mesial to it. This tooth also has a mesiodistally elongate tubercle in the centre of the mesial occlusal groove, on the lingual side, which is possibly associated with this trait. This is a continuation of the mesial ridge of the mesiolingual cusp, which curves round towards the central fossa. The site is worn on PN1. The most appropriate Korenhof type codes are given in Table 9.35.

Forms of this trait found on Middle Pleistocene teeth are: a transverse ridge, as in PN4, linked to either or both the mesial margin and the median paracone ridge; a ridge running distally from the median paracone ridge; and crests across the mesial occlusal groove. Because of the level of wear, it is difficult to see the sources of the crests. They can be at the mesial end of the groove or central. In one case (Atapuerca-SH AT10, third molar) the median paracone ridge bifurcates to produce two crests, and this is in addition to a transverse ridge. Just over half the Middle Pleistocene teeth have these crests. Crests at the mesial end of the groove occur on earlier Middle Pleistocene first to third molars, and on later Middle Pleistocene first molars. Crests on later Middle Pleistocene third molars are all at the centre of the groove, and this type also occurs on Middle Pleistocene first and second molars.

Of the teeth studied that are relatively unworn, only the Steinheim second and third molars (and one first molar) appear not to have any form of this trait. All the Krapina teeth exhibit this trait. Most have a transverse ridge, as described for PN4, which may be attached to the mesial margin, and/or the median paracone ridge, or neither. Frequently these have offshoots (also as described for PN4) that form crests across the mesial occlusal groove (normally at the mesial end, and only on first and second molars). Ridges may be multiple and some go distally instead of mesially. In Table 9.36 the frequencies given are of crests (mesial or central) across the mesial groove.

MESIAL MARGINAL RIDGE (25)

The occlusal groove passes over the mesial margin on the two Pontnewydd first molars. In the third molars, the margin is uninterrupted on PN17 (groove does not pass over it) and intersected by the occlusal groove on PN19. None of the mesial grooves continues onto the mesial face (the site is worn on PN1). In almost all the Middle Pleistocene and Krapina teeth the occlusal groove passes over the mesial margin.

DISTAL MARGINAL RIDGE (25)

The distal occlusal groove passes over the distal margin on all the Pontnewydd teeth, apart from PN4 on which the margin is intersected. On PN12 the groove continues a little way onto the distal surface, and on the two third molars it goes halfway down. It does not continue on PN1 or PN4. Of the Middle Pleistocene upper molars studied, 20% have intersected distal margins and in 70% the occlusal groove passes over the distal margin. The latter is also the case in all but three KDP upper molars. The posterior fovea is pit-like in 30% of the Middle Pleistocene upper molars and half the KDP upper molars but not on the Pontnewydd teeth.

BUCCAL AND LINGUAL OCCLUSAL GROOVES (25)

The buccal occlusal groove cuts the buccal margin on PN4 and PN1, and goes over it on PN12 and on the two third molars. It only continues onto the buccal surface (halfway) on PN19. The lingual occlusal groove goes over the margin on PN4 and PN12, and cuts the margin on PN19 (site worn on PN1 and groove

| PN no.<br>Tooth type: | PN11<br>Left, 1st | PN15<br>Right, 2nd | PN16<br>Right, 3rd | PN21<br>Right, 3rd |
|---|---|---|---|---|
| Groove pattern | 'X' | 'Y' | 'Y' | '+' |
| Cusp 5 | 5,B | 4,B | 3,Medial | 3,B |
| Cusp 6 | 0 | 0 | 0 (worn) | 1 |
| Cusp 7 | 1A | 1A & 2 | 0 | 1A |
| Protostylid | 2 | 0 | 0 | 1 |
| Deflecting wrinkle | 0 | 0 | 0 | 0 |
| Mid trigonid crest | 1 | 1 | 1 | 0 |
| Distal trigonid crest | 0 | 0 | 0 | 1 |
| Anterior fovea | 3 | 3 | 2 | 4 |
| Posterior fovea | 0 | 0 | Slight (worn) | 0 |
| Mesial margin | Present | Present | Broken | Absent |
| Wrinkling | Mild | Worn | Mild | Distinct |
| Relative cusp sizes | MB>ML><br>DL<br>>DB>C5 | MB>ML>DB<br>>DL>C5>C7 | MB>DB>DL<br>>C5 (no ML) | MB>ML>DB<br>>C5>DL>C6 |
| Enamel extensions | 0 | 0.5 | Broken | Broken |
| Buccal vertical grooves | Absent | Absent | Positions A &<br>C | Positions A-E |

*Table 9.37. Crown morphology, lower molars, Pontnewydd Middle Pleistocene.*

absent on PN17). It continues onto the lingual surface on PN4 as an irregular 3.5 mm groove, then as a fine groove to the cervix; and on PN12 as a groove to the cervix, with a bridge across the centre. It does not continue onto the lingual surface on PN19, and does not reach the cervix on PN1.

WRINKLING (15)
Of the Pontnewydd teeth, only PN17 and PN19 exhibit any wrinkling, on the mesiobuccal and distobuccal cusps, and on the mesiolingual cusp of PN19. Just under half of Middle Pleistocene upper molars have some level of wrinkling but it is found in nearly all KDP upper molars.

PROMINENT OCCLUSAL RIDGES/GROOVES
On both PN17 and PN19 there are prominent median ridges on the mesiobuccal cusp (paracone). On PN19 the mesial and median ridges on the distobuccal cusp (metacone) are also well developed, with a fissure between them.

BUCCAL ASPECT
All the Pontnewydd upper molars have a lingual inclination of the buccal surface (slight on PN4). The surface is convex on all teeth (mildly on PN17) other than PN1, which has a slight basal prominence. The lingual inclination of the buccal surface of PN19 is greater than that of PN17.

LINGUAL ASPECT
Both the Pontnewydd first molars have a convexity and buccal inclination of the lingual surface. The buccal inclination is greater on PN12 than on PN4. The hypocones on both teeth are distinctly swollen. The lingual surface extends beyond the line of the cervix. On the third molars the lingual surface is curved sharply buccally. The buccal inclination on PN17 is considerably greater than that on PN19. The lingual surface of PN1 is also convex (site worn).

MESIAL AND DISTAL ASPECTS
The mesial and distal surfaces of Pontnewydd teeth are generally

vertically convex. On PN19 the convexity is slight but on the distal surface of PN12 it is pronounced. The lower half of the mesial surface of PN12 is flared. The distal surface of PN17 has a mesial inclination.

OCCLUSAL GROOVE PATTERNS
Distolingual occlusal groove – PN4, PN12, PN1: at the lingual end the groove divides into two, the mesial part ascending the mesiolingual cusp. At the distal end a ridge protrudes from the distal side of the distobuccal cusp, buccal to the posterior fovea, between two grooves ascending the distobuccal cusp.
Hypocone – The mesiodistal occlusal groove continues as a trace on the hypocone on PN4 and PN1, but is deep on PN12, with a lesser mesiodistal groove buccal to it.
Central fossa – On PN4, PN12: each has four grooves emanating from the central fossa – distal up the oblique ridge, lingual up the protocone, buccal, mesial. On PN17 this is as with PN4 and PN12 except that it has offshoots from the buccal groove that go up the paracone and the metacone, and one that runs from the mesial groove up the protocone. On PN19 the seven grooves listed under PN17 all emanate from the central fossa. An additional two grooves ascend the paracone from the buccal groove. The groove ascending the metacone is fissure-like between two pronounced ridges. There is a crest across the lower end of this. Of the grooves ascending the protocone, one delineates the mesiodistal tubercle lingual to the mesial occlusal groove, and the other passes between the protocone and the metaconule. The distal groove splits into three to delineate the hypocone and cusp 5.
Other – on both PN17 and PN19 there is a buccolingual groove on the paracone, mesial to the median ridge, which joins the mesial occlusal groove. On PN19 there is a pit where they join at the anterior fovea. There is also a pit on PN17 but it is on the slope of the paracone. Four short mesiodistal grooves ascend the mesial margin of PN17.

ENAMEL EXTENSIONS (26)
These are not found on the Pontnewydd upper molars, or on any of the Middle Pleistocene upper molars studied. There are small

| PN no. Tooth type: | PN8 Right, second | PN2 Right, third |
|---|---|---|
| Occlusal outline | Rounded rectangle, cusps rounded | As PN8, distal surface rounded |
| Trigonid V talonid | Trigonid = talonid | Talonid > trigonid |
| Groove pattern | 'X' | 'X' |
| Cusp 5 | 0 | 4, buccal |
| Cusp 6 | 0 | 0 |
| Cusp 7 | 0 | 0 |
| Protostylid | 1 (very small) | 1 (on MB corner) |
| Deflecting wrinkle | 0 | 0 |
| Mid trigonid crest | 0 (trace) | 0 |
| Distal trigonid crest | 0 | 0 |
| Anterior fovea | 3, medial | 0 |
| Posterior fovea | Pit | Pit |
| Mesial margin | Absent, single groove | Absent, single groove |
| Distal margin | Groove does not go over | Groove goes over |
| Buccal furrow | Well defined, to halfway down tooth. Ridge from base of groove to cervix | Mild, to one third way down tooth. Slight crest over at occlusal margin |
| Cusp 5 furrow | - | Mild, to one third way down tooth |
| Wrinkling | Absent | Mild, all cusps |
| Prominent ridges | None | None |
| Occlusal tubercles/crests | Absent | MD elongate tubercle, centre mesial groove, from ML cusp |
| Occlusal pits | None | None |
| Relative cusp sizes | MB>DL>DB>ML | MB>DL>ML>C5>DB(reduced) |
| Buccal aspect | MB: Convex, top inclines lingually DB: Curves lingually | Convex, top MB cusp very inclined lingually |
| Lingual aspect | Swollen | Convex, top inclined buccally |
| Mesial face | Convex | Convex |
| Distal face | Convex, top very inclined mesially | Convex |
| Enamel extensions | 0.5 | 0 |
| Pearls | 0 | 2 mm vertical, buccal surface |
| Buccal vertical grooves | Absent | Absent |
| B/L surface crenulated | Mild | Mild |

*Table 9.38. Crown morphology, lower molars, Pontnewydd Mesolithic.*

enamel extensions (trace level, 0.5 mm) on one KDP first molar and one KDP third molar. The presence/absence of pearls cannot reliably be determined on the casts used.

### Lower permanent molars

*First – PN11 (left); Second – PN15 (right), PN13 (right) and Third – PN16 (right), PN21 (right)*

These teeth are compared with earlier Middle Pleistocene: Arago 2, 69, 10/32 (Individual 6), 13 and Mauer; later Middle Pleistocene: Ehringsdorf (adult and juvenile), Montmaurin (mandible and 2D3) and Atapuerca-SH (casts: AT1, AT2, AT11, AT13, AT14, AT21, AT75; descriptions: AT22/AT101 (Individual XV), AT30, AT43 (with AT2, Individual II), AT100, AT141, AT142, AT143, plus tables for occurrence of cusps 5, 6 and 7 in Bermúdez de Castro (1993); and Krapina (17 KDPs).Details of the morphology of the Pontnewydd lower molars are given in Tables 9.37 (Middle Pleistocene) and 9.38 (Mesolithic). Trait frequencies and value ranges for teeth in the samples used for comparison are given in Table 9.39. The following discussion only

relates to the Pontnewydd Middle Pleistocene teeth. Because of the level of wear on the tooth, PN13 is not referred to.

Occlusal shape

The occlusal outline of all the Pontnewydd lower molars is a rounded rectangle. The distal ends of the third molars are distinctly rounded and the distolingual corner of PN21 is slightly abbreviated, as is also found in Atapuerca-SH third molars. The distolingual cusp on the third molars is reduced in size compared with the first and second molars. In the greater part of the Middle Pleistocene sample the mesial and distal halves of the tooth (the trigonid and the talonid) have the same buccolingual dimension, and this is the case with all but one of the Pontnewydd teeth. The talonid is wider in five Middle Pleistocene teeth, and in eleven the trigonid is wider. At Krapina the talonid is wider in 90% of KDP first molars, 60% of second molars and 40% of third molars. Of the Pontnewydd teeth, the talonid is wider on PN11.

| Trait | M1 EMP | M1 LMP | M1 KR | M2 EMP | M2 LMP | M2 KR | M3 EMP | M3 LMP | M3 KR |
|---|---|---|---|---|---|---|---|---|---|
| Groove pattern =Y | 1/2 | 5/5 | 6/7 | 3/4 | 3/6 | 7/12 | 1/3 | 2/9 | 2/7 |
| Cusp 5 >0 | 2/2 | 11/13 | 12/12 | 4/4 | 9/14 | 11/11 | 3/3 | 10/14 | 5/6 |
|  | 5 | 3-4 | 2-5 | 5-5+ | 2-3 | 2-5 | 3-4 | 2-3 | 1-4 |
| Cusp 6 >0 | 1/2 | 1/10 | 5/6 | 0/4 | 2/12 | 5/9 | 2/2 | 3/12 | 2/5 |
| Cusp 7 >0, Exc. 1a | 0/2 | 3/11 | 5/11 | 1/4 | 3/12 | 3/11 | 1/2 | 4/11 | 8/9 |
|  |  | 3 | 2-3 | 3 |  | 1-2 | 1 | 1-2 | 1-4 |
| Protostylid >1 | 0/2 | 0/6 | 2/13 | 0/4 | 1/4 | 3/13 | 0/2 | 0/6 | 2/8 |
|  | 0-1 | 0-1 | 0,2,3 | 0-1 | 0,1,3 | 0,1,4,6 | 0-1 | 0-1 | 0,1,5,6 |
| Deflecting wrinkle >0 | 0/2 | 2/3 | 4/9 | 1/4 | 1/4 | 2/11 | 1/2 | 2/6 | 2/7 |
|  |  | 1-2 | 1 | 2 | 2 | 1 | 3 | 2 | 2 |
| Mid trigonid crest | 1/2 | 7/7 | 12/13 | 2/4 | 5/5 | 13/13 | 0/2 | 5/8 | 8/8 |
| Distal trigonid crest | 1/2 | 1/3 | 1/9 | 1/4 | 0/4 | 2/13 | 1/2 | 2/6 | 2/8 |
| Anterior fovea >2 | 1/2 | 5/6 | 11/12 | 2/4 | 2/5 | 10/11 | 2/2 | 3/8 | 6/8 |
|  | 0,3 | 2-3 | 2-4 | 1-4 | 1-4 | 2-4 | 4 | 1-4 | 2-4 |
| Posterior fovea | 0/2 | 1/6 | 2/7 | 1/4 | 0/5 | 0/9 | 1/2 | 0/7 | 0/5 |
| Mesial margin | 2/2 | 6/7 | 10/13 | 2/4 | 4/6 | 8/13 | 0/2 | 2/8 | 2/7 |
| Wrinkling | - | 0/2 | 7/7 | 3/3 | 3/4 | 8/8 | 2/2 | 4/8 | 5/5 |
| Enamel extensions >0 | 1/3 | 2/7 | 4/8 | 1/5 | 2/6 | 2/9 | 0/3 | 0/5 | 0/4 |
|  | 1 | 0.5,1 | 0.5,1 | 0.5 | 0.5,1 | 0.5,1 |  |  |  |
| Buccal vertical grooves | 1/2 | 3/7 | 8/13 | 2/4 | 4/6 | 13/13 | 1/2 | 5/6 | 8/8 |

Number of specimens with trait over number of specimens scored. Range of grades found shown below.

*Table 9.39. Crown morphology, lower molars, comparative data.*

GROOVE PATTERN (27)

The 'X' groove pattern on PN11 is unusual for a first molar. It is only otherwise seen on Arago 13 and in one KDP. The other first molars all have 'Y' groove patterns. About half the second molars, and a quarter of the third molars, in the sample studied have a 'Y' groove pattern (a similar proportion in both Middle Pleistocene teeth and KDPs), as do PN15 and PN16. Of the remaining teeth, two thirds of the second molars and all the KDP third molars have an 'X' pattern, but two thirds of Middle Pleistocene third molars, in common with PN21, have a '+' pattern.

CUSP 5 (28)

Only two European Middle Pleistocene first molars are known without a cusp 5, both from Atapuerca-SH. Five second molars from Atapuerca-SH are without a cusp 5 (and two reported for Arago by Bermúdez de Castro (1988; 1993) but not included in the comparative sample), and third molars without a cusp 5 are found at Atapuerca-SH (three), Ehringsdorf (adult), and Krapina (one KDP). The size of cusp 5 on PN11 is large for the later Middle Pleistocene first molars observed (no grades are published for Atapuerca-SH teeth). Similarly, the size of cusp 5 on PN15 is large for a later Middle Pleistocene second molar. However, grade 3 (intermediate size) cusp 5s on third molars, as seen on PN16 and PN21, are also found at Atapuerca-SH, Montmaurin and Ehringsdorf. For each tooth type, the higher grades of cusp 5 occur both on earlier Middle Pleistocene teeth and on Krapina teeth. Cusp 5s are buccally placed on nearly all first molars studied (exceptions are Atapuerca-SH AT2 and one KDP) but predominantly medially placed on Middle Pleistocene second and third molars.

CUSP 6 (29)

Of the later Middle Pleistocene cusp 6s, four are found at Montmaurin and Ehringsdorf (occurring on over half the teeth) and only two at Atapuerca-SH (under 10%). For Krapina the incidence is much higher, at 60% of KDPs overall, against 20% for the Middle Pleistocene, the frequency reducing from first to third molars. Generally, the cusp 6s observed on the Middle Pleistocene and Krapina teeth are small, as is the one on PN21 (no size grades published for Atapuerca-SH). The largest Middle Pleistocene cusp 6s are on third molars.

CUSP 7 (30)

The cusp 7s observed on the Middle Pleistocene teeth reduce in size from first and second to third molars. No grades are published for Atapuerca-SH. Krapina cusp 7s vary in size, the largest (and, at 90%, the greatest frequency) being found on third molars. Occurrence rates for other Middle Pleistocene and KDP lower molars are between 25% and 45%. Overall occurrence rates of grade 1A, which is not properly a cusp 7 (see Scott and Turner 1997 and description in Appendix A), are approximately one quarter for Middle Pleistocene teeth and one third for KDPs. The grade 1A cusp 7 on PN21 is very faint.

PROTOSTYLID (31)

The occurrences of a protostylid on Pontnewydd teeth are a grade 2 on PN11 and a very small pit (grade 1) in the buccal groove of PN21. This is in line with the findings for Middle Pleistocene teeth, only one of which has an expression of protostylid greater than grade 1. Nevertheless, whilst slight, the protostylid on PN11 would be scored as present ('present' being grade 2 and above). The grade 1s are either as found on PN21, or pits on the mesial corner of the buccal surface, and are commoner on Middle Pleistocene teeth than in KDPs. Krapina teeth, conversely, have protostylids up to grade 6, the occurrence rate for above grade 1 increasing from first molars to second/third molars. (PN16 has a number of small shallow pits on the buccal surface that can be seen with a 10× magnifying glass. These are immediately mesial to the buccal groove, at 3.5–4.5 mm above the cervix, and may be associated with this trait).

## DEFLECTING WRINKLE (32)

Deflecting wrinkles are found in approximately one third of the Middle Pleistocene teeth and KDPs studied. The only grade 3 is on a third molar. Grade 1 only occurs on first and second molars.

## MID TRIGONID CREST (33)

PN11 and PN15 have weakly formed mid trigonid crests, whilst that on PN16 is very robust. This trait is very common amongst the teeth in the sample and, in particular, is present on all the later Middle Pleistocene first and second molars, and on all Krapina molars, with the possible exception of one first molar. There are fewer occurrences (about 50%) in earlier Middle Pleistocene teeth, and on later Middle Pleistocene third molars.

## DISTAL TRIGONID CREST (34)

Of the Pontnewydd teeth, this trait is only encountered, in a mild form, on PN21 (in place of a mid trigonid crest). It is found in around 40% of Middle Pleistocene first and third molars but only in 15% of second molars. At Krapina the overall rate of occurrence is lower. A number of Krapina teeth have crests that run across the mesial occlusal groove from a mesial cusp to a distal cusp or cusp 7. These are not scored as distal trigonid crests.

## ANTERIOR FOVEA (35)

The anterior foveae on Pontnewydd teeth are all placed centrally. This trait is present in all but one of the Middle Pleistocene teeth (Mauer right first molar) but its size is very variable. It occurs at grade 1 on the Mauer right second molar, one Atapuerca-SH second molar and most Atapuerca-SH third molars. Anterior foveae on third molars from other Middle Pleistocene sites occur at up to grade 4. The anterior foveae of Krapina teeth are more consistent in size, and on average larger, on second and third molars (all above grade 1). On Atapuerca-SH teeth the anterior fovea is always buccally placed (unlike Pontnewydd), apart from one first molar on which it is placed centrally.

## POSTERIOR FOVEA (36)

There is a faint, lingually placed, posterior fovea on PN16. This trait is present in few of the teeth studied, only otherwise being seen at Arago, Montmaurin and Krapina. It is found on three first molars and on one second and one third molar (both the latter being earlier Middle Pleistocene).

## MESIAL MARGIN (37)

The mesial margin is present as a wide flat tubercle on both PN11 and PN15 but is absent on PN21 (site absent on PN16). The mesial occlusal groove passes over the mesial border, as a single groove on PN21, and as two grooves, one each side of the marginal tubercle, on PN11 and PN15. On PN11 the margin is wedge shaped. The proportion of Middle Pleistocene teeth and KDPs with a mesial margin (present as a ridge or one or more tubercles) reduces markedly from first to third molars.

## DISTAL MARGIN (38)

The distal margin is present on PN16, with the distal occlusal groove passing over it, and is absent on PN21. On PN11 and PN15 the sites are worn. Of the third molars that are sufficiently unworn to determine this trait, the margin is present on most of the Middle Pleistocene teeth, with the distal occlusal groove going over it, but absent in KDPs.

## BUCCAL FURROWS

No peculiarities are present in the buccal face furrows of the Pontnewydd teeth. Traits such as widening of the central furrow, tubercles/ridges in the furrow, and crests across the furrow, occur in a quarter of the Middle Pleistocene sample and a little over a third of the KDPs. In the KDPs the frequency reduces from first molars to third molars. The central buccal furrows on the Pontnewydd teeth are well defined and go halfway down the buccal face. The cusp 5 furrows reach one third of the way down the buccal face. They are well defined on the first and second molars, PN11 and PN15, but very weak on the two third molars, PN16 and PN21. None of the furrows reaches as far as the cervix.

## WRINKLING (15)

Occlusal areas on the Pontnewydd lower molars that have sufficiently little wear all exhibit wrinkling (distobuccal and distolingual cusps and cusp 5 on PN11, mesiobuccal and distobuccal cusps on PN16, and all cusps on PN21). The wrinkling is mild on PN11 and PN16 but distinct on PN21. Wrinkling (mainly mild) is found on all the earlier Middle Pleistocene teeth and KDPs with relatively little wear but only in just half of the later Middle Pleistocene teeth. Prominent ridges occur medially on the mesiolingual cusps of PN15, PN16, and PN21.

## OCCLUSAL TUBERCLES AND CRESTS

Occlusal tubercles and crests observed on Pontnewydd lower molars (other than mid and distal trigonid crests) are:
All – low crest over the buccal occlusal groove at the central fossa (slight on PN16 and PN21);
PN11 – mesiodistally elongate tubercle on the lingual side of the anterior fovea. Crest between hypoconid and hypoconulid, in the centre of the cusp 5 occlusal groove (site worn);
PN21 – mesiodistally elongate crest across the lingual side of the anterior fovea, between the mesial margin and the mesiobuccal cusp.

All of these crests are seen at other sites. The crest over the buccal occlusal groove at the central fossa is found at Arago (AR13 first molar and AR32 second molar), Montmaurin (first molar), Atapuerca-SH (first molars AT1 and AT2) and Krapina (three first molars and two second molars). The anterior fovea crest/tubercle is also found on the Ehringsdorf juvenile first and second molars, all three Arago 13 molars and the Atapuerca-SH AT75 third molar (in this case a mesiodistal tubercle in the mesial occlusal groove at the anterior fovea). A crest between the hypoconid and hypoconulid at the centre of the cusp 5 occlusal groove occurs in the Montmaurin first molars. Crests at the mesial end of this groove are seen at Ehringsdorf and Krapina.

## OCCLUSAL PITS

Both third molars, PN16 and PN21, have a number of small pits appearing on cusps. PN16 has one pit on the mesiolingual cusp, two on the distolingual cusp and two on cusp 5. PN21 has one pit on the distolingual cusp, one on the distobuccal cusp and two on cusp 5. On PN11, PN15 and PN16 there is a widening in the centre of the buccal occlusal groove to form a pit.

## RELATIVE CUSP SIZES

The sequence of cusp sizes for Pontnewydd teeth were calculated using ImageJ software (Rasband 1997–2008) and are shown in Table 9.37. For comparison, the average cusp size sequences for Atapuerca-SH teeth (excluding cusps 5, 6 and 7) taken from Bermúdez de Castro (1988) are; first molars: MB>ML>DL>DB, second molars: MB>DB>ML>DL, third molars: MB>ML>DB>DL. There is good agreement for first and third molars but not for the second molar, though there is an

| Position | Mesiobuccal cusp | | Distobuccal cusp | | Cusp 5 |
| | Mesial (A) | Distal (B) | Mesial (C) | Distal (D) | Mesial (E) |
|---|---|---|---|---|---|
| **PN16** | Shallow | - | Shallow | - | - |
| **PN21** | Shallow | Two, deep | Deep | Shallow | Very faint |

*Table 9.40. Positions of buccal surface vertical grooves on Pontnewydd lower third molars.*

Atapuerca-SH second molar with the same cusp size sequence as PN15. Of note is the fact that the distobuccal cusp is predominantly the smallest in the Atapuerca-SH first molars, as in PN11, but the distolingual cusp is the smallest in nearly all cases in the second and third molars at both sites. Trefný (2005) studied relative cusp sizes in samples of Middle Pleistocene, Krapina and European Neanderthal molars and found similar mean size sequences in lower first and second molars to those of Atapuerca-SH (though in his first molar Middle Pleistocene sample the distobuccal cusp is larger than the distolingual cusp).

BUCCAL ASPECT
Both PN11 and PN15 have a slightly swollen buccal surface on the distobuccal cusp. On all the Pontnewydd teeth the buccal surface is convex and inclines lingually. None of the Pontnewydd teeth has any trace of a cingulum.

LINGUAL ASPECT
The Pontnewydd teeth all have at least a mild convexity of the lingual surface and that of PN21 is distinctly swollen. PN16 has a slight buccal inclination of the lingual surface that is not found in the other teeth. On all the Pontnewydd teeth the lingual surface extends beyond the line of the cervix.

MESIAL AND DISTAL ASPECTS
The lower halves of the mesial surfaces of the Pontnewydd teeth are inclined sharply mesially and the upper halves are near vertical or, in the case PN21, have a distal inclination. The distal surfaces are upright and mildly convex (distinctly convex on PN21).

ENAMEL EXTENSIONS (26)
PN15 has a slight enamel extension of 0.5 mm, and a very small pearl, on the buccal surface. Enamel extensions occur, at mainly trace (0.5 mm) or 1 mm level, on Middle Pleistocene and Krapina first and second molars, but none occur on third molars. The presence/absence of pearls cannot reliably be determined on the casts studied.

BUCCAL SURFACE VERTICAL GROOVES (39)
Both Pontnewydd third molars exhibit these grooves, which can occur in five positions on the buccal surface (Table 9.40).

There is a strong ridge between the two grooves at position B on PN21, and also between the grooves at positions C and D. These grooves are commoner on Middle Pleistocene second and third molars than on first molars. The frequency of occurrence, as a percentage of the maximum number possible (five on each tooth), is 10% for first molars, 35% for second molars and 45% for third molars. The grooves are most frequently found in positions A and B, and least frequently in position E. 60% of Middle Pleistocene molars have one or more grooves. These grooves are commoner amongst KDPs, occurring on over half the first molars and on all second and third molars. As with Middle Pleistocene teeth the frequency of occurrence increases between first molars and second/third molars (average of 30% of positions on first

molars and 55% on second and third molars) and the positions in which grooves are found decreases in frequency from position A to position E.

More than one groove in a position is rare. The Montmaurin mandible third molar has two grooves in position B, as with PN21, as also does the Arago 6 second molar, and two KDP third molars have two grooves each in positions A and B. One Krapina second molar has an additional groove between positions C and D.

### Upper deciduous fourth premolar
#### PN4 (right)
This tooth is compared with Krapina (five KDPs). Details of the morphology of PN4 are given in Table 9.35.

OCCLUSAL SHAPE
PN4, and all the Krapina teeth, are mildly rhomboid in shape, with the rounded hypocone protruding slightly distally.

METACONE (16)
The metacone of PN4 is size grade 3.5 against grade 4 for all the KDPs.

HYPOCONE (17)
As with the metacone, the hypocone of PN4 is smaller than those of the KDPs, grade 3.5 against grades 4 and 5.

CUSP 5 (19)
There is no cusp 5 present on PN4, nor on any of the Krapina teeth.

CARABELLI'S TRAIT (20)
The Carabelli's trait is well developed on PN4 (grade 5) and in the KDPs (grades 4–7). The trait exhibited is as normally defined for more recent teeth but, in addition to this, the teeth have a wide, and usually deep, vertical pit placed behind, and at the tip of, the cusp or enamel protrusion. This pit is circular or mesiodistally elongate in the Krapina teeth. In three KDPs there is a distinct cusp on the rim of the pit. In the other two KDPs the rim is near horizontal. On the worn Ehringsdorf fourth deciduous premolar there is a distinct Carabelli's cusp (1.5 mm diameter) with a small amount of dentine exposure, but no pit behind it (Vlček 1993). On PN4 the trait is in the form of a wide and long horizontal groove (approximately 1.5 mm mesiodistally and 0.3 mm buccolingually), with a horizontal rim and a downward breach of this at the mesial end. This is very similar to some of the Carabelli's traits described for Krapina permanent upper first molars.

PARASTYLE (21)
There is a mild expression of this trait on PN4, as found on the PN4 first permanent molar. In all the KDPs there is a similar expression, i.e. two vertical grooves but no cusp. In two KDPs this appears on both the mesiobuccal and distobuccal cusps.

OBLIQUE RIDGE (22)
The oblique ridge on PN4 is wide and continuous, with dentine exposure down the centre. The Krapina oblique ridges are also all continuous.

METACONULE (23)
There is no trace of a metaconule on PN4. One KDP has a slight distal prominence on the oblique ridge.

DISTAL MARGINAL RIDGE (25)
The distal margin of PN4 is deeply intersected by the distal occlusal groove (as also found on the PN4 first permanent molar). It does not continue onto the distal surface. In contrast, in the five KDPs this groove may or may not cross over the distal margin but does not intersect it.

BUCCAL AND LINGUAL OCCLUSAL GROOVES (25)
The buccal occlusal groove on PN4 cuts the buccal margin but does not continue onto the buccal surface. The lingual occlusal groove goes over the lingual margin and continues for 2.0 mm onto the lingual surface. In both cases there are similarities to the permanent molar.

BUCCAL ASPECT
On PN4 the buccal surface is convex and has a slight lingual inclination.

LINGUAL ASPECT
The lingual face of PN4 is convex and has a buccal inclination that is greatest on the mesiolingual cusp. As with the permanent teeth, the lingual surface extends beyond the line of the cervix.

MESIAL AND DISTAL ASPECTS
Both the mesial and distal aspects of PN4 are convex.

ENAMEL EXTENSIONS (26)
There are no enamel extensions or pearls on PN4 nor any enamel extensions in any of the KDPs. The presence/absence of pearls cannot reliably be determined on the casts studied.

OCCLUSAL GROOVES
Most occlusal grooves on PN4 are obliterated. A slight ridge protrudes from the distal side of the oblique ridge, buccal to the posterior fovea, with a groove on the buccal side ascending the metacone. There is a deep central fossa with buccal, mesial and distal grooves leaving it.

Traits that cannot be determined on PN4 because of wear are: additional cusps on mesial marginal ridge (18); anterior transverse ridge (24); mesial marginal ridge interrupted (25); wrinkling (15) and prominent occlusal ridges.

## Discussion – morphology of Middle Pleistocene permanent teeth

*Dental traits of European Middle Pleistocene hominins*
Bermúdez de Castro (1988) lists the outstanding dental traits of European Middle Pleistocene hominins. As they relate to Pontnewydd teeth, these are:

LOWER INCISORS
• Strong tuberculum linguale (cingulum);

• marked lingual inclination of buccal face.
These are both found on PN10.

LOWER THIRD PREMOLAR
• Asymmetry of the crown.
The crowns of the three Pontnewydd lower third premolars are very similar in shape to those of other European Middle Pleistocene hominins, in particular the Mauer, Ehringsdorf juvenile and Atapuerca-SH AT2 specimens.

UPPER FIRST MOLAR
• Strong development of the hypocone.
The hypocones on both PN4 and PN12 are very large. That on PN4 is the same size as those found at Atapuerca-SH, Arago (AR21), Biache, Bilzingsleben, Petralona, Steinheim and Visogliano, and the slightly smaller one on PN12 is the same size as that on the Arago 9 specimen. The hypocone on PN4, in particular, is above the size range on the ASU reference plaque, which represents the variation observed on recent human teeth.

UPPER AND LOWER MOLARS
• Radicular and supraradicular taurodontism;
• swelling of the buccal faces.
Supraradicular taurodontism occurs in all the Pontnewydd permanent molars with roots, other than PN13, at a similar level to that found in Atapuerca-SH teeth and in the Mauer, Montmaurin, Ehringsdorf juvenile, Bilzingsleben, Steinheim and Bau de l'Aubesier specimens. The level of taurodontism described for the Gran Dolina hominins (Hominids 1 and 3), with bifurcation of the roots of upper molars at 4–5 mm beyond the cervix (Bermúdez de Castro *et al.* 1999b), is milder than that found in the Pontnewydd and Atapuerca-SH upper molars. However, the third molar of the more recently reported Hominid 7 from Gran Dolina is stated as being meso-taurodont, whilst the second molar appears to be hypo-taurodont (description and photographs in Carbonell *et al.* 2005). This therefore confirms the early emergence of this trait. All the Pontnewydd molars have either a basal bulge or a convexity of the whole buccal surface. There is, though, a greater tendency for the lingual surface (also convex) to extend beyond the line of the cervix.

Also listed are firstly; traits shared by eastern Asian and north-west African Middle Pleistocene hominins yet not present in European Middle Pleistocene hominins (but see below regarding Gran Dolina):
• Buccal cingulum on premolars and molars;
• strong molarization of lower fourth premolar (*i.e.* an enlarged occlusal area and possibly an additional buccal cusp);
• two roots on lower premolars.
None of these traits are found on the Pontnewydd teeth.

Secondly; traits frequently absent in the European Middle Pleistocene hominins:
• Invariable presence of cusp 5, and a 'Y' fissure (groove) pattern, on lower molars.
All the Pontnewydd lower molars with sufficiently little

wear to tell have cusp 5s. However, only PN15 and PN16 have a 'Y' fissure pattern. In fact, of the Middle Pleistocene teeth in the comparative sample, 80% have cusp 5s and just 50% have 'Y' fissure patterns. For lower first molars alone, the proportion is 85% for both traits. Cusp 5 and a 'Y' fissure pattern are present on all the Gran Dolina lower first and second molars (Bermúdez de Castro *et al.* 1999b, Carbonell *et al.* 2005). All the lower first molars in Bailey's (2002b) sample of *Homo erectus* have a 'Y' fissure pattern but only 90% of second molars. Again though, all the first and second molars have cusp 5s. In Irish and Guatelli-Steinberg's (2003) pooled sample of gracile African fossil hominins, 95% of second molars have a 'Y' fissure pattern but all have a cusp 5. Presence of cusp 5 and 'Y' fissure pattern are considered to be the primitive traits in hominin teeth (*e.g.* Weidenreich 1937). The above illustrates how loss of cusp 5 is only becoming apparent in the European Middle Pleistocene, whereas second molars without a 'Y' fissure pattern can be seen in early hominins.

Thirdly; traits sometimes present, but usually less marked, in the European Middle Pleistocene hominins:
• Secondary crenulation and fissuration (wrinkling). Wrinkling is present on the unworn parts of the Pontnewydd lower molars. Two of the upper molars have prominent ridges on the occlusal surface and also wrinkling. In the sample studied, 65% of Middle Pleistocene lower molars exhibit wrinkling but only 45% of upper molars.

Bermúdez de Castro *et al.* (1999b), in discussing the Gran Dolina teeth, identify certain dental traits which are common to *Homo heidelbergensis*, *Homo neanderthalensis* and *Homo sapiens*, and which differentiate them from other fossil hominins, including Gran Dolina *Homo antecessor*. (Comments on Gran Dolina Hominid 7 are taken from descriptions and pictures in Carbonell *et al.* 2005):
Absence of buccal cingulum in mandibular canines and premolars (can also be absent in *Homo ergaster*) (present on Gran Dolina teeth) – The Pontnewydd teeth do not have cinguli and nor do the other later Middle Pleistocene teeth studied, but mild cinguli are present on the Mauer and Arago 13 lower third premolars (as noted by Bermúdez de Castro *et al.* 1999b). The Middle Pleistocene teeth can have mesial and distal vertical grooves on the buccal surface (double shovelling), which may be a relic of the cingulum or an entirely separate trait.
Mild asymmetry of the occlusal shape of lower third premolars against strong asymmetry for other hominins – The Pontnewydd lower third premolars are mildly asymmetric, in line with other European Middle Pleistocene teeth, as noted above, and unlike the strongly asymmetric Gran Dolina Hominid 1 lower third premolar that exhibits a prominent distolingual projection of the crown (the talonid). In contrast, the lower third premolar of Gran Dolina Hominid 7 has greater symmetry because the talonid is smaller.
Talonid on lower third premolar small or absent (present on Gran Dolina lower third premolars but less prominent on Hominid 7 than on Hominid 1) – The talonid is absent on the Pontnewydd lower third premolars and not seen on

the other Middle Pleistocene teeth studied.
Single-rooted lower premolars – For two-rooted forms, the classification used by Bermúdez de Castro *et al.* (1999b) differentiates between, on the one hand, the various configurations found in *Australopithecus afarensis, Homo habilis, Homo ergaster* and in Gran Dolina Hominid 1 (that for Gran Dolina being unlike the others) and, on the other, the Tomes' root found in Asian *Homo erectus* and in African Middle Pleistocene hominins (and in modern humans). It is not clear if the single two-rooted lower third premolar reported for Krapina (Smith 1976b) is a Tomes' root or not. None of the Krapina lower premolars that are not in place are two-rooted (S. E. Bailey, pers. comm.). Although not complete, there is no sign of bifurcation or any grade of Tomes' root on the Pontnewydd lower third premolars, and this is also the case (with one exception that has two radicals) for the Atapuerca-SH lower premolars (Martinón-Torres *et al.* 2007a). Of the other European Middle Pleistocene lower premolars in the sample, the two-rooted form occurring at Gran Dolina is found at Arago (AR13) (Bermúdez de Castro 2003a) but the remainder appear to be single rooted. Unlike Hominid 1, the roots of both premolars of Gran Dolina Hominid 7 are single rooted, there being a Tomes' root bifurcation of the lower half in the third premolar. Additionally, the lower third and fourth premolars in the very early (1,200,000–1,100,000 years ago) Sima del Elefante (Atapuerca, Spain) ATE9-1 specimen are single rooted and have the grooves associated with the lower grades of Tomes' root (Carbonell *et al.* 2008). The world range for Tomes' root on lower third premolars (grades 4–7) in recent humans is 0–38.7%, the highest frequencies being observed in sub-Saharan Africans (Scott and Turner 1997).
Hypoconulid (cusp 5) in the mandibular first and second molars can be absent, less so in the first molar than in the second (present on Gran Dolina teeth) – The Pontnewydd lower first and second molars both have cusp 5s. Second molars in the Middle Pleistocene sample without cusp 5s are only seen at Arago and Atapuerca-SH and, for first molars, only at Atapuerca-SH.

Bermúdez de Castro *et al.* (1999b) consider that the presence of cinguli on lower premolars, a strongly asymmetrical crown and well-developed talonid on the lower third premolar, and complex root morphology of lower premolars, together with wrinkling on posterior teeth, as found in the Gran Dolina hominins, to be plesiomorphic (*i.e.* primitive characteristics) for the genus *Homo*. Carbonell *et al.* (1995) add to this:
Buccal and lingual faces of all post-canine teeth quite swollen by the presence of a conspicuous basal prominence – The Pontnewydd premolars all have convex buccal and lingual surfaces. The lower third premolars have particularly swollen lingual faces and a slight basal prominence on the buccal surface (most developed on PN7). Of the molars, only PN1 has a basal prominence (buccal) but some buccal and lingual surfaces are distinctly swollen.
Lingual cusp of lower premolars is mesial to the buccal cusp – This is the case on PN5 but not on the Pontnewydd lower

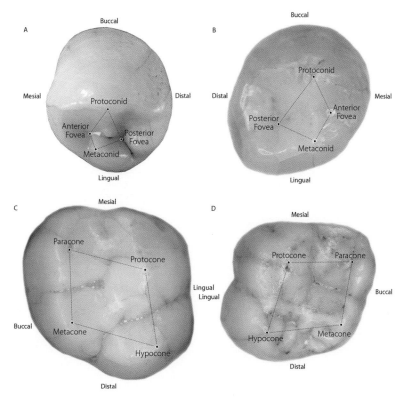

*Figure 9.44. Occlusal polygons: A) lower third premolar; B) lower fourth premolar; C–D) upper molars.*

third premolars. Generally, in the comparative sample as at Pontnewydd, the principal or only lingual cusp of lower third premolars is not mesial to the buccal cusp, but that of lower fourth premolars is.

### Neanderthal dental traits
Certain traits and aspects of occlusal shape have been identified as being characteristic of Neanderthal teeth:

LOWER THIRD PREMOLAR
Gómez-Robles *et al.* (2008) have studied the occlusal shape of lower third premolars and the form of their occlusal polygon (formed by linking the buccal and principal lingual cusps (the protoconid and the metaconid) and the anterior and posterior foveae) (see Figure 9.44) using geometric morphometrics and have defined three forms:

- An archaic form, found in early African and Asian hominins, having an asymmetric oval outline in a mesiobuccal/distolingual direction, a well-developed protruding talonid and a large occlusal polygon;
- two derived forms. The talonid is reduced or absent in both and, largely as a result, the outline is more symmetric and regular. *Homo heidelbergensis* (sample made up of European specimens only) and *Homo neanderthalensis* generally have a small, lingually placed, occlusal polygon as a consequence of the tip of the buccal cusp migrating lingually towards the centre of the tooth. They also tend to have a convexity of the distal surface and a concavity or flattening of the mesial surface. In modern humans the occlusal polygon is large and centrally placed and the occlusal outline is approximately circular.

The Pontnewydd lower third premolars are typical of *Homo heidelbergensis* and *Homo neanderthalensis* in having a smooth and near circular outline and a small, lingually placed, occlusal polygon. Gómez-Robles *et al.* (2008) comment on the particularly diminutive occlusal polygon in the Atapuerca-SH population compared to others. The tip of the buccal cusp is well within the lingual half of the tooth on both PN6 and PN7 and, due to this, the Pontnewydd teeth appear to be similar in that respect to the lower third premolars of Atapuerca-SH. This situation is reflected in the high angles between buccal and lingual cusps found for Pontnewydd lower third premolars.

LOWER FOURTH PREMOLAR
- Multiple lingual cusps;
- continuous transverse crest across the sagittal sulcus;
- asymmetry of crown when viewed occlusally because of mesiolingual flattening;
- principal lingual cusp (metaconid) placed mesially.

The last three traits occurring together, or in pairs, is considered to be typically Neanderthal by Bailey (2002a), 59% of Bailey's (2002a) Neanderthal sample having the three traits and 35% having two traits. In contrast, fewer than 3% of an anatomically modern human sample had two traits and none had three. In the Middle Pleistocene comparative sample, the figures are 30% and 50% respectively. The three traits appear to be present on Gran Dolina Hominid 7 (picture in Carbonell *et al.* 2005). All four traits occur on PN5. Mesially placed principal lingual cusps are seen on all the specimens in the Middle Pleistocene sample, and

| | African Plio-Pleistocene EAFHOM X (SD) | Gran Dolina H1&H3 X | Homo erectus X (SD) | Pontnewydd | Pontnewydd | Middle Pleistocene X (SD) | Krapina X (SD) | Le Moustier 1 X | Neanderthal X (SD) | Homo sapiens Early X (SD) | Upper Palaeolithic X (SD) | Recent X (SD) |
|---|---|---|---|---|---|---|---|---|---|---|---|---|
| **FIRST MOLAR** | | | | | | | | | | | | |
| *OCCLUSAL POLYGON ANGLES* | | | | PN4 | PN12 | | | | | | | |
| No. in sample | | | 2 | | | | | | 17 | 4 | 5 | 19–32 |
| Protocone | | | 105.3 | 113 | 110 | | | | 106.1 (5.2) | 109.0 (4.5) | 106.3 (4.4) | 104.5–114.6 |
| Paracone | | | 75.2 | 74 | 78 | | | | 66.7 (6.7) | 72.5 (2.5) | 71.1 (2.7) | 68.0–73.6 |
| Metacone | | | 96.8 | 108 | 105 | | | | 118.0 (10.0) | 102.0 (1.9) | 110.3 (4.9) | 102.3–106.4 |
| Hypocone | | | 82.0 | 65 | 67 | | | | 69.0 (6.1) | 79.6 (6.1) | 73.3 (4.8) | 70.9–79.7 |
| *RELATIVE CUSP AREAS (PERCENT)* | | | | | | | | | | | | |
| No. in sample | 8 | | 3 | | | 5 | 7 | | 18 | 7 | 12 | 59 |
| Protocone | 28.2 (1.4) | 29.3 | 31.4 (1.1) | 31.9 | 32.2 | 32.0 (2.9) | 30.2 (1.8) | 29.4 | 29.7 (2.4) | 31.4 (2.0) | 31.8 (1.7) | 31.0 (2.0) |
| Paracone | 22.0 (1.8) | 22.9 | 26.0 (2.3) | 26.1 | 26.1 | 23.4 (2.7) | 24.2 (2.2) | 22.4 | 25.4 (2.1) | 24.9 (2.0) | 25.8 (2.7) | 25.8 (2.1) |
| Metacone | 25.8 (1.7) | 24.8 | 21.4 (3.3) | 20.4 | 21.6 | 22.3 (1.3) | 22.5 (2.5) | 22.0 | 21.0 (1.5) | 21.6 (1.6) | 23.0 (1.6) | 22.9 (1.8) |
| Hypocone | 24.2 (2.4) | 22.8 | 21.2 (2.4) | 21.6 | 20.1 | 22.4 (2.8) | 23.1 (2.0) | 26.2 | 23.8 (2.2) | 22.1 (4.2) | 19.5 (3.1) | 20.5 (2.5) |
| *RATIO OF OCCLUSAL POLYGON AREA TO CROWN BASE AREA (PERCENT)* | | | | | | | | | | | | |
| No. in sample | | | 2 | | | | | | 17 | 4 | 5 | 24 |
| Value | | | 32.9 | 25.0 | 26.5 | | | | 26.7 (1.8) | 33.3 (2.7) | 32.7 (1.9) | 37.5 (5.4) |
| *RATIO OF BUCCAL TO LINGUAL OCCLUSAL POLYGON LENGTH* | | | | | | | | | | | | |
| | 0.78 | | | 0.89 | 0.90 | 0.71 | | | 0.69 | | | 1.09–1.19 |
| **SECOND MOLAR** | | | | PN1 | | | | | | | | |
| *RELATIVE CUSP AREAS (PERCENT)* | | | | | | | | | | | | |
| No. in sample | 3 | | 3 | | | 4 | 5 | | 11 | 3 | 7 | 79 |
| Protocone | 33.2 (3.7) | 34.1 | 31.0 (5.9) | 39.3 | | 34.6 (3.0) | 35.4 (3.6) | 30.3 | 31.9 (2.1) | 33.8 (2.2) | 41.7 (5.4) | 35.0 (3.8) |
| Paracone | 26.9 (0.3) | 25.6 | 27.1 (1.3) | 25.8 | | 25.2 (3.9) | 30.3 (2.0) | 27.9 | 28.4 (2.9) | 25.0 (1.7) | 30.1 (2.7) | 29.3 (2.5) |
| Metacone | 20.0 (1.9) | 21.4 | 22.8 (3.2) | 19.6 | | 22.4 (3.4) | 22.2 (3.5) | 21.3 | 21.2 (1.7) | 18.7 (1.8) | 19.8 (3.3) | 21.0 (2.5) |
| Hypocone | 19.1 (2.7) | 18.9 | 19.2 (2.8) | 15.3 | | 17.8 (4.0) | 12.1 (6.7) | 20.5 | 19.0 (3.7) | 22.5 (2.1) | 8.5 (4.6) | 14.7 (5.4) |
| **THIRD MOLAR** | | | | PN17 | PN19 | | | | | | | |
| *RELATIVE CUSP AREAS (PERCENT)* | | | | | | | | | | | | |
| No. in sample | 2 | | | | | | 6 | | | | | 32 |
| Protocone | 29.5 (1.0) | | | 54.4 | 46.7 | | 35.5 (3.1) | 38.7 | | | | 38.8 (4.2) |
| Paracone | 26.3 (2.3) | | | 31.0 | 31.5 | | 33.8 (2.4) | 28.0 | | | | 33.7 (2.7) |
| Metacone | 27.9 (5.1) | | | 14.6 | 16.9 | | 21.9 (3.7) | 23.4 | | | | 21.6 (4.8) |
| Hypocone | 16.4 (1.8) | | | 0.0 | 4.9 | | 8.8 (6.8) | 9.9 | | | | 10.4 (6.8) |

Occlusal Polygon Angles, Relative Cusp Areas and Ratio of Occlusal Polygon Area to Crown Base Area: EAFHOM; *H habilis, H ergaster. Homo erectus*; M1 Bailey (2004), M2 Bailey (2002b). Middle Pleistocene; Arago, Rabat, Steinheim. Neanderthal, *H sapiens* Early & *H sapiens* Upper Palaeolithic. Modern; M1 Polygon Angles, San, Sotho, Asiatic Indians, Whites and Papago Indians, M1 remainder Bailey *et al.* (2008a), M2 Bailey 2002b, M3 Rajhrad. Ratio of Buccal to Lingual Occlusal Polygon Length: EAFHOM; *H habilis*. Middle Pleistocene (*H heidelbergensis*); Arago, Atapuerca-SH, Pontnewydd, Steinheim. Neanderthal; Krapina, Pinilla del Valle, Kůlna, Le Moustier, St Césaire, Sidrón, Tabūn. Modern; as for M1 Polygon Angles.

*Table 9.41. Upper molar occlusal polygons and relative cusp base areas.*

multiple lingual cusps and transverse crests are frequently found, but asymmetry of the crown because of mesiolingual flattening is less common, only occurring in one third of the teeth.

Bailey and Lynch (2005) consider symmetry of the crown to be the primitive state and a high frequency of asymmetry to be a derived characteristic in Neanderthals. However, Martinón-Torres *et al.* (2006), using a larger sample, conclude that the primitive state is an elongated, sub-rectangular outline, with a bulging talonid and a mesially displaced principal lingual cusp. The symmetrical outline seen in modern humans, with a reduced or absent talonid, is the derived form. Using the results of the morphometric analysis performed by Martinón-Torres *et al.* (2006), the occlusal shape of PN5, and the position and shape of its occlusal polygon (formed by linking the buccal and principal lingual cusps and the anterior and posterior foveae, see Figure 9.44), can be seen, by comparing it to their figure 4, to be intermediate in position along the first and second axes of their principal components analysis, the area in which most of the European Middle Pleistocene specimens analysed fall. Martinón-Torres *et al.* (2006) also show that the relative size of the occlusal polygon, compared to the total occlusal area of the crown, decreases over time. At 10.7%, the relative size of the occlusal polygon of PN5 is below the means of all the groups analysed, but within one standard deviation of all but the earliest, and close to the means of 10.94% and 11.27% for *Homo heidelbergensis* and *Homo neanderthalensis* respectively.

LOWER MOLARS
• Mid trigonid crest (Bailey 2002a).
Of the Pontnewydd lower molars, PN11, PN15 and PN16 exhibit this trait but the third molar PN21 does not. It is found in over two-thirds of the Middle Pleistocene sample. As noted below, the incidence of this trait increases from earlier Middle Pleistocene through to Krapina.

UPPER MOLARS
Bailey (2004) identifies aspects of the shape of upper first molars that are typical in Neanderthals as against anatomically modern humans:
• The markedly skewed shape, with the lingual cusps being distinctly distal to the buccal cusps;
• internally placed cusps, leading to a relatively small occlusal polygon area (the area of the irregular four-sided figure formed by linking the four cusp tips, see Figure 9.44);
• an occlusal polygon that is narrower distally than mesially;
• a relatively larger hypocone and smaller metacone.
(Modern human upper first molars tend to be squarer in shape, have cusp tips placed nearer the periphery of the occlusal face and have smaller hypocones). It is considered by Bailey (2004) that this distinctive morphology may be derived in Neanderthals. Gómez-Robles *et al.* (2007) used geometric morphometric methods to explore the occlusal

shape of this tooth in an enlarged sample of hominins, from the Pliocene through to modern humans, and also identified a unique morphology in Neanderthals. The distinguishing features are distal displacement of the lingual cusps, and a bulging protrusion of the hypocone, leading to a rhomboidal occlusal polygon and a skewed external outline, which is seen to a lesser degree in European Early and Middle Pleistocene populations. Gómez-Robles *et al.* (2007) conclude that the primitive hominin shape, also seen in modern humans, is of a near square occlusal polygon, and a round occlusal outline, without any particular cusp protrusion.

Table 9.41 contains measurements relating to the occlusal polygons and cusp base areas of Pontnewydd upper molars, calculated using ImageJ software (Rasband 1997–2008). Cusp 5s, when present, are included in the area of the metacone, in line with the method used by Trefný (2005). Relative cusp areas for East African *Homo* (EAFHOM) come from Wood and Engleman (1988), for Middle Pleistocene, Krapina and Le Moustier (and recent *Homo sapiens* for third molars) from Trefný (2005) and for Gran Dolina H1 and H3 from Bermúdez de Castro *et al.* (1999b). Ranges of mean occlusal polygon angles, and ratios of buccal to lingual occlusal polygon length (distance between paracone and metacone tips compared to distance between protocone and hypocone tips) for five recent human groups come from Morris (1986). Figures for the remaining ratios of buccal to lingual occlusal polygon length come from Gómez-Robles *et al.* (2007). Other comparative data come from Bailey (2004) and Bailey *et al.* (2008a) for first molars and Bailey (2002b) for second molars. The Neanderthal samples are widely defined and include, amongst others, Krapina and Le Moustier. Pontnewydd is included in Bailey's (2002b) Neanderthal sample and in Gómez-Robles *et al.* (2007) *Homo heidelbergensis* (Middle Pleistocene) sample. Trefný's (2005) Middle Pleistocene sample is predominantly of European sites but also includes Rabat.

Upper first molars – of the occlusal polygon angles, those of the PN4 and PN12 hypocones are similar to the Neanderthal sample mean figure, but those for the paracone have greater similarity to other populations. The Pontnewydd protocone and metacone angles are closer to each other (5° apart on each tooth) than is the case in the Neanderthal sample, and in this respect are similar to *Homo erectus* and *Homo sapiens*. The reason for this is the greatly enlarged Neanderthal metacone angle. The metacone angles of the Pontnewydd teeth are intermediate between *Homo erectus* and Neanderthals, and those of the protocone higher than both.

The relative cusp areas for PN4 and PN12 are most comparable overall to those of *Homo erectus*, and similar to the Middle Pleistocene and Krapina samples. They contrast with EAFHOM and Gran Dolina in having relatively larger mesial cusps and smaller distal cusps. The metacones are relatively small, as is also seen in the Neanderthals and early *Homo sapiens,* but the hypocones are not as relatively large as is the case in Neanderthals, and particularly compared to the late Neanderthal from Le Moustier. The sequence of cusp sizes in PN4 and PN12 reflects those seen in the Middle Pleistocene and Krapina samples (protocone >paracone >hypocone ≈ metacone) but with the paracone relatively larger compared to the metacone and hypocone. It contrasts with the sequence in the Le Moustier teeth, where the hypocone is the second largest cusp. (See Bailey *et al.* 2008b and Quam *et al.* 2009 for comments on the evolution of cusp proportions in hominin upper first molars).

The ratios of occlusal polygon area to total crown base area in PN4 and PN12 are similar to that of the Neanderthal sample and small compared to other populations, reflecting the internal placement of cusps mentioned above. The buccal lengths of the occlusal polygons in PN4 and PN12 are shorter than the lingual, as is also seen in other groups, with the exception of recent *Homo sapiens*, where the reverse applies (Gómez-Robles *et al.* (2007) give a figure of 0.73 for a mixed sample of Upper Palaeolithic and recent humans). However, the two lengths are more nearly equal than is the case in *Homo habilis* (EAFHOM), *Homo heidelbergensis* or Neanderthals. Bailey (2004) finds that in most Neanderthals the distal width of the occlusal polygon is narrower than the mesial width. The reverse applies in the Pontnewydd upper first molars, as it also does in Bailey's (2004) *Homo erectus* sample. In recent humans the two widths are very similar (Morris 1986). There are therefore a number of differences between Pontnewydd and Neanderthal upper first molars, particularly in the shape and proportions of the occlusal polygon. Bailey (2004) considers that the position of the metacone is principally responsible for the shape differences between Neanderthal and modern human upper first molars, it being placed more mesially and lingually in Neanderthals. The positioning of this cusp can also explain most of the differences between the Pontnewydd and Neanderthal occlusal polygons.

Upper second and third molars – as with the first molar, the mesial cusps of the EAFHOM upper third molars are relatively smaller than is found in later material and the distal cusps relatively larger. In upper second molars the trend is less evident. For both second and third upper molars the sequence of cusp sizes is consistently protocone >paracone >metacone >hypocone, with the exception of early *Homo sapiens* second molar, where the hypocone is larger than the metacone, and EAFHOM third molar, where the metacone is larger than the paracone. The relatively large size of the protocone compared to other populations (excepting Upper Palaeolithic upper second molars) is noticeable in Pontnewydd upper second and third molars, as are the relatively small upper third molar metacones. In other respects PN1 fits well with the Middle Pleistocene sample. The paracone of the Krapina second molar is relatively larger than in PN1 but, for the third molar, the relative size is similar to those of PN17 and PN19. The relative size of the hypocone of PN1 is intermediate between the *Homo erectus* and Krapina means but smaller than in the Neanderthal sample and at Le Moustier.

## Trends in trait grades and frequencies

Certain differences can be seen in terms of size grades of traits, and changes in incidence of traits, between earlier and later Middle Pleistocene, and between all/later Middle Pleistocene and Krapina. Because of the small sample size, these are necessarily tentative and no statistical analysis has been attempted. They are summarized in Table 9.42 and the more significant differences are described here, followed by a discussion of the traits exhibited by Pontnewydd teeth.

### LOWER LATERAL INCISOR

Angle of inclination of the buccal surface to the vertical – the mean of the angles found in the teeth from Krapina is higher than the range of values occurring in the four Middle Pleistocene specimens measured.

Other changes can be seen as relating to the strengthening of the incisors, and the increase in their occlusal area, through the Middle Pleistocene, discussed by Wolpoff (1979) and Bermúdez de Castro (1988; 1993):

Shovelling – there is a greater degree of shovelling on the Krapina teeth than in Middle Pleistocene specimens, grade 2 being present in three quarters of KDPs but only on one Middle Pleistocene tooth, the remainder being grades 0 or 1.

Lingual median longitudinal ridge – this is more strongly developed on Krapina lateral incisors, being at grade 2 in the majority of KDPs but only at this grade on a single Middle Pleistocene specimen (Mauer).

Flaring – whilst all the teeth in the sample show distal flaring, only the Krapina teeth also predominantly show mesial flaring.

### PREMOLARS

Mesiobuccal swelling – lower premolars – amongst lower third premolars this trait occurs in over half the later Middle Pleistocene specimens, and in both the earlier Middle Pleistocene specimens, but is less frequently found in KDPs. In lower fourth premolars it is only seen in the earlier Middle Pleistocene specimens.

Position of buccal cusp – upper fourth premolar – at Krapina the buccal cusp is predominantly placed medially but on most Middle Pleistocene teeth it is placed mesially.

Rotation of lingual aspect of buccal cusp in a mesiobuccal/ distolingual direction – lower third premolar – this is apparent on the later Middle Pleistocene and Krapina teeth but not on the earlier Middle Pleistocene teeth.

Multiple lingual cusps – upper fourth premolar and lower premolars – in upper fourth premolars this trait is only found at Krapina. In lower third premolars, 30% of later Middle Pleistocene specimens and KDPs have multiple cusps but neither of the earlier Middle Pleistocene specimens does. Multiple lingual cusps on lower third premolars are also not found at Gran Dolina, nor in the sample of *Homo erectus* teeth used by Bailey (2002b). In lower fourth premolars, one-third of Middle Pleistocene specimens have single lingual cusps but all KDPs have multiple lingual cusps.

Position of principal lingual cusp – lower third premolar – the lingual cusp is predominantly placed distally on the Middle Pleistocene teeth but medially on Krapina teeth.

Angle to the horizontal between buccal cusp and principal lingual cusp – lower premolars – this measurement is intended to show how prominent the buccal cusp is in relation to the lingual cusp. The two later Middle Pleistocene lower third premolars measured are mid-range and top of range for the total sample. Similarly, the later Middle Pleistocene lower fourth premolars are at the higher end of the range, with the earlier Middle Pleistocene specimens towards the bottom of the range. The lowest values for lower fourth premolars are found at Krapina.

Additional buccal occlusal ridges – upper and lower fourth premolars – 90% of KDP upper fourth premolars have a bifurcated median ridge but only one-third of Middle Pleistocene specimens. Both mesial and distal ridges occur on earlier Middle Pleistocene and Krapina upper and lower fourth premolars, but mesial ridges do not occur in the later Middle Pleistocene specimens. No distal ridges occur on later Middle Pleistocene upper fourth premolars, but are present on all later Middle Pleistocene lower fourth premolars.

Marginal ridges – upper fourth premolar and lower premolars – the rate of interruption of both mesial and distal margins on upper fourth premolars increases slightly going from Middle Pleistocene to Krapina. The distal marginal ridge is interrupted in over 50% of KDP lower third premolars but not in any of the Middle Pleistocene specimens. The mesial margin is interrupted on all Middle Pleistocene lower fourth premolars but not in all KDPs.

Occluso-lingual grooves/clefts – lower premolars – distal clefts on lower third premolars predominate over mesial in Middle Pleistocene teeth, whilst only mesial clefts occur on Krapina teeth. In lower fourth premolars, mesial clefts occur more frequently in KDPs than in Middle Pleistocene specimens.

Double shovelling – upper fourth premolar and lower premolars – mesial and distal double shovelling occurs at up to grade 3 at Krapina but not above grade 2 on Middle Pleistocene teeth. In lower third premolars, distal double shovelling is more frequent, and mesial less frequent, in KDPs than in Middle Pleistocene specimens. All KDP lower fourth premolars have distal double shovelling but only half of Middle Pleistocene lower fourth premolars.

CUSP SIZE CHANGES

Table 9.43 shows the average cusp size grades calculated for upper molar metacone, hypocone and cusp 5, and for lower molar cusp 5.

Metacone – in upper first molars there is a decrease in average size between later Middle Pleistocene and Krapina, and in upper second molars from earlier Middle Pleistocene through later Middle Pleistocene to Krapina. However, in upper third molars the average size remains the same.

Hypocone – there is no change apparent in upper first molars, the hypocones being consistently very large throughout. The hypocone sizes on upper second and third molars are more variable, and there is a decrease in average size between earlier Middle Pleistocene and later Middle Pleistocene/Krapina.

Upper molar cusp 5 – there is a decrease in the average size of upper first molar cusp 5s between the Middle Pleistocene and Krapina but not within the Middle Pleistocene. In upper second and third molars there is a decrease going from earlier Middle Pleistocene through later Middle Pleistocene to Krapina.

Lower molar cusp 5 – the sizes of lower first and second molar cusp 5s are very consistent within earlier Middle Pleistocene and later Middle Pleistocene specimens, and there is a clear decrease in average size between the two, particularly in the second molar. However, there is no further decrease in size between later Middle Pleistocene and Krapina. In lower third molars there is no decrease in size between earlier and later Middle Pleistocene, but there is between later Middle Pleistocene and Krapina.

If Atapuerca-SH is placed in the earlier Middle Pleistocene group, the result is that the earlier and later groups become more similar, with no change in average size apparent between earlier and later Middle Pleistocene in any of the above, other than a decrease in size of upper molar cusp 5 in third molars, and of

lower molar cusp 5 in second molars, as already described (mean figures unchanged), and an increase in size of upper second molar metacones (mean figures 4 and 5 respectively).

UPPER MOLARS

Carabelli's trait – Smith (1989) notes that Near Eastern and European Neanderthals frequently have some expression of Carabelli's trait on second and third molars, as well as on the first, whereas, in an 'early *sapiens*' group, Carabelli's trait is usually limited to the first molar. Smith (1989) also notes that McCown and Keith (1939) considered that the presence of Carabelli's trait on most molars was one of the morphological characteristics of Neanderthals. Of the Middle Pleistocene teeth, it is found at grades above zero on all Biache and Steinheim molars and on the Bilzingsleben first molar, but does not occur on all Arago, Petralona, Visogliano, Pesada or Atapuerca-SH molars, thus it is not as prevalent at the earlier sites. However, unless Atapuerca-SH is put in the earlier Middle Pleistocene group, the difference is not clear-cut. At all sites where both teeth are present, the trait is found on second or third molars but not always both. The earlier sites are therefore exhibiting this Neanderthal characteristic. There is, though, a clear increase in frequency between Middle Pleistocene and Krapina. For first, second and third molars the percentage occurrence rates at any level are 90/60/40 for Middle Pleistocene against 100/90/80 for KDPs. True Carabelli cusps (grades 5–7) are commoner on KDP first molars than on Middle Pleistocene first molars, but the reverse is true for second molars.

Oblique ridge – the oblique ridge is absent on all Middle Pleistocene third molars but is found (present or divided) in 60% of KDP third molars.

Metaconule – Grade 2 metaconules are only found on Middle Pleistocene teeth.

Anterior transverse ridge crests – there is a slightly higher incidence of anterior transverse ridge in KDPs than in Middle Pleistocene specimens, but a lower incidence of the associated crests. There are no crests on Krapina third molars or later Middle Pleistocene second molars.

LOWER MOLARS

Groove pattern – two thirds of Middle Pleistocene third molars have a '+' groove pattern but no Krapina third molars.

Cusps 5 and 6 – there is an increase in the occurrence of both cusps between the Middle Pleistocene and Krapina on first and second molars.

Cusp 7 – cusp 7s are more frequently found on KDP third molars than on Middle Pleistocene third molars, and higher grades are present.

Protostylid – this trait is only found at levels up to grade 3 on Middle Pleistocene teeth but higher grades are seen on Krapina second and third molars. If grade 1s are included (scored as described in Appendix A), the occurrence rates for protostylids on first and second molars are considerably higher in Middle Pleistocene teeth than in KDPs.

Deflecting wrinkle – grade 2/3 deflecting wrinkles only occur on third molars at Krapina but are also found on Middle Pleistocene first and second molars.

Mid trigonid crest – this crest is nearly ubiquitous on Krapina molars and later Middle Pleistocene first and second molars, but not in earlier Middle Pleistocene specimens nor later Middle Pleistocene third molars. (Weidenreich (1937) noted the existence of trigonid crests in all anthropoids but considered these to be secondary acquisitions. In support of this, he pointed out that the crests in the molars of *Dryopithecus*, *Australopithecus* and fossil orang are only in the form of coarse wrinkles and that

| Earlier Middle Pleistocene | Later Middle Pleistocene | PN | Krapina |
|---|---|---|---|
| | *1. Lower lateral incisor* | | |
| | Shovelling found | ✓ | More pronounced |
| | Double shovelling found | ✗ | |
| | Distinct labial convexity | ✓ | |
| Grade 2 | Lingual median ridge often present, grade 1 | ✓ | Most grade 2 |
| | Distal flaring but none mesial* | ✓ | Also mesial |
| | Marked lingual inclination of buccal surface* | ✓ | More pronounced |
| | Strong cingulum* | ✓ | |
| | | | |
| | *2. Upper fourth premolar* | | |
| | Buccal cusp larger than lingual | ✓ | |
| | Buccal cusp placed mesially | ✗ | Mainly medial |
| | Single lingual cusp* | ✓ | Multiple cusps found |
| | Principal lingual cusp placed mesially* | ✓ | |
| Both found | No mesial or distal buccal occlusal ridges* | - | Both found |
| | Median buccal occlusal ridge can be bifurcated (<½) | ✗ | 90% bifurcated |
| | Sagittal sulcus interrupted | ✓ | |
| | Distal margin interrupted more frequently than mesial | ✓ | Both more frequent |
| | Accessory marginal tubercles found (<½) | ✗ | |
| | Double shovelling, stronger mesially | ✓ | More pronounced |
| | | | |
| | *3. Lower third premolar* | | |
| | Occlusal outline circular with mesiolingual flattening, principal ling cusp < buccal cusp & at most ling point* | ✓ | |
| | Mesiobuccal swelling | ✓ | Less frequent |
| | Buccal cusp placed medially & pronounced m & d borders | ✓+ | |
| No rotation | Lingual faces buccal cusps rotated | ✓ | |
| | Mesial & distal occlusal marginal ridges present* | ✓ | |
| None | Multiple lingual cusps (<½) | ✓ | |
| | Principal lingual cusp placed distally | ✗+ | Mainly medial |
| Less pronounced | Tip of buccal cusp migrated towards lingual surface and high angle between buccal & lingual cusps* | ✓ | |
| Not distal on all | Distal buccal occlusal ridge but not mesial* | ✓ | |
| | No bifurcation of median buccal occlusal ridge* | ✓ | |
| | Sagittal sulcus interrupted* | ✓+ | |
| | Mesial & distal margins not interrupted* | ✓ | 55% distal interrupted |
| | Mesial occluso-lingual groove occasionally a distinct cleft (<½) | ✓ | |
| | Distal occluso-lingual groove frequently a distinct cleft | ✓ | None found |
| | Double shovelling (<½) | ✓ | Distal > ½, mesial < ½ |
| | No talonid* | ✓ | |
| 2-rooted found | Single rooted* | ✓ | 2-rooted found |
| | | | |
| | *4. Lower fourth premolar* | | |
| Less frequent | Mesiolingual occlusal flattening | ✓ | |
| Present | Mesiobuccal swelling absent* | ✓ | |
| | Buccal cusp placed mesially | ✗+ | |
| | Weak mesial & strong distal occlusal marginal ridges | ✓ | |
| | Single/multiple lingual cusps (up to 5) | ✓ | All multiple |
| | Principal lingual cusp placed mesially* | ✓ | |
| | Most lingual cusp immediately distal to principal lingual cusp. Principal (largest) cusp most mesial | ✓ | |
| Less pronounced | Buccal cusp larger and higher than principal lingual cusp* | ✓ | Not always higher |
| And mesial, dist not always pres. | Distal buccal occlusal ridge but not mesial* | ✓ | And mesial, distal not always present |
| | Median buccal occlusal ridge bifurcated | ✗ | |
| | Sagittal sulcus interrupted | ✓ | |
| Not all lower | Posterior fovea wider and lower than anterior fovea* | ✓ | Not all lower |
| | Mesial margin always interrupted*, distal occasionally, mesial frequently a cleft | ✓ | Mesial not interrupted on all |
| | Occluso-lingual grooves present but generally not clefts | ✓ | Higher frequency of mesial cleft |
| | Double shovelling, stronger mesially | ✓ | More pronounced, distal on all |
| | No molarization* | ✓ | |
| 2-rooted found | Single rooted* | - | |

| Earlier Middle Pleistocene | Trait | PN | Krapina |
|---|---|---|---|
| | **5. Premolars and molars** | | |
| Present on lwr 3rd premolars | No cinguli | ✓ | |
| | Supraradicular taurodontism on molars, most pronounced on upper molars | ✓ | Present on premolars. More pronounced on molars, & radicular present |
| On all lower molars | Swelling of molar buccal faces | ✓ | |
| | Wrinkling present on upper molars (<½) & lower molars. Generally absent on premolars | ✓ | On all upper and 80% lower 4th premolars. All upper & lower molars except one upper 1st |
| | **6. Upper molars** | | |
| | Occlusal outline of first molars rhomboid/square, second molars irregular rhomboid/rectangular, third molars oval/triangular | ✓ | |
| | Incipient 'Neanderthal' occlusal morphology of first molar, including distinctive distally protruding hypocone* | ✓ | More pronounced |
| Above grade 3 | Second & third molar hypocones variable | ✓ | |
| | Relative sizes of first molar cusps: protocone > paracone > hypocone ≈ metacone | ✓ | |
| More frequent | Mesial marginal cusps sometimes present (<½) & can be large | ✗ | More frequent, freq increases 1st to 3rd |
| Large, also multiple on 2nd | Cusp 5 frequently present (all 3rd molars*). Can be multiple on 3rd molars (<½) | ✓ | Also multiple on 2nd |
| Not always on 1st | Carabelli's trait present at some level on all 1st molars*, > ½ 2nd & < ½ 3rd. Freq grades > 2 decrease from 1st to 3rd. True Carabelli cusps present | ✓ | Higher frequency > 0 |
| Not all 1st | Small parastyle present on all 1st molars*, <½ 2nd & ½ 3rd | ✓ | |
| | Oblique ridge present on first molar, present/divided on second molar, absent on third molar* | ✓ | All grades present on third molar |
| | Grade 2/3 Metaconule occasionally present (<½). No grade 3 on 1st, no grade 2 on 3rd. | ✓ | Only single grade 3 on a 2nd, no grade 2 |
| On all | Anterior transverse ridge present on all 1st*, most 2nd & 3rd | ✓ | On all |
| Also on 2nd | Anterior transverse ridge crests over mesial occlusal groove present on 1st & 3rd, not 2nd | ✓ | Lower frequency & decreasing frequency 1st to 3rd, none on 3rd |
| | Mesial & distal margins interrupted | ✓ | |
| | No enamel extensions* | ✓ | Trace found on 2 teeth |
| | **7. Lower molars** | | |
| | Occlusal outline square/rectangular, some m/d rounding, especially on 3rd molars | ✓ | |
| | Talonid width decreases rel to trigonid from 1st to 3rd | ✓ | Talonid relatively wider |
| C5 pres on all. Large cusps on 1st & 2nd molars | Cusp 5 and 'Y' groove pattern not invariably present, 'Y' pattern frequency decreases from 1st to 3rd molars. '+' pattern on 3rd molars | ✓+ | Cusp 5 present on all 1st & 2nd. All 'X' pattern on 3rd |
| | Cusp 5 buccally placed on 1st, medial on 2nd & 3rd | ✓+ | |
| Higher frequency | Cusp 6 found at low frequency (<½) | ✓ | Higher frequency |
| | Cusp 7 found at low frequency (<½) | ✓ | Higher freq, & higher grades, on third molar |
| | Cusp 7 grade 1A (metaconid) found (<½) | | |
| To grade 1 only | Protostylid at low level only (to grade 3) | ✓+ | Higher grades, to gr 6 |
| Grade 3 on one 3rd | Deflecting wrinkles found at grades 1-2 (<½) | ✗ | No grade 2 on 1st & 2nd |
| Not always on 1st to 3rd | Mid trigonid crest always present on 1st & 2nd molars* but less frequently on 3rd | ✓ | Present on all 3rd also |
| | Distal trigonid crest occasionally present (<½) | ✓ | Lower frequency |
| Also grade 0 on 1st | Small (grade 1) anterior foveae found on 2nd & 3rd (<½) | ✗ | All high grades (>1) |
| | Posterior fovea occasionally present (<½) | ✓ | |
| | Mesial margin present on 1st & 2nd molars but <½ on 3rd. Frequency decreases 1st to 3rd | ✓ | |
| | Enamel extensions present to grade 1 only (<½) on 1st & 2nd molars | ✓ | |
| | Buccal vertical grooves present, increasing freq first to third molar, decreasing freq positions A to E | ✓ | Higher frequency, present on all 2nd & 3rd |

Trait found on over 50 per cent of teeth unless otherwise stated. '*' indicates found on all teeth in sample including Pontnewydd. Under PN: ✓/✗; present/absent, '+'; see comments on differences in text. Only significant differences are noted under 'Earlier Middle Pleistocene' and 'Krapina'

Table 9.42. Summary of morphological traits of European Later Middle Pleistocene teeth showing these traits found at Pontnewydd and differences found in Earlier Middle Pleistocene and Krapina teeth.

| Cusp | Tooth | Earlier Mid Pleistocene | Later Mid Pleistocene | Total Mid Pleistocene | Krapina |
|---|---|---|---|---|---|
| Metacone | $M^1$ | 5 | 5 | 5 | 4 |
| | | (3, 4-5+) | (7, 4-5+) | (10, 4-5+) | (11, 3.5-5) |
| | $M^2$ | 5 | 4 | 4 | 3.5 |
| | | (5, 3.5-5) | (5, 3-5) | (10, 3-5) | (11, 3-4) |
| | $M^3$ | 3.5 | 3.5 | 3.5 | 3.5 |
| | | (3, 2-4) | (4, 3-4) | (7, 2-4) | (7, 3-4) |
| Hypocone | $M^1$ | 5+ | 5+ | 5+ | 5+ |
| | | (3, 5+) | (7, 5+) | (10, 5+) | (11, 4-5++) |
| | $M^2$ | 5 | 3.5 | 4 | 3.5 |
| | | (5, 4-5+) | (5, 1-5) | (10, 1-5+) | (10, 1-5) |
| | $M^3$ | 3.5 | 3 | 3 | 3 |
| | | (3, 3.5) | (5, 1-3.5) | (8, 1-3.5) | (5, 2-4) |
| Upper molar cusp 5 | $M^1$ | 4 | 4 | 4 | 2 |
| | | (1, 4) | (2, 3-4) | (3, 3-4) | (6, 1-3) |
| | $M^2$ | 4 | 3 | 4 | 2 |
| | | (4, 4-5) | (2, 2-4) | (6, 2-5) | (7, 1-3) |
| | $M^3$ | 5 | 4 | 4 | 3 |
| | | (2, 4-5+) | (2, 3-4) | (4, 3-5+) | (3, 2-4) |
| Lower molar cusp 5 | $M_1$ | 5 | 4 | 4 | 4 |
| | | (2, 5) | (6, 3-4) | (8, 3-5) | (12, 2-5) |
| | $M_2$ | 5 | 3 | 4 | 3 |
| | | (4, 5-5+) | (5, 2-3) | (9, 2-5+) | (11, 2-5) |
| | $M_3$ | 3 | 3 | 3 | 2 |
| | | (3, 3-4) | (5, 2-3) | (8, 2-4) | (5, 1-4) |

Number in sample, and range of values found, shown in brackets below mean.

*Table 9.43. Mean size grades of cusps.*

they are absent in *Parapithecus*. He considered the absence of any direct connection between protoconid and metaconid, as found in the majority of '*Sinanthropus*' molars, to be the real primitive stage. Against this, Zubov (1992) reports finding mid trigonid crests in *australopithecines, Homo habilis* and *Homo erectus mauritanicus*).

Distal trigonid crest – this trait occurs at a slightly higher overall frequency in Middle Pleistocene specimens than in KDPs.

Anterior fovea – the lower grades (0 and 1) of anterior fovea only occur on Middle Pleistocene teeth, particularly on second and third molars.

Buccal vertical grooves – these grooves occur at a higher frequency in KDPs than in Middle Pleistocene specimens.

All these variations, apart from groove pattern, cusp 7 and distal trigonid crest, can be identified on second molars.

WRINKLING

There is a considerable increase in the frequency of wrinkling between Middle Pleistocene and Krapina on upper and lower fourth premolars and upper molars. In lower molars, all of the earlier Middle Pleistocene specimens and KDPs exhibit wrinkling, but only half of the later Middle Pleistocene specimens.

*Conclusions regarding trends in trait grades and frequencies*

A secular decrease in the size of upper molar metacones, hypocones and cusp 5s, and lower molar cusp 5s, is apparent going from earlier Middle Pleistocene to Krapina. This is generally most marked in second molars. The decrease in the size of these cusps fits with the overall decrease observed in the size of posterior teeth over the

Pleistocene (Brace 1967; Smith 1977; Wolpoff 1982). The upper third molar is the only posterior tooth in Wolpoff's European late Middle to early Late Pleistocene sample that is larger than the corresponding Arago tooth (mean crown area of 127 mm$^2$ against 118 mm$^2$). However, it can be seen from Table 9.4 that, whilst there is a decrease in the crown areas of all upper molars (in particular the second molar) between the earlier and later Middle Pleistocene, there is an increase between the later Middle Pleistocene and Krapina. The same can be seen for lower molars (Table 9.6). Therefore, it might be expected to find a decrease in size of the metacone and hypocone (and also possibly lower molar cusp 5) going from earlier to later Middle Pleistocene, and then an increase going from later Middle Pleistocene to Krapina. As it is, there is a decrease in size of the metacone on upper first and second molars at the end of the Middle Pleistocene (Table 9.43). The decrease in size of the hypocone on the upper second and third molars (no change on the first molar) between earlier and later Middle Pleistocene is as would be expected. An approximate relationship can be found between crown area and metacone grade, but not between crown area and hypocone grade.

Trefný (2005) came to similar conclusions whilst investigating molar cusp sizes – a distinct decrease in size of upper second molar hypocones and metacones, and lower second molar cusp 5s, between the Middle Pleistocene as a whole and Krapina but, in upper first molars, a slight increase in size in hypocones and metacones and only a small decrease in size in lower first molar cusp 5s.

Many of the traits are found at higher grades, or at a greater frequency, on Krapina teeth than on Middle Pleistocene teeth:

Lower lateral incisor – stronger shovelling, lingual median longitudinal ridges and flaring; buccal surfaces more angled.

Premolars – greater frequency of multiple lingual cusps, of bifurcated buccal median ridges, and of interruption of marginal ridges by the sagittal sulcus; greater degree and frequency of double shovelling.

Upper molars – Carabelli's trait at a higher frequency, oblique ridge found on third molars.

Lower molars – greater frequency of cusps 5, 6 and 7, of mid trigonid crest and of buccal vertical grooves; stronger protostylids and only higher grades of anterior foveae present.

Wrinkling – greater prevalence on upper and lower fourth premolars and upper and lower molars.

Certain traits reduce in frequency between the Middle Pleistocene and Krapina, namely: mesiobuccal swelling, and presence of distal clefts, on lower third premolars; grade 2 metaconules; grade 2/3 deflecting wrinkles; and distal trigonid crests.

Because of the small number of earlier Middle Pleistocene teeth in the sample, changes between earlier and later Middle Pleistocene are less clearly seen. Some traits appear to be at a different level in the later Middle Pleistocene in comparison with both the earlier Middle Pleistocene and Krapina. These are:

- A high angle between buccal and lingual cusps on lower premolars;
- different frequency of mesial and distal additional buccal occlusal ridges on upper and lower fourth premolars;
- wrinkling not found on all lower molars.

Other differences between earlier and later Middle Pleistocene are:

- Lower third premolar – rotation of lingual aspect of buccal cusp, presence/absence of multiple lingual cusps, presence/absence of cingulum;
- lower fourth premolar – presence/absence of mesiobuccal swelling;
- lower molars – frequency of mid trigonid crest and of cusps 5, 6 and 7.

If Atapuerca-SH is grouped with earlier Middle Pleistocene sites, the differences become less distinct.

### Affinities of Pontnewydd teeth

The Pontnewydd teeth are very similar to other later Middle Pleistocene teeth in terms of shape, traits present and their grades. Where, in the previous sections, there is shown to be variation in the grade or presence/absence of traits, the Pontnewydd teeth are, in most cases, in good agreement with the values for later Middle Pleistocene teeth or Middle Pleistocene teeth in total. In particular:

LOWER LATERAL INCISOR
This shows a faint lingual median longitudinal ridge and no mesial flaring.

UPPER FOURTH PREMOLAR
This has a single lingual cusp; the buccal occlusal median ridge not bifurcated; and a low level of double shovelling.

LOWER PREMOLARS
Angles between cusps are at the high end of the range for the sample; there is a low level of double shovelling (not above grade 2); and there is pronounced mesiobuccal swelling on PN6 but none on PN5. On third premolars: there is rotation of the lingual aspect of the buccal cusp; multiple lingual cusps; distal marginal ridges not interrupted; predominance of distal clefts; and no cinguli. On PN5: only a distal buccal occlusal ridge is present; the mesial margin is interrupted; and there is no wrinkling.

UPPER MOLARS
These have similar sizes of metacones, of hypocones (not PN1), and of cusp 5s on third molars. Grade 2 metaconule is present. The oblique ridge is absent on the third molars. An anterior transverse ridge crest is present on third molar PN19. Only PN17 and PN19 have wrinkling and fissuration.

LOWER MOLARS
On third molars: cusp 5s are of similar size (see below); and there is a '+' groove pattern on PN21. There is no cusp 6 on the first molar (unlike most KDPs) and no cusp 7 on third molars (also unlike most KDPs). The protostylid is only found at trace level (up to grade 2) (see below). The mid trigonid crest is present on first and second molars but not on PN21. There are no buccal vertical grooves present on second molars (present in all KDPs).

There are a few differences between Pontnewydd teeth and other Middle Pleistocene teeth:

PN6 (LOWER THIRD PREMOLAR)
This is the only tooth in the whole sample (Middle Pleistocene and Krapina) on which there is no ridge across the sagittal sulcus.

PN7 (LOWER THIRD PREMOLAR)
Both cusps are mesially placed. Only Arago 13 has a mesially placed buccal cusp, and one KDP a mesially placed lingual cusp.

PN5 (LOWER FOURTH PREMOLAR)
The buccal cusp is medially placed, as it is in Arago 13 and two KDPs, but in none of the other teeth in the sample.

PN1 (UPPER SECOND MOLAR)
The grade of hypocone on this tooth is only otherwise found on upper first molars and earlier Middle Pleistocene upper second molars.

PN11 (LOWER FIRST MOLAR)
The 'X' groove pattern on this tooth is only found on two other lower first molars in the sample – Arago 13 and one KDP. The other first molars all have a 'Y' groove pattern.

PN11 (LOWER FIRST MOLAR) AND PN15 (LOWER SECOND MOLAR)

The cusp 5s are of a higher grade than those measured on other corresponding later Middle Pleistocene teeth. That on PN11 is of the same grade as those found on the two earlier Middle Pleistocene lower first molars, and the grades of both are found amongst KDPs.

The placing of the cusps on PN7 and PN5, and the groove pattern on PN11, are found in Arago 13 and in some KDPs but on none of the other later Middle Pleistocene teeth. Nonetheless, as noted before, there are dissimilarities in occlusal shape between the Arago and Pontnewydd premolars. The above differences may only be apparent because of small sample sizes, as also may other minor variations.

*Gran Dolina teeth*

Details of the morphology of the Gran Dolina teeth are taken from descriptions and photographs in Bermúdez de Castro *et al.* (1999b), Bermúdez de Castro and Sarmiento (2001) and Carbonell *et al.* (2005). In certain respects they fit in with the trends identified but in others not.

LOWER LATERAL INCISORS

The angle of inclination of the buccal surface to the vertical on both Gran Dolina lower lateral incisors is 35°, which is similar to the values found on Krapina teeth. Both incisors have distinct mesial and distal shovelling (at least grade 2), and one has mesial as well as distal flaring. The other just has distal flaring. One also appears to have a grade 2 lingual median ridge. The teeth therefore have greater similarities to Krapina teeth than to Middle Pleistocene teeth in these respects. They are similar to most teeth in the sample in having distinct labial convexity and prominent cinguli.

PREMOLARS

As observed in Middle Pleistocene teeth, the Gran Dolina upper fourth premolars both have single lingual cusps, as do the lower third and fourth premolars, which also have well developed talonids. The angles to the horizontal between buccal cusp and principal lingual cusp on Hominid 1 are: lower third premolar, 15°; lower fourth premolar, 10°. The angle of the lower third premolar is lower than those of the Middle Pleistocene and Krapina teeth, and that of the lower fourth premolar is the same as the earlier Middle Pleistocene teeth. The lingual cusp is mesially placed on both upper and lower Gran Dolina premolars. In comparison, none of the Middle Pleistocene lower third premolars has a principal lingual cusp that is so mesially placed, but the principal lingual cusp is mesial on all lower fourth premolars and also on upper fourth premolars. The buccal cusp is mesial on one Gran Dolina upper fourth premolar and medial on the other. In Middle Pleistocene upper fourth premolars the buccal cusp can also be mesial or medial. The buccal cusp is mesial on all Gran Dolina lower premolars. In Middle Pleistocene lower premolars, the buccal cusp is only mesial on Arago 13 and Pontnewydd PN7 third premolars (medial on the others),

but is mesial on most lower fourth premolars (not Arago 13 or Pontnewydd PN5). The mesial and distal marginal ridges of the Gran Dolina lower third premolars appear to be uninterrupted, as found on Middle Pleistocene lower third premolars (but not in all KDPs), and there are well defined occluso-lingual grooves/clefts. There is therefore a reasonable level of similarity between Gran Dolina and Middle Pleistocene teeth in terms of specific traits, but with some differences. Other points of similarity of Gran Dolina teeth to Middle Pleistocene teeth are: upper fourth premolars – shallow interruption of sagittal sulcus (which appears to be double in both Hominid 1 teeth), with the straight sagittal sulcus passing over it; mesial marginal tubercle present; mesial and distal margins interrupted. Lower third premolars – slight mesiobuccal prominence; sagittal sulcus interrupted (very mesially). Lower fourth premolars – mesiobuccal prominence as found on earlier Middle Pleistocene teeth (Mauer and Arago 13 specimens) but not on later Middle Pleistocene teeth (this trait is also absent on the earlier Sima del Elefante ATE9-1 lower fourth premolar (Carbonell *et al.* 2008)); mild mesiolingual flattening; posterior fovea largest and lowest; but, unlike Middle Pleistocene teeth, the mesial marginal ridge does not appear to be interrupted on Hominid 1, although it is on Hominid 7. Neither the third nor fourth lower premolars appear to have mesial or distal buccal occlusal ridges, nor bifurcation of the median ridge of the buccal cusp, but a distal ridge and a bifurcated median ridge both occur on the upper fourth premolars.

CUSP SIZE CHANGES

The photographs of the upper first and second molars from Hominid 1 show large metacones (grade 5) and hypocones (grade 5+) but the hypocone on the Hominid 3 first molar is smaller. There are no cusp 5s on Hominid 1 upper first molars, but there appear to be cusp 5s on the Hominid 3 upper first molar and Hominid 1 upper second molar, both at grade three. The cusp 5s on the Hominid 1 lower first and second molars are grade 5. Apart from upper molar cusp 5s, these grades are at the top end of the range of values found for earlier Middle Pleistocene teeth and are consistent with the changes in size over time described above.

UPPER MOLARS

The Gran Dolina upper second molar has an anterior transverse ridge, as found on most Middle Pleistocene teeth, and a crest across the mesial occlusal groove at the central fossa. This tooth has two intersections of the oblique ridge, forming what appears to be a metaconule cusp in the centre (although this could just be wrinkling). The oblique ridge is continuous on the Hominid 1 first molars but almost interrupted on the Hominid 3 first molar. Expressions of Carabelli's trait on Gran Dolina upper molars are mild, a pit on both first and second molars, similar to the grades found in Atapuerca-SH and Pontnewydd teeth.

LOWER MOLARS

There are many points of similarity of Gran Dolina Hominid

1 lower molars with Middle Pleistocene teeth. There are cusp 5s on all three molars; no cusp 6s; cusp 7 on the second molar (small, grade2/3) and on the third molar; no protostylids visible (but there is a distal deflection of the buccal groove on the second molar); no buccal vertical grooves; mid trigonid crest slight on the first molar but definite on the second molar, and also a mild distal trigonid crest on the second molar; small anterior fovea, and also a posterior fovea, present on the first molar, and a larger anterior fovea present on the second molar; 'Y' groove pattern on both first and second molars. The first molar appears to have a mesial margin but not the second molar. Both the second and third Gran Dolina Hominid 1 lower molars are wrinkled (the second mildly; the first molar is worn), as are the upper premolars and molars and the lower third premolar. The lower molars of Hominid 7 appear to have similar occlusal features to those of Hominid 1.

There is debate over whether the Atapuerca-SH population is a continuation of the Gran Dolina population, or partly or wholly replaced it (Bermúdez de Castro *et al.* 2003a; Bermúdez de Castro *et al.* 2004a; Martinón-Torres *et al.* 2007a). This has been intensified by the discovery of earlier dates for Atapuerca-SH (Bischoff *et al.* 2003; 2007). Specifically, from the dental perspective, there is the question of whether there could have been such a considerable change in tooth size, and in the morphology of the lower premolars, over such a short period, although, taking the smaller size of Hominid 7 teeth into account, the size difference is not as great as at first appeared. Bermúdez de Castro *et al.* (1999b; 2003a; 2004a) list differences between the Gran Dolina TD6 and Atapuerca-SH populations. These relate to the morphological differences described above and, in addition, for both upper and lower teeth, the relationship in the breadth of incisors to posterior teeth, and the relative sizes of first and second molars. Bermúdez de Castro *et al.* (1999b) also point out the difference in relative sizes of anterior and posterior teeth, anterior teeth from Atapuerca-SH being relatively larger than those from Gran Dolina. However, as noted above, the distinctive features of lower premolars are not as pronounced in Hominid 7 as they are in Hominid 1, and Hominid 7 has a higher level of taurodontism than has Hominid 1.

Martinón-Torres *et al.* (2006; 2007a) identify certain morphological similarities between the teeth of the two populations. There is a particular form of shovelling seen in the upper lateral incisors of some Neanderthals and at Atapuerca-SH, described as 'triangular shovel shape', that is found in an incipient form at Gran Dolina and in certain *Homo erectus* specimens. The shape of upper and lower canines at both Atapuerca-SH and Gran Dolina is a derived form that is unlike the primitive form seen in early fossil hominins. The transverse crest in lower fourth premolars, and the mesial (mid) trigonid crest on lower first and second molars, are common amongst Neanderthals and at Atapuerca-SH, and are seen at Gran Dolina, but are rare in modern humans. There are aspects of the shape of the upper first molar, described by Bailey (2004) as being typical in Neanderthals and unlike modern humans, which are seen at Atapuerca-SH and at Gran Dolina. The occlusal shape of the Gran Dolina lower fourth premolars has aspects in common with Middle Pleistocene teeth and Neanderthals. Primitive traits such as the mesially placed metaconid and asymmetry are retained, but there is reduction of the buccal portion of the talonid and in the lingual side of the tooth. This is in contrast to a more centrally placed metaconid and symmetrical outline in modern humans.

Bermúdez de Castro *et al.* (1999b; 2003a; 2004a) note aspects of the teeth of the Arago 13 specimen that are intermediate between Gran Dolina and Atapuerca-SH. On the one hand; large teeth, trace cingulum on the lower third premolar, and a lower fourth premolar root of the same form as that found at Gran Dolina but, on the other; the lower third premolar more symmetrical and without a talonid.

Carbonell *et al.* (1999) consider the archaeological arguments for replacement against continuity. Developed Mode 1 (Oldowan) lithic technologies in Europe, as seen at Gran Dolina, were replaced by developed African Mode 2 (Acheulian) technologies, as seen at Atapuerca-SH, between 500,000 and 600,000 BP, without going through the early African Mode 2 development stage. The earliest dates for both Mode 1 and Mode 2 occur in Africa, and here there is a smooth progression from Mode 1 to the archaic forms of Mode 2. The nature of the difference between the two modes in Europe, the Mode 2 industries lacking archaic characteristics, indicates that the change between them could not have been as a result of natural evolution. Moreover, some European sites have Mode 1 stratigraphically above Mode 2. Carbonell *et al.* (1999) considered, therefore, that this change, which in their view took 100,000–200,000 years to complete, was because of cultural diffusion or migration from Africa, possibly from the African Rift System.

An argument in favour of continuity is the remarkable proportionality between the occlusal measurements of the Gran Dolina and Atapuerca-SH premolar and molar teeth. Table 9.44 shows the percentage differences from Gran Dolina hominins to the Atapuerca-SH means for premolars and molars. It can be seen that the figures for mesiodistal measurements, and for buccolingual measurements, are very similar between upper third and fourth premolars, and between lower third and fourth premolars. Furthermore, for Gran Dolina Hominid 1, the figures for upper and lower first molar mesiodistal measurements, and buccolingual measurements, are very similar, and likewise for second molars.

*Possible east/west division of sites*
There are traits whose distribution suggests the possibility of an east/west split of the sites in the sample. In particular, the German sites, and Biache in the Pas-de-Calais, appear to form a geographical cluster.

| | Mesiodistal | | Buccolingual | |
|---|---|---|---|---|
| | Premolars | | | |
| | **P³** | **P⁴** | **P³** | **P⁴** |
| Hominid 1 | 5 | 5 | 9 | 11 |
| Hominid 3 | 10 | - | 12 | 10 |
| | **P₃** | **P₄** | **P₃** | **P₄** |
| Hominid 1 | 10 | 12 | 16 | 16 |
| Hominid 7 | 1 | 5 | 8 | 9 |
| | Hominid 1 molars | | | |
| | Mesiodistal | | Buccolingual | |
| | **Upper** | **Lower** | **Upper** | **Lower** |
| First molar | 8 | 8 | 12 | 12 |
| Second molar | 18 | 19 | 12 | 15 |

*Table 9.44. Percentage differences between dimensions of Gran Dolina teeth and Atapuerca-SH means.*

| | **Talonid › Trigonid** | **Trigonid = Talonid** | **Trigonid › Talonid** |
|---|---|---|---|
| First molar | 12 | 9 | 0 |
| Second molar | 10 | 9 | 4 |
| Third molar | 3 | 6 | 7 |

*Table 9.45. Relative widths of trigonid and talonid on Middle Pleistocene and Krapina lower molars.*

| | **Talonid › Trigonid** | | **Trigonid = Talonid** | | **Trigonid › talonid** | |
|---|---|---|---|---|---|---|
| | East | West | East | West | East | West |
| First molar | 80% | 15% | 20% | 85% | 0% | 0% |
| Second molar | 65% | 0% | 35% | 50% | 0% | 50% |
| Third molar | 30% | 0% | 50% | 15% | 20% | 85% |

*Table 9.46. Relative widths of trigonid and talonid on Middle Pleistocene and Krapina lower molars split between east and west.*

RELATIVE WIDTHS OF TRIGONID AND TALONID ON LOWER MOLARS

In those teeth in which the trigonid (the mesial half of the tooth) and the talonid (the distal half of the tooth) are not the same width buccolingually, the talonid is wider in:

- Mauer (first and second molars);
- Ehringsdorf adult (second molar);
- Ehringsdorf juvenile (second molar);
- Atapuerca-SH AT2 (first molar);
- Krapina KDPs (10 first molars, 7 second molars, 3 third molars).

and the trigonid is wider in:

- Mauer (third molar);
- Arago (AR13 second and third molars; AR32 second molar);
- Ehringsdorf adult (third molar);
- Montmaurin (second and third molars);
- Atapuerca-SH (AT1 second and third molars; AT13 third molar; AT75 third molar).

Data are taken from Weidenreich (1937) for the Mauer and Ehringsdorf specimens and from casts for the remainder.

Table 9.45 gives the figures for the total sample of Middle Pleistocene and Krapina teeth. It can be seen that there is a progression from first to third molars, the talonid becoming relatively narrower and the trigonid relatively wider.

This trend appears to be more pronounced in the more western sites. Second molars with a wider trigonid come from Atapuerca-SH, Montmaurin and Arago, whilst those with a wider talonid come from Mauer, Ehringsdorf and Krapina. Third molars with a wider talonid come from Krapina. This is shown in Table 9.46.

In the Gran Dolina Hominid 1 lower molars, the talonid is wider than the trigonid in the first molar and the trigonid is wider than the talonid in the second molar, which fits with the above.

VARIATIONS IN CROWN INDEX OF POSTERIOR TEETH

Of the later Middle Pleistocene specimens, those of Biache, Steinheim, Bilzingsleben and Ehringsdorf tend to have low crown indices (*i.e.* narrow teeth) in premolars and molars compared with Atapuerca-SH, Pesada and Montmaurin. This is found in particular teeth – upper fourth premolars, upper second and third molars, lower third premolars and lower first and second molars. Teeth not affected are – upper first molar, lower fourth premolar and lower third molar. All the affected teeth have crown indices at least one standard deviation below the Atapuerca-SH mean values and 80% are below the ranges of values occurring at Atapuerca-SH. In lower third premolars, upper and lower second molars, and upper third molars, seven of nine teeth are over two standard deviations below the relevant Atapuerca-SH mean. All the Montmaurin and Pesada teeth are within the Atapuerca-SH range, and all the Pontnewydd teeth other than PN1 (upper second molar), PN19 (upper third molar) and PN20 (lower third premolar), which are below range. (PN1 and PN20 are over one standard deviation below the Atapuerca-SH mean and PN19 over two). The teeth affected include all three teeth that show a distinct decrease in size compared with Gran Dolina Hominid 1 – lower third premolar and upper and lower second molars – and these are amongst the most affected.

The pattern is seen at Krapina in a less extreme form. All the Krapina means for crown index, other than those for lower fourth premolar and lower third molar, are below those of Atapuerca-SH, and the differences are most pronounced for upper second and third molars. The trend is reversed in Neanderthals, all the Neanderthal means being above those of Krapina, and all except upper third molar being above those of Atapuerca-SH. The upper third premolar shows a similar pattern, but with the crown index of the Montmaurin upper third premolar (129) being smaller than the mean (but within range) of Atapuerca-SH (134). This in turn, though, is above the mean of Krapina (132) and below the mean of Neanderthals (141), in line with the above. However, the value for the Biache upper third premolar (136) is higher than that of Atapuerca-SH.

MORPHOLOGY OF BIACHE AND STEINHEIM TEETH

The Biache and Steinheim specimens are distinctive in that the upper first molars of both specimens have grade three parastyles. These only occur at grade two or below on other Middle Pleistocene upper molars. They also show higher grades of Carabelli's trait (grades 5 and above) than are found at Petralona, Visogliano, Atapuerca-SH, Pesada or Pontnewydd (but are present at Arago). In addition, the Bilzingsleben upper first molar (C1) described by Mania and Vlček (1981) appears from the photograph to have a worn grade 5 Carabelli's cusp.

The position of Pontnewydd is intermediate in terms of trigonid and talonid widths, and of crown index, and similar to western sites in terms of lack of development of parastyles and Carabelli's trait.

*Dating of the Montmaurin mandible*
The size of the cusp 5s on the molars of this mandible suggests a later, rather than an earlier, Middle Pleistocene date. Grades 3 and 2 on first and second molars respectively are at the low ends of the ranges for later Middle Pleistocene teeth and compare with grades 5/5+ on the earlier Middle Pleistocene teeth. Grades 1–3 on lower third molars compare with grades 2 and 3 on other later Middle Pleistocene teeth, and grades 3 and 4 on the earlier Middle Pleistocene teeth.

There are no traits present that might suggest an earlier Middle Pleistocene date, *e.g.* lack of a mid trigonid crest on first or second molars. There are also no traits suggesting affinities with Krapina, *e.g.* presence of a large protostylid. This fits with some views on the age of this fossil (reviewed in Stringer *et al.* 1984).

*Arago 21*
Stringer *et al.* (1984) group western European fossils into three in terms of modern human or Neanderthal apomorphies (*i.e.* advanced characteristics). In this, Arago 13 is placed with Mauer and Bilzingsleben as having no apomorphies and Arago 21 is placed with Steinheim, Montmaurin, Atapuerca-SH and others as having more debatable affinities.

The metacone sizes on the upper first to third molars of Arago 21 (4, 3.5/3 and 2 respectively) are smaller than those on the other earlier Middle Pleistocene teeth, and would fit better with the ranges of values found for the later Middle Pleistocene sample. In contrast, the hypocone grade of 3.5 on the third molar is relatively large and the same as that on the Petralona specimen, larger than those on the later Middle Pleistocene teeth other than Biache and Pesada. The sizes of the cusp 5s on second and third molars are also large (grade 4) but this grade is found on both earlier and later Middle Pleistocene teeth.

*Comparisons with recent human teeth*
It is noteworthy that almost all the crown morphological traits studied here, and described by the authors listed in Appendix A as occurring on recent teeth, occur on these Middle Pleistocene teeth. Exceptions are:

- odontomes, not found;
- hypocone absence on upper molars (grade 0). The lowest grade found is grade 1;
- parastyle, only found at low grades (to grade 3);
- protostylids, only found at trace level (to grade 3) but found at higher grades on Krapina teeth;
- enamel extensions, only found on lower molars and not above grade 1.

Irish and Guatelli-Steinberg (2003) have studied African fossil hominins – *Paranthropus, Australopithecus,* and *Homo* (*habilis, rudolfensis, ergaster/erectus* and indeterminate) – and found no odontomes, no hypocone absence (grades 0 and 1) on upper second molars and no enamel extensions on upper first molars, and concluded that these were derived traits and not ancestral. Parastyles on upper third molars at any grade were only found in *Australopithecus africanus*. Odontomes are a rare trait in recent teeth, principally occurring on East Asian and American teeth at a frequency of up to 7% (Scott and Turner 1997).

Bailey (2002b) notes traits that are missing on Neanderthal and other fossil hominin lower premolars – more than two lingual cusps, and presence of a buccal cusp bifurcated median ridge, on lower third premolars, and the lack of a well-defined lingual cusp on either lower premolar – and suggests that these are possibly modern human derived traits. They are not found in the Middle Pleistocene sample, or at Krapina. Traits are mostly present in the form described but there is greater variation in double shovelling and anterior transverse ridge. Scott and Turner (1997) review occurrence rates for certain traits in recent populations. These traits are listed below, along with the occurrence rates for the Middle Pleistocene sample (including the Pontnewydd teeth). Also given is the rate for mid trigonid crest (Wu and Turner 1993):

- Hypocone absence, upper second molar, grades 0–1; 10%;
- cusp 5, upper first molar, grades 1–5; 55%;
- Carabelli's trait, upper first molar, grades 5–7; 20%;
- enamel extensions, upper first molar, grades 2–3; 0%;
- groove pattern, lower second molar, 'Y'; 65%;
- hypoconulid (cusp 5) absence, lower first molar, grade 0; 15%;
- hypoconulid absence, lower second molar, grade 0; 25%;
- cusp 6, lower first molar, grades 1–5; 15%;
- cusp 7, lower first molar, grades 1–4; 20%;
- deflecting wrinkle, lower first molar, grade 3; 0%;
- distal trigonid crest, lower first molar, present; 35%;
- mid trigonid crest, lower first molar, present; 90%.

Most of the occurrence rates are within the ranges reported for recent teeth, the rate for cusp 5 absence on lower first molars being a little above (recent human range 0–10%), and that for grade 3 deflecting wrinkle on lower first molars being a little below (recent human range 5–40%). The two exceptions are mid trigonid crest (as noted by Bailey 2001; 2002a) and distal trigonid crest. The occurrence rates for these traits in recent teeth are very much lower, at 0–13% and 0–20% respectively. The rates for upper first molar cusp 5, lower second molar 'Y' groove pattern, and lower first molar cusp 7, are at the high end of ranges for recent teeth and similar to those found in sub-Saharan teeth. Scott and Turner (1997) identify three crown traits for which sub-Saharan Africans occupy an extreme position – 'Y' groove pattern, cusp 7 and mesial canine ridge. The high occurrence rate for upper first molar cusp 5 is shared with Sahul-Pacific. The lack of enamel extensions is unlike Sino-American and Sunda-Pacific groups (as is the frequency for cusp 6). Other groups have rates of 10% or under for enamel extensions. The rate for hypoconulid absence on lower first molars is similar to that of western Eurasia but the rate for lower second molars is more similar to other groups. The occurrence rates for the remaining traits are not specific to particular recent groups.

Ludwig (1957) published rates of occurrence of certain traits on lower fourth premolars for recent humans, split into ethnic groups. These traits are listed below, along with the rates of occurrence for the Middle Pleistocene sample:

- Single lingual cusp; 30%;
- two lingual cusps; 30%;
- three or more lingual cusps; 40%;
- buccal cusp – additional mesial ridge only; 0%;
- buccal cusp – additional distal ridge only; 70%;

- buccal cusp – both mesial and distal additional ridges; 15%;
- buccal cusp – median ridge bifurcated; 55%;
- sagittal sulcus interrupted; 75%.

The occurrence rates for additional distal ridges are higher than those for additional mesial ridges in recent humans, as they are in the Middle Pleistocene. The occurrence rate for Middle Pleistocene 'distal ridge only' is at the top of the range of 30–70% for recent humans. The rate for median ridge bifurcated is higher for the Middle Pleistocene (recent humans 5–40%), as is that for multiple lingual cusps (noted by Bailey 2002a for Neanderthals). The 'recent human' range for three or more lingual cusps is only 0–5% (Ludwig did not observe more than three lingual cusps in his sample) and the range for single cusps is 45–100%. The other occurrence rates are within the ranges for recent humans.

Bailey (2002b) investigates the occurrence of a number of other traits in groups of fossil hominin teeth and a range of contemporary anatomically modern human groups. These are listed below, along with the percentage frequency found in the Middle Pleistocene sample. In all those marked by an asterisk, the frequency for the trait in the Middle Pleistocene sample is above the range of frequencies found in the contemporary human groups.

- Upper fourth premolar – mesial and/or distal additional ridges on buccal cusp; 50%, buccal cusp median ridge bifurcated; 30%*, mesial accessory marginal tubercles; 20%, distal accessory marginal tubercles; 15%;
- Lower third premolar – multiple lingual cusps; 35%, position of principal lingual cusp; 55% distal*, mesial additional ridge on buccal cusp; 0%, distal additional ridge on buccal cusp; 85%*, sagittal sulcus interrupted; 100%*;
- Lower fourth premolar – mesiolingual occlusal flattening; 40%*, multiple lingual cusps; 70%, position of principal lingual cusp; 100% mesial*;
- Upper first molar – mesial marginal cusps; 40%;
- Upper second molar – mesial marginal cusps; 65%, cusp 5; 60%, Carabelli's trait above grade 2; 50%*;
- Lower first molar – anterior fovea present at any grade; 90%*;
- Lower second molar – cusp 6; 10%, cusp 7; 30%*, deflecting wrinkle (grades 1–3); 20%*, mid trigonid crest; 80%*, distal trigonid crest; 10%*, anterior fovea present at any grade; 100%*.

Certain aspects of the lower third premolar reflect the findings for the lower fourth premolar – additional distal ridges on the buccal cusp more frequent than additional mesial ridges (as with recent human teeth) and frequency of additional distal ridges higher than the range found in contemporary modern groups. Similarly, the lower second molar is like the lower first molar in having high frequencies of cusp 7, mid trigonid crest, distal trigonid crest and anterior fovea. In almost all cases where the frequency of a trait in the Middle Pleistocene sample is above those found in contemporary modern human groups, Bailey (2002b) finds the same is the case for a sample of

| Trait | African Fossil Hominins  % | European Middle Pleistocene  % | Krapina  % |
|---|---|---|---|
| Hypocone absence, $M^2$, grades 0-1 (D) | 0 | 10 | 10 |
| Cusp 5, $M^1$, grades 1-5 (A) | 70 | 55 | 65 |
| Carabelli's cusp, $M^1$, grades 5-7 (A) | 40 | 20 | 70 |
| Parastyle, $M^3$, grades 1-5 | 5 | 50 | 55 |
| Enamel extension, $M^1$, grades 2-3 (D) | 0 | 0 | 0 |
| Odontome present, premolars (D) | 0 | 0 | 0 |
| No. of lingual cusps, $P_4$, grades 2-9 | 80 | 70 | 100 |
| Groove pattern, $M_2$, equals 'Y' (A) | 95 | 65 | 60 |
| Cusp 5 absent, $M_2$, grade 0 (D) | 0 | 25 | 0 |
| Cusp 6, $M_1$, grades 1-5 | 5 | 15 | #85 |
| Cusp 7, $M_1$, grades 1-4 (exc 1A) (A) | 60 | 20 | *45 |
| Protostylid, $M_1$, grades 1-6 | 55 | 55 | 15 |
| Deflecting wrinkle, $M_1$, grade 3 (D) | 0 | 0 | 0 |
| Mid trigonid crest present, $M_1$ | 55 | 90 | 90 |
| Distal trigonid crest present, $M_1$ (D) | 10 | 35 | 10 |
| Anterior fovea, $M_1$, grades 2-4 | 95 | 90 | 100 |

The figures for African fossil hominins have been rounded to the nearest five per cent
European Middle Pleistocene includes Pontnewydd but excludes Gran Dolina
# This figure is higher than those given by Irish (1998) and Bailey (2000) for the occurrence rate of cusp 6 on lower first molar at Krapina.
* The higher figure quoted in Stringer *et al.* (1997) includes grade 1A.

*Table 9.47. Morphological crown traits in African fossil hominins compared with European Middle Pleistocene and Krapina teeth.*

Neanderthals. Exceptions are sagittal sulcus interrupted on lower third premolars, distal trigonid crest on lower first molars and deflecting wrinkle on lower second molars. (See also Coppa *et al.* (2005) and Bailey (2006) for a discussion on Neanderthal tooth morphology).

*Comparisons with African and Asian fossil hominin teeth*

Irish and Guatelli-Steinberg's (2003) pooled sample of gracile African fossil hominins – *Australopithecus africanus* and *Homo* (*habilis, rudolfensis, ergaster/erectus* and indeterminate) – is compared with the European Middle Pleistocene and Krapina samples in Table 9.47.

Scores for traits considered by Irish and Guatelli-Steinberg (2003) to be ancestral (marked [A] in Table 9.47) are generally lower in the European Middle Pleistocene and Krapina samples than in the African sample, particularly in the European Middle Pleistocene. Traits that Irish and Guatelli-Steinberg (2003) consider to be derived (marked D in Table 9.47) are either absent in the Middle Pleistocene and Krapina samples or (with two exceptions) at a low level. Major differences are – the higher scores for cusp 5 absence on lower second molars, and distal trigonid crest on lower first molars, in the Middle Pleistocene; the high scores for Carabelli's cusp on upper first molars, and cusp 6 on lower first molars, at Krapina; the low score for protostylid on lower first molars at Krapina, which is because of a lack of any at grade 1; and the increase in the scores for parastyle on upper third molars, and mid trigonid crest on lower first molars, in both the Middle Pleistocene and the Krapina samples.

Wood and Engleman (1988) studied upper premolars and

upper molars in similar samples of African fossil hominins – EAFHOM (*Homo habilis* and *ergaster*) and SAFGRA (*Australopithecus africanus*) and found that:

- The median longitudinal fissure (sagittal sulcus) in upper fourth premolars is usually uninterrupted, unlike the Middle Pleistocene and Krapina samples;
- cusp 5 occurs on all three molars other than EAFHOM first molars, and is found on all third molars, the frequency increasing from first to third. The highest frequency of occurrence in the Middle Pleistocene sample is also on the third molar;
- Carabelli's trait occurs at above trace level on all three molars (other than in EAFHOM first molars), as found in the Middle Pleistocene and Krapina samples, but, contrary to these, occurs at higher frequencies on second and third molars than on first molars. In addition, unlike the later teeth, the highest grade is in the form of an enamel shelf (cingulum) rather than being a cusp;
- the oblique ridge is present (continuous or divided) on all EAFHOM molars, but divided on all SAFGRA first molars, and divided or absent on SAFGRA second and third molars. The pattern is not, therefore, as clear-cut as in the Middle Pleistocene sample.

Wood and Abbott (1983) studied the lower molars in the same samples and noted that:

- Second and third lower molars predominantly either have 'Y' or '+' groove patterns, as is the case with the Middle Pleistocene third molars;
- the incidence of cusp 6 on lower molars increases distally, none being found on first molars. Again this is reflected in the Middle Pleistocene sample, where

the greatest frequency of cusp 6 is on third molars;

- cusp 7s are similarly less frequent on first molars than on second and third molars, with none on SAFGRA first molars;
- well-developed protostylids occur on all three lower molars, the highest frequency being on the third molar, like Krapina but completely unlike the Middle Pleistocene sample.

Wood and Uytterschaut (1987) studied the lower premolars in the same samples and noted that:

- Lower third premolars only have a single lingual cusp and lower fourth premolars have no more than two lingual cusps, unlike the Middle Pleistocene and Krapina samples;
- the position of lingual cusps on both premolars is predominantly distal, as found with the third premolar in the Middle Pleistocene sample but not with the fourth premolar. The EAFHOM sample, in particular, has no mesially placed lingual cusps on either premolar, and all the lingual cusps on the fourth premolars are distally placed;
- the median longitudinal fissure (sagittal sulcus) is absent or interrupted on all third premolars, but either uninterrupted or interrupted on fourth premolars, both as with the later teeth;
- mesiobuccal and distobuccal marginal grooves (double shovelling) are found on both premolars, most frequently on the third premolar, and more frequently distally than mesially on the fourth premolar, the reverse of the situation in the Middle Pleistocene sample. Mesiolingual and distolingual grooves are also present, at a lower frequency.

Robinson (1956) had previously studied the sample of *Australopithecus africanus* and observed traits that can be found on later teeth:

- Lingual median ridges occur on lower lateral incisors;
- upper fourth premolars have mesial and distal buccal grooves (double shovelling) associated with a buccal cingulum;
- an anterior crest joining the paracone and protocone can occur on upper first and third molars, defining a distinct anterior fovea (as found on Middle Pleistocene and Krapina teeth in association with the anterior transverse crest);
- single or double metaconule cusps can occur on upper third molars;
- posterior foveae can occur on lower first molars;
- it appears, from the illustration, that there is a mesiodistal crest across the anterior fovea on a lower molar, as seen in later teeth. Some anterior foveae are double.

Bailey (2002b) has studied a sample of east and north African and Chinese *Homo erectus* and recorded a number of other traits:

- Crown asymmetry, because of mesiolingual flattening, of lower third and fourth premolars. Not ubiquitous for either tooth;

- additional mesial and distal occlusal ridges on buccal cusps of upper and lower premolars, and buccal median ridge bifurcated on upper premolars. Distal ridges are more frequently found than mesial ridges on lower premolars, as also recorded for Middle Pleistocene and Krapina teeth;
- sagittal sulcus sometimes, but not always, interrupted on lower third and fourth premolars. The rate of interruption is lower than in the Middle Pleistocene teeth (80 against 100% for the third premolar and near 40 against 75% for the fourth premolar) ;
- mesial accessory marginal tubercles on upper fourth premolars. (Mesial tubercles are also the most common in the Middle Pleistocene and Krapina samples);
- mesial marginal cusps on upper second molars;
- deflecting wrinkle at grades 1–3 on lower first and second molars, the frequency being higher on first molars, as found on Middle Pleistocene and Krapina teeth.

Bailey (2002b) concludes that, since these traits are found on both Neanderthal and anatomically modern human teeth, they can be considered as being primitive characteristics. The lingual cusp on lower third premolars is predominantly centrally placed in this sample, unlike the Wood and Uytterschaut (1987) samples and the Middle Pleistocene sample. It is normally placed mesially on lower fourth premolars, as with all the Middle Pleistocene and Krapina teeth but again unlike the Wood and Uytterschaut (1987) samples. Hypocones are present on all upper second molars, as found in Irish and Guatelli-Steinberg's (2003) pooled sample of gracile African fossil hominins. The frequency of cusp 6s is higher on lower second molars than on first molars, as observed in EAFHOM and SAFGRA samples but, unlike these, occurs at a frequency of near 30% on first molars. Distal trigonid crests only occur on lower second molars (third molars not scored) and then only at a rate of near 10%. Grade 0 anterior foveae (*i.e.* absent), as is seen on the Mauer lower first molar, are found on both first and second molars.

The increase over time in the number of cusps on lower premolars is evident in lower third premolars. Wood and Uytterschaut's (1987) samples have single lingual cusps, as does Bailey's (2002b) sample of *Homo erectus* and, likewise, the Gran Dolina teeth. The Middle Pleistocene sample can have up to two lingual cusps (on Atapuerca-SH and Pontnewydd teeth), as is the case with the Krapina teeth and Bailey's (2002b) Neanderthal sample. More than two lingual cusps are only seen in anatomically modern humans (see comments in Bailey 2002b). Similarly, lower fourth premolars in Wood and Uytterschaut's (1987) samples have no more than two lingual cusps, likewise Gran Dolina (single cusps), whereas multiple lingual cusps are found in the Middle Pleistocene and Krapina samples (and in modern humans).

There is, therefore, a considerable level of continuity apparent in the above, the majority of traits studied being ancestral.

## *Asian influences on the Pleistocene colonization of Europe*

Martinón-Torres *et al.* (2007b) have analysed non-metric crown morphological traits of late Pliocene and Pleistocene hominins from Africa, Asia and Europe using a sample of over 5,000 teeth. Both phenetic analysis (based on 51 traits) and cladistic analysis (based on nine traits) grouped Asian *Homo erectus* with European Pleistocene species and separated these from African species. The exception to this was that the cladistic analysis placed the Dmanisi hominins closer to the African species. These authors identify contrasting aspects of the African and Eurasian anterior and posterior dentitions. The Eurasian anterior dentition is more robust than the African, with greater expression of 'mass additive' traits such as shovel shape and canine mesial ridge. Conversely, the African posterior dentition has the 'mass additive' traits, *e.g.* higher frequencies of accessory cusps than is found in Eurasians. Other traits also have very different frequencies in the two groups, for instance mid trigonid crest, and transverse crest in lower fourth premolars, occur more often in the Eurasian group than in the African group. These authors conclude that 'the evolutionary courses of the Eurasian and the African continents were relatively independent for a long period' and that 'the genetic impact of Asia in the colonization of Europe during the Early and Middle Pleistocene was stronger than out of Africa'.

Rolland (1992), in investigating the archaeological and geographical evidence, concludes that the hypothesis of an 'out of central Asia' route for the early colonization of Europe is more cohesive than other options and without data incompatibility. It would also identify hominin dispersal with the Galerian faunal dispersal from Asia into Europe. Rolland (1992) considers that this conclusion provides the only plausible explanation for European non-handaxe (Mode 1) industries (see also Aguirre and Carbonell 2001). In contrast, Lycett and Cramon-Taubadel (2008) argue that the presence of Mode 1 industries in Europe could be the result of skills loss in small groups, due to complex cultural elements not being passed on to subsequent populations, and point to the presence of 'Acheulian-like' elements in Mode 1 industries such as the Clactonian of Britain as supporting this interpretation.

Several authors have linked the Gran Dolina hominins to Chinese Middle Pleistocene fossils and *Homo erectus* from Java, and therefore consider that they are descended from the earliest emigrants out of Africa (reviewed in Aguirre and Carbonell 2001; Aguirre 2007). Bermúdez de Castro *et al.* (1997; 1999b), though, see the Gran Dolina fossils as having a place mid-way between *Homo ergaster* and *Homo heidelbergensis* (based in large part on dental characteristics). Bermúdez de Castro *et al.* (2007) compared the dental morphology of the Gran Dolina hominins to North African Middle Pleistocene populations (principally the contemporary site of Tighennif and the later site of Rabat) and concluded from this, and from the shape of the mandibles, that they are distinct hominin lineages, the North African group having greater similarity to *Homo ergaster* than to the

Gran Dolina fossils. Unlike the North African group, Gran Dolina hominins have certain derived dental characteristics that are seen in European Middle Pleistocene specimens and in *Homo neanderthalensis*. The recently reported mandible ATE9-1 from Sima del Elefante at Atapuerca, 'the first hominin of Europe', dated at 1,200,000–1,100,000 BP, has been provisionally grouped with the Gran Dolina hominins (Carbonell *et al.* 2008). These authors similarly suggest that, from the form of the mandible, the first settlement of Western Europe could be from the east and related to an early expansion out of Africa.

## Conclusions to the chapter

### *Measurements*

The measurements given for the occlusal outline of European permanent teeth show a decrease in tooth size through the Middle Pleistocene that is most marked in upper and lower second molars and lower third premolars and, to a lesser extent, lower fourth premolars. This trend, though, is reversed in going from the later Middle Pleistocene to the site of Krapina. A decrease in size of the upper premolars (principally in length) is evident in the later European Neanderthal sample, compared with earlier material.

The Pontnewydd teeth measurements (with the exception of PN12) are more consistent, in terms of relative size, with other individual later Middle Pleistocene and Atapuerca-SH material than they are with earlier or later material. For instance, they show a similar relative decrease in size compared with Hominid 1 from the earlier site of Gran Dolina. However, with the exception of the very small PN12, they are generally large compared with individual later Middle Pleistocene and Atapuerca-SH teeth, and are more consistently within the range of sizes found in teeth from earlier Middle Pleistocene sites. The upper fourth premolar, and the lower first and second molars, are particularly large compared with those of Atapuerca-SH. With certain exceptions (notably the small size of Neanderthal upper fourth premolars), the Pontnewydd teeth are similar in size to the means of the Krapina and Neanderthal samples. This is most evident in the lower teeth. PN12 is smaller than all the other individual Middle Pleistocene teeth and those from Krapina, but within the range of values found at Atapuerca-SH and in the Neanderthal sample.

The decrease in size in the Middle Pleistocene is generally more marked in the decrease of breadth, leading to narrower teeth. In contrast, in the Pontnewydd upper and lower second molars (and those of Atapuerca-SH and Krapina), the decrease in length compared with the Gran Dolina Hominid 1 teeth is greater.

The Pontnewydd teeth are similar in shape to the means of Atapuerca-SH, Krapina and Neanderthals, but with some exceptions that are notably narrower – one upper third molar compared with Atapuerca-SH, one lower third premolar compared with Krapina and both lower third molars compared with Neanderthals. They tend to be narrower than the Gran Dolina and earlier Middle Pleistocene individual specimens and similar in shape to the later Middle Pleistocene individual specimens.

The sizes and shapes of the different Pontnewydd teeth (other than PN12) are seen to be very consistent when compared with other individual specimens and the means of groups. This suggests that they come from a closely related group of individuals.

A tentative explanation for the large difference in size of the two upper first molars, PN4 and PN12, and the small size of PN12 compared with other teeth, is sexual dimorphism. As a result of comparing Pontnewydd tooth sizes with those of Atapuerca-SH; PN12, and the smaller of the upper third molars (PN19), are considered to be possibly female and the remainder possibly male.

A Penrose size and shape coefficient test demonstrates that the Pontnewydd teeth have the greatest affinity in terms of shape to those of Atapuerca-SH and, to a slightly lesser extent, Krapina, and least to Neanderthals and early Upper Palaeolithic. The greatest affinity in terms of size is to Krapina, with scarcely any difference apparent. The shape distances from Pontnewydd, and from Atapuerca-SH, to Krapina, Neanderthals and EUP are similar to each other and indicate a secular trend.

Certain other measurements and indices show a progression from early hominins to recent humans – length/crown height index (decreasing), root robusticity (decreasing), ratio of crown area divided by root robusticity (increasing), root length (decreasing). For the Pontnewydd Middle Pleistocene teeth:

- The length/crown height indices calculated for third molars and lower premolars are lower than the means for 'Sinanthropus' but within the range of means for groups of recent humans. Those of the premolars are similar to those measured from Atapuerca-SH;
- root robusticities are (with the exception of upper second molar PN1, which is higher) within the range of values found in 'Sinanthropus' and above the means for recent human teeth. Apart from PN12, they are high compared with those of the few Atapuerca-SH teeth measured and those of the Ehringsdorf specimens;
- the ratio of crown area to root robusticity is low, lower in all cases than the means for 'Sinanthropus' and well below the mean figures for recent teeth;
- root lengths of both Pontnewydd and Atapuerca-SH teeth are similar to the range of values reported for 'Sinanthropus', below the values for Gran Dolina and earlier teeth, and above, or at the high end of the ranges of, the mean lengths of recent teeth.

The deciduous tooth (PN4) is relatively small compared with the PN4 permanent tooth. Its crown area (corrected for wear) is mid-way between the means of a 'late Middle/early Late Pleistocene' sample and a late Neanderthal sample. Its crown index is the same as the mean of the Krapina sample. The uncorrected measurements are nearly identical to a similarly worn tooth from Ehringsdorf. The root length and root robusticity figures are high compared with the means for recent teeth.

The Mesolithic teeth are consistent in size with a sample of European Mesolithic male teeth and well above the means for recent European teeth. The root robusticity, and ratio of crown area to root robusticity, of PN2 are similar to the means for recent teeth, and the length/crown height index of this tooth is nearly identical to the mean for recent European teeth.

## Wear

The horizontal wear of the Pontnewydd molars is consistent with that encountered in a sample of European Middle and Late Palaeolithic teeth. The form of the wear seen on the molars is similar to that found at Atapuerca-SH and at other Middle Pleistocene sites. It is unlike that found at Krapina and at the earlier Middle Pleistocene sites of Mauer and Petralona. There is cupped (concave) wear of the enamel, and the phase 1 facets tend to be larger than the phase 2 facets and display a greater degree of wear. This suggests a diet requiring a shearing action rather than a crushing action (*e.g.* leaf stems and other fibrous material rather than seeds and nuts, *etc.*). The degree of phase 1 facet wear on the Pontnewydd teeth is at the top end of the spectrum for later Middle Pleistocene teeth. Wear is from distal to mesial on lower molars (the reverse of that encountered at Krapina and on the Mauer specimen) and from mesial to distal on upper molars. Exposed dentine is worn normally (unlike the two earlier sites of Mauer and Petralona, at which the dentine is excavated out). The rate of wear appears to be similar to that of Atapuerca-SH but higher than on certain other later Middle Pleistocene specimens, *e.g.* Biache, Steinheim and Ehringsdorf, and higher than at Krapina. The flat wear seen on the lower incisor, PN10, is unlike the rounded wear found on many Neanderthal teeth. Polished areas occur on occlusal surfaces, as well as clearly visible pitting and buccolingual scratches. The level of chipping is high in comparison with other reference groups, and there is evidence of split teeth, suggesting the presence of hard objects in the diet. The type and pattern of chipping on some teeth (especially on the lingual surface of lower first molar PN11 and on the buccal cusp of lower fourth premolar PN5), the presence of 'cut-marks' on the lower lateral incisor and lower fourth premolar, and a groove on lower second molar PN13, is suggestive of non-masticatory use. The buccal and lingual surfaces have predominantly vertical scratch-marks but also horizontal, and some areas of polish. Subvertical grooves occur on several of the interproximal facets. These are considered to be typical of Neanderthals, and are similar in form and frequency to those at other reference sites.

## Oral health and pathology

Oral health appears to be good, with only a trace of dental calculus on one tooth and, as would be expected, no caries. In addition, the bite appears to be normal, there being only mild misalignment. Nevertheless, the dentition is very uneven, all the erupted premolars being distally tilted and/or rotated, the crypt of one upper premolar misaligned, one lower premolar possibly impacted and another possibly transposed. Mild hypoplasia occurs on four teeth (this is at a higher rate than that found at Atapuerca-SH but lower than in a sample of Neanderthals), and mild hypercementosis on the roots of two teeth. There are a series of grooves of unknown origin on the mesial surface of the root trunk of the lower first molar PN11, and polish on the mesial surface of the root trunk of the upper second molar PN1.

### Number of individuals

When ageing the Middle Pleistocene teeth, and grouping them into individuals, two approaches were taken; firstly, a normal recent human dental development pattern was assumed, but with an occlusal eruption age of 15 for third molars, and the eruption of second molars preceding the eruption of premolars; secondly, a late Neanderthal dental development pattern based principally on juveniles from the sites of Scladina and Le Moustier with teeth at a similar stage of development to those at Pontnewydd. The 17 teeth plus a tooth fragment can be grouped into a minimum of five individuals: based on recent human dental development criteria: two 11 year olds, a 12–13 year old, an 18–20 year old and a mature adult; based on late Neanderthal dental development criteria: an 8.5 year old, a 9 year old, an 11–11.5 year old, a 14–16 year old and a mature adult. One 11/9 year old is tentatively put as being female and the others tentatively as male. The maximum possible number of individuals is sixteen (nine juveniles/adolescents, five young adults and two mature adults). The age range is in line with those found at Atapuerca-SH and Krapina. The two Mesolithic teeth are considered to have come from the same individual, an adolescent aged 14–15 years.

The find-spots for the teeth indicate a lack of mixing within the Lower Breccia that, along with the good condition of the teeth, suggests that their original position was probably within the cave and that they have only travelled a short distance. However, the small proportion of the theoretical number of teeth discovered, along with the almost complete lack of bone, suggests that the remains in their original location were probably already fragmentary, although still discrete within individual.

### Morphology

#### Roots

The roots of the Pontnewydd teeth are very similar in form to those of Atapuerca-SH teeth, specific morphological characteristics being found on both. Taurodontism occurs in all the Pontnewydd molars with roots, apart from one lower molar (PN13). The degree of taurodontism is similar to that encountered in many other later Middle Pleistocene teeth and, as with Atapuerca-SH, is greater in the upper molars than in the lower molars. The Middle Pleistocene teeth studied only have the milder supraradicular form of taurodontism, not the more extreme radicular and total taurodontism seen in Krapina teeth and in certain later Neanderthals.

#### Crown

The overall characteristics of the Pontnewydd teeth are very similar to other later Middle Pleistocene teeth, which, in most respects, form a cohesive group. Earlier Middle Pleistocene teeth can, in some cases, be different in appearance (*e.g.* Arago lower premolars).

Traits defined as being common to European Middle Pleistocene hominins, such as marked lingual inclination of the buccal face of lower incisors, and large hypocones on upper first molars, are all found on the Pontnewydd teeth. Other traits defined as being shared by eastern Asian and north-west African Middle Pleistocene teeth, but not seen in European Middle Pleistocene teeth, such as buccal cinguli on premolars and molars, and two-rooted lower premolars, are absent. Pontnewydd teeth have certain traits which differentiate *Homo heidelbergensis* and *Homo neanderthalensis* from Gran Dolina and other fossil hominins, in particular related to lower premolars, *e.g.* mild against strong asymmetry of lower third premolars. Traits commonly encountered on Neanderthal teeth, such as mid trigonid crest and asymmetry of the lower fourth premolar crown, are found on the Pontnewydd teeth and other Middle Pleistocene teeth. Others, such as the shape and proportions of the occlusal polygon in upper first molars, differ. The relatively large size of the protocone on Pontnewydd upper second and third molars is notable.

Certain traits show a variation in occurrence over time. Some differences can be seen between earlier and later Middle Pleistocene teeth; for instance, on earlier teeth, the presence of a mesiobuccal swelling on lower fourth premolars, and a lower incidence of mid trigonid crest. A few traits appear to be at a different level in later Middle Pleistocene teeth compared with earlier and later teeth, *e.g.* angle between buccal and lingual cusps on lower premolars, and the extent of wrinkling on lower molars. Many traits occur at a higher level or greater frequency at Krapina (*e.g.* multiple lingual cusps on premolars, Carabelli's trait and protostylids) but others are less frequent (*e.g.* metaconules). There is a clear secular progression seen in the average sizes of metacones, hypocones and upper and lower cusp 5s.

With some exceptions, the traits found on the Pontnewydd teeth are consistent with those found on later Middle Pleistocene teeth, as against earlier Middle Pleistocene or Krapina teeth. Exceptions include small differences in lower premolars, the presence of a large hypocone on the upper second molar PN1, and large cusp 5s on lower molars. The last two of these are in accord with the fact that the Pontnewydd teeth are large compared with other later Middle Pleistocene teeth.

The Atapuerca-SH teeth fit better with later Middle Pleistocene teeth than with earlier Middle Pleistocene teeth in that, if they are included with the 'later' group, the differences between 'earlier' and 'later' are clearer cut.

In comparing the Gran Dolina teeth with Middle Pleistocene teeth, certain traits in the Gran Dolina teeth confirm the trends seen in later teeth, *e.g.* large metacones, hypocones and lower molar cusp 5s, low angles between

| Cusp location | Tribosphenic system name | Dental anthropology name |
|---|---|---|
| **Upper** | | |
| Mesiolingual | Protocone | Cusp 1 |
| Mesiobuccal | Paracone | Cusp 2 |
| Distobuccal | Metacone | Cusp 3 |
| Distolingual | Hypocone | Cusp 4 |
| **Lower** | | |
| Mesiobuccal | Protoconid | Cusp 1 |
| Mesiolingual | Metaconid | Cusp 2 |
| Distobuccal | Hypoconid | Cusp 3 |
| Distolingual | Entoconid | Cusp 4 |

_Table 9.48. Molar cusp terminology (after Hillson 1996)._

buccal and lingual cusps on lower premolars, a mesiobuccal prominence on the lower fourth premolar, and single lingual cusps on premolars. However, the reverse applies with the lower second incisors. These have a greater similarity to those of Krapina. A number of traits commonly found on Middle Pleistocene teeth occur on the Gran Dolina teeth, _e.g._ mid trigonid crest. The proportionality of occlusal dimensions between Gran Dolina specimens and Atapuerca-SH means could be taken as evidence of continuity between the two populations.

There is tentative evidence of an east/west split of Middle Pleistocene and Krapina teeth, shown in:

- The relative width of trigonid and talonid on lower molars, particularly second molars, the talonid tending to be wider at the eastern sites and the trigonid at the western sites;
- variations in crown index, teeth from more eastern sites having a tendency to be narrower (_i.e._ lower crown indices);
- the similarities between Biache, Steinheim and Bilzingsleben in the development of Carabelli's trait and parastyles, as against most other Middle Pleistocene sites.

Pontnewydd teeth are intermediate.

Almost all the studied morphological traits that have been described as occurring in recent human teeth are found on the Middle Pleistocene teeth. A few, though, are only found at a low level (_e.g._ parastyles, protostylids and enamel extensions) and others are altogether absent (_e.g._ bifurcated median ridge, and more than two lingual cusps, on lower third premolars). In comparison to recent teeth, the occurrence rates for mid and distal trigonid crests are high on Middle Pleistocene teeth; as are those for median ridge bifurcated on upper and lower fourth premolars, and multiple lingual cusps on lower fourth premolars, amongst others. Certain traits occur at a higher rate than in recent humans on second molars, _e.g._ cusp 7. The rates for upper first molar cusp 5, 'Y' groove pattern on lower second molars, and cusp 7 on lower first molars, are similar to modern sub-Saharan teeth, but groups to which there are similarities vary between different traits. A large number of the traits studied are found in samples of African fossil

hominins and therefore are considered to be ancestral, whilst others, such as three cusped upper second molars and four cusped lower second molars, are not and are therefore thought to be derivative.

Despite the small number of teeth in the Pontnewydd sample, these are very informative because, in general, they are well-preserved, relatively unworn, and represent a good range of teeth, at least for the posterior dentition. They are also among the best-dated dental samples for the Middle Pleistocene.

## Appendix A

### _Molar cusp terminology (after Hillson 1996)_

Described in Table 9.48

### _Descriptions of morphological traits_

References referred to below against particular traits are:

| | |
|---|---|
| A: | Turner _et al._ (1991) |
| | Scott and Turner (1997) |
| B: | Jordan _et al._ (1992) |
| C: | Kraus and Furr (1953) |
| D: | Ludwig (1957) |
| E: | Kanazawa _et al._ (1990) |
| F: | Reid and Van Reenen (1995) |
| G: | Wood and Engleman (1988) |
| H: | Korenhof (1960) |
| I: | Weidenreich (1937) |
| J: | Zubov (1992) |
| K: | Wu and Turner (1993) |
| L: | Grine (1981) |
| M: | Lasker (1950) |

Where a trait is scored as present or absent, '0' is entered for absent and '1' for present.

_1 Shovelling_

Teeth: upper and lower incisors and canines.

Definition: the presence of lingual marginal ridges.

Scoring: scored in terms of the strength of the ridges; 0 (none), 1–6 (faint to marked shovel) and 7 (barrel-shaped) for upper incisors, and 0 (none) and 1–3 (faint to marked shovel) for

lower incisors. Additionally, the ridges can be scored as being non-convergent (near vertical) or convergent (ridges nearly in contact at the cingulum).
Reference plaques: ASU UI1, UI2 and lower I shovelling.
Reference: A.

*2 Double shovelling*
Teeth: upper and lower incisors, canines and premolars.
Definition: the presence of labial marginal ridges. These are separated from the body of the tooth by single shallow vertical grooves.
Scoring: 0 (none), 1–6 (faint to extreme double shovel). The mesial and distal sides are scored separately for the present study.
Reference plaque: ASU UI1 double shovelling.
References: A, C.

*3 Labial convexity*
Teeth: upper and lower incisors.
Definition: the labial surface of the incisor, when viewed from the occlusal aspect, can range from being essentially flat to showing a pronounced degree of convexity.
Scoring: 0 (flat) to 4 (pronounced convexity).
Reference plaque: ASU UI1 curvature.
Reference: A.

*4 Lingual median longitudinal ridge*
Teeth: lower incisors and canines.
Definition: a longitudinal ridge in the centre of the lingual surface. This may be on the lower part of the lingual surface only or reach the occlusal edge.
Scoring: 0 (not present), 1 (ridge not continuous), 2 (ridge continuous from cingulum to occlusal edge).
Reference plaque: none.
Reference: M.

*5 Mesial and distal flaring*
Teeth: lower incisors.
Definition: the mesial and distal margins of lower incisors may be vertical (in line with the root) or flared mesially/distally.
Scoring: flaring present/absent. Mesial and distal margins scored separately.
Reference plaque: none.
Reference: B.

*6 Positions of cusps*
Teeth: upper and lower premolars.
Definition: the positions of the buccal and principal lingual cusps in relation to the buccolingual longitudinal axis of the tooth at the cervix. (This differs from the definition used for the position of the lingual cusp(s) by Kraus and Furr (1953) and Ludwig (1957). They determined its position relative to the long axis of the median occlusal ridge of the buccal cusp).
Scoring: for each cusp; 1 (mesial), 2 (distal), 3 (medial).
Reference plaque: none.
Reference: none.

*7 Additional buccal occlusal ridges*
Teeth: upper and lower premolars.
Definition: the occlusal surface of the buccal cusp may have accessory transverse ridges in addition to the median ridge. These are roughly parallel to, and shorter than, the median ridge, and may be mesial or distal. The median ridge itself may have a uniform appearance throughout its course, or it may divide near its base into two or more secondary ridges.

Scoring: present/absent. Mesial ridge, distal ridge and median ridge bifurcated are each scored separately. Ridges at trace level, which are only visible on newly erupted teeth, are not scored.
Reference plaque: none.
References: C, D, A2.

*8 Sagittal sulcus interrupted (premolar transverse crest)*
Teeth: upper and lower premolars.
Definition: the mesiodistal occlusal developmental groove may be continuous, or be interrupted by one or, very rarely, more enamel ridges connecting the buccal and lingual cusps.
Scoring: groove continuous (0) or interrupted (1) and, if a ridge is present, the lingual cusp to which it connects and whether or not it reaches its tip.
Reference plaque: none.
References: C, D.

*9 Marginal ridges interrupted*
Teeth: upper and lower premolars.
Definition: the sagittal sulcus may end in the anterior/posterior fovea, leaving the marginal ridge uninterrupted, or a continuation may pass over or through the marginal ridge.
Scoring: 0 (ridges continuous), 1 (mesial marginal ridge interrupted), 2 (distal marginal ridge interrupted), 3 (both marginal ridges interrupted).
Reference plaque: none.
Reference: B.

*10 Odontomes*
Teeth: upper and lower premolars.
Definition: a cone-like projection that emanates from the median occlusal ridge of the buccal cusp.
Scoring: present/absent.
Reference plaque: none.
Reference: A.

*11 Lingual ridging/grooving*
Teeth: upper and lower premolars.
Definition: multiple vertical ridging/grooving of the lingual surface, mainly towards the centre.
Scoring: present/absent.
Reference plaque: none.
Reference: none.

*12 Accessory marginal tubercles*
Teeth: upper premolars.
Definition: an accessory cusp on the marginal ridge, at the mesial and/or distal ends of the sagittal sulcus. These are only scored if they are strongly separated from both buccal and lingual cusps.
Scoring: present/absent. Mesial and distal cusps recorded separately.
Reference plaque: none.
Reference: A.

*13 Lingual cusp variation*
Teeth: lower premolars (also noted for upper premolars).
Definition: the number of lingual cusps present and their size relative to each other.
Scoring: the ASU system records the number of cusps present, up to three, and their relative size. A (no lingual cusp), 0 (one lingual cusp), 1 (one or two lingual cusps), 2–7 (two lingual cusps and their relative size, with mesial relatively very large at code 2, distal at code 7 and cusps of equal size at code 4), 8–9 (three lingual cusps, cusps of equal size at code 8, mesial cusp much larger than medial and/or distal at code 9).

Reference plaques: ASU LP1 cusp and LP2 cusp.
References: A, (C and D).

### 14 Occluso-lingual grooves
Teeth: lower premolars.
Definition: a groove that passes from the occlusal surface onto the lingual aspect of the tooth. Generally, this will be between lingual cusps. The groove may be in the form of a distinct cleft.
Scoring: number of a) mesiolingual or medial and b) distolingual grooves recorded separately, and whether or not they are clefts.
Reference plaque: none.
Reference: C.

### 15 Wrinkling
Teeth: upper and lower premolars and molars.
Definition: additional multiple occlusal ridges present and/or normal occlusal ridges distorted. In this study, additional ridges and bifurcated ridges on lingual cusps of premolars are scored as wrinkling.
Scoring: recorded as mild (1) or distinct (2) and by cusp. Prominent normal ridges are recorded separately.
Reference plaque: none.
Reference: none.

### 16 Metacone
Teeth: upper molars.
Definition: the distobuccal cusp scored for presence/absence and size.
Scoring: 0 (absent), 1 (attached ridge is present but no free apex), 2, 3, 3.5, 4, 5 (cusp present, from faint cuspule to very large). Scored as 5+ or 5++ if size exceeds grade 5 on reference plaque.
Reference plaque: ASU metacone (cusp 3).
Reference: A.

### 17 Hypocone
Teeth: upper molars.
Definition: the distolingual cusp scored for presence/absence and size.
Scoring: as for metacone.
Reference plaque: ASU hypocone (cusp 4).
Reference: A.

### 18 Mesial marginal cusps
Teeth: upper molars.
Definition: there are three types of accessory tubercle that may appear on the mesial margin:
1. Mesial paracone tubercle – expressed as an independent part of the mesial accessory ridge of the paracone.
2. Protoconule – hypertrophied mesial accessory ridge of the protocone, with an independent cusp tip.
3. Mesial accessory tubercle – on mesial marginal ridge, between mesial paracone tubercle and protoconule.
Scoring: each cusp scored as present/absent, and size recorded using reference plaque for upper molar cusp 5.
Reference plaque: none.
References: A2, E.

### 19 Cusp 5 (postentoconule)
Teeth: upper molars.
Definition: may be present on the distal marginal ridge, between the metacone and the hypocone, usually delimited by two adjacent grooves on the distal aspect of the tooth. Multiple cusps may be found, especially on third molars.
Scoring: 0 (absent), 1–5 (size grade of cusp, faint cuspule to

medium sized cusp). Scored as 5+ if size exceeds grade 5 on reference plaque.
Reference plaque: ASU UM cusp 5.
Reference: A.
Note: there has been confusion over the name of this cusp and several authors have wrongly referred to it as the metaconule. See Scott and Turner (1997) and Reid and Van Reenen (1995) for a discussion on this and also Hershkovitz (1971) for a general discussion on cusp homologues.

### 20 Carabelli's trait
Teeth: upper molars.
Definition: a feature appearing on the lingual or mesiolingual surface of the protocone.
Scoring: 0 (site smooth), 1 (groove present), 2 (pit, not in lingual groove), 3–4 (Y-shaped depression), 5–7 (small to large cusp).
Reference plaque: Zoller Laboratory Carabelli's cusp.
Reference: A.

### 21 Parastyle
Teeth: upper molars.
Definition: a feature appearing on the buccal surface of the paracone, and sometimes on the buccal surface of the metacone.
Scoring: scored in either position; 0 (sites smooth), 1 (pit in or near buccal groove), 2–5 (small to very large cusp), 6 (free peg-shaped crown).
Reference plaque: ASU parastyle.
Reference: A.
Note: grade 2 is described as a small cusp with an attached apex, but on the reference plaque it is very distinctive. There is an intermediate feature between grades 1 and 2, consisting of two vertical grooves, which are not convergent, with a bulge between them but no clearly defined cusp. For the present study, this has been scored as grade 2 and distinct cusps with a free apex as grade 3 or above.

### 22 Oblique ridge
Teeth: upper molars.
Definition: the ridge connecting the protocone and the metacone may be continuous, divided by a developmental groove or absent.
Scoring: 1 (ridge continuous, developmental groove may pass over it), 2 (ridge divided in two by developmental groove), 3 (ridge absent).
Reference plaque: none.
References: G, H.

### 23 Metaconule
Teeth: upper molars.
Definition: crescent shaped swellings on the side of the oblique ridge (usually distal, sometimes mesial), or a small, single or double cuspule situated on the oblique ridge (or on the site of the oblique ridge).
Scoring: 0 (absent), 1 (slight curve on side of oblique ridge), 2 (distinct curve), 3 (isolated single or double cuspule).
Reference plaque: none, but pictures in reference.
Reference: F.

### 24 Anterior transverse ridge
Teeth: upper molars.
Definition: a complex of traits, principally relating to the median (lingual) ridge of the paracone (mesiobuccal cusp). The most common form is defined by Jordan et al. (1992) as 'an elongated cusp-like prominence extending diagonally from the mesiobuccal

corner between the mesial marginal ridge and the triangular ridge of the mesiobuccal cusp'. This is equivalent to the lingual paracone tubercle defined by Kanazawa *et al.* (1990). Korenhof (1960) defines five forms:

1. Lingual paracone ridge connects with the mesial marginal ridge (may link to mesial paracone tubercle or mesial accessory tubercle).
2. Distinct ridge, mesially from the lingual paracone ridge, not connected with the marginal ridge and not directed distally.
3. Complete crest from tip of paracone to mesial marginal ridge.
4. Uninterrupted connection from tip of the paracone to tip of the protocone.
5. C-shaped crest between two localities on the mesial marginal ridge.

In other variations; a) the prominence may not be connected to the lingual paracone ridge, b) it may be double, c) it may run distally and d) an offshoot running lingually may form a crest across the mesial end of the mesial occlusal groove.

Scoring: Korenhof type, whether prominence is/is not connected to mesial marginal ridge or lingual paracone ridge, and variations described above, including combinations.
Reference plaque: none.
References: B, E, H.

### 25 Marginal ridges interrupted
Teeth: upper molars.
Definition: the buccal, lingual, mesial and distal marginal ridges may be continuous (uninterrupted), or the occlusal groove may pass either over the margin or through it. The anterior and posterior foveae may or may not be pit-like.
Scoring: 0 (marginal ridge continuous), 1 (occlusal groove passes over margin), 2 (margin intersected by occlusal groove). Deep pits in anterior or posterior foveae separately recorded as present/absent.
Reference plaque: none.
References: B, H.

### 26 Enamel extensions/pearls
Teeth: upper and lower molars.
Definition: enamel extensions are projections of the enamel border (which is normally horizontal) in an apical direction, usually on the buccal side, sometimes lingual and sometimes distal. Pearls are islands of enamel found on roots, which are not attached to the crown.
Scoring: enamel extensions on buccal side of crown; 0 (absent), 0.5 (trace <1 mm long), 1–2 (*c.* 1 or 2 mm long), 3 (4+ mm long). Pearls; present/absent.
Reference plaque: none.
Reference: A.

### 27 Groove pattern
Teeth: lower molars.
Definition: the pattern formed by the occlusal fissures. Recorded in terms of which major cusps are in contact.
Scoring: Y; cusps 2 and 3 (mesiolingual and distobuccal) are in contact
+; cusps 1 to 4 are all in contact
X; cusps 1 and 4 (mesiobuccal and distolingual) are in contact.
Reference plaque: none.
Reference: A.

### 28 Cusp 5 (hypoconulid)
Teeth: lower molars.

Definition: occurs on the distal occlusal aspect between the hypoconid and the entoconid. A single cusp in this position is assumed to be a cusp 5.
Scoring: 0 (no occurrence), 1–5 (size grade, very small to very large). Scored as 5+ if size exceeds grade 5 on reference plaque. Position of cusp also recorded (medial/buccal).
Reference plaque: ASU LM cusp 5.
Reference: A.
Note: Some authors (*e.g.* Bermúdez de Castro 1993) score a single distal cusp as a cusp 6 if it is derived from the distal lobe of the entoconid.

### 29 Cusp 6 (entoconulid)
Teeth: lower molars.
Definition: occurs on the distal occlusal aspect lingual to cusp 5.
Scoring: scored by size relative to cusp 5; 0 (absent), 1 and 2 (cusp 6 smaller), 3 (cusps equal in size), 4 and 5 (cusp 6 larger).
Reference plaque: ASU LM cusp 6.
Reference: A.

### 30 Cusp 7 (metaconulid)
Teeth: lower molars.
Definition: occurs in the lingual groove between the metaconid and the entoconid.
Scoring: 0 (absent), 1 (faint cusp and associated additional lingual groove), 1A (tipless cusp occurs as a bulge on the lingual surface of cusp 2), 2–4 (small to large cusp with a free apex).
Reference plaque: ASU cusp 7.
Reference: A.
Note: grade 1A may occur with grades 1–4. Some authors do not consider grade 1A to be a true cusp 7, preferring the term post-metaconulid (Scott and Turner 1997).

### 31 Protostylid
Teeth: lower molars.
Definition: a paramolar cusp found on the buccal surface of the protoconid, and normally associated with the buccal groove between cusps 1 and 3.
Scoring: 0 (absent), 1 (pit occurs in the buccal groove), 2 (buccal groove is curved distally), 3–6 (groove extending mesially from buccal groove with increasing strength), 7 (cusp with free apex).
Reference plaque: Zoller Laboratory protostylid.
Reference: A.
Note: a pit or pits (placed horizontally) or a short horizontal groove, occurring on the mesiobuccal corner of the buccal surface, may also be treated as a trace protostylid.

### 32 Deflecting wrinkle
Teeth: lower molars.
Definition: constriction or distal deflection of the median ridge of the metaconid.
Scoring: 0 (absent, ridge straight and either runs to the developmental groove between the mesial cusps or to the central fossa), 1 (mid-point constriction), 2 (deflection), 3 ('L' shaped deflection, with median ridge making contact with cusp 4).
Reference plaque: ASU deflecting wrinkle.
Reference: A.

### 33 Mid trigonid crest
Teeth: lower molars.
Definition: the median ridges of the mesial cusps (protoconid and metaconid) link to form a crest across the mesial occlusal groove.

Scoring: present/absent. The reference plaque differentiates between crests with a sharp edge and those with a rounded edge.
Reference plaques: ASU LM and dlm mid trigonid crest.
References: J, K.

### 34 Distal trigonid crest

Teeth: lower molars.
Definition: the distal ridges of the protoconid and the metaconid link to form a crest across the mesial occlusal groove.
Scoring: present/absent.
Reference plaque: Hanihara deciduous l. second molar d. trigonal crest.
References: A, J.

### 35 Anterior fovea

Teeth: lower molars.
Definition: a buccolingually elongate fossa, lying immediately distal to the mesial border on the occlusal surface, and bounded distally by the mesial or median ridges of the mesial cusps.
Scoring: 0 (absent), 1–4 (increasing depth and length of fossa).
Reference plaque: ASU anterior fovea LM1.
Reference: A.

### 36 Posterior fovea

Teeth: lower molars.
Definition: a fossa (pit or buccolingual groove) lying immediately mesial to the distal border on the occlusal surface. This may be placed centrally or lingually.
Scoring: present/absent.
Reference plaque: none.
Reference: L.

### 37 Mesial margin

Teeth: lower molars.
Definition: the mesial margin may be present as an enamel ridge, or as one or more tubercles, or be absent. It may have one or more grooves passing over it.

Scoring: margin present or absent. Number of grooves passing over margin recorded.
Reference plaque: none.
Reference: B.

### 38 Distal margin

Teeth: lower molars.
Definition: the distal margin between cusp 4 and cusps 3/5/6 (as present) may be present or absent, and may or may not be crossed by the distal occlusal groove.
Scoring: 0 (margin present, distal groove does not pass over it), 1 (margin present and distal groove passes over it), 2 (margin absent).
Reference plaque: none.
Reference: B.

### 39 Buccal surface vertical grooves

Teeth: lower molars.
Definition: vertical grooves may occur on the buccal surfaces of the protoconid, the hypoconid and cusp 5. They are wide and well-defined, and run the whole height of the crown. On the protoconid and the hypoconid they may occur mesially and/or distally and may be multiple.
Scoring: scored as present/absent in each of five positions, A to E (cusp 1 mesial, cusp 1 distal, cusp 3 mesial, cusp 3 distal, cusp 5 mesial). Additional grooves and ridges recorded.
Reference plaque: none.
Reference: I.

### 40 Crenulations

Teeth: all teeth.
Definition: on recent teeth the enamel near the cingulum on the buccal and/or lingual surfaces may have a crenulated appearance.
Scoring: present/absent.
Reference plaque: none.
Reference: none.

# 10. Pontnewydd Cave: the Characterization, Petrology, Taphonomy and Interpretation of the Archaeological Finds

*Stephen Aldhouse-Green, Richard E. Bevins, Heather Jackson, Rick Peterson and Elizabeth A. Walker with a note by Tim Young*

*Study of the character and taphonomy of the artefact assemblage at Pontnewydd Cave suggests that the bulk of the hominin occupation took place outside the modern cave system, although not necessarily outside the Pleistocene system. Hard rocks were used for making many of the 1,284 artefacts recovered from Pontnewydd; alongside a small flint component. The majority of the raw materials used would have been locally available and need not have been transported far by the hominins. Many different debris flow movements have moved artefacts from this original site of deposition. The surviving assemblage is technologically very consistent and may represent a single extended phase of occupation, or possibly a palimpsest of short occupations.*

## The taphonomy and interpretation of the lithic artefacts

*Stephen Aldhouse-Green, Rick Peterson and Elizabeth A. Walker*

### Densities of artefacts in the cave and their interpretation

The currently accessible area of the debris flow-filled Main Cave runs 30 m from the entrance to the Cross Rift. It is easy to map changing frequencies of artefacts between these two points using the numbered component of the grid squares to define a succession of metre-wide transects running from north to south. Table 10.1 shows that the greatest concentrations of finds occur where side passages enter the Main Cave from the south. The difficulties of working in these generally narrow side passages – in particular, a lack of space and the frequent problem of avoiding excavating in one's own shadow – means that we have not achieved a complete view of the immediate source of the deposits which now fill them. It is clear, however, that both the South-East Fissure and the Cross Rift run on a slight downhill gradient from the Main Cave. The South-East Fissure can also be seen to narrow rapidly as it moves south from the Main Cave. It is likely, therefore, that the side passages were infilled from the Main Cave, rather than from their entrances in the external southern cliff face. Accordingly, the higher densities of finds in these 'side passage zones' most probably relates to the locally larger quantities of sediment available for excavation in these areas.

### The characterization of the artefacts

The typological analysis of the artefacts at Pontnewydd was a primary concern of the 1984 monograph (Green 1984b). Our focus now lies more closely with the *langage sans paroles* of the artefacts: in other words, with our capacity to use the evidence of the context, condition, chronology, typology and raw materials in order to enable us to understand their taphonomies equally in the use of the site by carnivores (including hominins) and in the sedimentary processes, in which the human and animal residues were eventually to become embedded. And all this is, of course, set against an evolutionary backdrop of climate, landscape, mammalian faunas, hominins, and of the cave itself.

With little doubt most, perhaps even all, of the rocks used for artefact manufacture – the commonest being rhyolite, fine silicic tuff, other tuffs, feldspar-phyric lava, ignimbrite and flint – have been moved often from quite distant sources by natural glacial action, in the form of boulders, cobbles or pebbles to the vicinity of the cave where they were accessed

| Grid squares | Upper Breccia & above | Lower Breccia | Intermediate complex | USG | Totals n | Totals % n=323 | Comment |
|---|---|---|---|---|---|---|---|
| 0 | 7 | 5 | - | - | 12 | 3.7 | 0–1 Cross Rift 4.9% |
| 1 | 5 | - | - | - | 5 | 1.5 | |
| 2 | 2 | - | - | - | 2 | 0.6 | 2–6 East Passage 13.3% |
| 3 | 7 | - | - | - | 7 | 2.2 | |
| 4 | 7 | 8 | - | - | 15 | 4.6 | |
| 5 | 6 | - | - | - | 6 | 1.9 | |
| 6 | 3 | 7 | 3 | - | 13 | 4.0 | |
| 7 | 37 | 50 | 2 | - | 89 | 27.5 | 7–8 SE Fissure 45.1% |
| 8 | 15 | 42 | - | - | 57 | 17.6 | |
| 9 | 2 | 12 | - | - | 14 | 4.3 | |
| 10 | 2 | 10 | - | - | 12 | 3.7 | |
| 11 | - | 2 | - | - | 2 | 0.6 | |
| 12 | 4 | 6 | - | - | 10 | 3.1 | 12–14 South Passage 9.5% |
| 13 | 1 | 16 | - | - | 17 | 5.2 | |
| 14 | 1 | 3 | - | - | 4 | 1.2 | |
| 15 | - | - | - | - | 0 | - | |
| 16 | - | - | - | - | 0 | - | |
| 17 | - | - | - | - | 0 | - | |
| 18 | - | - | - | 1 | 1 | 0.3 | |
| 19 | - | 2 | - | - | 2 | 0.6 | |
| 20 | 12 | 1 | 1 | 1 | 15 | 4.6 | 20–21 South Fissure 14.7% |
| 21 | 27 | 6 | - | - | 33 | 10.2 | |
| 22 | 6 | - | - | - | 6 | 1.9 | |
| 23 | - | - | - | - | 0 | - | |
| 24 | - | - | - | - | 0 | - | |
| 25 | - | - | - | - | 0 | - | |
| 26 | 1 | - | - | - | 1 | 0.3 | |
| **Totals** | **145** | **170** | **6** | **2** | **323** | | |

See figure 6.2 for a map of the numbered grid squares and the metre-wide transects which they subtend.
Note that the central axis of the Guard Chamber runs from square 27 westwards to square 30.

*Table 10.1. Pontnewydd Cave, Areas BCDF all artefacts showing varying frequency with depth into the cave.*

by the hominins. There is evidence of deliberate selection of raw materials by the Pontnewydd hominins, who also re-thought their knapping strategies in the light both of the varying sizes of the cobbles or pebbles available, as also of the flaking characteristics of the different rocks used (Green 1988). Thus, bifaces and other heavy-duty tools were preferentially made of rhyolite and feldspar-phyric lava, whereas scrapers show high incidences of the use of flint and fine silicic tuff. There is some evidence too that fine silicic tuff – which, of all the volcanic rocks, most closely approaches the flaking qualities of flint – was brought to the site in the form of roughed-out cores which were later removed by the tool-makers for re-use elsewhere. Most or all other raw materials seem to have been readily available at or near the cave and to have been worked on

the spot and then abandoned. There is no evidence from earlier Palaeolithic Wales for trade or exchange, with the possible exception of fine silicic tuff at Pontnewydd where, in any event, transport may have been very local, since glacially derived pebbles are involved and the rock is known to occur in the pre-archaeological levels of the cave itself. This evidence for no more than a very local traffic in raw materials during earlier Palaeolithic times is consistent with what is known from Europe, where 50 km would normally be the limit of such activity (Stringer and Gamble 1993, 174). Low levels of movement of this order are supported by a recent study mapping the occurrences of artefacts deemed to be the result of the activities of individual specialists or maybe 'schools' (Hardaker 2006); the maximum distance was 44 km. Consideration is given

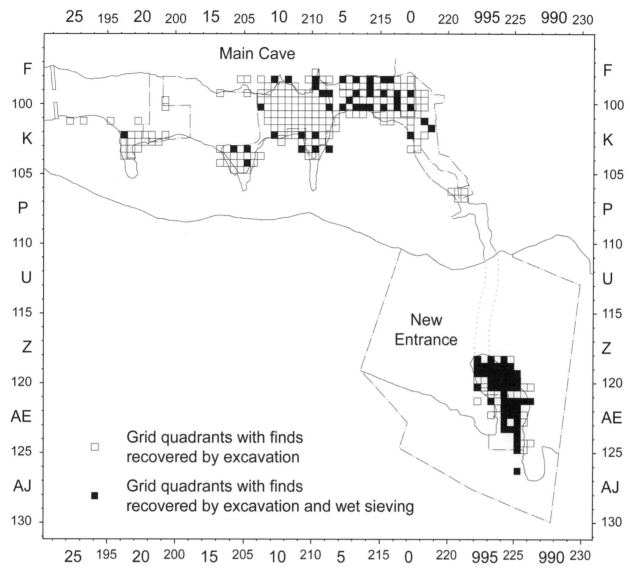

*Figure 10.1. Pontnewydd Cave. Recovery of artefacts, hominin remains and fauna from stratified deposits in the Main Cave and the New Entrance.*

elsewhere in this volume (Aldhouse-Green chapter 13) to the possibility that a small number of andesite artefacts may have been introduced from elsewhere by human agency.

A further possibility is that selected artefacts, thought to be beautiful or powerful or simply useful, were hidden in special places in the landscape either singly or in caches. We may note here Potts's argument (1988) for the existence of raw material caches spaced across the landscape at Olduvai Gorge as early as the beginning of the Pleistocene. Such 'stores', if re-discovered much later, may have provided templates for the reproduction of obsolete artefact forms.

### Taphonomy

Study of the patterning of the lithics, hominin remains and fauna within the debris flow layers has the potential to increase understanding of the nature of the original Pleistocene occupation at Pontnewydd. Throughout this section only finds recovered by excavation from *in situ*

cave deposits have been considered and, in consequence, artefacts, hominins and fauna from the Dump deposits in Area A have been excluded.

Several factors must be borne in mind when attempting to identify and interpret any patterning in the distributions of artefacts and fauna. The most important of these is the sampling strategy applied in each of the excavated areas of the cave. Figure 10.1 shows how the increasing use of wet-sieving in the later seasons of the fieldwork has led to a much higher proportion of finds from Area F and, especially, from the New Entrance. This has particular and obvious implications for the recovery of the smaller pieces of lithic debitage as well as for the smaller faunal species. Another important factor is the possibility that more massive objects may have been transported differentially in the debris flows, moving either more or less than lighter pieces, and so distorting the distributions. Figure 10.2 shows the distribution of *in situ* lithic finds from the cave, with the pieces divided into three categories by mass. The distribution of finds appears to be independent of mass.

| Find no. | Context | Specimen | Pres. type | Comment |
|----------|---------|----------|------------|---------|
| F21 | Upper Breccia | Bear left $M_1$ | III | Displays clear mark from a stone blade but stands alone as evidence for a Last Glacial human presence |
| D3960 | Lower Breccia | Bear vertebra | I | Certain: cut-marks indicate skinning |
| D1569 | Lower Breccia | Cervid canine | I | Certain |
| D1632 | Lower Breccia | Horse metapodial | I | Possible: cut-marks indicate filleting |
| D3813 | Silt beds/Lower Breccia interface | Horse podial | ? | 'Charred'; most likely context is Lower Breccia |
| H3235 | Layer 34 | Indeterminate | n/a | Chop-marks visible |

*Table 10.2. Certain and possible cut-marked bones.*

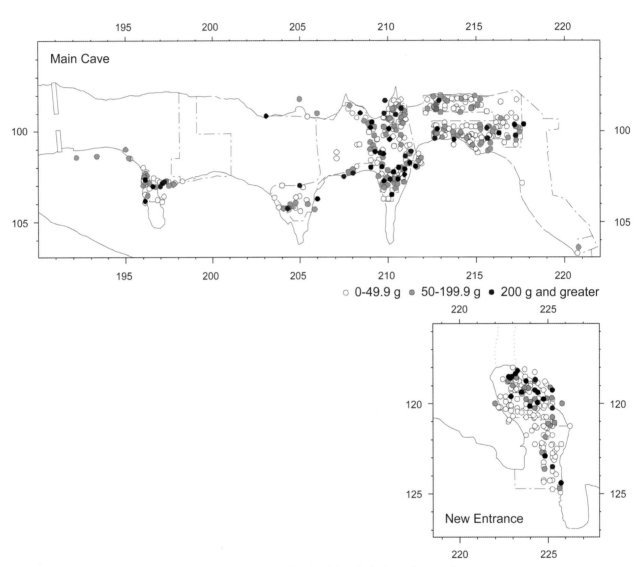

*Figure 10.2. Distribution of* in situ *lithic finds from the cave by mass.*

*The taphonomy of tool-use at Pontnewydd*

Visual examination of a limited number of the Pontnewydd faunal specimens by Jill Cook, Roger Jacobi and Ruth Charles during 1998 led to agreement that just six specimens display unequivocal evidence for human modification (Table 10.2). The quantity of bones displaying human modification is therefore small when seen as a proportion of the faunal remains found at Pontnewydd.

The marks that are visible are, however, important to our understanding of the use of stone tools by the hominins at Pontnewydd. Lyman has noted that humans will exploit animals to extract resources, be they energy (food), or materials for tools or clothing (1994, 294). The cut-marks on a bear vertebra, D3960, are consistent with skinning and bear skins would have provided a useful resource for clothing. A horse metapodial, D1632, has cut-marks

| Find no. | Context | Specimen | Pres. type |
|----------|---------|----------|------------|
| D4318 | Upper Breccia | Bear left radius (gnawed) | I |
| F542 | Upper Breccia | Bear deciduous canine | III |
| F283 | Upper Breccia | Bear deciduous canine | III |
| F1122 | Upper Breccia | Reindeer metacarpal | III |
| F1500 | Upper Breccia | Bear deciduous canine | III |
| F5207 | Lower Breccia | Bear deciduous canine | I |
| D94 | Lower Breccia | Bear left $M_2$ | I |
| D386/7 | Lower Breccia | Bear left metapodial | I |
| D2559 | Lower Breccia | Horse cuneiform | I |
| D5074 | Lower Breccia | Bear left incisor | I |
| D4578 | Lower Breccia | Bear right $M_2$ | I |
| C126 | Lower Breccia | Horse left metapodial | I |
| B47 | 'Breccia' | Horse left unciform | I |
| B2 | 'Breccia' | Reindeer phalange (gnawed) | III |

*Table 10.3. Possible 'cut-marked bones', but more likely to be natural.*

close to the proximal articulation which are indicative of filleting, the removal of meat from the bone for food. One charred horse podial indicates the incorporation of this one specimen into a fire, either natural or deliberate, at some stage in its history. An indeterminate bone found in the New Entrance deposits has chop-marks visible on it. These features are generally associated with axe use for dismembering of carcasses (Binford 1981, 110). Cut-marks on teeth are less commonly referenced in the literature, as the cranium tends mainly to be used for the extraction of the tongue for food and the rest of it is discarded. Two teeth do however, show cut-marks, these are a canine tooth of an undetermined cervid and a lower first molar of a bear. The latter is significant for it comes from a Last Glacial context with the preservation type typical of such a context. This makes it the sole evidence from the site for a human presence at this date. A further six specimens originating from the Upper Breccia were examined but were all rejected as displaying cut-marks and instead the marks were agreed to be natural (Table 10.3). This leaves it open to question if the single cut-mark on the bear molar from the Upper Breccia is indeed genuine. The specimens that were rejected as natural were disregarded due to the complex taphonomic history of the bones that were transported in the debris flow events. A large amount of the surface layers of the bones has been removed during the processes of emplacement of the deposits within the cave and the presence of sharp stones and angular clasts may also have left their mark on some of these specimens. The taphonomic history of the specimens and the destructive forces of the debris flow events have wreaked their havoc on the faunal assemblage, as noted by Currant (chapter 8, this volume). It is therefore fair to assume that there were once many more bones amongst the original assemblage that were used by the hominins, but which have now lost all traces of their past use due to subsequent taphonomic processes.

*Taphonomy of the lithic assemblage*

ROLLING AND TRANSECTUAL FREQUENCIES
Examination of the degree of 'rolling' exhibited by the artefacts (Green 1988), led to three conclusions:

- That the degree of rounding increased with distance from the entrance into the Main Cave;
- that, even so, such differences could not be shown to be significant in a statistical sense;
- that the likely cause was *in situ* solutional rounding rather than rolling during transport into the cave by natural agencies.

However, the latter interpretation was based on the scanning electron microscopy study of only two artefacts (Green 1984b, 115). Further study is needed, but we would now favour the 'rolling hypothesis' on the grounds that the intensity of the rounding of the artefacts co-varies with distance into the Main Cave.

PROVENANCES AND BIOGRAPHIES OF THE LITHIC ARTEFACTS
Sedimentary studies indicate that the lithic material at Pontnewydd was likely to have been moved into the cave from sites outside the Main and New Entrances (Mourne and Case chapter 5, this volume). Thus, it seems probable that we are dealing with the remains of relatively short-lived occupations of restricted areas (Green 1984b, 114) outside the present cave system; although not necessarily outside the Pleistocene system. One piece of evidence which seemed to hint at a longer timescale for Pontnewydd was that of artefacts which had been re-struck through a patinated surface which had developed over earlier working. However, study of such re-worked pieces (Table 10.4) shows the following provenances:

- Main Cave unstratified    2
- Main Cave Upper Breccia    1
- New Entrance Stalagmite spread (20, 22)    1
- New Entrance Limestone Breccia (23, 24, 26)    4

In other words, not one of these artefacts comes from a certain Middle Pleistocene context, nor can any be demonstrated to be of that age on typological grounds. Indeed, one could not wholly rule out the possibility that these artefacts may be of Last Glacial Neanderthal age.

THE CHAÎNE OPÉRATOIRE
Comparing the distributions of cores and debitage with those for formal tools and retouched pieces (Figure 10.3), it

| Find no. | Context | Description | Material/ condition | L | B | Th | Wt |
|---|---|---|---|---|---|---|---|
| A149 | Unstratified | Crude core (retouched through patina) | Rhyolitic tuff | 60 | 55 | 25 | 86.9 |
| A532 | BD | Disc core (2 phases of patina) | Fine silicic tuff | 62 | 55 | 18 | 58.8 |
| D160 | UB | Flake (chipped through patina) | Fine silicic tuff | 42 | 38 | 11 | 23 |
| H758 | 20 | Chunk | | 52 | 49 | 21 | 459 |
| H1965 | 24 | Bifacially retouched piece; Bordes 50 | Flint; fresh condition | 34 | 27 | 12.5 | 11 |
| H3197 | 26 | Single convex side-scraper Bordes 10 | Baked shale | 36 | 21 | 15 | 8.4 |
| H767 | 23 | Flake, struck from patinated piece | Fine silicic tuff | 17 | 18 | 3 | 1.0 |
| H2606 | 26 | Crude core | Ignimbrite | 95 | 67 | 41.5 | 244.3 |

*Table 10.4. Artefacts which show retouch through patina.*

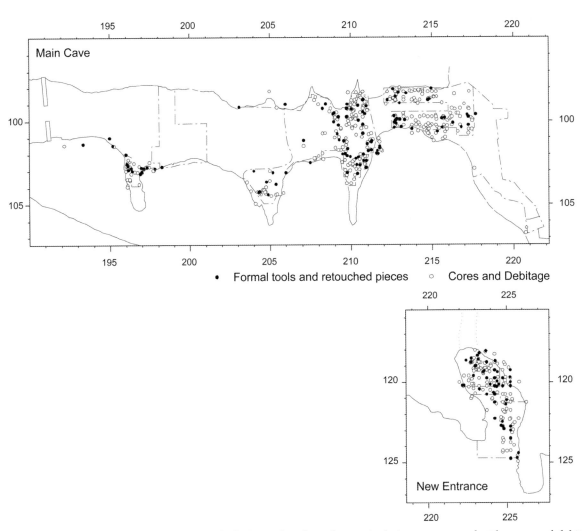

*Figure 10.3. Distributions of* in situ *lithic finds. Formal tools and retouched pieces contrasted with cores and debitage.*

appears that both primary reduction and finishing of lithics was taking place at *locales* outside both the Main Cave and the New Entrance. Both topographically at Pontnewydd, and sequentially through all the main debris flows, there is no apparent distinction between these stages of artefact production. This could suggest that the material belongs to an assemblage from a single *locale* which has been transported to many different parts of the deeper recesses of the cave system.

| Principal artefact types | Main Cave | | New Entrance ULB | ULB | MG | MG |
|---|---|---|---|---|---|---|
| | Nos. | % | Nos. | % | Nos. | % |
| Biface trimming flakes | 18 | 2.4 | 2 | 0.7 | 0 | 0 |
| Bifaces | 62 | 8.2 | 4 | 1.4 | 0 | 0 |
| Biface fragments | 3 | 0.4 | 0 | 0 | 0 | 0 |
| Biface roughouts | 5 | 0.7 | 0 | 0 | 0 | 0 |
| Chips and spalls | 37 | 4.9 | 49 | 17.3 | 19 | 50.0 |
| Choppers/chopping tools | 6 | 0.8 | 1 | 0.4 | 0 | 0 |
| Chunks | 38 | 5.1 | 15 | 5.3 | 3 | 7.9 |
| Cleaver | 2 | 0.3 | 0 | 0 | 0 | 0 |
| Cores, miscellaneous | 23 | 3.1 | 13 | 4.6 | 0 | 0 |
| Core fragments | 12 | 1.6 | 2 | 0.7 | 2 | 5.2 |
| Discoidal cores | 41 | 5.4 | 4 | 1.4 | 0 | 0 |
| Flakes | 241 | 32.0 | 41 | 14.5 | 1 | 2.7 |
| Flake fragments | 113 | 15.0 | 106 | 37.5 | 5 | 13.1 |
| Hammerstones | 1 | 0.1 | 0 | 0 | 7 | 18.4 |
| Levallois cores | 13 | 1.7 | 1 | 0.4 | 0 | 0 |
| Levallois flakes | 47 | 6.3 | 24 | 8.5 | 0 | 0 |
| Levallois blades | 3 | 0.4 | 2 | 0.7 | 0 | 0 |
| Levallois points | 3 | 0.4 | 0 | 0 | 0 | 0 |
| Mousterian point | 2 | 0.3 | 0 | 0 | 0 | 0 |
| Microlith | 1 | 0.1 | 0 | 0 | 0 | 0 |
| Naturally backed knives | 10 | 1.2 | 2 | 0.7 | 0 | 0 |
| Notches/Denticulates | 7 | 0.9 | 4 | 1.4 | 0 | 0 |
| Other retouched artefacts | 25 | 3.3 | 2 | 0.7 | 0 | 0 |
| Scrapers, end | 1 | 0.1 | 0 | 0 | 0 | 0 |
| Scrapers, side | 37 | 4.9 | 11 | 3.9 | 1 | 2.7 |
| Truncated blades | 3 | 0.4 | 0 | 0 | 0 | 0 |
| **Totals** | **754** | | **283** | | **38** | |

Re-deposited finds from Area A, including the microlith, are listed here.

*Table 10.5. Frequency of principal artefact and debitage types from the Main Cave and New Entrance. ULB = Upper Limestone Breccia (Layers 23 to 26); MG = Mudstone Gravel (Layers 33 to 38).*

FRAGMENTATION AND DISTINCTIONS BETWEEN THE MAIN CAVE AND THE NEW ENTRANCE

The compositions of the lithic assemblages from both sites appear to be generally similar. Table 10.5 shows the typology of artefacts from both sites, both as absolute counts and as percentages. The only substantial difference lies in the proportion of fragmentary debitage from the two sites, with fragments being much more common in the New Entrance than in the Main Cave. This is very unlikely to represent a genuine distinction between the two assemblages but is more likely to be an 'artefact' of the change in sieving strategy discussed above, leading to a higher recovery of the very small fragmentary debitage. The fragmentary debitage recovered from the Main Cave is similarly biased towards areas which were excavated in later seasons.

The data were re-studied without fragmentary debitage to establish whether the distortion of the totals by this material was masking more subtle differences between the two assemblages (Figures 10.4 and 10.5). Once again, most artefacts were represented with broadly comparable frequencies at both sites, further strengthening the hypothesis that all the Pontnewydd material was

originally part of a single assemblage. However, one category of artefact differed in frequency between the two sites: bifaces were more common in the Main Cave. This distinction appears to be genuine and to require explanation. It may be that differential transportation of the artefacts to their present locations in the Main Cave and New Entrance has affected the composition of the assemblages. However, there does not seem any compelling reason why just bifaces should be affected in this way. Given the general similarity of the assemblages it seems more likely that the distinction between the two sites is a result of differential spatial patterning at the activity areas where the lithic artefacts originally accumulated.

*Distinctions between major debris flow events in the Main Cave*

The distribution of lithics within the major debris flows (Figure 10.6) highlights several important distinctions between the Main Cave and the New Entrance. In the Main Cave, both Lower and Upper Breccias appear to have transported worked stone pieces. More artefacts came from the Lower Breccia, but a substantial number were recovered from the Upper Breccia (see Tables 10.1

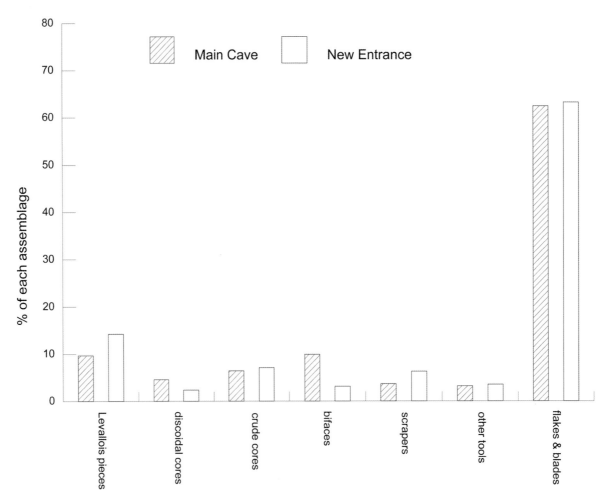

*Figure 10.4. The typology of* in situ *lithic artefacts in the Main Cave and the New Entrance, excluding fragmentary debitage. Totals expressed as percentages of the total assemblage for each area.*

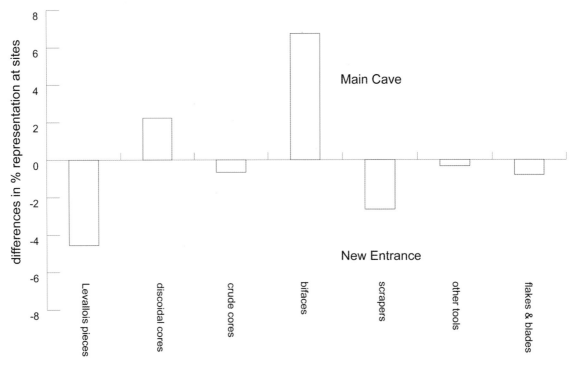

*Figure 10.5. Differences between the lithic assemblages in the Main Cave and the New Entrance, excluding fragmentary debitage. 0 = equal percentage representation at both sites.*

|  | LB & Ic (n) | LB & Ic (%) | UB & UB/SB (n) | UB & UB/SB (%) |
|---|---|---|---|---|
| Levallois pieces | 21 | 9.25 | 19 | 10.73 |
| Discoidal cores | 11 | 4.85 | 8 | 4.52 |
| Crude cores | 14 | 6.17 | 13 | 7.34 |
| Bifaces | 28 | 12.33 | 11 | 6.22 |
| Scrapers | 8 | 3.52 | 5 | 2.83 |
| Other tools | 10 | 4.41 | 3 | 1.69 |
| Flakes and blades | 135 | 59.47 | 118 | 66.67 |
| **Totals** | 227 | 100.00 | 177 | 100.00 |

Ic = Intermediate complex; LB = Lower Breccia; UB = Upper Breccia;
UB/SB = Upper Breccia with Silt beds.

*Table 10.6. Typology of lithic artefacts from the Main Cave debris flows.*

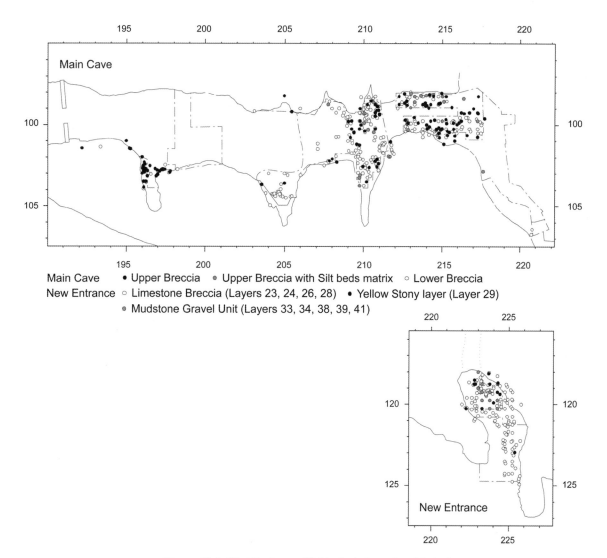

*Figure 10.6. Distributions of lithic finds in major debris flows.*

and 10.6). Both debris flows also seem to have moved material similar distances and in roughly the same direction. The low number of Upper Breccia finds from the South Passage (Area C) arises from the small amount of this context which has survived in this area. The compositions of the assemblages moved by the two debris flows are generally similar (Figures 10.7 and 10.8) with the only distinctions being a significantly higher proportion of bifaces in the Lower Breccia and Intermediate complex and a significantly higher proportion of flakes in the Upper Breccia. This is likely to be a product of the mechanics of the debris flows (Collcutt 1984, 54–61). Denser pieces, such

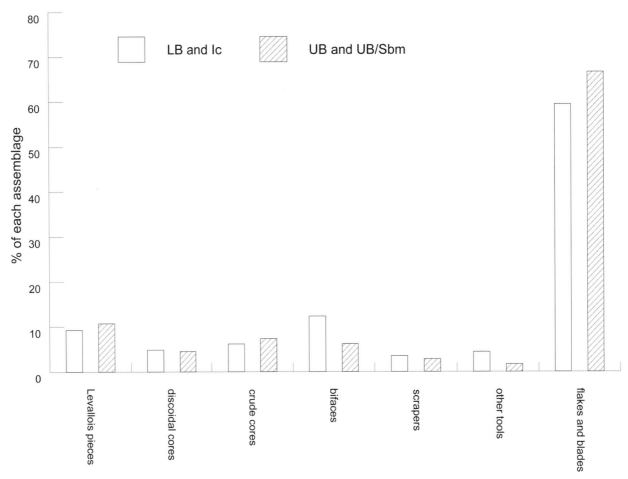

*Figure 10.7. The typology of lithic artefacts in the Lower and Upper Breccias, excluding fragmentary debitage. Totals expressed as percentages of the total number of artefacts in both contexts.*

*Figure 10.8. Differences between the lithic assemblages in the Lower and Upper Breccias, excluding fragmentary debitage. 0 = equal percentage representation in both contexts.*

| | Mudstone Gravel (n) | Mudstone Gravel (%) | Yellow Stony layer (n) | Yellow Stony layer (%) | Limestone Breccia (n) | Limestone Breccia (%) |
|---|---|---|---|---|---|---|
| Levallois pieces | 0 | 0.00 | 0 | 0.00 | 35 | 15.69 |
| Discoidal cores | 0 | 0.00 | 0 | 0.00 | 6 | 2.69 |
| Crude cores | 2 | 28.57 | 0 | 0.00 | 15 | 6.73 |
| Bifaces | 0 | 0.00 | 4 | 66.66 | 4 | 1.79 |
| Scrapers | 0 | 0.00 | 0 | 0.00 | 12 | 5.38 |
| Other tools | 0 | 0.00 | 1 | 16.67 | 8 | 3.59 |
| Flakes and blades | 5 | 71.43 | 1 | 16.67 | 143 | 64.13 |
| **Totals** | 7 | 100.00 | 6 | 100.00 | 223 | 100.00 |

Table 10.7. Typology of artefacts from the New Entrance debris flows.

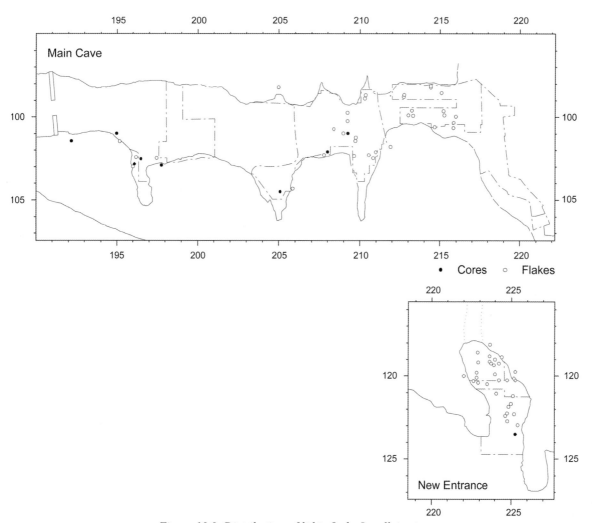

Figure 10.9. Distribution of lithic finds, Levallois pieces.

as bifaces, presumably behaved like other sub-spherical coarse particles within the original Lower Breccia debris flow. A complex system of recycling keeps the particles in a debris flow poorly sorted, allowing the flow to move. Struck flakes are both less dense and much flatter than the rest of the particles in a debris flow. For this reason a proportion of the struck flakes would tend to 'float' on the top of the flow, escaping the recycling process. Consequently, when the upper layers of the Lower Breccia were eroded by the Upper Breccia debris flow, the lithics incorporated into the more recent layers would contain a much higher proportion of flakes.

*Distinctions between major debris flow events in the New Entrance*

In the New Entrance most of the artefacts came from the Limestone Breccia with very few from other contexts (Table 10.7). The numbers of finds from the earlier debris flows at the New Entrance are too small to admit of meaningful comparisons with other debris flow events.

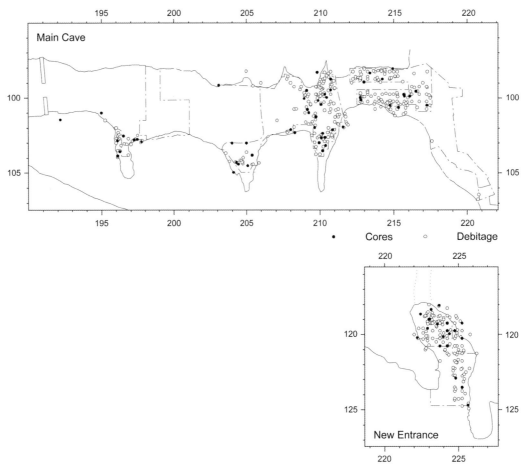

*Figure 10.10. Distribution of lithic finds, cores and debitage.*

All the flows in the New Entrance were emplaced after the Last Interglacial (see Aldhouse-Green and Peterson chapter 6, this volume) and appear to have flowed into the New Entrance from the south, in contrast to the surficial Layer 20 which is both coeval and co-extensive with the Upper Breccia, and the Limestone Breccia layers. However, the presence of both Middle Pleistocene fauna and thermoluminescence dates of the same antiquity on artefacts from within these debris flows (see Aldhouse-Green and Peterson chapter 6, this volume), clearly indicate that the New Entrance debris flows are made up of much older material, probably stored in now destroyed parts of the cave system before being emplaced. In particular, we should note that sedimentological considerations (see Mourne and Case chapter 5, this volume) suggest that the mudstone gravel layers (33–41) were derived from the Lower Breccia.

*Distributions of major artefact classes*
The Pontnewydd assemblage is dominated by bifaces, scrapers and Levallois products (Green 1984b, 115; Green *et al.* 1989, 45; Aldhouse-Green 1993, 49). Given the derived nature of the deposits it was not expected that any patterns would be detectable in the distributions of individual classes of artefacts. This has generally proved to be the case. However, the distribution of Levallois products

(Figure 10.9) would seem to reflect an apparent pattern of Levallois flakes travelling further in the debris flow than Levallois cores. Even so, the relatively low numbers of finds involved means that this is unlikely to be significant. Indeed, it is noticeable that no such pattern is visible when all cores are plotted with all debitage (Figure 10.10). Figure 10.11 shows the distribution of bifaces in the excavated areas of the cave. As discussed above, they were much more common in the Main Cave. There is little evidence of patterning in the distribution other than this numerical distinction between the Main Cave and New Entrance. Similarly and unsurprisingly, the distribution of scrapers (Figure 10.12) shows no evidence of any structuring.

### How many phases of occupation?

In 1998, a paper published by Aldhouse-Green entitled 'the archaeology of distance' contained a suggestion that differing frequencies of tool types in the Main Cave and New Entrance might be evidence for two phases of occupation. This proposal was limited in its scope and took no account of evidence from the Intermediate complex of an early human presence, so our question now is whether there had been three – or, perhaps, one should say at least three – periods of human presence?

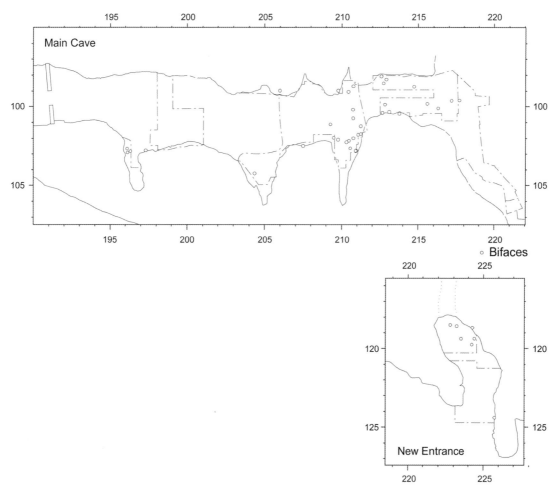

*Figure 10.11. Distribution of* in situ *lithic finds in all layers, Bifaces.*

*Finds from the Intermediate complex*

The archaeological evidence for Middle Pleistocene settlement from the Main Cave comes from the two layers immediately above the Upper Sands and Gravels, namely the Intermediate complex and the Lower Breccia. The Intermediate complex, whatever interpretation one puts on its chronostratigraphic integrity (see Mourne and Case chapter 5 and Currant chapter 8, this volume), contains a number of interglacial faunal species and, so, stands apart from the artefactually productive and hominin-rich Lower Breccia where jumbled together, stratified but *ex situ*, are derived artefacts and once associated food and other modified bones, and carnivore accumulations. Their age is known within the limits of the Uranium-series and thermoluminescence (TL) dating methods and is given a *terminus ante quem* by determinations on a stalagmitic floor formed on the surface of the Lower Breccia yielding statistically consistent ages of 215,000±36,000 BP (Schwarcz 1984, 91–92) and 224,000+41,000/–31,000 BP (Ivanovich *et al.* 1984). Dates probably contemporary with the occupation are provided by TL determinations on burnt flint artefacts from the Main Cave respectively of 200,000±25,000 BP and 269,000±37,000 BP, neither statistically distinguishable from the other. An estimated age of *c.* 225,000 BP for human presence signalled by the

discoveries in the Lower Breccia of the Main Cave would, therefore, seem reasonable.

Artefactual, hominin and faunal finds are sparse within the Intermediate complex but all undoubtedly occur there (Table 10.8). There are five artefactual finds from Area D and three from Area F, plus a solitary find from the South Fissure (Area B). The Levallois blade from Area B (B395) would be inconsistent with Currant's interpretation of elements of the fauna as being of MIS 9 age. Indeed, the presence of a probable biface trimming flake and a discoidal core within the Intermediate complex would see the techno-culture of the Pontnewydd hominins as being very similar both in the Intermediate complex and in the Lower Breccia.

*Finds from the New Entrance*

Some 40 m from the Main Cave, excavations 1987–1995 revealed a new entrance buried under up to 6 m of scree and solifluction deposits. The solifluction produced one very weathered biface (H9) which must have originated from a *locale* on the hill *above* Pontnewydd Cave. This entrance has proved to contain a sequence of debris flows relatively rich in artefacts and fauna, and with one securely stratified hominin tooth. Sedimentological analysis indicates that the immediate sources of the flows in both the Main

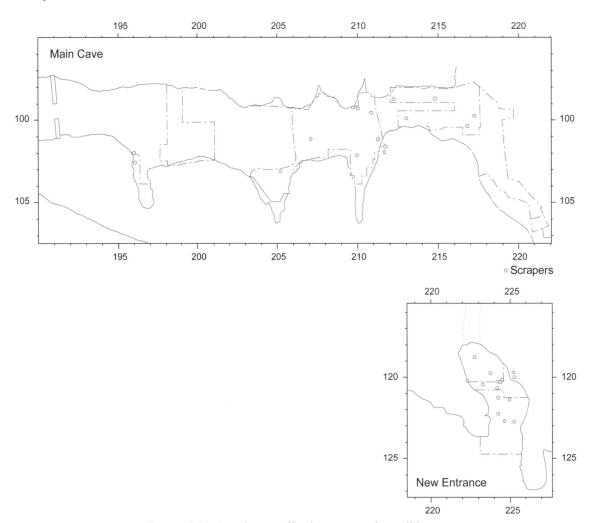

*Figure 10.12. Distribution of* in situ *scrapers from all layers.*

| Find no. | Layer | Type name | Raw material | Wt | Square | Z |
|----------|-------|-----------|--------------|-----|--------|---|
| B395 | Int. | Levallois blade | Dacite | 54.2 | K20 | 99.09 |
| D687 | BI | Discoidal core | Flint | 29.7 | I 9 | 98.97 |
| D1853 | BI | Chunk | Rhyolite | 45.5 | J8 NE | 99.00–98.95 |
| D3944 | BI | Flake fragment | Carboniferous Chert | 14.6 | H7 NW | 99.02 |
| D3948 | BI | Flake | Flint | 1 | H7 NW | 99.01 |
| D4708 | OI | Flake (probably biface trimmer) | Crystal lithic tuff | 37.2 | K7 NE | 98.81 (15 cm deep in layer) |
| F3263 | BI | Chunk | Crystal tuff | 13.2 | G2 SW | 99.18 |
| F4048 | BI | Chip | Fine silicic tuff | 0.2 | G4 SW | 98.90–98.88 |
| F7063 | BI | Chunk | Flint | 0.9 | H2 SE | 99.12–99.01 |

Key to layer abbreviations: Int. = Intermediate complex; BI = Buff Intermediate;
OI = Orange Intermediate; LBc = Lower Breccia, layer c.

*Table 10.8. Fnds from the Intermediate complex.*

Cave and the New Entrance lie outside of their respective modern entrances. Thus, it is likely that substantial external occupation has taken place in at least two separate areas. Sedimentological analysis has identified the Mudstone Gravel unit (Layers 33–41) as being, plausibly, re-worked Lower Breccia sediment of comparable age and origin. If that is the case, the artefactually much richer Upper Limestone Breccia of the New Entrance may possibly

| Expected frequencies | Observed frequencies Main Cave | Expected frequencies New Entrance (ULB) |
|---|---|---|
| Bifaces (including roughouts and fragments) | 9.3% | 26.3% (observed = 1.4%) |
| Levallois (including cores, flakes, blades and points) | 8.8 % | 24.9% (observed = 9.6%) |
| Side-scrapers | 4.9 % | 13.9% (observed 3.9%) |

*Table 10.9. Main Cave and New Entrance observed and expected artefact frequencies.*

| Main Cave Type | Rank | % | Nos. |
|---|---|---|---|
| Flakes | 1 | 37.6 | 241 |
| Flake fragments | 2 | 17.6 | 113 |
| Bifaces | 3 | 9.7 | 62 |
| Levallois flakes | 4 | 7.3 | 47 |
| Discoidal cores | 5 | 6.4 | 41 |
| Chunks | 6 | 5.9 | 38 |
| Chips and spalls | 7 | 5.8 | 37 |
| Scrapers, side | 8 | 5.8 | 37 |
| Other retouched artefacts | 9 | 3.9 | 25 |
| | | **Total** | **641** |

If the Main Cave were used as benchmark then:
- bifaces would be 7 times less common than expected (EF = 29)
- scrapers would be only 0.7 times less common (EF = 17)
- Levallois flakes would be just 1.1 commoner than expected (EF = 22)

*Table 10.10. The nine most commonly occurring types in the Main Cave.*

| New Entrance Type | Rank | % | Nos. |
|---|---|---|---|
| Flake fragments | 1 | 39. 0 | 111 |
| Chips and spalls | 2 | 23.9 | 68 |
| Flakes | 3 | 14.7 | 42 |
| Levallois flakes | 4 | 8.4 | 24 |
| Chunks | 5 | 6.3 | 18 |
| Scrapers, side | 6 | 4.2 | 12 |
| Discoidal cores | 7 | 1.4 | 4 |
| Bifaces | 8 | 1.4 | 4 |
| Other retouched artefacts | 9 | 0.7 | 2 |
| | | **Total** | **285** |

*Table 10.11. The nine most commonly occurring artefact types in the New Entrance.*

contain the debris of a younger occupation. If one takes the numerically much richer assemblage from the Main Cave as the 'gold standard', it is possible to compute figures for the New Entrance in respect of the expected frequencies of the principal Palaeolithic artefact types (Tables 10.9–10.11).

Here we present a comparative analysis of the New Entrance artefacts (Tables 10.9–10.11) with that already published from the Main Cave (Green 1984b). Looking at the main categories only, the New Entrance figures reveal the presence of only two certain bifaces (both heavily rolled), an incidence of only 2% compared with 14% in the Main Cave. The New Entrance has produced ten pieces in total – bifaces, roughouts and trimming flakes – which relate to the manufacture or use of bifaces, but Pleistocene stratified finds include only two finished bifaces: one of quartz from Layer 24 of the Limestone unit and one of crystal lithic tuff from the underlying Yellow Stony Layer 29 (Table 10.12). Both areas display relatively high frequencies of side-scrapers and Levallois debitage, but the higher values come from the New Entrance. 'Pseudo-tools', genuine artefacts further modified by pressure in debris flows or by earlier cryoturbation, figure prominently in both analyses. Thermoluminescence dating of burnt flint from the New Entrance by Debenham has produced

ages of 214,000±21,000 BP; 173,000±20,000 BP and 179,000±22,000 BP. The latter two ages, whilst statistically indistinguishable from the earliest result of 214,000 BP and the Main Cave determinations, nonetheless suggest the possibility of a younger age for a New Entrance assemblage in which bifaces formed a very minor component and where the products of Levallois technology and side-scrapers were dominant.

## Artefact petrology
*Heather Jackson and Richard E. Bevins*

The early hominin visitors to Pontnewydd Cave left behind lithic artefacts comprising a hard rock industry of which flint is only a minor component. 1,284 artefacts were recovered during excavation at the cave along with many more natural clasts which were systematically collected during the excavations due to their similarity to the material from which the artefacts were made. Analysis of these two groups of material has led to a thorough study of the raw materials represented, their origin and their use by their Palaeolithic makers (Jackson 2002).

## Methodology
*Artefact identification*

All the artefacts recovered from the cave were examined in order to compile a database to link the lithological information with the typological work and create a complete description for each artefact. Specimens previously identified (Bevins 1984; Green 1988) were first examined in hand specimen. The unidentified artefacts were then

| Find no. | Context | Find | Raw material | Degree of rolling | Whole / broken |
|---|---|---|---|---|---|
| H9 | 6/8 | Biface – amygdaloid | Dacite | high | whole |
| H1276 | U/S | Biface | Ignimbrite | | |
| H3022 | 23 | Biface (? unfinished) | Silicic tuff | fresh | whole |
| H3142 & H3374 | 23 | Flake (? biface trimmer) | Pumice crystal tuff | fresh | broken |
| H2117 | 23 | Biface trimmer | Rhyolitic tuff | slightly rolled | whole |
| H507 | 24 | Biface | Quartz | slightly rolled | whole |
| H2858 | 24/26 | Biface roughout | Ignimbrite | slightly rolled | whole |
| H2135 | 29 | ? Failed biface | Tuffaceous sandstone | very rolled | whole |
| H2416 | 29 | Biface – lanceolate | Crystal lithic tuff | very rolled | whole |
| H2771 | 29b | ? Unfinished biface | Tuffaceous sandstone | fresh | whole |

Stratified finds include only two finished bifaces: one of quartz from Layer 24 and one of crystal lithic tuff from Layer 29.

*Table 10.12. The New Entrance bifaces and biface roughouts and trimming flakes.*

also examined in hand specimen and given an approximate identification. Many artefacts, including all less than 30 mm in length, were further examined using a binocular microscope, particularly if there was any doubt over their initial identification, or if the artefact displayed only a small surface area for examination. In accordance with the International Union of Geological Sciences (IUGS) classifications, the artefacts were then grouped into distinct lithological categories for this site.

*Sampling programme*

In order to clarify the hand specimen identifications and to provide sufficient information for provenance studies, 82 artefacts were selected for the creation of thin sections from which determinations of provenance could be attempted using a petrological microscope. Much of the raw material has undergone low grade metamorphism and associated recrystallization. Alteration of the material has therefore taken place, resulting in a loss of primary textural characteristics and the generation of new surface features. After the material had been discarded by its users it was subjected to transport and modification within debris flows. This process resulted in most of the artefacts acquiring weathered surfaces in addition to the cortical surfaces already present, which further complicated identification from hand specimen alone. Selection of the artefacts for thin section was undertaken in a manner that attempted to limit the quantity as far as possible, while maintaining a statistically representative sample, and to use artefacts which were damaged in order to limit the aesthetic damage to the collection. Artefacts were selected which characterized the subtle variations shown by each rock type represented. In cases where classification was uncertain, a thin section was proposed.

POLISHED THIN SECTION PREPARATION

Thin section preparation was undertaken in the Rock Preparation Laboratory in the Department of Geology, National Museum of Wales. A thin slice (5 mm) was removed from the artefact edge using a microtome saw, leaving a cut which was back-filled with paste. One surface was polished and bonded onto a microscope slide with Epoxy resin, then ground and polished until the slice was 30 μm thick. At this thickness most minerals are transparent and can therefore be viewed by transmitted light microscopy. Using polarized light, minerals can then be identified and their inter-relationships and orientations studied. The thin section was finished by polishing, rather than by addition of a cover slip. This leaves the section undamaged for potential further analysis. Reflected, as well as transmitted light, microscopy may also be used on polished thin sections, which permits the identification of opaque minerals. On the basis of hand specimen, and where available transmitted light microscopic investigation each artefact was attributed a specific identification, and a likely source was suggested where possible.

**Classification of the rocks**

Rock names adopted have generally followed conventions such as those established by the International Union of Geological Sciences; however variations have been adopted in this study in order to emphasize particular lithological attributes of the Pontnewydd assemblage. The resulting classification of the rock types represented by the artefacts found at Pontnewydd Cave shows that each artefact can be classified into one of eleven main groups, several of which can be sub-divided into tighter groupings. These are:

## I. Rhyolite

Silica rich (>69% $SiO_2$) volcanic rocks. The mineral assemblage is usually quartz, alkali feldspar and plagioclase feldspar (the latter two minerals typically in a ratio >1:2). Biotite, hornblende and zircon are common accessory minerals. Rhyolite can be considered the extrusive equivalent of granite.

## II. Rhyolitic tuff

These pyroclastic rocks consist of 100–75% fragmented volcanic material, ejected into either the atmosphere or under water during explosive volcanic activity as solid fragments, which are fractured during the eruption. Upon consolidation this material becomes a pyroclastic rock. Tuffs typically contain a predominance of fragments between 20 mm and 1/16 mm in diameter. Fine tuffs are dominated by fragments of less than 1/16 mm. Tuffs and ashes may be further qualified by their fragmental composition. The sub-groups within this category derive their names from the characteristic fragments which constitute each tuff.

i)   Crystal tuff – crystal fragments are the most abundant constituent.
ii)  Crystal lithic tuff – contains both crystal and lithic fragments in approximately equal proportions. These lithic fragments may be previously erupted lava *etc.*
iii) Lithic tuff – lithic fragments are more abundant than crystal or vitric fragments.
iii) Vitric tuff – shards of glass and pumice are more abundant than either crystal or lithic fragments.
iv)  Fine silicic tuff – a specific tuff, occurring as small fragments usually no more than 5 cm², consisting almost entirely of a crypto-crystalline silicic matrix. It produces a good conchoidal fracture, and is usually dark in colour.
v)   Silicic tuff – light coloured tuff, chert-like in appearance, within which a degree of banding is often clearly visible.

## III. Ignimbrite

Ignimbrites are deposited by a pyroclastic flow, a hot suspension of particles and gases that flows rapidly from a volcano. They are dacitic or rhyolitic in composition. Ignimbrites consist of a poorly sorted mixture of tuffaceous material (including pumice, crystals, lithics and glass shards). The temperature of emplacement of a pyroclasitc flow can vary considerably. If the pyroclastic flow is relatively cold then the resultant ignimbrite is commonly a poorly sorted mass of crystals, lithics and vitric fragments, although some sorting usually occurs, especially towards the base of the resultant deposit. If the pyroclastic flow retains heat within itself then textural modifications occur as glass shards and pumice fragments become plastic and weld themselves together or deform around lithic and crystal fragments. The resultant ignimbrite has a 'streaky' texture termed eutaxitic, or if extreme parataxitic, a texture that resembles a primary flow foliation seen in many rhyolitic lavas.

## IV. Feldspar-phyric lava

A volcanic rock containing feldspar phenocrysts in a silicic matrix. This classification does not fall within IUGS parameters, but is used here for clarity because it is such a distinctive lithology in the Pontnewydd assemblage.

## V. Basalt

A volcanic rock of mafic composition, consisting mainly of calcic plagioclase feldspar, pyroxene (usually clinopyroxene), and opaque minerals (usually Fe-Ti oxides). Olivine and minor interstitial quartz may be present.

## VI. Andesite

Andesite is a volcanic rock, of intermediate composition, which is often porphyritic in texture. The mineral assemblage is typically dominated by plagioclase feldspar, either or both clinopyroxene and orthopyroxene, and sometimes hornblende and/or biotite. However, there is a problem over attribution of the term 'andesite' in the Pontnewydd assemblage. In fresh rocks andesites are distinguished from basalts by their higher contents of $SiO_2$, a slightly lower colour index value, and plagioclase feldspars which are richer in the albite component. All of the Pontnewydd basalts/andesites have been affected by low grade metamorphism, in which the rock colour alters (primarily through the crystallization of chlorite replacing original mafic minerals – hence the term 'greenstones'), plagioclase feldspar is altered to albite and $SiO_2$ contents may be affected by element mobility. Many of the 'andesites' of the English Lake District, for example, are now recognized as being basalts or basaltic andesites. Caution is therefore required in calling certain Pontnewydd artefacts 'andesites'; they could equally be altered basalts or basaltic andesites.

## VII. Dacite

A volcanic rock composed of quartz and sodic plagioclase with minor amounts of biotite and/or hornblende and/or pyroxene. Chemically equivalent to granodiorite.

## VIII. Dolerite

A basic intrusive rock intermediate in grain size between basalt and gabbro and composed essentially of plagioclase, pyroxene (usually clinopyroxene) and opaque minerals (usually Fe-Ti oxides), often with an ophitic texture. Olivine may also be present.

## IX. Microdiorite

An intermediate intrusive rock consisting of less than 50% anorthitic plagioclase, commonly hornblende and often with biotite or minor augite.

## X. Baked shale

A low grade metamorphosed argillaceous rock, resulting from either contact or regional metamorphism.

## XI. Sandstone

Several sandstone types, including epiclastic and tuffitic

sandstones, are present in the Pontnewydd assemblage, namely:

i) Micaceous sandstone.

ii) Tuffaceous sandstone/tuffite – containing between 75% and 25% pyroclastic material (the remainder being epiclastic material). Average clast size ranges between 2 mm and 1/16 mm.

iii) Volcaniclastic sandstone – immature sandstone made up of igneous lithic fragments, crystals *etc.*, often chlorite-rich.

## *Statistical analyses*

Once the lithology of each artefact had been determined, a number of statistical analyses were conducted for each rock type represented in the Pontnewydd artefact assemblage. The Chi-squared test was conducted on three groupings, namely on unfragmented non-debitage tools, on debitage types and also on fragmented tools. This established whether the percentage of artefacts made from each type of rock was significantly different from the distribution that would be expected if no selection had taken place (all the tests were undertaken at the 5% level; Jackson 2002). The $Chi^2$ analysis showed that the differences in rock use for each artefact type were statistically significant, and that there was also a significant difference between the rock types used to make bifaces and those used in the rest of the lithic assemblage. It also showed that the rock types found as flakes are not representative of the assemblage as a whole, which may suggest that the tools were manufactured elsewhere and only part of the flaked waste was incorporated in the debris flows.

In addition, f-test and t-test analyses were undertaken in order to determine whether it was possible to show statistically if different artefacts of different shapes and sizes were manufactured from different lithologies. Measurements of selected continuous variables were taken on all the artefacts; length measurements were taken along the mid-axis perpendicular to the bulb of percussion and width measurements at the maximum width perpendicular to the length measurement. Thickness measurements were taken at the thickest point of the flake. Using these measurements f-tests were carried out on pairs of logged data on each possible combination of rock types for each of the following categories: length (mm), width (mm), and thickness (mm), weight (g), length/width ratio and thickness/length ratio. The results of the f-test determined on which categories the t-test could be implemented for each pair of rock types (ibid.).

Due to the small size of all flint artefacts, they could not be compared statistically with the rest of the assemblage using a t-test. Artefacts of fine silicic tuff therefore had the most significant differences in all mean dimensions to each and every other rock type. Study of the length of the artefacts showed that the mean length of artefacts of crystal lithic tuff, feldspar-phyric lava and ignimbrite were statistically similar to each other, and that artefacts of rhyolite lava and rhyolitic tuff were also of statistically similar lengths.

## *Discussion of results*

### *Raw materials*

The raw materials used at the site (Bevins 1984; Clayton 1984; Aldhouse-Green *et al.* 2004) are all allochthonous and have probably reached the cave or its vicinity through the processes of glacial, periglacial and fluvial transport. The lithologies are very similar to those in unworked specimens in the cave deposits, and the vast majority of these in turn closely match the Ordovician rocks in Snowdonia and the Arenig Mountains of Gwynedd, as noted previously by Bevins (1984) and Jackson (2002). A small number, five in total, possibly match better with a Lake District source, as discussed in some detail below.

The study of Jackson (2002) attributed particular sources for a small number of artefacts. Many more artefacts have attributes which suggest a source in the Lower Palaeozoic sequences of Snowdonia, but a more detailed provenance was not possible.

The raw material was obtained in the form of cobbles not normally greater than 250–300 mm in maximum dimension (Green 1984b). The size of the raw material and its quality has influenced the dimensions and refinement of the implements that could be produced. Fracture cleavages – microfaults resulting from compression and low-grade metamorphism of the source area rock strata – form parallel planes of weakness which may be discontinuous through the rock and even occur in different planes in a single pebble. A large number of *accidents de Siret* (Tixier *et al.* 1980) occur amongst the artefacts and occurred during experimental knapping of these rock types, where flakes spilt into two pieces more or less following the axis of percussion. The rock types used in the greatest quantities are rhyolite and ignimbrite. It is not known whether this is a reflection of their availability in the local landscape, as no comparative external deposits have been (or can now be) studied. Geomorphological studies by Livingston (Livingston 1986) were not able to correlate any extant drift deposits with those from Pontnewydd, and in any case the inhomogeneity of the drift would also render such comparisons spurious. Analysis of exotic pebbles from the Upper and Lower Sands and Gravels provides the only possible comparison (Bevins 1984).

### Flint

Flint is the classic rock type for Palaeolithic tools in Britain and there is a close correlation, with the exception of Pontnewydd, between the distribution of Palaeolithic sites and the occurrence of flint-bearing gravel deposits (Roe 1968). At Pontnewydd, however, only 9.5% of the worked material found in the Main Cave is flint, although in the New Entrance, the frequency is 20.2% (Table 10.13). Flint that appears at the site is small, and the majority (89%) of small debitage (chunks, chips and spalls) is made of flint, which supports the suggestion (Green 1984b) that knapping took place in proximity to the cave. The majority of the flint found at the site has been used to make retouched flakes (17%). The other two artefact types which dominate the flint distribution are core fragments (17%) and tool fragments (11.5%); these numbers show that flint at Pontnewydd was a valuable resource and was therefore exploited until it reached a state in which it was too fragmentary to be of further use. This value was probably due to its scarcity and the relative difficulty of finding flint of suitable size in the local till deposits (something which neither the author (Jackson 2002) nor Livingston (1986) succeeded in doing). Unlike most of the raw materials used for artefact manufacture, flint is absent in the basal units of the cave deposits, but it may have been available nearby in the drift (Clayton 1984) or the local river gravels, as many pieces show evidence of water transport. The west coast of Scotland (480 km to the north) is a likely source of the 'coalesced lephispheric' and 'skeletal rich' flints (ibid.). Flint is present in the green silt layer in Cefn Caves (Green 1986, 38–39; Green and Walker 1991, 44–47) in a pre-Last Interglacial context.

## QUARTZITE

Quartzite is the most common alternative to flint and forms a major part of most African industries. African research (Leakey *et al.* 1972) has shown that quartzite tools, when used for skinning and cutting meat, retain a sharp edge far longer than tools manufactured from volcanic rocks. Experimental knapping work (Moloney *et al.* 1988) has shown that 59% of quartzite flakes are recognizable as artefacts, compared to 98% of flint flakes and sometimes only 14% of volcanic debitage (Newcomer 1984). However, both quartz and quartzite are poorly represented at Pontnewydd (2.3%). They are mainly used for cores, and constitute 20% of the miscellaneous core assemblage. Quartzite is chemically similar to the silicic volcanic rocks that are used for the majority of the artefacts, but is probably less abundant in the local drift deposits.

## OTHER SEDIMENTARY ROCKS

Sandstone and siltstone at Pontnewydd constitute 5.2% of the total assemblage and were mainly used for discoidal cores (18%), retouched flakes (11%) and biface trimming flakes (11%). Chert and baked shale account for only 2.5% of the non-debitage total assemblage, and their greatest use was for side-scrapers (9.1%).

## VOLCANIC MATERIALS

80% of the worked material at Pontnewydd is volcanic material comprising altered igneous, pyroclastic or volcaniclastic material. For the most part this material is highly silicic and therefore tough and suitable for knapping; however, it has an inherent weakness, namely its pervasive spaced cleavage. Volcanic rocks were often used for Palaeolithic artefacts. They are best known in East Africa, for example the use of basalt, andesite, trachyte, phonolite and nephelinite in the Olduvai Gorge (Leakey *et al.* 1972). In Chile, Pleistocene people used basalt, felsite and ignimbrite (Lanning 1970).

|  | Main Cave | | | | | | | | | | New Entrance | |
|  | Totals A | % A | Totals B/C | % B/C | Totals D | % D | Totals F | % F | Totals Main Cave | % Main Cave | Totals | % |
| --- | --- | --- | --- | --- | --- | --- | --- | --- | --- | --- | --- | --- |
| Flint/Chert | 15 | 10.3 | 9 | 15.3 | 9 | 7.6 | 4 | 5.8 | 37 | 9.5 | 22 | 20.2 |
| Ignimbrite | 17 | 11.7 | 5 | 8.5 | 15 | 12.7 | 13 | 18.8 | 50 | 12.8 | 14 | 12.8 |
| Rhyolite | 22 | 15.2 | 7 | 11.9 | 16 | 13.6 | 9 | 13.0 | 54 | 13.8 | 5 | 4.6 |
| Rhyolitic tuff | 13 | 9.0 | 2 | 3.4 | 19 | 16.1 | 7 | 10.1 | 41 | 10.5 | 18 | 16.5 |
| Fine silicic tuff | 34 | 23.4 | 12 | 20.3 | 12 | 10.2 | 7 | 10.1 | 65 | 16.6 | 8 | 7.3 |
| Feldspar-phyric lava | 15 | 10.3 | 10 | 16.9 | 16 | 13.6 | 9 | 13.0 | 50 | 12.8 | 6 | 5.5 |
| Crystal tuff | 5 | 3.4 | 4 | 6.8 | 8 | 6.8 | 4 | 5.8 | 21 | 5.4 | 11 | 10.1 |
| Crystal lithic tuff | 9 | 6.2 | 3 | 5.1 | 4 | 3.4 | 6 | 8.7 | 22 | 5.6 | 6 | 5.5 |
| Tuff | 3 | 2.1 | 0 | 0.0 | 4 | 3.4 | 0 | 0.0 | 7 | 1.8 | 1 | 0.9 |
| Quartzite | 0 | 0.0 | 0 | 0.0 | 4 | 3.4 | 1 | 1.4 | 5 | 1.3 | 7 | 6.4 |
| Sand/siltstone | 6 | 4.1 | 4 | 6.8 | 7 | 5.9 | 4 | 5.8 | 21 | 5.4 | 5 | 4.6 |
| Andesite/dacite | 3 | 2.1 | 2 | 3.4 | 3 | 2.5 | 0 | 0.0 | 8 | 2.0 | 2 | 1.8 |
| Microdiorite | 1 | 0.7 | 0 | 0.0 | 1 | 0.8 | 5 | 7.2 | 7 | 1.8 | 4 | 3.7 |
| Basalt | 2 | 1.4 | 1 | 1.7 | 0 | 0.0 | 0 | 0.0 | 3 | 0.8 | 0 | 0.0 |
| **Totals** | **145** | | **59** | | **118** | | **69** | | **391** | | **109** | |

*Table 10.13. Raw materials by area.*

The volcanic lithologies found at Pontnewydd are fine silicic tuff (13.9%), ignimbrite (12.4%), feldspar-phyric lava (12.2%), rhyolitic tuff (11.2%), rhyolite lava (11%), crystal tuff (8.5%), crystal lithic tuff (5.4%), microdiorite (2.9%) and andesite (2.1%).

## Rhyolite and feldspar-phyric lava

Rhyolite and feldspar-phyric lava crystallize from a liquid state and are fine grained to very fine grained holocrystalline, isotropic rocks, unlike the tuffs and sedimentary rocks which typically possess bedding, are weaker and thus are more likely than the other rock types present to develop multiple fracture cleavages. This may explain the similar artefact range and implement frequency for rhyolite and feldspar-phyric lava (Green 1988). They are mainly used for heavy-duty tools such as bifaces, choppers and cleavers, as well as Levallois products. Rhyolite is mainly used for bifaces (23%), and Levallois flakes (19%). Indeed 17% of all bifaces found at Pontnewydd are made from rhyolite.

Feldspar-phyric lava is mainly used for bifaces (19%) and Levallois flakes (11%), but is also substantially utilized for tool reuse (11%). This may be due to its relatively holocrystalline and isotropic nature and hence its ability to retain an edge without shattering. Although used in the largest quantity for bifaces, feldspar-phyric lava still constitutes 17% of the scraper population, and 20% of the number of reused tools are made from feldspar-phyric lava, a percentage second only to fine silicic tuff.

Rhyolitic tuff has a similar chemical composition to rhyolite but is commonly finely laminated and tends to be very fine grained, having formed from ash. It is composed of a variable mixture of crystals, lithic fragments, pumice and former glass shards. It is mainly used for bifaces (19%) and Levallois flakes, and a number of biface trimming flakes on this material have also been found (9%). In experimental work on flint, basalt, volcanic tuff, dolerite, quartzite, diorite, granite and limestone from Africa the rhyolitic tuff proved the easiest to flake (Moloney 1988). Other experiments have established some degree of correlation between the silica content of a material and its suitability for the production of good bifaces (Newcomer 1984; 1988). Several of the rhyolite artefacts contain features which suggest that they derive from localities in Snowdonia.

## Andesite

The fine grain size of andesite allows for refined secondary working and production of first-class tools (MacRae and Moloney 1988, 95–102).

The original description of 'andesite' (but see the discussion earlier in this section over the use of the term andesite) from Pontnewydd by Bevins (1984) was based on two samples, B310 and A74/1. Both samples show petrographical features which are different from the bulk of the Pontnewydd samples. It was for this reason they were sub-characterized and subject to thin section investigation. The original description separated these two samples in view of the fact that they are more basic in character than the vast

majority of Pontnewydd lithologies which are predominantly silicic. They are, however, altered, and have appearances typical of Lower Palaeozoic basic to intermediate volcanic rocks, which is thought to be the age of the silicic volcanic rock component of the Pontnewydd assemblage.

Petrographic analysis confirmed the low grade metamorphic character of the rocks, with a green, pleochroic fibrous mineral with moderate birefringence present in both samples. Optically this appears to be actinolite or ferro-actinolite. In one sample (A74/1) it occurs chiefly in a thin veinlet, whilst in B310 it occurs partly in pseudomorphs after mafic phenocrysts and also pervasively replacing the fine grained rock groundmass. Sample B310 is porphyritic, with altered plagioclase phenocrysts which show the former presence of chemical zoning. A74/1 is also porphyritic but this sample is heavily altered and the phenocrysts are not so well preserved as in the other sample investigated. Importantly, such features are typical of calc-alkaline rocks and a possible Lake District provenance was placed on the 'andesites'.

When these original descriptions were made there were two key drivers in the provenance attribution. Firstly, whilst the Lake District Lower Palaeozoic volcanic rocks (the Borrowdale Volcanic Group) were known to be calc-alkaline in chemistry, no calc-alkaline volcanic rocks had been hitherto recorded in the Snowdon area of Wales. Secondly, and seemingly contradictory, neither actinolite nor ferro-actinolite had been recorded from the Lake District in a low grade metamorphic context, but had been from parts of the North Wales Lower Palaeozoic sequences, albeit sparingly (Roberts 1981).

Since those original attributions there have been developments which necessitate a re-appraisal of the original considerations. Firstly, more detailed investigations into the low grade metamorphic character of the Borrowdale Volcanic Group has led to the identification of actinolite in the western part of the succession, occurring in basalts and andesites. It is thought to be a result of contact metamorphism by the Eskdale and Ennerdale granite/granophyre intrusions (Bevins *et al.* 1985; Allen *et al.* 1987; Meller 1997; Millward *et al.* 2000).

In addition, as a result of an extensive mapping, petrological and geochemical investigations carried out across the Snowdon area by the British Geological Survey in the mid to late 1980s, it has become apparent that parts of the Llewelyn Volcanic Group, most notably the Foel Fras Complex, have calc-alkaline characteristics (Ball and Merriman 1989; Howells *et al.* 1991). Significantly, the Foel Fras Volcanic Complex rocks contain a green, pleochroic actinolite or ferroactinolite. So the possibility is that the two 'andesites' could have been sourced in either the Lake District or Snowdonia.

Because of the potential significance of a provenance being determined for these two 'andesites', permission was requested to section and investigate three other artefacts from Pontnewydd Cave that have been identified as 'andesites'. These are samples D1440, D45790 and A684. All three samples are altered, like the two previously investigated Pontnewydd 'andesites'. All are porphyritic, with the phenocrysts chiefly being plagioclase feldspar which is variably altered, although in places original plagioclase is preserved which shows original compositional zoning. Sample D45790 shows the presence of microphenocrysts of fresh clinopyroxene, sometimes occurring in glomeroporhyritic clusters, along with chlorite-replaced pseudomorphs after another mafic phase, most probably orthopyroxene. Sample A684 contains spectacular, fresh, twinned and compositionally zoned clinopyroxene phenocrysts. Actinolite or ferroactinolite is present in coarse patches associated with chlorite and epidote is sample D1440, whilst biotite is an abundant phase in the groundmass of sample D45790. The primary mineralogical characteristics are again typical of low grade metamorphic rocks, especially those of the Lake District. For example, none of the Foel Fras Complex sequences contain clinopyroxene-phenocrystic lavas, whilst in addition the abundance and distribution of actinolite/ferroactinolite in sample B310 resembles a contact metamorphic effect rather than a low grade regional metamorphic effect. The presence of biotite in sample D45790 may well also be related to a contact metamorphic effect.

On balance therefore, a Lake District source is preferred for these 'andesites'. This is partly based on the phenocryst assemblages described above, as well as the metamorphic mineral assemblages being perhaps indicative of contact metamorphism rather than regional metamorphism. This also accords with the presence of a small number of granite cobbles present in the Pontnewydd Cave assemblage, and also reported from the nearby Cae Gwyn Cave deposits (R. E. Bevins unpublished data). These have been likened to the predominantly pink-coloured Eskdale and Ennerdale granitic and granodioritic intrusive rocks exposed in the western area of the Lake District, around Eskdale and Ennerdale. Significantly, these intrusions have produced thermal contact metamorphic aureoles in the adjacent Borrowdale Volcanic Group rocks which pass outwards from a highest temperature biotite-bearing zone to a lower temperature actinolite-bearing zone, beyond which the volcanic rocks show an abundance of the alteration mineral epidote. All of these characteristics are therefore consistent with these 'andesites' and the rarer granites and granodioritic rocks being derived from the English Lake District.

## TUFFS

Tuffs are well known for their use in the production of Neolithic axes, such as the British Group VI artefact material. Tuffs are deposited in beds and have a propensity to part along bedding planes or where deformed and fine grained commonly possess a cleavage. Crystal lithic tuff is the least homogenous lithology of all the tuff types present at Pontnewydd and the least suitable for the production of fine artefacts. The occupants of Pontnewydd appear to have been aware of these characteristics, as crystal lithic tuff is not used in large quantities and then mainly for the production of bifaces (25%) and Levallois flakes (14%). Crystal tuff is a relatively homogeneous and isotropic material, which is

used for Levallois flakes (25%) and retouched flakes (12%), and some bifaces (12%). Crystal tuff makes up 15.6% of the Levallois products, a similar percentage to rhyolite and feldspar-phyric lava (14.3%). This would not necessarily be expected on petrological grounds, but is probably due to their alteration under low grade metamorphism, which has changed many of their constituent minerals and possibly homogenized them to some extent.

Although similar to tuffs in composition, ignimbrites are typically welded rather than bedded; this recrystallization makes them more similar to rhyolites than tuffs in terms of their thermal history and hence properties. This may explain why ignimbrites were rarely used for Levallois products, but primarily for disc cores (14%), crude cores (14%) and producing retouched flakes (13%). Ignimbrite dominates the discoidal core assemblage, providing 20% of the total. Welded ignimbrites are highly durable but also have a high degree of homogeneity because of recrystallization during welding, making them extremely tough and therefore difficult to flake unless they have suffered some degree of weathering (Newcomer 1984). Jackson (2002) proposed a source in the Llewelyn Volcanic Group for several of the tuffs found at Pontnewydd.

Fine silicic tuff is finely bedded and therefore large cobbles are less likely to survive. Despite this, the greatest number of artefacts (13.9%) are made of this material. Fine silicic tuff is mainly used for retouched flakes (18%), Levallois flakes (15.5%) and tool reuse (12%). Fine silicic tuff provides a high percentage of Levallois artefacts (14%), scrapers (13%) and tool reuse (23%); the low mean size of these artefacts reflects the raw material size. There is a scarcity of cores made of fine silicic tuff. This may reflect a removal from the site of cores, or the bringing to the site of already roughed out artefacts, also demonstrated by the lack of cortex on these artefacts (Green 1988). There are several potential sources for the fine silicic tuff, and we have not yet been able to establish which of these were actually used.

The artefacts of both fine silicic tuff and flint have a high breakage frequency. This may be because these materials have similar properties, even when broken, are more easily recognizable as artefacts, or because they occur as small pebbles, which are more likely to become flawed during transport.

### Choice of raw material

The choice of raw material at Pontnewydd is dependent upon three main factors, namely its suitability for a purpose, the ease with which it can be worked, and its availability.

The physical properties of the rock determine how well a sharp cutting edge will be retained, or how long a hammerstone may stand up to repeated impacts. Stones that fracture conchoidally are the most desirable for flaking, and fracture is influenced by the percentage of silica within a raw material; for example both flint and obsidian, with their high silica content, fracture conchoidally. A second advantageous feature in a raw material is homogeneity leading to rock isotropy. A homogenous, isotropic rock

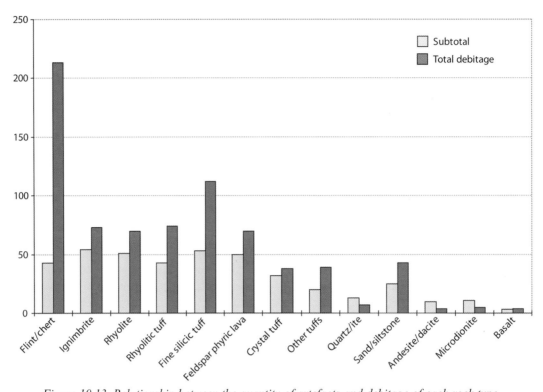

*Figure 10.13. Relationship between the quantity of artefacts and debitage of each rock type.*

lacks differences in texture, cracks, planes, flaws and other obstacles to the force of impact that passes through the material when struck. The best rocks for knapping are therefore usually cryptocrystalline in nature, as in theory larger crystals will divert the impact force from its path. Rocks must also contain a degree of elasticity in order to carry the force through the body of material and produce a flake. The Lithic Grade Scale was developed by experimental flint-knappers (Callahan 1979) to give some indication as to how easily certain rocks may be worked. Under this system, almost all the materials worked at Pontnewydd are described as hard to work. Even within petrological groups, the suitability of rocks for knapping may be highly variable, depending on their speed of cooling, their homogeneity, any metamorphism that they may have suffered, and hence any secondary minerals which have developed especially sheet silicates such as chlorite and white mica. The final choice of material is often a compromise as the most durable rock may also be the hardest to work.

Chi-squared analysis of the assemblage at Pontnewydd demonstrates that the raw materials were not used in equal proportions for all artefact types, and that the proportion of raw material used for each artefact type does not parallel the total use of that raw material throughout the assemblage (Aldhouse-Green *et al.* 2004, 97). Comparison of rock type data for each category with the distribution of rock types used for bifaces illustrated some interesting differences (ibid. 98). In all the categories that could be accurately tested, bifaces had a significantly different profile of rock use. They were preferentially made on feldspar-phyric lava, rhyolite lava and rhyolitic tuff, the rock types that,

on the basis of petrological considerations, should lead to the least refinement compared to the fine grained silicic tuffs. This difference extended to 'chunky' products such as crude cores, many of which were made of ignimbrite, the most highly silicic of the larger non-flint materials in the assemblage, but also the hardest to work. Levallois products were made of the less common rock types, crystal tuff and microdiorite. These rocks are less silicic (and hence slightly softer) than many of the other rocks available, but are extremely homogeneous, and seem to fracture less frequently. Scrapers are most commonly made from feldspar-phyric lava, fine silicic tuff and flint, whilst retouched flakes are most commonly made from fine silicic tuff and flint.

Taken as a whole, the above information indicates that there was a degree of selectivity in the rock types that were used for tool manufacture at Pontnewydd (Figure 10.13 and Table 10.14). The major differences appear to lie in cores, bifaces, Levallois products and side-scrapers. The notable difference in the frequency of chips may be due to the greater production of small debitage during the manufacture of some tools (Newcomer 1984). Alternatively it may result from the greater visibility of both worked flint and fine silicic tuff compared with the coarser materials at the site and is certainly due, in part, to the enhanced wet-sieving programme adopted at the site during the later excavation seasons.

*Selection of blanks*
Many of the artefacts at Pontnewydd show evidence of manufacture by striking flakes off pebbles, rather than angular blocks, and the shape of the blanks available

| | % Artefact frag. | % Core | % Discoidal core | % Biface | % Levallois product | % Scraper | % Retouched flake | % Reworked artefact | % Flake | % Small debitage | Total no. of artefacts |
|---|---|---|---|---|---|---|---|---|---|---|---|
| Flint | 31.8 | 28.8 | 10.0 | 2.5 | 6.0 | 12.2 | 20.8 | 15.0 | 18.1 | 69.9 | 303 |
| Rhyolite lava | 9.1 | 13.6 | 6.0 | 17.7 | 14.0 | 10.2 | 5.7 | 0.0 | 11.5 | 2.6 | 128 |
| Rhyolitic tuff | 9.1 | 5.1 | 10.0 | 15.2 | 11.0 | 8.2 | 9.4 | 10.0 | 10.6 | 5.7 | 130 |
| Feldspar-phyric lava | 4.5 | 8.5 | 14.0 | 19.0 | 13.0 | 16.3 | 3.8 | 17.5 | 11.1 | 2.6 | 132 |
| Fine silicic tuff | 0.0 | 1.7 | 14.0 | 8.9 | 15.0 | 14.3 | 24.5 | 20.0 | 13.8 | 9.8 | 170 |
| Crystal tuff | 4.5 | 3.4 | 4.0 | 8.9 | 13.0 | 10.2 | 9.4 | 15.0 | 6.8 | 2.1 | 90 |
| Ignimbrite | 18.2 | 18.6 | 20.0 | 8.9 | 7.0 | 8.2 | 15.1 | 10.0 | 11.7 | 2.1 | 135 |
| Siltstone | 13.6 | 15.3 | 12.0 | 6.3 | 5.0 | 6.1 | 5.7 | 5.0 | 7.3 | 4.1 | 89 |
| Crystal lithic tuff | 9.1 | 3.4 | 0.0 | 10.1 | 5.0 | 4.1 | 3.8 | 2.5 | 5.6 | 1.0 | 59 |
| Andesite & dacite | 0.0 | 1.7 | 6.0 | 2.5 | 1.0 | 4.1 | 1.9 | 2.5 | 0.7 | 0.0 | 15 |
| Microdiorite | 0.0 | 0.0 | 4.0 | 0.0 | 10.0 | 6.1 | 0.0 | 2.5 | 2.8 | 0.0 | 33 |
| **Totals** | 100 | 100 | 100 | 100 | 100 | 100 | 100 | 100 | 100 | 100 | 1284 |

*Table 10.14. Summarized data showing percentage of each tool type made on each raw material.*

must have played a part when deciding which materials to work (Fish 1979). White (1995) suggested that the shape of bifaces in southern Britain is largely dependent on the dimensions of the primary form of the raw materials, namely that the shape of the biface is determined by the shape and size of the blank. Ashton and McNabb (1994) were able to reconstruct the size and shape of large cutting tool blanks and therefore indicate to what extent shape had affected the finished artefact. At Pontnewydd, fine silicic tuff occurs in tabular fragments, which provide the perfect blanks, whereas the majority of rhyolite available would have been in the form of glacially rounded pebbles. The size of the rhyolite cobbles available may have limited the possibilities for thinning and refining, resulting in thicker pieces (Moloney *et al.* 1988). When experimentally flaking both glacially weathered pebbles and river-washed cobbles from the Pontnewydd area the rounded cobbles were found to be more homogeneous and hence possessed fewer flaws than those directly from the glacial drift. It is likely that rather than extracting materials directly from the glacial drift, cobbles would have been collected from talus slopes at the base of the limestone cliffs or from stream-bed deposits. It is worth remembering that the effects of solifluction processes, vegetation and snow cover would have made different areas within the Elwy valley suitable for collecting materials at different times of year. Also, immediately following de-glaciation there would most probably have been an abundance of high energy streams and rivers moving massive amounts of glacially transported debris so it would have been a very dynamic environment.

Many experiments, both formal and informal, have been conducted on the viability of non-flint materials for knapping (Jones 1979; Toth 1982; Newcomer 1984; MacRae and Moloney 1988) and on the influence of raw material on morphology in the Acheulian (Clark 1980; Toth 1982; Ashton and McNabb 1994; White 1995). Jones (1979) replicated bifaces and cleavers from Olduvai Gorge and suggested that raw material fracture properties and least-effort flaking strategies influenced aspects of biface morphology. By making and then using bifaces of basalt and phonolite, he indicated that hominins had responded to the raw materials' mechanical properties by varying the intensity of retouch performed on them. This had the result of making some of the artefacts appear 'cruder' than others, a point that is paralleled in the assemblage at Pontnewydd.

These studies were first given impetus by the suggestion (Clark 1980; Strauss 1980; Villa 1983) that the physical properties of the raw material influenced the type of tool produced, thereby causing lithic assemblage variability. Experimental knapping work performed on quartzite (Moloney *et al.* 1988) has demonstrated some interesting points, which may be equally applicable to other highly silicic, holocrystalline, isotropic materials such as rhyolite. This work suggests that the nature of the raw material means that the strongest and sharpest edge is formed by the removal of the first few flakes, and the unpredictability of the material may limit continued flaking and therefore result in the production of a less complicated tool. Some of the observations made during these experiments apply particularly to the Pontnewydd assemblage (Jackson 2002). Primarily it was found that very hard follow-through blows were necessary to detach flakes, the best results being achieved using a combination of a large boxwood hammer and an ignimbrite hammerstone. Internal flaws in the material, which were not immediately noticeable, continually hampered flaking. Newcomer's (1984) experiments seem to demonstrate that the raw materials at Pontnewydd did not limit the tool types present; rather they may have limited the possible levels of refinement.

Not all the erratics that occur in drift in the Elwy valley area were used for artefact manufacture. Those largely avoided include local limestones and shales, weak, weathered granites and basic igneous rocks, which would have been unsuitable for knapping; an element of choice has therefore been exhibited.

It can be seen that the raw materials differ between the Main Cave and the New Entrance (Table 10.13). However, they differ in detail also between the stratified areas of the Main Cave (Areas B, C, D, F, of which B is closest to the entrance and F deepest into the system). Thus the rocks most commonly used as raw materials for artefacts are B/C – fine silicic tuff; D – rhyolitic tuff; F – ignimbrite. The rock type most frequently found in the New Entrance is flint, but this comprises mainly small debitage; otherwise

the next three rock types found there in descending order of frequency are rhyolitic tuff, ignimbrite and crystal tuff – a result very similar to the range of the Main Cave. It is clear, however, that the taphonomic contexts of deposition and recovery in these two areas were different and this is undoubtedly a key factor in their differentiation.

A review of the frequencies of artefact types in the Main Cave and the New Entrance shows variation which may be explicable in terms of chronology, as previously proposed (Aldhouse-Green 1998, 140–141; Aldhouse-Green *et al.* 2004, 102), but which may also be interpreted either in terms of spatial variation in activities or in stochastic terms, arising from the potentially complex taphonomic history of the debris flows from which the artefacts were recovered (Table 10.15). Study of the different areas of the Main Cave (Table 10.13) shows a predictable variation which may be interpreted in the terms set out above. There is, however, less difference between these individual areas than between the Main Cave and the New Entrance (Table 10.15). The chronological evidence, such as it is, would make sense of the New Entrance assemblage as a fully Middle Palaeolithic industry, in which bifaces, if not actually derived, are relatively rare.

## Note on the results of a search for haematite specimens amongst the lithics from Pontnewydd Cave

*Tim Young*

All the residues from the Lower Breccia with a sieve size of >9 mm have been examined for possible specimens of haematite. None of these contained any 'exotics', defined for working purposes on site as all rocks excluding limestone and mudstone. In addition, approximately 70% of the 'exotics' collection has been examined, including any non-Lower Breccia material contained therein (Table 10.16). The total yield of haematite material with grain size greater than approximately 6 mm was only 47.5 g. Of this three pieces (4.6 g) came from the Upper Breccia, one piece (19.8 g) from the Silt beds and five pieces from the Lower Breccia (23.1 g). In addition there were various smaller soft red grains from various contexts which were too small for hand lens identification.

| *Principal Artefact Types* | *Main Cave* | | *New Entrance* | |
|---|---|---|---|---|
| | *No.* | *%* | *No.* | *%* |
| Bifaces | 70 | 23.6 | 4 | 5.5 |
| Choppers/chopping tools | 6 | 2.0 | 1 | 1.4 |
| Discoidal cores | 41 | 13.8 | 4 | 5.5 |
| Levallois cores | 13 | 4.4 | 1 | 1.4 |
| Miscellaneous cores | 35 | 11.8 | 17 | 23.3 |
| Levallois flakes, blades, points | 53 | 17.8 | 26 | 35.6 |
| Side-scrapers | 37 | 12.5 | 12 | 16.4 |
| Notches/denticulates | 7 | 2.4 | 4 | 5.5 |
| Other retouched artefacts | 25 | 8.3 | 2 | 2.7 |
| Naturally backed knives | 10 | 3.4 | 2 | 2.7 |
| **Total** | **297** | | **73** | |

*Table 10.15. Artefact frequencies in the Main Cave and New Entrance.*

| *Find no.* | *Grid square* | *Context* | *Height below S.D.* | *Weight* | *Description* |
|---|---|---|---|---|---|
| F661 | H1 SW | UB | 99.84-99.74 | 2.4 g | Fibrous crust |
| Unnum. | I7 SE | LB | 99.25-99.15 | 6.4 g | Haematite with quartz |
| D1823 | J6 NW | Sb | 99.70-99.60 | 19.8 g | Haematite with quartz & calcite |
| D2155 | J7 SW | LB | 99.38-99.28 | 0.9 g | Haematite with quartz |
| D4952 | G7 SW | LB | 99.19 | 5.2 g | Haematite with quartz |
| D2096 | I7 NW | LB | 99.10-99.00 | 5.5 g | Haematized sandstone |
| D888g | I7 | UB | 99.60 | 0.6 g | Haematite with quartz (broken from below) |
| D888d | I7 | UB | 99.60 | 1.6 g | Haematite with quartz (broken from above) |
| D3572 | J6 NW | LB | 99.30-99.20 | 5.1 g | Haematized sandstone |

*Table 10.16. Haematite samples.*

The material could be divided into several petrographic types. The most important was a quartz-bearing haematite ore (34.7 g) total, but there were also iron oxides derived from oxidation of iron sulphides, and what appeared to be haematized sandstones. There was, in addition to the rest of the haematite material, one pebble of Ordovician sedimentary ironstone, which could have been derived from Snowdonia or Anglesey (context: World War II Dump). All the haematitic material occurred apparently as water-worn pebbles.

On casual inspection the origin of this material was not apparent, larger pieces would be required before the textures would be useful. Potential source areas include fissures and caves within the Carboniferous Limestone of North Wales where Triassic/Jurrasic haematites are locally developed (*e.g.* in Dyserth Quarry, 8 km east of Pontnewydd (SJ 095702). The distribution of such features outside the major quarries is currently not known, and would require primary fieldwork to determine. Similar material could also be glacially-derived from Cumbria, where almost identical ores occur on the opposite side of the Morecambe Bay basin. It seems likely that these sources could be differentiated chemically in appropriate material, but there is little comparative data currently available (compared, for instance with the large body of data now constructed for the Bristol Channel Orefield).

Given the small size of the pieces, their rounded pebble form, and the low levels of abundance, there is no evidence as to whether these materials were, or were not, derived through human agency. The pilot study tells us that pigments were present but there is so far no evidence that they were introduced by humans. In order to determine whether this material may have been derived by human agency, it would be necessary either to locate humanly modified pieces or to demonstrate that the Pontnewydd haematite clasts were unlikely to have originated in the contemporary Pleistocene drift. A conclusion that ochres were in use at Pontnewydd over 200,000 years ago would be exciting. However, just as significant would be a conclusion that such ores were available locally but were not used by the hominins at the cave.

## Conclusions

*Stephen Aldhouse-Green, Rick Peterson*
*and Heather Jackson*

The present cave is a fragment of a much larger Pleistocene system. The surviving lithics were probably moved several times from their original source, and some elements of these movements can be reconstructed. Before 220,000 BP, the Lower Breccia moved material eastwards into the present Main Cave at least as far as the Cross Rift, and probably through to the New Entrance. Further flows moved material from the south of the present New Entrance in the direction of the surviving cave. The fresher condition of the lithic artefacts in the New Entrance flow suggests

that their degree of movement was less in this part of the system than was the case with the Main Cave.

Lithic material was also transported in at least four Devensian debris flows. The Upper Breccia debris flow in the Main Cave is mainly composed of limestone scree but seems to have re-worked material from within the Lower Breccia, probably including material which had originally come to rest in now destroyed sections of the cave system to the west. In the New Entrance, the Mudstone Gravel may be correlative with the Lower Breccia. The Yellow Stony layer debris flow, which overlay it, seems to have originated in a now lost source to the south. However, the last of these debris flows, which resulted in the formation of the Limestone Breccia, transported large amounts of material from this second source into the New Entrance.

Whether the raw materials at Pontnewydd (with the exception of the andesites) derived directly from the glacial till or were collected from the banks of the River Elwy, it is clear that they would have been readily available within the local 'foraging radius' (Mellars 1996). This is consistent with the raw material procurement patterns on Middle Palaeolithic sites in south-western France (Geneste 1988; Turq 1988) which reveal a strong predominance of material derived from very local sources. In addition, all stages of the lithic reduction sequence at Pontnewydd are represented, from the initial importation of cobbles to the production of finished tools. This indicates that knapping took place at the cave and is consistent with the use of raw materials derived from the most local foraging zone of 4–5 km from the site (Geneste 1988). It is likely that cobbles were subjected to trial flaking before transportation back to the cave, because as with many glacially weathered rocks, it would be difficult to tell the texture from the outward appearance of a pebble.

Whether the Pontnewydd hominins made their artefacts at one *locale* or several it is likely to be the remains of a relatively short-lived set of practices. The technological similarity of the artefacts allows the material to be regarded as the product of a single group of hominins. The only possible exception to this is the relative paucity of bifaces from the New Entrance which may represent either a degree of patterning in the lithic scatter at the original *locale(s)* or a chronological distinction. Unfortunately, no conclusion is possible at this stage for the potential use of ochre by hominins at Pontnewydd.

## Catalogue of illustrated artefacts from Pontnewydd

*Stephen Aldhouse-Green and Elizabeth A. Walker*

In the select catalogue which follows, the artefacts are presented typologically.

The attributes recorded for use in the artefact analyses were devised with the particular circumstances of Pontnewydd in mind (Table 10.17).

| *The following attributes were recorded* |
|---|
| I Curatorial<br>    1. Find no.<br>    2. Year of excavation |
| II Stratigraphy<br>    3. Layer<br>    4. 0.5 metres grid square<br>    5. Height relative to site datum (SD = 100.00, OD = 90.473) |
| III Raw material<br>    6. Raw material |
| IV Typology<br>    7. Name<br>    8. Type number (after Bordes) |
| V Condition<br>    9. Burnt<br>    10. Fresh<br>    11. Slightly rolled 21–40%<br>    12. Heavily rolled > 40%<br>    13. Edge chipped<br>    14. Ancient damage through patina |
| VI Colouration<br>    15. Patina<br>    16. Stained |
| VII Completeness<br>    17. Whole (estimated > 90% complete)<br>    18. Broken (< 90% complete) |
| VIII Cortex<br>    19. 90–100% (of any one surface, or both cumulatively as % of overall artefact surface.<br>    20. 50–90%<br>    21. 10–49%<br>    22. < 10% |
| IX Dimensions<br>    23. Length – on bulbar axis (expressed as 'length +' of variable<br>    24. Breadth – at right angles to bulbar axis (expressed as 'breadth +' of variable)<br>    25. Thickness (maximum)<br>    26. Weight – grammes to nearest 0.1gr (expressed as 'weight +' of variable) |
| X Non-Levallois removal<br>    27. Flake<br>    28. Blade<br>    29. Spall<br>    30. Chunk<br>    31. Chip |
| XI Core types<br>    32. Discoidal<br>    33. Levallois<br>    34. Indeterminate (*i.e.* too fragmentary to determine)<br>    35. Crude |
| XII Flat butt type<br>    36. Absent<br>    37. Removal (deliberately in antiquity)<br>    38. Plain<br>    39. Dihedral<br>    40. Faceted<br>    41. Soft hammer<br>    42. Punctiform<br>    43. Mixed |
| XIII Levallois removals<br>    44. Flake<br>    45. Flake-blade<br>    46. Point |
| XIV Style of retouch<br>    47. Thick<br>    48. Demi-Quina<br>    49. Abrupt<br>    50. Scaler<br>    51. Parallel<br>    52. Sub-parallel<br>    53. Inverse<br>    54. Bifacial<br>    55. Retouch (ancient) through patina |

*Table 10.17. Attributes recorded for use in analysis.*

**Figure 10.14**      **A547**

| Curatorial | 1 | 95.35H/2.A547 |
|---|---|---|
| | 2 | 1995 |
| Stratigraphy | 3 | Area A (Boyd Dawkins' Dump) Layer 2 |
| Raw material | 6 | Siliceous tuff |
| Typology | 7 | Biface |
| Condition | 12 | Heavily rolled |
| Completeness | 17 | Whole |
| Cortex | 22 | None |
| Dimensions | 23 | Length = 75.6 mm |
| | 24 | Breadth = 46.3 mm |
| | 25 | Thickness = 16.2 mm |
| | 26 | Weight = 52.2 g |

A small pointed biface made on a flake. The tool has been trimmed on both faces; in some places the flake removals have left a series of stepped fractures on the surface of the tool. There is some edge chipping caused during abrasion and the flake scar surfaces are heavily rolled.

**Figure 10.14**      **D4959**

| Curatorial | 1 | 88.166H/2.D4959 |
|---|---|---|
| | 2 | 1988 |
| Stratigraphy | 3 | Lower Breccia – Silt bed matrix |
| | 4 | Grid square K7SE |
| | 5 | 99.27 m |
| Raw material | 6 | Silicic tuff (thin section 224) |
| Typology | 7 | Cleaver |
| Condition | 12 | Heavily rolled |
| Colouration | 16 | Some staining |
| Completeness | 17 | Whole |
| Cortex | 21 | 10% coverage |
| Dimensions | 23 | Length = 102.0 mm |
| | 24 | Breadth = 86.3 mm |
| | 25 | Thickness = 27.0 mm |
| | 26 | Weight = 231.4 g |

A biface made on a cobble fashioned to a flat cleaver end. The original pebble surface survives at the thick, cortical butt but the rest of the tool has been well thinned and trimmed on both faces.

**Figure 10.14**      **A533**

| Curatorial | 1 | 95.35H/2.A533 |
|---|---|---|
| | 2 | 1995 |
| Stratigraphy | 3 | Area A (Boyd Dawkins' Dump) Trench II, Layer 2 |
| Raw material | 6 | Rhyolitic tuff |
| Typology | 7 | Biface |
| Condition | 12 | Heavily rolled |
| Completeness | 18 | 85% complete |
| Cortex | 21 | Coverage over 20% of surface |
| Dimensions | 23 | Length = 116.0 mm |
| | 24 | Breadth = 65.8 mm |
| | 25 | Thickness = 35.7 mm |
| | 26 | Weight = 236.1 g |

A biface made on a pebble. The pebble surface survives over part of the tool. There are several hinged fractures around the area where the knapper attempted to remove the cortex. The tool is missing part of its butt and has heavily rolled flake scars.

**Figure 10.14**      **A766**

| Curatorial | 1 | 95.35H/2.A766 |
|---|---|---|
| | 2 | 1995 |
| Stratigraphy | 3 | Area A (World War II Dump) Trench II, Layer 1 |

| Raw material | 6 | Rhyolite |
|---|---|---|
| Typology | 7 | Biface |
| Condition | 12 | Heavily rolled |
| Completeness | 17 | 70% complete |
| Cortex | 22 | 5% coverage |
| Dimensions | 23 | Length = 66.1 mm |
| | 24 | Breadth = 54.5 mm |
| | 25 | Thickness = 31.9 mm |
| | 26 | Weight = 117.8 g |

A small finely flaked biface which is missing its tip. The break that removed the tip is ancient but the tool has also experienced recent damage on one side where a number of flakes have been removed from its edge. The surface of the biface has a series of stepped fractures on the surface.

**Figure 10.15**      **D4445**

| Curatorial | 1 | 87.93H/1.D4445 |
|---|---|---|
| | 2 | 1987 |
| Stratigraphy | 3 | Lower Breccia |
| | 4 | Grid square K7NE |
| | 5 | 99.50 m |
| Raw material | 6 | Rhyolitic tuff |
| Typology | 7 | Biface |
| Condition | 12 | Heavily rolled |
| Completeness | 17 | 95% complete |
| Cortex | 22 | None |
| Dimensions | 23 | Length = 75.2 mm |
| | 24 | Breadth = 65.1 mm |
| | 25 | Thickness = 38.4 mm |
| | 26 | Weight = 201.9 g |

A small, thick biface very crudely shaped with stepped fractures and a very irregular shape. The tip is missing, from an ancient break, and the flake scars are very heavily rolled.

**Figure 10.15**      **D4938**

| Curatorial | 1 | 88.166H/2.D4938 |
|---|---|---|
| | 2 | 1988 |
| Stratigraphy | 3 | Lower Breccia – Silt bed matrix |
| | 4 | Grid square K7SE |
| | 5 | 99.35 m |
| Raw material | 6 | Feldspar-phyric lava |
| Typology | 7 | Biface |
| Condition | 12 | Heavily rolled |
| Completeness | 18 | 70% complete |
| Cortex | 22 | None |
| Dimensions | 23 | Length = 98.5 mm |
| | 24 | Breadth = 57.3 mm |
| | 25 | Thickness = 31.7 mm |
| | 26 | Weight = 194.4 g |

A neatly made pointed biface with thinned and trimmed butt. It is missing part of one side due to an ancient break. The tool has very heavily weathered flake scars.

**Figure 10.15**      **A652**

| Curatorial | 1 | 95.35H/2.A652 |
|---|---|---|
| | 2 | 1995 |
| Stratigraphy | 3 | Area A (Boyd Dawkins' Dump) Layer 2 from safety baulk/east section |
| | 5 | 98.55 m |
| Raw material | 6 | Crystal lithic tuff |
| Typology | 7 | Biface |
| Condition | 12 | Very heavily rolled |
| Completeness | 17 | Whole |
| Cortex | 21 | 40% coverage |

| Dimensions | 23 | Length = 154.1 mm |
| | 24 | Breadth = 116.6 mm |
| | 25 | Thickness = 43.3 mm |
| | 26 | Weight = 919.7 g |

A large unfinished biface that has been roughly flaked to shape on both faces and at the butt. One face is cortical. The biface has experienced some minor recent damage on one face, otherwise is complete. It has very heavily rolled flake scars.

**Figure 10.16**                    **D4786**

| Curatorial | 1 | 88.166H/2.D4786 |
| | 2 | 1988 |
| Stratigraphy | 3 | Lower Breccia – Red Clay matrix |
| | 4 | Grid square H5 |
| | 5 | 99.50 m |
| Raw material | 6 | Fine silicic tuff |
| Typology | 7 | Biface |
| Condition | 12 | Very heavily rolled |
| Completeness | 17 | Complete |
| Cortex | 21 | 20% coverage |
| Dimensions | 23 | Length = 146.9 mm |
| | 24 | Breadth = 101.7 mm |
| | 25 | Thickness = 45.7 mm |
| | 26 | Weight = 715.2 g |

A large biface made on a stone cobble. The pebble surface survives on one face towards the butt. Both faces are neatly flaked although there are a few stepped fractures present on both faces.

**Figure 10.16**                    **D5406**

| Curatorial | 1 | 93.40H/2.D5406 |
| | 2 | 1993 |
| Stratigraphy | 3 | Lower Breccia |
| | 4 | Grid square K8SE |
| | 5 | 99.20–99.17 m |
| Raw material | 6 | Ignimbrite |
| Typology | 7 | Biface |
| Condition | 12 | Heavily rolled |
| Completeness | 17 | Complete |
| Cortex | 21 | 10% coverage |
| Dimensions | 23 | Length = 98.6 mm |
| | 24 | Breadth = 67.0 mm |
| | 25 | Thickness = 42.2 mm |
| | 26 | Weight = 271.7 g |

A pointed biface that has been carefully trimmed over one face. The tool has some cortex surviving on one side and the tool is fashioned into a point that has been thinned. The biface has a thick butt and heavily rolled flake scars.

**Figure 10.17**                    **D4785**

| Curatorial | 1 | 88.166H/2.D4785 |
| | 2 | 1988 |
| Stratigraphy | 3 | Lower Breccia |
| | 4 | Grid square H7NW |
| | 5 | 99.43 m |
| Raw material | 6 | Crystal lithic tuff |
| Typology | 7 | Biface |
| Condition | 12 | Heavily rolled |
| Completeness | 17 | Complete |
| Cortex | 21 | 40% coverage |
| Dimensions | 23 | Length = 120.4 mm |
| | 24 | Breadth = 92.4 mm |
| | 25 | Thickness = 67.3 mm |
| | 26 | Weight = 860.3 g |

A cortical cobble modified to a thick point at one end whilst retaining the original pebble surface over much of one side and

the butt. The flaking is stepped and the tool has had very little trimming over one face.

**Figure 10.17**                    **F2925**

| Curatorial | 1 | 89.168H/2.F2925 |
| | 2 | 1989 |
| Stratigraphy | 3 | Lower Breccia (a) |
| | 4 | Grid square I4NE |
| | 5 | 99.72 m |
| Raw material | 6 | Flow-banded rhyolite (thin section 212) |
| Typology | 7 | Biface |
| Condition | 11 | Slightly rolled |
| Completeness | 17 | Complete |
| Cortex | 21 | 20% coverage |
| Dimensions | 23 | Length = 94.8 mm |
| | 24 | Breadth = 68.0 mm |
| | 25 | Thickness = 38.5 mm |
| | 26 | Weight = 251.1 g |

A complete pointed biface with stepped fractures on one face running through the cortex. The tool has more regular flaking elsewhere over both faces. The pebble cortex surface survives over part of one face of the tool and the flake scars are slightly rolled.

**Figure 10.17**                    **H507**

| Curatorial | 1 | 88.166H/2.H507 |
| | 2 | 1988 |
| Stratigraphy | 3 | Layer 24 |
| | 4 | Grid square AA994SW |
| | 5 | 99.25 m |
| Raw material | 6 | Quartz |
| Typology | 7 | Biface |
| Condition | 12 | Rolled |
| Completeness | 17 | Complete |
| Cortex | 22 | None |
| Dimensions | 23 | Length = 79.8 mm |
| | 24 | Breadth = 44.2 mm |
| | 25 | Thickness = 29.7 mm |
| | 26 | Weight = 93.6 g |

A small rolled pointed biface made on a flake of quartz. The ventral surface is flat with few flake removals taken from it, whilst the dorsal is very heavily worked and shaped.

**Figure 10.18**                    **D4871**

| Curatorial | 1 | 88.166H/2.D4871 |
| | 2 | 1988 |
| Stratigraphy | 3 | Lower Breccia |
| | 4 | Grid square G7SE |
| | 5 | 99.26 m |
| Raw material | 6 | Feldspar-phyric lava |
| Typology | 7 | Biface |
| Condition | 12 | Heavily rolled |
| Completeness | 18 | 90% complete |
| Cortex | 21 | 40% coverage |
| Dimensions | 23 | Length = 146.6 mm |
| | 24 | Breadth = 105.8 mm |
| | 25 | Thickness = 41.6 mm |
| | 26 | Weight = 819.3 g |

A biface made on a tabular piece of stone. One face is largely cortical, although has been trimmed around part of its edge. The other face is heavily flaked. The tip of the biface is missing, broken in antiquity.

**Figure 10.18** F2860

| Curatorial | 1 | 89.168H/2.F2860 |
| | 2 | 1989 |
| Stratigraphy | 3 | Lower Breccia (c) |
| | 4 | Grid square I4NW |
| | 5 | 99.38 m |
| Raw material | 6 | Ignimbrite |
| Typology | 7 | Biface |
| Condition | 11 | Slightly rolled |
| Completeness | 18 | 70% complete |
| Cortex | 22 | 30% coverage |
| Dimensions | 23 | Length = 78.2 mm |
| | 24 | Breadth = 63.3 mm |
| | 25 | Thickness = 33.6 mm |
| | 26 | Weight = 146.8 g |

A biface fragment with some stepped fracturing on one face. The piece has a break across the butt, which is missing. This is an ancient break. The tool has a cortical surface on one side, the rest of the tool is carefully flaked.

**Figure 10.18** H2135

| Curatorial | 1 | 94.38H/2.H2135 |
| | 2 | 1994 |
| Stratigraphy | 3 | Layer 29 |
| | 4 | Grid square AA995SE |
| | 5 | 98.72 m |
| Raw material | 6 | Tuffaceous sandstone |
| Typology | 7 | Biface |
| Condition | 12 | Heavily rolled |
| Completeness | 18 | 70% complete |
| Cortex | 21 | 40% coverage |
| Dimensions | 23 | Length = 79.3 mm |
| | 24 | Breadth = 52.5 mm |
| | 25 | Thickness = 33.1 mm |
| | 26 | Weight = 164.3 g |

A possible failed biface fragment which is missing its tip. It has one domed thick side which has been very heavily flaked. The other side is cortical and flat. This side has had some trimming at the butt.

**Figure 10.19** F4490

| Curatorial | 1 | 94.38H/2.F4490 |
| | 2 | 1994 |
| Stratigraphy | 3 | Lower Breccia |
| | 4 | Grid square G5NE |
| | 5 | 99.31 m |
| Raw material | 6 | Ignimbrite |
| Typology | 7 | Biface |
| Condition | 12 | Heavily rolled |
| Completeness | 17 | 95% complete |
| Cortex | 21 | 10% coverage |
| Dimensions | 23 | Length = 144.1 mm |
| | 24 | Breadth = 81.0 mm |
| | 25 | Thickness = 36.5 mm |
| | 26 | Weight = 430.3 g |

A biface that has been heavily rolled. It has cortex surviving towards the butt on one face whilst there are some carefully removed thinning flakes from the other face, particularly near the tip of the tool.

**Figure 10.19** H2771

| Curatorial | 1 | 95.35H/2.H2771 |
| | 2 | 1995 |
| Stratigraphy | 3 | Layer 29b |
| | 4 | Grid square AB993NW |

| | 5 | 98.29 m |
| Raw material | 6 | Tuffaceous sandstone |
| Typology | 7 | Biface on a flake |
| Condition | 11 | Slightly rolled |
| Completeness | 17 | Complete |
| Cortex | 21 | 30% coverage |
| Dimensions | 23 | Length = 95.7 mm |
| | 24 | Breadth = 67.2 mm |
| | 25 | Thickness = 30.0 mm |
| | 26 | Weight = 158.5 g |

A thin irregularly shaped, unfinished biface made on a flake with step fractured trimming flake removals along one edge. The cortical pebble surface only survives around the butt area. It is slightly rolled.

**Figure 10.19** H3022

| Curatorial | 1 | 95.35H/2.H3022 |
| | 2 | 1995 |
| Stratigraphy | 3 | Layer 23 |
| | 4 | Grid square AG992SW |
| | 5 | 98.70 m |
| Raw material | 6 | Silicic tuff (thin section 256) |
| Typology | 7 | Biface |
| Condition | 11 | Slightly rolled |
| Completeness | 17 | Complete |
| Cortex | 21 | 35% coverage |
| Dimensions | 23 | Length = 74.4 mm |
| | 24 | Breadth = 48.0 mm |
| | 25 | Thickness = 27.4 mm |
| | 26 | Weight = 105.7 g |

An unfinished biface made on a flake. The tool has a cortical dorsal surface with some trimming along the edge. The ventral side is mainly unmodified, apart from a few flake removals. The original pebble surface covers most of the dorsal face. There is concreted sediment adhering to areas of the tool.

**Figure 10.20** F4888

| Curatorial | 1 | 94.38HH/2.F4888 |
| | 2 | 1994 |
| Stratigraphy | 3 | Lower Breccia (c) |
| | 4 | Grid square I1NW |
| | 5 | 99.45 m |
| Raw material | 6 | Crystal vitric tuff (thin section 208) |
| Typology | 7 | Biface |
| Condition | 12 | Heavily rolled |
| Completeness | 17 | Complete |
| Cortex | 21 | 40% coverage |
| Dimensions | 23 | Length = 124.2 mm |
| | 24 | Breadth = 61.5 mm |
| | 25 | Thickness = 28.6 mm |
| | 26 | Weight = 256.1 g |

An unfinished pointed biface. The tool is asymmetrical with an off-centre tip and has a very crudely flaked butt. It is made on a lenticular-shaped pebble and the original cobble surface survives over most of one face and on one side. It has been heavily rolled.

**Figure 10.20** H9

| Curatorial | 1 | 86.31H/2.H9 |
| | 2 | 1986 |
| Stratigraphy | 3 | From solifluction layers 6/8 which sealed the New Entrance |
| | 5 | c. 93.00 m |
| Raw material | 6 | Dacite (thin section 209) |

| Typology | 7 | Biface |
|---|---|---|
| Condition | 12 | Very heavily rolled |
| Colouration | 16 | Stained in patches |
| Completeness | 17 | Complete |
| Cortex | 22 | None |
| Dimensions | 23 | Length = 136.4 mm |
|  | 24 | Breadth = 84.9 mm |
|  | 25 | Thickness = 37.2 mm |
|  | 26 | Weight = 400.3 g |

A large and very heavily weathered pointed biface with surface staining in places. The tool has a stepped appearance to several of its flake scars.

**Figure 10.21**    H2416

| Curatorial | 1 | 95.35H/2.H2416 |
|---|---|---|
|  | 2 | 1995 |
| Stratigraphy | 3 | Layer 29 |
|  | 4 | Grid square AA993SW |
|  | 5 | 98.76 m |
| Raw material | 6 | Crystal lithic tuff (thin section 280) |
| Typology | 7 | Biface |
| Condition | 12 | Heavily rolled |
| Completeness | 17 | Complete, but in two pieces |
| Cortex | 22 | None |
| Dimensions | 23 | Length = 154.1 mm |
|  | 24 | Breadth = 77.7 mm |
|  | 25 | Thickness = 44.0 mm |
|  | 26 | Weight = 512.5 g |

A large pointed biface that has had recent damage towards its tip. It is flaked extensively over both faces and is heavily rolled.

**Figure 10.21**    H2039

| Curatorial | 1 | 94.38H/2.H2039 |
|---|---|---|
|  | 2 | 1994 |
| Stratigraphy | 3 | Layer 23 |
|  | 4 | Grid square AC992NW |
|  | 5 | 99.70–99.60 m |
| Raw material | 6 | Crystal tuff |
| Typology | 7 | Chopping tool |
| Condition | 11 | Slightly rolled |
| Completeness | 17 | Complete |
| Cortex | 20 | 60% coverage |
| Dimensions | 23 | Length = 102.0 mm |
|  | 24 | Breadth = 71.0 mm |
|  | 25 | Thickness = 48.5 mm |
|  | 26 | Weight = 417.4 g |

A cobble of tuff modified into a simple chopping tool by the removal of some large alternating flakes from each face. This has created a basic cutting edge. The tool is slightly rolled and the cortical pebble surface survives over much of the butt.

**Figure 10.22**    A537

| Curatorial | 1 | 95.35H/2.A537 |
|---|---|---|
|  | 2 | 1995 |
| Stratigraphy | 3 | Area A (Boyd Dawkins' Dump) Trench II, Layer 2 |
| Raw material | 6 | Rhyolitic tuff |
| Typology | 7 | Levallois flake |
| Condition | 12 | Heavily rolled |
| Completeness | 17 | Complete |
| Cortex | 22 | 5% coverage |
| Dimensions | 23 | Length = 68.9 mm |
|  | 24 | Breadth = 43.0 mm |
|  | 25 | Thickness = 14.8 mm |

|  | 26 | Weight = 51.9 g |
|---|---|---|
| Butt type | 38 | Plain |
| Levallois removals | 44 | Flake |

A Levallois flake struck from a partially cortical core. There are traces of cortex on one edge of the dorsal surface. The flake has one recent chip from the ventral face. It is heavily rolled and has a plain, thick striking platform with a pronounced bulb of percussion.

**Figure 10.22**    A566

| Curatorial | 1 | 95.35H/2.A566 |
|---|---|---|
|  | 2 | 1995 |
| Stratigraphy | 3 | Area A (Boyd Dawkins' Dump) Trench II, Layer 2 |
| Raw material | 6 | Rhyolitic tuff |
| Typology | 7 | Single-straight side-scraper made on a Levallois flake |
| Condition | 12 | Heavily rolled |
| Completeness | 17 | Complete |
| Cortex | 22 | None |
| Dimensions | 23 | Length = 83.9 mm |
|  | 24 | Breadth = 73.5 mm |
|  | 25 | Thickness = 15.1 mm |
|  | 26 | Weight = 99.8 g |
| Butt type | 38 | Plain |
| Levallois removals | 44 | Flake |
| Style of retouch | 50 | Scalar |

A single-straight side-scraper made on a Levallois flake with marginal retouch running along one edge. The retouch is scalar in form.

**Figure 10.22**    F1772

| Curatorial | 1 | 88.166H/2.F1772 |
|---|---|---|
|  | 2 | 1988 |
| Stratigraphy | 3 | Upper Breccia – Silt bed matrix |
|  | 4 | Grid square G2SW |
|  | 5 | 99.50 m |
| Raw material | 6 | Microdiorite |
| Typology | 7 | Levallois flake |
| Condition | 12 | Very heavily rolled |
| Completeness | 17 | Complete |
| Cortex | 22 | None |
| Dimensions | 23 | Length = 69.9 mm |
|  | 24 | Breadth = 64.5 mm |
|  | 25 | Thickness = 14.7 mm |
|  | 26 | Weight = 69.5 g |
| Butt type | 39 | Dihedral |
| Levallois removals | 44 | Flake |

A Levallois flake which has been very heavily rolled. It has recent minor edge damage. The flake has a very pronounced bulbar scar on the ventral surface.

**Figure 10.22**    F2805

| Curatorial | 1 | 89.168H/2.F2805 |
|---|---|---|
|  | 2 | 1989 |
| Stratigraphy | 3 | Lower Breccia |
|  | 4 | Grid square H4SW |
|  | 5 | 99.44 m |
| Raw material | 6 | Microdiorite |
| Typology | 7 | Single-straight side-scraper made on a Levallois flake |
| Condition | 12 | Heavily rolled |
| Completeness | 17 | Complete |
| Cortex | 22 | None |
| Dimensions | 23 | Length = 51.1 mm |

| | 24 | Breadth = 45.5 mm |
| --- | --- | --- |
| | 25 | Thickness = 13.7 mm |
| | 26 | Weight = 40.9 g |
| Butt type | 38 | Plain |
| Levallois removals | 44 | Flake |
| Style of retouch | 49 | Abrupt |

A heavily rolled single-straight side-scraper made on a Levallois flake. The retouch is very marginal along one edge. The flake has a very pronounced bulb of percussion.

**Figure 10.22**     **D4434**

| Curatorial | 1 | 87.93H/1.D4434 |
| --- | --- | --- |
| | 2 | 1987 |
| Stratigraphy | 3 | Lower Breccia |
| | 4 | Grid square K7NE |
| | 5 | 99.54 m |
| Raw material | 6 | Fine silicic tuff (thin section 219) |
| Typology | 7 | Levallois flake |
| Condition | 12 | Heavily rolled |
| Completeness | 17 | 95% complete |
| Cortex | 22 | None |
| Dimensions | 23 | Length = 61.7 mm |
| | 24 | Breadth = 46.5 mm |
| | 25 | Thickness = 10.1 mm |
| | 26 | Weight = 26.5 g |
| Butt type | 39 | Dihedral |
| Levallois removals | 44 | Flake |

A Levallois flake with heavily rolled flake scars. There is some ancient damage on both sides of the flake and an area of one side is missing. The flake has a very pronounced bulb of percussion.

**Figure 10.22**     **F1340**

| Curatorial | 1 | 87.93H/1.F1340 |
| --- | --- | --- |
| | 2 | 1987 |
| Stratigraphy | 3 | Upper Breccia |
| | 4 | Grid square I2SE |
| | 5 | 99.81 m |
| Raw material | 6 | Microdiorite |
| Typology | 7 | Levallois flake |
| Condition | 12 | Heavily rolled |
| Completeness | 17 | Complete |
| Cortex | 22 | None |
| Dimensions | 23 | Length = 90.7 mm |
| | 24 | Breadth = 57.3 mm |
| | 25 | Thickness = 14.0 mm |
| | 26 | Weight = 71.6 g |
| Butt type | 38 | Plain |
| Levallois removals | 44 | Flake |

A Levallois flake with some edge damage. Some of the damage is from excavation and some is ancient chipping. The flake scars are heavily rolled. The flake has a plain platform and a very highly pronounced bulb of percussion.

**Figure 10.22**     **F1876**

| Curatorial | 1 | 88.166H/2.F1876 |
| --- | --- | --- |
| | 2 | 1988 |
| Stratigraphy | 3 | Upper Breccia – Silt bed matrix |
| | 4 | Grid square G3NW |
| | 5 | 99.52 m |
| Raw material | 6 | Fine silicic tuff |
| Typology | 7 | Levallois flake |
| Condition | 12 | Very heavily rolled |
| Colouration | 16 | Stained |
| Completeness | 17 | Complete |
| Cortex | 22 | None |

| Dimensions | 23 | Length = 64.9 mm |
| --- | --- | --- |
| | 24 | Breadth = 50.5 mm |
| | 25 | Thickness = 11.1 mm |
| | 26 | Weight = 38.2 g |
| Butt type | 40 | Facetted |
| Levallois removals | 44 | Flake |

A very heavily rolled flake, so much so that the flake scars are very smooth and rounded. There is some surface staining on the flake and there are traces of concreted sediment adhering to areas of both the dorsal and ventral surfaces. The flake has a very highly pronounced bulb of percussion.

**Figure 10.23**     **H236**

| Curatorial | 1 | 87.93H/1.H236 |
| --- | --- | --- |
| | 2 | 1987 |
| Stratigraphy | 3 | Layer 23 |
| | 4 | Grid square AC992SW |
| | 5 | 99.56 m |
| Raw material | 6 | Tuff |
| Typology | 7 | Levallois flake (thin section 213) |
| Condition | 11 | Slightly rolled |
| Completeness | 17 | Complete |
| Cortex | 22 | None |
| Dimensions | 23 | Length = 63.6 mm |
| | 24 | Breadth = 58.6 mm |
| | 25 | Thickness = 9.0 mm |
| | 26 | Weight = 40.3 g |
| Butt type | 38 | Plain |
| Levallois removals | 44 | Flake |

A Levallois flake with slightly rolled flake scars. The tool has some concreted sediment adhering to its dorsal surface. There is some recent damage at its distal end. It has a plain striking platform and a very pronounced bulb of percussion.

**Figure 10.23**     **H351**

| Curatorial | 1 | 88.166H/1.H351 |
| --- | --- | --- |
| | 2 | 1988 |
| Stratigraphy | 3 | Layer 24 |
| | 4 | Grid square AA994SE |
| | 5 | 99.40 m |
| Raw material | 6 | Crystal tuff |
| Typology | 7 | Levallois point |
| Condition | 11 | Slightly rolled |
| Completeness | 17 | Complete |
| Cortex | 22 | None |
| Dimensions | 23 | Length = 59.0 mm |
| | 24 | Breadth = 58.6 mm |
| | 25 | Thickness = 9.6 mm |
| | 26 | Weight = 34.6 g |
| Butt type | 39 | Dihedral |
| Levallois removals | 46 | Point |

A Levallois point made on a flake with some minor ancient damage around its edges. There are traces of concreted sediment adhering to its surface. The piece has a dihedral platform.

**Figure 10.23**     **H940**

| Curatorial | 1 | 88.166H/2.H940 |
| --- | --- | --- |
| | 2 | 1988 |
| Stratigraphy | 3 | Layer 28 |
| | 4 | Grid square HA |
| | 5 | 98.61 m |
| Raw material | 6 | Flint |
| Typology | 7 | Levallois blade |
| Condition | 11 | Slightly rolled |
| Colouration | 15 | White patina |

| Completeness | 17 | Complete |
| Cortex | 22 | None |
| Dimensions | 23 | Length = 46.5 mm |
| | 24 | Breadth = 22.9 mm |
| | 25 | Thickness = 6.5 mm |
| | 26 | Weight = 6.2 g |
| Levallois removals | 45 | Flake-blade |

A Levallois blade with marginal irregular edge chipping on both faces. The blade has a white patination.

**Figure 10.23** — **H754**

| Curatorial | 1 | 88.166H/2.H754 |
| | 2 | 1988 |
| Stratigraphy | 3 | Layer 20 |
| | 4 | Grid square AB995NE |
| | 5 | 98.98 m |
| Raw material | 6 | Rhyolitic tuff |
| Typology | 7 | Levallois flake |
| Condition | 12 | Heavily rolled |
| Completeness | 18 | 50% complete |
| Cortex | 22 | None |
| Dimensions | 23 | Length = 37.7 mm |
| | 24 | Breadth = 15.1 mm |
| | 25 | Thickness = 5.1 mm |
| | 26 | Weight = 3.1 g |
| Levallois removals | 44 | Flake |

A Levallois flake that has broken along its length. The flake scars are heavily rolled and it has a damaged striking platform. There are a few ancient chips along the edge of the flake.

**Figure 10.23** — **H525 conjoining with H685**

| Curatorial | 1 | 88.166H/2.H685 and H525 |
| | 2 | 1988 |
| Stratigraphy | 3 | Layer 26 |
| | 4 | Grid square HA |
| | 5 | 98.92 m and 98.91 m |
| Raw material | 6 | Fine rhyolitic tuff |
| Typology | 7 | Levallois flake |
| Condition | 11 | Slightly rolled |
| Completeness | 17 | 95% complete |
| Cortex | 22 | None |
| Dimensions | 23 | Length = 105.9 mm |
| | 24 | Breadth = 41.6 mm |
| | 25 | Thickness = 8.1 mm |
| | 26 | Weight = 34.1 g |
| Butt type | 38 | Plain |
| Levallois removals | 45 | Flake-blade |

A Levallois blade that has been broken into two pieces. The break is recent and probably happened during excavation. There is recent damage on one side of the blade on the ventral surface. It has been struck from a plain striking platform and has a pronounced bulb of percussion.

**Figure 10.23** — **H658**

| Curatorial | 1 | 88.166H/2.H658 |
| | 2 | 1988 |
| Stratigraphy | 3 | Layer 26 |
| | 4 | Grid square AA994SE |
| | 5 | 99.01 m |
| Raw material | 6 | Flint |
| Typology | 7 | Levallois flake fragment |
| Condition | 11 | Slightly rolled |
| Colouration | 15 | White patination |
| Completeness | 18 | 50% complete |
| Cortex | 22 | None |

| Dimensions | 23 | Length = 41.4 mm |
| | 24 | Breadth = 33.5 mm |
| | 25 | Thickness = 9.6 mm |
| | 26 | Weight = 10.4 g |
| Butt type | 43 | Mixed |
| Levallois removals | 44 | Flake |

A Levallois flake fragment that has suffered damage recently and in antiquity. The distal end of the flake is missing from an ancient break. The flake has been slightly rolled and has edge damage. It has a white patination and a complex, heavily prepared striking platform.

**Figure 10.23** — **H2460**

| Curatorial | 1 | 95.35H/2.H2460 |
| | 2 | 1995 |
| Stratigraphy | 3 | Layer 26 |
| | 4 | Grid square AB993 |
| | 5 | 99.15–98.95 m |
| Raw material | 6 | Flow-banded rhyolite |
| Typology | 7 | Levallois flake fragment |
| Condition | 12 | Heavily rolled |
| Completeness | 18 | 65% complete |
| Cortex | 22 | None |
| Dimensions | 23 | Length = 45.3 mm |
| | 24 | Breadth = 44.1 mm |
| | 25 | Thickness = 9.3 mm |
| | 26 | Weight = 21.4 g |
| Butt type | 38 | Plain |
| Levallois removals | 44 | Flake |

A Levallois flake fragment that is missing its distal end due to damage in antiquity. There is also a recent chip removed from the same broken edge. The flake scars are all heavily weathered and the flake has a very pronounced bulbar scar.

**Figure 10.23** — **H2346**

| Curatorial | 1 | 95.35H/2.H2346 |
| | 2 | 1995 |
| Stratigraphy | 3 | Layer 26 |
| | 4 | Grid square AC993NW |
| | 5 | 99.20–98.90 m |
| Raw material | 6 | Ignimbrite |
| Typology | 7 | Levallois flake fragment |
| Condition | 12 | Heavily rolled |
| Completeness | 18 | 70% complete |
| Cortex | 22 | None |
| Dimensions | 23 | Length = 62.6 mm |
| | 24 | Breadth = 56.8 mm |
| | 25 | Thickness = 13.4 mm |
| | 26 | Weight = 41.8 g |
| Butt type | 36 | Absent |
| Levallois removals | 44 | Flake |

A Levallois flake fragment with heavily weathered flake scars and some concreted sediment adhering to both the surfaces. The distal end and part of the striking platform broke in antiquity.

**Figure 10.23** — **H3055**

| Curatorial | 1 | 95.35H/2.H3055 |
| | 2 | 1995 |
| Stratigraphy | 3 | Layer 24 |
| | 4 | Grid square AE992NW |
| | 5 | 99.18 m |
| Raw material | 6 | Tuff (thin section 254) |
| Typology | 7 | Retouched Levallois flake |
| Condition | 12 | Heavily rolled |
| Completeness | 17 | Complete |

| Cortex | 21 | 10% coverage |
|---|---|---|
| Dimensions | 23 | Length = 56.5 mm |
| | 24 | Breadth = 52.6 mm |
| | 25 | Thickness = 17.5 mm |
| | 26 | Weight = 49.5 g |
| Butt type | 38 | Plain (cortical) |
| Levallois removals | 44 | Flake |
| Style of retouch | 49 | Abrupt |

A Levallois flake with a small area of abrupt retouch. The flake has heavily weathered flake scars and has a cortical pebble surface surviving at its proximal end. There are remnants of concreted sediment adhering to parts of the dorsal surface.

| **Figure 10.24** | | **H3242** |
|---|---|---|
| Curatorial | 1 | 95.35H/2.H3242 |
| | 2 | 1995 |
| Stratigraphy | 3 | Layer 24 |
| | 4 | Grid square AF992W |
| | 5 | 99.80–98.79 m |
| Raw material | 6 | Ignimbrite |
| Typology | 7 | Levallois core |
| Condition | 11 | Slightly rolled |
| Completeness | 17 | Complete |
| Cortex | 22 | 5% coverage |
| Dimensions | 23 | Length = 88.5 mm |
| | 24 | Breadth = 74.8 mm |
| | 25 | Thickness = 54.5 mm |
| | 26 | Weight = 425.2 g |
| Core type | 33 | Levallois |

An unstruck Levallois core. It has slightly rolled surfaces and some traces of cortex on its underside. One face is steep-sided and dome-shaped, the other is flat and has been prepared.

| **Figure 10.24** | | **D4911** |
|---|---|---|
| Curatorial | 1 | 88.166H/2.D4911 |
| | 2 | 1988 |
| Stratigraphy | 3 | Lower Breccia |
| | 4 | Grid square K7SW |
| | 5 | 99.20 m |
| Raw material | 6 | Feldspar-phyric lava |
| Typology | 7 | Core |
| Condition | 12 | Heavily rolled |
| Completeness | 17 | Complete |
| Cortex | 22 | 5% coverage |
| Dimensions | 23 | Length = 119.6 mm |
| | 24 | Breadth = 96.3 mm |
| | 25 | Thickness = 72.9 mm |
| | 26 | Weight = 778.0 g |
| Core type | 35 | Crude |

A thick core made on a cobble that has been flaked all around its edges. It has heavily weathered and rolled flake scars and traces of cortex on one surface only.

| **Figure 10.25** | | **F2422** |
|---|---|---|
| Curatorial | 1 | 89.168H/2.F2422 |
| | 2 | 1989 |
| Stratigraphy | 3 | Upper Breccia – Silt bed matrix |
| | 4 | Grid square G4SW |
| | 5 | 99.44 m |
| Raw material | 6 | Fine silicic tuff |
| Typology | 7 | Discoidal core |
| Condition | 12 | Heavily rolled |
| Completeness | 17 | Complete |
| Cortex | 21 | 20% coverage |
| Dimensions | 23 | Length = 61.0 mm |

| | 24 | Breadth = 49.3 mm |
|---|---|---|
| | 25 | Thickness = 25.6 mm |
| | 26 | Weight = 89.6 g |
| Core type | 32 | Discoidal |

A discoidal core with traces of pebble cortex on one side. The core has been re-worked on an older artefact, possibly a broken biface.

| **Figure 10.25** | | **F2486** |
|---|---|---|
| Curatorial | 1 | 89.168H/2.F2486 |
| | 2 | 1989 |
| Stratigraphy | 3 | Lower Breccia |
| | 4 | Grid square G4NW |
| | 5 | 99.23 m |
| Raw material | 6 | Fine silicic tuff |
| Typology | 7 | Discoidal core |
| Condition | 12 | Heavily rolled |
| Completeness | 17 | Complete |
| Cortex | 21 | 40% coverage |
| Dimensions | 23 | Length = 75.3 mm |
| | 24 | Breadth = 70.1 mm |
| | 25 | Thickness = 16.5 mm |
| | 26 | Weight = 118.5 g |
| Core type | 32 | Discoidal |

A discoidal core that has a substantial area of abrasion-scratched pebble cortex on one side. Both faces have been worked; one only on its edges. All the flake scars are very heavily rolled. There is some concreted sediment adhering to the top of the core.

| **Figure 10.25** | | **H3115** |
|---|---|---|
| Curatorial | 1 | 95.35H/2.H3115 |
| | 2 | 1995 |
| Stratigraphy | 3 | Layer 23 |
| | 4 | Grid square AE993SE |
| | 5 | 98.95 m |
| Raw material | 6 | Ignimbrite |
| Typology | 7 | Discoidal core |
| Condition | 11 | Slightly rolled |
| Completeness | 17 | Complete |
| Cortex | 22 | None |
| Dimensions | 23 | Length = 84.3 mm |
| | 24 | Breadth = 69.5 mm |
| | 25 | Thickness = 21.2 mm |
| | 26 | Weight = 142.4 g |
| Core type | 32 | Discoidal |

A discoidal core with slightly worn flake scars with traces of concreted sediment adhering to the flaked face. The piece has been carefully shaped and is without cortex. The core has one face which is dome-shaped and has flake scars radiating out from all directions. The other side is very flat and is unmodified. The core may have been created from a thick flake.

| **Figure 10.25** | | **H192** |
|---|---|---|
| Curatorial | 1 | 87.93H/1.H192 |
| | 2 | 1987 |
| Stratigraphy | 3 | Layer 23 |
| | 4 | Grid square AB994 |
| | 5 | 99.50–99.40 m |
| Raw material | 6 | Rhyolitic tuff |
| Typology | 7 | Discoidal core |
| Condition | 11 | Slightly rolled |
| Completeness | 17 | Complete |
| Cortex | 21 | 40% coverage |
| Dimensions | 23 | Length = 63.9 mm |
| | 24 | Breadth = 54.4 mm |

| | 25 | Thickness = 20.4 mm |
| | 26 | Weight = 70.7 g |
| Core type | 32 | Discoidal |

A discoidal core with slightly weathered flake scars. One side retains a cortical coverage and has been trimmed around the edges, the other is more heavily worked and is dome-shaped in cross-section.

| **Figure 10.25** | | **H2068** |
| Curatorial | 1 | 94.38H/2.H2068 |
| | 2 | 1994 |
| Stratigraphy | 3 | Layer 23/24 |
| | 4 | Grid square AB992NW |
| | 5 | 99.80–99.30 m |
| Raw material | 6 | Feldspar-phyric lava |
| Typology | 7 | Discoidal core |
| Condition | 12 | Heavily rolled |
| Completeness | 17 | Complete |
| Cortex | 22 | 5% coverage |
| Dimensions | 23 | Length = 60.1 mm |
| | 24 | Breadth = 57.7 mm |
| | 25 | Thickness = 24.8 mm |
| | 26 | Weight = 108.5 g |
| Core type | 32 | Discoidal |

A heavily weathered discoidal core with both faces carefully prepared for the removal of flakes. One face has several step fractures over it; the other has had a flake removed from across the centre of the core. There are some traces of cortex on the edge of one face.

| **Figure 10.25** | | **H314** |
| Curatorial | 1 | 88.166H/2.H314 |
| | 2 | 1988 |
| Stratigraphy | 3 | Layer 24 |
| | 4 | Grid square AA994SE |
| | 5 | 99.37 m |
| Raw material | 6 | Fine silicic tuff |
| Typology | 7 | Discoidal core |
| Condition | 11 | Slightly rolled |
| Completeness | 17 | Complete |
| Cortex | 21 | 30% coverage |
| Dimensions | 23 | Length = 68.0 mm |
| | 24 | Breadth = 64.8 mm |
| | 25 | Thickness = 34.5 mm |
| | 26 | Weight = 169.7 g |
| Core type | 32 | Discoidal |

A slightly weathered discoidal core that has been prepared around its entire edge. One face is dome-shaped and has remnants of cortex on it. The other face is flatter and more heavily worked. These removals are irregular in form. There are traces of concreted sediment adhering to the surfaces of the core.

| **Figure 10.26** | | **A532** |
| Curatorial | 1 | 95.35H/2.A532 |
| | 2 | 1995 |
| Stratigraphy | 3 | Area A (Boyd Dawkins' Dump) Trench II, Layer 2 |
| Raw material | 6 | Fine silicic tuff (thin section 211) |
| Typology | 7 | Core |
| Condition | 12 | Heavily rolled |
| Completeness | 17 | Complete |
| Cortex | 22 | None |
| Dimensions | 23 | Length = 60.9 mm |
| | 24 | Breadth = 55.2 mm |
| | 25 | Thickness = 17.3 mm |

| | 26 | Weight = 57.4 g |
| Core type | 35 | Crude |

A core re-worked through an older patinated flake. The core has heavily weathered flake scars and is complete. It has had little working on either surface.

| **Figure 10.26** | | **H552** |
| Curatorial | 1 | 88.166H/2.H552 |
| | 2 | 1988 |
| Stratigraphy | 3 | Layer 26 |
| | 4 | Grid square HA |
| | 5 | 99.21 m |
| Raw material | 6 | Tuff (thin section 266) |
| Typology | 7 | Core |
| Condition | 11 | Slightly rolled |
| Completeness | 17 | Complete |
| Cortex | 21 | 40% coverage |
| Dimensions | 23 | Length = 83.3 mm |
| | 24 | Breadth = 56.2 mm |
| | 25 | Thickness = 34.5 mm |
| | 26 | Weight = 169.4 g |
| Core type | 35 | Crude |

An irregularly shaped crude core made on a cobble of tuff. The core retains much of its pebble surface on one face, whilst the other has had some flake removals struck from it. The flake scars are slightly rolled.

| **Figure 10.26** | | **D5837** |
| Curatorial | 1 | 94.38H/2.D5837 |
| | 2 | 1994 |
| Stratigraphy | 3 | Lower Breccia |
| | 4 | Grid square G8NE |
| | 5 | 99.25 m |
| Raw material | 6 | Rhyolite |
| Typology | 7 | Globular core |
| Condition | 12 | Heavily rolled |
| Completeness | 17 | Complete |
| Cortex | 20 | 50% coverage |
| Dimensions | 23 | Length = 115.1 mm |
| | 24 | Breadth = 94.2 mm |
| | 25 | Thickness = 80.0 mm |
| | 26 | Weight = 822.1 g |
| Core type | 35 | Crude |

A core made on a thick rhyolite cobble half covered with cortex. The flake scars are heavily weathered.

| **Figure 10.27** | | **H2858** |
| Curatorial | 1 | 95.35H/2.H2858 |
| | 2 | 1995 |
| Stratigraphy | 3 | Layer 24 or 26 |
| Raw material | 6 | Ignimbrite (thin section 207) |
| Typology | 7 | Crude core |
| Condition | 11 | Slightly rolled |
| Completeness | 17 | Complete |
| Cortex | 21 | 10% coverage |
| Dimensions | 23 | Length = 103.7 mm |
| | 24 | Breadth = 53.3 mm |
| | 25 | Thickness = 41.2 mm |
| | 26 | Weight = 192.7 g |
| Core type | 35 | Crude |

A crude core of irregular shape with slightly weathered flake scars and traces of sediment adhering to the surface in patches.

| **Figure 10.27** | | **H151** |
| Curatorial | 1 | 87.93H/2.H151 |

|  |  |  |
|---|---|---|
|  | 2 | 1987 |
| Stratigraphy | 3 | Layer 20 |
|  | 4 | Grid square AC994NE |
|  | 5 | 99.77 m |
| Raw material | 6 | Quartz |
| Typology | 7 | Core |
| Condition | 12 | Heavily rolled |
| Completeness | 17 | Complete |
| Cortex | 21 | 20% coverage |
| Dimensions | 23 | Length = 68.4 mm |
|  | 24 | Breadth = 66.1 mm |
|  | 25 | Thickness = 55.2 mm |
|  | 26 | Weight = 225.9 g |
| Core type | 35 | Crude |

A core made on a quartz cobble with some of the original pebble surface surviving. All of the flake scars on the core are crude and coarse due to the difficult flaking properties of this rock.

| **Figure 10.28** |  | **A515** |
|---|---|---|
| Curatorial | 1 | 88.166H/2.A515 |
|  | 2 | 1988 |
| Stratigraphy | 3 | Area A Unstratified |
| Raw material | 6 | Crystal tuff |
| Typology | 7 | Side-scraper |
| Condition | 12 | Heavily rolled |
| Colouration | 16 | Some staining |
| Completeness | 17 | Complete |
| Cortex | 22 | None |
| Dimensions | 23 | Length = 40.5 mm |
|  | 24 | Breadth = 34.8 mm |
|  | 25 | Thickness = 11.0 mm |
|  | 26 | Weight = 18.2 g |
| Butt type | 36 | Absent |
| Style of retouch | 50 | Scalar |

A scraper with retouch running along one length in an irregular pattern. This is mostly marginal, but there are some areas where it is invasive. This retouch is scalar in form. There is also some more irregular retouch along the other edge. The proximal end of the flake is missing and the tool has some staining on the dorsal surface.

| **Figure 10.28** |  | **F5680** |
|---|---|---|
| Curatorial | 1 | 95.35H/2.F5680 |
|  | 2 | 1995 |
| Stratigraphy | 3 | Lower Breccia (c) |
|  | 4 | Grid square I1NE |
|  | 5 | 99.19 m |
| Raw material | 6 | Rhyolitic tuff |
| Typology | 7 | Side-scraper with bifacial retouch |
| Condition | 12 | Heavily rolled |
| Completeness | 17 | Complete |
| Cortex | 22 | None |
| Dimensions | 23 | Length = 73.0 mm |
|  | 24 | Breadth = 51.7 mm |
|  | 25 | Thickness = 26.0 mm |
|  | 26 | Weight = 100.2 g |
| Butt type | 36 | Absent |
| Style of retouch | 50 | Scalar |

A possible core that has steep but marginal retouch running along one edge giving it a convex retouched edge. There is limited retouch on the ventral surface at the same position.

| **Figure 10.28** |  | **F2796** |
|---|---|---|
| Curatorial | 1 | 89.168H/2.F2796 |
|  | 2 | 1989 |

| Stratigraphy | 3 | Lower Breccia |
|---|---|---|
|  | 4 | Grid square H4SW |
|  | 5 | 99.48 m |
| Raw material | 6 | Fine silicic tuff |
| Typology | 7 | Side-scraper made on a Levallois flake |
| Condition | 12 | Heavily rolled |
| Completeness | 17 | Complete |
| Cortex | 22 | None |
| Dimensions | 23 | Length = 71.0 mm |
|  | 24 | Breadth = 57.0 mm |
|  | 25 | Thickness = 20.2 mm |
|  | 26 | Weight = 84.6 g |
| Butt type | 38 | Plain |
| Levallois removals | 44 | Flake |
| Style of retouch | 50 | Scalar |

A single side-scraper with invasive scalar retouch running along one edge. The scraper is made on a Levallois flake which has a plain striking platform. It has been struck with a hard hammer and has a very pronounced bulb of percussion and bulbar scar.

| **Figure 10.28** |  | **H132** |
|---|---|---|
| Curatorial | 1 | 87.93H/2.H132 |
|  | 2 | 1987 |
| Stratigraphy | 3 | Layer 23 |
|  | 4 | Grid square AC994SE |
|  | 5 | 99.49 m |
| Raw material | 6 | Feldspar-phyric lava (thin section 248) |
| Typology | 7 | Convergent convex double side-scraper |
| Condition | 12 | Heavily rolled |
| Completeness | 18 | 50% complete |
| Cortex | 22 | None |
| Dimensions | 23 | Length = 44.6 mm |
|  | 24 | Breadth = 42.2 mm |
|  | 25 | Thickness = 11.0 mm |
|  | 26 | Weight = 23.1 g |
| Butt type | 36 | Absent |
| Style of retouch | 50 | Scalar |

A scraper with steep retouch along one edge and shallow retouch on the other. The two areas of retouch are scalar and the retouch is marginal. The tool is missing its tip in an ancient break and it has heavily weathered flake scars. The bulbar end is also missing, lost in antiquity.

| **Figure 10.28** |  | **H1151** |
|---|---|---|
| Curatorial | 1 | 88.166H/2.H1151 |
|  | 2 | 1988 |
| Stratigraphy | 3 | Layer 26 |
|  | 4 | Grid square AC993SE |
|  | 5 | 98.93 m |
| Raw material | 6 | Feldspar-phyric lava |
| Typology | 7 | Single-straight side-scraper on a Levallois flake |
| Condition | 12 | Heavily rolled |
| Completeness | 17 | Complete |
| Cortex | 22 | None |
| Dimensions | 23 | Length = 55.6 mm |
|  | 24 | Breadth = 34.4 mm |
|  | 25 | Thickness = 12.0 mm |
|  | 26 | Weight = 32.5 g |
| Butt type | 38 | Plain |
| Levallois removals | 44 | Flake |
| Style of retouch | 50 | Scalar |

A single-straight side-scraper made on a Levallois flake. The retouch is marginal, scalar and is shallow along one edge. The flake is struck from a plain striking platform and the piece has no cortex. It displays heavily weathered flake scars.

**Figure 10.28**         **H1678**

| Curatorial | 1 | 89.168H/2.H1678 |
|---|---|---|
| | 2 | 1989 |
| Stratigraphy | 3 | Layer 36 |
| | 4 | Grid square AB994SE |
| | 5 | 99.73–99.60 m |
| Raw material | 6 | Ignimbrite |
| Typology | 7 | Single-straight side-scraper |
| Condition | 11 | Slightly rolled |
| Completeness | 17 | Complete |
| Cortex | 21 | 20% coverage |
| Dimensions | 23 | Length = 61.7 mm |
| | 24 | Breadth = 45.0 mm |
| | 25 | Thickness = 19.7 mm |
| | 26 | Weight = 54.8 g |
| Butt type | 38 | Plain |
| Style of retouch | 53 | Inverse |

A single-straight side-scraper with a cortical natural backing at one side. The cortex covers 20% of the tool's surface to provide a natural backing to it. The retouch is shallow but moderately invasive on a straight edge parallel to the cortical length. This is mostly on the ventral surface. The dorsal surface has also been flaked. The flake scars are slightly weathered and the tool is complete.

**Figure 10.28**         **H3197**

| Curatorial | 1 | 95.35H/2.H3197 |
|---|---|---|
| | 2 | 1995 |
| Stratigraphy | 3 | Layer 26 |
| | 4 | Grid square AD993NE |
| | 5 | 99.14 m |
| Raw material | 6 | Baked shale |
| Typology | 7 | Single convex side-scraper made on a Levallois blade |
| Condition | 12 | Heavily rolled |
| Completeness | 17 | 50% complete |
| Cortex | 22 | None |
| Dimensions | 23 | Length = 36.5 mm |
| | 24 | Breadth = 21.6 mm |
| | 25 | Thickness = 10.2 mm |
| | 26 | Weight = 8.3 g |
| Butt type | 36 | Absent |
| Levallois removals | 44 | Flake |
| Style of retouch | 50 | Scalar |

A single convex side-scraper made on a Levallois blade with scalar retouch which is steep and moderately invasive on one edge. The blade is broken and is missing its proximal edge. The flake scars are heavily weathered and no cortex survives.

**Figure 10.28**         **H1926**

| Curatorial | 1 | 94.38H/2.H1926 |
|---|---|---|
| | 2 | 1994 |
| Stratigraphy | 3 | Layer 24 |
| | 4 | Grid square AC993SW |
| | 5 | 99.30–99.20 m |
| Raw material | 6 | Baked shale (thin section 270) |
| Typology | 7 | Single convex side-scraper fragment |
| Condition | 11 | Slightly rolled |
| Completeness | 17 | 60% complete |
| Cortex | 22 | None |
| Dimensions | 23 | Length = 49.4 mm |
| | 24 | Breadth = 23.4 mm |
| | 25 | Thickness = 13.4 mm |
| | 26 | Weight = 14.2 g |
| Butt type | 36 | Absent |
| Style of retouch | 50 | Scalar |

A scraper fragment that has broken along its length in antiquity. The retouched edge is convex but the retouch is irregular, in places moderately invasive and in others very marginal. The flake scars are slightly weathered.

**Figure 10.28**         **H1935**

| Curatorial | 1 | 94.38H/2.H1935 |
|---|---|---|
| | 2 | 1994 |
| Stratigraphy | 3 | Layer 24 |
| | 4 | Grid square AC993NW |
| | 5 | 99.20–99.00 m |
| Raw material | 6 | Feldspar-phyric lava |
| Typology | 7 | Single-straight side-scraper |
| Condition | 12 | Heavily rolled |
| Completeness | 17 | 90% complete |
| Cortex | 21 | 45% coverage |
| Dimensions | 23 | Length = 57.3 mm |
| | 24 | Breadth = 44.8 mm |
| | 25 | Thickness = 17.3 mm |
| | 26 | Weight = 54.0 g |
| Butt type | 36 | Absent |
| Style of retouch | 50 | Scalar |

A single-straight side-scraper with marginal, shallow and straight retouch running along one edge. The other edges have also been prepared to give the tool a form of backing. Cortex survives over much of the dorsal surface. The piece has an ancient break at its butt, where it is missing the platform.

**Figure 10.28**         **H3001**

| Curatorial | 1 | 95.35H/2.H3001 |
|---|---|---|
| | 2 | 1995 |
| Stratigraphy | 3 | Layer 20 |
| | 4 | Grid square AE993NW |
| | 5 | 99.42–99.35 m |
| Raw material | 6 | Crystal tuff |
| Typology | 7 | Side-scraper fragment |
| Condition | 11 | Slightly rolled |
| Completeness | 18 | 75% complete |
| Cortex | 22 | None |
| Dimensions | 23 | Length = 45.4 mm |
| | 24 | Breadth = 32.4 mm |
| | 25 | Thickness = 11.2 mm |
| | 26 | Weight = 19.3 g |
| Butt type | 36 | Absent |
| Style of retouch | 50 | Scalar |

A side-scraper fragment broken during excavation. The scraping edge is convex and has steep, scalar retouch which terminates in recent breaks at both ends of the tool.

**Figure 10.28**         **H3229**

| Curatorial | 1 | 95.35H/2.H3229 |
|---|---|---|
| | 2 | 1995 |
| Stratigraphy | 3 | Layer 23 |
| | 4 | Grid square AE993SE |
| | 5 | 98.99–98.90 m |
| Raw material | 6 | Microdiorite |
| Typology | 7 | Single-convex side-scraper made on a burnt Levallois flake |

| Condition | 11 | Slightly rolled |
|---|---|---|
| Completeness | 17 | Complete |
| Cortex | 22 | None |
| Dimensions | 23 | Length = 74.7 mm |
| | 24 | Breadth = 59.0 mm |
| | 25 | Thickness = 18.3 mm |
| | 26 | Weight = 83.2 g |
| Butt type | 38 | Dihedral |
| Levallois removals | 44 | Flake |
| Style of retouch | 49 | Abrupt |

A burnt single-convex side-scraper made on a Levallois flake. The scraping edge has steep abrupt retouch that is marginal to invasive yet irregular around the scraping edge. The flake has a dihedral striking platform.

| **Figure 10.28** | | **D4335** |
|---|---|---|
| Curatorial | 1 | 87.93H/1.D4335 |
| | 2 | 1987 |
| Stratigraphy | 3 | Lower Breccia |
| | 4 | Grid square K8NE |
| | 5 | 99.58 m |
| Raw material | 6 | Crystal lithic tuff |
| Typology | 7 | Convex transverse scraper |
| Condition | 11 | Slightly rolled |
| Completeness | 17 | Complete |
| Cortex | 21 | 30% coverage |
| Dimensions | 23 | Length = 70.3 mm |
| | 24 | Breadth = 59.6 mm |

| | 25 | Thickness = 20.0 mm |
|---|---|---|
| | 26 | Weight = 77.3 g |
| Butt type | 38 | Plain |
| Style of retouch | 50 | Scalar |

A finely shaped transverse scraper with scalar retouch along its convex end. The tool is made on an abrasion scratched cortical pebble.

| **Figure 10.28** | | **A739** |
|---|---|---|
| Curatorial | 1 | 95.35H/2.A739 |
| | 2 | 1995 |
| Stratigraphy | 3 | Area A (World War II Dump) Trench II, Layer 1 |
| Raw material | 6 | Flint |
| Typology | 7 | Microlith |
| Condition | 10 | Fresh |
| Colouration | 15 | White patina |
| Completeness | 17 | Complete |
| Cortex | 22 | None |
| Dimensions | 23 | Length = 20.0 mm |
| | 24 | Breadth = 4.7 mm |
| | 25 | Thickness = 4.1 mm |
| | 26 | Weight = 0.3 g |
| Style of retouch | 51 | Parallel |

A later Mesolithic flint microlith of a curved back form. The retouch is along one edge and is steep, running the entire length of the tool. There are traces of concreted sediment adhering to parts of the surface of the tool.

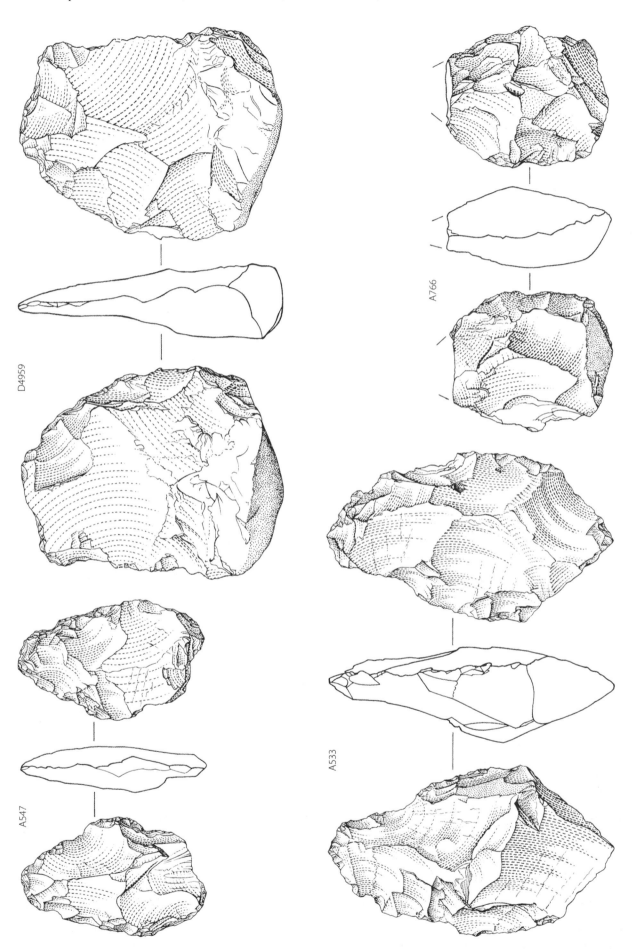

*Figure 10.14. Bifaces.*

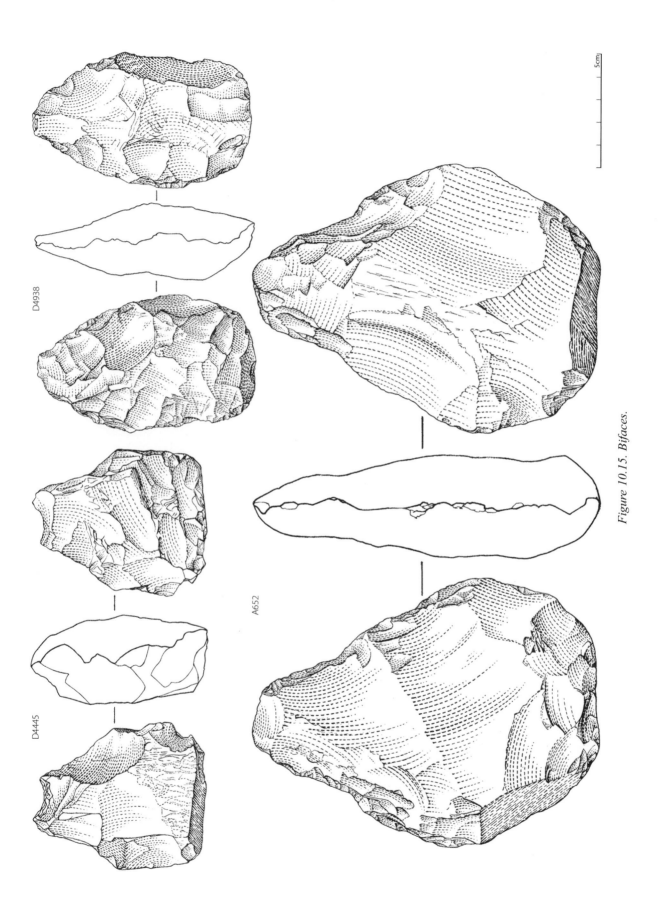

*Figure 10.15. Bifaces.*

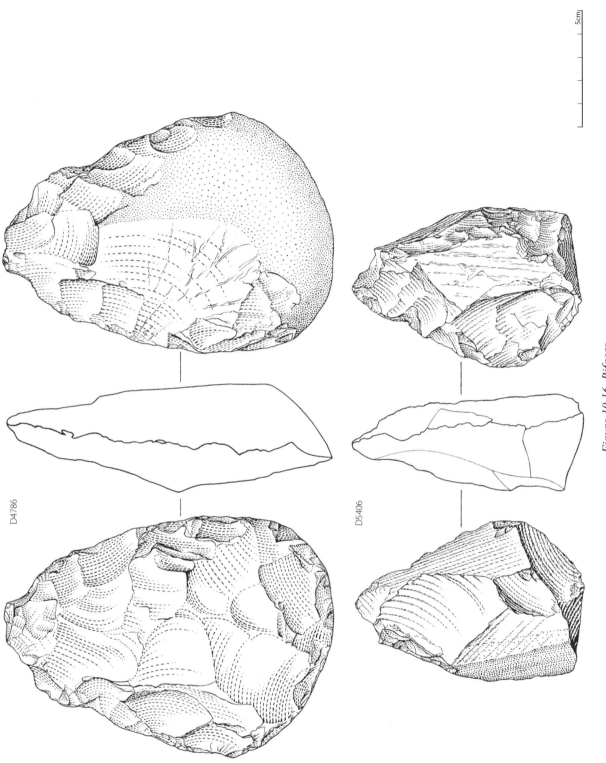

D4786

D5406

*Figure 10.16. Bifaces.*

5cm

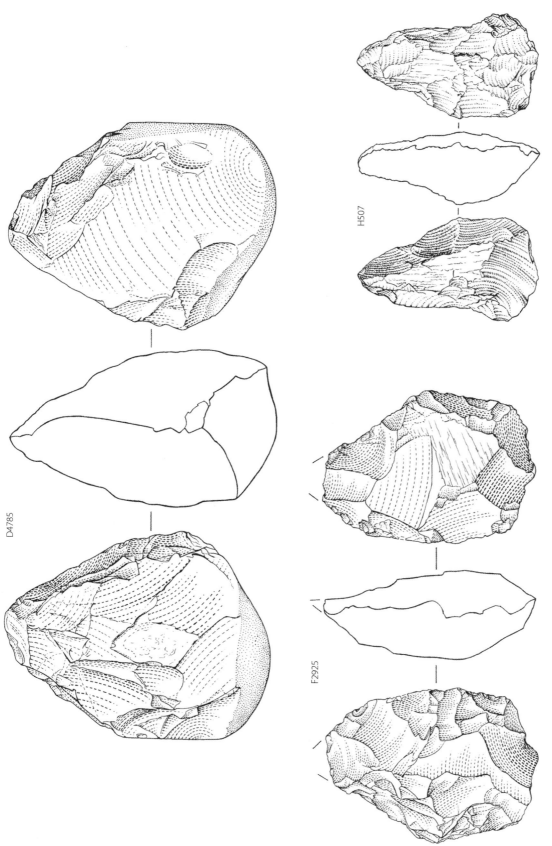

*Figure 10.17. Bifaces.*

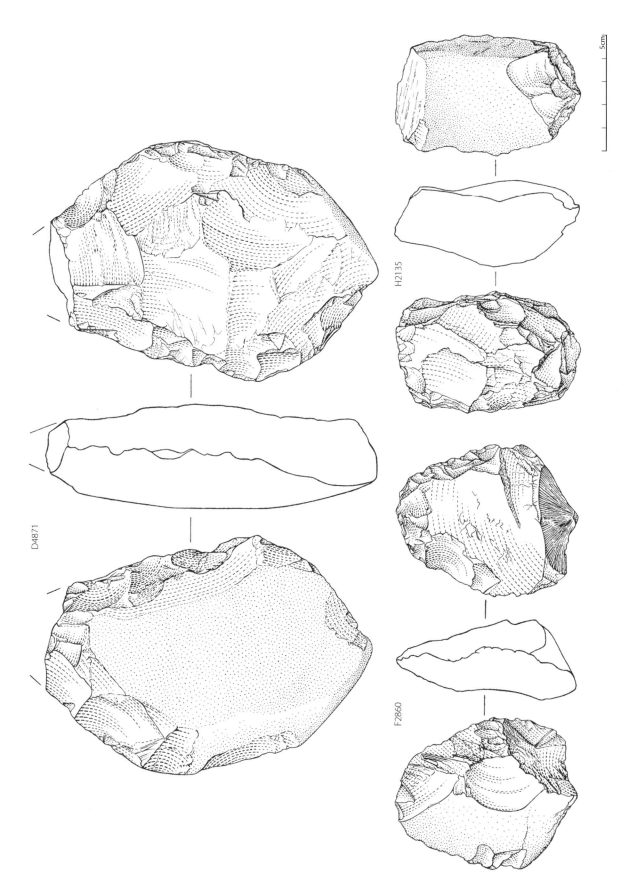

*Figure 10.18. Bifaces.*

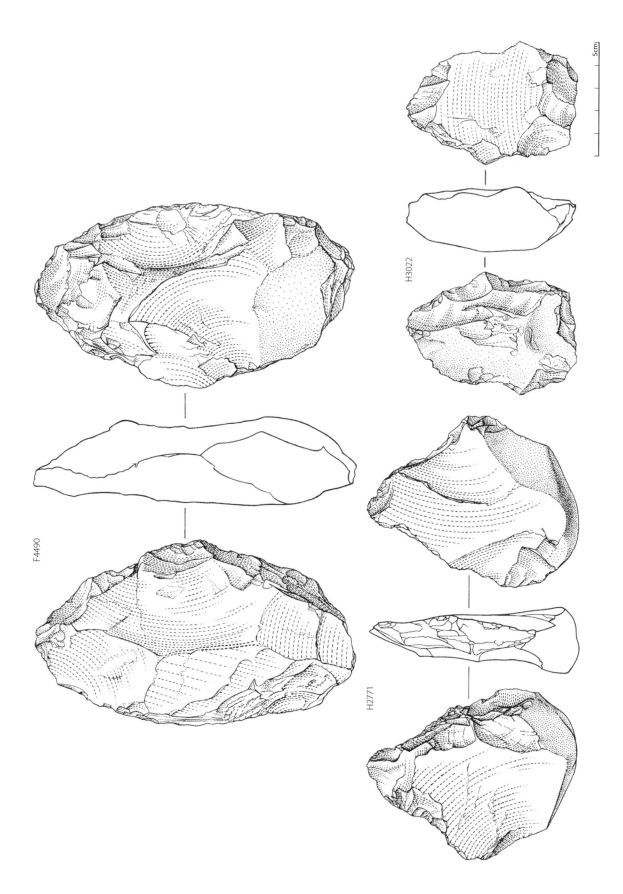

F4490

H3022

H2771

*Figure 10.19. Bifaces.*

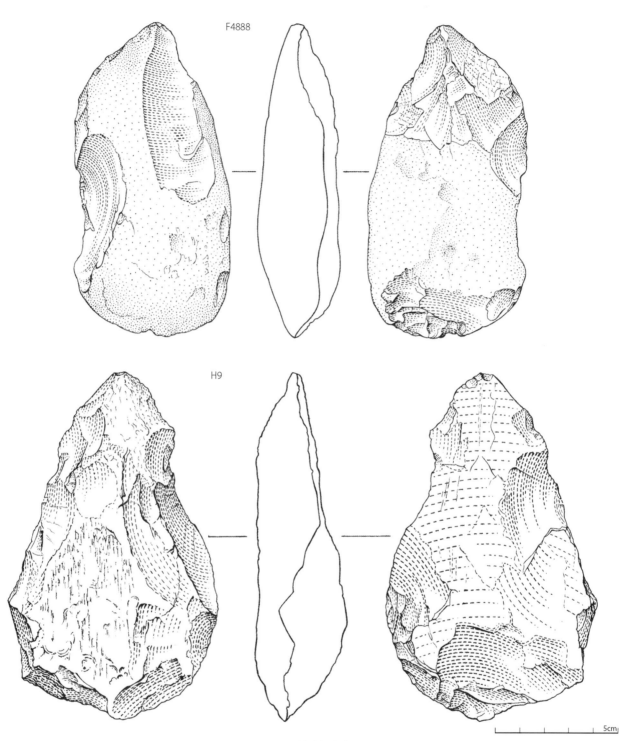

F4888

H9

5cm

*Figure 10.20. Bifaces.*

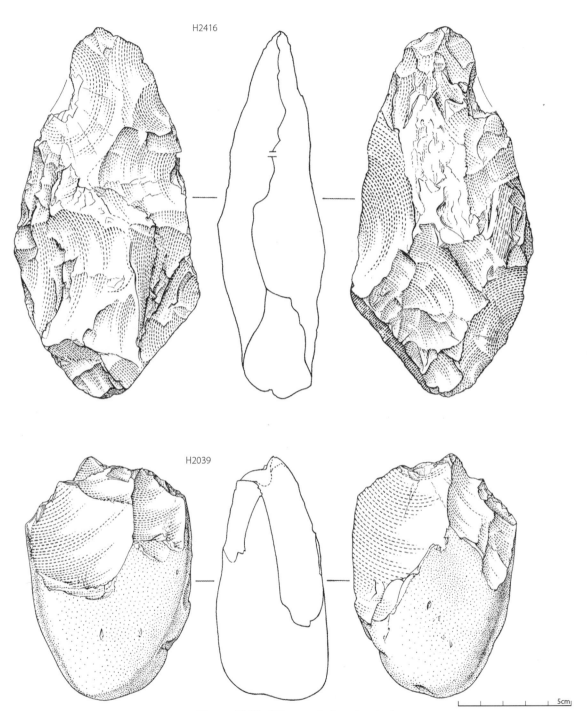

H2416

H2039

5cm

*Figure 10.21. Biface and chopping tool.*

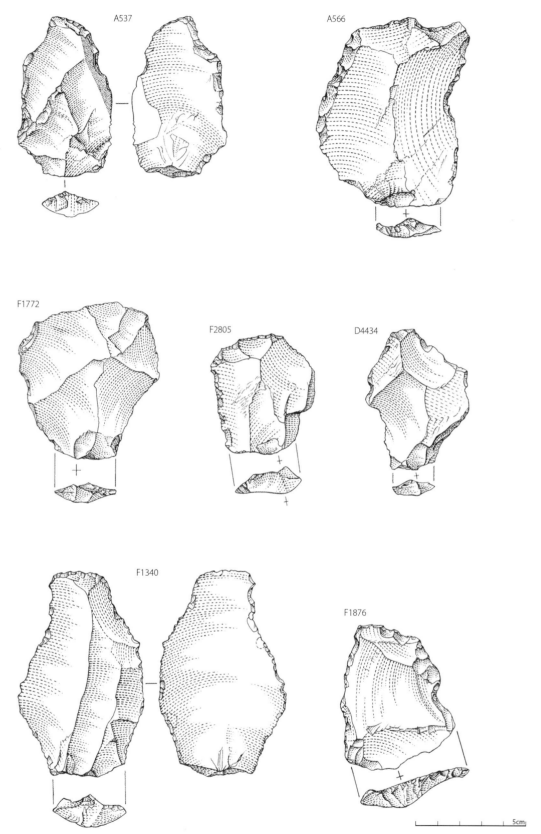

*Figure 10.22. Levallois products.*

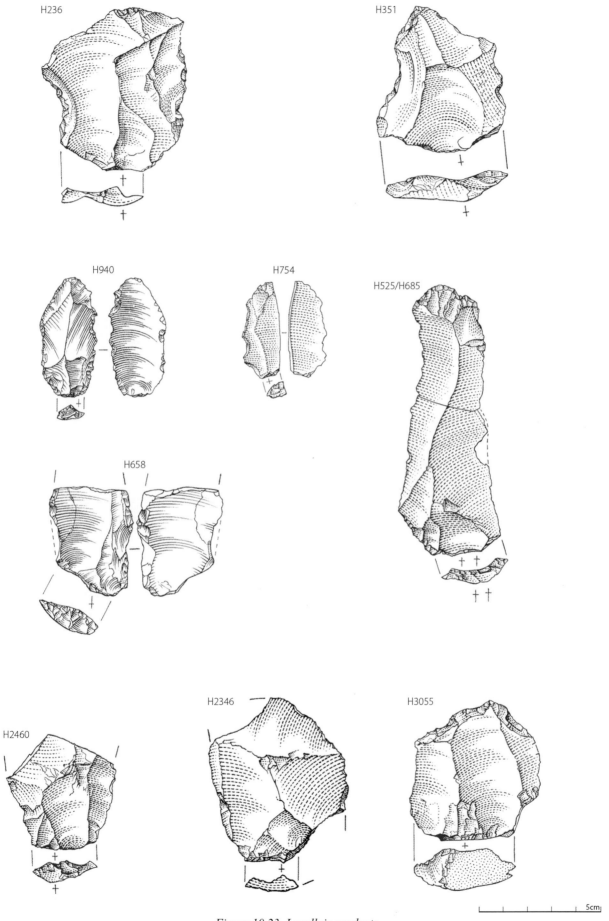

*Figure 10.23. Levallois products.*

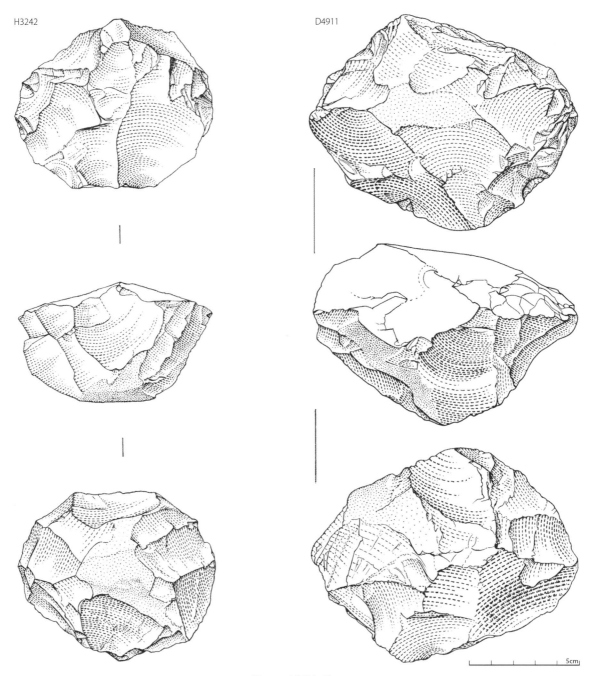

*Figure 10.24. Cores.*

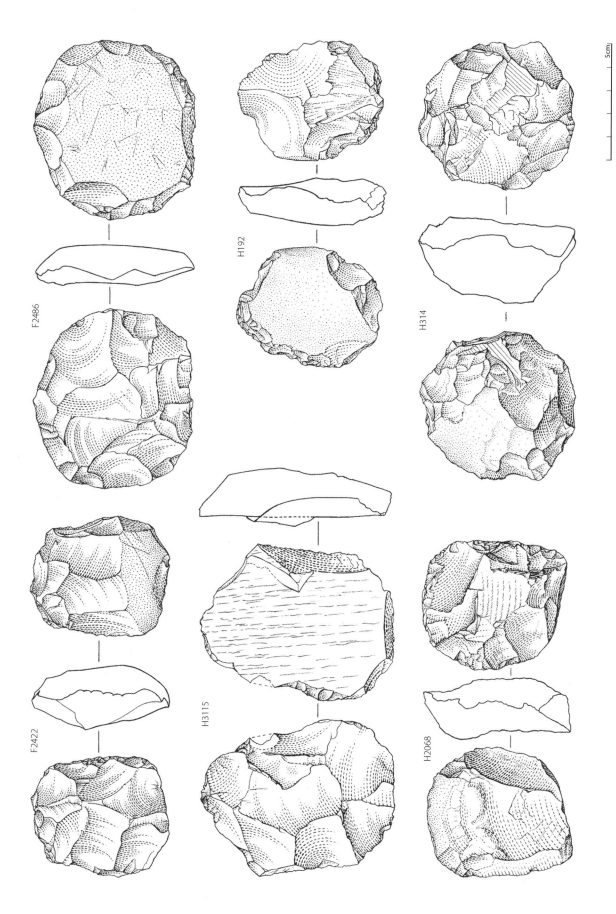

F2486

H192

H314

F2422

H3115

H2068

5cm

*Figure 10.25. Cores.*

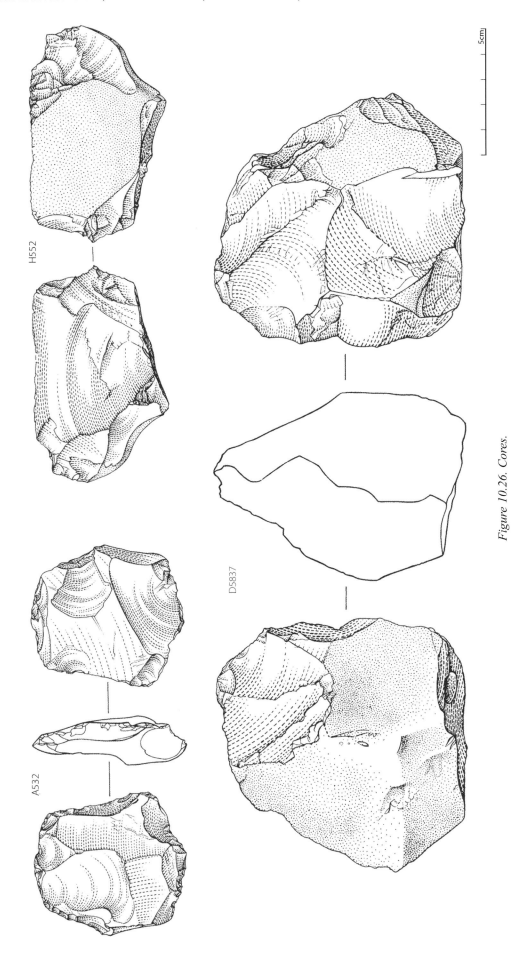

*Figure 10.26. Cores.*

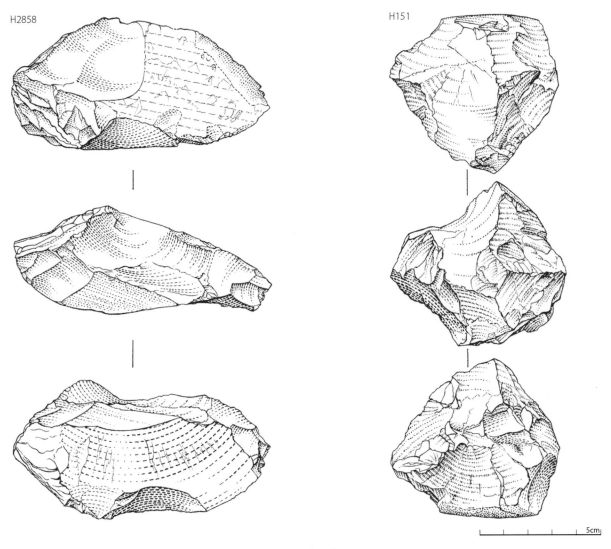

*Figure 10.27. Cores.*

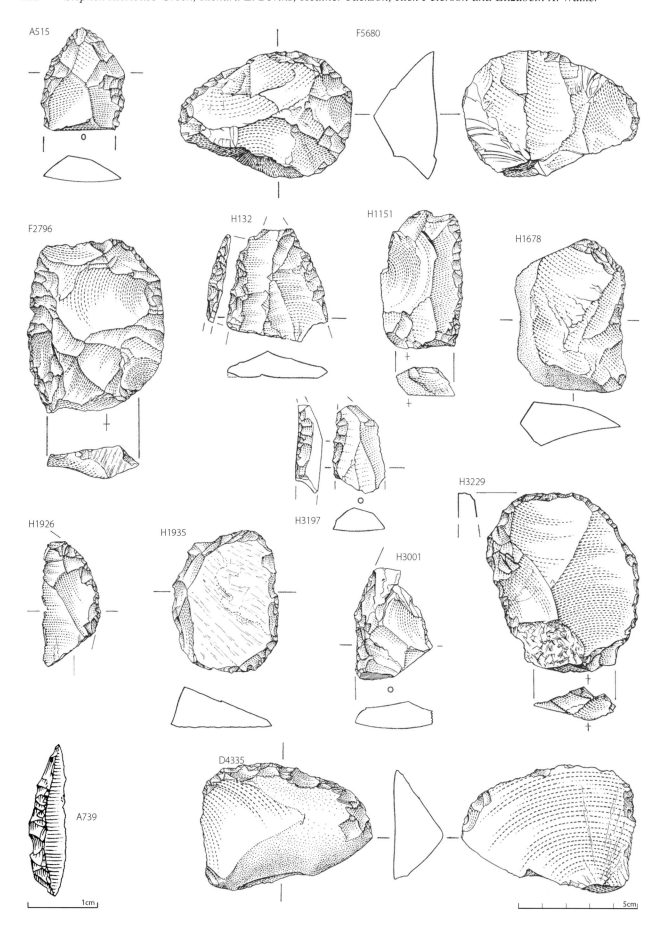

*Figure 10.28. Scrapers and microlith.*

# 11. Dating

*Nicholas C. Debenham, Tim Atkinson, Rainer Grün, Nick Hebden, Thomas Higham, Rupert Housley, Paul Pettitt, Ed Rhodes, Peter Rowe and Li Ping Zhou*

*This chapter falls into two parts. The first is focused primarily on dating the Middle Pleistocene occupation and deals with the application of thermoluminescence (TL) and Uranium series dating to stalagmites, and so to chronostratigraphy. It also considers the application of TL to burnt flints and explores, with some success, the use of electron spin resonance (ESR) for bone dating. The second part deals with the radiocarbon dating of the Devensian fauna. The overall aim was to establish evidence for temporal patterning in the taxonomically diverse faunal record from the Upper Breccia in order to relate these to taphonomic, ecological and climatic factors that could have influenced the biomass, faunal composition and animal biodiversity of the surrounding environs to the site.*

## Thermoluminescence dating of flint, stalagmite and sediment from Pontnewydd Cave

*Nicholas C. Debenham*

### Introduction

Thermoluminescence (TL) has been applied to the dating of flints, stone, stalagmites and sediment from Pontnewydd Cave. While details of the date measurements differ between these four types of material, the same general principles underlie all these methods. In fact, the date measurement involves two distinct procedures. The first is the TL examination of the sample, in which it is used as a dosimeter to measure the quantity of ionising radiation that it has received since the event to be dated. The second set of measurements allows an assessment of the rate at which the radiation dose was received, which, combined with the TL data, produces the elapsed time. The general principles of TL date measurement are explained below. Separate sections describe the TL examination and the dose rate assessment procedures. The last section discusses the TL dates obtained for the various materials excavated from Pontnewydd Cave.

### General principles of TL dating

Many crystalline materials share the potential for being used as dosimeters, capable of recording the doses of ionising radiation to which they have been exposed. Ionising radiation is present in varying intensities in all environments. Alpha, beta and gamma radiation originates from naturally occurring radioactive nuclides, such as uranium, thorium and potassium, while cosmic radiation is generated when high-energy particles are incident on the Earth's atmosphere. When crystals are exposed to the energy of these radiations, their electronic structures are re-arranged in a variety of ways. Most of these re-arrangements are temporary. However, some of the alterations persist for very long periods, and effectively form a long-term memory of the quantity of radiation which the crystal has absorbed. The radiation dose thus recorded is termed the palaeodose.

Thermoluminescence is one means of obtaining a read-out of the crystalline dosimeter. As the crystal is progressively heated, a luminescence is produced. This emission of light results from the release of radiation energy which has been absorbed, and subsequently retained, by the crystal. The intensity of the luminescence is thus related to the palaeodose, and a measurement of this dose can be obtained from observations of the material's present-day TL intensity (or natural TL), and of its response to known doses of radiation. These measurements can determine the palaeodose with a precision which is typically between $\pm4\%$ and $\pm8\%$.

For the TL observations to be useful as a measurement of age, the following two requirements must be satisfied; (i) the event to be dated must cause the removal of all (or nearly all) of the pre-existing TL, and (ii) it must be possible to make an assessment of the rate at which the material absorbed radiation energy since the initial event

| Sample | Find no. | Lab ref. | Layer | Square | Height | Dated by |
|---|---|---|---|---|---|---|
| **Main Cave Areas B, C, D, F, and G** | | | | | | |
| Stal (i/s)[1] | B409 | 226g1 | LSG 3 | K17 | | OxTL |
| Stal (i/s)[1] | B556 | PND42 | LSG | Deep Sounding | 97.48 | BMTL |
| Stal (i/s) | D188 | 226a1 | LT | H5 | | OxTL |
| Stal[2] | D471 | 226e6 | On LB | G9 | 99.45 | OxTL |
| Stal (i/s) | D604 | 226e14 | On LB | J9 | 99.67 | OxTL |
| Stal (i/s) | D1693 | 226h3 | On LB | G10 | | OxTL |
| Stal (i/s) | D1711 | 226h21 | On LB | J7 | | OxTL |
| Stal (i/s) | F2264 | PND37 | On Pond | G2 NE | 99.73 | BMTL |
| Stal (i/s) | G75 | PND47 | Site G[3] | GA0997SE | 99.8 | BMTL |
| Stal (d) | B111 | 226a8 | Int/Br | K21 | 99.07 | OxTL |
| Stal (d) | B396 | 226e4 | Base of Br | K20 | 99.07 | OxTL |
| Stal (d) | B0b:1 | 226f2 | Base of Br | K21 | | OxTL |
| Stal (d) | B0b:2 | 226f1 | Base of Br | K21 | | OxTL |
| Stal (d) | D292 | 226e13 | UB | K10 | 99.69 | OxTL |
| Stal (d) | D446 | 226e9 | UB | H8 | 99.78 | OxTL |
| Flint (d) | D4367 | PND25 | Top of LB | K8 NE | 99.49 | BMTL |
| **New Entrance Area H** | | | | | | |
| Sediment (i/s) | H196 | PND23 | Scree 12 | | 103.03 | BMTL |
| Flint (d) | H598 | PND33 | 26 | AB994 NE | 99.03 | BMTL |
| Flint (d) | H1036 | PND32 | 28 | AB994 NW | 98.80–98.70 | BMTL |
| Stal (i/s) | H1713/2 | PND41 | 31 | AA994 SE | 98.22–98.14 | BMTL |
| Stal (d) | H1724 | PND43 | Scree; 50 | AC991 SW/NW | | BMTL |
| Stal (d) | H1725 | PND44 | Scree; 50 | AC991 SW/NW | | BMTL |
| Stone (d) | H2312 | PND62 | 26 | AB993S/AC993N | 99.15–99.00 | QTLS |
| Stal (d) | H3150 | PND66 | 39 | AC994 NW | 97.09 | QTLS |

Abbreviations: (i/s) = *in situ*; (d) = derived; LSG = Lower Sands and Gravels; LT = Laminated Travertine; UB = Upper Breccia; LB = Lower Breccia; Br = Breccia; Int = Intermediate; OxTL = Research Laboratory for Archaeology, Oxford; BMTL = British Museum, Department of Scientific Research; QTLS = Quaternary TL Surveys, Nottingham.

Notes:  1 Interstitial calcite; 2 Probably *in situ*; 3 Stalagmitic floor between 2 and 3.

*Table 11.1. Locations and descriptions of samples dated by TL.*

occurred. The first requirement is fulfilled when, for instance, flint or stone is heated, stalagmite crystallizes, or sediment is deposited and exposed to light. Because the TL is zeroed (or greatly reduced) by these occurrences, the palaeodose evaluated from the present-day TL intensity can be interpreted as the quantity of radiation absorbed since the date of the event. Provided that the mean rate at which the radiation dose was received can also be evaluated, the date may be calculated.

For an assessment of the mean dose rate to be possible, the sample should ideally have lain undisturbed during its history. Furthermore, enough of the burial environment should be preserved to allow the contribution it has made to the sample's dose rate to be measured. This last condition is particularly important for flint and stalagmite samples, because the radiation dose received from the environment is often greater than that which the sample administers to itself.

In addition to the above conditions, it is required that the stored TL be adequately stable and that it does not saturate. The long-term stability of the TL has already been mentioned as a basic necessity, ensuring that there is no significant loss of the TL signal before it is measured in the laboratory. Saturation of the TL refers to the situation whereby, after a high dose of radiation, the TL capacity of the material is reached, and further doses produce no increase of TL intensity. Clearly, both instability and saturation prevent an accurate evaluation of the palaeodose, and therefore limit the age range over which the TL method may be applied.

None of the samples from Pontnewydd Cave, whether flint, stalagmite or sediment, have been limited by TL saturation. This is evident from the fact that further doses of artificial radiation, added to the palaeodose, have in all samples produced TL intensities well in excess of the natural TL. The loss of TL through decay cannot be so directly observed; it can only be deduced from wider studies comparing TL dates obtained from different materials, from comparisons with dates measured by other methods, or from correlations of date frequency distributions with known climatic fluctuations. In the case of flint, the evidence suggests that no significant loss of TL through decay has occurred since Marine Isotope Stage (MIS) 7. For stalagmites of this age, if an instability is present its effect is not larger than the typical TL date error limit, or 15%. In contrast, the TL dating of sediments is severely limited by instability to the last 150,000 years.

### Palaeodose evaluations

Table 11.1 lists the stratigraphic details and find locations of twenty-four samples of stalagmite, sediment, flint and

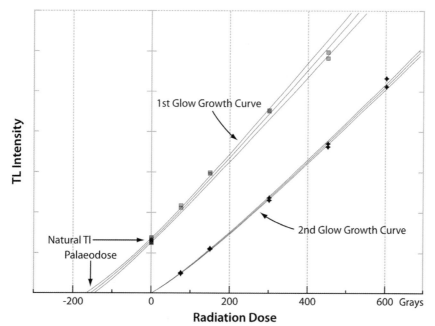

*Figure 11.1. TL measurements of stalagmite, H3150 (PND66), showing the natural and first glow intensities (squares) and second glows (crosses) fitted by supralinear growth curves. The curve used to extrapolate the first glow data is derived from the second glow growth curve by translation along the dose axis and scaling on the intensity axis. The palaeodose is evaluated where the extrapolated curve meets the dose axis.*

stone which have been dated by TL. While procedures for measuring palaeodoses are similar for flint, stone and stalagmite, they are to some extent different for sediment. To prepare the former materials, the outer 2 mm of each piece are cut away to remove those parts that have been exposed to light and to the alpha and beta activity of the burial soil. The interior piece is then crushed, and two different grain sizes are selected for TL examination. Large grains, of size 75–125 μm, are sprinkled onto stainless steel discs. Fine grains (approximately 2–10 μm) are deposited from suspension in acetone onto aluminium discs.

The set of large grain discs is used for the main palaeodose evaluation. About half of the discs are irradiated with varying doses from a beta radiation source, while the rest are left un-irradiated. The TL intensities of the un-irradiated discs yield the natural TL level. Together with the emissions of the irradiated discs, these measurements are referred to as the first glows, and they demonstrate the growth of TL intensity as increasing radiation doses are added to the palaeodose. The palaeodose is evaluated by extrapolating the growth of the TL backward to zero intensity.

For both flint and stalagmite, palaeodose evaluation is complicated by the fact that the growth of TL vs. radiation dose follows a non-linear curve. Clearly, it is necessary to know how the TL accumulated while the sample was buried, and this is discovered by a further set of TL measurements, known as the second glows. Following the first glow measurements, sample discs are re-irradiated with various doses to induce new TL signals in them. The growth of TL vs. dose in the subsequent second glows then provides the template for extrapolating the first glow data. This method of palaeodose evaluation is illustrated

in Figure 11.1, which compares the first and second glow growth curves of the stalagmite, H3150 (PND66).

Alpha radiation produces TL in a manner different from that in which beta and gamma radiations act. In particular, the TL producing efficiency of alphas relative to other rays varies between different samples of flint or stalagmite. This relative efficiency is expressed as a b-value, which is measured by comparing the intensities of TL induced by known doses of alpha and beta radiations. Because alpha rays have very low penetration, thinly deposited fine grain discs must be used for this measurement. Table 11.2 lists the b-values obtained.

For sediment dating, a slightly different procedure is used for the palaeodose evaluation. The date of deposition is measurable because one of the TL signals present in sediments is greatly reduced, or bleached, by the exposure to daylight which accompanies the event. Care must be taken when collecting sediments for TL dating to avoid light exposure, and outer parts of the sample, which may have been exposed, are subsequently removed. Fine grains are selected and deposited onto a set of aluminium discs for TL examination.

About half of these discs are used for natural and first glow TL measurements, as described for flint and stalagmite. The rest of the discs are exposed to daylight for a few days to remove the bleachable part of the TL signal, and are then irradiated with various beta or alpha doses to regenerate their TL signals. After measurement of these TL emissions, it is possible to evaluate the dose which regenerates a TL intensity equal to that of the natural material. This quantity of radiation, which is termed the natural regeneration dose, can be identified with the

| Sample | Find no. (Lab ref.) | Lab ref. | Palaeodose (Grays) | b-Value (Gy.μm²) | Internal dose rate (Gy/ka) | External dose rate (Gy/ka) | TL Age (ka BP) |
|---|---|---|---|---|---|---|---|
| **Main Cave Areas B, C, D, F and G** | | | | | | | |
| Stal | B409 | 226g1 | 243 ± 17 | 3.80 | 0.43 | 0.88 | 210 ± 70 |
| Stal | B556 | PND42 | 146 ± 7 | 2.30 | 0.489 | 0.88 | 115 ± 46 |
| Stal | D118 | 226a1 | 22 ± 11 | 3.77 | 0.38 | 0.62 | 27 ± 14 |
| Stal | D471 | 226e6 | 227 ± 27 | 3.65 | 0.59 | 0.77 | 188 ± 35 |
| Stal | D604 | 226e14 | 207 ± 20 | 2.57 | 0.14 | 0.82 | 222 ± 42 |
| Stal | D1693 | 226h3 | 174 ± 12 | 2.81 | 0.41 | 0.68 | 177 ± 30 |
| Stal | D1711 | 226h21 | 172 ± 14 | 2.37 | 0.20 | 0.86 | 173 ± 23 |
| Stal | F2264 | PND37 | 121 ± 9 | 2.48 | 0.253 | 0.595 | 141 ± 29 |
| Stal | G75 | PND47 | 88 ± 5 | 1.29 | 0.122 | 0.988 | 87 ± 14 |
| Stal | B111 | 226a8 | 160 ± 19 | 4.36 | 0.84 | 0.96 | 115 ± 21 |
| Stal | B396 | 226e4 | 200 ± 15 | 6.51 | 1.61 | 1.09 | 107 ± 15 |
| Stal | B0b:1 | 226f2 | 162 ± 17 | 7.11 | 1.02 | 1.05 | 108 ± 18 |
| Stal | B0b:2 | 226f1 | 143 ± 17 | 4.62 | 0.59 | 1.05 | 113 ± 19 |
| Stal | D292 | 226e13 | 134 ± 19 | 3.17 | 0.41 | 0.73 | 139 ± 29 |
| Stal | D446 | 226e9 | 134 ± 34 | 2.83 | 0.14 | 0.61 | 196 ± 54 |
| Flint | D4367 | PND25 | 298 ± 30 | 1.33 | 0.225 | 0.884 | 269 ± 37 |
| **New Entrance Area H** | | | | | | | |
| Sediment | H196 | PND23 | 155 ± 26 | 0.99 | 2.956 | 0.940 | 32 ± 6 |
| Flint | H598 | PND33 | 173 ± 15 | 2.35 | 0.205 | 0.761 | 179 ± 22 |
| Flint | H1036 | PND32 | 247 ± 17 | 1.89 | 0.631 | 0.794 | 173 ± 20 |
| Stal | H1713/2 | PND41 | 178 ± 11 | 4.02 | 0.868 | 1.105 | 101 ± 25 |
| Stal | H1724 | PND43 | 103 ± 5 | 3.43 | 0.154 | 0.534 | 154 ± 36 |
| Stal | H1725 | PND44 | 86 ± 5 | 3.53 | 0.276 | 0.432 | 130 ± 29 |
| Stone | H2312 | PND62 | 452 ± 17 | 2.70 | 1.300 | 0.783 | 214 ± 21 |
| Stal | H3150 | PND66 | 155 ± 8 | 3.98 | 0.228 | 0.518 | 226 ± 21 |

Notes. Uncertainties in the b-value lie mostly in the range from ±8% to ±24%; those for the internal dose rate, from ±10% to ±23%; and those for the external dose rate, from ±7% to ±22% (excepting samples B409 and B556, whose external dose rates have uncertainties of approximately ±35%). The internal dose rate gives the present-day effective dose rate due to alpha and beta radiations; the external dose rate is that due to gamma and cosmic radiations.

*Table 11.2. TL date measurements of samples from Pontnewydd Cave.*

palaeodose by virtue of the observation that bleaching does not alter the efficiency of TL production. The palaeodose shown in Table 11.2 for the sediment H196 (PND23) is the natural regeneration dose of beta radiation, while the b-value shows its relationship to the alpha dose which had the same effect.

### Dose rate assessments

The radiation dose absorbed by a TL sample during its period of burial is composed of two parts. The internal dose is that imparted by the short-ranged alpha and beta rays originating within the sample. The external, or environmental, dose is mainly due to gamma rays which are emitted by the surrounding soil, and which can penetrate up to 30 cm before losing energy in the TL sample. The external dose also includes a small contribution from cosmic rays. Flint and stalagmite generally have a low content of radioactivity, and in consequence, the absorbed palaeodose is often dominated by the external gamma dose. Therefore, the confidence with which the external dose rate can be assessed is the principal factor in determining the precision of the date measurement.

The typical cave environment is extremely inhomogeneous in its radioactive content. The recovery of the TL sample inevitably results in some destruction of its burial environment, and it is sometimes difficult to assess accurately the external dose rate to which the sample was exposed. Where possible, use is made of surviving sections of the burial soils which can, with varying degrees of confidence, be taken as representative of the destroyed deposit. The error limits of the date measurements listed in Table 11.2 mainly reflect the uncertainty of the external dose rate assessment. Most notably, the very low dating precision for the interstitial calcites from the Lower Sands and Gravels is due to the large variability of gamma dose rate within this deposit.

Most of the external dose rate assessments in this study were performed by means of capsules containing a sensitive TL dosimeter (calcium fluoride). The capsules were buried for approximately one year in the burial soils, and at the end of this time the dose absorbed by the calcium fluoride was measured. Alternatively, external dose rates were measured using a portable gamma spectrometer. This method not only avoids the delay inherent in the use of capsules, but also identifies the sources of the gamma rays. Internal dose rates were measured in the laboratory by observing the alpha activities of the TL samples, and by analysis of their potassium contents. Assessments of the present-day internal and external dose rates are shown in Table 11.2.

### TL Dates

The TL measurements, described above, yield the present

natural TL intensity of the examined material, and the manner in which the TL increased with radiation exposure. The dose rate assessments allow us to calculate how the radiation dose accumulated with time. By combining these measurements, the age of the material can be obtained as the length of time required for the different forms of radiation to induce TL levels which sum to the observed natural intensity. In the case of stalagmitic material, allowance must be made for the changing internal dose rate which results from the increasing presence of thorium-230 and its decay products. (This phenomenon provides the basis of the uranium series disequilibrium dating method.) The external dose rate may also vary with time, mainly as a consequence of varying water content in the burial deposits. The water acts as a radiation shield, absorbing gamma energy which might otherwise be received by the TL sample. It is therefore necessary to estimate a range of values within which the average past water content of the deposits is likely to have lain. The uncertainty associated with this range is incorporated in the error limits of the TL date measurement.

The calculated TL dates are listed in Table 11.2. The quoted error limits include all sources of error, both random and systematic, and represent the 68% confidence level. Four TL dates refer to the heating of flint or stone. If this heating did not coincide with the human occupation itself, it must certainly have occurred while the material remained at ground surface. The TL date of the flint, D4367, lies separate from an otherwise tight grouping formed by the other three (H598, H1036 and H2312). However, taking its error limits into account, there is insufficient evidence from TL dates for proposing more than a single period of occupation. The weighted mean of the four dates yields a best estimate of 196,000±19,000 BP for the heating of the flint and stone pieces. This is in good agreement with the TL date of 200,000±25,000 BP obtained for the flint D687 (OxTL 226d1) by Huxtable (1984).

The dated stalagmitic material falls mainly into two categories; that formed *in situ*, which provides a chronological marker in the stratigraphy, and derived material, whose formation must pre-date the deposit within which it occurs. A third category comprises the interstitial calcites, B409 and B556, which must have formed after the deposition of the Lower Sands and Gravels. Together with the uranium series disequilibrium dates on stalagmite from the cave, the TL dates serve to constrain the chronology of the various emplacements, and to relate the stratigraphic units uncovered in the Main Cave with those in the New Entrance.

Among the *in situ* stalagmites, samples D471, D604, D1693 and D1711 all formed on top of the Lower Breccia in the Main Cave. Their TL dates are mutually consistent and indicate an age of formation between 170,000 and 200,000 BP. This is earlier than the formation of the derived stalagmite from Layer 31 in the New Entrance, H1713, whose TL date places it in the Last Interglacial (this stalagmite had been erroneously interpreted as *in situ* in Aldhouse-Green 1995). The derived pieces of

stalagmitic floor (B111, B396, B0b:1 and B0b:2) form a clearly defined set of samples. Their TL dates are closely grouped, suggesting that all pieces derived from the same formation, and indicate a Last Interglacial age for the floor. They were published in Schwarcz (1984) as having been found at the base of the Breccia in the Main Cave or at its boundary with the Intermediate unit. But this was commented on by Green (1984, 30) where he suggests that these stalagmites can only be referred to somewhere in the Upper Breccia/Intermediate sequence as a whole.

The TL date of sediment, H196, relates to the scree deposition which covered the New Entrance.

## Speleothem U-Series dating: University of East Anglia alpha spectrometry results

*Peter Rowe, Tim Atkinson and Nick Hebden*

### Sampling

Most speleothem samples were collected by the archaeological team during the course of excavation, although a few were collected by the authors under the supervision of Stephen Aldhouse-Green.

### Sample selection and treatment

Typically 20–60 g of calcite were used for dating. Selected layers of interest were cut from the main calcite body using diamond-edged circular or diamond wire saws, avoiding dirt bands (hiatuses) and vuggy areas as far as possible, and crushed to a powder in a tungsten mill.

### Chemical procedures

The calcite powder was slowly added to 1–2 litres of constantly stirred dilute (1M) nitric acid solution to which had been added a weighed amount of spike solution which was in secular equilibrium ($^{228}Th/^{232}U = 1.027$). Following dissolution and subsequent filtering to remove insoluble detritus (generally <1%), the solution was boiled to reduce volume and remove dissolved $CO_2$. A few milligrams of $FeCl_3$ was added and the pH of the solution raised to ~9 to co-precipitate uranium and thorium with $Fe(OH)_3$. The bulk of the supernate was decanted and the precipitate centrifuged down before being dissolved in a few millilitres of 9M HCl and passed through a pre-washed anion exchange column (Bio-Rad AG 1-X8 100–200 mesh) to separate uranium and thorium isotopes. These were then further purified from interfering elements on additional exchange columns in 7M $HNO_3$ and the final eluate evaporated and electroplated in ammonium sulphate solution onto stainless steel discs for counting.

### Alpha spectrometry

The isotopes were counted on EG&G Ortec 576A alpha spectrometers with efficiencies of ~36% and resolution of 10MeV (FWHM). Several thousand counts were accumulated under the main isotopic peaks of interest to minimize age errors. The raw spectrometric data were background corrected and input to a computer programme to iteritively solve the $^{230}$Th/$^{234}$U age equation.

### *Results*

Table 11.3 summarizes the results for the 9 samples analysed.

### Discussion

The speleothem growth phases recorded by these samples correspond, within the dating errors, to interglacial or interstadial periods (Table 11.3). F5084a is beyond the range of the dating method (>300,000 years ago) and no conclusion can be reached regarding this sample. A517 is heavily contaminated with detritus and the corrected age of 81,500 (MIS 5a) is an estimated age based on assumptions about the thorium isotopic composition of the detritus (see Table 11.3). It is possible that its true age is younger and that it grew during an interstadial phase in MIS 3. Although the ages of D5901 and H2217 do not precisely correspond with warm phases, the dating errors easily allow the former to be correlated with MIS 5e and the latter with MIS 7.3 or 7.5. H2216 has an apparent age of 269,400 BP, placing it in MIS 8. Whilst this may be the case since it is not known to have been a period of extensive lowland glaciation in the British Isles, the dating errors allow correlation with MIS 9 but suggest it is unlikely to date from MIS 7.5.

### Electron Spin Resonance dating of tooth enamel from Pontnewydd Cave

*E. J. Rhodes, R. Grün and L. P. Zhou*

### *Introduction*

Electron Spin Resonance (ESR) age estimates have been derived for several mammal teeth or tooth fragments collected from excavations within Pontnewydd Cave (Table 11.4). ESR dating was undertaken in two campaigns. One series of tooth samples was prepared and measured by Rainer Grün (RG series samples), while the second series was prepared and measured jointly by Ed Rhodes and Li Ping Zhou (EJR-LPZ series). A similar approach for sample preparation and analysis was adopted in both campaigns, and determinations were made using similar ESR measurement parameters. The results form an internally coherent group of age estimates, despite significant variations in internal uranium content between several samples.

Although hydroxyapatite from teeth contains a strong ESR signal from which precise values of equivalent dose can be measured, teeth absorb uranium during burial from ground water (Grün and Invernati 1985). Uncertainty in the pattern of uranium uptake, besides its spatial distribution within each of the different tooth materials (enamel, dentine, cement), leads to uncertainty in the final ESR age estimates. Uranium uptake can be modelled (Grün

*et al.* 1988), though such models may not accurately reflect the reality of uranium migration, particularly in cave environments (Grün 2009b). Additionally, recent research casts some doubt on the validity of conventional ESR equivalent dose determinations and suggests that ESR age underestimates may be encountered (Joannes-Boyau and Grün 2011). Notwithstanding these caveats, we present the ESR age determinations made for samples from Pontnewydd Cave.

### *Sample preparation and measurement*

Samples were prepared by cutting one or more panels of enamel from each tooth, recording the initial thickness, then grinding the outer layers to remove the surface (see Table 11.4 for details). The remaining enamel was ground using an agate pestle and mortar, and sieved. A subsample was removed for U content analysis. For the single enamel samples removed from teeth E80 and E81 (EJR-LPZ series), the remaining enamel was divided into 4 different grain size fractions, to assess whether there were any systematic variations in accumulated dose value. Each sample was weighed out into 10 equal aliquots to within ±0.5%, and these were administered a range of different gamma dose values.

Room temperature X-band ESR measurements (9.16 GHz) were made using a microwave power of 2mW, modulation frequency of 100kHz and modulation amplitude of 0.5mTpp. For the RG sample series, measurements were made using a Bruker 100 ER spectrometer at McMaster University, Canada (sample D2312 only) or a JEOL RE1X at Cambridge, U.K., while for the EJR-LPZ series samples, determinations were performed using a small bench-top Bruker spectrometer at Royal Holloway, University of London.

### *Age estimation*

For both measurement series, equivalent dose values were determined using a conventional multiple aliquot additive dose procedure (Grün 1989). Additive dose curves were constructed for each group of aliquots by fitting an exponential function and extrapolating to zero ESR signal intensity in order to derive an equivalent dose estimate. Age calculations were performed using the DATA program of Grün (2009) using the parameters shown in Table 11.4, and incorporating the most recent values for beta attenuation, uncertainty propagation, energy conversion and other factors. Internal uranium concentrations for enamel and dentine were measured by delayed neutron counting at XRAL, Ontario, Canada. Sediment U, Th and K concentrations were measured by instrumental neutron activation analysis (INAA), also performed at XRAL. Gamma dose rates were not measured directly, but were calculated based on U, Th and K concentrations of sediment from appropriate locations within the cave. Sediment beta dose rates were based on sediment collected with each tooth, or from values measured from the appropriate horizon.

| Sample lab. ref. | Site ref. | Yield U % | Yield Th % | U ppm | $\frac{234U}{238U}$ | Error | $\frac{230Th}{234U}$ | Error | $\frac{230Th}{232Th}$ | Error | Age (ka) uncorrected | Age (ka) corrected | Marine Isotope Stage |
|---|---|---|---|---|---|---|---|---|---|---|---|---|---|
| UEA771 | F773 Top* | 71 | 74 | 0.69 | 1.0841 | 0.0153 | 0.6844 | 0.0141 | 267.0 | 39.0 | 122.4+5.2/-4.9 | 122.4+5.2/-4.9 | 5e |
| UEA772 | A517 | 83 | 27 | 0.32 | 1.0358 | 0.0221 | 0.6186 | 0.0180 | 2.6 | 0.1 | 103.8+5.7/-5.3 | 81.5+6.4/-6.1** | 5a |
| UEA773 | F50084a | 79 | 30 | 0.48 | 1.1148 | 0.0240 | 1.0761 | 0.0311 | 6.3 | 0.2 | >350 | >350*** | --- |
| UEA774 | F4894 | 77 | 55 | 0.31 | 1.1326 | 0.0158 | 0.9154 | 0.0183 | 74.0 | 8.2 | 237.3+20.3/-16.9 | 237.3+20.3/-16.9 | 7.5 |
| UEA775 | D5901 Base | 55 | 47 | 0.76 | 1.0489 | 0.0184 | 0.7240 | 0.0198 | 90.5 | 10.3 | 137.4+8.6/-7.9 | 137.4+8.6/-7.9 | 5e |
| UEA644 | D4698 | 46 | 71 | 0.90 | 1.0713 | 0.0231 | 0.6657 | 0.0326 | 100.3 | 10.4 | 116.8+10.6/-9.7 | 116.8+10.6/-9.7 | 5e |
| UEA646 | F2996 | 47 | 55 | 0.49 | 1.1151 | 0.0219 | 0.8581 | 0.0362 | 215.9 | 37.1 | 197.5+25.1/-20.6 | 197.5+25.1/-20.6 | 7.1 |
| UEA683 | H2216 | 52 | 30 | 0.39 | 1.1006 | 0.0120 | 0.9408 | 0.0184 | 18.2 | 0.8 | 269.4+24.0/-19.9 | 265.3+28.5/-22.4 | 9? |
| UEA684 | H2217 | 51 | 5 | 1.16 | 1.0662 | 0.0147 | 0.8880 | 0.0256 | 88.9 | 8.4 | 224.8+23.2/-19.2 | 224.8+23.2/-19.2 | 7.3/7.5 |

Errors are 1 s.d. based on counting statistics. Samples with ($^{230}$Th/$^{232}$Th) ratios <20 are detritally contaminated and calculated uncorrected ages therefore are maximum possible ages. Corrected ages for these samples are calculated assuming that the initial ($^{230}$Th/$^{232}$Th) value of the contaminanating detritus was 0.8, representing an average crustal value assuming equilibrium in the $^{238}$U decay chain. * F773: the dated sample is one of several stalagmite bosses on the upper surface of this flowstone; the base of F773 has not been dated because its internal structure is quite complex, it is generally vuggy, and it contains several broken pieces of older stalagmite that have fallen and been incorporated within the younger calcite.
** A517: this sample is heavily contaminated with detritus and a corrected age is very sensitive to choice of ($^{230}$Th/$^{232}$Th)$_{initial}$ value and although the Marine Isotope Stage 5a corrected age is plausible, the true age could be younger and lie within MIS 3. *** F50084a: This sample is heavily thorium contaminated and correction using a ($^{230}$Th/$^{232}$Th)$_{initial}$ ratio ≤4 does not produce a finite age.

*Table 11.3. U-series dating results.*

| Lab. code | Find no. | Layer | Grid square | X | Y | Depth below S.D. | Description |
|---|---|---|---|---|---|---|---|
| **EJR-LPZ series samples** | | | | | | | |
| E75a | F2853 | LBc | I1NE | | | 99.32–99.22 | *Stephanorhinus* sp. tooth fragment |
| E78a | D2909 | LB | H9NE | 45 | 78 | 99.24 | *Stephanorhinus* sp. tooth fragment |
| E80a, b, c, d | C286 | LB | L13NW | 44 | 49 | 99.01 | *Stephanorhinus kirchbergensis* tooth fragment |
| E81a, b, c, d | C189 | LB | M13NE | 47 | 68 | 99.37 | *Stephanorhinus* sp. tooth fragment |
| E82a, b | B440 | | K22SW | 65 | 6 | 99.44 | *Stephanorhinus* sp. tooth fragment |
| **RG series samples** | | | | | | | |
| 394 | D2312 | LB | J7SW | | | 99.05–98.95 | Unidentified tooth |
| 570 | H428 | 24 | AB994NW | 37 | 12 | 99.25 | ? Bovid tooth |
| 589 | D358 | LB | H9SW/SE | | | | *Stephanorhinus* sp. tooth |
| 590 | C119 | LB | M13NW | | | 99.13 | *Stephanorhinus* sp. tooth fragment |
| 591 | D2121 | LB | I7NW | | | 99.10–99.00 | *Cervus elaphus* M$_3$ |

*Table 11.4. ESR sample locations and descriptions.*

## *Dating results*

ESR age estimates, and the parameters used in their calculation are presented in Table 11.5, integrating samples from both sample series and listing the results in approximate stratigraphic order within the cave. Following the usual format adopted for ESR, age estimates are presented based on different models of uranium migration into the teeth, specifically on early uptake (EU) and linear uptake (LU) models. Additionally, age estimates assuming a recent uptake (RU) model are presented. It should be noted that these uptake models implicitly assume that all uranium in a given tooth sub-sample was acquired from ground water in a uniform fashion, a condition not likely to pertain in reality.

The age estimates mostly lie in the range of 100–300 ka. No single uptake model provides ages that are entirely consistent, though the recent uptake (RU) ages have the smallest fractional variation between results.

## *Discussion and conclusions*

A striking feature of the ESR age estimates is the consistency between the two sample series, measured at different times using different equipment. However, variation exists for the age estimates of teeth nominally from the same horizon. For the samples from the Lower Breccia (layer LB in Table 11.5), the variation between samples represented by one standard deviation is around twice the mean uncertainty value for the recent uptake model age estimates.

Several caveats to these conventional ESR age estimates have been mentioned above. These include differences in uranium uptake pattern experienced by different teeth and within single teeth, leading to apparent age variation, and also recently described problems associated with differential response of tooth enamel ESR centers to beta and gamma radiation (Joannes-Boyau and Grün 2011). This latter effect may lead to age underestimates of up to 30%; variations in magnitude may exist between species and the effect may possibly also be dependent on age and tooth type. The complexities of cave stratigraphy should also be borne in mind when considering these results.

In summary, ESR age estimates for 11 teeth or tooth fragments provide ages between 90±6 ka and 232±14 ka (EU), 108±8 ka to 274±19 ka (LU) or 132±12 ka to 322±29 ka (RU). Problems associated with the conventional ESR dating approach used here that have only recently been identified, besides better understood issues of complex uranium uptake and migration within teeth, render these age estimates difficult to interpret in a more detailed manner. However, future ESR dating application, for example incorporating laser ablation ICP-MS uranium determinations and investigation of the relative contributions of different $CO_2-$ radicals responsible for the ESR signal, may be able to overcome these current limitations.

## A summary of the chronological evidence from Pontnewydd Cave

*Nicholas C. Debenham*

### *Introduction*

The programme of absolute age measurements on materials excavated from Pontnewydd Cave has had two principal objectives. These are (i) to date the human occupation of the site, and (ii) to date the emplacement of the remains of that occupation within the cave. Regarding the date of occupation, the most direct evidence is provided by thermoluminescence (TL) date measurements on five heated archaeological flints which derived from the cave deposits. For the second objective, the clearest indications are provided by measurements on *in situ* stalagmitic formations, especially those which mark the interval between the Lower Breccia and Upper Breccia emplacements. A total of thirty-one samples of *in situ* stalagmite were dated using the uranium series disequilibrium technique, of which nine were also dated by TL. In addition, date measurements were performed on forty-three samples of derived materials, including stalagmitic fragments, bone and teeth, by means of U-series, TL and electron spin resonance (ESR) procedures.

Tables 11.6 and 11.7 list details of the available dating evidence for *in situ* and derived samples, respectively. The data are sub-divided according to the stratigraphic unit to which they relate, and then ordered by find number of the dated sample. Summaries of the data are presented graphically in Figures 11.2 and 11.3. Uncertainties attached to the date measurements are expressed by the error limits which accompany the central date values. In the present data sets, error limits refer to the 68% confidence level. When comparing dating evidence from a variety of measurement techniques, it is useful to distinguish three categories of uncertainty. The first source of uncertainty is directly related to the measurement procedures in the laboratory and field. These measurement errors, whether random or systematic, are quantifiable by normal scientific methods and should always be included in the calculation of the date error limits.

The second category includes estimated corrections that are applied to the date calculations. Examples of these adjustments are the detrital thorium correction in the U-series method, and the correction of the dose-rate assessment in TL dating to allow for possible long-term variations in environmental factors. Where such corrections are applied, the additional uncertainty that they introduce should also be included in the date error limits. The third category of uncertainty arises from the possible invalidity of assumptions which form the basis of the dating method. In TL dating of stalagmites, it is assumed that the speleothem has not partly or wholly re-crystallized since its original formation. In U-series dating, the stalagmite is assumed to be a perfect time capsule, and that no uranium or thorium has passed into or out of the sample during its history. The effects on measured dates caused by failures of these assumptions are unquantifiable, and are therefore

| Find no. | Lab. code | De (Gy) | De error (Gy) | U-EN (ppm) | U-DE (ppm) | U-SED (ppm) | Th-SED (ppm) | K-SED (%) | Gamma dose rate (µGy/a) | Water in sediment (%) | Enamel thickness (µm) | Removed either side (µm) | ESR age estimates EU (ka) | EU error (ka) | LU (ka) | LU error (ka) | RU (ka) | RU error (ka) |
|---|---|---|---|---|---|---|---|---|---|---|---|---|---|---|---|---|---|---|
| H428 | 570A | 254 | ± 7 | 1.17 | 54.3 | 5.81 | 13.0 | 2.25 | 1370 | 20 | 1230 | 20 | 102 | ± 7 | 124 | ± 9 | 153 | ± 14 |
| | 570B | 219 | ± 7 | 1.11 | 54.3 | 5.81 | 13.0 | 2.25 | 1370 | 20 | 1350 | 20 | 90 | ± 6 | 108 | ± 8 | 132 | ± 12 |
| H359 | E83A1 | 207 | ± 7 | 0.30 | 51.2 | 6.23 | 7.2 | 1.22 | 630 | 15 | 2335 | 115 | 186 | ± 14 | 227 | ± 18 | 280 | ± 26 |
| F2853 | E75A | 445 | ± 13 | 0.40 | 91.1 | 13.2 | 11.5 | 2.13 | 1370 | 15 | 1500 | 100 | 177 | ± 13 | 217 | ± 17 | 269 | ± 25 |
| D2909 | E78A | 276 | ± 9 | 0.30 | 45.8 | 14.2 | 12.3 | 2.13 | 1050 | 15 | 1680 | 100 | 155 | ± 11 | 179 | ± 14 | 206 | ± 18 |
| D2312 | 394 | 227 | ± 6 | 0.17 | 8.96 | 9.47 | 16.0 | 2.93 | 880 | 20 | 800 | 20 | 140 | ± 9 | 149 | ± 11 | 163 | ± 13 |
| | 394A | 312 | ± 9 | 0.13 | 29.1 | 9.47 | 16.0 | 2.93 | 880 | 20 | 900 | 20 | 170 | ± 11 | 196 | ± 14 | 224 | ± 18 |
| | 394B | 306 | ± 11 | 0.53 | 15.1 | 9.47 | 16.0 | 2.93 | 880 | 20 | 700 | 20 | 160 | ± 16 | 181 | ± 15 | 204 | ± 18 |
| D358 | 589A | 447 | ± 6 | 0.10 | 31.2 | 9.47 | 16.0 | 2.93 | 880 | 10 | 850 | 25 | 232 | ± 14 | 271 | ± 18 | 316 | ± 26 |
| | 589B | 452 | ± 14 | 0.43 | 31.6 | 9.47 | 16.0 | 2.93 | 880 | 10 | 740 | 20 | 210 | ± 14 | 253 | ± 17 | 306 | ± 25 |
| | 589C | 431 | ± 14 | 0.30 | 32.5 | 9.47 | 16.0 | 2.93 | 880 | 10 | 1050 | 25 | 232 | ± 15 | 274 | ± 19 | 322 | ± 29 |
| D2121 | 591A | 258 | ± 7 | 0.09 | 3.73 | 9.47 | 16.0 | 2.93 | 880 | 10 | 1900 | 50 | 215 | ± 17 | 222 | ± 18 | 227 | ± 19 |
| | 591C | 267 | ± 6 | 0.01 | 3.73 | 9.47 | 16.0 | 2.93 | 880 | 10 | 1900 | 50 | 228 | ± 18 | 232 | ± 19 | 235 | ± 20 |
| C286 | E80A1 | 290 | ± 10 | 0.20 | 20.8 | 19.6 | 11.3 | 1.90 | 880 | 15 | 1900 | 120 | 214 | ± 17 | 234 | ± 19 | 253 | ± 22 |
| | E80A2 | 291 | ± 11 | 0.20 | 20.8 | 19.6 | 11.3 | 1.90 | 880 | 15 | 1900 | 120 | 214 | ± 17 | 234 | ± 20 | 254 | ± 23 |
| | E80A3 | 290 | ± 11 | 0.20 | 20.8 | 19.6 | 11.3 | 1.90 | 880 | 15 | 1900 | 120 | 214 | ± 17 | 234 | ± 19 | 253 | ± 23 |
| | E80A4 | 293 | ± 12 | 0.20 | 20.8 | 19.6 | 11.3 | 1.90 | 880 | 15 | 1900 | 120 | 216 | ± 18 | 236 | ± 20 | 255 | ± 23 |
| C189 | E81A1 | 230 | ± 6 | 1.40 | 42.7 | 19.6 | 11.3 | 1.90 | 880 | 15 | 2000 | 120 | 127 | ± 9 | 159 | ± 11 | 202 | ± 18 |
| | E81A2 | 226 | ± 7 | 1.40 | 42.7 | 19.6 | 11.3 | 1.90 | 880 | 15 | 2000 | 120 | 126 | ± 9 | 157 | ± 12 | 199 | ± 18 |
| | E81A3 | 229 | ± 7 | 1.40 | 42.7 | 19.6 | 11.3 | 1.90 | 880 | 15 | 2000 | 120 | 127 | ± 9 | 159 | ± 12 | 202 | ± 18 |
| | E81A4 | 225 | ± 7 | 1.40 | 42.7 | 19.6 | 11.3 | 1.90 | 880 | 15 | 2000 | 120 | 125 | ± 9 | 156 | ± 11 | 198 | ± 18 |
| C119 | 590A | 254 | ± 7 | 0.36 | 63.5 | 19.6 | 11.3 | 1.90 | 880 | 10 | 1500 | 50 | 140 | ± 9 | 171 | ± 12 | 213 | ± 18 |
| | 590B | 247 | ± 6 | 0.68 | 49.3 | 19.6 | 11.3 | 1.90 | 880 | 10 | 1600 | 50 | 140 | ± 9 | 170 | ± 12 | 210 | ± 18 |
| B440 | E82A1 | 298 | ± 8 | 1.00 | 134 | 19.6 | 11.3 | 1.90 | 880 | 15 | 2320 | 115 | 143 | ± 10 | 190 | ± 14 | 262 | ± 23 |
| | E82A2 | 293 | ± 10 | 0.80 | 111 | 19.6 | 11.3 | 1.90 | 880 | 15 | 2010 | 110 | 145 | ± 11 | 188 | ± 14 | 257 | ± 23 |

Table 11.5. *ESR age estimates and parameters used in age calculations. All uncertainties shown are 1 sigma uncertainty values; 5% uncertainty was used for internal U concentrations (enamel and dentine); 10% uncertainty was used for sediment U, Th and K concentrations and sediment gamma dose rate values. A uniform internal and sediment water content value of 15% was used, and samples were assumed to be buried at 20 m depth for cosmic dose rate estimation. Age estimates are presented for early uptake (EU), linear uptake (LU) and recent uptake (RU) of internal uranium; see text for discussion of the relative merits of these age calculations.*

| Find no. (Sample no.) | Layer | Square | Depth S.D. | Age ka | Method | Dated by | Notes |
|---|---|---|---|---|---|---|---|
| A517 (UEA772) | --- | F37 | 99.78 | 103.8 +5.7/-5.3 | U u | UEA | Stalagmite on north wall of the Entrance outside the Guard Chamber |
| D188 (226a1) | LT | H6 | --- | 81.5 +6.4/-6.1* | U c | RLA | * Sensitive to (230Th/232Th)init value |
|  |  |  |  | 13 +7/-6 | U c | RLA | Laminated travertine |
|  |  |  |  | 32 +12/-11 | U c |  |  |
|  |  |  |  | 15 ± 7 | U c |  | Mean of 3 U-series dates: 17 ± 5 ka |
|  |  |  |  | 27 ± 14 | TL |  |  |
| D4698 (UEA644) | --- | G10NE | 100.50 | 116.8 +10.6/-9.7 | U c | UEA | High level wall stalagmite (North Passage) |
| D5901:base (UEA775) | --- | K7NE | 100.50 | 137.4 +8.6/-7.9 | U c | UEA | High level wall stalagmite (South East Fissure) |
| G75 (PND47) | On LB | GAO997SE | 99.8 | 87 ± 14 | TL | BM | Stalagmitic floor above Lower Breccia |
| F2264 (PND37) | On Sb | G2NE | 99.73 | 141 ± 29 | TL | BM | Stalagmite |
| B274 | On LB | J22NW | 99.85 | 230 +21/-20 | U u | MCM | Flowstone over Lower Breccia |
|  |  |  |  | 217 +24/-20 | U c |  |  |
| C0 (MCM-78852) | On LB | M13SE | 99.33 | 189 ± 12 | U u | MCM | Stalagmite Boss |
|  |  |  |  | 177 ± 12 | U c |  |  |
| C133 (Root of C0) | On LB | M13SE | 99.33 | >350 | U u | MCM | Interstitial calcite crust |
| D312 : top | On LB | K9NW | 99.54-99.64 | 89.3 ± 2.7 | U u | MCM | Base of stalagmitic pillar and part of apron |
| D312 : base |  |  |  | 95.7 ± 4.3 | U u |  | Mean of 2 dates: 91.1 ± 2.9 ka |
| D471 (226e6) | On LB | H7SE | 99.45 | 174 +35/-27 | U c | RLA | Stalagmite |
|  |  |  |  | 188 ± 35 | TL | RLA |  |
| D534 : 2 | On LB | H11NE | 99.50 | 227 ± 13 | U u | MCM | Stalagmitic pillar |
| D534 : 3 |  |  |  | 300 +54/-37 | U u |  | Mean of 2 dates: 232 ± 19 ka |
| D604 (226e14) | On LB | J9 | 99.67 | 161 ± 11 | U u | MCM | Stalagmitic boss |
|  |  |  |  | 222 ± 42 | TL | RLA |  |
| D642 | On LB | I7NW | 99.44 | 95 ± 7 | U u | MCM | Stalagmitic boss |
|  |  |  |  | 83 ± 9 | U c |  |  |
| D1288B:upper | On LB | J7NW | 99.68 | 196 +27/-22 | U u | MCM | Stalagmitic floor |
| D1288B:middle |  |  |  | 257 +60/-40 | U u |  | D1288B: mean of 3 dates: 215 ± 36 ka |
| D1288B:lower |  |  |  | 193 +21/-18 | U u |  |  |
| D1288C:upper | On LB | J7NW | 99.68 | 184 +26/-22 | U | AEA | Stalagmitic floor |
| D1288C:upper (HAR 2255) |  |  |  | 285 +71/-45 | U | AEA | Upper: mean of 3 dates: 225 +44/-32 ka |
| D1288C:upper (HAR 5612) |  |  |  |  |  |  |  |
| D1288C:upper (HAR 5624) |  |  |  | 205 +35/-27 | U | AEA |  |
| D1288C:middle (HAR 2256) |  |  |  | 262 +69/-44 | U | AEA |  |
| D1288C:middle (HAR 5610) |  |  |  | 238 +44/-33 | U | AEA | Middle: mean of 4 dates: 218 +39/-29 ka |

| Sample | Location | Grid ref | Level | Date | Method | Dated by | Description |
|---|---|---|---|---|---|---|---|
| D1288C:middle (HAR 5622) | | | | 183 +20/-17 | U | AEA | |
| D1288C:middle (HAR 5623) | | | | 188 +25/-21 | U | AEA | Lower: mean of 2 dates: 229 +41/-32 ka |
| D1288C:lower (HAR 2257) | | | | 239 +41/-31 | U | AEA | |
| D1288C:lower (HAR 5621) | | | | 218 +42/-31 | U | AEA | D1288C: mean of 9 dates: 223 +40/-31 ka |
| D1288D:base | On LB | J7SW | 99.68 | 218 +33/-26 | U | MCM | |
| D1693 (226h3) | On LB | G10 | | 176 +29/-23 | U c | RLA | Stalagmitic floor |
| | | | | 177 ± 30 | TL | RLA | |
| D1711 (226h21) | On LB | J7 | | 302 +inf/-74 | U c | RLA | Stalagmitic floor |
| | | | | 173 ± 23 | TL | RLA | |
| F1058 | On LB | H1SW | | 100.4 +4.4/-4.2 | U c | AEA | Stalagmite B. Cross Rift. Locally thin *in situ* floor on Lower Breccia (in East Passage) |
| F2996 (UEA646) | | G2NW | 99.73 (top) | 197.5 +25.1/ -20.6 | U c | UEA | Stalagmite A. East Passage. Wall stalagmite on north side of cave |
| F4894 (UEA774) | | G2SE | 99.54 | 237.3 +20.3/ -16.9 | U c | UEA | Stalagmite B |
| F5383 (J5629) | On LB | I2NE | 99.77-99.75 | 193 ± 12 | U c | AEA | Stalagmitic pillar (top) |
| F5417 (J5632) | On LB | I2NE | 99.65-99.60 | 134 ± 27 | U c | AEA | Stalagmitic boss 220 x 190 x 50 mm thick |
| F5579:base (J5634) | On LB | G5NW | 99.53 | 121 ± 9 | U c | AEA | Stalagmitic pillar 130 mm high on small base (100x70mm) |
| F5579:base (J5628) | | | | 131 ± 5 | U c | | As above. Separate measurement on another aliquot from same final solution. Mean of 2 dates: 129±5 ka |
| F5579:top (J5979) | On LB | G5NW | 99.53 | 88 ± 3 | U c | AEA | As above |
| F6050 (J5631) | On LB | I2NE | 99.80–99.68 | 86 ± 6 | U c | AEA | Stalagmitic pillar (lower part) |
| B409 (226g1) | LSG 3 | K17 | | 243 +91/-48 | U c | RLA | Interstitial calcite concretion |
| | | | | 210 ± 70 | TL | RLA | |
| B556 (PND42) | LSG | Deep sounding | 97.48 | 115 ± 46 | TL | BM | Interstitial calcite concretion |
| H196 (PND23) | Scree; 12 | | 103.03 | 32 ± 6 | TL | BM | Sediment |
| H3202 (J5627) | (42) | AC993NW/AC994NE | 96.50 | 91 ± 7 | U | AEA | *In situ* floor below Mudstone Gravel (38); fragment 20-25 mm thick |
| H3221 (J5630) | (43) | AB994SE | 96.95 | 85 ± 9 | U | AEA | Fragment of flowstone on bedrock below Mudstone Gravel |

Layers: LT = Laminated Travertine; Sb = Silt beds; LB = Lower Breccia; LSG = Lower Sands and Gravels.

Method: U u = Uranium series disequilibrium - uncorrected for detrital Th; U c = Uranium series disequilibrium - corrected for detrital Th; TL = Thermoluminescence.

Dated by: MCM = Henry Schwarz, Dept of Geology, McMaster University, Canada; AEA = Miro Ivanovich and Angela Rae, Atomic Energy Authority, Harwell, Oxford, UK; UEA = Peter Rowe and Timothy Atkinson, School of Environmental Sciences, UEA; RLA = Nick Debenham, Research Laboratory for Archaeology, Oxford University; BM = Nick Debenham and Mona Winter, British Museum, London; QTLS = Nick Debenham, Quaternary TL Surveys, Nottingham.

*Table 11.6. Pontnewydd Cave in situ samples.*

| Find no. (Sample no.) | Layer | Square | Depth S.D. | Age ka | Method | Dated by | Notes |
|---|---|---|---|---|---|---|---|
| B260 | RCE | K20 | 99.73 | 307 +44/-55 | U u | MCM | Porous flowstone |
| B262 | RCE | K20 | 99.74 | 179 ± 12 | U u | MCM | Stalactite |
| B275 | Interface of RCE /UB | K20 | 99.69 | 132 ± 4 | U u | MCM | Stalagmite clast |
| Boa (MCM-78850) | UB1 | K20 | | 149 ± 9 | U u | MCM | Flowstone clast |
| BOb : 1 (MCM-78851) (226f2) | UB1 | K21 | | 236 +80/-46 | U c | RLA | Flowstone |
| | | | | 130 ± 7 | U u | MCM | |
| | | | | 108 ± 18 | TL | RLA | |
| BOb : 2 (226f1) | UB1 | K21 | | 244 +88/-46 | U c | RLA | Flowstone |
| | | | | 204 ± 20 | U u | MCM | |
| | | | | 113 ± 19 | TL | RLA | |
| B111 : 1-2 (226a8) | UB/Ic | K21 | 99.07 | 104 +14/-13 | U c | RLA | Stalagmite block |
| | | | | 143 +20/-17 | U c | RLA | Mean of 2 U-series dates: 118 +14/-13 ka |
| | | | | 115 ± 21 | TL | RLA | |
| B148 | UB | L21 | 99.28 | 209 ± 16 | U u | MCM | Stalagmite clast |
| B279 | UB | K20 | 99.62 | 227 +24/-20 | U u | MCM | Stalagmite clast |
| B396 : 1-2 (226e4) | UB (base) | K20 | 99.07 | 118 +17/-15 | U c | RLA | Stalagmite |
| | | | | 106 +15/-13 | U c | RLA | Mean of 2 U-series dates: 111 +15/-13 ka |
| | | | | 107 ± 15 | TL | RLA | |
| B440 (E82-A) | UB1 | K22SW | 99.44 | 143 ± 10 | ESR e | LPZ/ER | Stephanorhinus sp. tooth fragment |
| | | | | 262 ± 23 | ESR r | | |
| | | | | 145 ± 11 | ESR e | LPZ/ER | Mean e: 144 ± 9 ka |
| | | | | 257 ± 23 | ESR r | | Mean r: 260 ± 19 ka |
| D187 | UB | 19NE | 99.30 | 125 ± 6 | U u | MCM | Stalactite |
| D292 : 1-2 (226e13) | UB | K10 | 99.69 | 160 +22/-18 | U c | RLA | Stalagmite |
| | | | | 185 +45/-31 | U c | RLA | Mean of 2 U-series dates: 165 +22/-18 ka |
| | | | | 139 ± 29 | TL | RLA | |
| D303 | UB | J8 | 99.87 | t: 18.0±0.8 s: 33.0+4.6/-4.4 | U | AEA | Bone: Vulpes vulpes (distal of end right femur) |
| D446 (226e9) | UB | H8 | 99.78 | 196 ± 54 | TL | RLA | Stalagmite |
| D472 | UB | I6 | 99.89 | t (cancellous): 25.7 ± 5.9 t (cortical): 14.2 ± 0.8 s: 222.9 +115.4/-58.0 | U | AEA | Bone: Ursus sp. ulna |

| Sample | Unit | Grid | Depth | Age | Method | Lab | Description |
|---|---|---|---|---|---|---|---|
| F375/431: base<br>:top | UB | H0NW | | 126 +8/-7<br>99 +8/-7 | U c<br>U c | AEA | Stalagmite boss.<br>Additional determination from surface of boss.<br>Mean of 2 dates: 113 ± 13 ka |
| F375/431: top | UB | H0NW | 100.25 | 133 ± 7 | U | MCM | Stalagmite boss, 42 cm thick. A core 34.9 cm deep was extracted by coring from upper surface of the boss |
| : middle<br>: base | | | | 105 ± 5<br>131 ± 5 | U<br>U | | Middle: between 10.0-15.7 cm deep<br>Mean of 3 dates: 121 ± 9 ka |
| F773: top (UEA771) | UB | G1SW/H1SW | 99.16-99.76 | 122.4+5.2/-4.9 | U | UEA | Rafted stalagmitic floor |
| D596 | UB / LB Interface | H8 | 99.42 | t: 16.0±6.9<br>s: 15.0±1.5 | U<br>U | AEA | Bone: *Rangifer tarandus* phalange. (lacking prox. epiphysis). |
| D6058 (J5631) | sSb | H8NE | top 99.50<br>base 99.46 | 122 ± 2 | U u | AEA | Inverted boss in base of Silt beds. Stalagmite boss and apron 70 x 70 x 33 mm (thick); incorporates soda straw stalactites |
| C119 (590a) | LB | M13NW | 99.13 | 140 ± 9<br>213 ± 18 | ESR e<br>ESR r | RG | *Stephanorhinus* sp. tooth fragment |
| (590b) | | | | 140 ± 9<br>210 ± 18 | ESR e<br>ESR r | RG | Mean e: 140 ± 8 ka<br>Mean r: 212 ± 16 ka |
| C189 (E81-A) | LB | M13NE | 99.37 | 127 ± 9<br>202 ± 18 | ESR e<br>ESR r | LPZ/ER | *Stephanorhinus* sp. tooth fragment |
| (E81-B) | | | | 126 ± 9<br>199 ± 18 | ESR e<br>ESR r | LPZ/ER | |
| (E81-C) | | | | 127 ± 9<br>202 ± 18 | ESR e<br>ESR r | LPZ/ER | |
| (E81-D) | | | | 125 ± 9<br>198 ± 18 | ESR e<br>ESR r | LPZ/ER | Mean e: 126 ± 7 ka<br>Mean r: 202 ± 14 ka |
| C286 (E80-A) | LB | L13NW | 99.01 | 214 ± 17<br>253 ± 22 | ESR e<br>ESR r | LPZ/ER | *Stephanorhinus kirchbergensis* tooth fragment |
| (E80-B) | | | | 214 ± 17<br>254 ± 23 | ESR e<br>ESR r | LPZ/ER | |
| (E80-C) | | | | 214 ± 17<br>253 ± 23 | ESR e<br>ESR r | LPZ/ER | |
| (E80-D) | | | | 216 ± 18<br>255 ± 23 | ESR e<br>ESR r | LPZ/ER | Mean e: 214 ± 13 ka<br>Mean r: 254 ± 15 ka |
| D358 (589a) | LB | H9SW/SE | | 232 ± 14<br>316 ± 26 | ESR e<br>ESR r | RG | *Stephanorhinus* tooth |
| (589b) | | | | 210 ± 14<br>306 ± 25 | ESR e<br>ESR r | RG | |
| (589c) | | | | 232 ± 15<br>322 ± 29 | ESR e<br>ESR r | RG | Mean e: 224 ± 11 ka<br>Mean r: 314 ± 22 ka |
| D809 | LB | J8 | 99.27 | t: 15.8 ± 0.9 | U | AEA | Bone: *Ursus* sp. ulna |
| D1585 | LB | H8SE | 99.20-99.10 | t: 147.1 +9.9 / | U | AEA | Bone: *Ursus* sp. metapodial |

| Sample | Phase | Square | Depth | Value | Method | Lab | Description |
|---|---|---|---|---|---|---|---|
| D2121 (591a) | LB | 17NW | 99.10-99.00 | 215 ± 17 / 227 ± 19 | ESR e / ESR r | RG | Tooth (M3) *Cervus elaphus* |
| (591b) | | | | 228 ± 18 / 235 ± 20 | ESR e / ESR r | RG | Mean e: 221 ± 15 ka / Mean r: 231 ± 17 ka |
| D2312 (394) | LB | J7SW | 99.05-98.95 | 140 ± 9 / 163 ± 13 | ESR e / ESR r | RG | Tooth |
| (394a) | | | | 170 ± 11 / 224 ± 18 | ESR e / ESR r | RG | |
| (394b) | | | | 160 ± 16 / 204 ± 18 | ESR e / ESR r | RG | Mean e: 153 ± 13 ka / Mean r: 189 ± 19 ka |
| D2909 (E78) | LB | H9NE | 99.24 | 155 ± 11 / 206 ± 18 | ESR e / ESR r | LPZ/ER | *Stephanorhinus* sp. tooth fragment |
| D4367 (PND25) | Top of LB | K8NE | 99.49 | 269 ± 37 | TL | BM | Heated flint, pebble fragment |
| F2853 (E75) | LBc | I1NE | 99.32-99.22 | 177 ± 13 / 269 ± 25 | ESR e / ESR r | LPZ/ER | *Stephanorhinus* sp. tooth fragment |
| B162 | Ic | L21 | 99.11 | 255 +89/-47 | U u | MCM | Calcite coating on block |
| D584 | LB/BI | J8 | 99.10 | T: 24.6 ± 1.2 | U | AEA | Bone: *Ursus* sp. phalange |
| D616 | BI/OI | J9 | 99.01 | T: 27.1 ± 3.8 | U | AEA | Bone: *Ursus* sp. phalange |
| D687 (226d1) | BI | I9NE | 98.97 | 200 ± 25 | TL | RLA | Heated flint, discoidal core |
| H1724 (PND43) | 50 | AC991SW/NW | | 154 ± 36 | TL | BM | Stalagmite |
| H1725 (PND44) | 50 | AC991SW/NW | | 130 ± 29 | TL | BM | Stalagmite |
| H3211:base[1] (J5634) | 20 | AE992NE | 99.98 | 83 ± 3 | U | AEA | Upper stalagmitic spread. Flowstone overlain by stalagmitic boss representing phase 2 |
| :base 2 (J5978) | | | | 83 ± 6 | U | AEA | As above: separate sample taken from different area of base |
| H359 (E83) | 24 | AA994SE | 99.40 | 186 ± 14 / 280 ± 26 | ESR e / ESR r | LPZ/ER | *Stephanorhinus* sp. tooth fragment |
| H428 (570a) | 24 | AB994NW | 99.25 | 102 ± 7 / 153 ± 14 | ESR e / ESR r | RG | ? Bovid tooth |
| (570 b) | | | | 90 ± 6 / 132 ± 12 | ESR e / ESR r | RG | Mean e: 95 ± 6 ka / Mean r: 141 ± 12 ka |
| H598 (PND33) | 26 | AB994NE | 99.03 | 179 ± 22 | TL | BM | Heated flint, fragment of artefact |
| H2312 (PND62) | 26 | AB993S/AC993N | 99.15-99.00 | 214 ± 21 | TL | QTLS | Heated flint, retouched flake fragment |
| H1036 (PND32) | 28 | AB994 NW | 98.80-98.70 | 173 ± 20 | TL | BM | Heated flint, flake |
| H2216 (UEA683) | (b) of core=29 | AB994SE | 97.15-97.00 | 269.4 +24.0 / -19.9 | U u | UEA | Stalagmite from the sediment core |
| | | | | 265.3 +28.5 / -22.4 | U c | | |
| H3096 (J5633) | 31 | AB994SE | 97.16 | 94 ± 3 | U | AEA | Derived stalagmitic floor in mudstone gravel. |

inexpressible in the quoted date error limits. However, since the effects generally differ from one dating technique to the next, an understanding of their scale may be gained by comparing the results from two or more methods.

### Heated flint

Among the worked flints which were excavated from archaeological contexts, five pieces were found to be datable by TL. Two of these were found in the Main Cave; D687 in the Intermediate complex, and D4367 in the top of the Lower Breccia. The remaining three pieces were from Area H; H598 and H2312 from Layer 26, and H1036 from Layer 28. To be datable by TL, materials need to be exposed to temperatures in excess of 400°C, and it is clear that pieces must be on or very close to the ground surface for such heating to occur. It is not always certain whether the heating has resulted from human agency or natural fires. However, where heated materials are artefacts or closely associated with archaeological remains, the probability that the fire was of human origin is increased. With the possible exception of D4367, the dated flints from Pontnewydd Cave are worked pieces.

The five TL dates form a reasonably coherent data set which yields a weighted mean value of 197,000±17,000 BP. This is the best estimate for the date at which the archaeological material found in the Intermediate complex and Lower Breccia (Main Cave) and in Layers 26 and 28 (New Entrance) was heated on the surface. It is certain that the emplacement of the deposits from which the flints derived must post-date this event.

### In situ *stalagmitic formations*

In the Main Cave, 29 samples of *in situ* travertine were dated by means of U-series and TL techniques. Twenty-three of these samples were taken from the stalagmitic floor which sealed the Lower Breccia, another four were attached to the cave walls at higher locations, and two were discovered in interstices within the Lower Sands and Gravels.

#### Stalagmite on the Lower Breccia Unit

The distribution of dates for the formation of the stalagmitic floor on the Lower Breccia is illustrated by the profile of date probabilities shown in Figure 11.4. The composition of the curve from U-series and TL data is also shown. It is clear that both methods support the interpretation that stalagmite formation occurred over an extended period of time. The precise form of the profile is not significant, depending as it does on a limited number of date determinations, but the curve appears to reveal episodes of enhanced stalagmite growth in MIS 7 and at the end of MIS 5. The low probability at the age of MIS 9 is expected given the presumption that Lower Breccia emplacement must post-date the heating of the flint artefacts (197,000±17,000 BP). However, there is a shoulder at approximately 225,000 BP on the profile of U-series dates which is inconsistent with this chronology.

| Sample | No. | Grid | Date | Method | Lab | Comment |
|---|---|---|---|---|---|---|
| DUP (J5633) | | | | | | Fragment 40 mm thick |
| H1713:top | | | 113 ± 7 | U | AEA | Mean of 2 dates: 97 ± 7 ka |
| AA994SE | 31 | 98.22-98.14 | 132.0+8.2/-7.6 | U | AEA | Derived stalagmite (previously identified as *in situ*) |
| :base (PND41) | | | 141.6+7.3/-6.8 | U | AEA | Mean of 2 U-series dates: 137.3 +5.5/-5.1 ka |
| | | | 101 ± 25 | TL | BM | |
| H2217 (UEA684) | (e) of core=38 | 95.90-95.80 | 224.8 +23.2/ -19.2 | U c | UEA | Stalagmite from the sediment core |
| AB994SE | | | | | | |
| H3150 (PND66) | 39 | 97.09 | 226 ± 21 | TL | QTLS | Stalagmite |
| AC994NW | | | | | | |

¹ These samples were recovered in cemented patches of Lower Breccia material which had been rafted within the Upper Breccia. See Green 1984, 96n.

Layer: RCE = Red Cave Earth; UB = Upper Breccia; Ic = Intermediate complex; BI = Buff Intermediate; OI = Orange Intermediate.

Age: t = total bone sample; s = surface of bone. [N.B. 'In general, Angela Rae regarded surface samples as the most reliable'.]

Method: U u = Uranium series disequilibrium - uncorrected for detrital Th; U c = Uranium series disequilibrium - corrected for detrital Th; TL = Thermoluminescence; ESR e = Electron Spin Resonance - assuming early uranium uptake; ESR r = Electron Spin Resonance - assuming recent uranium uptake.

Dated by: MCM = Henry Schwarz, Dept of Geology, McMaster University, Canada; AEA = Miro Ivanovich and Angela Rae, Atomic Energy Authority, Harwell, Oxford, UK; UEA = Peter Rowe and Timothy Atkinson, School of Environmental Sciences, UEA; RLA = Joan Huxtable, Nick Debenham and Mona Winter, Research Laboratory for Archaeology, Oxford University; BM = Nick Debenham, British Museum, London; QTLS = Nick Debenham, Quaternary TL Surveys, Nottingham; LPZ/ER = Li Ping Zhou, University of Cambridge, and Ed Rhodes, University of London, Egham; RG = Rainer Grun, Australian National University, Canberra.

*Table 11.7. Pontnewydd Cave derived samples.*

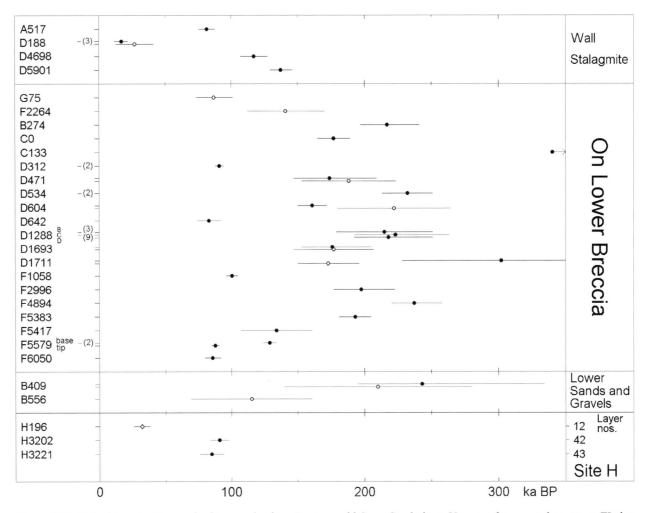

*Figure 11.2. Date determinations on* in situ *samples from Pontnewydd Cave. Symbols:* ● *U-series date on stalagmite;* ○ *TL date on stalagmite;* △ *TL date on heated flint;* ■ *U-series date on bone;* □ *ESR date on tooth;* ◇ *TL date on sediment. In general, one date is given for each sample. A mean date formed from a number of date determinations is indicated by giving the number in parantheses. Two or more dates for a single sample are shown if they were produced by different techniques, or by different laboratories, or if different parts of the sample were dated with significantly different results.*

Examining data from the Lower Breccia stalagmites more closely, it is found that only three out of the twenty-three samples (C133, D1711 and F4894) gave dates earlier than the heated flints to the extent that their error limits do not overlap, and that the discrepant dates are all from U-series measurements. The question therefore arises whether there are effects intrinsic to either U-series or TL methods that could account for this discrepancy. The uncertainties relevant to this question are those described in the introduction as of the third category, i.e. those which, resulting from failures of the basic assumptions, cannot be expressed in the date error limits. Comparisons between U-series and TL measurements on identical stalagmites present the best prospect for detecting such uncertainties.

Among the chronological data for Pontnewydd Cave, there are fourteen examples of U-series dates which can be directly compared with TL determinations. In six of the fourteen pairs, there is disagreement between the two measurements to the extent that their error limits do not

overlap. This is a greater number than would be expected on statistical grounds. In all except one of the six discrepant pairs, the U-series ages are greater than the TL dates. This pattern accords with the view that TL measurements on stalagmites are prone to underestimate the true age while U-series dates tend to overestimation. In the case of TL, the explanation recognises that re-crystallization of the calcite after its original formation can reduce the measured age. Similarly, re-crystallization presents problems for U-series measurements. Discussing the dating of sample D534, Henry Schwarcz (1984) has referred to the possible leaching of radiogenic Th-230 from the surrounding limestone and its introduction into the stalagmite, thus causing the U-series date to over-estimate the true age. These effects are probably sufficient to account for both the observed pattern of TL and U-series comparisons, and the discrepancy between the alternative Lower Breccia emplacement dates as set, respectively, by the TL dates on heated flint, and by U-series measurements on *in situ* stalagmites. As a corollary, it should be inferred that a greater weight can be given to

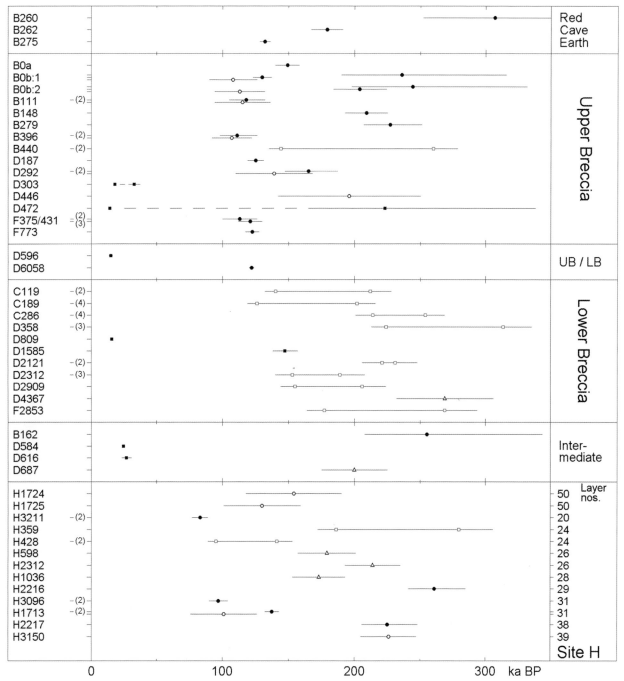

*Figure 11.3. Date determinations on derived materials from Pontnewydd Cave. Symbols: ● U-series date on stalagmite; ○ TL date on stalagmite; △ TL date on heated flint; ■ U-series date on bone; □ ESR date on tooth; ◊ TL date on sediment. In general, one date is given for each sample. A mean date formed from a number of date determinations is indicated by giving the number in parantheses. Two or more dates for a single sample are shown if they were produced by different techniques, or by different laboratories, or if different parts of the sample were dated with significantly different results.*

the eight cases in which the U-series dates and their TL counterparts are in agreement.

*Wall attached speleothem*
Four speleothems from *in situ* positions above the Lower Breccia were dated. Among them, two stalagmites attached to the cave wall (D4698 and D5901) produced U-series dates which are older than the youngest stalagmites on top of the Lower Breccia. At first sight, therefore, the dates appear

to be conflicting. Both samples were located in Area D of the Main Cave (D4698 in the North Passage, and D5901 in the South-East Fissure) at an altitude approximately one metre above the stalagmitic floor on the Lower Breccia. Their U-series dates and error limits cover the range from 146,000 BP to 105,000 BP. It is interesting to note that no other *in situ* stalagmite from Area D has produced a date which encroaches upon this age range. Thus, D471, D534, D604, D1288, D1693 and D1711 all have lower age limits

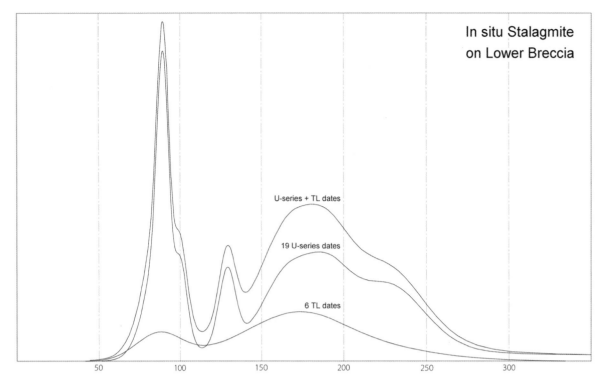

*Figure 11.4. Distribution of date probabilities for* in situ *stalagmites on top of the Lower Breccia (Main Cave).*

greater than 146,000 BP, while the date ranges of D312 and D642 are confined between 94,000 and 74,000 BP. It is not impossible, therefore, that in Area D a deposit temporarily covered the stalagmitic floor on the Lower Breccia to a depth of 1 m, and that D4698 and D5901 are the only remaining fragments of the stalagmites which formed on it.

### Lower Sands and Gravels

Three date measurements were performed on calcite concretions in interstitial positions within the Lower Sands and Gravels. Assuming that the samples formed soon after the emplacement of the unit, they should not post-date by far the Intermediate and Lower Breccia emplacements. The TL date of sample B556 appears to conflict with this interpretation. However, two facts argue against the acceptance of this measurement as entirely reliable. Firstly, the technical difficulty in establishing a reliable environmental dose-rate introduced a large degree of imprecision which may not be fully reflected in the error limits; and secondly, its interstitial location meant that the calcite was especially prone to re-crystallization.

It is concluded, therefore, that the evidence provided by date measurements on *in situ* stalagmitic material within the Main Cave shows no major inconsistencies with the chronology given by the heated flints. It points to a finding that the emplacement of the archaeological remains within the cave took place during MIS 7, soon after the human occupation.

### New Entrance

At the New Entrance, two *in situ* stalagmites produced date measurements; H3202 from Layer 42, and H3221 from Layer 43. The dates reveal that both samples are contemporaneous with the latest phase of stalagmitic growth on the Lower Breccia. This evidence, which forms the strongest link between the stratigraphies in the two entrances, is discussed below.

## Derived materials

Date measurements were performed on 43 samples of various materials derived from deposits in the Main Cave and the New Entrance. They serve to test the proposed chronology of events at Pontnewydd Cave. The basis of the tests assumes that no material found within a unit can post-date the emplacement of the unit. This assumption is valid in the absence of bioturbation and mechanical disturbance.

### Red Cave Earth and Upper Breccia Units

The emplacement of the Upper Breccia occurred as a debris flow which demolished parts of the stalagmitic floor on the Lower Breccia and incorporated fragments of it in the deposit. As expected, therefore, age determinations on 16 speleothems recovered from the Upper Breccia and Red Cave Earth show a date distribution similar to that of the source material. According to the measured dates, no parts of the stalagmitic floor sealing the Lower Breccia formed after approximately 85,000 BP. However, this growth terminus is possibly the result of a cooling climate rather than Upper Breccia emplacement. A much younger age for the Upper Breccia is suggested by the presence of one bone (D303) which is dated by U-series analysis to the range 18,000–33,000 BP.

*Lower Breccia and Intermediate Units*

A total of fifteen samples derived from units in the Main Cave which, prior to the Upper Breccia emplacement, had been sealed by the stalagmitic floor on top of the Lower Breccia. Therefore, these samples are expected to pre-date the emplacement of the Lower Breccia at approximately 200,000 BP. This chronology is also supported by faunal studies. According to Andy Currant (pers. comm.), the identification of rhinoceros tooth fragments as belonging to *Stephanorhinus kirchbergensis* places them at a date at or before late MIS 7. In fact, only four of the age determinations are inconsistent with this interpretation.

The four discrepant dates were all obtained by U-series analyses of bone samples (D809, D1585, D584, D616) which derived from the Lower Breccia and Intermediate deposits. If correct, their dates would imply that the emplacements of these units were late Devensian or Holocene events. It is impossible to reconcile these very recent dates with the U-series and TL measurements of *in situ* stalagmites formed on the Lower Breccia. Table 11.7 shows the results of U-series analyses performed on different components of the same bone. There is often inconsistency between the results of these repeated analyses, suggesting that the bone has not maintained its integrity as a closed system. A judgement in favour of the chronology based on stalagmites can be justified considering the degree of coherence between U-series and TL measurements on them, and the correlation of the date distribution with climatic events.

*New Entrance*

Out of a total of sixteen dated samples from the New Entrance excavations, thirteen were derived materials, including stalagmitic fragments, teeth and flint. The paucity of *in situ* samples and the limited extent of the excavation allow only a tentative interpretation of the data.

The three *in situ* samples comprise one sediment and two stalagmites. The sediment sample (H196) was collected from scree which covered the entrance, and provides a minimum age of approximately 32,000 BP for the underlying deposits. The two *in situ* stalagmites, H3202 and H3221, were found in Layers 42 and 43, respectively, which places them stratigraphically beneath all other dated materials from Area H. They have produced U-series dates of approximately 85,000–91,000 BP, and therefore appear to be contemporaneous with the youngest stalagmitic formations on the Lower Breccia in the Main Cave. On this evidence, a case may be made for interpreting the overlying deposits as similar in age and nature to the Upper Breccia. The dates of samples derived from these layers can be viewed in the light of this suggestion.

Eight of the derived samples from Area H are stalagmitic fragments which have been dated by means of U-series and TL. The youngest stalagmite (H3211) is very similar in age to the youngest formation on the Lower Breccia. Likewise, the oldest stalagmitic fragment (H2216), dated by U-series analysis to approximately 260,000 BP, is similar in age to the oldest speleothem from the Upper Breccia. As noted

above, three samples of heated flint from Area H (H598, H2312 and H1036) produced TL dates which are consistent with the dates of two flints from the Lower Breccia and Intermediate units. Finally, two measurements by ESR on teeth (H359 and H428) yielded results similar to those of corresponding material derived from the Lower Breccia.

Thus, the material types and dates obtained from Area H resemble a palimpsest of those found in the Upper and Lower Breccias and in the Intermediate complex. In the Main Cave, the debris flow which emplaced the Upper Breccia broke the stalagmitic floor sealing the Lower Breccia and channelled into the underlying unit. The Upper Breccia therefore incorporates not only parts of the floor but also a certain amount of material that had been sealed beneath it. In the New Entrance, it appears that a similar process has occurred, the only difference being that the original units have been mixed to a considerably greater extent than was the case in the Main Cave.

## Last Glaciation faunas: the radiocarbon determinations

*Paul Pettitt, Rupert Housley and Thomas Higham*

### Introduction

Pontnewydd is famous for being the earliest known humanly occupied site in Wales due to the presence of early Neanderthal cultural and anatomical remains from MIS 7, approximately one quarter of a million years ago. In the context of this part of the investigation programme, however, the early occupation is not the focus. Instead the radiocarbon dating programme relates to a later period, from ~41,000–21,000 BP (*i.e.* MIS 3 and early MIS 2), and is specifically concerned with the faunal history of the site rather than with the archaeology. Here, by examining the temporal patterning in the Upper Pleistocene fossil bone assemblages from the Upper Breccia, we seek to elucidate changing faunal composition, biodiversity and biomass within the Pontnewydd region over a period of ~20,000 years. The resulting trends are compared to similar data from other late Pleistocene localities in Wales and the adjoining western regions of the British 'peninsula' with the aim of answering a series of questions concerning the role of carnivore predation as an agent of bone accumulation in the cave, the identification of temporally-discrete faunal communities in the surrounding area, and the influence changing climate may have had on the faunal record in the Upper Breccia.

Over the past two decades the Oxford Radiocarbon Accelerator Unit (ORAU) has been responsible for making 57 AMS measurements on Middle Devensian Pleistocene fauna from Pontnewydd. Prior to 2001 Oxford had made a total of nine measurements on fauna from the cave, a single determination measurement (by John Gowlett) in 1986 on a femur of *Ursus* sp. (OxA-1025; Hedges *et al.* 1987) was followed by a further seven dates in 1993 (made by Rupert Housley) on a variety of taxa and faunal elements (OxA-4367 to -4373) and a single determination made by Paul

Pettitt in 1996 on woolly rhinoceros (OxA-6267; Hedges *et al.* 1996). But in 2001 financial support from the Natural Environment Research Council permitted the dating of two large series of Upper Breccia specimens. It was found that many of the bones tested were so poorly preserved that a fair proportion of the first batch failed to yield adequate amounts of collagen (details below). Hence, a second series was sampled for processing and dating in 2003–2004. From this combined programme a further 48 dates were obtained. Given technological and methodological advances in dating and sample pre-treatment methodologies between 1986 and 2004, it is not surprising that some potential for bias exists in this mixed data set, so in this report careful attention is given to this aspect of the research.

### *Aims of the study*

The radiocarbon dating programme must be seen in the context of the wider aims of the Pontnewydd project as a whole. Thus, the Pontnewydd project forms part of the 'Palaeolithic Settlement of Wales Research Programme'. Its objectives have been to investigate, interpret and communicate:

- The nature and chronological patterning of Palaeolithic human presence at the periphery of the Pleistocene world;
- how evidence of this kind may be preserved in regions subjected to such a huge natural destructive process as glaciation;
- the social behaviour of hominins, including their relationship with the landscape, climate and changing faunas, mobility, and the exploitation of raw materials.

However, the specific $^{14}$C sampling and analysis objectives that this programme aimed to investigate were as follows:

1) To identify changing patterns of faunal composition, biodiversity and biomass intensity over the period 40,000–20,000 BP.
2) To seek to identify from this, reasons for a scarce human presence (attested perhaps by a single cut-marked tooth) from the Upper Breccia context at Pontnewydd, which is composed of accumulations probably brought into the cave by the action of bears, wolves and foxes.
3) To compare Pontnewydd with relevant coeval assemblages – including those from the nearby sites of Ffynnon Beuno and Cae Gwyn – where there is evidence for both human and hyaena presence, both of which are lacking from Pontnewydd.
4) To examine whether the bear and wolf presences can be differentiated chronologically.
5) To establish whether the accumulations of herbivore remains primarily coincide with the pattern of wolf presence at the cave.
6) To examine whether original spatial and chronological configurations of animal bones in the cave can be retrieved.

The overall aim with the $^{14}$C dating at Pontnewydd was thus to establish evidence for temporal patterning in the taxonomically diverse faunal record from the Upper Breccia in order to relate these to taphonomic, ecological and climatic factors that could have influenced the biomass, faunal composition and animal biodiversity of the surrounding environs of the site.

### *Methodology*

Radiocarbon dating close to the background limit is challenging because it becomes increasingly difficult to distinguish autochthonous radiocarbon from exogenous or contaminant radiocarbon as the proportion of remaining $^{14}$C significantly declines. Because of this all radiocarbon dates tend to cleave asymptotically towards 40,000–50,000, the so called 'radiocarbon barrier' (Chappell *et al.* 1996). Developments in sample chemistry at Oxford over the past 5–10 years have, however, led to increased confidence in dates for samples which approach background limits, or are within the overall time range of MIS 3 (Higham *et al.* 2006). The use of improved pre-treatment methods, including ultrafiltration, has enabled the extraction of better quality collagen from even poorly preserved bone (~1% wt collagen) (Higham *et al.* 2006). Ultrafiltration has been applied to all of the Pontnewydd dates produced since 2001 and the methodology is now described before comparing with the measurements made in the 1980s and 1990s.

### *Current Oxford $^{14}$C methodology*

Each of the bones dated from Pontnewydd 2001–2004 was sampled by Tom Higham using an NSK Electer GX drill with a tungsten carbide drill. Ideally, 500 mg was taken, but for some samples, the bones were too small to enable this amount to be taken and consequently some bones comprised a much smaller starting weight (Table 11.8). The bones were all pre-treated manually, initially with decalcification using 0.5M HCl, removal of humates using 0.1 M NaOH, then re-acidification using 0.5M HCl. Each step was interspersed with distilled water rinses. The samples were gelatinized in weakly acidic water (pH3) at 75°C in an incubator for 20 hours, and the supernatant recovered using an EziFilter™. The supernatant was further treated by ultrafiltration using a Vivaspin™ 30 kD MWCO ultrafilter (see Bronk Ramsey *et al.* 2004; Higham *et al.* 2006). The >30 kD fraction was freeze-dried and retained for AMS dating. Samples of ultrafiltered gelatine are denoted by the prefix 'AF' in Tables 11.8 and 11.9 (one sample was not pre-treated further and was dated as filtered gelatine only because it produced a very low yield of collagen. This is termed 'AG' in Table 11.8). The ultrafilter removes low molecular weight particles, including degraded and broken up collagen fragments, salts, and small non-collagenous contaminants and in our experience produces collagen of a higher 'quality' when compared with other preparation methods (principally assessed by C:N ratios and %C and %N on combustion).

Samples of pre-treated bone gelatine were combusted and analysed using a Europa Scientific ANCA-MS system consisting of a 20–20 IR mass spectrometer interfaced to a Roboprep CHN sample converter unit operating in continuous flow mode, using He carrier gas. This enables the measurement of $\delta^{15}N$ and $\delta^{13}C$, nitrogen and carbon contents, and C:N ratios. $\delta^{13}C$ values in this paper are reported with reference to VPDB and $\delta^{15}N$ results are reported with reference to AIR. Graphitization was by reduction of $CO_2$ over an iron catalyst in an excess $H_2$ atmosphere at 560°C (Bronk Ramsey and Hedges 1999; Bronk Ramsey *et al.* 2000). The Oxford AMS radiocarbon instrumentation has been described by Bronk Ramsey and Hedges (1999), Bronk Ramsey *et al.* (2000) and Bronk Ramsey *et al.* (2004).

### Preservation state

The first series of samples dated at ORAU in 2002 produced collagen which ranged from 0.2–7.6 wt% collagen, with a mean of 2.0±1.9 wt.%. The threshold for acceptance at ORAU is 1 wt.% collagen (equivalent to 10 mg collagen/g bone), therefore many of the samples we extracted collagen from were on the margin of acceptability. In general, the Pontnewydd bone was poorly preserved.

The samples identified in Table 11.8 with bold in the pretreatment yield column are those that had values of less than 1 wt% collagen. In many instances these produce 'greater than' ages because of the low yield and its function in influencing the background limit for AMS dating. Another major problem in the first series of AMS dates analysed in 2002 was that the majority of bones analysed failed to yield any extractable collagen, and were therefore failed. There were 25 successful AMS dated samples obtained from the first batch (which include two dates on the same animal, noted on Table 11.8), and 25 samples that failed to provide collagen (Table 11.10).

In the light of this excessively high failure rate, ORADS was asked for permission to allow further dating to go ahead. To reduce the failure rate, a systematic programme of screening bones was undertaken by Tom Higham. Percent nitrogen analysis (%N) and C:N atomic ratios were measured from small amounts (*c.* 10–15 mg bone powder) of bone from specimens housed in the National Museum of Wales, Cardiff in 2003. Under most circumstances, percent nitrogen is a reasonable correlate for remaining protein, since nitrogen originates from the proteinaceous fraction of the bone, rather than the hydroxyapatite (Brock *et al.* 2010). However, an acceptably high %N value does not always correlate with a high collagen yield, since the quality of the collagen and its degree of alteration is not being measured and degraded or broken-up collagen will not be extractable using the ultrafiltration technique applied at ORAU. Nevertheless, it was hoped that %N analysis would reduce the failure rate.

The results are shown in Figure 11.5 and the data is given in Table 11.11. Figure 11.5 shows a reasonably good correlation between %N and C:N. As %N decreases, particularly below 1%, the ratio of carbon to nitrogen increases. Generally speaking, C:N ratios of whole bone above 5 are indicative of either the addition of humic complexes or the diagenetic alteration of the bone, for example by deamination. The combination of high C:Ns and low %N is indicative of poor bone protein preservation coupled with the presence of carbon from other sources, for example humic or sediment matrices. Samples that have a %N value below about 1% and a C:N >5 were therefore not expected to be dateable. Modern bone has a %N of *c.* 4–4.5% depending on species. 1%N under ideal circumstances, then, would correlate with *c.* 25% remaining collagen. In reality this is almost never obtained when pre-treating bones because of the difficulties in obtaining 100% efficiency in collagen yield and the likelihood that at least some of the collagen will be degraded and not recoverable. Samples below these cut-offs were not, therefore, sampled further for chemistry and AMS dating, whilst those above it were sampled in Cardiff for dating in 2004 (see Table 11.11).

The screening resulted in a much higher success rate for the analysed bones. Only 11% of the second group of samples failed (see Table 11.12), compared with >50% for the first series. In addition, the collagen yields improved markedly in the second series. The uncalibrated radiocarbon results are given in Table 11.9 and plotted by species in Figure 11.6.

### Earlier Oxford methodologies

Earlier Oxford dates were obtained using an amino acid method or an ion-exchanged gelatine method. The first involved dating purified amino acids (ORAU laboratory code for this was AC). The bone was decalcified and the insoluble residue hydrolyzed and treated with activated charcoal, before the separation of the amino acids from inorganic solutes with cation-exchange columns and Dowex 50W-X8 resin (Gillespie and Hedges 1983; Gillespie *et al.* 1984). This method was used for all dates obtained prior to 1989. The ion-exchanged gelatine (code AI) method superseded this. The bone was decalcified, often utilizing a continuous-flow apparatus (see Hedges *et al.* 1989; Law and Hedges 1989). A sodium hydroxide wash was applied to attempt to remove humic contaminants. The insoluble collagen was gelatinized and purified using an ion-exchange column with BioRad AGMP-50 resin. This method was used until 2000 when it was abandoned because of concerns regarding the possibility of column resin bleed and the difficulty in excluding this as a potential contaminant (see also Burky *et al.* 1998). The method itself, with this exception, was a substantial step forward in bone pre-treatment chemistry, and a variant of it is now being tested in order to date single amino acids in Oxford.

### Comparison/calibration

At the time of writing, there is no agreed way to calibrate radiocarbon dates from the Middle to Upper Palaeolithic. There is no agreed curve for the period prior to 26,000

| Find no. | Species | Identification | OxA | $^{14}C$ age BP | error | CN | $\delta^{13}C$ | $\delta^{15}N$ | Use wt. (mg) | Pret. yld (mg) | % C | pcode |
|---|---|---|---|---|---|---|---|---|---|---|---|---|
| D477 | cf. *Lepus timidus* | pelvis (left) | 11666 | 33200 | 1900 | 3.3 | -20.0 | -0.2 | 150 | 2.4 | 40.38 | AF |
| D2990 | *Lepus timidus* | pelvis (left) | 11565 | 21330 | 140 | 3.4 | -19.2 | 3.8 | 1400 | **12.1** | 20.00 | AF |
| S209 | *Dicrostonyx* | mandible | 11667 | >22700 | | | -21.8 | | 160 | **0.4** | 33.00 | AF |
| F3025 | *Vulpes sp.* | humerus | 11501 | 27120 | 210 | 3.2 | -18.7 | 4.8 | 1020 | 30 | 30.75 | AF |
| F4510 | *Vulpes vulpes* | humerus | 11502 | 27350 | 250 | 3.3 | -18.7 | 6.1 | 660 | 12.9 | 38.18 | AF |
| D315 | *Vulpes vulpes* | mandible (right) | 11668 | 26300 | 1100 | 3.1 | -20.2 | 9.1 | 100 | 1.6 | 31.81 | AF |
| F1508 | *Canis lupus* | caudal vertebra | 11566 | 26950 | 210 | 3.4 | -18.6 | 5.5 | 450 | 25.4 | 55.79 | AF |
| F1516 | *Canis lupus* | caudal vertebra | 11682 | 27790 | 210 | 3.3 | -19.3 | 8.4 | 700 | 53.6 | 34.03 | AF |
| D425 | ? *Canis lupus* | upper right incisor | 11608 | 24470 | 170 | 3.4 | -19.8 | 13.8 | 500 | 15.5 | 41.45 | AF |
| F1186 | *Rangifer tarandus* | humerus (left) | 11669 | >36700 | | 3.5 | -20.0 | 5.2 | 450 | **1.9** | 43.00 | AF |
| D1786 | *Rangifer tarandus* | humerus (right) | 11670 | >40200 | | 3.3 | -18.4 | 2.5 | 410 | **2.8** | 42.14 | AF |
| D1063 | *Rangifer tarandus* | tibia | 11671 | >35400 | | 3.4 | -19.7 | 3.0 | 460 | **2.4** | 41.04 | AF* |
| F970 | *Rangifer tarandus* | tibia | 11672 | 31800 | 1000 | 3.3 | -17.7 | 3.0 | 487 | **3.5** | 40.91 | AF |
| F1397 | *Ursus sp.* | fibula | 11673 | 34400 | 2500 | 3.4 | -20.5 | 9.2 | 449 | **1.9** | 38.47 | AF |
| F1306** | *Ursus arctos* | humerus (right) | 11503 | 32900 | 800 | 3.3 | -19.8 | 10.9 | 486 | 5.2 | 42.21 | AF |
| F1163** | *Ursus arctos* | humerus (left) | 11674 | >37400 | | 3.3 | -19.9 | 10.6 | 481 | **1.8** | 42.11 | AF |
| F435 | *Ursus sp.* | humerus (right) | 11675 | 32100 | 1600 | 3.4 | -20.3 | 10.7 | 502 | **2.3** | 41.17 | AF |
| D884 | *Ursus sp.* | femur (right) | 11504 | 32150 | 700 | 3.3 | -19.7 | 10.7 | 500 | 5.8 | 40.21 | AF |
| D1240 | *Ursus sp.* | ulna | 11505 | 28650 | 650 | 3.3 | -20.8 | 10.4 | 509 | **3.9** | 39.67 | AF |
| F1258 | *Ursus sp.* | second phalange | 11676 | >36800 | 1900 | 3.3 | -20.6 | 7.5 | 442 | **2.2** | 40.14 | AF |
| F1511 | *Ursus sp.* | second phalange | 11677 | 41600 | 1900 | 3.4 | -19.7 | 9.3 | 248 | 6.9 | 40.42 | AF |
| F1823 | *Ursus sp.* | second phalange | 11506 | 31260 | 320 | 3.3 | -19.4 | 10.9 | 453 | 16.9 | 41.43 | AF |
| F1394 | *Anser anser* | femur (right) | 12651 | 28230 | 170 | 3.2 | -21.0 | nd | 640 | 34.8 | 39.54 | AF |
| F835 | *Anas platyrhyncos* | humerus (left) | 12363 | 28210 | 150 | 3.3 | -14.0 | 10.1 | 700 | 27.4 | 40.61 | AF |
| F2232 | cf. *Branta bernicla* | femur (right) | 12381 | 25950 | 220 | 3.2 | -15.9 | 7.5 | 220 | 23.6 | 40.22 | AG |

*Table 11.8. AMS Radiocarbon results for the first series of samples dated at ORAU in 2002.*

All samples are of ultrafiltered gelatine (code AF, with the exception of AF* which refers to a solvent pre-wash to remove conservation material such as glues) with the exception of OxA-12381, which is filtered gelatine (code AG). $\delta^{13}C$ values are reported with reference to VPDB with a measurement precision of ± 0.2‰. $\delta^{15}N$ values are reported with reference to AIR. %C is the amount of carbon produced upon the combustion of the gelatine in an elemental analyser. Pret[reatment] Y[ie] ld samples in bold are those with a %wt. collagen value that is below 1%, which is the minimum threshold for acceptance at ORAU, Find numbers followed by ** denotes duplicate measurements from the same bone.

| Find no. | Species | Identification | OxA | Date | error | CN | δ13C | δ15N | Use weight (mg) | Pret.yld. (mg) | % C | pcode |
|---|---|---|---|---|---|---|---|---|---|---|---|---|
| D427 | cf. *Lepus timidus* | pelvis (left) | 13947 | 28680 | 170 | 3.2 | -20.2 | 2.8 | 500 | 22.85 | 41.19 | AF |
| D455 | *Lepus* sp. | astragalus (right) | 13948 | 23110 | 100 | 3.3 | -19.9 | 1.3 | 560 | 41.8 | 42.72 | AF |
| D994 | *Vulpes* sp. | tibia (left) | 13983 | 25500 | 140 | 3.3 | -19.2 | 6.3 | 580 | 21.25 | 43.54 | AF |
| D1154 | *R. tarandus* | first phalange | 13984 | 25210 | 120 | 3.2 | -18.4 | 3.1 | 600 | 25.2 | 39.56 | AF |
| D1206 | *Lepus timidus* | astragalus (left) | 13985 | 23840 | 100 | 3.4 | -19.9 | -0.8 | 520 | 37.6 | 43.82 | AF |
| D4382 | *Vulpes* sp. | scapula (left) | 13986 | 25450 | 140 | 3.3 | -19.0 | 5.9 | 500 | 24 | 42.93 | AF |
| F447 | *Vulpes vulpes* | metatarsal | 13987 | 29490 | 170 | 3.3 | -19.8 | 9.4 | 720 | 54.2 | 43.41 | AF |
| F775 | cf. *Panthera* sp. | second phalange | 13988 | 40000 | 600 | 3.2 | -18.9 | 11.2 | 740 | 21.35 | 41.68 | AF |
| F1010 | *Ursus arctos* | rt maxilla and premaxilla | 13990 | 34020 | 360 | 3.2 | -18.9 | 11.0 | 440 | 15.7 | 41.15 | AF |
| F1010 | *Ursus arctos* | rt maxilla and premaxilla | 13989 | 33560 | 330 | 3.2 | -18.9 | 10.9 | 380 | 17.7 | 42.92 | AF |
| F1014 | ? *Panthera leo* | phalange | 13991 | 40300 | 750 | 3.2 | -18.9 | 10.7 | 640 | 16 | 43.76 | AF |
| F1018 | *Ursus* sp. | second phalange | 13992 | 29790 | 180 | 3.2 | -19.5 | 10.0 | 760 | 28.6 | 41.67 | AF |
| F1828 | *R. tarandus* | metacarpal (left) | 13993 | 30240 | 230 | 3.2 | -18.5 | 3.2 | 780 | 17.5 | 42.91 | AF |
| F4831 | cf. *Ursus* sp. | long bone shaft | 13994 | 30780 | 390 | 3.2 | -19.6 | 9.9 | 854 | 14.9 | 37.75 | AF |
| F7041 | *Vulpes* sp. | metapodial | 14049 | 33700 | 600 | 3.4 | -20.6 | -1.6 | 540 | 7.9 | 45.39 | AF |
| F1629 | *Vulpes vulpes* | scapula (left) | 14050 | 26820 | 140 | 3.3 | -19.4 | 8.5 | 660 | 37.5 | 40.06 | AF |
| F1684 | *Lepus* sp. | scapula | 14051 | 25670 | 150 | 3.4 | -20.5 | 0.2 | 600 | 21 | 44.58 | AF |
| F1898 | *R. tarandus* | right mandible | 14052 | 39600 | 900 | 3.4 | -18.6 | 3.1 | 822 | 11 | 44.51 | AF |
| F1964 | *Lepus* sp. | calcaneum (right) | 14053 | 30870 | 240 | 3.3 | -20.5 | -1.5 | 920 | 18.6 | 28.67 | AF |
| F2149 | *Ursus* sp. | carpal | 14054 | 36100 | 800 | 3.5 | -19.0 | 9.5 | 772 | 7.4 | 39.41 | AF |
| F2549 | *R. tarandus* | astragalus (left) | 14055 | 41400 | 1400 | 3.3 | -18.4 | 3.0 | 860 | 8.9 | 33.79 | AF |
| F2881 | *Cervus* sp. | podial | 14056 | 30020 | 170 | 3.4 | -18.3 | 2.5 | 840 | 66.1 | 47.59 | AF |
| F4796 | *Lepus timidus* | calcaneum | 14057 | 38800 | 600 | 3.4 | -20.4 | 1.7 | 860 | 16.9 | 43.14 | AF |

Note that F1010 was dated twice as part of the ORAU QA programme. All of the samples dated in this table were above 1% wt. collagen with the exception of OxA-14054 that was marginally below (0.96%).

*Table 11.9. Second series of AMS dates on bone from Pontnewydd.*

| OxA no. | Find | Species | Identification |
|---|---|---|---|
| 13362 | F422 | *Dicrostonyx* | mandible |
| 13363 | S209 | *Dicrostonyx* | mandible |
| 13364 | S210 | *Dicrostonyx* | mandible |
| 13365 | F1116 | *Vulpes vulpes* | calcaneum (right) |
| 13366 | F1344 | cf. *Vulpes vulpes* | femur (right) |
| 13370 | F1224 | *Vulpes vulpes* | mandible (right) |
| 13371 | F600 | *Equus* sp. | first phalange |
| 13372 | D296 | *Equus* sp. | lunate (left) |
| 13373 | C340 | *Equus* sp. | metapodial |
| 13374 | B336 | *Equus* sp. | podial |
| 13377 | D1343 | *Canis lupus* | cuboid (left) |
| 13378 | F1302 | cf. *Canis lupus* | radius |
| 13380 | D156 | *Rangifer tarandus* | astragalus (left) |
| 13381 | F915 | *Rangifer tarandus* | astragalus (right) |
| 13382 | F1390 | *Rangifer tarandus* | calcaneum (left) |
| 13383 | F1418 | *Rangifer tarandus* | calcaneum (left) |
| 13384 | F308 | *Rangifer tarandus* | calcaneum (right) |
| 13385 | F556 | *Rangifer tarandus* | calcaneum (right) |
| 13386 | F1275 | *Rangifer tarandus* | cuneiform |
| 13387 | D431 | *Rangifer tarandus* | cuneiform (right) |
| 13388 | F1329 | *Rangifer tarandus* | humerus (right) |
| 13391 | C18 | *Rangifer tarandus* | radius (right) |
| 13399 | F1802 | *Ursus* sp. | femur (right) |
| 13401 | B457 | *Ursus* sp. | tibia |
| 13405 | F4622 | *Ursus* sp. | second phalange |

*Table 11.10. List of Pontnewydd samples from the Upper Breccia submitted to Oxford for dating in the first batch that failed during the chemical pre-treatment process.*

cal. BP (Reimer *et al.* 2004). In an attempt to gauge approximately the calendrical equivalent ranges for the new radiocarbon series, therefore, we have, tentatively 'compared' (see van der Plicht *et al.* 2004) our results against the Cariaco Basin record of Hughen *et al.* (2006). The Cariaco $\delta^{18}O$ dataset is tuned to the Hulu Cave $\delta^{18}O$ speleothem record of Wang *et al.* (2001), which has the advantage of having been dated reliably using a series of U/Th dates. A new interim calibration curve spanning 0–55,000 BP is expected to be published in 2010 (Reimer, pers. comm.). 'Calibrated' ages prior to 26,000 cal. BP, therefore, are tentative comparisons, essentially. Because of such uncertainty about comparisons we work below with both uncalibrated and calendrically compared ages.

### The dating programme

#### Selection of the dating samples

The earlier $^{14}C$ analyses undertaken in 1986 and 1993 had demonstrated that the faunal assemblage in the Upper Breccia at Pontnewydd fell well within the limits of modern AMS dating techniques, for the initial results indicated bone accumulation during the Middle Devensian, in the 25,000–35,000 BP age range. In terms of sample suitability for a dating study, the fauna from the Upper Breccia had been well excavated and recorded, and unlike projects on some other British Pleistocene sites that have relied on museum

| Find no. | Burn wt. (mg) | Wt. N (mg) | % N | CN | Sampled for AMS dating? |
|---|---|---|---|---|---|
| H95 | 19.6 | 0.028 | 0.14 | 64.18 | n |
| H225 | 22.1 | 0.023 | 0.1 | 46.5 | n |
| H1958 | 19.2 | 0.017 | 0.09 | 78.96 | n |
| H2310 | 19 | 0.018 | 0.1 | 66.83 | n |
| H2470 | 13.8 | 0.012 | 0.08 | 87.62 | n |
| D427 | 7.5 | 0.13 | 1.7 | 4.49 | y |
| D455 | 4.2 | 0.107 | 2.5 | 4.43 | y |
| D465 | 9.6 | 0.219 | 2.3 | 4.4 | y |
| D994 | 10.8 | 0.116 | 1.1 | 5.26 | y |
| D1109 | 5.4 | 0.002 | 0.04 | 48.26 | n |
| D1154 | 7.7 | 0.186 | 2.4 | 4.46 | y |
| D1206 | 12 | 0.259 | 2.2 | 4.62 | y |
| D4382 | 12.8 | 0.296 | 2.3 | 4.14 | y |
| D45060 | 13.3 | 0.342 | 2.6 | 3.86 | y |
| F447 | 12.5 | 0.35 | 2.8 | 3.83 | y |
| F684 | 6.6 | 0.054 | 0.8 | 5.83 | n |
| F775 | 7.7 | 0.246 | 3.2 | 3.78 | y |
| F995 | 4.6 | 0.152 | 3.3 | 3.75 | y |
| F1010 | 18.6 | 0.492 | 2.6 | 3.9 | y |
| F1014 | 7.1 | 0.242 | 3.4 | 3.66 | y |
| F1018 | 5 | 0.148 | 3 | 3.81 | y |
| F1279 | 7.9 | 0.125 | 1.6 | 4.31 | y |
| F1367 | 7.2 | 0.023 | 0.3 | 13.37 | n |
| F1780 | 15.5 | 0.018 | 0.1 | 51 | n |
| F1828 | 6.2 | 0.17 | 2.7 | 4.05 | y |
| F4608 | 15.2 | 0.354 | 2.3 | 4.13 | y |
| F4831 | 6.6 | 0.206 | 3.1 | 3.81 | y |
| F7041 | 7.7 | 0.188 | 2.4 | 4.03 | y |
| D4605 | 5 | 0.115 | 2.3 | 4.38 | y |
| D5282 | 8.25 | 0.004 | 0.05 | 39.36 | n |
| D5951 | 4.1 | 0.088 | 2.2 | 4.19 | y |
| F1197 | 14.3 | 0.184 | 1.3 | 3.96 | y |
| F1629 | 8.8 | 0.19 | 2.2 | 3.99 | y |
| F1684 | 8.7 | 0.173 | 2 | 4.31 | y |
| F1748 | 8.1 | 0.213 | 2.6 | 3.79 | y |
| F1779 | 4.4 | 0.135 | 3.1 | 3.91 | y |
| F1819 | 4.1 | 0.067 | 1.6 | 4.75 | y |
| F1872 | 10.75 | 0.035 | 0.3 | 10.05 | n |
| F1886 | 4.75 | 0.134 | 2.8 | 3.99 | y |
| F1898 | 12.8 | 0.265 | 2.1 | 4.23 | y |
| F1907 | 6.85 | 0.234 | 3.4 | 3.81 | y |
| F1964 | 14.3 | 0.302 | 2.1 | 4.29 | y |
| F2149 | 10.75 | 0.257 | 2.4 | 4.21 | y |
| F2335 | 8.1 | 0.196 | 2.4 | 4.14 | y |
| F2355 | 5.4 | 0.135 | 2.5 | 4.07 | y |
| F2549 | 7 | 0.15 | 2.2 | 4.14 | y |
| F2881 | 7.4 | 0.217 | 2.9 | 3.94 | y |
| F4773 | 16.1 | 0.009 | 0.06 | 49.72 | n |
| F4796 | 9.7 | 0.232 | 2.4 | 4.16 | y |
| F5521 | 5.5 | 0.066 | 1.2 | 5.44 | y |

The bone powder samples were measured using an elemental analyser interfaced with an isotope ratio mass spectrometer. The CN is the atomic ratio of carbon to nitrogen. %N refers to the percentage of nitrogen in the bone powder. At ORAU, we estimate a value >0.76% as being adequate for further chemical pre-treatment to extract collagen (Brock *et al.* 2010). For CN atomic ratios on whole bone, values of around 3.5–6.0 are acceptable. An indication is given of whether the bone was sampled for further dating, or failed at this juncture.

*Table 11.11. Results of bone screening for the Pontnewydd fauna selected for dating.*

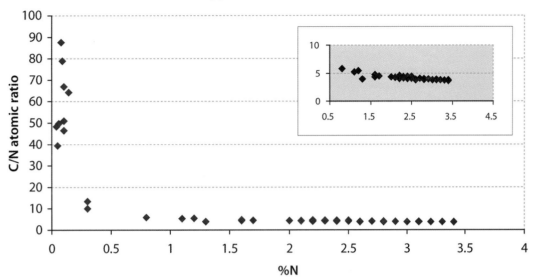

Figure 11.5. Results of bone screening. %N values are plotted against C:N atomic ratios for whole bones analysed from the Pontnewydd site. See Table 11.9 for the data. Bones yielding <1% N and with CNs > ~5 (see inset) were not selected for AMS dating.

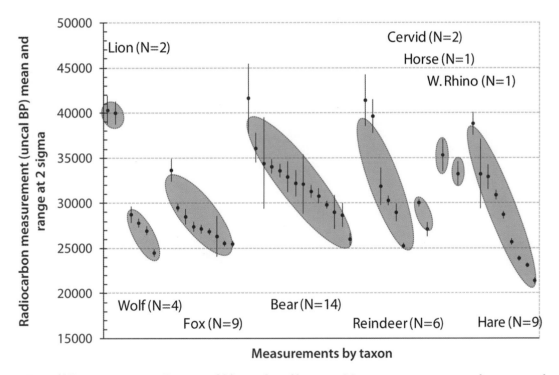

Figure 11.6. Finite ¹⁴C measurements on Pontnewydd fauna plotted by taxon. Measurements are expressed as mean and range at 2σ. Dashed ovals show parsimonious readings of age ranges by taxonomic group. Infinite measurements have been excluded.

| OxA no. | Find | Species | Identification |
|---------|------|---------|----------------|
| 15926 | D595 | *Vulpes vulpes* | radius |
| 15929 | F1779 | *Ursus* sp. | second phalange |
| 15930 | F1819 | *Rangifer tarandus* | second phalange |
| 15931 | F1886 | *Ursus* sp. | second phalange |
| 15938 | F5521 | *Lepus* sp. | calcaneum |

Table 11.12. Failed samples from the second batch of fauna submitted to ORAU from Pontnewydd Cave.

finds from old excavations, there would be no problems of contamination from recently applied preservatives.

During excavation the Upper Breccia (shown in the section drawing in Figure 6.5) was observed to extend over a distance of at least 35 linear metres from the Main Entrance inwards to the East Passage. From there, it continued in modified form as far as the New Entrance (shown on the plan in Figure 6.1). Fabric studies (Collcutt 1984) showed that the deposit had formed as the result of debris flow and was emplaced from the direction of the Main Entrance. Because of this mode of emplacement, no chronological or spatial information for the associated faunal accumulation is expected. In consequence, the only means of understanding the patterning of use of the cave is by applying radiocarbon. The intermingling of different-aged material in a debris flow ruled out the conventional *biostratigraphic* approach, but the large number of identifiable faunal specimens provided an alternative methodology, which may be best described as the *dynamic* approach. This involved making multiple radiocarbon age determinations on different faunal species in order to construct an age profile of changing faunal representation and biomass with time. This had previously been used at Paviland Cave (Aldhouse-Green 2000; Pettitt 2000; Turner 2000), which was investigated during the infancy of archaeology and where, unlike Pontnewydd, no clear stratigraphic records were made during these 'excavations'. At Pontnewydd the intention was to adopt a similar approach to Paviland but for different reasons; here it was to be used as a way to address the problem of multi-aged material in a mixed debris flow where stratigraphic position had no necessary bearing on the age of the specimen.

The selected dating samples represented bone from the Upper Breccia that displayed the characteristic Upper Breccia preservation type III (Currant 1984 and Currant chapter 8, this volume). The decision to confine the selection to those specimens was to ensure that no potentially intrusive faunal elements to the Upper Breccia were included, whether representing later intrusions or earlier re-worked specimens, which might confuse the subsequent interpretation. Species with preservation characteristic of the Upper Breccia included *Dicrostonyx torquatus* (collared lemming), *Lemmus lemmus* (Norwegian lemming), *Lepus* cf. *timidus* (arctic hare), *Canis lupus* (wolf, most likely the prime faunal accumulator), *Vulpes vulpes* (red fox), *Ursus arctos* (brown bear, the commonest species), *Equus ferus* (horse), *Coelodonta antiquitatis* (woolly rhinoceros), *Rangifer tarandus* (reindeer), *Ovibos moschatus* (musk ox, only rarely present), and a number of avifaunal taxa. The faunal collection from the Upper Breccia comprised most of the typical elements of an MIS 3 assemblage as identified by Currant and Jacobi (1997; 2001). It was distinctive however, in that it lacked the spotted hyaena, so common on many other MIS 3 sites, and was instead dominated by the wolf, *Canis lupus*, which was an important agent responsible for introducing the bone assemblage to the cave (see Scott chapter 8, this volume). There was also a disproportionately high frequency of bear remains from the deposit, which may reflect the relatively frequent use of the cave as a den for hibernating bears. The total absence of hyaenas at first sight seemed surprising, given their common role in accumulating bones in caves during the Pleistocene (including locally in the Elwy valley at Cefn Cave at ~34,000 BP), but an explanation may be that hyaenas became less frequent in localized areas after 30,000 BP. In any event, it was important to rule in, or out,

regional chronological patterning of carnivore presences in this study.

The rationale behind the choice of potential specimens from the cave involved the selection of as many suitable samples as possible relative to species frequency within the collection. The MNI (Minimum Number of Individuals) approach produced too few individuals for most species whereas an MNE (Minimum Number of Elements) approach yielded too many specimens for a realistic resource-limited project. Accordingly, MNE sample sizes were trimmed to produce a species balance based for the most part on post-cranial material, selecting those specimens that were best suited to the radiocarbon sampling process. It was possible that, in some cases, two specimens from the same individual may have been dated, but our view was that the destructive and selective nature of bone preservation within a cave debris flow deposit, particularly where carnivores have been involved in the first instance, actually make it highly unlikely that more than one specimen from an individual would survive to be excavated. Repetition of this nature, in any case, would not affect our database, which seeks to reconstruct chronological patterning of taxa, rather than relative abundance in any one period.

## Results

Tables 11.13 and 11.14 list the radiocarbon determinations from the Upper Breccia at Pontnewydd. The dates are firstly presented in order of age (youngest to oldest) and then 'calibrated' and grouped by species. As we have noted above, many additional samples were submitted to the ORAU under the NERC dating programme but could not be dated due to having failed in the chemical pre-treatment stage (Tables 11.10 and 11.12). It is particularly unfortunate that so many of the *Rangifer*, *Equus* and *Dicrostonyx* specimens failed in comparison with the small number of specimens of the same taxa which were successfully age measured. For reindeer the overall age distribution may be discernible, but for horse and collared lemming the age patterning remains tentative due to an inadequate number of determinations.

The Pontnewydd Upper Breccia [14]C results span an age range from 25,000–55,000 calendar years BP (*c.* 24,500–41,500 [14]C BP). They support the sedimentological and fabric analyses that suggest the Upper Breccia incorporated material of many different ages. In archaeological terms the determinations coincide with the Early Upper Palaeolithic – and perhaps a phase of the Mousterian – although at Pontnewydd the faunal assemblage cannot be linked with clear evidence for human activity. At best the Upper Breccia may be coeval with these archaeological period(s), but no direct human presence may be demonstrated save for a single cut-marked tooth. This is dissimilar to the Goat's Hole, Paviland, where humans were present (Pettitt 2000, 67) although a similarity is shared in that at both sites the process of faunal accumulation seems to have ceased prior to the onset of the Last Glacial Maximum.

| OxA | Species | Description | Find no. | Context | CN ratio | δ¹³C (‰) | Date | Error |
|-----|---------|-------------|----------|---------|----------|----------|------|-------|
| 11565 | *Lepus timidus* | Pelvis (left) | D2990 | UB | 3.4 | -19.2 | 21330 | 140 |
| 11667 | *Dicrostonyx torquatus* | Mandible | S209 | UB | n/a | -21.8 | >22700 | |
| 13948 | *Lepus* sp. | Astragalus (right) | D455 | UB | 3.3 | -19.9 | 23110 | 100 |
| 13985 | *Lepus timidus* | Astragalus (left) | D1206 | UB | 3.4 | -19.9 | 23840 | 100 |
| 11608 | *Canis lupus* | Upper right incisor | D425 | UB | 3.4 | -19.8 | 24470 | 170 |
| 13984 | *Rangifer tarandus* | First phalange | D1154 | UB | 3.2 | -18.4 | 25210 | 120 |
| 13986 | *Vulpes* sp. | Scapula (left) | D4382 | UB | 3.3 | -19.0 | 25450 | 140 |
| 13983 | *Vulpes* sp. | Tibia (left) | D994 | UB | 3.3 | -19.2 | 25500 | 140 |
| 14051 | *Lepus* sp. | Scapula | F1684 | UB/SB | 3.4 | -20.5 | 25670 | 150 |
| 12381 | cf. *Branta bernicla* | Femur (right) | F2232 | UB/SB | 3.2 | -15.9 | 25950 | 220 |
| 4367 | *Ursus* sp. | Femur | F126 | UB | n/a | -21.3 | 25970 | 330 |
| 11668 | *Vulpes vulpes* | Mandible (right) | D315 | UB | 3.1 | -20.2 | 26300 | 1100 |
| 14050 | *Vulpes vulpes* | Scapula (left) | F1629 | UB/SB | 3.3 | -19.4 | 26820 | 140 |
| 11566 | *Canis lupus* | Caudal vertebra | F1508 | UB | 3.4 | -18.6 | 26950 | 210 |
| 4373 | *Cervus* sp. (medium sized) | Calcaneum (right) | H231 | 20 | n/a | -20.3 | 27070 | 360 |
| 11501 | *Vulpes* sp. | Humerus | F3025 | UB | 3.2 | -18.7 | 27120 | 210 |
| 11502 | *Vulpes vulpes* | Humerus | F4510 | UB | 3.3 | -18.7 | 27350 | 250 |
| 11682 | *Canis lupus* | Caudal vertebra | F1516 | UB | 3.3 | -19.3 | 27790 | 210 |
| 12363 | *Anas platyrhyncos* | Humerus (left) | F835 | UB | 3.3 | -14.0 | 28210 | 150 |
| 12651 | *Anser anser* | Femur (right) | F1394 | UB | 3.2 | -21.0 | 28230 | 170 |
| 4372 | *Vulpes vulpes* | Radius (left) | F829 | UB | n/a | -19.6 | 28470 | 410 |
| 11505 | *Ursus* sp. | Ulna | D1240 | UB | 3.3 | -20.8 | 28650 | 650 |
| 13947 | *Lepus* cf. *timidus* | Pelvis (left) | D427 | UB | 3.2 | -20.2 | 28680 | 170 |
| 4369 | cf. *Canis lupus* | Radius (left) | D3048 | UB | n/a | -20.0 | 28730 | 420 |
| 4368 | *Rangifer tarandus* | Radius and ulna | D176 | UB | n/a | -17.8 | 28950 | 450 |
| 1025 | *Ursus arctos* | Femur (left) | F1024 | UB | n/a | n/a | 29000 | 800 |
| 13987 | *Vulpes vulpes* | Left third metatarsal | F447 | UB | 3.3 | -19.8 | 29490 | 170 |
| 13992 | *Ursus* sp. | Second phalange | F1018 | UB | 3.2 | -19.5 | 29790 | 180 |
| 14056 | *Cervus* sp. | Podial | F2881 | UB/SB | 3.4 | -18.3 | 30020 | 170 |
| 13993 | *Rangifer tarandus* | Metacarpal (left) | F1828 | UB | 3.2 | -18.5 | 30240 | 230 |
| 13994 | cf. *Ursus* sp. | Long bone shaft | F4831 | UB | 3.2 | -19.6 | 30780 | 390 |
| 14053 | *Lepus* sp. | Calcaneum (right) | F1964 | UB/SB | 3.3 | -20.5 | 30870 | 240 |
| 11506 | *Ursus* sp. | Second phalange | F1823 | UB | 3.3 | -19.4 | 31260 | 320 |
| 11672 | *Rangifer tarandus* | Tibia | F970 | UB | 3.3 | -17.7 | 31800 | 1000 |
| 11675 | *Ursus* sp. | Humerus (right) | F435 | UB | 3.4 | -20.3 | 32100 | 1600 |
| 11504 | *Ursus* sp. | Femur (right) | D884 | UB | 3.3 | -19.7 | 32150 | 700 |
| 4371 | *Lepus timidus* | Calcaneum | F1520 | UB | n/a | -21.3 | 32870 | 660 |
| 11503 | *Ursus arctos* | Humerus (right) | F1306 | UB | 3.3 | -19.8 | 32900 | 800 |
| 6267 | *Coelodonta antiquitatis* | Terminal phalange | F4515 | UB | n/a | -21.2 | 33200 | 650 |
| 11666 | cf. *Lepus timidus* | Pelvis (left) | D477 | UB | 3.3 | -20.0 | 33200 | 1900 |
| 13989 | *Ursus arctos* | Right maxilla & premaxilla | F1010 | UB | 3.2 | -18.9 | 33560 | 330 |
| 14049 | *Vulpes* sp. | Metapodial | F7041 | UB | 3.4 | -20.6 | 33700 | 600 |
| 13990 | *Ursus arctos* | Right maxilla & premaxilla | F1010 | UB | 3.2 | -18.9 | 34020 | 360 |
| 11673 | *Ursus* sp. | Fibula | F1397 | UB | 3.4 | -20.5 | 34400 | 2500 |
| 4370 | *Equus ferus* | Third phalange | D447 | UB | n/a | -20.6 | 35270 | 860 |
| 11671 | *Rangifer tarandus* | Tibia | D1063 | UB | 3.4 | -19.7 | >35400 | |
| 14054 | *Ursus* sp. | Carpal | F2149 | UB/SB | 3.5 | -19.0 | 36100 | 800 |
| 11669 | *Rangifer tarandus* | Humerus (left) | F1186 | UB | 3.5 | -20.0 | >36700 | |
| 11676 | *Ursus* sp. | Second phalange | F1258 | UB | 3.3 | -20.6 | >36800 | |
| 11674 | *Ursus arctos* | Humerus (left) | F1163 | UB | 3.3 | -19.9 | >37400 | |
| 14057 | *Lepus timidus* | Innominate (right) | F4796 | UB/SB | 3.4 | -20.4 | 38800 | 600 |
| 14052 | *Rangifer tarandus* | Right mandible | F1898 | UB/SB | 3.4 | -18.6 | 39600 | 900 |
| 13988 | cf. *Panthera* sp. | Second phalange | F775 | UB | 3.2 | -18.9 | 40000 | 600 |
| 11670 | *Rangifer tarandus* | Humerus (right) | D1786 | UB | 3.3 | -18.4 | >40200 | |
| 13991 | cf. *Panthera leo* | Phalange | F1014 | UB | 3.2 | -18.9 | 40300 | 750 |
| 14055 | *Rangifer tarandus* | Astragalus (left) | F2549 | UB/SB | 3.3 | -18.4 | 41400 | 1400 |
| 11677 | *Ursus* sp. | Second Phalange | F1511 | UB | 3.4 | -19.7 | 41600 | 1900 |

*Table 11.13. Radiocarbon age determinations on faunal specimens from the Upper Breccia (UB) and UB/SB at Pontnewydd Cave.*

| OxA | Species | Conventional radiocarbon age (BP) | Standard error (1 σ) | Comparison age (68.2% prob.) | | Comparison age (95.4% prob.) | |
|---|---|---|---|---|---|---|---|
| | | | | from | to | from | to |
| **Carnivores** | | | | | | | |
| 13988 | *? Panthera sp.* | 40000 | 600 | 44318 | 43050 | 45192 | 42628 |
| 13991 | *? Panthera leo* | 40300 | 750 | 44964 | 43170 | 45342 | 42652 |
| 4369 | cf. *Canis lupus* | 28730 | 420 | 33970 | 32762 | 34216 | 32284 |
| 11682 | *Canis lupus* | 27790 | 210 | 32822 | 32016 | 32860 | 31960 |
| 11566 | *Canis lupus* | 26950 | 210 | 31932 | 31608 | 32838 | 31350 |
| 11608 | *Canis lupus* | 24470 | 170 | 29770 | 29074 | 29802 | 28586 |
| 14049 | *Vulpes vulpes* | 33700 | 600 | 39952 | 37476 | 40190 | 36328 |
| 13987 | *Vulpes vulpes* | 29490 | 170 | 34270 | 33682 | 34958 | 33370 |
| 4372 | *Vulpes vulpes* | 28470 | 410 | 33342 | 32298 | 34000 | 32116 |
| 11502 | *Vulpes vulpes* | 27350 | 250 | 32840 | 31650 | 32848 | 31614 |
| 11501 | *Vulpes vulpes* | 27120 | 210 | 31964 | 31638 | 32846 | 31580 |
| 14050 | *Vulpes vulpes* | 26820 | 140 | 31930 | 31580 | 31968 | 31346 |
| 11668 | *Vulpes vulpes* | 26300 | 1100 | 32836 | 29992 | 33956 | 29056 |
| 13983 | *Vulpes* sp. | 25500 | 140 | 30928 | 30208 | 31312 | 29842 |
| 13986 | *Vulpes vulpes* | 25450 | 140 | 30920 | 30006 | 31294 | 29830 |
| **Omnivores** | | | | | | | |
| 11677 | *Ursus* sp. | 41600 | 1900 | 47166 | 43148 | 55190 | 42560 |
| 11674 | *Ursus arctos* | >37400 | | Date out of range | | | |
| 11676** | *Ursus* sp. | >36800 | | ... | 47250 | ... | 43370 |
| 14054 | *Ursus* sp. | 36100 | 800 | 41962 | 40498 | 42570 | 39444 |
| 11673** | *Ursus* sp. | 34400 | 2500 | 42022 | 36306 | 51624 | 34258 |
| 13990 | *Ursus arctos* | 34020 | 360 | 39994 | 38304 | 40178 | 37608 |
| 13989 | *Ursus arctos* | 33560 | 330 | 38914 | 37514 | 39956 | 36366 |
| 11503 | *Ursus arctos* | 32900 | 800 | 38586 | 36294 | 39994 | 35532 |
| 11504 | *Ursus* sp. | 32150 | 700 | 37978 | 35510 | 38632 | 35006 |
| 11675 | *Ursus* sp. | 32100 | 1600 | 38734 | 34996 | 41166 | 34028 |
| 11506 | *Ursus* sp. | 31260 | 320 | 35854 | 35028 | 35890 | 34614 |
| 13994 | Possible *Ursus* sp. | 30780 | 390 | 35842 | 34542 | 35862 | 34352 |
| 13992 | *Ursus* sp. | 29790 | 180 | 34390 | 34052 | 34994 | 33428 |
| 1025 | *Ursus arctos* | 29000 | 800 | 34288 | 32760 | 34992 | 32070 |
| 11505 | *Ursus* sp. | 28650 | 650 | 34002 | 32318 | 34326 | 32006 |
| 4367 | *Ursus* sp. | 25970 | 330 | 31326 | 30452 | 31580 | 30386 |
| **Herbivores** | | | | | | | |
| 14055 | *Rangifer tarandus* | 41400 | 1400 | 45710 | 43172 | 48860 | 42592 |
| 11670** | *Rangifer tarandus* | >40200 | | ... | 52787 | ... | 52786 |
| 14052 | *Rangifer tarandus* | 39600 | 900 | 44202 | 42604 | 45262 | 42404 |
| 11669** | *Rangifer tarandus* | >36700 | | ... | 49530 | ... | 43366 |
| 11671** | *Rangifer tarandus* | >35400 | | 55940 | 42590 | ... | 42190 |

| 11672 | *Rangifer tarandus* | 31800 | 1000 | 37974 | 35004 | 39294 | 34318 |
|---|---|---|---|---|---|---|---|
| 13993 | *Rangifer tarandus* | 30240 | 230 | 34926 | 34322 | 35020 | 34236 |
| 4368 | *Rangifer tarandus* | 28950 | 450 | 34028 | 32958 | 34324 | 32312 |
| 13984 | *Rangifer tarandus* | 25210 | 120 | 30376 | 29852 | 30408 | 29806 |
| 14056 | *Cervus* sp. | 30020 | 170 | 34970 | 34238 | 34996 | 34098 |
| 4373 | *Cervus* sp. | 27070 | 360 | 32012 | 31592 | 32848 | 31328 |
| 4370 | *Equus ferus* | 35270 | 860 | 41216 | 39328 | 42172 | 38612 |
| 6267 | *C. antiquitatis* | 33200 | 650 | 38726 | 36362 | 39962 | 35886 |
| 14057 | *Lepus timidus* | 38800 | 600 | 43252 | 42330 | 44162 | 42154 |
| 11666 | *Lepus* cf. *timidus* | 33200 | 1900 | 40110 | 35688 | 42566 | 34448 |
| 4371 | *Lepus timidus* | 32870 | 660 | 38550 | 36126 | 39898 | 35624 |
| 14053 | *Lepus* sp. | 30870 | 240 | 35844 | 34692 | 35860 | 34532 |
| 13947 | *Lepus* cf. *timidus* | 28680 | 170 | 33334 | 32762 | 33950 | 32326 |
| 14051 | *Lepus* sp. | 25670 | 150 | 31286 | 30396 | 31324 | 30226 |
| 13985 | *Lepus timidus* | 23840 | 100 | 29172 | 28418 | 29400 | 28230 |
| 13948 | *Lepus* sp. | 23110 | 100 | 28518 | 27788 | 28526 | 27776 |
| 11565 | *Lepus timidus* | 21330 | 140 | 25858 | 25104 | 25892 | 25082 |
| 11667 | *Dicrostonyx torquatus* | >22700 | | ... | 31680 | ... | 30618 |
| **Birds** | | | | | | | |
| 12651 | *Anser anser* | 28230 | 170 | 33036 | 32300 | 33214 | 32228 |
| 12363 | *Anas platyrhyncos* | 28210 | 150 | 32924 | 32300 | 33212 | 32222 |
| 12381 | cf. *Branta bernicla* | 25950 | 220 | 31314 | 30460 | 31550 | 30410 |

\*\* Comparison age may extend out of range.

The results are 'compared' against the Cariaco Basin record of Hughen *et al.* (2006) as described in the text in the absence at the time of writing of an internationally agreed calibration curve. Comparison data is shown in 68.2 and 95.4% probability ranges. In some instances, the ages are close to the limit of the comparison curve, and these problematic cases are given with a double asterisk. Where 'greater than' ages were obtained, these are compared by using the results in Fraction Modern (fM) notation rather than as conventional radiocarbon ages BP. This is not as straightforward as interpreting a comparison age for a finite determination because it becomes increasingly difficult to justify the assumption that each year is equally likely as another within the range covered over long time ranges but they do allow us to consider an upper comparison age limit for the result, which is of some use.

*Table 11.14. List of radiocarbon determinations from Pontnewydd Cave grouped by broad type.*

## AMS radiocarbon dating and faunal biostratigraphy at Pontnewydd

Table 11.14 presents calibrated ranges (at 68.2 and 95.4% probability ranges) by faunal taxa. Overall, the resulting faunal age ranges span some 20,000 $^{14}$C years from ~41,000 to ~21,000 BP, with the majority falling within some 13,000 $^{14}$C years between ~38,000 and ~25,000 BP. We discuss here the chronological patterning for carnivores and herbivores, before comparing these with other pertinent data from the western parts of the British peninsula.

### Carnivores

Four carnivore taxa were selected for dating – lion, wolf, red fox, and a brown bear/unspecified bear (to include an omnivore), and 31 dates in total pertain to these. The bears (represented by 16 samples) appear relatively early in the sequence of dated fauna, around or before 40,000 BP, and seem to have had a fairly continuous presence in the region down to at least 26,000 BP. On the basis of one dated sample, fox seems also to have appeared as early, although only two samples predate ~28,000 BP and the majority of dates for this taxon cluster around 28,000–26,000 BP. This may simply reflect the effects of sampling bias on a relatively continuous record of red fox in the region from at least 40,000 BP, or sparse populations of this taxon before ~28,000 BP. The record for lion and wolf is more intermittent. The two dated specimens classifiable as lion fall relatively early in the sequence (~40,000 BP). Wolf (represented by four samples) occupies a relatively narrow age range between ~29,000 and ~25,000 BP, suggesting that it may have been a relatively late addition to the regional carnivore taxa (but see Scott chapter 8, this volume).

*Herbivores*

Five herbivore taxa are represented among the dated fauna, and 23 dates pertain to these. Reindeer appear relatively early (around or before 40,000 BP) and persist until ~25,000 BP, although the main cluster of dates for this taxon are ~33,000–30,000 BP. *Lepus* appears from this time (by or after 35,000 BP, possibly as early as 40,000 BP) and persists latest of all of the dated taxa, present in the region down to the Last Glacial Maximum. By contrast to these two taxa the record for woolly rhinoceros, horse and an unspecified cervid are far more patchy and given the lack of dates for these taxa one cannot make any sound inferences about the dates that do exist. The one dated sample of woolly rhinoceros (*Coelodonta antiquitatis*) belongs to the later group at ~33,000 BP, and the single sample of horse is not much earlier at ~35,000 BP. By contrast, the two samples of unspecified cervid are later, spanning ~30,000–27,000 BP.

While it must be remembered that the radiocarbon dates are only sampling the taxa present at the cave, some general observations can be made. Taking the results at face value, there seems to have been a major restructuring of the faunal community around 40,000 BP. Prior to this, lion, bear, and possibly red fox, seem to have been the only carnivore accumulators at the site, and the only dated herbivores reindeer. Shortly after, however, there is a rise in taxonomic diversity, at least from ~37,000 BP, with the concentration of the major series of dates on bear and the possible persistence of red fox, and among the herbivores the appearance of wild horse, woolly rhino and *Lepus*. Somewhat later, perhaps around 29,000 BP, additional changes seem to have involved the floruit of red foxes and the appearance of wolves, possibly in the context of the diminution or disappearance of bear. The two dated cervids fall into this phase, and the only herbivorous taxon that persists through it is *Lepus*. It may also be significant that the three examples of directly dated birds (not plotted) fall into the ~25,000 to ~28,000 BP time range. With the exception of one date, on *Lepus* at ~23,000 BP, no dates are younger than ~24,000 BP, which may reflect increasingly severe conditions in the region as climate declined towards the Last Glacial Maximum.

Thus, in terms of the questions outlined above, the radiocarbon results suggest a major rise in taxonomic diversity before or around 35,000 BP, possibly coincident with the disappearance of lion and the rise of bear, and another re-structuring some time after 29,000 BP, after which wolf appears to have been sympatric with red

fox although bear had probably declined in numbers or disappeared. The wolves and foxes appear to have been the main accumulators of the unspecified cervids, later reindeer, and hares, whereas the only dated candidates for the accumulation of wild horse and woolly rhinoceros are the red fox and bear. Finally, and with only two exceptions, none of the specimens sampled in the radiocarbon programme date younger than ~24,000 BP.

In Figure 11.7, we show a plot of the comparison ages, produced using OxCal 4.1 and the record from the Cariaco Basin (Hughen *et al.* 2006). The data is compared against the NGRIP GICC05 $\delta^{18}$O climate record of Svensson *et al.* (2006) and Andersen *et al.* (2006) in order to provide a tentative comparison against a climatic record. The data confirm the observations already made above, but what is immediately apparent are the wide uncertainties associated with many of the comparison ages. This makes a precise association with climatic signals quite difficult, and we refrain from doing so for this reason.

### Wider comparisons

It is important to see the faunal assemblage from the Upper Breccia in the context of the wider British Upper Pleistocene faunal biostratigraphy. Currant and Jacobi (1997; 2001) have proposed a five stage mammalian chronostratigraphy that extends from the Last Interglacial (MIS 5e) to the Last Glacial Maximum (MIS 2). The first 'Joint Mitnor' mammalian assemblage zone (MAZ) contains temperate elements such as *Hippopotamus amphibious*, and is represented by sites like Trafalgar Square, London and Joint Mitnor Cave, Devon. The next 'Bacon Hole' mammalian assemblage zone, equated with the later sub-stages of MIS 5 (5a–d), is marked by the disappearance of the temperate elements and the presence of roe deer, mammoth and northern vole. The third mammalian assemblage zone, represented by the MIS 4 levels at Banwell Bone Cave, is characterized by a relatively impoverished suite of taxa dominated by bison and reindeer. This is succeeded by the MIS 3 'mammoth steppe' Middle Devensian fauna, formalized as the 'Pin Hole' (cave) mammalian assemblage zone (that replaces Coygan Cave, now no longer available for study), which is noted for its relative species diversity. This MAZ is punctuated by a mammalian assemblage interzone corresponding to the Dimlington Stadial, *i.e.* the early part of MIS 2. Mammalian fossils do exist for this period although are relatively rare, and at present, there is no available locality with sufficient biostratigraphic integrity to use as a type site. It can be noted, however, that a number of AMS radiocarbon dates on hyaena bones from Creswell Crags and its surrounding region span this period (see Currant and Jacobi 2001). The fifth, and last, mammalian assemblage zone that Currant and Jacobi (2001) propose is represented by the MIS 2 fauna of Gough's Cave that has red deer and horse well represented.

The dated Upper Breccia fauna from Pontnewydd spans later MIS 3 to the beginning of MIS 2, *i.e.* Currant

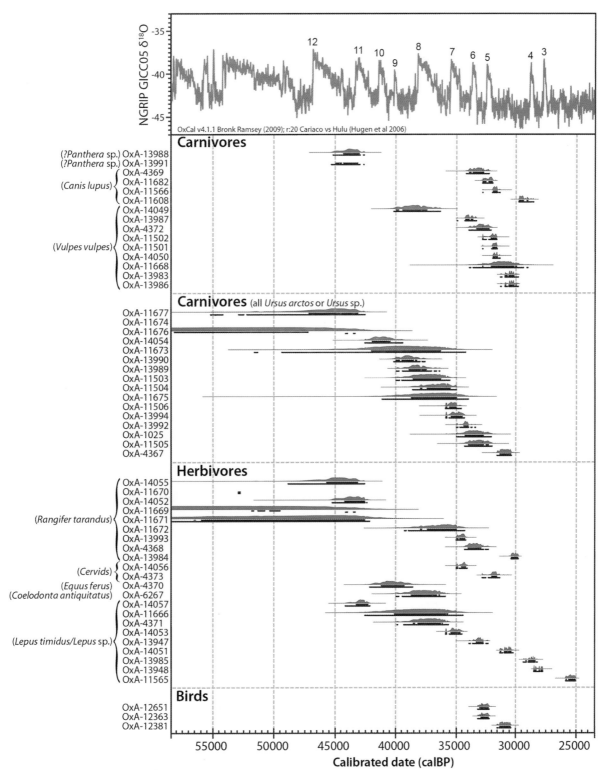

*Figure 11.7. Plot of comparison age ranges (cal. BP, Cariaco vs. Hulu; Hughen* et al. *2006) deriving from identified faunal specimens dated at Pontnewydd. The age determinations show identified taxon, which have been grouped into carnivore, omnivore, herbivore or avian categories. The BGRIP GICC08σ¹⁸O climate record is shown for comparative purposes. This illustration was made using OxCal 4.1 (Bronk Ramsey 2009).*

and Jacobi's Pin Hole MAZ and, possibly the Dimlington Stadial mammalian interzone. The dated Pontnewydd fauna shares elements with the scheme of Currant and Jacobi (2001) although differences may be observed. We have discussed above the uncalibrated $^{14}$C measurements

by faunal taxa shown in Figure 11.6. It can be seen that, overall, the dates span the period ~25,000 – ~40,000 BP, and the abrupt termination of dates at the end of MIS 3/Pin Hole MAZ presumably reflects the marked deterioration of climate into the Dimlington Stadial. Taking the dated

| Site | Species | Ref. no. | δ¹³C | Date |
|---|---|---|---|---|
| Coygan Cave | *Rangifer tarandus* | BM-499 | $\delta^{13}$C unavailable | 38684 +2713/- 2024 BP |
| Coygan Cave | *Coelodonta antiquitatis* | OxA-2509 | $\delta^{13}$C unavailable | 24620 ± 320 BP |
| Little Hoyle | *Crocuta crocuta* | OxA-1491 | Estimated $\delta^{13}$C -21.0 used. | 34590 ± 1500 BP |
| Little Hoyle | *Rangifer tarandus* | OxA-1028 | No measured $\delta^{13}$C | 29200 ± 700 BP |
| Little Hoyle | *Ursus arctos* | ANU-4347 | $\delta^{13}$C unavailable | 20080 ± 1120 BP |
| Little Hoyle | *Ursus arctos* | ANU-4350 | $\delta^{13}$C unavailable | 20800 ± 910 BP |
| Little Hoyle | *Ursus arctos* | ANU-4348 | $\delta^{13}$C unavailable | 18240 ± 1260 BP |
| Little Hoyle | *Ursus arctos* (laboratory intercomparison of ANU-4348) | OxA-2508 | $\delta^{13}$C -18.3‰ | 23550 ± 290 BP |
| Ogof-yr-Ychen | *Coelodonta antiquitatis* | Birm-340 | $\delta^{13}$C unavailable | 22350 ± 620 BP |
| Ffynnon Beuno 11 | *Equus ferus* | Failed No collagen | | |
| Ffynnon Beuno 6 | *Coelodonta antiquitatis* | OxA-9020 | $\delta^{13}$C -19.3‰ | 28030 ± 340 BP |
| Ffynnon Beuno 21 | *Rangifer tarandus* | Failed No collagen | | |
| Ffynnon Beuno 13 | *Mammuthus primigenius* | OxA-9008 | $\delta^{13}$C -20.9‰ | 27870 ± 340 BP |
| Ffynnon Beuno 51 | *Cervus elaphus* | Failed No collagen | | |
| Ffynnon Beuno 29 | *Bos sp./Bison* sp. | OxA-8998 | $\delta^{13}$C -20.0‰ | 24450 ± 400 BP |
| Ffynnon Beuno | *Mammuthus primigenius* | Birm-146 | $\delta^{13}$C unavailable | 18000 ±1400/- 1200 BP |
| Cae Gwyn | *Mammuthus primigenius* | OxA-8314 | $\delta^{13}$C -21.6‰ | 41800 ± 1800 BP |
| Cae Gronw | *Ursus* sp. | OxA-6335 | $\delta^{13}$C -20.1‰ | 35100 ± 1500 BP |
| Cae Gronw | *Rangifer tarandus* | OxA-5990 | $\delta^{13}$C -19.4‰ | 20200 ± 460 BP |
| Bacon Hole | *Ursus* sp. | OxA-5699 | $\delta^{13}$C -20.3‰ | 33200 ± 950 BP |
| Bacon Hole | *Ursus* sp. | OxA-6022 | $\delta^{13}$C -20.5‰ | 31500 ± 1200 BP |

*Table 11.15. Conventional (Birm; BM; ANU) and AMS radiocarbon measurements on fauna from Welsh caves other than Pontnewydd.*

fauna from Pontnewydd at face value it might suggest that the onset of severe conditions caused the localized extinction of most MIS 3 faunal taxa; however one looks at it a dramatic impoverishment seems evident. In terms of the specific taxa, eight of the dated fauna from Pontnewydd are found in the type locality of Pin Hole cave, Creswell (Currant and Jacobi 2001, table 5), with Pin Hole lacking only a cervid other than reindeer or *Megaloceros*.

Compared with Pin Hole, Pontnewydd lacks mammoth, *Megaloceros, Bison* and two mustelids, although a highly fragmentary bovid tooth from the Upper Breccia Silt beds matrix (identification A. Currant and E. Walker pers. comm.) may indicate the presence of *Bison* but it is not taxonomically identifiable. Despite the taxonomic

similarity, however, diversity is relatively low in the Pontnewydd fauna compared with Pin Hole (nine taxa as opposed to 15) and is the same as that for the 'impoverished' fauna of the preceding Bacon Hole MAZ, with which it shares five taxa (*Canis lupus, Vulpes vulpes, Ursus* sp., *Rangifer tarandus* and *Lepus* sp.). Taxonomically, then, the Pontnewydd MIS 3 dated fauna are somewhat intermediate between the preceding Bacon Hole MAZ of MIS 4 and the Pin Hole MAZ of MIS 3 with which they should be biostratigraphically equated. This could be significant, for example in demonstrating a degree of geographical variability within mammalian assemblage zones.

We now move to more specific comparisons with MIS 3/2 sites. Table 11.15 presents the small number of existing

| | Pontnewydd | Paviland |
|---|---|---|
| *Panthera leo* | * | |
| *Canis lupus* | * | * |
| *Vulpes vulpes / Alopex lagopus* | * | * |
| *Crocuta crocuta* | | * |
| *Ursus* sp. | * | * |
| *Rangifer tarandus* | * | * |
| Cervid | * | * |
| *Equus ferus* | * | * |
| *Coelodonta antiquitatis* | * | * |
| Bovid | | * |
| *Megaloceros giganteus* | | * |
| *Mammuthus primigenius* | | * |
| *Lepus* sp. | * | |
| *Homo sapiens* | | * |

*Table 11.16. Taxonomic composition at Pontnewydd and Paviland between ~37 and ~25 Kyr BP. Shading denotes the presence of a taxon at one site which is known from the other.*

| Site | No. Taxa > 37 kyr BP | No. Taxa <37 kyr BP |
|---|---|---|
| Pontnewydd | 4 | 8 |
| Paviland | 0 or 2 | 11 |

*Table 11.17. Taxonomic diversity at Pontnewydd and Paviland prior to and after ~37 kyr BP.*

measurements from Welsh caves other than Paviland, which we discuss below. There are serious doubts about the reliability of the majority of these measurements in the light of recent re-dating of several key specimens by new samples using ultrafiltration, but the few dates that exist on taxonomically identifiable bones from Ffynnon Beuno, Coygan Cave, Little Hoyle and Ogof-yr-Ychen probably support the broad picture (Aldhouse-Green *et al.* 1995). That is to say they show dated faunas that appear ~40,000 BP and with some evident biostratigraphic turnover shortly thereafter. At Coygan, reindeer may have persisted after 37,000 BP (BM-499) and woolly rhinoceros dates possibly to well after (OxA-2509); however Higham *et al.* (2006) consider this latter date to be inaccurate due to extremely low collagen preservation. At Little Hoyle, hyaena has been dated to 34,590±1,500 BP (OxA-1491), reindeer to 29,200±700 (OxA-1028), and brown bear to considerably later (ANU-4347, ANU-4350, ANU-4348 and OxA-2508). Again, we have doubts about the reliability of these results due to low collagen yields and less than adequate pre-treatment chemistry in the earliest days of the Oxford Laboratory. The latter result, for instance, that of the brown bear (OxA-2508 at 23,550±290 BP) is a case in point. The original sample yielded only 0.3% collagen when it was dated in 1989 using ion-exchanged gelatine. On the basis of this, Higham and Jacobi (unpub.) re-dated this specimen and obtained an older result (25,860±350 BP; OxA-X-2288-32). The result was given an OxA-X- result because of a continued problem of low collagen yields (640 mg of bone was treated but only 4.7 mg of gelatine was obtained). This is less than 10 mg and below 1% weight collagen. Other parameters, including the CN atomic ratio (3.3), were acceptable. Only woolly rhinoceros is dated

at Ogof-yr-Ychen (Birm-340; 22,350±620 BP) and again we would be very cautious about the reliability of a date measured early in the practice of radiocarbon, and of such a relatively young age for this taxon. Finally, at the type site of the Bacon Hole MAZ, the taxonomically poor faunal assemblage containing reindeer, wolverine and bear noted above has yielded dates of 33,200±950 BP (OxA-5699) and 31,500±1,200 BP (OxA-6022) both on right second molars of *Ursus* sp. (Hedges *et al.* 1996).

The large number of radiocarbon dates on fauna, human remains and humanly modified faunal material from Goat's Hole Cave at Paviland, Gower, renders it the best biostratigraphy to compare to Pontnewydd. Forty-five measurements have been produced for this site (Pettitt 2000) in the context of a major re-examination of the site and its collections (Aldhouse-Green 2000). The results span a broadly comparable time range to those from Pontnewydd, in this case from ~36,000 BP to ~25,000 BP. Although there are some taxonomic differences – the presence of hyaena at Paviland for example – some broad similarities exist.

Table 11.16 compares the fauna represented at the two sites for the period ~37,000 to ~25,000 BP. With 12 faunal taxa (including humans) Paviland is taxonomically richer than Pontnewydd (nine, lacking humans), although it can be seen that the two sites share seven taxa (three carnivores – wolf, fox and bear, and four herbivores – reindeer, cervid, horse and woolly rhinoceros). At each site all of these taxa overlap chronometrically, with the exception of equids and unspecified cervids, which in both cases are dated earlier at Pontnewydd, although one should not place too much emphasis on this given the small number of dates on these taxa at both sites (a total of three dates for each

| OxA | Species | Description | Find no. | Context | $\delta^{13}C$ | Date |
|---|---|---|---|---|---|---|
| **Soldier's Hole** | | | | | | |
| 691 | *Rangifer tarandus* | Calcaneum | | Unit 4 | | >34500 |
| 692 | *Rangifer tarandus* | Phalange | 13 phal | Unit 4 | | 29300 ± 1100 |
| 693 | *Rangifer tarandus* | Astragalus | 14 astrag | Unit 4 | | >35,000 |
| 1957 | *Rangifer tarandus* | Humerus | LL 7811 | Unit 4 | | 41700 ± 3500 |
| 2471 | *Rangifer tarandus* | Phalange (repeat of – OxA-692) | 13 phal | Unit 4 | | 29900 ± 450 |
| 1777 | Bovid | Tibia | | Unit 4 | | >42900 |
| **Bench Tunnel Cavern, Brixham** | | | | | | |
| 13512 | *Crocuta crocuta* | Right dentary – repeat of OxA-1620/5961 (see Jacobi *et al.* 2006) AF method | | | -18.4 | 36800 ± 450* |
| 13324 | *Crocuta crocuta* | Right dentary – repeat of OxA-1620 AG method (see Jacobi and Higham, in prep.) | | | -18.5 | 37500 ± 900* |
| **Creswell Crags\*\*\*** | | | | | | |
| 3417 | *Rangifer tarandus* | Cut-marked partial tibia indicative of human presence | | | -17.8 | 37200 ± 1300 |
| **Pin Hole Cave, Creswell Crags** | | | | | | |
| 4754 | *Crocuta crocuta* | Pre-maxillary | | 66/9'(P.8) | | 37800 ± 1600 |
| 3405 | *Rangifer tarandus* | Antler, worked, indicative of human presence | | Main passage, 3'3" | -17.7 | 31300 ± 550 |
| 3406 | *Rangifer tarandus* | Antler | | Main passage, 69/6' | -17.7 | 37450 ± 1050 |
| 3407 | *Rangifer tarandus* | Antler | | Main passage, 66/4' | -19.7 | 34360 ± 750 |
| 3409 | *Rangifer tarandus* | Antler | | Main passage, 67/5' | -17.6 | 34120 ± 750 |
| **Robin Hood Cave, Creswell Crags** | | | | | | |
| 3455 | *Coelodonta antiquitatis* | Tooth | +7969 | Uncemented screes | -20.0 | 29300 ± 480 |
| **The Arch, Creswell Crags** | | | | | | |
| 5797 | Bovid | Right M3 | AH7 | | -21.0 | 23140 ± 340 |
| **Ash Tree Cave, Derbyshire** | | | | | | |
| 4104 | *Coelodonta antiquitatis* | Calcaneum | AI, 27 | Stony cave earth | -20.3 | 30250 ± 550 |
| 4105 | *Coelodonta antiquitatis* | Right ulna | BII, 8+9 | Stony cave earth | -19.8 | 31300 ± 600 |
| 5798 | *Crocuta crocuta* | Right P4 | | | -19.1 | 25660 ± 380 |
| **Kent's Cavern, Torquay\*\*** | | | | | | |
| 4435 | *Cervus elaphus* | Molar | 11 | Vestibule | | 28060 ± 440 |
| 4436 | *Rangifer tarandus* | Tooth | B 6'9" | Vestibule | -19.7 | 27780 ± 400 |
| 4437 | *Vulpes vulpes* | Right mandible | C 5'6" | Vestibule | -20.9 | 23680 ± 300 |
| 4438 | *Vulpes vulpes* | Right mandible | B/c 6'0" | Vestibule | -23.5 | 28700 ± 600 |
| 5693 | *Rangifer tarandus* | Left calcaneum | 2084, 3/21/1'/6b | Vestibule | -18.1 | 27820 ± 500 |
| 5694 | *Rangifer tarandus* | Right calcaneum | 2024, 3/17/3'/IL | Vestibule | -17.9 | 28880 ± 440 |
| 5695 | *Canis lupus* | Left scapula | 1881, | Vestibule | -18.2 | 26300 ± 340 |

| | | | 3/2/4'/6L | | | |
|---|---|---|---|---|---|---|
| 5696 | *Megaloceros* sp. | Distal femur | B 8'4" | Vestibule | -20.9 | 23080 ± 260 |
| 13965 | *Coelodonta antiquitatis* | Cranial fragment (repeat of OxA-6108; see Jacobi *et al*. 2006) | C 9'6" | Vestibule | -20.1 | 37200 ± 550 |
| **Uphill Quarry, Somerset** | | | | | | |
| 13716 | *Rangifer tarandus* | Lozangic *sagaie* indicative of human presence (repeat of OxA-8408; Jacobi *et al*. 2006) | | | -17.5 | 31730 ± 250* |
| **Hyaena Den, Wookey, Somerset** | | | | | | |
| 13803 | Unidentified | Bone or antler *sagaie* indicative of human presence (repeat of OxA-3451; Jacobi *et al*. 2006). | | | -19.2 | 31550 ± 340* |
| 4782 | *Cervus elaphus* | Incisor, cut-marked, indicative of human presence | HDH, 1992, V10, 2 | Cave earth, north side of cave mouth | -18.9 | 40400 ± 1600 |
| 5701 | *Rangifer tarandus* | Antler | UHDNW, 1994, K17 | Top of stony cave earth in fissure at southern side of cave | -18.9 | 31450 ± 550 |
| 5702 | *Ursus* sp. | Canine | UHDNW, 1994, K17 | Top of stony cave earth in fissure at southern side of cave | -18.9 | 32750 ± 700 |
| 5703 | *Equus ferus* | Tooth | HDHS, 1994, K15 | Bottom of stony cave earth in fissure at southern side of cave | -20.8 | 37700 ± 1200 |
| 5704 | *Canis lupus* | Canine | HDHS, 1994, I14, 6b | Sandy-silts at southern end of cave | -18.7 | 39100 ± 1300 |

Sources: Gowlett *et al*. 1986; Hedges *et al*.1994; Higham *et al* 2006; Jacobi *et al*. 2006; Jacobi 1999.
*Indicates that previous measurements exist for these samples which were produced prior to ultrafiltration at Oxford. Results shown are re-measurements on ultrafiltered samples. See Higham *et al*. 2006 for discussion.
**We omit the existing direct AMS radiocarbon date on a human mandible from Kent's Cavern.
*** We also omit AMS radiocarbon measurements on hyaenas from Church Hole and Robin Hood Cave, Creswell Crags, which were previously published in Hedges *et al*. 1996 but which, after re-dating of samples pre-treated with ultrafiltration are now demonstrably older than the range of dated Pontnewydd fauna (>40,000 BP: Higham *et al*. 2006). We do, however, include a hyaena specimen from Pin Hole. The determination from The Arch at Creswell Crags is likely to be aberrant. Jacobi and Higham attempted to re-date this and obtained no collagen, implying that the initial date is almost certainly problematic.

*Table 11.18. $^{14}C$ determinations from other Late Pleistocene contexts in the west of Britain.*

site). Differences between the two sites can mainly be explained by the presence of additional taxa at Paviland, which saw hyaena denning from ~28,000 BP and the presence of bovids and *Megaloceros* prior to ~27,000 BP, and mammoth (with the exception of one tooth, in the form of humanly-modified ivory artefacts) between 30,000 and 24,000 BP, and Gravettian humans at around ~29,000 BP (Jacobi and Higham 2008). By contrast, both lion and *Lepus* are entirely absent from the fauna (dated and undated) of Paviland.

At Paviland, a parsimonious reading of the faunal age ranges would suggest no dated species earlier than ~35,000 BP, although taking age ranges into account woolly rhinoceros and reindeer may have been present as early as ~37,000 BP. Even in this scenario, taxonomic diversity more than quadrupled after 37,000 BP. Table 11.17 compares taxonomic diversity at the two sites, from which it can be seen that at Pontnewydd the diversity doubles after 37,000 BP. A closer reading of the age distributions of the fauna at Paviland (Pettitt 2000) suggested a major faunal restructuring ~28,000 BP, as represented by the apparent appearance of human groups, as represented by the burial of the 'Red Lady' at 29,000 BP, in the context of the disappearance of woolly rhinoceros and bovids (and probably *Megaloceros*) and the appearance of wild horse and mammoth. With regard to the carnivores it is interesting that wolf makes its first dated appearance at Paviland by ~28,000 BP, approximately the time it is first dated at Pontnewydd. This re-structuring could, in addition, be reflected at Pontnewydd with the floruit of fox (present, but poorly-dated at Paviland), appearance of cervid, and possible disappearance of bear. One must perhaps not make too much of these broad faunal changes, although the fact that at both sites *broad* faunal turnovers and re-structurings coincide around 37,000 and 28,000 BP and dated records effectively cease ~25,000 BP is of interest.

Radiocarbon dates from other sites from western England or those on a latitudinal parallel with Pontnewydd are also pertinent to the results, and in this light we include dated samples from Devon (Bench Tunnel Cavern, Kent's Cavern), Somerset (Soldier's Hole, Hyaena Den, Uphill Quarry) and Derbyshire (Pin Hole, Robin Hood Cave, The Arch, and Church Hole at Creswell Crags, Ash Tree Cave). These are presented in Table 11.18. As so few dates exist for fauna from these sites little can be said by way of comparison, but as with the Welsh sites broad agreement can be observed. Seven taxa dated from Pontnewydd can be found varyingly among these sites, and in five cases (fox, reindeer, bear, wolf and cervid (in the case of the latter equating the unspecified cervid at Pontnewydd with red deer)) their broad age ranges overlap and place them within the Pin Hole MAZ. With the exception of the lack of humans at Pontnewydd (see below), which in addition to Paviland are attested at the western English sites around ~32,000–30,000 BP (Hyaena Den, Uphill Quarry) and on typological grounds at Creswell around ~28,000 BP (the *Font Robert* points from Pin Hole), the only fauna conspicuously lacking among the dated examples from western English sites is *Lepus*. All one can really say is that the dated fauna from Pontnewydd is certainly not inconsistent with Pin Hole MAZ dated faunas from elsewhere in the west of Britain.

There are a series of dated faunal specimens from several cave sites in Ireland with which the Pontnewydd Upper Breccia assemblage may be compared. These were dated by the Oxford Laboratory in the early and mid 1990s, using the then prevailing chemical pre-treatment methods involving ion-exchanged gelatine, and reported by Woodman *et al.* (1997). The most relevant sites with Pleistocene faunas that pre-date the Last Glacial Maximum include Castlepook and Foley Caves in Co. Cork, Ballynamintra and Shandon Caves in Co. Waterford. The range of taxa is very relevant to the Pontnewydd Upper Breccia, however, there are current questions concerning the validity of some of these determinations. The Oxford laboratory is currently undertaking a small re-dating programme of some of the Shandon and Castlepook determinations and although it is premature to go into details there are indications that some of the older results reported in Woodman *et al.* (1997) are biased and the ages misleading. For these reasons we have omitted detailed discussion of this evidence. Further work,

involving ultrafiltration methods, will probably clarify the situation in the near future.

### Concluding remarks

One major question is why there is no evidence of the presence of humans at Pontnewydd, during the period in which Gravettian activity at Paviland left, among other things, the burial of the 'Red Lady'. At Paviland, human remains and humanly-modified artefacts thought to be associated with a Gravettian occupation, were once interpreted as dating to the range ~24,000 to 28,000 BP, although the presence of diagnostically Aurignacian artefacts at the site presumably indicates occupation prior to this time, perhaps around 32,000 BP on the basis of a direct AMS radiocarbon date on a diagnostic lozangic antler point from Uphill Quarry Cave 8 (OxA-13716 at 31,730±250 BP). The amount of Gravettian material recovered from the site, however, is not great, and one must remember that diagnostic Gravettian material (in the form of *Font Robert* points) has only been recovered from nine British sites (Jacobi 1999). One might infer from this that humans were present in Britain only sporadically, and a parsimonious interpretation of the diagnostic artefacts (*Font Robert* points, which on the continent are securely dated to around 29,000) suggests brief human incursions in this period alone. The intriguing find and date obtained for the human humerus attributed to the Eel Point Cave at the western end of Priory Bay on the north side of Caldey Island, South Wales (Schulting *et al.* 2005) suggests human presence took place once more by 24,500 BP. This is towards the end of a time of extremely cold temperatures and suggests perhaps that Gravettians had become better adapted to colder conditions (presumably with improved shelter, organization and clothing) to allow settlement in much harsher environments. What is confusing is the lack of Late Gravettian lithic remains in the British Isles. The most northerly diagnostic Gravettian artefacts have been found in Pin Hole cave at Creswell Crags, but this of course does not mean that Gravettian groups penetrated as far to the north-west as Pontnewydd. The reason for their absence could thus be one of simple distance. The radiocarbon evidence from Pontnewydd indicates that red fox, wolf, bear, birds, reindeer, cervids and hares were present in the period in which the *Font Robert* phase of the Gravettian belongs, and at Paviland in this specific period the only herbivores dated are *Bos* and mammoth. We would have liked to include the horse vertebrae spatula from Paviland here although despite re-dating using ultrafiltration these still appear to be contaminated and therefore minimum ages. Faunal impoverishment, therefore, does not seem to be a sensible explanation for the lack of human presence at Pontnewydd.

Finally we ask again the questions which we posed at the outset:

1.  *To identify changing patterns of faunal composition, biodiversity and biomass intensity over the period*

*40–20,000 BP.* There seems to have been major faunal restructuring around 29,000 BP, in the form of the appearance of a taxonomically-richer Pin Hole MAZ, followed by a disappearance of this faunal MAZ around 25,000 BP. These results are broadly similar to those observed at Paviland, and the few dates available from other sites are consistent with this patterning.

2. *To seek to identify from this, reasons for a scarce human presence (attested perhaps by a single cut-marked tooth) from the Upper Breccia context at Pontnewydd, which is composed of accumulations probably brought into the cave by the action of bears, wolves and foxes.* The results demonstrate the persistence of fox, wolf and, particularly, bear at Pontnewydd, albeit in the absence of hyaena. This may alone suggest why the cave was not attractive to humans. Traces of Early Upper Palaeolithic humans in Britain are remarkably rare, and it is only with the Late Upper Palaeolithic after ~13,000 BP that a good sample exists. We note the absolute lack of Late Glacial faunas among the dated sample from Pontnewydd, which may suggest the unavailability of the cave for habitation at the time.

3. *To compare Pontnewydd with relevant coeval assemblages – including those from the nearby sites of Ffynnon Beuno and Cae Gwyn – where there is evidence for both human and hyaena presence, both of which are lacking from Pontnewydd.* Paviland Cave is the only site available with a suitably large suite of dates on faunal taxa, and shares a number of similarities with Pontnewydd, including faunal turnover (= a rise in taxonomic diversity consistent with the appearance

of a Pin Hole MAZ) around 29,000 BP. The poor database of radiocarbon measurements from other sites is consistent with this. Differences, amounting only to greater taxonomic diversity at Paviland, possibly reflect regional differences (perhaps latitudinal) and these possibly had an effect on the presence of humans in the south but not in the north.

4. *To examine whether the bear and wolf presences can be differentiated chronologically.* It appears that they can. A parsimonious reading of age ranges for these taxa suggest that by the time wolf appears ~29,000 BP bear populations in the cave were diminished, possibly gone.

5. *To establish whether the accumulations of herbivore remains primarily coincide with the pattern of wolf presence at the cave.* It appears not. With the exception of *Lepus* sp. the herbivore taxa accumulated earlier than the known age range of wolf in the cave, and a number of specimens of *Lepus* itself pre-date wolf. The accumulation of reindeer, cervid, and the individual specimens of horse and woolly rhino occurred in the period that fox and bear were using the cave, and probably pre-date the accumulation of wolf.

6. *To examine whether original spatial and chronological configurations of animal bones in the cave can be retrieved.* Despite a large number of failures in the dating of faunal specimens due to lack of collagen, a good degree of success has been evident in the reconstruction of faunal turnover in the cave which is of a pattern observable elsewhere (at Paviland) and which is consistent with the scatter of more isolated results from other caves in the region.

# 12. Stable Isotope Analyses of Animal Bone from Pontnewydd Cave

## Mandy Jay, Vaughan Grimes and Michael P. Richards

*Carbon, nitrogen and oxygen isotope analyses ($\delta^{13}C$, $\delta^{15}N$ and $\delta^{18}O$) of bone collagen and phosphate were undertaken with a view to investigating aspects of diet, environment and climate on samples of herbivore (hare and reindeer), omnivore (bear and fox) and carnivore (lion); with carbon and nitrogen ratios alone available from separate analyses undertaken as part of the radiocarbon dating programme also being available from deer, wolf and mallard.*

## Carbon, nitrogen and oxygen stable isotope analysis

Stable isotope analysis has been applied to bones from the Upper Breccia at Pontnewydd Cave which date to the period from around 40,000 to 20,000 BP. Such analysis of skeletal remains can be used for a range of purposes, including the reconstruction of diet, interpretation of local environments and the study of the movement of individuals (Ambrose 1993; Katzenberg 2000; Sealy 2001; Hedges *et al.* 2004). Different chemical elements are generally used for each purpose, with carbon and nitrogen employed mainly for investigating diet, and oxygen for studying climate and long-distance mobility. Combining the different elements within one study, however, can help to clarify the data and aid interpretation.

The chemical content of skeletal tissues is dependent upon that of the food and water consumed by the animal. These in turn are affected by the environment in which the plants at the base of any foodweb have originated (*e.g.* the local climate and soil attributes). It is these relationships which allow stable isotope analysis to be used in the interpretation of past environments, diets and mobility patterns.

### Carbon and nitrogen

Carbon and nitrogen analyses are the best understood of the isotopic techniques available. These chemical elements are usually employed for dietary reconstruction, with dietary studies of archaeological material dating back several decades (*e.g.* Vogel and van der Merwe 1977; Tauber 1981), but they can also contribute to our understanding of past environments (*e.g.* Richards and Hedges 2003; Stevens and

Hedges 2004). The analysis of both elements is best applied to the organic collagen fraction of bone, although carbon analysis of bone carbonate is sometimes undertaken (*e.g.* Lee-Thorp and Sponheimer 2003). In most cases, issues relating to burial environment contamination and diagenetic alteration make the more chemically robust collagen the fraction of choice. Collagen is built up from the elements which are present in food, but more particularly from the amino acids which make up the protein content of that food (Ambrose and Norr 1993; Ambrose 2000).

The technique involves measuring the ratio of two isotopes for each element ($^{12}C$ and $^{13}C$; $^{14}N$ and $^{15}N$) and comparing the resultant data with the values which might be expected for a particular trophic level within a foodweb. The isotopic values calculated are given in units ‰ (per mil, or parts per thousand) and are shown as $\delta^{13}C$ and $\delta^{15}N$ values. In a typical system, the collagen values for a consumer will increase by 3–5‰ over the consumed (or prey) for $\delta^{15}N$ and by somewhere around 1‰ for $\delta^{13}C$. The analysis is dependent upon an understanding of geographical and temporal differences which must be expected in background environments. Precipitation levels, sunlight availability, temperature, salinity and carbon dioxide levels are all likely to affect the values obtained and will all vary across time and space. It is also necessary to have as much background information and as many isotopic data as possible from the animals (terrestrial, marine and fresh water) which would have been present at the time of the accumulation of the assemblage being investigated. This is very often a limiting factor in the analysis, particularly when working with Palaeolithic material for which preservation may be poor and material scarce.

Collagen has a long turn over period (Libby *et al.* 1964;

Stenhouse and Baxter 1979; Wild *et al.* 2000; Hedges *et al.* 2007), so that the signatures obtained will not be affected by short-term variations in dietary consumption patterns, except in the case of very young mammals which may retain a signal relating to their mothers' milk (Schurr 1998; Fuller *et al.* 2006).

## Oxygen

Oxygen isotope analyses are usually employed for the investigation of climate change and the possibility of tracking mobile individuals across climatic zones. The bone fraction of choice here is phosphate extracted from bone mineral, the alternative being carbonate which is thought to be more likely to be affected by diagenetic alteration (Kolodny and Luz 1991). The isotope ratio analysed is that between $^{18}O$ and $^{16}O$, and the values obtained from mammalian bone phosphate ($\delta^{18}O_p$) are related to the oxygen isotopes in precipitation ($\delta^{18}O_{precip}$) via drinking water. $\delta^{18}O_{precip}$ values are in turn strongly influenced by environmental and geographic parameters, such that lower (more negative) values occur in colder environments, at higher latitudes and altitudes, and with increased continentality (Dansgaard 1964). The $\delta^{18}O_p - \delta^{18}O_{precip}$ relationship has therefore been widely used by researchers in reconstructing past climates (Longinelli 1984; Luz and Kolodny 1985; Genoni *et al.* 1998; Iacumin *et al.* 2004) and, increasingly, to detect human and animal migration (White *et al.* 2004).

## Methodology

### Carbon and nitrogen

The data discussed in this report have been produced partly by the authors at the University of Bradford, and partly at the Oxford Radiocarbon Accelerator Unit (ORAU) in the course of the production of dates. The methods described below are those used at Bradford, but are similar to those used at ORAU (see Pettitt *et al.* chapter 11, this volume for a discussion of their methods) and, in particular, both involve the use of ultrafiltration during collagen extraction.

The samples used were drilled powder, rather than whole bone fragments, this allowing the choice of a precise sampling site on the bone in agreement with the curator of the material. Initial screening tests were undertaken to check collagen preservation by measuring the percentage of nitrogen and the atomic C:N ratios prior to dating and isotopic analysis. This is discussed further in the radiocarbon dating chapter (see Pettitt *et al.* chapter 11, this volume). Work was continued only on those samples which showed evidence of good preservation. In some cases, it was not possible for the Bradford team to obtain samples from bones with good preservation since dating was the priority activity and the entire fragment was used in that process. Whilst ORAU carbon and nitrogen data were available from all dated samples, this restricted the number of samples from which oxygen data are available.

The methods used for collagen extraction follow those of Richards and Hedges (1999), with the addition of an ultrafiltration stage (Brown *et al.* 1988). The samples were demineralized in 0.5 M HCl, gelatinized in pH 3 water at 70°C and filtered with Ezee® filters. The retained supernate was then ultrafiltered to 30 kD, the smaller (and more degraded) collagen fraction being discarded and those molecules over 30 kD being retained. The collagen yields listed in Table 12.1 should be considered in the light of this ultrafiltration stage, since the process reduces the yields normally to be expected by ensuring discard of the more degraded collagen fragments.

The supernate was lyophilized and the resultant collagen sample was analysed using either a Europa Scientific Geo 20/20 isotope ratio mass spectrometer coupled to a Roboprep elemental analyser, or a Thermo Finnigan DELTAplusXL coupled to a Flash EA 1112. The values obtained are the average of two replicates, where possible, but collagen yields were low and this was only the case for eight of the samples listed in Table 12.1. Analytical error is considered to be ±0.2‰ for each of carbon and nitrogen. The international standards against which the sample values are calculated are VPDB and AIR for carbon and nitrogen respectively.

## Oxygen

The method used to extract phosphate from the bone mineral was adapted from that of O'Neil *et al.* (1994) and Stephan (2000). The powder samples were treated with 2.5% sodium hypochlorite and 0.125M sodium hydroxide to remove possible organic and humic acid contaminants, respectively. They were then reacted with HF to remove calcium as a $CaF_2$ precipitate, leaving a phosphoric acid solution. This was then neutralized in 2M potassium hydroxide and reacted with a buffered silver amine solution over heat to precipitate silver phosphate crystals, which were weighed, filtered and then analysed using a Thermo Finnigan DELTAplusXL isotope ratio mass spectrometer coupled to a TC/EA (Bremen, Germany). The values obtained are the average of two replicates and have been normalized to three in-house standards according to the normalization procedures discussed in Vennemann *et al.* (2002). Analytical error is considered to be ±0.4‰. The international standard against which the sample values are calculated is VSMOW.

## Pontnewydd Cave results

The isotopic data for carbon, nitrogen and oxygen which were obtained at the University of Bradford on 20 samples are presented in Table 12.1, along with the available radiocarbon dates and sample details. The carbon and nitrogen values obtained by the Oxford Radiocarbon Accelerator Unit on a further 26 samples are listed in the section in this volume which discusses the dates (see Pettitt *et al.* chapter 11, this volume).

Figure 12.1 depicts the carbon and nitrogen values

| Sample code | Find no. | Species | Sample details | Radiocarbon date OxA | Date (BP) | δ13C (‰) | δ15N (‰) | δ18Op (‰) | C:N (atomic) | %C | %N | Collagen yield (%) |
|---|---|---|---|---|---|---|---|---|---|---|---|---|
| PONT 1 | F1779 | Bear (*Ursus* sp.) | 2nd phalange. Upper Breccia–Silt beds. | | Not dated | -20.5 | 8.3 | 15.9 | 3.5 | 41.4 | 14.0 | 0.9 |
| PONT 2 | F2549 | Reindeer (*Rangifer tarandus*) | Left astragalus. Upper Breccia–Silt beds. | 14055 | 41400 ± 1400 | -19.3 | 3.3 | 15.7 | 3.3 | 40.9 | 14.3 | 1.1 |
| PONT 3 | F1898 | Reindeer (*Rangifer tarandus*) | Right mandibular ramus. Upper Silt beds. | 14052 | 39600 ± 900 | Bad C:N | Bad C:N | 16.8 | 9.0 | 41.5 | 5.4 | 0.2 |
| PONT 4 | F4831 | Bear (*Ursus* sp.) | Bone shaft. Upper Breccia. Note that this was originally identified as '?reindeer', but reconsidered by Andy Currant following isotopic analysis and is now thought to be probably bear. | 13994 | 30780 ± 390 | -20.7 | 9.7 | 14.3 | 3.6 | 38.3 | 12.5 | 0.6 |
| PONT 5 | F2149 | Bear (*Ursus* sp.) | Carpal. Upper Breccia–Silt beds | 14054 | 36100 ± 800 | -20.0 | 9.3 | 15.3 | 3.5 | 39.8 | 13.3 | 0.7 |
| PONT 6 | F1014 | Lion (*Panthera leo*) | Phalange. Upper Breccia. | 13991 | 40300 ± 750 | -19.5 | 10.5 | 15.0 | 3.3 | 40.8 | 14.5 | 1.4 |
| PONT 7 | F1886 | Bear (*Ursus* sp.) | 2nd phalange. Upper Breccia–Silt beds. | | Not dated | -20.4 | 9.9 | 15.6 | 3.5 | 39.9 | 13.4 | 0.8 |
| PONT 8 | F775 | Bear (*Ursus* sp.) | 2nd phalange. Upper Breccia. | 13988 | 40000 ± 600 | -19.6 | 10.6 | 14.7 | 3.3 | 40.0 | 14.0 | 1.0 |
| PONT 9 | F1018 | Bear (*Ursus* sp.) | 2nd phalange. Upper Breccia. | 13992 | 29790 ± 180 | -19.8 | 9.5 | 15.0 | 3.4 | 36.9 | 12.5 | 0.8 |
| PONT 10 | D1154 | Reindeer (*Rangifer tarandus*) | 1st phalange. Upper Breccia. | 13984 | 25210 ± 120 | -19.1 | 2.9 | 15.1 | 3.5 | 41.8 | 14.1 | 2.3 |
| PONT 11 | F5521 | Hare (*Lepus* sp.) | Calcaneum. Upper Breccia/Sb (Silt bed). | | Not dated | -21.1 | 6.0 | 16.7 | 3.4 | 37.4 | 12.9 | 1.8 |
| PONT 12 | F4796 | Hare (*Lepus* sp.) | Innominate. Upper Breccia/Sb (Silt bed). Note that this was originally identified as fox, but reconsidered by Andy Currant following isotopic analysis and is now thought to be hare. | 14057 | 38800 ± 600 | -21.1 | 1.6 | 16.7 | 3.3 | 37.3 | 13.1 | 2.0 |
| PONT 13 | F1964 | Hare (*Lepus* sp.) | Right calcaneum. Upper Breccia–Silt beds. | 14053 | 30870 ± 240 | -21.2 | -0.2 | 16.2 | 3.4 | 38.6 | 13.4 | 2.2 |
| PONT 14 | D427 | Hare (*Lepus* sp.) | Left innominate. Upper Breccia. | 13947 | 28670 ± 170 | -20.8 | 3.0 | 16.9 | 3.5 | 40.6 | 13.6 | 1.6 |
| PONT 15 | D5951 | Fox (*Vulpes vulpes*) | Proximal radius. Upper Breccia (Silt beds) | | Not dated | -20.5 | 9.3 | 17.3 | 3.4 | 39.4 | 13.4 | 1.0 |
| PONT 16 | D994 | Fox (*Vulpes vulpes*) | Shaft of left tibia. Upper Breccia. | 13983 | 25500 ± 140 | -20.2 | 6.6 | 15.7 | 3.6 | 40.9 | 13.2 | 1.1 |
| PONT 17 | F447 | Fox (*Vulpes vulpes*) | Metatarsal. Upper Breccia. Note that this was originally identified as hare, but reconsidered by Andy Currant following isotopic analysis and is now considered to be fox. | 13987 | 29490 ± 170 | -20.2 | 8.7 | 17.1 | 3.4 | 39.2 | 13.6 | 1.7 |
| PONT 18 | F1828 | Reindeer (*Rangifer tarandus*) | Left metacarpal. Upper Breccia. | 13993 | 30240 ± 230 | -18.7 | 2.8 | 15.4 | 3.2 | 38.8 | 14.0 | 0.4 |
| PONT 19 | F1819 | Reindeer (*Rangifer tarandus*) | 2nd phalange. Upper Breccia–Silt beds | | Not dated | -19.3 | 1.7 | 15.3 | 3.4 | 39.4 | 13.6 | 0.5 |
| PONT 20 | F1010 | Bear (*Ursus arctos*) | Right maxilla & pre-maxilla. Upper Breccia. | 13989 | 33560 ± 330 | -18.8 | 10.2 | 15.2 | 3.3 | 35.3 | 12.4 | 0.6 |

*Table 12.1. Isotopic data produced at Bradford for C, N and O, sample details and available radiocarbon dates for material from Pontnewydd.*

Note: Isotopic data are averages of two separate replicates where collagen yields made this possible (PONT 5, 7, 10–14, 17). The replication for PONT 20 was very poor and the value shown here is that for the replicate which showed the better %C and %N, although the C:N ratio for the second replicate was similarly at 3.3.

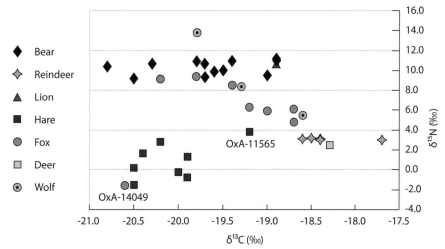

*Figure 12.1. Carbon and nitrogen values produced at Oxford at the time of radiocarbon dating, for those samples which resulted in reliable dates (excluding a mallard). These include 15 of the 20 samples analysed at Bradford. OxA-14049 and OxA-11565 are highlighted as a fox and a hare for which there are probable confusions in identification, based on the isotopic data.*

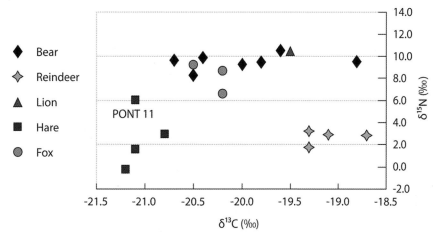

*Figure 12.2. Carbon and nitrogen values from the Bradford laboratory (19 values, including four which are not in Figure 12.1). These are the samples which are also depicted in Figure 12.3, with associated oxygen values. PONT 11 is highlighted as a hare which may be misidentified, based on the isotopic data.*

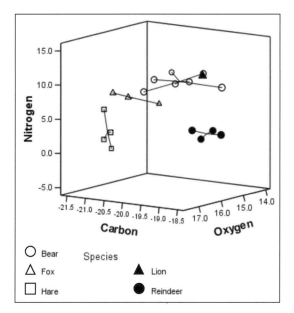

*Figure 12.3. Carbon, nitrogen and oxygen values produced at Bradford for 19 samples.*

obtained at Oxford for those samples which produced non-problematic dates (excluding the mallard). The diagram includes the Oxford values for 15 of the samples for which Bradford values are also available, in order to ensure that any slight inter-laboratory differences do not skew the data (such differences are generally within the range which might be expected for multiple processing of the same sample, but this approach eliminates any question of systematic differences between the laboratories). Figure 12.2 shows the Bradford values on 19 samples (excluding the one which produced a poor C:N value in that laboratory). Figure 12.3 is a three-dimensional scatter-plot showing the carbon, nitrogen and oxygen values obtained at Bradford on 19 samples. Figures 12.4 and 12.5 show nitrogen and oxygen over time for those samples with radiocarbon dates available.

## Species identification

The species identification for three of the samples (PONT 4, 12 and 17 (F4831, F4796 and F447) – probable bear,

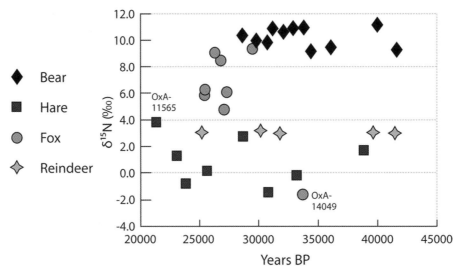

*Figure 12.4. Nitrogen values for species where n > 5, from the Oxford data, plotted against the radiocarbon date. OxA-14049 and OxA-11565 are highlighted as a fox and a hare for which there are probable confusions in identification, based on the isotopic data.*

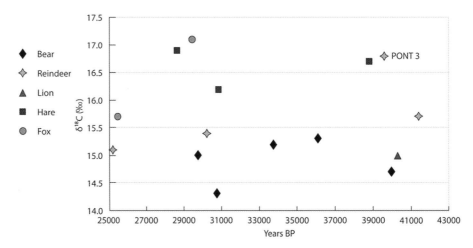

*Figure 12.5. Oxygen data for all samples for which both dates and δ¹⁸O values are available. The chart includes the reindeer (PONT3) which has a collagen C:N ratio outside of the acceptable range.*

hare and fox; previously reindeer, fox and hare respectively) were reconsidered by Currant following initial analysis, since anomalous isotopic data suggested that the original identifications may have been incorrect. All three were re-classified at that stage (see Table 12.1) and the figures presented here show the revised species. Similarly, although there are no oxygen data available for OxA-11565 (hare D2990) or OxA-14049 (fox F7041), their positions in figure 12.1 might indicate that these have been confused, hare with fox and fox with hare. PONT 11 (F5521; undated) is another hare which might also be worth reconsidering on the basis of the high nitrogen value (Figure 12.2).

Whilst it is not reasonable to suggest that isotopic analysis should be used to identify bones to individual species in any routine way, it is interesting to note the situation here. A reconsideration of fragmentary material may be possible if the confusion is likely to be between animals of differing trophic levels. At Pontnewydd, both

the known and possible confusions are between carnivores, omnivores and herbivores; although it is also clear that even a confusion between herbivorous hare and reindeer would be picked up isotopically (despite original confusion between animals of such different sizes being obviously unlikely). This situation may be of interest in the consideration of an animal bone assemblage where the material is very fragmentary and there was a specific question which related to species proportions at a particular site.

## Discussion

The most obvious pattern in these data relates to species identification. It is clear from the figures that, even when there is some overlap between species in the carbon and nitrogen data (*e.g.* the three foxes shown in Figure 12.2 overlap with the bear data), adding in the oxygen values refines the division. At least part of the reason for the relatively clear species distinctions seen here is that the animals are all from the same site. The environmental differences which will occur across space when different sites are investigated are likely to cause blurring in all three isotopic systems. In this case, it would also appear that such differences over time are not clearly present. When considering the possibility of seeing purely environmental changes over time at this site, it is best first to consider the purely herbivorous species, so that differences in the carbon and nitrogen signals which may be due to individual differences in omnivorous behaviour are excluded from the variability to be considered. The herbivorous species for which there are a number of samples from Pontnewydd Cave are reindeer and hare.

There is no systematic trend in the carbon, nitrogen or oxygen values over time for those species, particularly if it is considered likely that OxA-11565 (D2990; no PONT number) and PONT 11 (F5521; undated) are foxes mis-identified as hares (see discussion of possible confusion over identifications above). Indeed, if those samples are excluded, the range of carbon values is only 1.3‰ for hares and 0.9‰ for reindeer (maximum, including all data from both laboratories), this being well within the level that might be expected for the same species at the same site and from the same period in time. The nitrogen variation in the reindeer is similarly low at 1.6‰, although it is higher for the hares at 4.5‰. The latter is more than would be expected if all other variables are ignored. Data from modern rabbits at seven locations throughout Britain (none of which had been affected by modern fertilizers) show a maximum range at any one site of 3.6‰ (Jay, unpublished data). If PONT 11 is a hare, rather than a fox, then the variation in $\delta^{15}N$ amongst the hares would increase to 7.5‰. Figure 12.4 shows the nitrogen values over time where there is a date (does not include PONT 11, therefore). There is no noticeable trend over time to be seen here, particularly if D2990 OxA-11565 is actually a fox.

The range of oxygen values in the reindeer is relatively low for four out of five samples, at 0.6‰ with a mean of 15.4‰. The fifth sample is the one with a poor C:N ratio for the collagen, such that it was discarded from the carbon and nitrogen data. It is quite possible that this is contaminated in some way, which may well affect the oxygen values, such that it would be conservative to exclude it from that data-set as well. The relatively limited range in $\delta^{18}O_p$ values for the Pontnewydd Cave reindeer samples is unusual when compared with the ranges seen in modern reindeer. Longinelli *et al.* (2003) noted considerable variation (>1.0‰) within modern reindeer samples obtained from the same geographic areas and suggested that herd migration and unique dietary adaptations to climatically severe habitats may account for their $\delta^{18}O_p$ variance. The atypical variation in the Pontnewydd Cave reindeer is further highlighted since they represent over 16,000 years of accumulation, as determined from their $^{14}C$ dates (see Figure 12.5), during which time fluctuations in global climate are known to have occurred (Jouzel *et al.* 1987; Johnsen *et al.* 1995). It is possible, however, that the values are recording the

optimal environmental conditions for the reindeer at each of their respective temporal episodes, in which case the limited range would be expected. In light of these issues, the Pontnewydd Cave reindeer $\delta^{18}O_p$ values remain difficult to interpret regarding climate reconstruction through time, especially given the small sample size.

The range for the hares is also relatively low, covering 0.7‰ with a mean value of 16.6‰. Bearing in mind that the analytical error for oxygen is considered to be ±0.4‰, these ranges for the reindeer and hares are not indicative of visible environmental differences and, once again, there is no noticeable pattern in the values through time.

Overall, the high nitrogen variability in the hares might well be due to a combination of factors. Firstly, environmental change may well be visible in this animal, but not with any clear temporal pattern. Secondly, it is possible that this small animal was being brought into the site by predators which had obtained it from a wide variety of source habitats, perhaps some of which were a significant distance away. Finally, it is possible that all of the hares need to be re-assessed in the light of the possible confusion in identification with foxes (see above).

The bears, which are relatively consistent in terms of nitrogen, but have a wide range of carbon values, may well have been consuming fish on a regular basis. The high $\delta^{15}N$ values are consistent with *Ursus arctos* found elsewhere in Britain at this time (*e.g.* Richards 2000 for Goat's Hole Cave, Paviland). The site is very close to the River Elwy, which is known today as being an excellent fishing ground for sea trout (*Salmo trutta trutta*). These spend their early lives in freshwater (1–5 years), before migrating to the sea to feed and grow and then returning to the river to spawn. Such a life history would involve the bears consuming fish with varying degrees of freshwater and marine signals, thus explaining the wide range of carbon values.

Figure 12.1 shows a number of foxes which similarly have high nitrogen values and more negative carbon values. This could be explained by a diet relatively high in aquatic foods, perhaps scavenging remains left by the bears, or else obtaining their own riverine foods, such as waterfowl. The Oxford data-set includes a mallard with a $\delta^{13}C$ value of -14.0‰ and $\delta^{15}N$ of 10.1‰. This would indicate that this particular bird was consuming marine-sourced foods (which have less negative carbon values and high nitrogen values), so that similar birds would not have been a major source of the fox diet. However, if birds which had concentrated on freshwater resources were available (*e.g.* mallards from an Iron Age site in Hampshire show appropriate values (Jay, unpublished data)), they might well make up some part of their diet.

The $\delta^{18}O$ ranges for bear and fox are much higher than for reindeer and hare, at 1.6‰ for both. This might well be indicative of animals which are consuming aquatic resources from both riverine and marine habitats, their $\delta^{18}O_p$ signatures reflecting the wide range in oxygen values from these varying water sources. The range in values for these animals might also, however, be accounted for if they lived at different altitudes throughout their life cycle.

The data-points for the lion cluster for all isotopic ratios with those for the bears. The identification of this bone has been checked by Currant and confirmed as *Panthera*. Whilst the lion would be expected to be a high-level carnivore, with the bears likely to be much more omnivorous, the different sources of animal protein involved may well have produced this equivalent result for the carbon and nitrogen isotope ratios. If the bears had been consuming fish, then this protein source would have had an elevated baseline $\delta^{15}N$ ratio, thereby enriching the bears' bone collagen in $^{15}N$ to a level equivalent to a lion, the latter having a much higher proportion of animal protein in the diet where that source was entirely terrestrial. This is also likely to be true if the bears were consuming large quantities of invertebrates, whilst the lion was not (Kelly 2000).

The lion $\delta^{15}N$ ratio is approximately 7‰ higher than the average for the reindeer and nearly 10‰ higher than that for the hares. These values are significantly higher than would be expected if the diet of the lion was entirely based on the herbivores represented here, the higher end of the expected range for a diet-consumer difference being 5‰ (*e.g.* Hedges and Reynard, 2007). In addition, the $\delta^{13}C$ values do not indicate a diet containing a high proportion of reindeer because the values for the latter are more enriched in $^{13}C$ than they are for the lion, whilst a normal diet-consumer difference would have the consumer around 1‰ more enriched than the prey. A diet containing a mixture of herbivore and bear might bring about the combination of $\delta^{15}N$ and $\delta^{13}C$ values seen for the lion, if bear might be seen as a possible prey animal at this time, but the analyses presented here obviously do not contain the full range of available prey species for a full evaluation to be considered. For instance, the very low $\delta^{15}N$ values for reindeer are also reflected at Goat's Hole Cave, Paviland (Richards 2000), whilst that site has isotopic data for *Bison/Bos* sp. which show much higher nitrogen isotope ratios. If such data were available from Pontnewydd, then these would make suitable suggestions for the lion diet. Neither the fox nor the wolf have contemporaneous dates, but a diet which contained significant proportions of omnivores or other carnivores might also produce the higher $\delta^{15}N$ value seen for this animal.

## Conclusions

The data obtained clearly separate the species analysed, particularly when all three isotopic systems are considered together. There is no apparent 'blurring' here to suggest visible environmental change over the period being investigated. The separation, together with a lack of any trend in the herbivore data over time (assuming the possibility of re-classification of hares/foxes), suggests that the animals sampled were living in very similar environments, or that the level of environmental change that existed was such that it is not possible to see it using these data. This is not to say that significant environmental change did not exist for the period from 40,000 to 20,000 BP, but that these animals were deposited at times during that period when conditions were very similar in terms of the isotopic signal from the skeletal material.

It is likely that the bears from this site were consuming fish on a regular basis and that some of the foxes were also consuming freshwater resources. The data from the lion reflects its status as a high-level carnivore.

In some circumstances, the ability to separate species using these three isotope systems together may have utility where the material from one site is fragmentary and perhaps difficult to identify. This would be particularly useful where the possible identification groups belonged to different trophic levels.

# 13. The Pontnewydd People, Their Cave and Their World

## Stephen Aldhouse-Green

*As an archaeologist, my interest in the hominin remains from Pontnewydd is focused on the people and their lives. A key question concerns the composition, with particular reference to age and gender, of the group(s) of Neanderthals who used the cave at Pontnewydd. But there are wider questions, too, and the research carried out both in the field and in the laboratory has produced some interesting results:*

**Proposal** *– Neanderthal society may have been divided, at least some of the time, into separate male and female groups.*
**Comment** *– based on late Neanderthal dental development criteria the Pontnewydd group contained at least one girl of 9 years old and four males, including one of 8.5 years old, one aged 11–11.5 years old; there was also one young adult male of 14–16 years and one mature adult male.*
- *The overall composition of the Pontnewydd Neanderthal group is suggestive of a task force.*

**Proposal** *– Neanderthals enjoyed a hypercarnivorous diet.*
**Comment** *– their diet at Pontnewydd seems to have included meat but with an important vegetarian component in the form of tough, fibrous material (see Compton and Stringer chapter 9, this volume).*
- *meat-eating and vegetarianism may have been seasonally based,*
- *the vegetarian element may suggest an interglacial context for the settlement.*

**Proposal** *– the hominin remains in Pontnewydd Cave had been deliberately placed in the cave either as disposals or burials.*
**Comment** *– there is a general acceptance that the Pontnewydd Neanderthals had been the subject of some form of mortuary activity but for so many to die in one place suggests prolonged or frequent periods of residence.*

*Pontnewydd presents the earliest known record of human ingress into Wales. This evidence of range expansion into north-western Britain, contrasts with the relatively parsimonious record of MIS 7 settlement in England, particularly when compared with earlier interglacials. It coincides also with both a technological watershed – the regular use of Levallois (or prepared core) technique – and with the evolution of early Neanderthals.*
- *I have also pursued some of the intrinsic problems that the use of caves would have presented to their primate and hominin users. These include issues of distribution – caves were only available in limited areas and, even then, may not have been accessible (depending on the precise state of cave-evolution/devolution and infill/erosion of cave sediments),*
- *differing orientation(s) of cave entrance(s) meant that individual caves might be preferentially used for settlement, burial or ritual,*
- *the natural internal structures of caves, and their dimensions, favoured occupations of caves by hominins and other carnivores: thus, bears frequently travelled far underground and marked their route both by urinating and by scratching on the walls with their claws. Caves frequently have entrance chambers, main passages, side passages, side chambers, and 'chimneys' and 'wells' which gave access to higher or lower levels of the cave-system,*
- *fire can be difficult to manage in caves where there may be powerful draughts or high levels of humidity. Clouds of smoke may form and be slow to disperse. Experiment suggests that winter may be the best time for cave-use,*
- *stalagmite is a key to climate and this is illustrated by a presentation of the complex Pontnewydd data.*

*The caves at Cefn have provided us with no evidence of an earlier human use than that indicated by the Late Upper Palaeolithic flint artefacts. It is reasonable to suppose that Cefn was at least visited by our early Neanderthals but that their visits were brief. It would seem therefore that it was Pontnewydd that was a special place that remained in the Neanderthal memory and was used and visited at various times.*

| SCENARIO I | | | | Mature | |
|---|---|---|---|---|---|
| Age in years | 8–5 | 11 | 14–16 | adult | Totals |
| Female | - | 1 | - | - | 1 |
| Male | 2 | - | 1 | 1 | 4 |
| Totals | 3 | - | 1 | 1 | 5 |

*Table 13.1. Pontnewydd Cave. scenario I: minimum numbers of hominins.*

| SCENARIO II | Juvenile/ | Mature | |
|---|---|---|---|
| Age in years | adolescents | adults | Totals |
| Female | 2 | - | 2 |
| Male | 7 | 7 | 14 |
| Totals | 9 | 7 | 16 |

*Table 13.2. Pontnewydd Cave. scenario II: maximum numbers of hominins.*

| Ages in years | <1 | 1 to <5 | 5 to <10 | 10 to <20 | 20 to <40 | 40+ | n | Comment |
|---|---|---|---|---|---|---|---|---|
| Sima de los Huesos | - | - | 3 | 17 | 10 | - | 30 | Male to female ratio 50:50 |
| | - | - | 10% | 56.7% | 33.3% | - | | |
| Pontnewydd | - | - | 2 | 2 | 1 | - | 5 | 5 = min. 16 = max. |
| | - | - | 40% | 40% | 20% | - | | |
| Krapina | - | 2 | 4 | 10 | 7 | - | 23 | |
| | - | 8.7% | 17.4% | 43.5% | 30.49% | - | | |
| Hortus | 1 | 1 | 5 | 3 | 8 | 5 | 23 | |
| | 4.3% | 4.3% | 21.7% | 13% | 34.8% | 21.7% | | |
| Vindija | - | - | - | - | 6 | 7 | 13 | |
| | | | | | 46.1% | 53.8% | | |
| Moula Guercy | - | - | 2 | 2 | 2 | - | 6 | |
| | - | - | 33.3% | 33.3% | 33.3% | | | |
| All sites nos. | 10 | 29 | 32 | 39 | 82 | 20 | 212 | |
| **All sites** | **4.7%** | **13.7%** | **15.1%** | **18.3%** | **38.7%** | **9.4%** | | |

After Trinkaus 1995; Defleur 1993, table 6, 219; Sima (Klein 1999); Pontnewydd (Compton and Stringer chapter 9, this volume); Moula-Guercy (Culotta 1999); Krapina (Oakley *et al.* 1971, 338–140); Hortus (Oakley *et al.* 1971, 120–122).

*Table 13.3. Age structure of Neanderthals and their European predecessors at cave sites.*

## The Pontnewydd people

As part of this social enquiry, a key question is the age and gender of the groups of Neanderthals who used the cave. But there are wider questions too that can lead to an interpretation of the lives of these people through an understanding of the processes by which the caves were formed, the emplacement of deposits within them, the cultural remains recovered from them and their use by other mammals at times in their past. Together all this provides glimpses of how early Neanderthals might have organized their lives; what, when and how they made use of the cave(s), and how their remains have come to be in our hands to undergo twenty-first century study so many millennia after their deaths.

The minimal and most plausible interpretation of the Pontnewydd hominin evidence (see Compton and Stringer chapter 9, this volume) is that it represents a group of five individuals: one 9 year old girl and four males – the latter are aged 8.5, 11–11.5 and 14–16 and one is a mature adult (Table 13.1 – scenario 1). The position scarcely changes,

except numerically, if one opts for the maximum number of individuals (Table 13.2– scenario II). Even then, there would only have been two females (both aged 11) out of a total of 16 individuals, and the pattern remains heavily weighted to the young.

The gender balance therefore argues against the hominin presence at Pontnewydd being that of a family and would more readily favour it as a task-specific group. One recalls here Binford's 'hard evidence' paper (1992) where he argues for largely separate, gender-based life-styles for Neanderthals. Olga Soffer's 'self-provisioning' theory (2000) presents a similar life strategy for female Neanderthals. If these interpretations were applied here, Pontnewydd might be seen as part of a wider male territory with a 'home-base' where the females were located, perhaps some distance away. But the presence even of a lone female (or two) in the Pontnewydd group would not seem to be consistent with this. There is one possibility that might explain the female presence; namely that, being pre-adolescent, she was possibly not viewed as gendered.

| PN hominin ref. nos. | Left upper | Left lower | Right upper | Right lower |
|---|---|---|---|---|
| 1, 12, 18 | 3 | | | |
| 4, 17, 19 | | | 3 | |
| 5, 7, 11, 20 | | 4 | | |
| 6, 10, 13, 15, 16, 21 | | | | 6 |
| **Totals** | **3** | **4** | **3** | **6** |

Note. PN9 is a fragment of very heavily worn, possibly upper molar (left/right not determined and so not included here). PN4 is a fragment with two teeth in place but is only counted once here.

*Table 13.4. Frequency of left/right (7:9) and upper/lower (6:10) tooth losses.*

| | UPPER | | | | | LOWER | | | | |
|---|---|---|---|---|---|---|---|---|---|---|
| **PN nos.** | I | C | P³ | P⁴ | M | I | C | P₃ | P₄ | M |
| 1 | | | | | ▼ | | | | | |
| 4 | | | | | ▼ | | | | | |
| 5 | | | | | | | | | | ▲ |
| 6 | | | | | | | | ▲ | | |
| 7 | | | | | | | | ▲ | | |
| 10 | | | | | | ▲ | | | | |
| 11 | | | | | | | | | | ▲ |
| 12 | | | | | ▼ | | | | | |
| 13 | | | | | | | | | | ▲ |
| 15 | | | | | | | | | | ▲ |
| 16 | | | | | | | | | | ▲ |
| 17 | | | | | ▼ | | | | | |
| 18 | | | | ▼ | | | | | | |
| 19 | | | | | ▼ | | | | | |
| 20 | | | | | | | | ▲ | | |
| 21 | | | | | | | | | | ▲ |
| **Total** | 0 | 0 | 0 | 1 | 5 | 1 | 0 | 3 | 1 | 5 |

Single-rooted teeth include incisors, canines, lower premolars, upper second premolars (P⁴). Upper first premolars (P³) and molars (m) have multiple roots. The ratio is 6:10 for both single:multiple roots and for upper:lower teeth.
Symbols: ▲ lower teeth; ▼ upper teeth.

*Table 13.5. Frequency of losses of permanent single-rooted and complex-rooted teeth.*

As we have seen the Pontnewydd hominins were seemingly a related task-group rather than a family group. If we examine the wider picture, we would note that what characterizes Neanderthals and sets them apart from other hominins is a high level of mortality among prime age adults. My presentation of the data – apart from inclusion of the necessary overview and analysis of Pontnewydd itself – is limited to European caves which have yielded the remains of at least ten individuals or where the data is of high quality (Table 13.3). If these results are meaningful, they seem to suggest that the life-span of the classic Neanderthals of the Last Glaciation was longer than had been the case with early Neanderthals, and that the modal value for death had moved from 'adolescent' to 'young adult'. The picture, then, is not one of a species headed for extinction but, rather, the converse.

## Early mortuary practices at Pontnewydd – the evidence and the argument

The earliest instance of the conscious disposal of the dead in Europe dates back to perhaps 500,000 years ago at Atapuerca in northern Spain. Here, a couple of dozen human bodies were found at the base of a shaft, known as the Sima de los Huesos or 'the abyss of bones'. A taphonomic analysis conducted by the excavators (Arsuaga *et al.* 1993) concluded that the accumulation of hominin remains could only have been 'anthropic or catastrophic'. The next site, in terms of chronology, that may have seen the deposition of corpses, similarly in the dark recesses of a cave, is Pontnewydd itself at around 225,000 years ago. The hominin remains, representing at least five separate individuals and perhaps as many as 16 people, were found almost entirely within a localized region (Figure 9.1), near the base of the Lower Breccia debris flow, both on the south side of the East Passage and within the

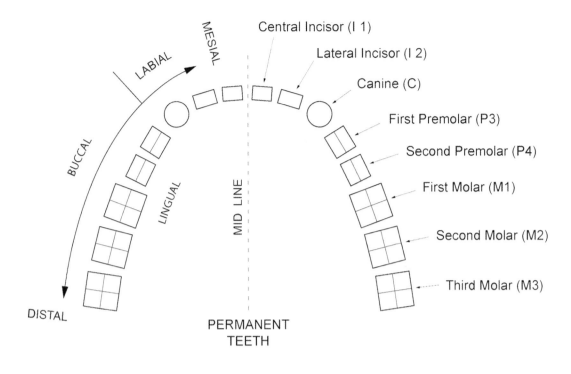

Figure 13.1. Deciduous and permanent dentitions.

South-East Fissure. They were found locally interstratified with a fauna, including remains of hibernating bears, which had accumulated *within* a cave (A. Currant pers. comm.). Analysis by Compton and Stringer (chapter 9, this volume) has led to the conclusion that the good condition of the hominin finds 'suggests that the original [place of accumulation or deposition] was inside the cave and that [the finds] have only travelled a short distance'. They argue, also, that it is clear that the remains were 'already fragmentary' before transport within the debris flows.

A further tooth (H2942), found twenty metres distant in the New Entrance, comes from a context suggestive of its derivation from a Lower Breccia deposit in the New Passage (Mourne and Case chapter 5, this volume). The evidence does not, of itself, admit of resolution as to the nature of the original context and mode of deposition, for the hominin

finds betray no evidence as to the manner of death of the people involved. The finds are too fragmentary to admit of direct evidence for cannibalism or defleshing rites by other hominins; likewise of processing by carnivores, although purely taphonomic factors – specifically, the durability of teeth – could also be invoked. The key fact is that the remains were localized, with one exception, to a small part of the cave and so may represent a single accummulation that was later dispersed. The occurrence of human remains is so rare at this period that chance accumulation does not provide a reasonable explanation. It is likely, therefore, that we are dealing with the disposal of a group of, perhaps related, individuals over a relatively short space of time, whether through deliberate disposal or simply from casual discard. Catastrophe, conflict or carnivores may all have had their part to play.

## Teeth and taphonomy

A simple analysis (Table 13.4) shows that the frequency of left to right teeth present is in the ratio 7:9, or nearly 50% for each. The presumption arising from this is that the teeth fell out naturally – and in a random manner – once they had become loosened *post mortem*. On this one measure, the range and patterning of the hominin remains present no evidence of ritual practices. However, when the evidence is approached differently, the results become more complex. Thus we may ask whether the teeth were lost equally from the upper and lower jaws (maxilla and mandible, respectively); and, second, whether single-rooted teeth were lost preferentially because they were less 'anchored' into the jaw (Figure 13.1; Table 13.5). If one can safely extrapolate from wider taphonomic data, it would seem that – on a scale from 'highly transportable' to 'no movement' – most cranial elements (including mandibles and teeth) move little if at all when subjected to fluvial action (Potts 1988, 66–67). If taphonomic reasons cannot be invoked to explain the discrepant ratio (below), it may be that depositional factors (involving humans) or, more likely, removal factors (involving carnivores or humans) are involved. In the event, analysis showed that the ratio of upper to lower teeth was not 50:50 but, rather, was 6:10. The inference is that the lower jaws had become separated from the crania. At the Anasazi pueblo site dated to around AD 1100 and located in the Mancos Canyon of Colorado in the American South-west the hominin remains recovered were the residues of conspecific consumption (cannibalism). Interestingly, mandibles were the 'most intact bone in the assemblage', possibly because of their 'lack of nutritional value'. It is certainly the case that sites defined by Defleur in his book on Mousterian burials (1993, 215) as *restes isolés* (dispersed human remains that could not be demonstrated as having once been interrred as burials (*restes en connexion*)) were typified by remains of the cranium, mandible and teeth. At Pontnewydd the individual teeth tell us much about the hominins from whom they came, yet afford less interpretation about how they died and were incorporated into the cave deposits. It may be that the more massive taurodont molars are likely to have survived preferentially, because of their inbuilt robusticity, but this is clearly only part of the story.

If we examine the evidence of bone chemistry and tooth damage for Neanderthal diet and eating habits, we encounter a surprise. Much of the scientific evidence has seemed to point to Neanderthal diet especially later as having been hypercarnivorous, yet the patterns of wear on the crowns of the Pontnewydd teeth seem to reflect a diet with a large shearing component. The implication is that the Pontnewydd diet was heavily vegetarian with a focus on such tough fibrous foods as leaf stems or twigs. Scratches on the molars may have arisen from the 'stuff and cut' method of eating, a practice in which the jaws hold the food in the manner of a vice or clamp, whilst pieces are cut off with a knife. In one case, cut-marks indicate that the individual was left-handed (PN10). There is also a high instance of chipping of the teeth, with all five

individuals and it had, moreover, occurred in life, as can be seen by the degree of rounding present on the fracture surfaces. This may have arisen from the chewing of bones (as practised by the recent Inuit) or, possibly, from some non-masticatory use (Compton and Stringer chapter 9, this volume). There is also some specific evidence in the form of vertical striations on the teeth for meat-eating.

## Artefacts, routeways and territory

The discoveries of artefacts and hominin remains of MIS 7 age at Pontnewydd Cave represent the earliest known human presence in Wales. Many – perhaps all – of the artefacts used were made of locally available raw materials (Jackson and Bevins chapter 10, this volume). However, the discovery, in the English Midlands, of a series of bifaces made of andesite associated with the deposits of the ancient Bytham River has implications for the settlement of Wales (Figure 13.2). This river was destroyed by Anglian ice *c.* 450,000 years ago during MIS 12, but until then, ran from Warwickshire, through Leicestershire and Lincolnshire, to meet the modern coast of East Anglia just south of Great Yarmouth. In the Middle Pleistocene it linked with the system of the Rhine and, so, afforded access into Britain from the very heart of Europe. Thus, the Bytham may once have been an important route for the penetration of early hominins into both northern and western Britain, unlike the ancestral Severn.

A number of andesite bifaces come from sites in the neighbourhood of Coventry where there is no unequivocal earlier glacial activity which could provide a natural context for transportation of their raw materials from their geological source area in the Lake District to the West Midlands. This has led to the suggestion (Wymer 1999, 115; Lang and Keen 2003; 2005) that the rocks the artefacts have been made on may have been moved by human agency to the localities where they were lost. There are only five andesite artefacts from Pontnewydd (Table 13.6), and none is from a secure Middle Pleistocene context, but their very rarity and their size and typology (two discoidal cores, one offset bifacial scraper, and two flakes), combined with the fact that two of the stratified specimens were found in very close proximity to each other at the mouth of the South-East Fissure may suggest that there was something special about them. This may have been colour. In terms of the materiality of the freshly fractured rocks, the colour of the andesites would have been green in contrast to the greys and blacks of the other raw materials (Jackson and Bevins chapter 10, and R. E. Bevins pers. comm.). This green rock could have been sourced directly from *in situ* deposits in the region of Ennerdale and Eskdale on the south-western margin of the Lake District or could have been collected from derived contexts in the Irish Sea plain between the Lake District and North Wales.

Whilst Pontnewydd, at a Latitude of 53° 15' N, remains the most north-westerly hominin site of its period in Eurasia, stray discoveries of bifaces from both open sites and caves at Settle (Victoria Cave) and Giggleswick

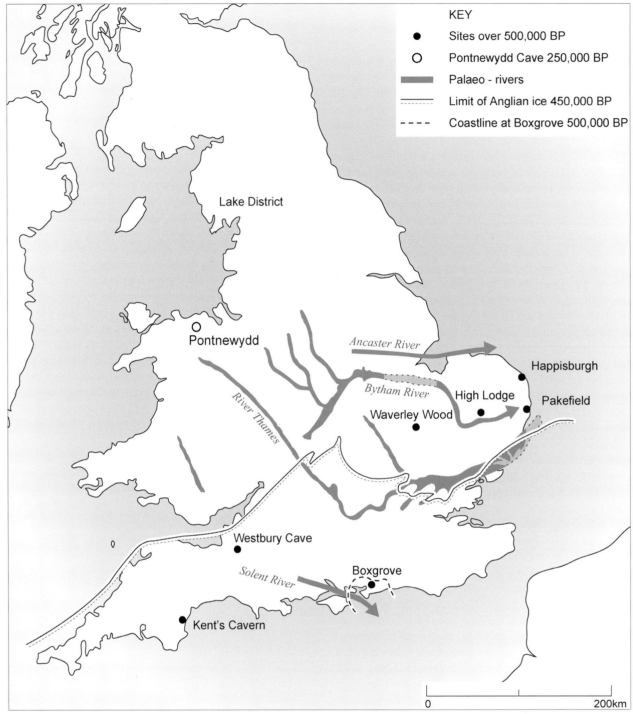

*Figure 13.2. Map of Bytham River.*

| Find no. | Artefact type | Context | Co-ordinates | Max. dimensions (mm) |
|----------|---------------|---------|--------------|----------------------|
| A74/1 | Discoidal core | BD dump | | 67 × 62.3 × 32 |
| A684 | Offset bifacial scraper | BD dump | I33SE | 65.5 × 91.6 × 23.2 |
| B310 | Large flake | UB | K20; 99.46 | 90.9 × 95.1 × 41.6 |
| D1440 | Discoidal core | UB | J7SE; 99.73 m | 90.5 × 82 × 34 |
| D45790 | Flake | UB | K7NE; 99.76–99.66 | 58.2 × 34.2 × 10.1 |

*Table 13.6. Andesite artefacts from Pontnewydd.*

|  | Main Cave | | New Entrance | |
| *Principal Artefact Types* | *No.* | *%* | *No.* | *%* |
|---|---|---|---|---|
| Bifaces | 70 | 23.6 | 4 | 5.5 |
| Choppers/chopping tools | 6 | 2.0 | 1 | 1.4 |
| Discoidal cores | 41 | 13.8 | 4 | 5.5 |
| Levallois cores | 13 | 4.4 | 1 | 1.4 |
| Miscellaneous cores | 35 | 11.8 | 17 | 23.3 |
| Levallois flakes, blades, points | 53 | 17.8 | 26 | 35.6 |
| Side-scrapers | 37 | 12.5 | 12 | 16.4 |
| Notches/denticulates | 7 | 2.4 | 4 | 5.5 |
| Other retouched artefacts | 25 | 8.3 | 2 | 2.7 |
| Naturally backed knives | 10 | 3.4 | 2 | 2.7 |
| **Total** | **297** | | **73** | |

*Table 13.7. Artefact frequencies in the Main Cave and New Entrance.*

(Kinsey Cave) show that areas as far to the north as 54° 30'N were settled – or at least visited – as far back as the age of Pontnewydd, if not much much earlier (Wymer 1988). Thus, it may be appropriate to think of Pontnewydd not only in terms of hominin territories extending southwards to the traditional continental homeland (Aldhouse-Green 1998), but also reaching to the north. Pontnewydd is around 400 km from the nearest point on the modern French coast and given the likely diameters of annual territories of mobile hunter-gatherers, the then British peninsula should perhaps be seen not just as an area available for seasonal extension of territory but, rather, as a region whose population might have been relatively static. Indeed, we are becoming increasingly aware that Pleistocene landscapes were hostile to faunal presence only during the very height of the glaciations. The implication is that, whilst climatic change may, at times, have driven hunter-gatherer populations out of the British Isles or have led to their local extinction, for most of the time groups of viable size established on the British peninsula could have remained permanently. Once the settlement of North Wales is perceived as part of a pattern extending a further 150 km northwards from Pontnewydd, this interpretation becomes all the more plausible (Figure 13.2).

## Contemporary settlement

On the basis of U-series dating, the occupation at Pontnewydd can be shown to be older than 225,000 years ago, since it is overlain by stalagmitic growth formed on the surface of the Lower Breccia (which contained the bulk of the archaeological and hominin finds). This dating is, furthermore, supported by TL determinations on burnt flint artefacts from the Lower Breccia, Intermediate, and from Layers 26 and 28 of the New Entrance, although the mean *terminus ante quem* of the New Entrance TL dates on burnt flint is younger at 197,000±17,000 BP. (For technical reasons, it is expected that TL results may be up to 15% too young and U-series results may be too old (Debenham chapter 11, this volume)).

England had been intermittently settled since perhaps one million years ago, but this is the earliest record of human ingress into Wales. This evidence of range expansion into north-western Britain, contrasts with the relatively thin record of MIS 7 settlement in England, particularly when compared with earlier interglacials (Ashton and Lewis 2002). It coincides also with both a technological watershed – the regular use of Levallois (or prepared core) technique – and with the evolution of early Neanderthals. It seems paradoxical that the appearance of these new people in far-flung territories, bearing the latest equipment, should occur at a time when people had become a rare sight in Britain generally. Indeed, the only two 'rich' sites in Britain at this time are Pontnewydd itself and Crayford in Kent. A case has been made (Aldhouse-Green 1998) for the existence of earlier and later phases of occupation at Pontnewydd Cave, centred on 225,000 and 175,000 years ago, represented by evidence from the Main Cave and New Entrances respectively (Table 13.7). It seems unlikely, because of the lack of resolution of the different dating methods involved, that it will be possible to reach a definitive conclusion on this. However, it is instructive to look more widely at broadly coeval assemblages in southern Britain. Here, I have selected sites which fall within a 'broad' time-range from *c.* 260,000–170,000 years ago, where there is evidence for integrity of context. The earliest sites – almost all limited to the lower Thames valley – tend to be of late MIS 8 to early MIS 7 age (260,000–230,000 years ago) and to be dominated by the products of Levallois technology (Table 13.8). By contrast, the sites from East Anglia, Sussex, and the Upper Thames tend to belong to the younger end of the MIS 7 interglacial and, so, are more likely to belong to the same phase as Pontnewydd, or just after. These late sites are generally noteworthy for their smaller size and mixtures of bifaces and Levallois technology (Table 13.9).

There is evidence, too, from south-western England – specifically from the Palaeolithic sites at Broom – situated on a low level terrace in the valley of the Axe, on the boundary of Devon and Dorset (Toms *et al.* 2005). Over many years of collecting, these sites have yielded a substantial assemblage of 1,800 artefacts, mostly bifaces

| Site | Context | Archaeology |
|------|---------|-------------|
| Norwood Lane, Southall | Possible kill site | Levallois pointed blade found 'near ... tusk, teeth and bones of mammoth' (Wymer 1999, 81). |
| Baker's Hole, Northfleet | Primary; sealed by Coombe Rock. | >100,000 Levallois flakes (typically centripetal) and cores; also bifaces. |
| Lion Pit, West Thurrock | Below a thick deposit of estuarine sand and gravel, above Coombe Rock. | Levallois industry resembling that at Baker's Hole. |
| Crayford | Primary at Stoneham's and Rutter's pits | Levallois cores and flakes (one on the jawbone of a woolly rhinoceros) – rich fauna. |
| West Drayton | ?Primary | Levallois flakes, blades and cores. |
| Yiewsley | ?Primary | Levallois flakes, blades and cores. |

*Table 13.8. Early Neanderthal sites in the Thames valley, southern Britain, broadly dated to c. 260,000–230,000 BP (late MIS 8/7c).*

| Site | Context | Archaeology |
|------|---------|-------------|
| Aveley, Essex | Interglacial sands | Flakes |
| Stanton Harcourt, Upper Thames | River channel | 5 Bifaces, 1 ?Levallois flake |
| Brundon, Stour valley, East Anglia | Primary context | Levallois cores, flakes and blades |
| Stoke Tunnel and Maidenhall, Ipswich, East Anglia | Fluviatile deposit of the River Orwell | Rare artefacts (including Levallois cores) |
| Stutton, Stour valley, East Anglia | Brickearth | Bifaces and Levallois blades |
| Norton, Sussex | Raised beach (?correlates with Brighton Raised Beach) | 'Sporadic artefacts' |
| Selsey Life-Boat Station, Sussex | Interglacial channel | Biface, Levallois core, flakes |
| Aveley, Essex | Interglacial silty clays | Levallois core, flakes |

*Table 13.9. Early Neanderthal sites in East Anglia, Sussex, and the Upper Thames valley, broadly dated to c. 250,000–175,000 BP (MIS 7c/early 6).*

and mostly of so-called Broom chert (Upper Greensand chert). Levallois material is virtually absent with only three such pieces recognized, but this lacuna cannot be for reasons of raw material constraints. Hosfield and Chambers (2009, 96) suggest that the rarity of Levallois technique – or its absence – may either reflect regional preference, or the bulk of the assemblage may pre-date the adoption of the Levallois technique, at least in southwestern Britain (Hosfield and Chambers 2002). Optical dating suggests that occupation may have spanned the period 340,000–221,000 years ago (broadly MIS 9–7) and, thus, may have represented 'a significant, long-lasting hominin presence in the region'. But it would be difficult, on the basis of the evidence revealed so far, to demonstrate whether the human presence was continuous or spasmodic. The most parsimonious, and therefore the 'best' result is that of 250,000±15,000 years ago; this yields a range at 2σ of 280,000–220,000 years ago. The site seems likely to be older than Pontnewydd but, clearly, the possibility of overlap cannot be ruled out. It may be, therefore,

that in some respects, Broom mirrors the situation of Pontnewydd: a site on the margins of the settlement of earlier Palaeolithic Britain, which was selected and regularly re-visited primarily on account of its abundant supplies of raw materials.

The distributional data seem to reflect a pattern of early sites where the humans exploited the lithic resources of the Thames valley, exposed in the open landscapes of MIS 8/earliest MIS 7, for large-scale or expedient production of Levallois blanks. Later settlement, in the temperate phase of MIS 7, may have been more diffuse with population groups smaller in size and with lithic resources harder to access. It is interesting that the putative MIS 6 occupation at Pontnewydd is characterized by a rarity of bifaces and an increase in Levallois, relative to frequencies in the Main Cave (Table 13.7). This would seem to be consonant with the suggestion (White and Pettitt 1995, 33–34) that Levallois technology was specifically adapted to a mobile, cold climate, life-style. In this scenario, Levallois cores would be transported and used for the production of a

| | Early MIS 7 woodland | Late MIS 7 open grassland | Pontnewydd Intermediate complex | Pontnewydd Lower Breccia |
|---|---|---|---|---|
| **Herbivores** | | | | |
| Straight-tusked elephant | **** | **** | | |
| Horse | **** | **** | **** | **** |
| Red deer | **** | **** | | **** |
| Bovid (Bison or Aurochs) | **** | **** | | **** |
| Bison | **** | | | |
| Aurochs | **** | | | |
| Fallow deer | **** | | | |
| Woolly mammoth | | **** | | |
| Mammoth (Ilford type) | | **** | | |
| Merck's rhinoceros | | **** | | **** |
| Narrow-nosed rhinoceros | | **** | **** | **** |
| Woolly rhinoceros | | **** | | |
| Giant deer | | **** | | |
| Musk ox | | **** | | |
| Roe deer | | | **** | |
| Beaver | | | **** | |
| **Carnivores** | | | | |
| Spotted hyaena | | **** | | **** |
| Wolf | | **** | **** | **** |
| Bear | | **** | **** | **** |
| Lion | | **** | | |
| Leopard | | **** | **** | **** |
| **Small mammals** | | | | |
| Mole | **** | | | |
| Bank vole | **** | | | |
| Water vole | | | **** | |
| Wood mouse | **** | | **** | |
| White-toothed shrew | **** | | | |
| Collared lemming | | **** | | |
| Ground squirrel | | **** | | |
| Norway lemming | | **** | | **** |
| Northern vole (large) | | **** | | **** |
| Water vole | | | | **** |
| Narrow-skulled vole | | | **** | **** |
| Pika | | | | **** |

Sources: Currant 1984; Schreve 2001; Scott 2001. After Aldhouse-Green 2004.

*Table 13.10. The environments of the Early Neanderthal occupation of Britain. 250,000–200,000 BP. Mammalian remains from Pontnewydd Cave compared with early and late MIS 7 faunas.*

number of forms (including points, blades and flakes) as need arose. The patterning of populations in the Palaeolithic of the British Isles has recently been the subject of critical evaluation (Ashton and Lewis 2002; White *et al.* 2006). These authors, and others cited by them, have emphasized the archaeological richness of MIS 9 and have seen this as a modal period when population peaked. But any settlement continuing into MIS 6 was brought to an abrupt end by climatic deterioration probably followed by actual glaciation around 150,000 years ago. This glacial event brought settlement in Britain as a whole to an end until the return of the Neanderthals after 60,000 years BP (Currant and Jacobi 2001).

The evidence of context shows therefore that, MIS 7a assemblages typically contain a mixture of bifaces and Levallois technology. Pontnewydd seems to stand alone as a potentially mid MIS 7 site and its remote situation and relatively large size may reflect the accessibility of Britain at this time – through lowered sea level – to cold-adapted and wide-ranging hunting bands, exploiting the rich game of the mammoth steppe. Unlike many sites with Levallois technologies, the artefacts found at Pontnewydd, particularly the Levallois cores, are heavily curated, rather like those at Crayford. Wymer's suggestion (1999, 80) that Levallois technique is preferentially a product of flint-rich areas is clearly applicable to lithic-rich resources of all kinds, for the technique is well-represented in the flint-poor but lithics-rich assemblage at Pontnewydd Cave where raw materials were clearly in plentiful supply (Green 1984; Newcomer 1984).

Pontnewydd Cave is the only Welsh site of its period where fauna has been preserved (Table 13.10). Other high quality comparative environmental evidence comes from the bones of Ice Age animals preserved in the sediments of limestone caves in western Britain. The British evidence for this early period has been summarized by Schreve (2001) and can be compared with Pontnewydd Cave, where two successive debris flow layers – the Intermediate complex and the Lower Breccia – may correlate with the early (MIS 7c) and later (MIS 7a) parts of the MIS 7 interglacial. In the early part of MIS 7, the indications are of a woodland environment, evidenced by such species as roe deer, beaver and wood mouse. Species known only to inhabit woodland were present also in late MIS 7 assemblages and include, at Pontnewydd, Merck's rhinoceros. But, even so, the domination of open-country species in this later period is well illustrated by the presence of horse, as also by narrow-nosed rhinoceros, lemmings and the northern vole.

## Cave formation and decay

It would be unwise to be dogmatic about which earlier Palaeolithic caves might have been in synchronous use within an area of landscape. It would be even more incautious to seek to reconstruct the secular patterning of cave-use over the last million years. The problem is that caves both appear and disappear through erosion and are liable to dissolve *pari passu* with the bedrock. This process is well-seen at a site like Westbury Cave on Mendip (Andrews *et al.* 1999). Again, it is easy to see how very transient will be the life-cycles of caves like Hoyle's Mouth and Little Hoyle in Pembrokeshire, with roofs now located a mere three to four metres below the local plateau surfaces. Many standard texts exist on the processes of cave-formation and decay (*e.g.* Gillieson 1996) and it is necessary, here, to refer only to the broad principles involved in the context of their interaction with the human use of caves.

Caves are most commonly found in limestone where they are formed by the action of underground water, opening joints in the bedrock to become cave fissures and passages. In time, the water-table falls leaving the cave-system dry. In time also, valley formation, as a consequence of fluvial action, may intersect what were once underground systems, thereby exposing caves and consequentially rendering them accessible for human and animal use. But, at just the same time as the caves are formed, the processes that will eventually lead to their destruction are already beginning. These are many and varied but, as already noted one such is the progressive dissolution of the limestone bedrock from the top down as a result of the action of carbonic acid. Rates of dissolution vary regionally and over time. To set the context in the Elwy valley, the highest of the sites studied here is Cae Gronw, located close to the top of the Cefn Bryn ridge, at 111 m O.D., whilst Pontnewydd lies lower at 90 m O.D., and Cefn at 70 m O.D. Valley down-cutting of the order of 20 m would have been needed to expose Pontnewydd, but the sequence at Cefn – based on the chronostratigraphical and biostratigraphical evidence – seems no older than that at Pontnewydd. Accordingly, 40

m or more of down-cutting of the valley may have taken place before the human occupation took place.

In the case of Westbury Cave on southern Mendip, the limestone bedrock was lowered by 25 m in around a million years – a rate of 25 mm per 1,000 years, or 2.5 m every 100,000 years (Stanton 1999, 18). In the Manifold valley of the Peak District, the rate of downcutting has been estimated at 50–60 mm per 1,000 years, broadly equivalent to 5 m every 100,000 years (Atkinson and Rowe 1992, 693–694). Data produced long ago by Boyd Dawkins (1874, 70), for the dissolution of Chalk rock and Oolitic limestone, yielded rates of around 23 mm every 1,000 years or 2.3 m every 100,000 years. Accordingly, leaving aside all other processes, the life history of many caves will be relatively short, even on the timescale of the presence of *Homo* in Britain or Europe. Indeed, looking beyond caves, it is worth noting that most 'observable relief' will generally be destroyed over a timescale of one to ten million years (Atkinson and Rowe 1992, 703).

If the rates of limestone dissolution quoted above are applicable to the Elwy valley, it is likely that bedrock has been lowered locally by the order of perhaps five to ten metres since the time when the cave became a focus of human activity. This figure refers only to the loss of bedrock from the plateau surface above the cave. But there is another process taking place at the same time, namely the retreat of the cliff faces from which the caves open. Physical and chemical processes are involved here and these have led to the regression of the cliff faces and the consequential loss of the original entrance chambers where settlement may once have taken place. We believe that we can quantify the scale of this retreat at the New Entrance at Pontnewydd where, recession of the order of at least ten metres has taken place over the last 100,000–200,000 years. At the Main Entrance, recession of at least seven metres has taken place since the cave was first exposed by glacial diversion of the valley of the palaeo-Elwy (Embleton 1960). This diversion has no context earlier than MIS 8 (303,000–245,000 years ago) in north-east Wales. Even, if one took the wider picture and made the assumption that the earliest glaciation known in Wales – the Penfro dated to MIS 16/12 (620,000–430,000 years ago) – must have impacted on north-eastern Wales as well, recession of the cliff-faces can only have begun after the exposure of the caves (Bowen 2005, 157–158; Thomas 2005).

Accordingly, it is difficult to accept Currant's argument (this volume, chapter 8) that elements of both the Pontnewydd and Cefn faunas may be of MIS 9 age. The environmental context for the most rapid retreats of the cliff-faces is likely to have been the glacial events of MIS 8, 6 and 2 (*c.* 275,000; 150,000 and 20,000). Taking the oldest date of 275,000 gives the slowest rate of recession, a figure of 35 mm per 1,000 years or 3.5 m every 100,000 years. This is likely to be a minimum figure because, in both cases, unroofed, fragmentary and horizontally truncated lengths of former cave passage are preserved externally in what is now a sub-aerial context. Accordingly, the overall scale of retreat is likely to have been greater. The present

| Find no. | Species | Layer | RU age and error |
|---|---|---|---|
| F2853 | *Stephanorhinus* sp. | LB | 269 ± 25 |
| D2909 | *Stephanorhinus* sp. | LB | 206 ± 18 |
| D2312 | Unidentified tooth | LB | 214 ± 18 mean of the two best results |
| D358 | *Stephanorhinus* sp. | LB | 316 ± 26 middle result of three |
| D2121 | *Cervus elaphus* | LB | 231 ± 20 mean result of two |
| C286 | *Stephanorhinus kirchbergensis* | LB | 253 ± 22 best result of four |
| C189 | *Stephanorhinus* sp. | LB | 200 ± 18 mean result of four |
| C119 | *Stephanorhinus* sp. | LB | 212 ± 18 mean result of two |
| B440 | *Stephanorhinus* sp. | Undifferentiated breccia | 260 ± 23 mean of two dates |

Table 13.11. Simplified ESR Determinations. Main Cave. Note: the term 'best result' refers to the determination with the smallest error term.

| Find no. | Species | Layer | RU age and error |
|---|---|---|---|
| H428 | ?Bovid tooth | 24 | 143 ± 13 |
| H359 | *Stephanorhinus* sp. | 24 | 280 ± 26 |

Table 13.12. Simplified ESR Determinations. New Entrance.

entrance-chamber at the mouth of the Main Cave is now less than five metres in horizontal depth. Overall at least 7–10 m has been lost since the Neanderthal presence at Pontnewydd and, in consequence, the nature of the shelter afforded at the cave entrances is now unknowable as Collcutt rightly noted (Collcutt 1984, 75–76).

## ESR dating

ESR was selected to help with one particular problem, namely the age of the faunas in the Lower Breccia of the Main Cave and in the New Entrance. Nine samples from the Lower Breccia have yielded the results set out in Table 13.11. Of these results, no fewer than seven lie between 200,000 and 260,000 BP and lend broad support to the interpretation of Pontnewydd as an MIS 7 site. The two results from Layer 24 (Table 13.12) of the New Entrance are insufficient for detailed interpretation but seem compatible with those from the Main Cave.

## The story of the stalagmite

Repeated human recolonizations of the north-western area of Eurasia were made possible by a combination of factors which included human social structure, clothing, shelter, and effective hunting techniques. Stalagmite is a key to climate. Rates of growth in recent stalagmite in English caves have been quoted at between 0.009 and 0.261 mm/year or between 9 and 261 mm/1000 years (Baker and Smart 1995). Other data give figures as high as between 6.07 mm/year and 7.66 mm/year for fast-growing speleothems in two Yorkshire caves (Gillieson 1996, 123). The formation of strongly crystalline stalagmite, as typically found at Pontnewydd, is suggestive of a largely

undisturbed and closed cave-environment whereas weaker, microcrystalline stalagmites are more characteristic of open and draughty caves (ibid. 118–119). The most massive stalagmites at Pontnewydd are those in the Cross Rift and New Passage, but even the thickest – F375 at 420 mm – might have formed over a period as short as 1,500 years, or as long as 47,000 years, using the growth rates quoted from Baker and Smart (1995).

## The Main Cave

Dating of stalagmites (Table 13.13) demonstrates that both the spatial configuration and scale of stalagmite-formation were quite different in MIS 7 and MIS 5. Thus, MIS 7 stalagmites, although forming areas of floor, are both discontinuous and relatively thin: they are to be found particularly in the East Passage, where dated to 224,000+41,000/–31,000 BP (D1288), and again in the Main Passage on the south wall of the cave, with an age of 217,000+24,000/–20,000 BP (B274).

A later phase of stalagmitic growth early in MIS 6 is attested by a nearly *in situ* boss (C0) in the South Passage, dated to 177,000±12,000 BP. Massive growth took place in the Cross Rift during MIS 5, which includes the Last Interglacial. Thereafter, in the absence of obvious biostratigraphic inputs of MIS 5 or 4, only small bosses and pillars seemed to have formed on the surface of the Lower Breccia. Of these, D642 with an age of 83,000±9,000 BP is typical. It is possible to argue, therefore, that a plug of Lower Breccia may have largely or totally blocked the entrance(s) to the cave from the time of the input of this debris flow until some point in the Middle Devensian. Moreover, it is possible to demonstrate that a situation when the cave was actually sealed obtained during the early Devensian, from 96,000 to 89,000 BP, plausibly MIS sub-stage 5c (Schwarcz 1984, 93–94).

The contexts of stalagmite-formation in the cave are complex in detail and the different episodes of speleothem formation, here numbered I–V, are reviewed in Table 13.13. Number I is the oldest and V the youngest, but the system is not necessarily sequential. There are two levels of major

| Name of stalagmite formation | Ref. no. | Selected dated samples | Location | Comment |
|---|---|---|---|---|
| Stalagmite lithozone | Ia | 217,000 BP (B274)<br>224,000 BP (D1288)<br>227,000 BP (D534:2) | East Passage | MIS 7 formations on Lower Breccia |
| Stalagmite lithozone | Ib | 197,000 BP (F296) | N wall of Area F | Stalagmite A |
| Stalagmite lithozone | Ic | 100,000 BP (F1058)<br>237,000 BP (F4894) | N wall of Area F | Stalagmite B |
| Stalagmite lithozone | Id | 177,000 BP (C0) | South Passage | MIS 6 isolated bosses |
| Stalagmite lithozone | Ie | 134,000 BP (F5417) | I2 NE | MIS 5 formations on Lower Breccia |
| Re-worked stalagmite from 'stalagmite lithozone' | If | 209,000 BP (B148)<br>179,000 BP (B262)<br>160,000 BP (D291)<br>126,000 BP (F375) base<br>122,000 BP (D6058)<br>99,000 BP (F375) top<br>83,000 BP (D642) | | Found in the Upper Breccia and in the New Entrance sequence |
| High Level stalagmite | II | 137,000 BP (D5901)<br>116,000 BP (D4698) | | |
| *In situ* stalagmite New Entrance | III | 91,000 BP (H3202)<br>83,000 BP (H3221) | | H3202 flowstone on bedrock<br>H3221 stalagmitic floor |
| Re-worked stalagmite New Entrance | IV | 218,000 BP (H2217)<br>132,000 BP (H1713)<br>83,000 BP (H3211) | | |
| External stalagmite Main Cave | V | 36,000 and 66,000 BP (A517) | Cemented onto external north wall of cave | |
| Laminated travertine | V | 13,000, 15,000 and 32,000 BP (D188) | | *In situ* |

*Table 13.13. Stalagmite formations and contexts.*

stalagmite formation in the Main Cave, both defined by Collcutt (1984):

- *The Stalagmite lithozone* formed on the surface of the Lower Breccia, thereby providing a minimum age for the underlying archaeological and hominin finds,
- the *Laminated Travertine*, formed on the surface of the Upper Clays and Sands, and probably of Holocene age.

*The Stalagmite lithozone*

This stalagmite formed on the surface of the Lower Breccia, in localized areas of the cave, from around 225,000 (phase Ia). There was some limited MIS 6 growth (Id). Growth during MIS 5, however, was on a much more massive scale, and was concentrated in the Cross Rift (Figure 6.8). A variety of processes, however, broke up even the thickest stalagmites, particularly in the Cross Rift and New Passage (If), facilitating in some cases their movement by the debris flow activity which was integral to the Upper Breccia event. Located on the north wall of the East Passage, close to the point where it emerges into the Cross Rift, is a stalagmitic floor (Ib) given the name 'Stal A' (Figure 6.16). The remarkable thing, obvious to all who viewed it in the field, was that – like a jigsaw puzzle – Stal A was clearly once part of a once contiguous floor (named 'Stal B') now lying 180 mm below the wall-stalagmite. Floor B (Ic) was heavily cracked and so may have fallen. It was possibly hanging before it fell, having been undercut by fluvial action. An alternative scenario would see the slumping of the floor as arising from dissolution of the bedrock floor of the cave (D. Case, pers. comm.). Other factors may have contributed; namely earthquake or landslide.

The evidence just quoted may be seen as part of a process (of Devensian age) of massive disruption, including faulting, of the East Passage MIS 5 floor combined with cracking of flowstone formations on the eastern roof of the Cross Rift. In South Wales, specifically at Hound's Hole on the Gower coast, just such a violent event caused a stalagmitic pillar to break and to lose its central part (Aldhouse-Green 2000, 10–13). Uranium-series determinations there suggest a *terminus post quem* of 85,000±10,000 BP. There is evidence, also, from Kent's Cavern, Devon that is suggestive of a severe earthquake event falling within the timespan 115,000–74,000 BP (Straw 1995, 202; 1996, 23). These 'evidences' may, indeed, all form part of earlier Devensian Pleistocene seismic activity that took place over a wide area of Britain

| Layer | Sample | Method | Ref. no. | Result |
|---|---|---|---|---|
| 50 | Derived stal. | TL | H1724 | 154,000 ± 36,000 BP |
| 50 | Derived stal. | TL | H1725 | 130,000 ± 29,000 BP |
| 20 | Cervid calcaneum | C14 | H231 | 27,070 ± 360 BP |
| 20 | Derived stal. | U-series | H3211 | 83,000 ± 3,000 BP |
| 26 | Burnt flint | TL | H598 | 179,000 ± 22,000 BP |
| 26 | Burnt stone | TL | H2312 | 214,000 ± 21,000 BP |
| 28 | Burnt flint | TL | H1036 | 173,000 ± 20,000 BP |
| [b] of core = ?29 | Derived stal. from core | U-series | H2216 | 229,000 ± 22,000 BP |
| 31 | Derived stal. | U-series | H3096 | 97,000 ± 7,000 BP |
| 31 | Derived stal. | TL | H1713 | 101,000 ± 25,000 BP |
| | | U-series | | 132,000 ± 8,000 BP |
| [e] of core = ?38 | Derived stal. from core B | U-series | H2217 | 224,000 ± 21,000 BP |
| 39 | Derived stal. | U-series | H3150 | 226,000 ± 21,000 BP |
| 42 | *In situ* stal. | U-series | H3202 | 91,000 ± 7,000 BP |
| 43 | *In situ* stal. | U-series | H3221 | 85,000 ± 9,000 BP |

*Table 13.14. Simplified New Entrance dates.*

from Devon to Derbyshire. The absence, at Hound's Hole, both of fauna and microfauna from the destruction layer associated with the broken pillar may suggest a rapid event, such as an earthquake (Ford 1997) or perhaps massive vibration caused by a landslip.

### Stalagmite II

This category (II) pertains to just two high level stalagmites, each of broadly Last Interglacial age (116,000 BP for D4698 and 137,000 BP in respect of D5901). These must have formed part of the same event as the MIS 5 growth of stalagmite in the Cross Rift but sit now, 'hanging' and cemented to the cave-wall, located respectively at 1.05 m (base of stalagmite 100.60 S.D.) and at 1.00 m (base of stalagmite at 100.50 S.D.) above the level where other contemporary stalagmite was forming on the surface of the Lower Breccia (Figure 6.9). Although seemingly anomalous, these speleothems probably formed on the surface of small patches of sediment stuck to the cave-wall. It may, indeed be more meaningful to view these formations as a part of the roof stalagmite which is present over a large area of the roof of the cave.

Stalagmite continued to form, at Pontnewydd, after MIS 5c but the intermittent filling of the cave with water – a process which led to the formation of the Silt beds – resulted in the formation of three or four lenses of 'proto-stalagmite' within the latter deposit. Plausibly, although impossible to demonstrate, these lenses of proto-stalagmite may be coeval with the *in situ* stalagmite preserved on the external north wall of the cave. The latter is likely to be of MIS 3 age, but the two results from it, of 36,000 and 67,000 BP, do not admit of a precise answer.

### The New Entrance

The relatively few U-series and TL dates on stalagmite from the New Entrance make interpretation difficult. The best approach is probably to include the three dates on burnt

flint, and the ESR dates on bone, and to assess the results from a stratigraphic perspective (Tables 13.12 and 13.14). It is clear that the archaeological and faunal contents of Layer 26 and below are coeval with the Lower Breccia, even if the *in situ* stalagmite dates suggest a complex history.

### Life of – and in – a cave

In tandem with the decay of the bedrock, sedimentary processes within caves lead to their progressive filling up (so that a once lofty cavern may become a small cave) or to their opening up (where the converse is true). In the excavation of archaeological cave sequences, recurring issues are the size of the entrance at any particular time and the accessibility of the cave. The possibility of the cave entrances being repeatedly blocked with natural plugs of debris flow is material to our understanding of the history of human and animal presences at Pontnewydd: thus, the height of an opening will affect the extent of the daylight entrance zone within a cave and, therefore, the potential space available for human activities for which daylight is preferred or essential. In contrast, darkness may have been preferred for some activities. These may have included sex, ritual, mortuary practices, expeditions underground to locate carnivores (hibernating or dead) who might be exploited for their skins and, maybe, *perigrinationes in tenebras amoris causa* (speleology for the fun of it).

The evidence for temperature and humidity, and for the generation of light and heat in caves, has been surveyed by Branigan and Dearne (1992, 8–12). Their results, based on data from Robin Hood Cave, Creswell Crags, and Poole's Cavern, Buxton, indicated that summer occupations were cold and damp whereas winter occupations were warm and dry. Experimental fires were lit in Robin Hood Cave in July and in December, located in both cases near the entrance and at the rear of the cave. The latter produced thick black smoke which filled the cave for seven hours. But whilst the fire near the entrance produced enough smoke in summer to make the cave uncomfortable for use after half an hour, there was little problem in winter. The location of the fire, fuel selected, shape and size of cave, and airflow regime were all important, but – if it is safe to generalize from such limited data – caves may have been most suited to winter use. A prediction follows from this, namely that to give maximum protection from cold north and east winds, and to gain maximum winter sunlight, preferred caves in the northern hemisphere will have been those orientated South to West.

## What the animals tell us

### The Middle Pleistocene faunas

Different animals (including humans) use caves in different ways.

*Hominins* use caves as landmarks and for shelter, warmth and raw materials; possibly also as a water supply. Food for cooking is brought to the site, stored, processed and cooked in separate areas. Acts of ritual may take place, including funerary ritual.

*Bears* use caves primarily for hibernation and for the raising of their young. Deaths may occur and the smell of rotting bear corpses may attract other carnivores. Bears do not introduce food to the site.

*Hyaenas* are virtually absent from Pontnewydd but are included here to be able to pose the question of their absence. Hyaenas present a totally different picture: food is brought to the site; cave-mouths and side-passages find favour as eating areas, plus some use for defecation (but, more usually, hyaenas will walk 20 m or more from the den before voiding their coprolites). Small caves, and awkward side passages of larger caves, are particularly liked by young hyaenas as places to 'scoff' food without challenge whilst the main chambers are used for denning. Hyaenas are largely nocturnal and so spend many of the hours of each day 'holed up' in the den and the young do not leave the den until they are 8 months old.

*Male wolves* deliver food to caves for the use of she-wolves in raising cubs. Wolves dislike treading in excrement and, accordingly their lairs are divided into three zones – activity, traffic and defecation. Lairs are normally occupied only in spring and early summer *and* in alternate years, because of smells. Wolves are not nocturnal species and the young stay only a short time in the den.

*Lions* are not common at Pontnewydd but where they had incorporated humans into their diet, they found them remarkably tasty (Andrews and Jalvo 1997, 214). A lion can eat between 18 and 30 kg of meat – or one human – at one sitting. Moreover, they frequently travel distances of up to half a kilometre in order to consume or cache their prey free from disturbance. A cave would be useful in this regard. However, it must be noted that a commonly cited example of lions caching human remains in caves (Patterson 1907, 155) has been convincingly reinterpreted as historical agro-pastoralist burial practice (Patterson 2004; Kusimba and Kusimba 2000).

We cannot, at present, extract the full story from the Lower Breccia at Pontnewydd but we can but flag up some questions and attempt some answers. Pontnewydd stands virtually alone as an MIS 7 cave on mainland Britain and it is, therefore, 'entitled' to be different. It is worth however seeking other sites of this broad period. The most obvious of these is Cefn but other caves, notably Kent's Cavern and Banwell Bone Cave, contribute to this story, Banwell in having leopard remains contemporary with those of Pontnewydd. Four bones from the Main Cave at Pontnewydd display certain or possible cut-marks or other human modification: horse, bear and cervid (Table 10.2). In the case of the bear, the cut-marks relate to the process of skinning and plausibly, therefore, to the exploitation of furs for clothing or other purposes. By contrast, the horse cut-marks arose from the filleting of horse-meat and clearly establishes Pontnewydd's status as a Palaeolithic source of *viande de cheval*. A cut-marked cervid tooth is suggestive of the removal of a delicacy such as the tongue. There is also a charred horse bone from a context probably (but not demonstrably) of Middle Pleistocene age. A single cut-marked bear tooth from the Upper Breccia presents the only plausible evidence for a Devensian human presence at Pontnewydd.

### Upper Pleistocene faunas

The fauna from the Upper Breccia at Pontnewydd is composed of the typical elements of MIS 3 faunas as identified by Currant and Jacobi (2001). It is distinctive however, in that it lacks the usually common spotted hyaena and, instead, the wolf, *Canis lupus* is present. There is also a significantly high frequency of the remains of bears from the deposit, which may reflect the use of the cave for hibernation. The total absence of hyaenas seems surprising given their role in accumulating bones in British Pleistocene caves, including locally in the Elwy valley at Cefn in the 35,000–32,000 years ago time range. However, behavioural arguments seem likely to be of relevance for it is well known that hyaenas both prefer smaller low-ceilinged caves and also use different parts of caves for different purposes (Pettitt 1997, 218; Mussi 2001, 150). Thus, cave-mouths and side-passages find favour as defecation and eating areas, whereas the main chamber(s) are used for denning. In the local context, both Pontnewydd and Cefn are relatively large caves. The same size factor may explain the rarity of hyaenas also in the frequently spacious caves of the Dordogne and Israel (Stringer and Gamble 1993, 159–160).

But chronology may be important here for Pettitt and colleagues (chapter 11, this volume) suggest that, in the later 30,000s, hyaena populations were thinning out. The evidence from Paviland is certainly in accord with this (Aldhouse-Green 2000, 232) and one sees, also, something similar in the mosaic patterning of the extinction of the Welsh wolf population in historic times: here, the distribution of *blaidd* place-names suggests marginalization to the uplands of central Wales before final extinction. But, it is not, I think mere happenstance that has led wolves,

| Species | | Comments |
|---|---|---|
| *Canis lupus* | wolf | $^{14}$C 28,500 BP; interpreted as prime accumulator |
| *Ursus arctos* | brown bear | $^{14}$C 29,000 & 26,000 BP; commonest species |
| *Vulpes vulpes* | red fox | $^{14}$C 28,500 BP |
| *Equus ferus* | horse | $^{14}$C 35,500 BP |
| *Coelodonta antiquitatis* | woolly rhino | $^{14}$C 33,000 BP; rare |
| *Rangifer tarandus* | reindeer | $^{14}$C 29,000 BP |
| *Ovibos moschatus* | musk ox | Rare |
| *Dicrostonyx torquatus* | collared lemming | |
| *Lemmus lemmus* | Norway lemming | |
| *Lepus* cf. *timidus* | Arctic hare | $^{14}$C 33,000 BP |

*Table 13.15. Upper Breccia fauna with characteristic UB preservation type.*

along paths no longer visited by hyaenas, to Pontnewydd Cave; the absence of competition was very helpful but the wolves knew a wolf cave (*ogof-y-blaidd*) when they encountered it. Thus, the Lupercal was a cave at the foot of the Palatine Hill in Rome where, according to legend, a she-wolf (Latin *lupa*) suckled the human twins, Romulus and Remus. It is also famous for its mention in Shakespeare's play *Julius Caesar* (iii.2):

> *you all did see that on the Lupercal*
> *I thrice presented him a kingly crown*
> *which he did thrice refuse*

Romulus became the legendary founder of Rome in 753 BC. The story may be a myth but the detail – bringing together the elements of a cave located at the *foot* of the hill *and* the use of the *cave* by a *female wolf* for raising her *dependent young* – is very accurate. If we look even further back, to Troy, we find in Homer's *Iliad* (*e.g.* I.4–5) that the role of canids and birds of prey in devouring the bodies of the slain was well-known to the ancient Greeks and work at Chauvet cave shows that most carnivores visit caves to search for carrion (Clottes 2003).

On the taphonomic front, one must remember that all of the original accumulations of bones have been shunted longitudinally into the cave-system by the action of debris flows. Reference to the model provided by the cave of Lunel-Viel in the Hérault may be of value here. Reinterpretation of the original excavation data has shown that there were two occupations: a human presence at the cave mouth and a hyaena den within the darkness zone fully ten metres into the system. It is by no means beyond the bounds of possibility that there may have been phases of activity by hyaenas at Pontnewydd, but evidenced only by remains which exist much deeper into the cave-system than the areas recently explored by excavation, a suggestion that has at least the merit of being testable by excavation. Excavation of the narrow side-passages at Pontnewydd, named the South Passage and the South-East Fissure, did not, however, yield either hyaena remains or evidence of hyaena activity.

The Devensian radiocarbon results are intriguing (Table 13.15). Red fox is common, particularly so in the 28,000–25,000 BP range. This is precisely where the geese and the ducks appear. The large number of hares

represented both as bones and as radiocarbon samples, may also have been accumulated by foxes. Stable isotope analysis (chapters 11 and 12) has proved useful in providing a means of confirming species identifications of often very fragmentary material. It has also demonstrated the likelihoods both of bears fishing for young sea-trout in the palaeo-Elwy and, also of foxes feasting on ducks and geese. The presences of bears from 40,000 to 26,000 BP, and of wolves from 29,000 to 24,000 BP, seem at face value to be largely complementary but, in reality, are illusory, for targeted taphonomic study by Kate Scott has identified reindeer bones with characteristic wolf modification at 30,240, 39,600 and 41,400 BP (Table 8.4). Bear-remains are unlikely to have accumulated at the site in any other context than hibernation, which implies that the cave was accessible. However, the woolly rhinoceros, horse and reindeer require a different explanation, that of accumulation by strong and powerful carnivores. These species would make an ideal three course meal for hyaenas, but the positive evidence of bone modification identifies denning she-wolves as the most likely agent (Currant 1984, 78) and Scott (chapter 8, this volume). One spin-off from the radiocarbon dating programmes for Paviland and Pontnewydd (Pettitt *et al.* chapter 11, this volume) has been the recognition of the marked contrast between herbivore/omnivore faunas of Gravettian age at the two sites. At Pontnewydd we have bear, birds, cervids and reindeer and at Paviland mammoth and bovid. These recall the importance of megaherbivores in Gravettian funerary ritual and suggest that the functions of the two caves at this time may have been very different.

Caves are sites that may have multiple functions. Thus, they may act as shelters or way-markers on long journeys. Again, caves are places where 'time elapsed is not time gone, but time accumulated' (Frame 2010, 225) and where the build-up of archaeological deposits may provide a record of the pattern of human presences. Such records are capable of interrogation and, so, of interpretation. In this early period, they may provide information on changing patterns of behaviour involving the use of caves and *abris* as natural shelters; the use of caves as receptacles for the bodies of the dead (so testifying to the world's earliest mortuary practices); and the use of caves for ritual practices.

|                              | *°C* | *Latitude* |
|------------------------------|------|------------|
| Pontnewydd Cave              | 10   | 53° N      |
| Kent's Cavern, Devon         | 11   | 50° N      |
| Arcy-sur-Cure (Grande Grotte)| 12   | 47° N      |
| Sima de los Huesos, Atapuerca| 13   | 42° N      |

*Table 13.16. Cave temperatures and latitude.*

## Cave use by primates and hominins

Reasons suggested for cave use by primates include security, shelter from bad weather, and access both to edible minerals and to water supply. A four year study of chacma baboons in the De Hoop Nature Reserve in South Africa involved monitoring their use of one particular cave known as Dronkvlei (Barrett *et al.* 2004, 215). The site lay at latitude 34° South, in a locality where the weather is hot and dry in summer and cold and wet in winter. The cave lacked sources of food or water and no correlation could be seen between the pattern of use of the cave and potential external risks from predators. Indeed, the cave was used in spite of the presence there of a Cape cobra which had killed two of the baboon troop.

The cave is accessed by means of a vertical shaft 5 m deep: at its base, lies a totally dark horizontal passage which runs for 40 m before it opens out into a large cavern 30 m in length. The baboons occupied sleeping areas – or more precisely sex, grooming and resting places in the inner cavern and, so, travelled some distance underground to reach these in complete darkness. How do we explain the use of this dark and dangerous cave? The answer seems to lie in thermoregulation, for heavier use of the cave in colder months demonstrated that keeping warm was a significant factor. The baboons clearly took advantage of the stable environment within the cave, normally within a degree of 17.5° C over any 24 hour period. At night, the temperature might be 5° C higher inside than outside the cave. We do not yet know what the thermo-neutrality watershed – the temperature where shivering starts – is for baboons but in the case of lightly clad humans, the optimum ambient temperature is 25° C and shivering starts at 13° C. Interestingly, it was more or less this figure that was 'retrodicted' in respect of the climate that the 1,500,000 year old *Homo erectus* skeleton known as the 'Turkana boy' would have would have experienced during life (Walker and Shipman 1996, 161). At Pontnewydd Cave, situated at a latitude of just over 53° N, the present-day temperature scarcely varies inside the cave, whether night or day or all year round, from a constant 10° C. In the winter, the cave seems delightfully warm. In the summer, the cave is cool – even cold – on a hot day. At any time of the year – even, indeed, when snow is lying on the ground – the west-facing mouth of the cave forms a natural sun-trap. Further to the south, at 50° N, we may note a constant temperature of 11° C for the show cave of Kent's Cavern (Anon. 2003, 18). At the Grande Grotte of Arcy-sur-Cure, situated in Burgundy at 47° N, a constant temperature of 12° C has been reported. The Sima de los Huesos deep underground

in northern Spain at 42° N achieves a constant temperature of 13° C (Table 13.16).

A study of the benefits of cave-use would require a study of caves, comprehensive but taken site by site, in order to evaluate the potential of the unique situation of each. But, as a generalization, it is probably fair to say that caves in Europe *selected* for settlement will generally have faced between south and west and, so, will have afforded maximum winter insolation and protection from cold winds. The movement of the sun shows differences which vary both according to latitude and time. In mid-summer the sun moves daily north-east to north-west from sunrise to sunset but, in mid-winter, movement from sunrise to sunset is from south-east to south-west. It has been a commonplace of the literature that south and west-facing caves in more northerly latitudes were favoured for occupation by Palaeolithic people. The selection of a cave with a southern or western aspect had clear gains in exposure to light and warmth of the sun and in shelter from cold northern and eastern winds. The discussion which follows draws upon a number of surveys and examines evidence both from European and local perspectives in the context of the study of cave and den use by primates and mammals.

Cave-use in far northern latitudes was studied some 40 years ago by the archaeologist, Lewis Binford, when he lived with the Nunamiut of inland North Alaska. These people were still hunters at that time and some 80% of their diet consisted of caribou. A number of key points emerged from Binford's study (1978, 489–490). First that caves in this region tend to be located in side valleys, but it was pointless for the local people to 'hole up' in these places and wait for the game to walk by because the animals knew that the hunters were camped in the caves and simply kept away. Second, wolves were reported by the Eskimo informants as preferring caves situated low down with easy access to the valley floor (Binford 1981, 198). Were this rubric to be applied to the Elwy valley caves, then Pontnewydd would emerge as a far more suitable wolf cave than Cefn. Third, the caves were of limited use in this region, because their positioning meant that they were far from the source of firewood provided by the trees which grew in the main river valleys. Fourth, the value of caves to the Nunamiut lay in their use as natural shelters which meant that the hunters did not need to transport tents when on expeditions. Thus, they were useful for well organized trapping and hunting parties which repeatedly used the same caves during particular seasons or for hunting particular species of game. In consequence, cave occupations tended to be small-scale but regularly repeated over long periods of time. Caves were the sites of transient camps, but were not used for long-term residential use.

At the open-air site of Hoxne, Suffolk, both artefacts and bone cease abruptly to one side of a north-east to south-west line which once probably marked the edge of the ancient Lake Hoxne. The settlement would, therefore, have been located on a broadly south-east facing shoreline (Wymer and Singer 1993, 119). In Brittany a range of open-air sites in different topographical situations has been recorded.

Three categories of Lower and Middle Palaeolithic sites were recognized by Monnier (1982), based upon analysis of data from 82 sites. These included, first, completely open sites (22%); second, open sites located very close to natural rock-shelters formed by boulders or cliffs (38%); and, third, true rock-shelters formed by marine cliffs (40%). Certain key characteristics for these sites were noted:

- Proximity to running water or springs (80%),
- vantage point (63%),
- situation adjacent to modern estuaries (25%), possibly reflecting their use as penetration routes for colonizing territories inland,
- rare inland sites (17%), mostly MTA, were located variously on plateaux (Bois-du-Rocher and Clos-Rouge) or on the sloping sides of valleys (Kervouster).

Consideration of the situation and aspect of Breton Lower and Middle Palaeolithic sites reveals some evidence of patterning. Thus, 29% of sites of pre-Last Interglacial age occur in totally open situations, compared with only 9% of Last Glacial Mousterian sites. Again, 53% of Last Glaciation Mousterian sites are undoubted rock-shelters, compared with 38% of the pre-Last Interglacial sites. Most other sites, respectively 33% and 38%, are sites that were open, but situated in close proximity to the shelter of cliffs or large boulders. Sites in such open positions were presumably selected for the degree of insolation and shelter that they afforded from cold east and north winds. All sites taken together display a modal south-western orientation, and none falls out of the south–south-east to west range. The orientation of rock-shelters was, of course, fixed, but we may note the following:

- Early rock-shelter sites in south-east to west range – observed frequency 75%; expected frequency 50%,
- Last Glaciation rock-shelter sites in south-east to west range – observed frequency 58%; expected frequency 43%,
- Lower and Middle Palaeolithic rock-shelters (including both Early and Last Glaciation sites) with an aspect in the range west to east-north-east, and so facing into potentially chill winds, total 21% against an expected frequency of 50%.

From these data we may infer a high degree of site-selection.

The region of the Caucasus is well known for its early open site of Dmanisi at *c.* 1,600,000 years ago. Many early Acheulian open air sites occur in this region at typical altitudes of between 1,500 and 2,500 m above present-day mean sea level (msl). Bifaces occur at these open air settlements. The earliest cave-use appears much later in the Middle Pleistocene, where the earliest sites have been described as Acheulian and currently date from *c.* 600,000–500,000 years ago. The caves involved are Azykh, Kudaro I, Kudaro III, Tsona, Akhshtyr and Treugol'naya (Doronichev 2000). Pollen analysis suggests between five and ten oscillations of climate at Azykh, Kudaro I and

Kudaro III. The use of fire is also part of the local story of cave-use. Thus, 'hearths' are recorded at Azykh in Acheulian levels, with layers of ash, the largest 10 m$^2$ by 0.26 m in thickness, reported from some sites. 'Hearths' are described also at Kudaro III (bed 5) and charcoal has been found in two levels of both Kudaro I and III. It is possible, of course, that these combustion events do not represent residues from sustained cave-occupations but, rather, arise from the use of fire to attack and drive off carnivores using caves as dens and, thereby, to deprive them of their kills (Boaz and Ciochon 2004, 120). Here, it is important to note that a 'wide spectrum of altitudinal belts' offered a correspondingly wide variety of game with, overall, more than 40 prey species known from the Acheulian levels of the caves and, even, from Kudaro I and III, possible evidence of fishing.

## Habitat preference: Pontnewydd or Cefn?

We have seen (Currant chapter 8, this volume) that a case can be made for the human occupation of Pontnewydd belonging to MIS 9, perhaps even MIS 11, rather than to MIS 7 as we have previously argued. The arguments hinge upon several notions, namely: that the Intermediate/Lower Breccia sequence in Pontnewydd is inverted, with the Lower Breccia originally predating the Intermediate but emplaced in reverse stratigraphic order and that the 'cave bear' fauna of the Lower Breccia should be of at least MIS 9 age, noting particularly the occurance at Cefn Caves of a macaque tooth which should be MIS 9 or older in age on the basis of British biostratigraphy. It is important to keep in view, however, the fact that the macaque tooth was stratified within early nineteenth century backfill. In later Victorian times, the cave became a sort of side show from whose 'tenebrous halls' a monster might emerge. This horror was later shown to be the corpse of a crocodile which had been sold off by a passing circus (Walker chapter 2, this volume). The first reaction of my very percipient late colleague, George Boon, on learning of the macaque was to suspect 'monkey business'. But the context of the tooth suggests that it is free of such taint.

The evidence from Pontnewydd is important because it demonstrates cave use by Middle Pleistocene hominins in Britain certainly by MIS 7, if not earlier. Pontnewydd is not, of course, the earliest such site and both Westbury Cave and Kent's Cavern present evidence of much earlier human presences either in or very close to these sites (Cook and Jacobi 1998; Andrews *et al.* 1999). MIS 11, however, presents no certain evidence of cave use. Indeed, all sites of this period seem to have been open sites located on river-edges rather than settlements on lake margins, or caves. The suggestion has been made (Ashton *et al.* 2005) that these may relate to the use of rivers as routes through areas of dense forest.

But why did the hunters occupy Pontnewydd and seemingly not other caves in the Elwy valley? Here, Pontnewydd provides a useful case study. The Main Cave faces due west and its often sunny entrance looks directly across and down into the valley, only 300 m wide at the level of the cave. The valley floor, at 40 m O.D, now lies *c.* 50 m below. However, it is possible that the palaeo-Elwy may have flowed closer to the level of the cave at the time of the Middle Pleistocene occupation (Embleton 1984, 29). It would seem unlikely, however, that it was ever much higher than 30 m above its present level during Stage 7 for, if it had been, the Middle Pleistocene depositional sequence of Cefn Cave, in many respects comparable to that of Pontnewydd, could not have formed (Green and Walker 1991, 44–47).

The Cefn cave-system, 700 m downstream, is much larger than Pontnewydd and would seem to afford a more spacious and comfortable residence. But there is no evidence of such use by hominins until 12,000 years ago (Figure 2.4). Later still, radiocarbon dates on unstratified human remains offer ages of 2,835±60 BP (OxA-6233) and 1,445±60 BP (OxA-6234) and clearly refer to Bronze Age and early medieval events. The main Cefn Cave is located halfway up a cliff which rises precipitously from the valley floor, now 35 m below. But, even so, the cave was clearly just as accessible in the Middle Pleistocene as now, as its use by hibernating bears attests. Yet, shelter alone was clearly not a sufficient reason for the use of Cefn by hominins. What Pontnewydd possessed and Cefn lacked were plentiful supplies of raw material for use in artefact manufacture, and easy access to the valley floor to intercept game (Aldhouse-Green 2001). This may tell us that Pontnewydd was a favoured place whereas Cefn was not. Certainly, the petrology of the Pontnewydd artefacts (Bevins 1984) shows that the raw materials recovered from the basal deposits of the cave precisely mirror the range of rocks used in the manufacture of the stone tools recovered from the Breccias (Green 1988; Aldhouse-Green 1998). It may be, therefore, that the availability of these rocks at Pontnewydd was a factor in its becoming a cyclically reoccupied or 'persistent place' (*sensu* Barton *et al.* 1995, 109–11).

The site of Pontnewydd Cave and its immediate surroundings had much to offer. It was a potential source of raw materials for stone tool manufacture. It lay adjacent to, or above, a river which could have provided a water supply both for humans and for prey animals. The river valley could have afforded a migration route for herbivores, but also probably had sources of raw material exposed in eroded river banks and additional caves and rock shelters to provide shelter along parts of its margins. The cave itself was both a shelter and a landmark, a place easily identified in the contemporary landscape, and so a readily identifiable goal as an overnight stop, rendezvous or quarry site. As a camp site, the rock walls offered shelter from the wind and the recovery of numerous burnt artefacts shows that encampment at the site was accompanied by the lighting of fires (although whether for security, cooking or warmth we cannot say). Perhaps, too, the cave was a place of mystery or fear or, even, just a convenient place to dispose of the dead.

So, we see a world where early Neanderthals – who had by now quietly developed brain insulation systems through their large noses and sinuses – were able to extend their ranges on the cold but game-rich steppes of northern Europe. That was how they reached Pontnewydd. If you live in a time of night cold and if, too, you're moving around a lot, then a cave becomes a 'des. res.', a place of choice. But caves are very different spaces from chimpanzee nests or 'centrifugal living spaces'. You can identify with your childhood cave. Perhaps – and perhaps for the first time – they offer a 'sense of place'. There is a word for this 'topophilia', meaning 'love of place'. Kolen (1999), in his brilliant study of 'hominids without homes' erects this concept, only to dismiss it. I think we do so at our peril. The late Gerald Durrell observed how animals captured for overseas zoos would remain in their cages, even at times when they could easily have escaped. Fear of the unknown strengthens even the most unlikely bonds. Perhaps, for this reason, the emotionally ambiguous idea of 'a sense of place' may provide a useful concept.

There is little published data available on the characterization of caves, rock-shelters and open-air sites as a basis for determining patterns of choice and variability of use. Relevant variables would include the precise situation of the site in relation to positioning in valleys, with particular reference to relative height, orientation, valley size and depth. It is important also to study archaeological caves in the full regional context of sites selected for intensive use, used to a lesser extent, or perhaps not at all. In this process, account has to be taken of sedimentological inputs (and removals) leading to changing floor levels and roof heights. Seemingly rich sites, in terms of the number of artefacts accumulated, may simply be sites where this acccumulation has taken place over a long period of time. Jacobi (2004) has demonstrated just such a scenario in the case of Gough's Cave, Cheddar. Sites of all types may preserve artefacts and distinctive stone tool-types serve as both as 'chronoliths' (time-based lithic forms) and as 'choraliths' (regionally varying lithic types). These *Gestalt* switches may suggest procurement strategies or map patterns of movement over time, with the identification of raw materials reflecting the geographical scale of that movement.

I have pursued here some of the intrinsic problems that the use of caves would have presented to their hominin users. Caves were only available in limited areas and, even then, may not have been accessible (depending on the precise state of cave-evolution/devolution and infill/erosion of cave sediments). They would have differing orientation(s) of cave entrance(s) which meant that individual caves might be preferentially used for settlement, burial, ritual *etc*; but these rules of thumb would not necessarily apply if caves were in short supply. The caves at Cefn have provided us with no clues for an earlier human use than that indicated by the Late Upper Palaeolithic flint blades found there. It is reasonable to suppose that Cefn was at least visited by our early Neanderthals but their visits were perhaps brief and no evidence survives of their presence. It would seem therefore, that it was Pontnewydd that was the special place that remained in the Neanderthal memory.

# Epilogue – The Glass Island

## Stephen Aldhouse-Green and Elizabeth A. Walker

*The Glass Island* is the title of a collection of poetry, remarkable for its imagery and sense of place, written by the poet Gladys Mary Coles, whom we met in the Prologue. The poems deal with the two themes of 'finds' and 'journeys'. As archaeologists, we are concerned with both. Thus, handaxes went on journeys as part of the picnic sets of their day, or they may have travelled – perhaps entering caves like Coygan – in the pockets of hyaena 'take-aways'. Perhaps too, they became lost or discarded, and became the subjects of further journeys. During these last journeys, they may have been encased in ice or, perhaps, hitched a ride as a clast in outwash gravel. When Stephen first joined the staff of the National Museum of Wales in 1976, only one handaxe open-air find had been published from Wales. Now, no fewer than eleven are known from the southern Welsh littoral, including two finds that are just over the border into England. The finds have been published by a variety of people, including A. D. Lacaille, Stephen Aldhouse-Green, and John Wymer. The traditional model of earlier Palaeolithic settlement, as focused on the south-eastern region of Britain, offers at best only a partial understanding of the geography of the early human settlement in Britain, for there clearly had been substantive settlement, now obliterated, in areas later scoured by ice-advance. The very latest discovery is a handaxe from Cwmbrân, Torfaen. This find has greatly influenced our thinking and will lead us to publish a re-assessment of this open-air material in the wider context of both western and northern Britain.

It is however, fair to say that without the research that this volume is concerned with there would remain just those handful of artefacts from Wales of Palaeolithic age. The open-air finds, whilst special and providing a memory of people at places across South Wales at specific times are now eclipsed by the quantity of evidence recovered from within Pontnewydd Cave. Writing in 2011 it seems remarkable that the artefacts and tooth published by Thomas McKenny Hughes in 1874 became forgotten. The tooth was forgotten to the extent that it can no longer be found. The artefacts he recovered, preserved in Cambridge, were also neglected and not studied as research moved into other areas, particularly the Palaeolithic of south-eastern England. It was here in the early twentieth century that attention focused on what were then considered to be the more important open-air sites and discoveries. 'Sites' including Swanscombe and Piltdown where there were thought to be richer pickings for the researchers were the focus of interest during this time. As such Wales was neglected. One hundred years is a long time for a rich cave like Pontnewydd to remain formally unexplored. It is therefore to Stephen's credit that the site was re-discovered, excavated and a new journey began. As the excavations proceeded, recovering hominin teeth and artefacts, the excitement that always surrounded the field seasons at Pontnewydd increased. The finds then began to embark on new journeys into laboratories, museum store rooms and galleries. They even make occasional journeys in ways these hominins could never have imagined; trips in trucks, aeroplanes and ferries to get them to continental Europe into exhibitions where they may sit locked in side-by-side with their relatives, enemies and ancestors in museum display cases. So their twenty-first century journey continues.

Poetry, art and music can help us to paint new mind pictures of the site and its discoveries. Pontnewydd Cave lying within poet Gerard Manley Hopkins' *Valley of the Elwy* is today reminiscent of the comforting home within the lovely woods, waters and meadows described therein. But it also makes us think of those past lives lived in the caves. So as is befitting the end of this wonderful journey we address our final words to the Pontnewydd people:

> Would it help us to learn
> what you are called in your forgotten
> language? Are not our jaws
> frail for the sustaining of the consonants'
> weight? Yet they were balanced
> on tongues like ours, echoed
> in the ears passages, in intervals when
> the volcano was silent. How
> tenderly did the woman handle
> them, as she leaned her haired body
> to yours? Where are the instruments
> of your music, the pipe of hazel, the
> bull's horn, the interpreters
> of your loneliness on this
> ferocious planet?

> R. S. Thomas – *Probing*

# References

Abbazzi, L., Fanfani, F., Ferretti, M. P. and Rook, L. 2000. New human remains of archaic *Homo sapiens* and Lower Palaeolithic industries from Visogliano (Duino Aurisina, Trieste, Italy). *Journal of Archaeological Science* 27, 1173–1186.

Aguirre, E. 2007. Atapuerca (Burgos, Northern Spain) – potential, progress and questions. *Courier-Forschungsinstitut Senckenberg* 259, 111–120.

Aguirre, E., Arsuaga, J. L., Bermúdez de Castro, J. M., Carbonell, E., Ceballos, M., Díez, C., Enamorado, J., Fernández-Jalvo, Y., Gil, E., Gracia, A., Martín-Nájera, A., Martínez, I., Morales, J., Ortega, A. I., Rosas, A., Sánchez, A., Sánchez, B., Sesé, C., Soto, E. and Torres, T. J. 1990. The Atapuerca sites and the Ibeas hominids. *Human Evolution* 5, N1, 55–73.

Aguirre, E. and Carbonell, E. 2001. Early human expansions into Eurasia: the Atapuerca evidence. *Quaternary International* 75, 11–18.

Aldhouse-Green, S. 1993. Lithic finds from Sudbrook. In S. Godbold and R. Turner *Second Severn Crossing Archaeological Response: Phase 1. The intertidal zone in Wales*, 45. Cardiff, Cadw.

Aldhouse-Green S. 1995. Cueva de Pontnewydd, Gales. Un yacimiento arqueológico con restos humanos del Pleistoceno Medio: revisión de la estratigrafía, dataciones, tafonomía y de su interpretación. In J. M. Bermúdez, J. -L. Arsuaga and E. Carbonell (eds). *Evolutión humain en Europa y los yacimientos de la Sierra de Atapuerca*, 37–55. Junta de Castilla y León, Actas 1.

Aldhouse-Green, S. H. R. 1998. The archaeology of distance: perspectives from the Welsh Palaeolithic. In N. M. Ashton, F. Healy and P. B. Pettitt (eds). *Stone Age Archaeology: essays in honour of John Wymer*, 137–145. Oxford, Oxbow Monograph 102.

Aldhouse-Green, S. (ed.). 2000. *Paviland Cave and the 'Red Lady': a definitive report*. Bristol, Western Academic and Specialist Press Ltd.

Aldhouse-Green, S. 2001. The colonisations and visitations of Wales by Neanderthals and Modern Humans. In A. Anderson, I. Lilley and S. O'Connor (eds). *Histories of Old Ages: essays in honour of Rhys Jones*, 225–235. Canberra, Coombs Academic Press, Australian National University.

Aldhouse-Green, S. H. R. 2004. The Palaeolithic. In M. J. Aldhouse-Green and R. Howell (eds). *Gwent County History. Volume I. Gwent in Prehistory and Early History,* 2–28. Cardiff, University of Wales Press.

Aldhouse-Green, S., Jackson, H. and Young, T. 2004. Lithics, raw materials and ochre: interrogation of data from the Middle Pleistocene hominid site of Pontnewydd Cave, Wales, Europe. In E. A. Walker, F. Wenban-Smith and F. Healy (eds). *Lithics in Action*, 93–104. Oxford, Lithic Studies Society Occasional Paper 8 and Oxbow Books.

Aldhouse-Green, S., Pettitt, P. and Stringer, C. 1996. Holocene humans at Pontnewydd and Cae Gronw Caves. *Antiquity* 70 (268), 444–447.

Aldhouse-Green, S., Scott, K., Schwarcz, H., Grün, R., Housley, R., Rae, A., Bevins, R. and Redknap, M. 1995. Coygan Cave, Laugharne, South Wales, a Mousterian site and hyaena den: a report on the University of Cambridge excavations. *Proceedings of the Prehistoric Society* 61, 37–79.

Al-Kindi, S., White, N., Sinha, M., England, R. and Tiley, R. 2003. Crustal trace of a hot convective sheet. *Geology* 31, 207–210.

Allen, P. M., Cooper, D. C. and Fortey, N. J. 1987. Composite lava flows in the English Lake District. *Journal of the Geological Society of London* 144, 945–960.

Ambrose, S. H. 1993. Isotopic analysis of paleodiets: methodological and interpretive considerations. In M. K. Sandford (ed.). *Investigation of Ancient Human Tissue: chemical analyses in anthropology*, 59–130. Langhorne, Pennsylvania, Gordon and Breach Science Publisher.

Ambrose, S. H. 2000. Controlled diet and climate experiments on nitrogen isotope ratios of rats. In S. H. Ambrose and M. A. Katzenberg (eds). *Biogeochemical Approaches to Paleodietary Analysis*, 243–259. New York, Kluwer Academic/Plenum.

Ambrose, S. H. and Norr, L. 1993. Experimental evidence for the relationship of the carbon isotope ratios of whole diet and dietary protein to those of bone collagen and carbonate. In J. B. Lambert and G. Grupe (eds). *Prehistoric Human Bone: archaeology at the molecular level*, 1–37. Berlin, Springer-Verlag.

Andersen, K. K., Svensson, A., Johnsen, S. J., Rasmussen, S. O., Bigler, M., Rothlisberger, R., Ruth, U., Siggaard-Andersen, M. -L., Steffensen, J. P., Dahl-Jensen, D., Vinther, B. M. and Clausen, H. B. 2006. The Greenland ice core chronology 2005, 15–42 ka. Part 1: constructing the time scale. *Quaternary Science Reviews* 25 (23–24), 3246–3257.

Anderson, M. A. and Stephens, M. A. 1972. Tests for randomness of directions against equitorial and bimodal alternatives. *Biometrika* 59, 613–621.

Andrews, C. W. 1920. Remains of the Great auk and Ptarmigan in the Channel Islands. *Annals of Natural History* 9 (6), 166.

Andrews, P., Cook, J., Currant, A. and Stringer, C. (eds). 1999. *Westbury Cave: the Natural History Museum Excavations 1976–1984*. Bristol, Western Academic and Specialist Press.

Andrews, P. and Fernandez-Jalvo, Y. 1997. Surface modifications of the Sima de los Huesos fossil humans. *Journal of Human Evolution* 33 (2–3), 191–217.

Anonymous 1863. Bone-cave at Cefn, Flintshire. *The Geologist* 6, 114.

Anonymous 1868. Index to Llyfr Coch Asaph. *Archaeologia Cambrensis* 23, 151–166; 329–339.

Anonymous 1959. *Dictionary of Welsh Biography down to 1940*. London, The Honourable Society of Cymmrodorion.

Anonymous 2003. *Kent's Cavern Souvenir Guide Book: Centenary Edition.* Torquay, Broglia Press.

Antoñanzas, R. L. and Bescós, G. C. 2002. The Gran Dolina site (Lower to Middle Pleistocene, Atapuerca, Burgos, Spain): new palaeoenvironmental data based on the distribution of small mammals. *Palaeogeography, Palaeoclimatology, Palaeoecology* 186 (3–4), 311–334.

Appleton, P. 1989. Limestones and caves of North Wales. In T. D. Ford (ed.). *Limestones and Caves of Wales*, 217–254. Cambridge, Cambridge University Press.

ApSimon, A. P. 1986. Picken's Hole, Compton Bishop, Somerset. Early Devensian bear and wolf den, and Middle Devensian hyaena den and Palaeolithic site. In S. N. Collcutt (ed.). *The Palaeolithic of Britain and its Nearest Neighbours: recent trends*, 55–56. Sheffield, Department of Archaeology and Prehistory, University of Sheffield.

Arsuaga, J. -L., Martinez, I., Gracia, A., Carretero, J. -M. and Carbonell, E. 1993. Three new human skulls from the Sima de los Huesos Middle Pleistocene in the Sierra de Atapuerca, Spain. *Nature* 362, 534–537.

Ashton, N. and Lewis, S. 2002. Deserted Britain: declining populations in the British late Middle Pleistocene. *Antiquity* 76, 388–396.

Ashton, N., Lewis, S., Parfitt, S. and White, M. 2005. Riparian landscapes and human habitat preferences during the Hoxnian (MIS 11) Interglacial. In AHOB 2005: *The Palaeolithic Occupation of Europe: programme and abstracts.* Quaternary Research Association annual discussion meeting held at the British Museum, 5th–6th January 2005.

Ashton, N. M. and McNabb, J. 1994. Bifaces in perspective. In N. M. Ashton and A. David (eds). *Stories in Stone*, 182–191. London, Lithic Studies Society Occasional Paper 4.

Atkinson, R. J. C. 1956. *Stonehenge.* London, Hamish Hamilton.

Atkinson, T. C. and Rowe, P. J. 1992. Applications of dating to denudation chronology and landscape evolution. In M. Ivanovich, and R. S. Harmon (eds). *Uranium Series Disequilibrium*, 669–703. Oxford, Oxford University Press.

Austen, J. H. (ed.). 1898. *Companion to St Asaph, with Map and Illustrations.* St Asaph, D. Hughes.

Bacher, A. 1967. *Vergleichend Morphologische Untersuchungen an Einzelknochen des Postkranialean Skeletts in Mitteleuropa Vorkommender Schwäne und Gänse.* Munchen, Institut für Palaeoanatomie, Domestikations-forschung und Geschichte der Tiermedizen, Universitat Munchen.

Bailey, S. E. 2000. Dental morphological affinities among Late Pleistocene and recent humans. *Dental Anthropology* 14, 1–8.

Bailey, S. E. 2001. Reconstructing Neandertal postcanine trait polarity: the cheek teeth speak. *Journal of Human Evolution* 40, A2.

Bailey, S. E. 2002a. A closer look at Neanderthal postcanine dental morphology: the mandibular dentition. *The Anatomical Record (New Anatomy)* 269, 148–156.

Bailey, S. E. 2002b. *Neandertal dental morphology: implications for modern human origins.* Unpublished PhD Dissertation, Arizona State University.

Bailey, S. E. 2004. A morphometric analysis of maxillary molar crowns of Middle–Late Pleistocene hominins. *Journal of Human Evolution* 47 (3), 183–198.

Bailey, S. E. 2005. Diagnostic dental differences between Neandertals and Upper Paleolithic modern humans: getting to the root of the matter. In E. Zadzinska (ed.). *Current Trends in Dental Morphology Research*, 201–210. Lodz, University of Lodz Press.

Bailey, S. E. 2006. Beyond shovel-shaped incisors: Neandertal dental morphology in a comparative context. *Periodicum Biologorum* 108 (3), 253–267.

Bailey, S. E. and Lynch, J. M. 2005. Diagnostic differences in mandibular P4 shape between Neandertals and anatomically modern humans. *American Journal of Physical Anthropology* 126 (3), 268–277.

Bailey, S. E., Glantz, M., Weaver, T. D. and Viola, B. 2008a. The affinity of the dental remains from Obi-Rakhmat Grotto, Uzbekistan. *Journal of Human Evolution* 55, 238–248.

Bailey, S. E., Quam, R. M. and Wood, B. A. 2008b. Evolution of M¹ cusp proportions in the genus *Homo. American Association of Physical Anthropologists,* Supplement 46, 62–63.

Baker, A. and Smart, P. L. 1995. Recent flowstone growth rates: field measurements in comparison to theoretical predictions. *Chemical Geology* 122, 121–128.

Ball, T. K. and Merriman, R. J. 1989. The petrology and geochemistry of the Ordovician Llewelyn Volcanic Group, Snowdonia, North Wales. *British Geological Survey Research Report*, SG/89/1.

Balter, V. and Simon, L. 2006. Diet and behavior of the Saint-Césaire Neanderthal inferred from biogeochemical data inversion. *Journal of Human Evolution* 51, 329–338.

Baring-Gould, S. 1903. *A Book of North Wales.* London, Methuen.

Barnatt, J. and Edmonds, M. 2002. Places apart? Caves and monuments in Neolithic and earlier Bronze Age Britain. *Cambridge Archaeological Journal* 12 (1), 113–129.

Barrett, M. J. 1977. Masticatory and non-masticatory uses of teeth. In R. V. S. Wright (ed.). *Stone Tools as Markers*, 18–23. Canberra, Australian Institute of Aboriginal Studies.

Barrett, P. H. 1974. The Sedgwick-Darwin geologic tour of North Wales. *Proceedings of the American Philosophical Society* 118 (2), 146–164.

Barrett, L., Gaynor, D., Randall, D., Mitchell, D. and Henzi, S. P. 2004. Habitual cave use and thermoregulation in chacma baboons (*Papio hamadryas ursinus*). *Journal of Human Evolution* 46, 215–222.

Barton, R. N. E., Berridge, P. J., Walker, M. J. C. and Bevins, R. E. 1995. Persistent places in the Mesolithic landscape: an example from the Black Mountain uplands of South Wales. *Proceedings of the Prehistoric Society* 61, 81–117.

Bartrum, P. C. 1993. *A Welsh Classical Dictionary: people in history and legend up to about A.D. 1000.* Aberystwyth, National Library of Wales.

Bassinot, F. C., Labeyrie, L. D., Vincent, E., Quidelleur, X., Shackleton, N. J. and Lancelot, Y. 1994. The astronomical theory of climate and the age of the Brunhes-Matuyama magnetic reversal. *Earth and Planetary Science Letters* 126, 91–108.

Battiau-Queney, Y. 1984. The pre-glacial evolution of Wales. *Earth Surface Processes and Landforms* 9, 229–252.

Bax, J. S. and Ungar, P. S. 1999. Incisor labial surface wear striations in modern humans and their implications for handedness in Middle and Late Pleistocene hominids. *International Journal of Osteoarchaeology* 9, 189–198.

Bayle, P., Braga, J., Mazurier, A., Radovčić, J. and Macchiarelli, R. 2007. Dental development patterns in Neandertals: a high-resolution 3D analysis. *American Association of Physical Anthropology* Supplement 44, 70.

Bayle, P., Braga, J., Mazurier, A. and Macchiarelli, R. 2008.

Dental development in the Neanderthal child of Roc de Marsal (Dordogne, France). *American Association of Physical Anthropology* Supplement 46, 65.

Bayle, P., Braga, J., Mazurier, A. and Macchiarelli. R, 2009. Dental development pattern of the Neanderthal child from Roc de Marsal: a high-resolution 3D analysis. *Journal of Human Evolution* 56, 66–75.

Beek, G. C. van 1983. *Dental Morphology, an Illustrated Guide, 2nd Edition.* Bristol, Wright.

Berger, G. W. 2009. Dating, luminescence techniques. In V. Gornitz (ed.). *Encyclopedia of Paleoclimatology and Ancient Environments*, 249–252. Dordrecht, Springer.

Bermúdez de Castro, J. M. 1986. Dental remains from Atapuerca (Spain) I metrics. *Journal of Human Evolution* 15, 265–287.

Bermúdez de Castro, J. M. 1988. Dental remains from Atapuerca/Ibeas (Spain) II morphology. *Journal of Human Evolution* 17, 279–304.

Bermúdez de Castro, J. M. 1993. The Atapuerca dental remains. New evidence (1987–1991) excavations and interpretations. *Journal of Human Evolution* 24, 339–371.

Bermúdez de Castro, J. M. and Aguirre, E. 1987. Los dientes del hombre fosil de Atapuerca. In E. Aguirre, E. Carbonell and J. M. Bermúdez de Castro (eds). *El hombre fosil de Ibeas y el Pleistoceno de la Sierra de Atapuerca I*, 327–358. Castilla y Leon, Junta de Castilla y Leon.

Bermúdez de Castro, J. M., Arsuaga, J. L., Carbonell, E., Rosas, A., Martínez, I. and Mosquera, M. 1997. A hominid from the Lower Pleistocene of Atapuerca, Spain: possible ancestor to Neandertals and modern humans. *Science* 276, 1392–1395.

Bermúdez de Castro, J. M., Bromage, T. G. and Fernández Jalvo, Y. 1988. Buccal striations on fossil human anterior teeth: evidence of handedness in the middle and early Upper Pleistocene. *Journal of Human Evolution* 17, 403–412.

Bermúdez de Castro, J. M. and Díez, J. C. 1995. Middle Pleistocene mortality pattern and fertility: the case of the Atapuerca hominids. *Revista Española de Paleontología* 10 (2), 259–272.

Bermúdez de Castro, J. M., Durand, A. I. and Ipina, S. L. 1993. Sexual dimorphism in the human dental sample from the SH site (Sierra de Atapuerca, Spain): a statistical approach. *Journal of Human Evolution* 24, 43–56.

Bermúdez de Castro, J. M., Martinón-Torres, M., Sarmiento, S. and Lozano, M. 2003a. Gran Dolina-TD6 versus Sima de los Huesos dental samples from Atapuerca: evidence of discontinuity in the European Pleistocene population? *Journal of Archaeological Science* 30, 1421–1428.

Bermúdez de Castro, J. M., Martinón-Torres, M., Sarmiento, S., Lozano, M., Arsuaga, J. L. and Carbonell, E. 2003b. Rates of anterior tooth wear in Middle Pleistocene hominins from Sima de los Huesos (Sierra de Atapuerca, Spain). *Proceedings of the National Academy of Sciences USA* 100 (21), 11992–11996.

Bermúdez de Castro, J. M., Martinón-Torres, M., Carbonell, E., Sarmiento, S., Rosas, A. van der, Made, J. and Lozano, M. 2004a. The Atapuerca sites and their contribution to the knowledge of human evolution in Europe. *Evolutionary Anthropology* 13 (1), 25–41.

Bermúdez de Castro, J. M., Martinón-Torres, M., Lozano, M., Sarmiento, S. and Muela, A. 2004b. Palaeodemography of the Atapuerca – Sima de los Huesos hominin sample: a revision and new approaches to the palaeodemography of the European Middle Pleistocene population. *Journal of Anthropological Research* 60 (1), 5–26.

Bermúdez de Castro, J. M., Martinón-Torres, M., Gómez-Robles, A., Prado, L. and Sarmiento, S. 2007. Comparative analysis

of the Gran Dolina-TD6 (Spain) and Tighennif (Algeria) hominin mandibles. *Bulletins et Mémoires de la Société d'Anthropologie de Paris* n.s., 19 (3–4), 149–167.

Bermúdez de Castro, J. M. and Nicolás, M. E. 1995. Posterior dental size reduction in hominids: the Atapuerca evidence. *American Journal of Physical Anthropology* 96, 335–356.

Bermúdez de Castro, J. M. and Nicolás, M. E. 1996. Changes in the lower premolar size sequence during hominid evolution. Phylogenetic implications. *Human Evolution* 11 (N3–4), 205–215.

Bermúdez de Castro, J. M. and Nicolás, M. E. 1997. Palaeodemography of the Atapuerca–SH Middle Pleistocene hominid sample. *Journal of Human Evolution* 33, 333–355.

Bermúdez de Castro, J. M. and Pérez, P. J. 1995. Enamel hypoplasia in the Middle Pleistocene hominids from Atapuerca (Spain). *American Journal of Physical Anthropology* 96, 301–314.

Bermúdez de Castro, J. M., Pérez-González, A., Martinón-Torres, M., Gómez-Robles, A., Rosell, J., Prado, L., Sarmiento, S. and Carbonell, E. 2008. A new early Pleistocene hominin mandible from Atapuerca-TD6, Spain. *Journal of Human Evolution* 55, 729–735.

Bermúdez de Castro, J. M. and Rosas, A. 2001. Pattern of dental development in Hominid XVIII from the Middle Pleistocene Atapuerca – Sima de los Huesos site (Spain). *American Journal of Physical Anthropology* 114, 325–330.

Bermúdez de Castro, J. M., Rosas, A., Carbonell, E., Nicolás, M. E., Rodríguez, J. and Arsuaga, J. L. 1999a. A modern human pattern of dental development in Lower Pleistocene hominids from Atapuerca-TD6 (Spain). *Proceedings of the National Academy of Sciences USA* 96, 4210–4213.

Bermúdez de Castro, J. M., Rosas, A. and Nicolás, M. E. 1999b. Dental remains from Atapuerca-TD6 (Gran Dolina site, Burgos, Spain). *Journal of Human Evolution* 37 (3–4), 523–566.

Bermúdez de Castro, J. M. and Sarmiento, S. 2001. Analyse morphométrique comparée des dents humaines de Gran Dolina (TD6) et de Sima de los Huesos d'Atapuerca. *L'Anthropologie* 105, 203–222.

Bermúdez de Castro, J. M., Sarmiento, S., Cunha, E., Rosas, A. and Bastir, M. 2001. Dental size variation in the Atapuerca-SH Middle Pleistocene hominids. *Journal of Human Evolution* 41, 195–209.

Berten, J. 1895. Hypoplasie des schmelzes (congenitale schmelzdefecte; erosionen). *Deutsche Monatsschrift für Zahnheilkunde* 13, 425–606.

Bevins, R. E. 1984. Petrological investigations. In H. S. Green *Pontnewydd Cave a Lower Palaeolithic Hominid Site in Wales: the first report*, 193–198. Cardiff, National Museum of Wales.

Bevins, R. E., Oliver, G. J. H. and Thomas, L. J. 1985. Low-grade metamorphism in the Paratectonic Caledonides of the British Isles. *Earth Evolution Sciences, Monograph Series* 1, 57–79.

Beynon, A. D. and Dean, M. C. 1988. Distinct dental development patterns in early fossil hominids. *Nature* 335, 509–514.

Billinghurst, S. A. 1928. Notes on the physiography and glaciology of north-east Carnarvonshire. *Geological Magazine* 65, 145–163.

Billy, G. 1982. Les dents humaines de la Grotte du Coupe-Gorge à Montmaurin. *Bulletins et Mémoires de la Société d'Anthropologie de Paris* 9, série XIII, 211–225.

Billy, G. and Vallois, H. V. 1977. La mandible Pré-Rissienne de Montmaurin. *L'Anthropologie* 81 (3), 411–458.

Binford, L. R. 1978. *Nunamiut Ethnoarchaeology.* New York, Academic Press.

Binford, L. R. 1981. *Bones: ancient men and modern myths.* New York, Academic Press.

Binford, L. R. 1992. Hard evidence. *Discover* February 1992, 44–51.

Bischoff, J. L., Fitzpatrick, J. A., Leon, L., Arsuaga, J. L., Falgueres, C., Bahain, J. J. and Bullen, T. 1997. Geology and preliminary dating of the hominid-bearing sedimentary fill of the Sima de los Huesos chamber, Cueva Mayor of the Sierra de Atapuerca, Burgos, Spain. *Journal of Human Evolution* 33 (2–3), 129–154.

Bischoff, J. L., Shamp, D. D., Aramburu, A., Arsuaga, J. L., Carbonell, E. and Bermúdez de Castro, J. M. 2003. The Sima de los Huesos hominids date to beyond U/Th equilibrium (>350 kyr) and perhaps to 400–500 kyr: new radiometric dates. *Journal of Archaeological Science* 30 (3), 275–280.

Bischoff, J. L., Williams, R. W., Rosenbauer, R. J., Aramburu, A., Arsuaga, J. L., Garcia, N. and Cuenca-Bescos G. 2007. High-resolution U-series dates from the Sima de los Huesos hominids yields 600+/+∞-66 kyrs: implications for the evolution of the early Neanderthal lineage. *Journal of Archaeological Science* 34, 763–770.

Black, G. V. 1902. *Descriptive Anatomy of the Human Teeth, 4th Edition.* Philadelphia, S. S. White Dental Manual Company.

Blatt, H., Middleton, G. and Murray, R. 1980. *Origin of Sedimentary Rocks.* New Jersey, Prentice-Hall.

Blockley, S. M. 2005. Two hiatuses in human bone radiocarbon dates in Britain (17000 to 5000 cal. BP). *Antiquity* 79, 505–513.

Blundell, D. J. and Waltham, D. A. 2009. A possible glacially-forced tectonic mechanism for late Neogene surface uplift and subsidence around the North Atlantic. *Proceedings of the Geologists' Association* 120 (2), 98–107.

Boaz, N. T. and Ciochon, R. L. 2004. *Dragon Bone Hill.* Oxford, Oxford University Press.

Bocherens, H., Billiou, D. and Mariotti, A. 1999. Palaeoenvironmental and Palaeodietary implications of isotopic biogeochemistry of last interglacial Neanderthal and mammal bones in Scladina Cave (Belgium). *Journal of Archaeological Science* 26, 599–607.

Bocquet-Appel, J. P. and Arsuaga, J. L. 1999. Age distribution of hominid samples at Atapuerca (SH) and Krapina could indicate accumulation by catastrophe. *Journal of Archaeological Science* 26 (3), 327–338.

Bond, G. and Lotti, R. 1995. Iceberg discharges into the North Atlantic on millennial time scales during the last glaciation. *Science* 267, 1005–1010.

Bond, G., Showers, W., Cheseby, M., Lotti, R., Almasi, P., de Menocal, P., Priore, P., Cullen, H., Hajdas, I. and Bonani, G. 1997. A pervasive millennial-scale cycle in North Atlantic Holocene and glacial climates. *Science* 278, 1257–1266.

Borges, J. L. 1975. *In Praise of Darkness.* London, Allen Lane.

Borges, J. L. 1981. The Circular Ruins In J. L. Borges *Labyrinths,* 72–75. London, King Penguin.

Borges, J. L. 2002. Las ruinas circulares. In J. L. Borges *Ficciones,* 56–65. Madrid, Alianza Editorial.

Boswell, P. G. H. 1949. *The Middle Silurian Rocks of North Wales.* London, Arnold.

Boule, M. and Vallois, H. V. 1957. *Fossil Men.* London, Thames and Hudson.

Bowen, D. Q. 1978. *Quaternary Geology: a stratigraphic framework for multidisciplinary work.* Oxford, Pergamon.

Bowen, D. Q. 1982. Surface morphology. In H. Carter (ed.). *National Atlas of Wales,* 1.3. Cardiff, University of Wales Press.

Bowen, D. Q. 1989. The Welsh landform. In D. H. Owen (ed.). *Settlement and Society in Wales: in memory of E. G. Bowen,* 27–44. Cardiff, University of Wales Press.

Bowen, D. Q. 1994. The land of Cardiganshire. In J. L. Davies and D. P. Kirby (eds). *Cardiganshire County History* 3–20. Cardiff, University of Wales Press.

Bowen, D. Q. 1999a. Only four major glaciations in the Brunhes chron? *International Journal of Earth Science (Geologische Rundschau)* 88, 276–284.

Bowen, D. Q. 1999b. Wales. In D. Q. Bowen (ed.). *A Revised Correlation of Quaternary Deposits in the British Isles.* London, Geological Society of London Special Report No. 23, 89.

Bowen, D. Q. 2005. South Wales. In C. A. Lewis and A. E. Richards (eds). *The Glaciations of Wales and Adjacent Regions,* 145–164. Almeley, Logaston Press.

Bowen, D. Q. 2010. Sea-level ~ 400 000 years ago (MIS 11): analogue for present and future sea-level? *Climate of the Past* 6, 19–29 and C128 1–6.

Bowen, D. Q., McCabe, A. M., Phillips, F. M., Knutz, P. C. and Sykes, G. A. 2002. New data for the Last Glacial Maximum in Great Britain and Ireland. *Quaternary Science Reviews* 21, 89–101.

Bowman, J. E. 1837. On the bone cave in Carboniferous limestone at Cefn in Denbighshire. *Report of the Sixth Meeting of the British Association for the Advancement of Science held at Bristol in August 1836* 5, 88–91.

Boyd Dawkins, W. 1874. *Cave Hunting, Researches on the Evidence of Caves Respecting the Early Inhabitants of Europe.* London, Macmillan and Co.

Boyd Dawkins, W. 1880. *Early Man in Britain and his Place in the Tertiary Period.* London, Macmillan and Co.

Brace, C. L. 1967. Environment, tooth form and size in the Pleistocene. *Journal of Dental Research* 46 (supplement to number 5), 809–816.

Brace, C. L. 1975. Reply to 'Did la Ferrassie I use his teeth as a tool?' – J. A. Wallace. *Current Anthropology* 16 (3), 396–397.

Brace, C. L. 1980. Australian tooth-size clines and the death of a stereotype. *Current Anthropology* 21, 141–153.

Bramwell, D. 1960. Some research into bird distribution in Britain during the Late Glacial and Post-glacial periods. *Merseyside Naturalists Trust Bird Report 1959–60,* 51–58.

Branigan, K. and Dearne, M. J. 1992. *Romano-British Cavemen.* Oxford, Oxbow Books.

Bridgland, D. R. and Schreve, D. C. 2004. Quaternary lithostratigraphy and mammalian biostratigraphy of the Lower Thames terrace system, south-east England. *Quaternaire* 15, 29–40.

British Geological Survey. 1973. *Denbigh, Sheet 107* (Drift Edition).

Brock, F., Higham, T., Ramsey, C. B. 2010. Pre-screening techniques for identification of samples suitable for radiocarbon dating of poorly preserved bones. *Journal of Archaeological Science* 37 (4), 855–865.

Bromage, T. G. and Dean, M. C. 1985. Re-evaluation of the age at death of immature fossil hominids. *Nature* 317, 525–527.

Bromwich, R. 1978. *Trioedd Ynys Prydein. The Welsh Triads.* 2nd edition. Cardiff, University of Wales Press.

Bronk Ramsey, C. and Hedges, R. E. M. 1999. Hybrid ion sources: Radiocarbon measurements from microgram to milligram. *Nuclear Instruments and Methods in Physics Research* B 123, 539–545.

Bronk Ramsey, C., Higham, T. F. G., Bowles, A. and Hedges, R. E. M. 2004. Improvements to the pretreatment of bone at Oxford. *Radiocarbon* 46 (1), 155–163.

Bronk Ramsey, C., Pettitt, P. B., Hedges, R. E. M., Hodgins, G. W. L. and Owen, D. C. 2000. Radiocarbon dates from the Oxford AMS system: Archaeometry Datelist 30. *Archaeometry* 42 (2), 459–479.

Brown, E. H. 1957. The physique of Wales. *Geographical Journal* 123, 208–221.

Brown, E. H. 1960. *The Relief and Drainage of Wales*. Cardiff, University of Wales Press.

Brown, E. H. and Cooke, R. U. 1977. Landforms and related glacial deposits in the Wheeler Valley area, Clwyd. *Cambria* 4, 32–45.

Brown, T. A., Nelson, D. E., Vogel, J. S. and Southon, J. R. 1988. Improved collagen extraction by modified Longin method. *Radiocarbon* 30 (2), 171–177.

Bull, P. A. 1984. Scanning electron microscope studies of sediments. In H. S. Green *Pontnewydd Cave a Lower Palaeolithic Hominid Site in Wales: the first report*, 77–87. Cardiff, National Museum of Wales.

Burky, R. R., Kirner, D. L., Taylor, R. E., Hare, P. E. and Southon, J. R. 1998. 14C Dating of bone using γ-carboxyglutamic acid and α-carboxyglycine (aminomalonate). *Radiocarbon* 40 (1), 11–20.

Callahan, E. H. 1979. The basics of biface knapping in the eastern fluted point tradition: a manual for flint knappers and lithic analysts. *Archaeology of Eastern North America* 7 (1), 1–213.

Callow, P. and Cornford, J. M. (eds). 1986. *La Cotte de Saint Brelade 1961–1978: excavations by C. B. M. McBurney 1961–1978*. Appendix F. Fauna from the deposits of the last cold stage at La Cotte de Saint Brelade. Norwich: Geo Books.

Campbell, S. and Bowen, D. Q. 1989. *Geological Conservation Review: Quaternary of Wales*. Peterborough, Nature Conservancy Council.

Campbell, T. D. 1925. *Dentition and Palate of the Australian Aboriginal*. Adelaide, University of Adelaide, Keith Sheridan Foundation.

Carbonell, E., Bermúdez de Castro, J. M., Arsuaga, J. L., Díez, J. C., Rosas, A., Cuenca-Bescós, G., Sala, R., Mosquera, M. and Rodríguez, X. P. 1995. Lower Pleistocene hominids and artifacts from Atapuerca-TD6 (Spain). *Science* 269, 826–829.

Carbonell, E., Bermúdez de Castro, J. M., Arsuaga, J. L., Allue, E., Bastir, M., Benito, A., Cáceres, I., Canals, T., Díez, J. C., van der Made, J., Mosquera, M., Ollé, A., Pérez-González, A., Rodríguez, J., Rodríguez, X. P., Rosas, A., Rosell, J., Sala, R., Vallverdu, J. and Vergés, J. M. 2005. An early Pleistocene hominin mandible from Atapuerca-TD6, Spain. *Proceedings of the National Academy of Sciences USA* 102 (16), 5674–5678.

Carbonell, E., Bermúdez de Castro, J. M., Parés, J. M., Pérez-González, A., Cuenca-Bescós, G., Ollé, A., Mosquera, M., Huguet, R., van der Made, J., Rosas, A., Sala, R., Vallverdú, J., García, N., Granger, D. E., Martinón-Torres, M., Rodríguez, X. P., Stock, G. M., Vergès, J. M., Allué, E., Burjachs, F., Cáceres, I., Canals, A., Benito, A., Díez, C., Lozano, M., Mateos, A., Navazo, M., Rodríguez, J., Rosell, J. and Arsuaga, J. L. 2008. The first hominin of Europe. *Nature* 452, 465–469.

Carbonell, E., Mosquera, M., Rodríguez, X. P., Sala, R. and van der Made, J. 1999. Out of Africa: the dispersal of the earliest technical systems reconsidered. *Journal of Anthropological Archaeology* 18 (2), 119–136.

Cassoli, P. F. 1978. L'avifauna pre-würmiana di Torre in Pietra, Lazio. *Quaternaria* 20, 429–440.

Cassoli, P. F. 1980. L'avifauna de Pleistocene superiore del Arene Candide, Liguria. *Memorie Instituto Paleontologia Umana*, n.s. 3, 155–234.

Cattani, L., Cremaschi, M., Ferraris, M. R., Mallegni, F., Masini, F., Scola, V. and Tozzi, C. 1991. Le gisement du Pléistocène Moyen de Visogliano (Trieste): restes humains, industries, environment. *L'Anthropologie* 95 (1), 9–36.

Chafetz, H. S. and Folk, R. L. 1984. Travertines: depositional morphology and the bacterially constructed constituents. *Journal of Sedimentary Petrology* 54, 289–316.

Chamberlain, A. T. 1996. More dating evidence for human remains in British caves. *Antiquity* 70, 950–953.

Chamberlin, T. C. 1897. The method of multiple working hypotheses. *Journal of Geology* 5, 837–848.

Chappell, J., Head, M. J. and Magee, J. 1996. Beyond the radiocarbon limit in Australian archaeology and Quaternary research. *Antiquity* 70, 543–552.

Clark, J., McCabe, A. M., Schnabel, C., Clark, P. U., McCarron, S., Freeman, S. H. T., Maden, C. and Xu, S. 2009. Cosmogenic [10]Be chronology of the last deglaciation of western Ireland, and implications for sensitivity of the Irish Ice Sheet to climate change. *Geological Society of America Bulletin* 121, 3–16.

Clark, J. D. 1980. Raw material and African lithic technology. In V. N. Misra, D. K. Chakrabarti and S. Sinha (eds). *Man and Environment* 4, 44–55.

Clark, J. W. and Hughes, T. McK. 1890. *The Life and Letters of the Reverend Adam Sedgwick: Volume I*. Cambridge, The University Press.

Clark, P. U., McCabe, A. M., Mix, A. C. and Weaver, A. S. 2004. Rapid rise of sea level 19,000 years ago and its global implications. *Science* 304, 1141–1144.

Clark, P. U., Dyke, A. S., Shakun, J. D., Carlson, J. D., Clark, J., Wohlfarth, B., Mitrovica, J. X., Hostetler, S. W. and McCabe, M. 2009. The Last Glacial Maximum. *Science* 325, 710–714.

Clayton, C. 1984. The flints. In H. S. Green *Pontnewydd Cave a Lower Palaeolithic Hominid Site in Wales: the first report*, 186–192. Cardiff, National Museum of Wales.

Clottes, J. (ed.). 2003. *Return to Chauvet Cave. Excavating the Birthplace of Art: the first full report*. London, Thames and Hudson.

Coles, B. 2006. *Beavers in Britain's Past*. Oxford, Oxbow Books.

Coles, G. M. 1992. *The Glass Island*. London, Duckworth and Co. Ltd.

Collcutt, S. N. 1984. The sediments. In H. S. Green *Pontnewydd Cave: a lower Palaeolithic hominid site in Wales: the first report*, 31–76. Cardiff, National Museum of Wales.

Combellack, M. 1988. *The Camborne Play*. Redruth, Dyllansow Truran.

Cook, J. and Jacobi, R. 1998. Observations on the artefacts from the Breccia at Kent's Cavern. In N. Ashton, F. Healy and P. Pettitt (eds). *Stone Age Archaeology: essays in honour of John Wymer*, 77–89. Oxford, Oxbow Books.

Cook, J., Stringer, C. B., Currant, A. P., Schwarcz, H. P. and Wintle, A. G. 1982. A review of the chronology of the European Middle Pleistocene hominid record. *Yearbook of Physical Anthropology* 25, 19–65.

Coppa, A., Grün, R., Stringer, C., Eggins, S. and Vargiu, R. 2005. Newly recognised Pleistocene human teeth from Tabun Cave, Israel. *Journal of Human Evolution* 49, 301–315.

Corruccini, R. S. 1973. Size and shape in similarity coefficients based on metric characters. *American Journal of Physical Anthropology* 38, 743–754.

Cramp, S. (ed.). 1988. *Handbook of the Birds of Europe, the Middle East and North Africa: birds of the western Palaearctic volume V.* Oxford, Oxford University Press.

Cramp, S. and Perrins, C. M. (eds). 1994. *Handbook of the Birds of Europe, the Middle East and North Africa: birds of the western Palaearctic volume VIII.* Oxford, Oxford University Press.

Cramp, S. and Simmons, K. E. L. (eds). 1977. *Handbook of the Birds of Europe, the Middle East and North Africa: birds of the western Palaearctic volume I.* Oxford, Oxford University Press.

Cramp, S. and Simmons, K. E. L. (eds). 1980. *Handbook of the Birds of Europe, the Middle East and North Africa: birds of the western palaearctic Volume II.* Oxford, Oxford University Press.

Culotta, E. 1999. Neanderthals were cannibals, bones show. *Science* 286, 118–119.

Cunha, E., Ramirez Rozzi, F., Bermúdez de Castro, J. M., Martinón-Torres, M., Wasterlain, S. N. and Sarmiento, S. 2004. Enamel hypoplasias and physiological stress in the Sima de los Huesos Middle Pleistocene hominins. *American Journal of Physical Anthropology* 125 (3), 220–231.

Currant, A. P. 1984. The mammalian remains. In H. S. Green *Pontnewydd Cave: a lower Palaeolithic hominid site in Wales: the first report,* 171–180. Cardiff, National Museum of Wales.

Currant, A. P. 1989. The Quaternary origins of the modern British mammal fauna. *Biological Journal of the Linnean Society* 38, 23–30.

Currant, A. P, and Jacobi, R. M. 1997. Vertebrate faunas from the British Late Pleistocene and the chronology of human settlement. *Quaternary Newsletter* 82, 1–8.

Currant, A. P. and Jacobi, R. M. 2001. A formal mammalian biostratigraphy for the Late Pleistocene of Britain. *Quaternary Science Reviews* 20, 1707–1716.

Dansgaard, W. 1964. Stable isotopes in precipitation. *Tellus* 16 (4), 436–468.

Davies, E. 1929. *The Prehistoric and Roman Remains of Denbighshire.* Cardiff, William Lewis Ltd.

Davies, E. 1949. *The Prehistoric and Roman Remains of Flintshire.* Cardiff, William Lewis Ltd.

Davies, E. 1959. *Flintshire Place-Names.* Cardiff, University of Wales Press.

Davies, F. J. and Ellis, B. M. 1960. *Caving in North Wales.* Shepton Mallet Caving Club, Occasional Paper 2.

Davies, G. L. 1969. *The Earth in Decay: a history of British geomorphology 1578–1878.* London, Macdonald and Co.

Davies, I. C. and Walker, R. G. 1974. Transport and deposition of resedimented conglomerates: the Cap Enrage Formation, Cambro-Ordovician, Gaspe, Quebec. *Journal of Sedimentary Petrology* 44, 1200–1216.

Davies, M. 1989. Cave archaeology in North Wales. In T. D. Ford (ed.). *Limestones and Caves of Wales,* 92–101. Cambridge, Cambridge University Press.

Day, M. H. 1986. *Guide to Fossil Man, 4th Edition.* Illinois, University of Chicago Press.

Day, M. L. (ed.). 1988. *The Story of Meriadoc, King of Cambria (Historia Meriadoci, Regis Cambrie).* New York and London, Garland Publishing Inc. Garland Library of Medieval Literature, series A.

Dean, C., Leakey, M. G., Reid, D. J., Shrenk, F., Schwartz, G. T., Stringer, C. and Walker, A. 2001. Growth processes in teeth distinguish modern humans from *Homo erectus* and earlier hominins. *Nature* 414, 628–631.

Dean, M. C., 2006. Tooth microstructure tracks the pace of human life-history evolution. *Proceedings of the Royal Society of London Series B* 273, 2799–2808.

Defleur, A. 1993. *Les Sepultures Mousteriennes.* Paris, C.N.R.S.

Delson, E. 1985. *Ancestors: the hard evidence.* New York, Alan R. Liss.

Dimock, J. F. (ed.). 1868. *Giraldi Cambrensis Opera VI. Itinerarium Kambriae et Descriptio Kambriae.* London, Longmans, Green, Reader and Dyer.

Doble, G. H. 1960. *The Saints of Cornwall. Part One. Saints of the Land's End District.* Truro, Dean and Chapter.

Doronichev, V. B. 2000. Lower Palaeolithic of the northern Caucasus. In D. Lordkipandze, O. Bar-Yosef and M. Otte. *Early Humans at the Gates of Europe.* Liege, ERAUL 92.

Drennan, M. R. 1929. The dentition of a Bushman tribe. *Annals of South African Museum* 24, 61–87.

Dreybrodt, W. 1996. Chemical kinetics, speleothem growth and climate. In S. E. Lauritzen (ed.). *Climate Change: the karst record, extended abstracts of a conference held at the Department of Geology, University of Bergen, Norway, August 1–4th 1996.* Norway: KWI Special Publication No. 2.

Dumančić, J., Kaić, Z. and Petrovečki, M. 2001. Evaluation of taurodontism in Krapina Neanderthals. In A. Brook (ed.). *Dental Morphology 2001,* 111-121. Sheffield, Sheffield Academic Press.

Dutton, A., Bard, E., Antonioli, F., Esat, T. M., Lambeck, K. and McCulloch, M. Y. 2009. Phasing and amplitude of sea-level and climate change during the penultimate interglacial, *Nature Geoscience* 2, 355–359.

Eastham, A. 1988. The season or the symbol: the evidence of swallows in the Palaeolithic of western Europe. *Archaeozoologia, Revue Internationale d'Archéologie* 2 (1.2), 243–252.

Edwards, N. 1991. The Dark Ages. In J. Manley, S. Grenter and F. Gale (eds). *The Archaeology of Clwyd,* 129–141. Mold, Clwyd County Council.

Egocheaga, J. E., Pérez-Pérez, A., Rodríguez, L., Galbany, J., Martínez, L. M. and Antunes, M. T. 2004. New evidence and interpretation of subvertical grooves in Neanderthal teeth from Cueva de Sidrón (Spain) and Figueira Brava (Portugal). *Anthropologie* 42 (1), 49–52.

Ellis, B. M. 1973. *British Cave Research Association Bulletin* 2 (Nov.), 30–32.

El Zaatari, S. 2007. Ecogeographic variation in Neandertal dietary habits: evidence from microwear texture analysis. *American Association of Physical Anthropology* Supplement 44, 105.

Embleton, C. E. 1960. The Elwy River system, Denbighshire. *Geographical Journal* 126, 318–334.

Embleton, C. E. 1961. The geomorphology of the Vale of Conway, North Wales, with particular reference to its deglaciation. *Transactions of the Institute of British Geographers* 29, 47–70.

Embleton, C. E. 1970. North eastern Wales. In C. A. Lewis (ed.). *The Glaciations of Wales and Adjoining Regions* 59–82. London, Longman.

Embleton, C. E. 1984. Location, setting and geomorphology. In H. S. Green. *Pontnewydd Cave: A lower Palaeolithic Hominid Site in Wales: the first report,* 23–29. Cardiff, National Museum of Wales.

Endicott, P., Ho, S., Metspalu, M. and Stringer, C. 2009.

Evaluating the mitochondrial timescale of human evolution. *Trends in Ecology and Evolution* 24, 515–521.

Endicott, P., Ho, S. Y. H. and Stringer, C. 2010. Using genetic evidence to evaluate four palaeoanthropological hypotheses for the timing of Neanderthal and modern human origins. *Journal of Human Evolution,* 59 (1), 87–95.

Érome, G. 1982. *Contribution à la connaissance éco-éthologique du castor (*Castor fiber*) dans la vallée du Rhône.* PhD thesis, Université Claude Bernard – Lyon 1.

Estalrich, A., Rosas, A., García-Vargas, S., García-Tabernero, A., Santamaría, D. and de la Rasilla, M. 2011. Brief communication: subvertical grooves on interproximal wear facets from the El Sidrón (Asturias, Spain) Neandertal dental sample. *American Journal of Physical Anthropology* 144, 154–161.

Evans, J. 1860. On the occurrence of flint implements in undisturbed beds of gravel, sand and clay. *Archaeologia* 38, 280–307.

Eyles, N. and McCabe, A. M. 1989. The Late Devensian (<22,000 BP) Irish Sea Basin: the sedimentary record of a collapsed ice sheet margin. *Quaternary Science Reviews* 8, 307–351.

Falconer, H. 1868. On the fossil remains found in Cefn Cave, near Bryn Elwy, North Wales (extracted from notes of a visit by the author to Cefn Cave on August 27 1859, 541–542. In C. Murchison (ed.) *Palaeontological Memoirs and Notes of the Late Hugh Falconer, A.M., M.D.* Vol. II. London, Robert Hardwicke.

Falguères, C., Yokoyama, Y., Shen, G., Bischoff, J. L., Ku, T. –L. and de Lumley, H. 2004. New U-series dates at the Caune de l'Arago, France. *Journal of Archaeological Science* 31 (7) 941–952.

Fiorenza, L., Kullmer, O., Bacso, S. and Schrenk, F. 2008a. Function and wear pattern analysis in Neanderthal and early *Homo sapiens* dentitions. *American Association of Physical Anthropology* Supplement 46, 96.

Fiorenza, L., Benazzi, S., Kullmer, O. and Schrenk, F. 2008b. Dental occlusion and wear pattern analysis in Neanderthals and early *Homo sapiens. Program and Abstracts of 14th International Symposium on Dental Morphology, Griefswald, Germany,* 7.

Fish, P. R. 1979. *The Interpretative Potential of Mousterian Debitage.* Arizona, Arizona State University Anthropological Research Papers 16.

Fisher, J. 1914. Some place-names in the locality of St Asaph. *Archaeologia Cambrensis* 69, 221–246.

Fisher, J. 1915. The discovery of the Cefn Caves. *Rhyl Journal,* 10 July 1915.

Fisher, J. (ed.). 1917. *Tours in Wales (1804–1813) by Richard Fenton.* London, Cambrian Archaeological Association.

Fishwick, A. 1977. The Conway Basin. *Cambria* 4, 56–64.

Ford, T. D. 1976. The geology of caves. In T. D. Ford, and C. H. D. Cullingford (eds). *The Science of Speleology,* 11–60. London, Academic Press.

Ford, T. D. 1997. Stalagmite sheets shattered by earthquakes. *Cave and Karst Science* 24 (3), 140–141.

Ford, D. C. and Ewers, R. O. 1978. The development of limestone cave systems in the dimensions of length and depth. *Canadian Journal of Earth Sciences* 15, 1783–1798.

Frame, J. 2010. *An Angel at My Table.* London, Virago Press.

Frayer, D. W. 1978. *The Evolution of the Dentition in Upper Palaeolithic and Mesolithic Europe.* Kansas, University of Kansas Publications in Anthropology no. 10.

Frayer, D. W. 1984. Biological and cultural change in the European Late Pleistocene and Early Holocene. In F. H. Smith and F. Spencer (eds). *The Origins of Modern Humans:*

*a world survey of the fossil evidence,* 211–250. New York, Alan R. Liss.

Fuller, B. T., Fuller, J. L., Harris, D. A. and Hedges, R. E. M. 2006. Detection of breastfeeding and weaning in modern human infants with carbon and nitrogen stable isotope ratios. *American Journal of Physical Anthropology* 129, 279–293.

Gamble, C. and Kruszynski, R. 2009. John Evans, Joseph Prestwich and the stone that shattered the time barrier. *Antiquity* 83, 461–475.

Garrod, D. A. E. 1926. *The Upper Palaeolithic Age in Britain.* Oxford, The Clarendon Press.

Gascoyne, M., Ford, D. C. and Schwarcz, H. P. 1983. Rates of cave and landform development in the Yorkshire Dales from speleothem age data. *Earth Surface Processes and Landforms* 8, 557–568.

Geneste, J. -M. 1988. Les industries de la Grotte Vaufrey: technologie du debitage, economie et circulation de la matiere premiere lithique. In J. -P. Rigaud *La Grotte Vaufrey: palaeoenvironnement, chronologie, activites humaines,* 441–517. Paris, Memoires de la Societé Préhistorique Française 19.

Genet-Varcin, E. 1976. Etude de dents humaines isolées provenant des Grottes de la Chaise de Vouthon (Charente), IV Les prémolaire. *Bulletins et Mémoires de la Société d'Anthropologie Paris* 3, série XIII, 243–259.

Genomi, L., Iacumin, P., Nikolaev, V., Gribchenko and Longinelli, A. 1998. Oxygen isotope measurements of mammoth and reindeer skeletal remains: an archive of Late Pleistocene environmental conditions in Eurasian Arctic. *Earth and Planetary Science Letters* 160, 587–592.

George, T. N. 1974a. The Cenozoic Evolution of Wales. In T. R. Owen (ed.). *The Upper Palaeozoic and Post-Palaeozoic Rocks of Wales* 341–372. Cardiff, University of Wales Press.

George, T. N. 1974b. *Prologue to a Geomorphology of Britain.* Institute of British Geographers Special Publication no.7, 113–125.

Gibbard, P. L. 1977. Pleistocene history of the Vale of St. Albans. *Philosophical Transactions of the Royal Society of London* B280, 445–483.

Gillespie, R. and Hedges, R. E. M. 1983. Sample chemistry for the Oxford high energy mass spectrometer. *Radiocarbon* 25 (20), 771–774.

Gillespie, R., Hedges, R. E. M. and Wand, J. O. 1984. Radiocarbon dating of bone by accelerator mass spectrometry. *Journal of Archaeological Science* 11, 165–170.

Gillieson, D. 1996. *Caves: processes, development and management.* Oxford, Blackwell.

Gleick, J. 1992. *Genius, the Life and Times of Richard Feynman.* New York, Pantheon.

Gómez-Robles, A., Martinón-Torres, M., Bermúdez de Castro, J. M., Margvelashvili, A., Bastir, M., Arsuaga, J. L., Pérez-Pérez, A., Estebaranz, F. and Martínez, L. M. 2007. A geometric morphometric analysis of hominin upper first molar shape. *Journal of Human Evolution* 53, 272–285.

Gómez-Robles, A., Martinón-Torres, M., Bermúdez de Castro, J. M., Prado, L., Sarmiento, S. and Arsuaga, J. L. 2008. Geometric morphometric analysis of the crown morphology of the lower first premolar of hominins, with special attention to Pleistocene *Homo. Journal of Human Evolution* 55, 627–638.

Gosse, J. C. and Phillips, F. M. 2001. Terrestrial *in situ* cosmogenic nuclides: theory and application. *Quaternary Science Reviews* 20, 1475–1560.

Gowlett, J. A. J. 2009. Boucher de Perthes: pioneer of Palaeolithic Prehistory. *Lithics* 30, 13–24.

Gowlett, J. A. J., Hedges, R. E. M., Law, I. A. and Perry, C. 1986. Radiocarbon dates from the Oxford AMS system: *Archaeometry* datelist 4. *Archaeometry* 28 (2), 206–221.

Green, H. S. 1981. The first Welshman: excavations at Pontnewydd. *Antiquity* 55, 184–195.

Green, H. S. 1983. La Grotte de Pontnewydd, Pays de Galles, Grande-Bretagne: un site du Paléolithique Inférieur avec des restes humains probablement Néandertaliens Archaíques. *L'Anthropologie* 87 (3), 417–419.

Green, H. S. 1984a. *Pontnewydd Cave: a Lower Palaeolithic Hominid Site in Wales: the first report*. Cardiff, National Museum of Wales.

Green, H. S. 1984b. The Palaeolithic artefacts. In H. S. Green *Pontnewydd Cave a Lower Palaeolithic Hominid Site in Wales: the first report*, 113–152. Cardiff, National Museum of Wales.

Green, H. S. 1986. The Palaeolithic settlement of Wales research project: a review of progress 1978–1985. In S. N. Collcutt (ed.). *The Palaeolithic of Britain and its Nearest Neighbours: recent trends*, 36–42. Sheffield, University of Sheffield.

Green, H. S. 1988. Pontnewydd Cave: the selection of raw materials for artefact-manufacture and the question of natural damage. In R. J. MacRae and N. Moloney (eds). *Non-Flint Stone Tools and the Palaeolithic Occupation of Britain*, 223–232. Oxford, British Archaeological Reports British Series 189.

Green, H. S., Bevins, R. E., Bull, P. A., Currant, A. P., Debenham, N., Embleton, C., Ivanovich, M., Livingston, H., Rae, A. M., Schwarcz, H. P. and Stringer, C. B. 1989. Le site acheuléen de la Grotte de Pontnewydd, Pays de Galles: géomorphologie, stratigraphie, chronologie, faune, hominids fossils, géologie et industrie lithique dans le contexte paléoécologique. *L'Anthropologie* 93, 15–52.

Green, H. S. and Currant, A. P. 1982. Early man in Wales: Pontnewydd Cave (Clwyd) and its Pleistocene fauna. *Nature in Wales* 1, 40–43.

Green, H. S., Stringer, C. B., Collcutt, S. N., Currant, A. P., Huxtable, J., Schwarcz, H. P., Debenham, N., Embleton, C., Bull, P., Molleson, T. I. and Bevins, R. E. 1981. Pontnewydd Cave in Wales – a new Middle Pleistocene hominid site. *Nature* 294, 707–713.

Green, H. S. and Walker, E. 1991. *Ice Age Hunters: Neanderthals and Early Modern hunters in Wales*. Cardiff, National Museum of Wales.

Grine, F. E. 1981. Occlusal morphology of the mandibular permanent molars of the South African Negro and the Kalahari San (Bushman). *Annals of the South African Museum* 86 (5), 157–215.

Groeneveld, H. T. and Kieser, J. A. 1987. An evaluation of the M-statistic in human odontomorphometric distance analysis. *International Journal of Anthropology* 2, 29–36.

Groeneveld, H. T. and Kieser, J. A. 1988. Odontometric differences between *Cercopithecus aethiops* populations: a simulation approach to estimating confidence limits for Penrose's Shape Coefficient. *International Journal of Primatology* 9 (1), 49–58.

Grün, R., Huang, P. -H., Wu, X., Stringer, C. B., Thorne, A. G. and McCulloch, M. 1997. ESR analysis of teeth from the palaeoanthropological site of Zhoukoudian, China. *Journal of Human Evolution* 32 (1), 83–91.

Guatelli-Steinberg, D. and Reid, D. J. 2008. What molars contribute to an emerging understanding of lateral enamel formation in Neandertals vs. modern humans. *Journal of Human Evolution* 54 (2), 236–250.

Guatelli-Steinberg, D., Reid, D. J., Bishop, T. A. and Larsen, C. S. 2005. Anterior tooth growth periods in Neandertals were comparable to those of modern humans. *Proceedings of the National Academy of Sciences USA*. 102 (40) 14197–14202.

Guatelli-Steinberg, D., Reid, D. J. and Bishop, T. A. 2007. Did the lateral enamel of Neandertal anterior teeth grow differently from that of modern humans? *Journal of Human Evolution* 52 (1), 72–84.

Hardaker, T. 2006. Two sets of twins re-united in Oxfordshire. *Lithics* 27, 74–82.

Hardy, B. L. 2010. Climatic variability and plant food distribution in Pleistocene Europe: implications for Neanderthal diet and subsistence. *Quaternary Science Reviews* 29 (5–6), 662–679.

Harris, A. N. 1947. *The Denudation Chronology of North-East Wales*, unpublished PhD thesis, London University.

Harrison, C. J. O. and Walker, C. A. 1977. A re-examination of the fossil birds from the Upper Pleistocene in the London Basin. *London Naturalist* 56, 6–9.

Haydenblit, R. 1996. Dental variation among four prehispanic Mexican populations. *American Journal of Physical Anthropology* 100, 225–246.

Hedges, R. E. M., Clement, J. G., Thomas, C. D. L. and O'Connell, T. C. 2007. Collagen turnover in the adult femoral mid-shaft: modeled from anthropogenic radiocarbon tracer measurements. *American Journal of Physical Anthropology* 133, 808–816.

Hedges, R. E. M., Housley, R. A., Bronk Ramsey, C. and van Kinken, G. J. 1994. Radiocarbon dates from the Oxford AMS system: *Archaeometry* datelist 18. *Archaeometry* 36 (2), 337–374.

Hedges, R. E. M., Housley, R. A., Law, I. A., Perry, C. and Gowlett, J. A. J. 1987. Radiocarbon dates from the Oxford AMS system: *Archaeometry* datelist 6. *Archaeometry* 29 (2), 289–306.

Hedges, R. E. M., Law, I. A., Bronk, C. R. and Housley, R. A. 1989. The Oxford accelerator mass spectrometry facility: technical developments in routine dating. *Archaeometry* 31, 99–113.

Hedges, R. E. M., Pettitt, P. B., Bronk Ramsey, C. and Klinken, G. J. van 1996. Radiocarbon dates from the Oxford AMS system. *Archaeometry* datelist 22. *Archaeometry* 38 (2), 391–415.

Hedges, R. E. M. and Reynard, L. M. 2007. Nitrogen isotopes and the trophic level of humans in archaeology. *Journal of Archaeological Science* 34 (8), 1240–1251.

Hedges, R. E. M., Stevens, R. E. and Richards, M. P. 2004. Bone as a stable isotope archive for local climatic information. *Quaternary Science Reviews* 23, 959–965.

Henry, A. G., Brooks, A. S. and Piperno, D. R. 2011. Microfossils in calculus demonstrate consumption of plants and cooked foods in Neanderthal diets (Shanidar III, Iraq; Spy I and II, Belgium). *Proceedings of the National Academy of Sciences* 108 (2), 486–491.

Hershkovitz, P. 1971. Basic crown patterns and cusp homologies of mammalian teeth. In A. A. Dahlberg (ed.). *Dental Morphology and Evolution*, 95–149. Illinois and Chicago, University of Chicago Press.

Hicks, H. 1884. On some recent researches in the bone-caves in Wales. *Proceedings of the Geologists' Association* 9 (1), 1–20.

Hicks, H. 1886a. Results of recent researches in some bone-caves in North Wales (Ffynnon Beuno and Cae Gwyn). *The Quarterly Journal of the Geological Society of London* 42, 3–19.

Hicks H. 1886b. Report of the committee consisting of Professor T. McK. Hughes, Dr H. Hicks, Messrs H. Woodward, E. G. Luxmoore, P. P. Pennant and Edwin Morgan, appointed for the purpose of exploring the caves of North Wales. *The Report of the Fifty-Sixth Meeting of the British Association for the Advancement of Science held at Birmingham in Sept. 1886*, 219–223.

Hicks H. 1886c. Letter – Periodicity of glacial epochs. *Nature* 34, July 8, 216.

Hicks, H. 1887. On some recent researches in bone-caves in Wales. *Proceedings of the Geologists' Association* 9, 1–20.

Higham, T. F. G., Jacobi, R. M. and Bronk-Ramsey, C. 2006. AMS Radiocarbon dating of ancient bone using ultrafiltration. *Radiocarbon* 48 (2), 179–195.

Hiiemae, K. M. 1978. Mammalian mastication: a review of the activity of the jaw muscles and the movements they produce in chewing. In P. M. Butler, and K. A. Joysey (eds). *Development, Function and Evolution of Teeth*, 359–398. London, Academic Press.

Hillis, R. S., Holford, S. P., Green, P. F., Doré, A. G., Gatliff, R., Stoker, M. S., Thomson, K., Turner, J. P., Underhill J. R. and Williams, G. A. 2008. Cenozoic exhumation of the southern British Isles. *Geology* 36, 371–374.

Hillson, S. 1996. *Dental Anthropology.* Cambridge, Cambridge University Press.

Hillson, S., Parfitt, S. and Stringer, C. 2006. Two hominin incisor teeth from the Middle Pleistocene site of Boxgrove, Sussex, England. In M. B. Roberts, S. A. Parfitt and M. I. Pope (eds). *The Archaeology of the Middle Pleistocene Hominin Site at Boxgrove, West Sussex, U.K. Excavations 1991–1996.* London, English Heritage Monograph Series.

Hodell, D. A., Evans, H. F., Channell, J. A. T. and Curtis, J. H. 2010. Phase relationships of North Atlantic ice-rafted debris and surface-deep climate proxies during the last glacial period. *Quaternary Science Reviews* 29, 3875–3886.

Hodgson, J. M. (ed.). 1974. *Soil Survey Field Handbook, describing and sampling soil profiles.* Soil Survey Technical Monograph no. 5. Harpenden, Rothamsted Experimental Station.

Holliday, D. W. 1993. Mesozoic cover over northern England: interpretation of apatite fission track data. *Journal of the Geological Society of London* 150, 657–660.

Hollingworth, S. E. 1931. The glaciation of western Edenside and adjoining areas and the drumlins of Edenside and the Solway Firth. *Quarterly Journal of the Geological Society of London* 87, 281–359.

Hosfield, R. T. and Chambers, J. C. 2002. The Lower Palaeolithic site of Broom: geoarchaeological implications of optical dating. *Lithics* 23, 33–42.

Hosfield, R. T. and Chambers, J. 2009. Genuine diversity? The Broom biface assemblage. *Proceedings of the Prehistoric Society* 75, 65–100.

Howell, F. C. 1960. European and northwest African Middle Pleistocene hominids. *Current Anthropology* 1, 195–232.

Howells, M. F., Reedman, A. J. and Campbell, S. D. G. 1991. *Ordovician (Caradoc) Marginal Basin Volcanism in Snowdonia (North-west Wales).* London, H.M.S.O. for the British Geological Survey.

Howells, W. W. 1975. Reply to 'Did la Ferrassie I use his teeth as a tool?' J. A. Wallace. *Current Anthropology* 16 (3), 397–398.

Hughen, K., Southon, J., Lehman, S., Bertrand, C. and Turnbull, J. 2006. Marine-derived $^{14}$C calibration and activity record for the past 50,000 years updated from the Cariaco Basin. *Quaternary Science Reviews* 25 (23–24), 3216–3227.

Hughes, P. D. 2002. Loch Lomond Stadial glaciers in the Aran and Arenig Mountains, North Wales, Great Britain. *Geological Journal* 37, 9–15.

Hughes, T. McK. 1885. Notes on the geology of the Vale of Clwyd. *Proceedings of the Chester Society of Natural Science* 3, 5–37.

Hughes, T. McK. 1887. On the drifts of the Vale of Clwyd and their relation to the caves and cave-deposits. *The Quarterly Journal of the Geological Society of London* 43, 73–120.

Hughes, T. McK. and Thomas, D. R. 1874. On the occurrence of felstone implements of the Le Moustier type in Pontnewydd Cave, near Cefn, St Asaph. *Journal of the Anthropological Institute* 3, 387–390.

Hughes, T. McK. and Williams Wynn, R. W. H. W. 1882. The results of recent further excavations in the caves of Cefn near St Asaph, North Wales. *Report of the Fifty-First Meeting of the British Association for the Advancement of Science held at York in August and September 1881*, 700.

Huxtable, J. 1984. Thermoluminescence (TL) studies on burnt flint and stones. In H. S. Green *Pontnewydd Cave a Lower Palaeolithic Hominid Site in Wales: the first report*, 106–107. Cardiff, National Museum of Wales.

Huybers, P. 2007. Glacial variability over the last two million years: an extended depth-derived age model, continuous obliquity pacing, and the Pleistocene progression. *Quaternary Science Reviews* 26, 37–55.

Iacumin, P., Nikolaev, V., Ramigni, M. and Longinelli, A. 2004. Oxygen isotope analyses of mammal bone remains from Holocene sites in European Russia: palaeoclimatic implications. *Global and Planetary Change* 40, 169–176.

Irish, J. D. 1993. Biological affinities of Late Pleistocene through modern African Aboriginal populations: the dental evidence. PhD Thesis, Arizona State University.

Irish, J. D. 1998. Ancestral dental traits in recent sub-Saharan Africans and the origins of modern humans. *Journal of Human Evolution* 34, 81–98.

Irish, J. D. and Guatelli-Steinberg, D. 2003. Ancient teeth and modern human origins: an expanded comparison of African Plio-Pleistocene and recent world dental samples. *Journal of Human Evolution* 45, 113–144.

Ivanovich, M., Rae, A. M. B. and Wilkins, M. A. 1984. Brief report on dating the *in situ* stalagmitic floor found in the east passage in 1982. In H. S. Green *Pontnewydd Cave a Lower Palaeolithic Hominid Site in Wales: the first report*, 98–99. Cardiff, National Museum of Wales.

Jackson, H. 2002. *Investigations into the Mineralogy and Petrology of the Artefacts and Sediments of the Lower Palaeolithic Site of Pontnewydd Cave, North Wales.* Unpublished M.Phil. thesis, University of Wales, Bangor.

Jacobi, R. 1999. Some observations on the British Early Upper Palaeolithic. In W. Davies and R. Charles (eds). *Dorothy Garrod and the Progress of the Palaeolithic*, 35–40. Oxford, Oxbow Books.

Jacobi, R. 2004. The Late Upper Palaeolithic lithic collection from Gough's Cave Cheddar, Somerset and human use of the cave. *Proceedings of the Prehistoric Society* 70, 1–92.

Jacobi, R. M. and Higham, T. F. G. 2008. The 'Red Lady' ages gracefully: new ultrafiltration AMS determinations from Paviland. *Journal of Human Evolution* 55, 898–907.

Jacobi, R. M., Higham, T. F. G. and Bronk-Ramsey, C. 2006. AMS radiocarbon dating of Middle and Upper Palaeolithic bone in the British Isles: improved reliability using ultrafiltration. *Journal of Quaternary Science* 21, 557–573.

Janis, C. M. 1984. Prediction of primate diets from molar wear patterns. In D. J. Chivers, B. A. Wood and A. Bilsborough (eds). *Food Acquisition and Processing in Primates*, 331–340. New York, Plenum Press.

Jansson, K. N. and Glasser, N. F. 2005. Palaeoglaciology of the Welsh sector of the British–Irish ice sheet. *Journal of the Geological Society of London* 162, 25–37.

Jenkins, D. A. 1984. Sand and clay mineralogy. In H. S. Green *Pontnewydd Cave: a Lower Palaeolithic Hominid Site in Wales: the first report*, 181–185. Cardiff, National Museum of Wales.

Jenkinson, R. D. S. 1984. *Creswell Crags. Late Pleistocene Sites in the East Midlands*. Oxford, British Archaeological Reports British Series 122.

Johnsen, S. J., Dahl-Jensen, D., Dansgaard, W. and Gundestrup, N. 1995. Greenland palaeotemperatures derived from GRIP bore hole temperature and ice core isotope profiles. *Tellus* 47B, 624–629.

Johnsen, T. F., Olsen, L. and Murray, A. (In press). OSL ages in central Norway support a MIS 2 interstadial (25–20 ka) and a dynamic Scandinavian ice sheet. *Quaternary Science Reviews*.

Jones, B. and MacDonald, R. W. 1989. Micro-organisms and crystal fabrics in cave pisoliths from Grand Cayman, British West Indies. *Journal of Sedimentary Petrology* 59, 387–396.

Jones, B. and Motyka, A. 1987. Biogenic structures and micrite in stalactites from Grand Cayman Island, British West Indies. *Canadian Journal of Earth Sciences* 24, 1402–1411.

Jones, G. and Jones, T. 2000. *The Mabinogion*. London, Everyman's Library.

Jones, O. T. 1937. On the sliding or slumping of submarine sediments in Denbighshire, North Wales, during the Ludlow period. *Quarterly Journal of the Geological Society of London* 93, 241–283.

Jones, P. R. 1979. Effects of raw materials on biface manufacture. *Science* 204, 815–816.

Jordan, R. E., Abrams, L. and Kraus, B. S. 1992. *Kraus' Dental Anatomy and Occlusion, 2nd Edition*. St Louis, Mosby Year Book.

Jouzel, J., Lorius, C., Merlivat, L. and Petit, J. -R. 1987. Abrupt climatic changes: the Antarctic ice record during the Late Pleistocene. In W. H. Berger and L. D. Labeyrie (eds). *Abrupt Climate Change*, 235–245. Dordrecht, Reidel Publishing.

Jouzel, J., Masson-Delmotte, V., Cattani, O., Dreyfus, G., Falourd, S., Hoffmann, G., Nouet, J., Barnola, J. M., Chappellaz, J., Fischer, H., Gallet, J. C., Johnsen, S., Leuenberger, M., Loulergue, L., Luethi, D., Oerter, H., Parrenin, F., Raisbeck, G., Raynaud, D., Schwander, J., Spahni, R., Souchez, R., Selmo, E., Schilt, A., Steffensen, J. P., Stenni, B., Stauffer, B., Stocker, T., Tison, J. -L., Werner, M. and Wolff, E. W. 2007. Orbital and millennial Antarctic climate variability over the last 800,000 years. *Science* 317, 793–796.

Kafka, F. 1978. *Wedding Preparations in the Country and Other Stories*. London, Penguin Books.

Kaidonis, J. A., Townsend, G. C. and Richards, L. C. 1992. Brief communication: interproximal tooth wear: a new observation. *American Journal of Physical Anthropology* 88, 105–107.

Kallay, J. 1970. A new classification of the taurodont teeth of the Krapina Neanderthal man. *Bulletin Scientifique (Yugoslavie)* 15, 2–3.

Kanazawa, E., Sekikawa, M. and Ozaki, T. 1990. A quantitative investigation of irregular cuspules in human maxillary permanent molars. *American Journal of Physical Anthropology* 83, 173–180.

Katzenberg, M. A. 2000. Stable isotope analysis: a tool for studying past diet, demography, and life history. In M. A. Katzenberg and S. R. Saunders (eds). *Biological Anthropology of the Human Skeleton*, 305–327. New York, Wiley-Liss.

Keene, H. J. 1966. A morphological and biometric study of taurodontism in a contemporary population. *American Journal of Physical Anthropology* 25, 208–209.

Kelly, J. F. 2000. Stable isotopes of carbon and nitrogen in the study of avian and mammalian trophic ecology. *Canadian Journal of Zoology* 78, 1–27.

Kelly, S. F. Spring 1967. Letter – as good as new. *The Speleologist* 2, 20–21.

Kennedy, G. E. 2005. From the ape's dilemma to the weanling's dilemma: early weaning and its evolutionary context. *Journal of Human Evolution* 48 (2), 123–145.

Kershaw, P. J. 1986. Radiocarbon dating of Irish Sea sediments. *Estuarine, Coastal and Shelf Science* 23, 295–303.

Kieser, J. A. 1990. *Human Adult Odontometrics, the Study of Variation in Adult Tooth Size*. Cambridge, Cambridge University Press, Cambridge Studies in Biological Anthropology.

Klein, R. G. 2009. *The Human Career, Human Biological and Cultural Origins 3rd Edition*. Chicago, University of Chicago Press.

Knight, J. 2001. Glaciomarine deposition around the Irish Sea basin: some problems and solutions. *Journal of Quaternary Science* 16, 405–418.

Knutz, P. C. 2000. *Late Pleistocene Glacial Fluctuations and Palaeogeography on the Continental Margin of North West Britain*. Unpublished PhD thesis, Cardiff University.

Knutz, P. C., Zahn, R. and Hall, I. 2007. Centennial-scale variability of the British Ice Sheet: implications for climate forcing and Atlantic meridional overturning circulation during the last deglaciation. *Paleoceanography* 22, PA 1207.

Kolen, J, 1999. Hominids without homes. In W. Roebrucks, and C. Gamble (eds). *The Middle Palaeolithic Occupation of Europe*, 139–173. Leiden, University of Leiden.

Kolodny, Y. and Luz, B. 1991. Oxygen isotopes in phosphates of fossil fish – Devonian to recent. In H. P. Taylor, J. R. O'Neil and I. R. Kaplan (eds). *Stable Isotope Geochemistry: a tribute to Samuel Epstein*, 105–119. San Antonio, Texas, The Geochemical Society, Special Publication no. 3.

Korenhof, C. A. W. 1960. *Morphogenetical Aspects of the Human Upper Molar*. Utrecht, Uitgeversmaatschappij Neerlandia.

Kraus, B. S. and Furr, M. L. 1953. Lower first premolars. Part 1. A definition and classification of discrete morphological traits. *Journal of Dental Research* 32, 554–564.

Kusimba, C. and Kusimba, S. 2000. Hinterlands and cities: archaeological investigations of economy and trade in Tsavo, southeastern Kenya. *Nyame Akuma* 54, 13–24.

Lacruz, R. S., Ramirez Rozzi, F. and Bromage, T. G. 2006. Variation in enamel development of South African fossil hominids. *Journal of Human Evolution* 51 (6), 580–590.

Lalueza-Fox, C. L. and Frayer, D. W. 1997. Non-dietary marks in the anterior dentition of the Krapina Neanderthals. *International Journal of Osteoarchaeology* 7, 133–149.

Lalueza-Fox, C. and Pérez-Pérez, A. 1993. The diet of the Neanderthal child Gibraltar 2 (Devil's Tower) through the study of the vestibular striation pattern. *Journal of Human Evolution* 24, 29–41.

Lalueza-Fox, C. and Pérez-Pérez, A. 1994. Cut marks and *post mortem* striations in fossil human teeth. *Human Evolution* 9 (N2), 165–172.

Lalueza, C., Pérez-Pérez, A. and Turbón, D. 1993. Microscopic study of the Banyoles mandible (Girona, Spain): diet, cultural activity and toothpick use. *Journal of Human Evolution* 24, 281–300.

Lambeck, K. 1996. Glaciation and sea level change of Ireland and the Irish Sea since Late Devensian/Midlandian time. *Journal of the Geological Society of London* 153, 853–872.

Lambeck, K. and Purcell, A. P. 2001. Sea-level change for Ireland and the Irish Sea since Late Devensian/Midlandian times. *Journal of the Geological Society* 152, 437–448.

Landeghem van, J. J., Wheeler, A. J. and Mitchell, N. C. 2009. Seafloor evidence for palaeo-ice streaming and calving of the grounded Irish Sea ice stream: implications for the interpretation of its final deglaciation phase. *Boreas* 38, 119–131.

Lang, A. T. O. and Keen, D. H. 2003. A further andesite handaxe from Waverley Wood quarry, Warwickshire. *Lithics* 24, 32–36.

Lang, A. T. O. and Keen, D. H. 2005. At the edge of the world, hominid colonisation and the Lower and Middle Palaeolithic of the West Midlands. *Proceedings of the Prehistoric Society* 71, 63–84.

Lanning, E. 1970. Pleistocene man in South America. *World Archaeology* 2, 90–111.

Lasker, G. W. 1950. Genetic analysis of racial traits of the teeth. *Cold Spring Harbor Symposia on Quantitative Biology* 15, 191–203.

Lavelle, C. L. B. 1970. Analysis of attrition in adult human molars. *Journal of Dental Research* 49 (4), 822–828.

Law I. A. and Hedges, R. E. M. 1989. A semi-automated bone pretreatment system and the pretreatment of older and contaminated samples. *Radiocarbon* 31, 247–253.

Leakey, R. E. F., Mungai, J. M. and Walker, A. C. 1972. New Australopithecines from East Rudolf, Kenya (11). *American Journal of Physical Anthropology* 36, 235–252.

Lebel, S. and Trinkaus, E. 2002. Middle Pleistocene human remains from the Bau de L'Aubesier. *Journal of Human Evolution* 43, 659–685.

Lee-Thorp, J. and Sponheimer, M. 2003. Three case studies used to reassess the reliability of fossil bone and enamel isotope signals for paleodietary studies. *Journal of Anthropological Archaeology* 22, 208–216.

Lefèvre, J. 1973. Etude odontologique des Hommes de Muge. *Bulletins et Mémoires de la Société d'Anthropologie de Paris* 10, série XII, 301–333.

Legoux, P. 1961. Remarques sur certains aspects de la mandibule de l'enfant d'Ehringsdorf. *Comptes Rendus des Séances de l'Academie des Sciences, Paris* 252 (12) (20.3.61), 1821–1823.

Leigh, R. W. 1925. Dental pathology of the Eskimo. *Dental Cosmos* 67, 884–898.

Lewis, C. A. 2005. Introduction. In C. A. Lewis, and A. E. Richards (eds). *The Glaciations of Wales and Adjacent Areas*, 1–16. Herefordshire, Logaston Press.

Lewis, C. L. E., Green, P. F., Carter, A. and Hurford, A. J. 1992. Elevated K/T palaeotemperatures throughout northwest England: three kilometres of Tertiary erosion? *Earth and Planetary Science Letters* 112, 131–148.

Libby, W. F., Berger, R., Mead, J. F., Alexander, G. V. and Ross, J. F. 1964. Replacement rates for human tissue from atmospheric radiocarbon. *Science* 146, 1170–1173.

Lindsay, J. F. 1968. The development of clast fabric in mudflow. *Journal of Sedimentary Petrology* 38, 1242–1253.

Linton, D. L. 1951. The Midland drainage, some considerations bearing on its origin. *The Advancement of Science* 7, (28) 449–456.

Livingston, H. J. 1986. *Quaternary Geomorphology of Part of the Elwy Valley and Vale of Clwyd, North East Wales.* Unpublished PhD thesis, King's College, University of London.

Livingston, H. J. 1990. Geomorphology of the Elwy Valley and Vale of Clwyd. In K. Addison, M. J. Edge and R. Watkins. *North Wales Field Guide*, 144–154. Coventry, Quaternary Research Association.

Longinelli, A. 1984. Oxygen isotopes in mammal bone phosphate: a new tool for paleohydrological and paleoclimatological research? *Geochimica et Cosmochimica Acta* 48, 385–390.

Longinelli, A., Iacumin, P., Davanzo, S. and Nikolaev, V. 2003. Modern reindeer and mice: revised phosphate-water isotope equations. *Earth and Planetary Science Letters* 214, 491–498.

Lordkipanidze, D., Jashashvili, T., Vekua, A., Ponce de Leon, M. S., Zollikofer, C. P., Rightmire, G. P., Pontzer, H., Ferring, R., Oms, O., Tappen, M., Bukhsianidze, M., Agusti, J., Kahlke, R., Kiladze, G., Martinez-Navarro, B., Mouskhelishvili, A., Nioradze M. and Rook, L. 2007. Postcranial evidence from early *Homo* from Dmanisi, Georgia. *Nature* 449, 305–310.

Love, K. M. and Chafetz, H. S. 1988. Diagenesis of laminated travertine crusts, Arbuckle Mountains, Oklahoma. *Journal of Sedimentary Petrology* 58, 441–445.

Lowe, J. J. and Walker, M. J. C. 1997. *Reconstructing Quaternary Environments* 2nd Edition. Harlow, Longman.

Ludwig, F. J. 1957. The mandibular second molars: morphologic variation and inheritance. *Journal of Dental Research* 36, 263–273.

Luedtke, B. 1979. The identification of sources of chert artefacts. *American Antiquity* 44, 744–757.

Lukacs, J. R. 1989. Dental palaeopathology: methods for reconstructing dietary patterns. In M. Y. Işcan and K. A. R. Kennedy (eds). *Reconstruction of Life from the Skeleton*, 261–286. New York, Alan R. Liss.

Lumley, M. A. de 1975. Ante-Neanderthals of western Europe. In R. H. Tuttle (ed.). *Palaeoanthropology, morphology and palaeoecology*, 381–387. The Hague, Mouton.

Luz, B. and Kolodny, Y. 1985. Oxygen isotope variations in phosphate of biogenic apatites, IV. Mammal teeth and bones. *Earth and Planetary Science Letters* 75 (1), 29–36.

Lycett, S. J. and Cramon-Taubadel, N. von 2008. Acheulean variability and hominin dispersals: a model-bound approach. *Journal of Archaeological Science* 35, 553–562.

Lyman, R. L. 1994. *Vertebrate Taphonomy*. Cambridge, Cambridge University Press.

Macchiarelli R., Bondioli L., Debénath A., Mazurier A., Tournepiche J. -F., Birch W. and Dean C. 2006. How Neanderthal molar teeth grew. *Nature* 444, 748–751.

Mackintosh, D. 1876. On the correlation of the deposits in Cefn and Pont-newydd caves with the drifts of the north-west of England and Wales. *The Quarterly Journal of the Geological Society of London* 32, 91–94.

MacNeice, L. 2001. *Louis MacNeice Poems Selected by Michael Longley*. London, Faber and Faber.

MacRae, R. J. and Moloney, N. 1988. *Non-Flint Stone Tools and the Palaeolithic Occupation of Britain*. Oxford, British Archaeological Report British Series 189.

Maddy, D. 1999. English Midlands. In D. Q. Bowen (ed.). A revised correlation of Quaternary deposits in the British Isles, 28–44. *Geological Society of London Special Report No. 23*.

Maddy, D., Lewis, S. G., Green, C. P. and Bowen, D. Q. 1995. Pleistocene Geology of the Lower Severn Valley, U.K. *Quaternary Science Reviews* 14, 209–222.

Mallegni, F., Bertoldi, F. and Carnieri, E. 2002. New Middle Pleistocene human remains from northern Italy. *Homo* 52 (3), 233–239.

Mania, D. and Vlček, E. 1981. *Homo erectus* in Middle Europe: the discovery from Bilzingsleben. In B. A. Sigmon and J. S. Cybulski (eds). *Homo erectus. Papers in honour of Davidson Black*, 133–151. Toronto, University of Toronto Press.

Marinos, G., Yannoulis, P. and Sotiriadis, L. 1965. Palaeoanthropological investigations of the Chalcidic Cave of Petralona. *Physics-Mathematics School. Aristotelion Panepistomion Thessalonika, Thessalonika* 9, 148–204.

Martinón-Torres, M., Bastir, M., Bermúdez de Castro, J. M., Gómez, A., Sarmiento, S., Muela, A. and Arsuaga, J. L. 2006. Hominin lower second premolar morphology: evolutionary inferences through geometric morphometric analysis. *Journal of Human Evolution* 50 (5), 523–533.

Martinón-Torres, M., Bermúdez de Castro, J. M., Bastir, M., Gómez-Robles, A., Sarmiento, S., Bastir, M., Muela, A. and Arsuaga, J. L. 2007a. Gran Dolina-TD6 and Sima de los Huesos dental samples: preliminary approach to some dental characters of interest for phylogenetic studies. In S. E. Bailey and J. -J. Hublin (eds). *Dental Perspectives on Human Evolution: state of the art research in dental paleoanthropology* 65–79. Springer, New York, Max Planck Institute subseries in Human Evolution.

Martinón-Torres, M., Bermúdez de Castro J. M., Gómez-Robles, A., Arsuaga, J. L., Carbonell, E., Lordkipanidze, D., Manzi, G. and Margvelashvili, A. 2007b. Dental evidence on the hominin dispersals during the Pleistocene. *Proceedings of the National Academy of Sciences USA* 104 (33), 13279–13282.

Maw, G., 1865. On some deposits of chert, white sand and clay in the neighbourhood of Llandudno, North Wales. *Geological Magazine* 2, 200–204.

McCabe, A. M. 2008. *Glacial Geology and Geomorphology: the landscapes of Ireland*. Edinburgh, Dunedin.

McCabe, A. M. and Clark, P. U. 1998. Ice sheet variability around the Atlantic Ocean during the last deglaciation. *Nature* 392, 373–377.

McCabe, A. M., Clark, P. U. and Clark, J. 2005. AMS [14]C dating of deglacial events in the Irish Sea Basin and other sectors of the British-Irish ice sheet. *Quaternary Science Reviews* 24, 1673–1690.

McCown, T. and Keith, A. 1939. *The Stone Age of Mount Carmel, Vol. II.* Oxford, Clarendon Press.

Meeson, R. A. 1966. *North Wales Caves*. Shropshire Mining Club Account no. 5.

Mellaart, J. 1967. *Catal Hüyük – a Neolithic town in Anatolia*. London, Thames and Hudson, new aspects of antiquity series.

Mellars, P. 1996. *The Neanderthal Legacy: an archaeological perspective from Western Europe*. Princeton, Princeton University Press.

Meller, N. 1997. The metamorphic history of the Borrowdale Volcanic Group, North-West England. Unpublished PhD thesis, University of Bristol.

Middleton Shaw, J. C. 1931. *The Teeth, the Bony Palate and the Mandible in Bantu Races of South Africa*. London, John Bale, Sons and Danielsson.

Mills, H. H. 1991. Three dimensional clast orientation in glacial and mass-movement sediments. *U. S. Geological Survey Open File Report* 90–128.

Millward, D., Johnson, E. W., Beddoe-Stephens, B., Young, B., Kneller, B. C., Lee, M. K., Allen, P. M., Branney, M. J., Cooper, D. C., Hirons, S., Kokellar, B. P., Marks, R. J., McConnell, B. J., Merrit, J. W., Molyneux, S. G., Petterson, M. G., Roberts, B., Rundle, C. C., Rushton, A. W. A., Scott, R. W., Spoer, N. J. and Stone, P. 2000. Geology of the Ambleside district. *Memoir of the British Geological Survey*, Sheet 38 (England and Wales).

Miyabara, T. 1916. An anthropological study of the masticatory system in the Japanese: (1) the teeth. *The Dental Cosmos* 58, 739–749.

Moldywarps Speleological Group, 1987. Journal 11.

Molnar, S. 1971. Human tooth wear, tooth function and cultural variability. *American Journal of Physical Anthropology* 34, 175–190.

Moloney, N. 1988. Experimental biface manufacture using non-flint lithic materials. In R. J. MacRae and N. Moloney (eds). *Non-Flint Stone Tools and the Palaeolithic Occupation of Britain*, 49–65. Oxford, British Archaeological Report British Series 189.

Moloney, N., Bergman, C., Newcomer, M. and Wenban-Smith, F. 1988. Experimental replication of bifacial implements using Bunter quartzite pebbles. In R. J. MacRae and N. Moloney (eds). *Non-Flint Stone Tools and the Palaeolithic Occupation of Britain*, 25–47. Oxford, British Archaeological Report British Series 189.

Monnier, J. -L. 1982. Le Paléolithique Inférieur et Moyen en Bretagne. Habitats et Économie des Matières Premières. *Bulletin de L'Association Française pour L'Étude du Quaternaire* 2 (3), 93–104.

Moore, G. W. and Sullivan, N. 1997. *Speleology: Caves and the Cave Environment*. St Louis, Cave Books.

Moorrees, C. F. A. 1957. *The Aleut Dentition*. Cambridge, Harvard University Press.

Morgan, A. V. 1973. The Pleistocene geology of the area north and west of Wolverhampton, Staffordshire, England. *Philosophical Transactions of the Royal Society of London* B265, 233–297.

Morris, D. H. 1986. Maxillary molar occlusal polygons in five human samples. *American Journal of Physical Anthropology* 70, 333–338.

Morris, R. H. (ed.). 1909. *Parochialia, Being a Summary of Answers to Parochial Queries in Order to a Geographical Dictionary, etc. of Wales issued by Edward Lhwyd. Part 1.* London, Cambrian Archaeological Association.

Morton, G. H. 1897. *The Geology of the Country Around Liverpool Including the North of Flintshire*. London, Philip.

Morwood, M. and Jungers, W. 2009. Conclusions: implications of the Liang Bua finds for hominin evolution and biogeography. *Journal of Human Evolution* 57, 640–650.

Murrill, R. I. 1981. *Petralona Man. A Descriptive and Comparative Study with New Important Information on Rhodesian Man.* Springfield, Charles C. Thomas.

Mussi, M. 2001. *Earliest Italy: an overview of the Italian Palaeolithic and Mesolithic*. New York, Kluwer Academic.

Neaverson, E. 1942. A summary of the records of Pleistocene and postglacial mammalian from North Wales and Merseyside. *Proceedings of the Liverpool Geological Society* 18 (3), 70–85.

Nelson, C. T. 1938. The teeth of the Indians of Pecos Pueblo. *American Journal of Physical Anthropology* 23, 261–293.

NESPOS Database 2010 /www.nespos.org.

Newcomer, M. H. 1984. Flaking experiments with Pontnewydd raw materials. In H. S. Green *Pontnewydd Cave a Lower Palaeolithic Hominid Site in Wales: the first report*, 153–158. Cardiff, National Museum of Wales.

Oakley, K. P., Campbell, B. G. and Molleson, T. I. 1971. *Catalogue of Fossil Hominids Part II: Europe.* London, Trustees of the British Museum (Natural History).

O'Connor, A. 2007. *Finding Time for the Old Stone Age: a history of Palaeolithic archaeology and Quaternary geology in Britain, 1860–1960.* Oxford, Oxford University Press.

Ogilvie, M. D., Curran, B. K. and Trinkaus, E. 1989. Incidence and patterning of dental enamel hypoplasia among the Neanderthals. *American Journal of Physical Anthropology* 79, 25–41.

Olejniczak, A. J., Smith, T. M., Feeney, R. N. M., Macchiarelli, R., Mazurier, A., Bondioli, L., Rosas, A., Fortea, J., de la Rasilla, M., Garcia-Tabernero, A., Radovčić, J., Skinner, M. M., Toussaint, M. and Hublin, J. -J. 2008. Dental tissue proportions and enamel thickness in Neandertal and modern human molars. *Journal of Human Evolution* 55 (1), 12–23.

O'Neil, J. R., Roe, L. J., Reinhard, E. and Blake, R. E. 1994. A rapid and precise method of oxygen isotope analysis of biogenic phosphate. *Israel Journal of Earth Sciences* 43, 203–212.

Orban, R. (ed.). 1990. *Hominid Remains, an Update – British Isles and East Germany (No 3).* Belgium, Department of Anthropology and Human Genetics, l'Université libre de Bruxelles.

Orme, N. 1996. *English Church Dedications: with a survey of Cornwall and Devon.* Exeter, University of Exeter Press.

Owen, M. (ed.) 2007. *Cofio'r Cefn – Cefn Remembered.* Cefn Meiriadog, Cefn Meiriadog Historical Society.

Parés, J. M., Pérez-Gonzalez, A., Weil, A. B. and Arsuaga J. L. 2000. On the age of the hominid fossils at the Sima de los Huesos Sierra de Atapuerca, Spain: palaeomagnetic evidence. *American Journal of Physical Anthropology* 111, 451–461.

Parfitt, S., Barendregt, R., Breda, M., Candy, I., Collins, M., Coope, G. R., Durbidge, P., Field, M., Lee, J., Lister, A., Mutch, R., Penkman, K., Preece, R., Rose, J., Stringer, C., Symmons, R., Whittaker, J., Wymer, J. and Stuart, A. 2005. The earliest record of human activity in Northern Europe. *Nature* 438, 1008–1012.

Parfitt, S. A., Ashton, N. M., Lewis, S. G., Abel, R. L., Coope, G. R., Field, M. H., Gale, R., Hoare, P. G., Larkin, N. R., Lewis, M. D., Karloukovski, V., Maher, B. A., Peglar, S. M., Preece, R., Whittaker, J. E. and Stringer, C. B. 2010. Early Pleistocene human occupation at the edge of the boreal zone in northwest Europe *Nature* 466, 229–233.

Patterson, B. D. 2004. *The Lions of Tsavo: exploring the legacy of Africa's notorious man-eaters.* New York, McGraw-Hill.

Patterson, J. H. 1907. *The Man-Eaters of Tsavo and Other East African Adventures.* New York, St Martin's Press.

Paxton, R. A. 1952. Notes on the Cefn Caves, St Asaph, Denbighshire, North Wales. *Cave Science* 3 (19), 120–121.

Pederson, P. O. 1949. The East Greenland Eskimo dentition. *Meddelelser om Grønland* 142, 1–256.

Pedley, M. 1992. Freshwater (phytoherm) reefs: the role of biofilms and their bearing on marine reef cementation. *Sedimentary Geology* 79, 255–274.

Pennant, T. 1991 reprint. *A Tour in Wales Volume II.* Wrexham, Bridge Books.

Pérez- Pérez, A., Espurz, V., Bermúdez de Castro, J. M., Lumley, M. A. de and Turbón, D. 2003. Non-occlusal dental microwear variability in a sample of Middle and Late Pleistocene human populations from Europe and the Near East. *Journal of Human Evolution* 44 (4), 497–513.

Pettitt, P. B. 1997. High resolution Neanderthals? Interpreting Middle Palaeolithic intrasite spatial data. *World Archaeology* 29 (2), 208–224.

Pettitt, P. B. 2000. The Paviland radiocarbon dating programme: reconstructing the chronology of faunal communities, carnivore

activity and human occupation. In S. H. R. Aldhouse-Green *Paviland Cave and the 'Red Lady': a definitive report,* 63–71. Bristol, Western Academic and Specialist Press Ltd.

Phillips, F. M., Bowen, D. Q. and Elmore, D. 1994. Surface exposure dating of glacial features in Great Britain using cosmogenic Chlorine-36: preliminary results. *Mineralogical Magazine* 58A, 722–723.

Pierson, T. C. 1980. Erosion and deposition by debris flows at Mt Thomas, North Canterbury, New Zealand. *Earth Surface Processes* 5, 227–247.

Pierson, T. C. 1981. Dominant particle support mechanisms in debris flows at Mt Thomas, New Zealand, and implications for flow mobility. *Sedimentology* 28, 49–60.

Piggott, S. 1985. *William Stukeley: an eighteenth century antiquary.* London, Thames and Hudson.

van der Plicht J., Beck, J. W., Bard, E., Baillie, M. G. L., Blackwell, P. G., Buck, C. E., Friedrich, M., Guilderson, T. P., Hughen, K. A., McCormac, F. G., Bronk Ramsey, C., Reimer, P. J., Reimer, R. W., Remmele, S., Richards, D. A., Southon, J. R., Stuiver, M. and Wehenmeyer, C. E. 2004. NOTCAL04 – Comparison/calibration 14C records 26–50 kyr BP. *Radiocarbon* 46, 1225–1238.

Poisson, P., Maureille, B., Couture, C., Tournepiche, J. -F. and Miquel, J. -L. 2002. Contribution à l'étude des sillons subverticaux intéressants des facettes interproximales. Applications aux dents Néandertaliennes de Rochelot. (Saint-Amant-de-Bonnieure, Charente, France). *Bulletins et Mémoires de la Société d'Anthropologie de Paris* n.s. 14 (1–2), 75–87.

Potts, R. 1988. *Early Hominid Activities at Olduvai.* New York, Aldine de Gruyter.

Powers, M. C. 1953. A new roundness scale for sedimentary particles. *Journal of Sedimentary Petrology* 23, 117–119.

Prestwich, J. 1860. On the occurrence of flint-implements, associated with the remains of animals of extinct species in beds of a late geological period, in France at Amiens and Abbeville, and in England at Hoxne. *Philosophical Transactions of the Royal Society of London* 150, 277–317.

Price, C. R. 2003. *Late Pleistocene and Early Holocene Small Mammals in South West Britain.* Oxford, British Archaeological Report British Series 347.

Pugh, E. 1816. *Cambria Depicta; a tour through North Wales.* London, E. Williams.

Quam, R., Bailey, S. and Wood, B. 2009. Evolution of M$^1$ crown size and cusp proportions in the genus *Homo. Journal of Anatomy* 214, 655–670.

Radovčić, J., Smith, F. H., Trinkaus, E. and Wolpoff, M. H. 1988. *The Krapina hominids. An Illustrated Catalog of Skeletal Collection.* Zagreb, Croatian Natural History Museum.

Ramirez Rozzi, F. V. and Bermúdez de Castro, J. M. 2004. Surprisingly rapid growth in Neanderthals. *Nature* 428 (6986), 936–939.

Ramsay, A. C. 1846. The denudation of South Wales and adjacent English counties. *Memoir of the Geological Survey of England and Wales* 1, 297–335.

Ramsay, A. C. 1852. On the superficial accumulations and surface-markings of North Wales. *Quarterly Journal of the Geological Society* 8, 371–376.

de Rance, C. E. 1888a. Notes on the Vale of Clwyd caves. *Proceedings of the Yorkshire Geological and Polytechnic Society* 11 (1), 1–20.

de Rance, C. E. 1888b. Age of Clwydian Caves. *The Geological Magazine* Decade III col. V (vii) July 1888, 300–303.

Rasband, W. S. 1997–2008. *ImageJ.* U. S. National Institutes of Health, Bethesda, Maryland, USA, http://rsb.info.nih.gov/ij/.

Rees, A. I. 1968, The production of preferred orientation in a concentrated dispersion of elongated and flattened grains. *Journal of Geology* 76, 457–465.

Rees Jones, G. 2007. The legend of Meiriadog. In M. Owen (ed.). *Cofio'r Cefn – Cefn Remembered*, 188–189. Cefn Meiriadog, Cefn Meiriadog Historical Society.

Reid, C. and Reenen, J. F. Van 1995. Remnants of the metaconule in recent man. In R. J. Radlanski and H. Renz (eds). *Proceedings of the 10th International Symposium on Dental Morphology*, 172–176. Berlin, C. and M. Brunne.

Reid, D. J. and Ferrell, R. J. 2006. The relationship between number of striae of Retzius and their periodicity in imbricational enamel formation. *Journal of Human Evolution* 50 (2), 195–202.

Reid, D. J., Guatelli-Steinberg, D. and Walton, P. 2008. Variation in modern human premolar enamel formation times: implications for Neandertals. *Journal of Human Evolution* 54 (2), 225–235.

Reimer, P. J. Baillie, M. G. L., Bard, E., Bayliss, A., Beck, J. W., Bertrand C. J. H., Blackwell, P. G., Buck, C. E., Burr, G. S., Cutler, K. B., Damon, P. E., Edwards, R. L., Fairbanks, R. G., Friedrich, M., Guilderson, T. P., Hogg, A. G., Hughen, K. A., Kromer, B., McCormac, G., Manning, S., Ramsey, C. B., Reimer, R. W., Remmele, S., Southon, J. R., Stuiver, M., Talamo, S., Taylor, F. W., van der Plicht, J. and Weyhenmeyer, C. E. 2004. IntCal04 terrestrial radiocarbon age calibration, 0–26 cal kyr BP. *Radiocarbon* 46, 1029–1058.

Richards, M. P. 2000. Human and faunal stable isotope analyses from Goat's Hole and Foxhole Caves, Gower. In S. Aldhouse-Green (ed.). *Paviland Cave and the 'Red Lady'*, 71–76. Bristol, Western Academic and Specialist Press.

Richards, M. P. and Hedges, R. E. M. 1999. Stable isotope evidence for similarities in the types of marine foods used by late Mesolithic humans at sites along the Atlantic coast of Europe. *Journal of Archaeological Science* 26, 717–722.

Richards, M. P. and Hedges, R. E. M. 2003. Variations in bone collagen δ¹³C and δ¹⁵N values of fauna from Northwest Europe over the last 40,000 years. *Palaeogeography, Palaeoclimatology, Palaeoecology* 193, 261–267.

Richards, M. P. and Trinkaus, E. 2009. Isotopic evidence for the diets of European Neanderthals and early modern humans. *Proceedings of the National Academy of Sciences* 106 (38), 16034–16039.

Rightmire, G. P., Lordkipanidze, D. and Vekua, A. 2006. Anatomical descriptions, comparative studies and evolutionary significance of the hominin skulls from Dmanisi, Republic of Georgia. *Journal of Human Evolution* 50, 115–141.

Rink, W. J., Schwarcz, H. P., Smith, F. H. and Radovčić, J. 1995. ESR ages for Krapina hominids. *Nature* 378, 24.

Roberts, B. 1981. Low grade and very low grade regional metabasic Ordovician rocks of Llyn and Snowdonia, Gwynedd. *Geological Magazine* 118, 189–200.

Robinson, J. T. 1956. *The Dentition of the Australopithecinae.* Pretoria, Transvaal Museum, Transvaal Museum Memoir No. 9.

Roe, D. A. 1968. *A Gazeteer of British Lower and Middle Palaeolithic Sites.* London, Council for British Archaeology Research Report 8.

Rolland, N. 1992. The Palaeolithic colonization of Europe: an archaeological and biogeographic perspective. *Trabajos de Prehistoria* 49, 69–111.

Rosas, A. 1995. Seventeen new mandibular specimens from the Atapuerca/Ibeas Middle Pleistocene Hominids sample (1985–1992). *Journal of Human Evolution* 28, 533–559.

Rosas, A., Martinez-Maza, C., Bastir, M., Garcia-Tabernero, A.,

Lalueza-Fox, C., Huguet, R., Estalrrich, A., Garcia-Vargas, S., de la Rasilla, M. and Fortea, J. 2007. Paleobiological aspects of El Sidrón (Asturias, Spain) Neandertals. *American Association of Physical Anthropology* Supplement 44, 202.

Rouffignac, C. de, Bowen, D. Q., Coope, G. R., Keen, D. H., Lister, A. M., Maddy, D. L., Robinson, J. E., Sykes, G. A. and Walker, M. J. C. 1995. Late Middle Pleistocene interglacial deposits at Upper Strensham, Worcestershire, England, 1995. *Journal of Quaternary Science* 10, 15–31.

Rowlands, B. M. 1955. *The Glacial and Postglacial Evolution of the Landforms of the Vale of Clwyd.* Unpublished M.A. thesis, Liverpool University.

Rowlands, B. M. 1970. *The Glaciation of the Arenig Region.* Unpublished Ph.D. thesis, Liverpool University.

Rowlands, B. M. 1971. Radiocarbon evidence of the age of an Irish Sea glaciation in the Vale of Clwyd. *Nature* 230, 9–11.

Rowlands, B. M. 1977. The Arenig region: a study in the Welsh Pleistocene. *Cambria* 6, 13–31.

Sanchez-Goñi, M. F. and Harrison, S. P. 2010. Millennial-scale variability and vegetation changes during the Last Glacial: concepts and terminology. *Quaternary Science Reviews* 21–22, 2823–2827.

Schoetensack, O. 1908. *Der Unterkiefer des* Homo heidelbergensis *aus den Sanden von Mauer bei Heidelberg.* Leipzig, Wilhelm Engelmann.

Schreve, D. C. 2001. Differentiation of the British late Middle Pleistocene interglacials: the evidence from mammalian biostratigraphy. *Quaternary Science Reviews* 20, 1693–1705.

Schulting, R. J., Trinkaus, E., Higham, T., Hedges, R., Richards, M. and Cardy B. 2005. A Mid-Upper Palaeolithic human humerus from Eel Point, South Wales, U.K. *Journal of Human Evolution* 48 (5), 493–505.

Schurr, M. R. 1998. Using stable nitrogen-isotopes to study weaning behavior in past populations. *World Archaeology* 193, 327–342.

Schwarcz, H. P. 1984. Uranium-series dating and stable isotope analyses of calcite deposits. In H. S. Green *Pontnewydd Cave a Lower Palaeolithic Hominid Site in Wales: the first report*, 88–97. Cardiff, National Museum of Wales.

Schwartz, J. H. and Tattersall I. 2002. *The Human Fossil Record Vol. 1 Terminology and Craniodental Morphology of Genus Homo (Europe).* New York, Wiley-Liss.

Scott, G. R. and Turner II, C. G. 1997. *The Anthropology of Modern Human Teeth.* Cambridge, Cambridge University Press, Cambridge Studies in Biological Anthropology.

Scott, K. 2001. Late Middle Pleistocene mammoths and elephants of the Thames Valley, Oxfordshire. In G. Cavarretta, P. Gioia, M. Mussi and M. R. Palomba (eds). *La Terra degli Elefanti: The World of Elephants*, 247–254. Rome, Proceedings of the First International Congress Rome, 16th–20th October 2001.

Sealy, J. 2001. Body tissue chemistry and palaeodiet. In D. R. Brothwell and A. M. Pollard (eds). *Handbook of Archaeological Sciences*, 269–279. Chichester, John Wiley and Sons.

Secord, J. A. 1991. The discovery of a vocation: Darwin's early geology. *The British Journal for the History of Science* 24, (part 1 no. 80), 133–157.

Sharp, R. P. and Nobles, L. H. 1953. Mudflow of 1941 at Wrightwood, Southern California. *Bulletin of the Geological Society of America* 64, 547–560.

Shaw, J. C. M. 1928. Taurodont teeth in South African races. *Journal of Anatomy* 62, 476–499.

Shen, G., Gao, X., Gao, B. and Granger, D. E. 2009. Age of

Zhoukoudian *Homo erectus* determined with [26]Al/[10]Be burial dating. *Nature* 458, 198–200.

Shennan, I., Bradley, S., Milne, G., Brooks, A., Bassett, S. and Hamilton, S. 2006. Relative sea-level changes, glacial isostatic modelling and ice-sheet reconstructions from the British Isles since the Last Glacial Maximum. *Journal of Quaternary Science* 21, 585–599.

Shone, W. 1894. Post-Glacial man in Britain. *The Geological Magazine* 4 (1) 78–80.

Siddall, M., Rohling, E. J., Almogi-Labin, A., Hemleben, Ch., Meischner, D., Schmelzer, I. and Smeed, D. A. 2003. Sea-level fluctuations during the last glacial cycle. *Nature* 423, 853–858.

Singer, R., Gladfelter, B. G. and Wymer, J. J. 1993. *The Lower Palaeolithic Site at Hoxne, England.* Chicago, University of Chicago Press.

Sissons, J. B. 1960. Erosion surfaces, cyclic slopes and drainage systems in southern Scotland and northern England. *Transactions of the Institute of British Geographers* 28, 23–38.

Skinner M. M. and Wood B. 2006. The evolution of modern human life history, a paleontological perspective. In K. Hawkes and R. P. Paine (eds). *The Evolution of Human Life History*, 331–400. Santa Fe, School of American Research Press.

Smiles, S. 2003. Record and reverie. In R. G. W. Anderson, M. L. Caygill, A. G. MacGregor and L. Syson (eds). *Enlightening the British: knowledge, discovery and the museum in the eighteenth century*, 176–181. London, The British Museum Press.

Smith, B. H. 1984. Patterns of molar wear in hunter-gatherers and agriculturalists. *American Journal of Physical Anthropology* 63, 39–56.

Smith, B. H. 1986. Dental development in *Australopithecus* and early *Homo*. *Nature* 323 (6086), 327–330.

Smith, B. H. 1994a. Sequence of emergence of the permanent teeth in *Macaca, Pan, Homo* and *Australopithecus*: its evolutionary significance. *American Journal of Human Biology* 6, 61–76.

Smith, B. H. 1994b. Patterns of dental development in *Homo, Australopithecus, Pan* and *Gorilla*. *American Journal of Physical Anthropology* 94, 307–325.

Smith, F. H. 1976a. On anterior tooth wear at Krapina and Ochoz. *Current Anthropology* 17 (1), 167–168.

Smith, F. H. 1976b. *The Neanderthal Remains from Krapina: a descriptive and comparative study.* Tennessee, Department of Anthropology, University of Tennessee, Report of Investigations number 15.

Smith, P. 1977. Selective pressures and dental evolution in hominids. *American Journal of Physical Anthropology* 47, 453–458.

Smith, P. 1989. Dental evidence for phylogenetic relationships of Middle Palaeolithic hominids. In B. Vandermeersch (ed.). *L'Homme de Neandertal Vol 7. L'Extinction*, 111–120. Liège, Université de Liège, Etudes et Recherches Archéologiques de l'Université de Liège number 34.

Smith, T. M. 2008. Incremental dental development: methods and applications in hominoid evolutionary studies. *Journal of Human Evolution* 54 (2), 205–224.

Smith, T. M., Harvati, K., Olejniczak, A. J., Reid, D. J., Hublin, J. -J. and Panagopoulou, E. 2009. Dental development and enamel thickness in the Lakonis Neanderthal molar. *American Journal of Physical Anthropology* 138, 112–118.

Smith, T. M., Reid, D. J., Olejniczak, A. J., Bailey, S. E., Glantz, M., Viola, B. and Hublin, J. -J. 2011. Dental development and age at death of a Middle Palaeolithic juvenile hominin from Obi-Rakhmat Grotto, Uzbekistan. In S. Condemi and G. -C. Weniger (eds). *Continuity and Discontinuity in the Peopling of Europe: one hundred fifty years of Neanderthal Study*, 155–164. Dordrecht, Springer.

Smith, T. M., Tafforeau, P., Reid, D. J., Grün, R., Eggins, S., Boutakiout, M. and Hublin, J. -J. 2007a. Earliest evidence of modern human life history in North African early *Homo sapiens*. *Proceedings of the National Academy of Sciences USA* 104 (15), 6128–6133.

Smith, T. M., Toussaint, M., Reid, D. J., Olejniczak, A. J. and Hublin J. -J. 2007b. Rapid dental development in a Middle Paleolithic Belgian Neanderthal. *Proceedings of the National Academy of Sciences USA* 104 (51), 20220–20225.

Soffer, O. 2000. The last Neanderthals. In D. Lordkipanidze, O. Bar-Yosef and M. Otte (eds). *Early Humans at the Gates of Europe*, 139–145. Liège, ERAUL 92.

Stanley, E. 1833. Memoir on a cave at Cefn in Denbigshire [sic] visited by the Rev. Edward Stanley, F.G.S., F.L.S., etc. *Edinburgh New Philosophical Journal* 14, 40–53.

Stanton, W. 1999. Early stages in the development of Westbury Cave. In P. Andrews, J. Cook, A. Currant and C. Stringer (eds). *Westbury Cave, The Natural History Museum Excavations 1976–1984*, 13–18. Bristol, Western Academic and Specialist Press.

Steers, J. A. 1956. *The Coastline of England and Wales.* Cambridge, Cambridge University Press.

Stefen, C. 2009. Intraspecific variability of beaver teeth (Castoridae: Rodentia). *Zoological Journal of the Linnean Society* 155, 926–936.

Stenhouse, M. J. and Baxter, M. S. 1979. The uptake of bomb [14]C in humans. In R. Berger and H. E. Suess (eds). *Radiocarbon Dating: proceedings of the ninth international conference in Los Angeles and La Jolla, 1976*, 324–341. Berkeley, University of California Press.

Stephan, E. 2000. Oxygen isotope analysis of animal bone phosphate: method refinement, influence of consolidants, and reconstruction of palaeotemperatures for Holocene sites. *Journal of Archaeological Science* 27, 523–535.

Stevens, R. E. and Hedges, R. E. M. 2004. Carbon and nitrogen stable isotope analysis of northwest European horse bone and tooth collagen, 40,000 BP–present: palaeoclimatic interpretations. *Quaternary Science Reviews* 23, 977–991.

Strahan, A. and de Rance, C. E. 1890. The geology of the neighbourhoods of Flint, Mold and Ruthin, (explanation of quarter-sheet 79 SE) *Memoir of the Geological Survey of England and Wales*. London, H.M.S.O.

Strauss, L. G. 1980. The role of raw materials in lithic assemblage variability. *Lithic Technology* 9 (3), 68–72.

Straw, A. 1995. Pengelly centenary lecture III. Kent's Cavern – whence and whither. *Transactions and Proceedings of the Torquay Natural History Society* 21 (4), 198–211.

Straw, A. 1996. The Quaternary record of Kent's Cavern – a brief reminder and update. *Quaternary Newsletter* 80, 17–25.

Stringer, C. B. 1981. The dating of European Middle Pleistocene hominids and the existence of *Homo erectus* in Europe. *L'Anthropologie* 19 (1), 3–14.

Stringer, C. B. 1984. The hominid finds. In H. S. Green, *Pontnewydd Cave a Lower Palaeolithic Hominid Site in Wales: the first report*, 159–176. Cardiff, National Museum of Wales.

Stringer, C. B. 1986. The British fossil hominid record. In S. N. Collcutt (ed.). *The Palaeolithic of Britain and its Nearest Neighbours: recent trends*, 59–61. Sheffield, Department of Archaeology and Prehistory, University of Sheffield.

Stringer C. 2002. Modern human origins – progress and prospects. *Philosophical Transactions of the Royal Society, London* (B) 357, 563–579.

Stringer, C. 2007. *Homo Britannicus*. London, Penguin.

Stringer, C. 2010. The changing landscapes of the earliest human occupation of Britain and Europe. In N. Ashton, S. Lewis and C. Stringer (eds). *The Ancient Human Occupation of Britain*. London, Elsevier.

Stringer, C. 2011. *The Origin of Our Species*. London, Allen Lane.

Stringer, C. and Andrews, P. 2011. *The Complete World of Human Evolution*. London, Thames and Hudson.

Stringer, C. B., Dean, M. C. and Martin, R. D. 1990. A comparative study of cranial and dental development within a recent British sample and among Neanderthals. In C. J. de Rousseau (ed.). *Primate Life History and Evolution*, 115–152. London, Wiley-Liss.

Stringer, C. B. and Gamble, C. S. 1993. *In Search of the Neanderthals: solving the puzzle of human origins*. London, Thames and Hudson.

Stringer, C. B., Howell, F. C. and Melentis, J. K. 1979. The significance of the fossil hominid from Petralona, Greece. *Journal of Archaeological Science* 6, 235–253.

Stringer, C. B., Hublin, J. J. and Vandermeersch, B. 1984. The origin of anatomically modern humans in western Europe. In F. H. Smith and F. Spencer (eds). *The Origins of Modern Humans – a world survey of the fossil evidence*, 51–135. New York, Alan R. Liss.

Stringer, C. B., Humphrey, L. T. and Compton, T. 1997. Cladistic analysis of dental traits in recent humans using a fossil outgroup. *Journal of Human Evolution* 32, 389–402.

Svensson, A., Andersen, K. K., Bigler, M., Clausen, H. B., Dahl-Jensen, D., Davies, S. M., Johnsen, S. J., Muscheler, R., Rasmussen, S. O., Rothlisberger, R., Steffensen, J. P. and Vinther, B. M. 2006. The Greenland ice core chronology 2005, 15–42ka. Part 2: comparison to other records. *Quaternary Science Reviews* 25 (23–24), 3258–3267.

Svensson, J. I., Heggen, H. P., Hufthammer, J., Mangerud, J., Pavlov, P. and Roebroecks, W. 2010. Geo-archaeological investigations of Palaeolithic sites along the Ural Mountains – on the northern presence of humans during the last Ice Age. *Quaternary Science Reviews* 29, 3138–3156.

Symonds, W. S. 1872. *Records of the Rocks*. London, John Murray.

Tanguy, B. 1999. Les Cultes de sainte Nonne et de saint Divy en Bretagne. In Y. Le Berre, B. Tanguy, and Y. -P. Castel. *Mystère Breton. Buez Santez Nonn – vie de sainte Nonne*. Minihi Levenez, C.R.B.C. and Minihi-Levenez, 9–31.

Tauber, H. 1981. ¹³C evidence for dietary habits of prehistoric man in Denmark. *Nature* 292 (23 July), 332–333.

Taylor, R. E. 2009. Radiocarbon dating. In V. Gornitz (ed.). *Encyclopedia of Paleoclimatology and Ancient Environments*, 863–869. Dordrecht, Springer.

Taylor, R. M. S. 1963. Cause and effect of wear of teeth – further non-metrical studies of the teeth and palate in Moriori and Maori skulls. *Acta Anatomica* 53 (1–2), 97–157.

Thomas, C. 1967. *Christian Antiquities of Camborne*. St Austell, H. E. Warne Ltd.

Thomas, D. R. 1872. Kereg the Tylluaine. *Archaeologia Cambrensis* 27, 160.

Thomas, D. R. 1883. *Y Cwtta Cyfarwydd: The Chronicle written by the famous Clarke, Peter Roberts, Notary Public, for the years 1607–1649*. London, Whiting and Co.

Thomas, D. R. c. 1894. *An Illustrated Handbook for Visitors to St Asaph, (Cathedral and Parish Church), Bodelwyddan and Cefn*. Rhyl, Pearce and Jones.

Thomas, G. S. P. 1985. The Late Devensian glaciation along the border of north-east Wales. *Geological Journal* 19, 125–142.

Thomas, G. S. P. 1989. The Late Devensian glaciation along the margin of the Cheshire-Shropshire Lowland. *Journal of Quaternary Science* 4, 167–181.

Thomas, G. S. P. 2005. North East Wales. In C. A. Lewis and A. E. Richards (eds). *The Glaciations of Wales and Adjacent Regions*, 41–58. Almeley, Logaston Press.

Thompson, J. L. and Illerhaus, B. 2005. 3-D-μCT analysis of the Le Moustier 1 Neandertal. In H. Ullrich (ed.). *The Neandertal Adolescent Le Moustier 1 – new aspects, new results*, 225–243. Berlin, Staatliche Museum.

Thompson, J. L. and Nelson, A. J. 2000. The place of Neanderthals in the evolution of hominid patterns of growth and development. *Journal of Human Evolution* 38, 475–495.

Tillier, A. -M. 1979. La dentition de l'enfant Moustérien Chateauneuf 2 découvert à l'Abri de Hauteroche (Charente). *L'Anthropologie* 83, 417–438.

Tixier, J., Inizan, M. L. and Roche, H. 1980. Les accidents de taillee. *Studia Praehistorica Belgica* 2 1982, 65–76.

Tobias, P. V. 1967. *Olduvai Gorge II: the cranium and maxillary dentition of Australopithecus (Zinjanthropus) boisei*. Cambridge, Cambridge University Press.

Tompkins, R. L. 1996. Relative dental development of Upper Pleistocene hominids compared to human population variation. *American Journal of Physical Anthropology* 99 (1), 103–118.

Toms, P. S., Hosfield, R. T., Chambers, J. C., Green, C. P. and Marshall, P. 2005. Optical dating of the Broom Palaeolithic sites, southwest England. In A.H.O.B. 2005: *The Palaeolithic Occupation of Europe: programme and abstracts*. Quaternary Research Association annual discussion meeting held at the British Museum, 5th–6th January 2005.

Tooley, M. J. 1974. Sea-level changes during the last 9000 years in north-west England. *Geographical Journal* 140, 18–42.

Toth, N. P. 1982. *The Stone Technologies of Early Hominids at Koobi Fora, Kenya: an experimental approach*. Unpublished PhD thesis, University of California, Berkeley.

Toulmin Smith, L. (ed.). 1906. *Leland's Itinerary in Wales Part IV*. London, George Bell and Sons.

Trefný, P. 2005. Size reduction of the Le Moustier 1 molars – a 2D analysis. In H. Ullrich (ed.). *The Neandertal Adolescent Le Moustier 1 – new aspects, new results*, 187–196. Berlin, Staatliche Museum.

Trimmer, J. 1838. On the discovery of the northern or diluvial drift containing fragments of marine shells covering the remains of terrestrial mammalia in Cefn Cave. *Report of the Eighth Meeting of the British Association for the Advancement of Science held at Newcastle in August 1838* 7, 86–87.

Trinkaus, E. 1978. Dental remains from the Shanidar adult Neanderthals. *Journal of Human Evolution* 7, 369–382.

Trinkaus, E. 1983. *The Shanidar Neandertals*. New York, Academic Press.

Trinkaus, E. 1995. Neanderthal mortality patterns. *Journal of Archaeological Science* 22 (1), 121–142.

Trinkaus, E., Marks, A. E., Brugal, J. P., Bailey, S. E., Rink, W. J. and Richter, D. 2003. Later Middle Pleistocene human remains from the Almonda karstic system, Torres Novas, Portugal. *Journal of Human Evolution* 45, 219–226.

Turner, A. 2000. The mammalian assemblage from Goat's Hole Cave, Paviland. In S. H. R. Aldhouse-Green *Paviland Cave and the 'Red Lady': a definitive report*, 133–140. Bristol, Western Academic and Specialist Press Ltd.

Turner II, C. G. 1987. Late Pleistocene and Holocene population history of east Asia based on dental variation. *American Journal of Physical Anthropology* 73, 305–321.

Turner II, C. G. and Cadien, J. D. 1969. Dental chipping in Aleuts, Eskimos and Indians. *American Journal of Physical Anthropology* 31, 303–310.

Turner, C. G., Nichol, C. R. and Scott, G. R. 1991. Scoring procedures for key morphological traits of the permanent dentition. In M. A. Kelley and C. S. Larsen (eds). *Advances in Dental Anthropology*, 13–31. New York, Clark Spencer, Wiley-Liss Inc.

Turq, A. 1988. Le Paléolithique inférieur et moyen en Haut-Agenais: état des recherches. *Revue de l'Agenais* 115, 83–112.

Twiesselmann, F. 1973. Évolution des dimensions et de la forme de la mandibule du palais et des dents de l'homme. *Annales de Palaeontologie (Vert)* 59 (2), 171–277.

Urzidil, J. 1968. *There Goes Kafka*. Detroit, Wayne State University Press.

Valdemar, A. E. 1970. A new assessment of the occupation of the Cefn Cave in relation to the Bont Newydd Cave and the River Elwy. *Transactions of the Cave Research Group of Great Britain* 12 (2) 109–112.

Valdemar, A. E. and Jones, R. D. 1970. An initial report on the archaeological and palaeontological caves and rock shelters in North Wales. *Transactions of the Cave Research Group of Great Britain* 12 (2) 99–107.

Vennemann, T. W., Fricke, H. C., Blake, R. E., O'Neill, J. R. and Colman, A. 2002. Oxygen isotope analysis of phosphates: a comparison of techniques for analysis of $Ag_3PO_4$. *Chemical Geology* 185, 321–336.

Villa, G. 1996. Hunter-Schreger band orientation in interproximal enamel of modern human molars with complex morphological traits. *Human Evolution* 11 (N1), 85–96.

Villa, G. and Giacobini, G. 1995a. Subvertical grooves of interproximal facets in Neanderthal posterior teeth. *American Journal of Physical Anthropology* 96, 51–62.

Villa, G. and Giacobini, G. 1995b. Interproximal wear of Neanderthal posterior teeth. Characteristics of subvertical grooves. In J. Mogi-Cecchi (ed.). *Aspects of Dental Biology: palaeontology, anthropology and evolution*, 177–182. Florence, International Institute for the Study of Man.

Villa, P. 1983. *Terra Amata and the Pleistocene Archaeological Record of Southern France*. Berkeley, Los Angeles, University of California Press.

Vincent, P. J., Wilson, P., Lord, T. C., Schnabel, C. and Wilcken, K. M. 2010. Cosmogenic isotope ($^{36}Cl$) surface exposure dating of the Norber erratics, Yorkshire Dales: further constraints on the timing of the LGM deglaciation in Britain. *Proceedings of the Geologists' Association* 121, 24–31.

Vinogradoff, P. and Morgan, F. (eds). 1914. *Survey of the Honour of Denbigh 1334*. London, British Academy.

Vlček, E. 1978. A new discovery of *Homo erectus* in Central Europe. *Journal of Human Evolution* 7, 239–251.

Vlček, E. 1993. Fossile menschenfunde von Weimar-Ehringsdorf. *Weimarer Monographien zur ur-und Frühgeschichte, band 30*. Weimar, Thüringisches Landesamt für Archäologische Denkmalpflege.

Vlček, E. and Mania, D. 1987. Funde von zähnen des *Homo erectus* aus dem travertin bei Bilzingsleben. 4 Mitteilung. *Jahresschrift für Mitteldeutsche Vorgeschichte, Halle* 70, 83–94.

Vogel, J. C. and van der Merwe, N. J. 1977. Isotopic evidence for early maize cultivation in New York State. *American Antiquity* 42 (2), 238–242.

Voous, K. H. 1960. *Atlas of European Birds*. New York, Thomas Nelson and Sons.

Wagner, G. A., Krbetschek, M., Degering, D., Bahain, J. -J., Shao, Q., Falguères, C., Voinchet, P., Dolo, J. -M., Garcia, T. and Rightmire, G. P. 2010. Radiometric dating of the type-site for *Homo heidelbergensis* at Mauer, Germany. *Proceedings of the National Academy of Sciences* 107 (46), 19726–19730.

Walker, A. and Shipman, P. 1996. *The Wisdom of Bones*. London, Weidenfeld and Nicholson.

Walker, E. A. 2009. Discoveries in Devon: the works of Father John MacEnery and William Pengelly. *Lithics* 30, 25–33.

Wallace, J. A. 1973. Tooth chipping in the Australopithecines. *Nature* 244, 117–118.

Walsh, P. 2001. *The Palaeogeography of the southern half of the British Isles and Adjacent Continental Shelf at the Palaeogene/ Neogene Boundary (g/n) and its Subsequent Modification: a reconsideration*. Katowice, Wydawnictwo Uniwersytetu Śląskiego.

Walsh, P. T., Boulter, M. C., Ijaba, M. and Urbani, D. M. 1972. The preservation of the Neogene Brassington Formation of the southern Pennines and its bearing on the evolution of Upland Britain. *Journal of the Geological Society of London* 128, 519–559.

Walsh, P. T., Boulter, M. C. and Morawawiecka, I. M. 1999. Chattian and Miocene elements in the modern landscape of western Britain and Ireland. In B. J. Smith, W. B. Whalley and P. A. Warke (eds). *Uplift Erosion and Stability: perspectives on long-term landscape development*, 45–63. London, Geological Society of London, special publication 162.

Walsh, P. T. and Brown, E. H. 1971. Solution subsistence outliers containing probable Tertiary sediment in North-east Wales. *Geological Journal* 7, 299–320.

Waltham, A. C., Simms, M. J., Farrant, A. R. and Goldie, H. S. 1997. *Karst and Caves of Great Britain*. Geological Conservation Review Series 12. London, Chapman and Hall.

Walton, R. E. 1996. Cracked tooth and vertical root fracture. In R. E. Walton and M. Torabinejad. *Principles and Practice of Endodontics*, 474–492. Philadelphia, Saunders.

Wang, Y. J., Cheng, H., Edwards, R. L., An, Z. S., Wu, J. Y., Shen C. -C. and Dorale, J. A. 2001. A high-resolution absolute-dated Late Pleistocene monsoon record from Hulu Cave, China. *Science* 294, 2345–2348.

Warren, P. T., Price, D., Nutt, M. J. C. and Smith, E. G. 1984. Geology of the country around Rhyl and Denbigh, *Memoir of the British Geological Survey*, sheets 95 and 107 and parts of sheets 94 and 106 (England and Wales). London, H.M.S.O.

Weidenreich, F. 1937. *The Dentition of Sinanthropus pekinensis: a comparative odontology of the hominids*. Palaeontologia Sinica, whole series number 101, new series D1.

Westaway, R. 2010. Cenozoic uplift of southwest England. *Journal of Quaternary Science* 25, 419–432.

White, C. D., Spence, M. W., Longstaffe, F. J. and Law, K. R. 2004. Demography and ethnic continuity in the Tlailotlacan enclave of Teotihuacan: the evidence from stable istope oxygen isotopes. *Journal of Anthropological Archaeology* 23, 385–403.

White, M. J. 1995. Raw materials and biface variability in Southern Britain: a preliminary examination. *Lithics* 15, 1–20.

White, M. and Pettitt, P. 1995. Technology of early Palaeolithic western Europe: an heuristic framework. *Lithics* 16, 27–40.

White, M., Scott, B. and Ashton, N. 2006. The Early Middle Palaeolithic in Britain: archaeology, settlement history and behaviour. *Journal of Quaternary Science* 21 (5), 525–541.

Wild, E. M., Arlamovsky, K. A., Golser, R., Kutschera, W., Priller, A., Puchegger, S., Rom, W., Steier, P. and Vycudilik, W. 2000. ¹⁴C dating with the bomb peak: an application to forensic medicine. *Nuclear Instruments and Methods in Physics Research, Section B – beam interactions with materials and atoms* 172, 944–950.

Wills, L. J. 1937. The Pleistocene history of the West Midlands. *British Association for the Advancement of Science Report of the Annual Meeting held 1937 in Nottingham, September 1–8,* 71–94.

Wills, L. J. 1938. The Pleistocene development of the Severn from Bridgnorth to the sea. *Quarterly Journal of the Geological Society of London* 94, 161–242.

Wills, L. J. 1952. *A Palaeogeographical Atlas of the British Isles and Adjacent Parts of Europe.* London, Blackie, London.

Williams, P. L., Warwick, R., Dyson, M. and Bannister, L. H. (eds). 1989 *Gray's Anatomy, 37th Edition.* Edinburgh, Churchill Livingstone.

Wolff, E. W., Chappellaz, J., Blunier, T., Rasmussen, S. O. and Svensson, A. 2009. Millennial-scale variability during the last glacial: the ice core record. *Quaternary Science Reviews* 21–22, 2828–2838.

Wolpoff, M. H. 1971. *Metric Trends in Hominid Dental Evolution.* Cleveland, Case Western Reserve University Studies in Anthropology 2.

Wolpoff, M. H. 1979. The Krapina dental remains. *American Journal of Physical Anthropology* 50, 67–114.

Wolpoff, M. H. 1980. Cranial remains of Middle Pleistocene European hominids. *Journal of Human Evolution* 9, 339–358.

Wolpoff, M. H. 1982. The Arago dental sample in the context of hominid dental evolution. In *L'Homo erectus et la place de l'Homme de Tautavel parmi les hominidés fossils,* 389–410. Nice, C.N.R.S. Congrés International de Paléontologie Humaine, 1st congrés, Pretirage, tome 1.

Wood, A. Unpublished. 1:25,000 maps of the Welsh coastline.

Wood, B. and Lonergan, N. L. 2008.The hominin fossil record: taxa, grades and clades. *Journal of Anatomy* 212, 354–376.

Wood, B. A. and Abbott, S. A. 1983. Analysis of the dental morphology of Plio-Pleistocene hominids. I. Mandibular molars: crown area measurements and morphological traits. *Journal of Anatomy,* 136 (1), 197–219.

Wood, B. A., Abbott, S. A. and Uytterschaut, H. 1988. Analysis of the dental morphology of Plio-Pleistocene hominids. IV. Mandibular postcanine root morphology. *Journal of Anatomy* 156, 107–139.

Wood, B. A. and Engleman, C. A. 1988. Analysis of the dental morphology of Plio-Pleistocene hominids. V. Maxillary postcanine tooth morphology. *Journal of Anatomy* 161, 1–35.

Wood, B. A. and Uytterschaut, H. 1987. Analysis of the dental morphology of Plio-Pleistocene hominids. III. Mandibular premolar crowns. *Journal of Anatomy* 154, 121–156.

Wood, M. 2003. *Franz Kafka.* Tavistock, Northcote House Publishers.

Wood, M. and Campbell, S. 1995. Flood for thought on the Great Orme. *Earth Heritage* 3, 15–19.

Woodcock, N. H. and Naylor, M. A. 1983. Randomness testing in three-dimensional orientation data. *Journal of Structural Geology* 5 (5), 539–548.

Woodman, P., McCarthy, M. and Monaghan, N. 1997. The Irish Quaternary Fauna Project. *Quaternary Science Reviews* 16, 129–159.

Wright, N. (ed.). 1985. *The Historia Regnum Britannie of Geoffrey of Monmouth: I: Bern, Burgerbibliothek, M.S. 568.* Cambridge, D. S. Brewer.

Wu, L. and Turner II, C. G. 1993. Brief communication: variation in the frequency and form of the lower permanent molar middle trigonid crest. *American Journal of Physical Anthropology* 91, 245–248.

Wyhe, J. van (ed.). 2009. *The Complete Work of Charles Darwin Online* (http://darwin-online.org.uk).

Wymer, J. J. 1988. A reassessment of the geographical range of Lower Palaeolithic activity in Britain. In R. J. MacRae, and N. Moloney (eds). *Non-Flint Stone Tools and the Palaeolithic Occupation of Britain,* 11–23. Oxford, British Archaeological Reports British Series no. 189.

Wymer, J. J. 1999. *The Lower Palaeolithic Occupation of Britain.* Salisbury, Wessex Archaeology and English Heritage.

Wymer, J. J. and Singer, R. 1993. Flint industries and human activity. In R. Singer, B. G. Gladfelter and J. J. Wymer (eds). *The Lower Palaeolithic Site at Hoxne, England,* 74–128. Chicago, University of Chicago Press.

Zubov, A. A. 1992. The epicristid or middle trigonid crest defined. *Dental Anthropology News* 6, 9–10.